Modern Social Problems

HOLT, RINEHART AND WINSTON
New York Chicago San Francisco Dallas
Montreal Toronto London Sydney

Modern Social Problems

Frank J. McVeigh
MUHLENBERG COLLEGE

with

Arthur B. Shostak
DREXEL UNIVERSITY

COPYRIGHT ACKNOWLEDGMENTS

We are grateful to the following authors and publishers for their permission to reprint copyrighted material in boxed excerpts within this text.

To Leontine R. Young for excerpts from *The Fractured Family* (New York: McGraw-Hill, 1973).

To Bradford C. Snell for excerpts from "American Ground Transport." Copyright © 1973 by Bradford C. Snell.

To the *New York Times* for excerpts from "Clearance," by Russell Baker, *New York Times Magazine* (June 16, 1974); and from "Waiting for the End," by Susan Jacoby, *New York Times Magazine* (March 31, 1974).

To *Change Magazine* for excerpts from James O'Toole, "The Reserve Army of the Underemployed," *Change Magazine* 7, 4 (May 1975).

To John Wiley & Sons, Inc. for excerpts from *The Cocktail Waitress: Woman's Work in a Man's World*, by James P. Spradley and Brenda Mann (New York: Wiley, 1975).

To Random House, Inc. for excerpts from *The American Health Empire*, by John Ehrenreich and Barbara Ehrenreich (New York: Vintage Books, 1971); from *Crisis in the Classroom*, by Charles Silberman (New York: Vintage Books, 1970); and from *Blaming the Victim*, rev. ed., by William Ryan (New York: Vintage Books, 1976).

Text design by Celine Brandes

Copyright © 1978 by Holt, Rinehart and Winston
All rights reserved

Library of Congress Cataloging in Publication Data

McVeigh, Frank J
  Modern social problems.

  Bibliographies
  Includes index.
  1. Social problems. I. Shostak, Arthur B., joint author. II. Title.
HN18.M23   362'.042   75-41863
ISBN 0-03-034821-8

890 032 9876543

Dedicated to my wife, Beverly, and to my mother, Viola C. Walk, who taught me everything I really know about love, marriage, and the family

Preface

Times have changed. During the 1960s it seemed that nothing was stable or settled. From demonstrations for civil rights to protests against the war in Vietnam, many young people were literally on the march. Universities came under seige. These events occurred just as millions born during the baby boom of the 1950s came of age. Some sociologists say that because of their growing numbers they felt they had the power (of numbers) to rebel against the established system; and rebel they did. They fought against racial injustice. Some defied the draft. Others protested the polluted environment. Some turned to drugs as an escape. Still others clamored and converged to demand equal rights for women. Police often overreacted to lawful protests and demonstrations by violating the life and liberty of protesting blacks and students. Students were killed at Kent State in Ohio and at Jackson State University in Mississippi.

It seemed to be like the era of the French Revolution, as described by Charles Dickens in *A Tale of Two Cities*: "It was the best of times, it was the worst of times. It was the spring of hope, it was the winter of despair."

But all that has changed—almost overnight, it seems. We have now passed our peaceful bicentennial celebration. Vietnam and the draft are in our past. We now talk of the "quiet campus," and students are again more interested in studies and careers than in social change or collective action. A new privatism and an affirmation of both traditional and new norms have set in among many of the young, and alcohol use has become more popular than narcotics or marijuana. The civil rights of minorities are no longer the burning issue. The birth rate has declined significantly in the last two decades, and schools are now worrying about future enrollments. Inflation, energy, and jobs are the issues that concern many Americans today.

All this suggests that what society perceives as a social problem changes rapidly over time. And what is in fact a social problem may be quickly slighted or shelved, though not solved, by society. This observation should give both scholars and students a better historical perspective of the problems that are still with us today, and of the steps that still must be taken to cope with them.

Every book in social problems has a problem of its own: how should the issues be presented and organized? Throughout this book, we have provided different definitions and alternative perspectives for analyzing social problems. In so doing, we have relied upon many different sociological and social theories, as well as presenting conservative, liberal, and radical perspectives. In structuring the book and ordering the problems, we have relied upon C. Wright Mills's distinction between "personal problems" and "social issues." Using that insight, we have organized this book into four parts:

1. Forming One's Biography: Personal Problems Leading to Social Issues
2. Groups, Immediate Social Environment, and Social Issues
3. Institutions and Social Issues
4. International Dimensions of Social Issues

This division attempts to organize social problems from the most immediate experience of individuals and groups to those of national and international scope. Part IV recognizes the insight of Robert Perrucci and Marc Pilisuk that social problems have an international dimension, as well as simply a societal base. The problems discussed in each part do not exhaust all the social problems that could have possibly been discussed. The last chapter offers a summary of and conclusions about social problems.

In order to structure significantly and meaningfully organize a large amount of material, each chapter (except the first and last) employs a logical outline for analyzing and understanding a social problem. This framework will be developed around the following headings:

1. Defining the Problem
2. Incidence and Prevalence of the Problem
3. Causes of the Problem
4. Proposed Solutions to the Problem
5. The Future of the Problem
6. Summary

An outline of each problem analyzed is presented at the beginning of each chapter.

In summary, then, we use theories and perspectives eclectically, in a fashion that sheds sharper light on each problem and, at the same time, integrates all the chapters by adhering to a major logical framework for every problem. This six-step conceptual outline organizes material in a logical and meaningful way so that readers and instructors can cover the same aspects of different problems. In this fashion, differences or similarities in the severity or seriousness of a problem can easily be compared. Each problem can be supplemented by lectures or visual aids, and students can be assigned papers to develop additional materials, following this same basic framework for a particular social problem. For example, it is possible for students to write new "futures" sections for 1980 or 1984. This framework should provide order and structure to their understanding and analysis, where otherwise there might be only a mishmash of facts, ideas, and insights. Finally, each chapter concludes with a brief description of books for further reading. There is also a list of periodicals; these are usually professional journals but we also include a few popular ones relevant to the problem discussed.

A special feature at the end of each chapter is a brief description of student career opportunities related to the social problem in that chapter. Names and addresses of organizations are supplied for students who wish to write for further information about certain careers.

F.J. McV.

Acknowledgments

No book is complete or completed without acknowledgments to all who made it possible.

My special thanks go to the friends and colleagues who read early drafts of particular chapters when the book was first taking shape. Sincere appreciation is due to George Hood, M.D., a former general practitioner and now medical consultant to the New Jersey Medicaid system, who made many excellent suggestions for improving the chapter on medical and health care. My appreciation also goes to Dr. Thomas Shey of the department of sociology at Fordham University, a long-time colleague and friend, who reviewed the chapters on ecology and population. I am also grateful to Griff Dudding, Dean of Adult Education, Lehigh County Community College, who examined the chapter on aging and the elderly.

I especially want to thank my friends and colleagues at Muhlenberg College: Dr. Joseph Francello, chairman of the department of sociology and anthropology, who read the chapter on changes in the family and sex roles; and Dr. Roger Baldwin, a specialist in criminology, who evaluated the chapter on crime and delinquency and administering justice. For the research assistance and other help received from former Muhlenberg sociology and social science students Julie Campbell, Bob Goodman, and Bryan Zeiner, I am grateful.

I express my appreciation and thanks to the administrators and faculty at Muhlenberg College: the Board of Trustees, President John Morey, Dean Harold Stenger, and all the members of the Faculty Personnel and Policy Committee, who granted me a leave of absence in the Fall semester of 1976 to complete the first draft of the manuscript. My thanks also to members of the Faculty Research Committee, who made available to me a grant for some photo research for the book.

My sincere thanks and appreciation are also given to the library staff of Muhlenberg College for their professional assistance.

I acknowledge and thank James Bergin, a fine editor, whose ideas, whenever there was a problem to overcome, were both inspirational and encouraging. The rewrite skills of Robert Heidel saved me from some errors in verbal structure and presentation.

My heartfelt acknowledgments and love go to my wife, Beverly, who typed the entire manuscript with patience, understanding, and devotion. Her suggestions for improvements were usually (though not always) heeded. I recognize the patience and understanding of my daughters, Linda and Evelyn, in learning what it means to have a father who is writing a book.

Last, my sincere thanks to my friend and colleague Arthur Shostak, who edited each chapter as it was written, and made suggestions for making this a better book.

F.J. McV.

Contents

1. Introduction to Social Problems 1
What Is a Social Problem? 3
Analyzing and Solving Social Problems 6
Contrasting Definitions of the Situation 9
How This Book Analyzes Social Problems 11
Career Opportunities 14
References 15
Suggested Readings 16

Part One FORMING ONE'S BIOGRAPHY: PERSONAL PROBLEMS LEADING TO SOCIAL ISSUES 18

2. Crime, Juvenile Delinquency, and Administering Justice 21
I. Defining Crime and Delinquency 23
Incidence and Prevalence of Crime and Delinquency 28
Causes of Crime and Delinquency 31
Proposed Solutions to Crime and Delinquency 36
The Future of Crime and Delinquency 42
Summary 43
II. Defining the Administration of Justice 44
Incidence and Prevalence of the Problems of Administering Justice 53
Causes of the Problems of Administering Justice 59

Proposals to Solve the Problems of Administering Justice   62
The Future of the Administering of Justice   67
Summary   69
Career Opportunities   71
References   72
Suggested Readings   80

3. Problems of Drug and Alcohol Abuse   83

I. Defining the Drug Problem   85
Incidence and Prevalence of Drug Use   91
Causes of the Drug Problem   96
Proposed Solutions to the Drug Problem   100
The Future of the Drug Problem   105
II. Defining the Alcohol Problem   106
Incidence and Prevalence of Alcohol Abuse   110
Causes of Alcohol Abuse   114
Proposed Solutions to Alcohol Abuse   115
The Future of Alcohol Abuse   118
Summary   121
Career Opportunities   121
References   122
Suggested Readings   126

4. Changes in the Family and Sex Roles   129

Defining the Changes in the Family and Sex Roles   131
Incidence and Prevalence of Changes in the Family and Sex Roles   142
Causes of the Changes in the Family and Sex Roles   154
Proposed Solutions to the Changes in the Family and Sex Roles   159
The Future of the Changing Family and Sex Roles   169
Summary   173

Career Opportunities 174
References 175
Suggested Readings 182

Part Two GROUPS, IMMEDIATE SOCIAL ENVIRONMENT, AND SOCIAL ISSUES 184

5. Urban and Suburban Problems 187

Defining the Urban and Suburban Problems 189
Incidence and Prevalence of Urban and Suburban Problems 192
Causes of Urban and Suburban Problems 198
Proposed Solutions to Urban and Suburban Problems
The Future of Our Cities and Suburbs 215
Summary 218
Career Opportunities 219
References 220
Suggested Readings 226

6. Poverty and Inequality 229

Defining Poverty and Inequality 231
Incidence and Prevalence of Poverty and Inequality 237
Causes of Poverty and Inequality 241
Proposed Solutions to Poverty and Inequality 247
The Future of Poverty and Inequality 253
Summary 256
Career Opportunities 257
References 258
Suggested Readings 262

7. Problems of Minorities in America 265

Defining the Minority Problem 267
Incidence and Prevelence of the Minority Problem 272

Causes of the Minority Problem   286
Proposed Solutions to the Minority Problem   290
The Future of the Minority Problem   297
Summary   300
Career Opportunities   301
References   302
Suggested Readings   309

8. Problems of Aging and the Elderly   311
Defining the Problems of Aging and the Elderly   313
Incidence and Prevalence of the Problems of Aging and the Elderly   325
Causes of the Problems of Aging and the Elderly   328
Proposed Solutions to the Problems of Aging and the Elderly   331
The Future of the Problems of Aging and the Elderly   335
Summary   339
Career Opportunities   340
References   341
Suggested Readings   345

Part Three   INSTITUTIONS AND SOCIAL ISSUES   346

9. Problems in Education   349
Defining the Problems of Education   351
Incidence and Prevalence of the Problems of Education   356
Causes of the Problems of Education   361
Proposed Solutions to the Problems of Education   369
The Future of the Problems of Education   375
Summary   381
Career Opportunities   382
References   383
Suggested Readings   388

10. Problems of Corporate Power and Work 391

Defining Corporate Institutions and Power 393

Incidence and Prevalence of Problems of Corporate Power and Work 397

Causes of the Problems of Corporate Power and Work 415

Proposed Solutions to Problems of Corporate Power and Work 419

The Future of Our Corporate Institutions and Work 428

The Future of Work and Its Problems 429

Summary 434

Career Opportunities 436

References 436

Suggested Readings 442

11. Problems of the Medical and Health-Care Institutions 445

Defining the Health-Care Problem 447

Incidence and Prevalence of the Health-Care Problem 458

Causes of the Health-Care Problem 465

Proposed Solutions to Health-Care Problems 470

The Future of the Health-Care Problem 475

Summary 480

Career Opportunities 481

References 482

Suggested Readings 486

12. Labeling and Treating Mental Illness 489

Definitions of Mental Illness 492

Incidence and Prevalence of the Mental-Illness Problem 500

Causes of the Mental-Illness Problem 506

Proposed Solutions to Mental-Illness Problems　512
　　　The Future of the Mental-Illness Problem　518
　　　Summary　520
　　　Career Opportunities　521
　　　References　521
　　　Suggested Readings　525

Part Four INTERNATIONAL DIMENSIONS OF SOCIAL ISSUES　526

13. Big Government and the Military　529
　　　Defining the Problems of Big Government　532
　　　Incidence and Prevalence of Big Government　535
　　　Causes of Big Government and Military Power　547
　　　Proposed Solutions to Problems of Big Government and the Military　553
　　　The Future of Big Government and the Military　562
　　　Summary　567
　　　Career Opportunities　568
　　　References　568
　　　Suggested Readings　573

14. Problems of Ecology and Population Growth　575
　　　I. Defining the Ecological Problem　577
　　　Incidence and Prevalence of the Ecological Problem　579
　　　Causes of the Ecological Problem　585
　　　The Future of Our Environment　594
　　　II. Defining the Problem of Population Growth　597
　　　Incidence and Prevalence of Population Growth　598
　　　Causes of the Problem of Population Growth　603
　　　Proposed Solutions to the Problem of Population Growth　607
　　　The Future of Population Growth　609

Summary   613
Career Opportunities   614
References   615
Suggested Readings   622

15. Summary and Conclusions   627
Conclusions   628
Outlook for the Future   630
References   632
Suggested Readings   633

Index   635

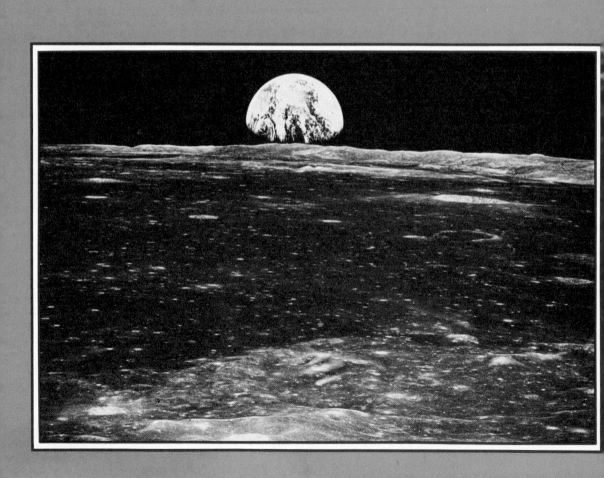

Introduction to Social Problems

INTRODUCTION
Cultural lag between technological progress and solving social problems.

DEFINITIONS
What is a social problem? Definitions by Richard Fuller and others.

Difficulties in defining social problems. Robert Merton's critique.

Robert Perruci and Marc Pilisuk's five factors affecting definitions of social problems.

Jerome Manis's new definition of social problems.

Primary, secondary, and tertiary problems.

ANALYZING AND SOLVING SOCIAL PROBLEMS
Six approaches used by sociologists.

Contrasting definitions of the situation.

How this book will deal with social problems.

The sociological imagination.

Personal troubles and social issues.

1 INTRODUCTION TO SOCIAL PROBLEMS

> We do not know what is happening to us and that is precisely the thing that is happening to us — **the fact** of not knowing what is happening to us.
>
> Ortega y Gasset, **Man and Crisis**, p. 119

As we enter the third century of our nation's existence, we still face a whole range of problems. But today the problems are somewhat different from those of 1776. We now live in a technological, rapidly changing, future-oriented society. We have taken giant steps in developing technology, but we lag behind in our ability to solve our social problems.

We live on an earth filled with problems, despite man's abilities to overcome earth's gravity by walking on the moon and by sending vehicles to explore the surface of Mars, our nearest neighbor in outer space. We are able to transport men and equipment millions of miles across outer space, but remain unable to master a system that can speed people across New York City or San Francisco. Although we explore outer space with ever more sophisticated equipment, millions turn to drugs and alcohol in desperate attempts to penetrate their own inner space. As we draw closer to understanding how the earth's life began and developed, we still have problems deciding how best to use the earth's environment. At the very moment we are making plans to house people in a space colony circling

Although we have developed the technological know-how to walk on the moon, a cultural lag remains between this knowledge and our ability to solve social problems on earth.

credit: Freelance Photographers Guild.

the earth, we are unable to implement plans for making houses available at prices young couples can afford.

As man's role in the universe becomes clearer and more certain, sex roles in our society become more confused and conflicting. We carefully nurse and analyze a handful of rocks and materials from outer space to understand the past, yet we tend to reject and ignore millions of elderly persons who are our chief social link with the past. So we achieve modern miracles with technology and discover new knowledge about life in space, while we displace millions of workers by applying our knowledge of new technology. As our world becomes a global village, socially linking and integrating all peoples of the earth, we still create racially segregated barriers and boundaries between black cities and white suburbs.

Our attitudes, values, and technological achievements in outer space contrast sharply with how much progress we still have to make in dealing with our social problems. Perhaps one of the reasons for this "cultural lag" (as sociologist William Ogburn called it) between technological progress and solving our social problems is that we cannot agree on the answers to two basic questions: (1) what *are* social problems? and (2) how should we analyze and attempt to solve them? Let us attempt an introductory answer to these questions, and look at the ways this book can help us to understand, analyze, and deal with social problems.

WHAT IS A SOCIAL PROBLEM?

Sociologists themselves disagree on what precisely constitutes a social problem. We can offer three definitions as an indication of the similarities and differences among sociologists.

The most widely accepted approach is founded upon Richard Fuller's definition of social problems, first offered in 1938. He wrote that "they represent a social condition which is regarded by a considerable number of individuals as undesirable, and hence these persons believe that something 'ought to be done' about the situation" (November 1938:419). This definition has both an objective and a subjective part. The persons may use objective facts or data to define a situation, such as an increase in abortion, as a problem. But, subjectively, some persons may not define this increase in abortion as a social problem.

Some sociologists, expanding upon Fuller's original concept, define social problems as "conditions deemed undesirable by large numbers of people" about which something can or should be done through some kind of collective social action (Manis, 1977:10).

Difficulties in Definitions

But there are difficulties inherent in these and similar definitions of social problems. It is assumed that society itself ultimately defines all social problems. For many years the ethical and moral standards of traditional Protestantism provided society with the implicit and explicit norms and values for determining what was or was not a social problem. According to sociologist Arthur Vidich, "under these standards social approval was given to the virtues of honesty, charity, sobriety, fidelity, monogamy, heterosexuality, work, self-control, self-discipline, and self-denial." By a simple process of reversal, "dishonesty and violence, divorce, infidelity, homosexuality, prostitution, illegitimacy, suicide, laziness, unemployment, loss of self-control through alcohol or drugs . . . and in general the refusal to accept existing social attitudes, became social problems" (Manis, 1976: vi). Some social problems are still defined in this way. Any serious deviance from accepted social and cultural norms (the mores) is usually considered a social problem.

Robert Merton, one of America's best-known sociologists, was among the first to point out difficulties with such definitions when he distinguished between manifest and latent social problems. A *manifest* problem is *recognized* by the public as a threat to major social values or norms. Crime is usually a manifest social problem. A *latent* social problem is one that is *unrecognized* as a threat to major social norms or values—such as the increased power of the military. This is one reason that definitions of what is or is not a social problem change over time. (Overpopulation and environmental pollution exemplify problems that have only recently become manifest. Alcohol and drinking—not alcoholism—is still pretty much a latent social problem.)

In addition to Robert Merton, sociologists Robert Perrucci and Marc Pilisuk see five major factors that affect our definitions of social problems:

1. Elites and groups in power, rather than the majority of the citizens, often define the problems.
2. Groups defining the problem may have a vested interest in labeling certain behavior or events as a problem.
3. There is a failure to define problems as coming from the social structure; instead, problems are defined as coming from personal characteristics.
4. Problems are defined strictly within the boundaries of a society or nation-state, without recognition or analysis of the problems on an international scale.
5. Current problems are so defined only after the public is made fully aware of them. Thus, the definition of social problems is past-oriented. Various parts of the social system that might produce problems in the future are ignored (1971: xvi–xvii).

Sociologists Malcolm Spector and John Kitsuse (1976) argue that social problems go through four stages, while Anthony Downs (1973: 108–9) sees five stages in what he calls the "Issue-Attention Cycle." They assume that through power, some vested interest group, speaking for a segment of the public, will define social problems.

A New Definition of Social Problems

To overcome the reliance on powerful interest groups or the public's own subjective feelings to define what constitutes a social problem, sociologist Jerome Manis has proposed a new definition of social problems. This one would use more objective and scientific means, rather than only the public's feelings, to gauge and determine what is and is not a social problem and just how serious a problem it is. Manis defines social problems as "those social conditions identified by scientific inquiry and values as detrimental to the well-being of human societies" (1977: 11). This definition envisions a much more central role for professionals and scholars, such as sociologists, psychologists, and political scientists, in defining social problems. It would also take into account the opinions of the public as "necessary but insufficient knowledge" for determining what is or is not a social problem. Sociological knowledge and scientific norms and values would be used so that the identification, nature, and seriousness of a social problem could be determined.

Manis's definition would be a far cry from merely relying upon the public's (or a public's) feelings. Nevertheless, there are pitfalls in such an objective, scientific approach to the definition of problems. Sociologists, even those with the best of intentions, cannot completely divorce their own values or beliefs in defining social problems. The best that can be hoped for is that conscious bias may be reduced and that a less subjective basis for defining problems will be used. In addition, attention can often be given to incipient social problems based upon the public's or a group's subjective feelings long before sufficient scientific evidence can be collected to verify a serious problem.

Using such a definition and a more objective approach, Manis maintains that sociologists and society would be better able to separate "primary," "secondary," and "tertiary" social problems. According to Manis, "primary social problems are influential social conditions which have multiple detrimental consequences for society." He classifies war, racism, and poverty as primary social problems, with their harmful effects defined as secondary or tertiary problems. Secondary social problems are "those harmful conditions resulting mainly from more influential social problems and in turn generating additional problems." Tertiary social problems are "harmful conditions which are, directly or indirectly, the results of more dominant problems" (1976: 18).

Figure 1-1 illustrates Manis's hypothesized connections between primary, secondary, and tertiary social problems.

In the "Defining" section of each chapter we will present various conflicting definitions of social problems to provide alternative perspectives by a variety of sociologists and segments of the public. A Millsian perspective, where appropriate, and others appear primarily under the "Causes" of each problem, while the more objective aspects of Manis's approach are incorporated into the "Incidence and Prevalence" section. "Proposed Solutions" to problems will discuss a variety of approaches that

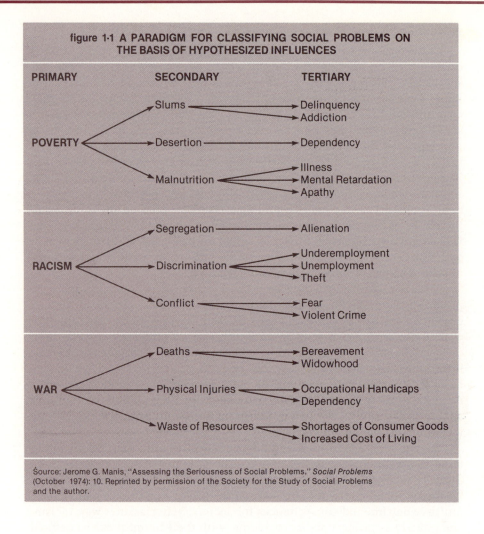

figure 1-1 A PARADIGM FOR CLASSIFYING SOCIAL PROBLEMS ON THE BASIS OF HYPOTHESIZED INFLUENCES

Source: Jerome G. Manis, "Assessing the Seriousness of Social Problems," *Social Problems* (October 1974): 10. Reprinted by permission of the Society for the Study of Social Problems and the author.

we believe should be included to understand the many proposals made by conservatives, liberals, and radicals to attempt to solve our social problems. Hence, throughout the book we combine an objective, scientific approach with the traditional subjective and social aspects of how social problems are defined.

ANALYZING AND SOLVING SOCIAL PROBLEMS

One reason for the lag between our technological progress and our inability to deal with social problems is a disagreement by sociologists, policy makers, and the public on how to define, analyze, and solve social problems. We shall be looking at a variety of perspectives by sociologists and nonsociologists, because before any social change can be made effectively, it must reflect the thinking of key policy makers or other segments of the public, as well as some sociologists.

Sociologists use different approaches in analyzing and offering solutions to our social ills. Among the most commonly accepted and recognized approaches, as summarized by McNall (1975: 7–8) and others are the following:

Social Pathology

According to the "social pathology" theory, social problems are caused by the poor, derelict, dependent, corrupt, and power-hungry persons both at the bottom and the top of society (although most problems come from those at the bottom). The solution to such social problems lies in educating or reeducating these groups. This approach equates problems with a social disease that, if eliminated, would make society function in a more nearly perfect way. It often assumes that, through "education," the social system can manage all problems (Berry, 1975: 104).

Social Disorganization

In this approach, sociologists see the breakdown or abuse of traditional social norms as the underlying cause of social problems. The "social disorganization" approach is built on the assumption that "society is a relatively persistent, stable structure; it is well-integrated, with every element having a function that helps maintain the system. Society has a consensus about its values" (Quinney, 1970: 9). The solution to social problems can be found in modifying parts of the system so that they function better. This usually means modifying individual behavior.

Value Conflicts

In this approach, sociologists contend that the difference in values lies at the basis of most social problems. Conflicts, personal and societal, arise when many sets of norms and values compete with one another in a rapidly changing culture and society. The "conflict model" (as opposed to the "social disorganization" model) assumes that "at every point society is subject to change; it displays dissension and conflict; every element contributes to change; and it is based on the coercion of some of its members by others" (Ibid., 9–10).

Society solves problems by equalizing power between conflicting groups. For unequal power serves only to maintain and prolong social problems by allowing the most powerful group to benefit from the social situation of the less powerful.

Deviant Behavior

From value conflicts, some sociologists began to focus on situations in which morals, norms, and laws were broken (just as the "social disorganization" approach had done). Here, emphasis is placed on the individual deviants involved in a problem, such as professional thieves, prostitutes, narcotic addicts, or delinquents, rather than on the social institutions and structures leading to such deviance. Although environmental conditions and circumstances are considered, the analysis focuses primarily on the deviant. This leads to what William Ryan calls "blaming the victim" (1976). Inadequate socialization and the person's unwillingness or inability to adhere to socially acceptable norms are viewed as the underlying cause of deviant behavior. The solution to all social problems lies in controlling the individual—by imprisonment, coercion, or reeducation.

Labeling Approach

Some sociologists examine how and why society tends to label certain behavior as deviant and other similar behavior as socially acceptable. For example, a young person who smokes a few marijuana cigarettes is labeled a deviant and a criminal; but the same young person can get drunk a few times, and people will say only that he has not yet learned to handle his liquor. The focus of the labeling approach is that deviant behavior is inherently neither functional nor dysfunctional for society; it is only the result of society's labeling that makes certain behavior a social problem.

This theory holds that deviance is due to society's creating rules or labels that designate certain behavior and certain persons as deviant. The labeling process may result in an intensification of a deviant role and impel persons to form or join a deviant subculture.

Whether a given act is deviant depends not on the nature of the act but on how other people react to it. Social problems change over time because the acts and targets of labeling change.

The solution to social problems becomes, then, a redefining or relabeling of behavior once considered a problem. For example, smoking marijuana in some states has now been relabeled (by law) as socially acceptable. Abortion and gambling have also been relabeled, although both were once considered very serious social problems.

Major Restructuring of Our Social Structure

This more radical sociological approach sees social problems as generated, nurtured, and developed by powerful elites that control our social structure and the whole society itself. To look at social pathology, social disorganization, deviant behavior, or labeling is to look at the results and symptoms caused by our existing elite-controlled social institutions and social structures. C. Wright Mills was one of the first scholars to point out

Social scientists test various theories and use diverse methodological approaches to analyze and understand social problems. Pictured here is Dr. Elisabeth Kübler-Ross, a social scientist who has called our attention to death and dying as a personal and social problem.

the difference between "personal problems" and "social issues" and to focus on our inequitable social institutions, instead of personal deviance, as the generator of social problems. The "primary" social problems stem from the way our society is structured and organized, and stacked against the poor, the minorities, and millions of desperate individuals who attempt to adapt to and survive within such an unjust social structure. The sociologists who follow this approach see the solutions to our social problems as a major overhaul or revolutionary change of our existing social structure. This requires radical institutional changes, with an eventual redistribution of income and power in our society.

Sociologists have found one of these six approaches, or a combination of them, to be useful tools for understanding, analyzing, and helping to solve our social problems. Each theory will be used where appropriate, and a combination of these approaches will be employed in discussing and analyzing social problems.

CONTRASTING DEFINITIONS OF THE SITUATION

Sociologist W. I. Thomas long ago pointed out the importance and necessity of taking into account the way in which the public (including sociologists) defines a situation. As he stated, "If men define situations as real, they are real in their consequences" (1923: 42). According to Thomas this applies at both the personal and social levels. When persons come to define or attempt to solve a social problem, they bring to bear certain conscious or unconscious ideologies, usually connected with their social status or group membership. These perspectives involve much more than just political labels or preference for a certain political party or candidate. According to Kenneth and Patricia Dolbeare, "ideologies are beliefs about the present nature of the world and the hopes one has for its future." They observe that "such beliefs and hopes, when integrated into a more or less coherent picture of (1) how the present social, economic, and political order operates; (2) why this is so, and whether it is good or bad; and (3) what should be done about it, if anything, may be termed an 'ideology'" (1971: 3). Thus, ideology affects how one defines and attempts to solve social problems.

In our society three major alternative ideologies (among others) are used to define and attempt to solve social problems. These ideological perspectives are conservative, liberal, and radical, according to the classification system of John Williamson, Jerry Boren, and Linda Evans (1974: v). Since these terms deal with ideology on a continuum, "often they can be classified equally well as optimistic or pessimistic or according to the perspectives of different interest groups" (Ibid.).

According to these three sociologists, conservative ideology is of two kinds in America today: "individualistic-conservatism, with the major emphasis on individual freedom, particularly freedom from government coercion, and organic conservatism, emphasizing a reverence for . . . society as the product of the traditions, institutions, and cumulative wisdom of the past" (Ibid., 8). Conservatives look for authority, social order, and freedom (within limits) and frequently oppose proposed changes by liberals or radicals as rash, revolutionary, or unnecessary. Social change may not be beneficial to society or individuals, they maintain. They support laissez-faire capitalism and the free-enterprise system, private property, and individual effort and initiative. They object to big government, social-welfare programs, and any outside interference with the free-enterprise system, unless it directly benefits business.

Liberal ideology also values individualism and freedom, but more emphasis is placed on civil liberties, due process, equality, and other rights "as means for protecting the individual against the power of the state" (Ibid., 10). The liberal view of power is referred to as "pluralism." Power seems to be dispersed among a wide range of interest groups rather than concentrated in the hands of a power elite or a ruling class. The result of pluralism is social reform, based on compromise. Liberal policies and proposals are likely to reflect the middle range of alternatives being presented to reform or change a social problem.

Social change, along with political stability and avoidance of violent conflict or radical changes in social structure, is the basic liberal objective.

The liberal "calls for reforms in the political and economic systems, but does not question the overall framework. He is quite willing to press for change using established procedures within the system," especially the federal government (Ibid., 12).

Radical ideology is referred to as Marxism or neo-Marxism. Its adherents believe that the economic structure of society basically determines social reality. It refers to thinkers who

> (1) see the character of economic organization as the basic factor in shaping a society's value system, social class structure, and political institutions and practices; (2) see a capitalist economy as creating profit-oriented, materialist values and a class structure in which wealthy owners constitute a ruling class that uses the power of the state, both at home and abroad, in exploitative and selfish ways; and (3) believe that such a social system is unjust, unnecessary, inconsistent with man's nature, and should be eliminated — peacefully or, if necessary, by force (Dolbeare and Dolbeare, 1971: 185).

The radical ideology points to great economic concentration of power and wealth in the major corporations and criticizes our economy for wasting so much money and resources on materialistic trinkets or on the military while neglecting basic human and material needs. Modern technology and bureaucracy, they argue, have benefited the power elites more than the masses.

HOW THIS BOOK ANALYZES SOCIAL PROBLEMS

As we present the definitions of and proposed solutions to social problems, the meanings behind these ideologies will be evident (implicitly or explicitly) whenever the terms conservative, liberal, or radical are used. In some chapters, other slightly different terms are utilized, such as "challengers" and "defenders" of the family or adherents to the "idealized model" and the "reality model" of medical care.

Williamson, Boren, and Evans maintain that deviance and social-disorganization theories "are commonly used by liberals and conservatives," while the conflict and "restructuring social structure" theories are used by radicals. This book employs a variety of sociological and social theories to explain social problems, since no one theory can claim to explain adequately all social issues. Our preference is for the liberal approach and the theoretical approaches of C. Wright Mills, especially to explain the root causes of many social problems. He and likeminded sociologists, such as Spector and Kitsuse, stress that inequality of power, which stems from our existing social structure, explains many of our present social problems. This theory will be developed and used in appropriate chapters, such as those concerning economic and political institutions.

When we describe and analyze social problems, we often have an ethnocentric view of issues, as though they affect our society alone. Sociologists must begin to develop a more global view of social problems. The Arabian Peninsula, most of the coastline of Africa from the Mediterranean Sea, and Antarctica can be seen in this first-ever view of the earth from outer space. Can you see the United States?

The Sociological Imagination

Since the four major parts of this book are based upon Mills's distinction between "personal troubles or problems" and "social issues," let us briefly explore this distinction. In *The Sociological Imagination* (1959), Mills wrote that modern man often feels trapped by his private life and "personal problems." But the reason for this frustration is that the individual fails to see the connection between his own life and what is happening in society.

So, Mills urged people to develop a quality of mind he called the "sociological imagination." If we use it, it enables us to grasp history and our own biography, as well as the social relationships between the two. For effective use of one's sociological imagination, three crucial questions (among others) must be asked and answered:

1. What is the structure of our society as a whole—its essential parts and their connections to one another?
2. Where does our society "stand in human history," and how is it changing?
3. What varieties of men and women presently prevail, and what kinds are coming to dominate?

These and other questions, and answers to them, enable a person to use "sociological imagination."

Personal Troubles and Social Issues

Another essential tool of the sociological imagination is to perceive and employ the distinction between "personal troubles" and "social issues." "Troubles" occur within the character of the individual and in his face-to-face relations with others in his immediate social setting (or "milieu," as Mills calls it). Thus, "troubles" are things that happen to individuals within limited areas of social life of which they are directly and personally aware. Personal problems or troubles are a private matter in which values cherished by an individual are felt to be threatened.

In sharp contrast, "social issues" involve matters that transcend the individual, his immediate social setting, and his personal character. Public issues concern the way many social settings are organized into the social institutions as a whole and the ways that different social "milieux" overlap and penetrate one another to form the structure of society and historical life. A "social issue" is a public matter, and cannot be clearly defined according to the personal experiences of individuals in their immediate social setting (unlike a "personal trouble").

A social issue often involves a crisis in social institutions and institutional arrangements, according to his analysis. Mills gives us some examples of the differences between "personal troubles" and "social issues" for the social problems of unemployment and marriage. He writes:

> Consider unemployment. When in a city of 100,000, only one man is unemployed, that is his personal trouble. . . . But when in a nation of 50 million employees, 15 million men are unemployed, that is an issue, and we may not hope to find its solution within the range of opportunities open to any one individual. The very structure of opportunities has collapsed. Both the correct statement of the problem and the range of possible solutions require us to consider the economic and political institutions of the society, and not merely the personal situation and character of a scatter of individuals. . . .
>
> Consider marriage. Inside a marriage a man and a woman may experience personal troubles, but when the divorce rate during the first four years of marriage is 250 out of every 1,000 attempts, this is an indication of a structural issue having to do with the institutions of marriage and the family and other institutions that bear upon them . . . (1959: 25–26).

His point is that one way to study social problems is to analyze the role of social structure and institutions in the causes and possible solutions of social issues. Of course, this is only one theoretical approach and method for studying social problems. Many other theories will be used throughout the book where appropriate.

According to Spector and Kitsuse, Mills failed to recognize that private troubles might be transformed into public issues. The most private trouble may become a social issue through some group's taking collective action to remedy an undesirable "personal" condition (Spector and Kitsuse, 1976: 8).

Let us turn our attention now to Part One of the book to see how personal problems often become society's problems and issues.

CAREER OPPORTUNITIES

Sociologists.

Sociologists study the many groups formed by people in society. They study the behavior and interaction of these groups; trace their origin and growth; analyze the influence of group activities on people; and identify, analyze, and help to solve social problems. Employment is expected to increase through the mid-1980s. Most new positions will be in college teaching (two- and four-year colleges). For further information write to: American Sociological Association, 1722 N St., N. W., Washington, D.C. 20036.

Social Workers.

Social problems have greatly expanded the need for social services. Social workers—through casework, group work, community organization, research, and administration—assist persons, families, and groups in using social services to solve their problems. Federal, state, county, and city government agencies employ about two-thirds of such workers. Rapid growth in employment is expected in future. Bilingual persons (particularly those who speak Spanish) have a great advantage when pursuing a career in social work. For further information write to: National Association of Social Workers, 600 Southern Building, 15th and H Sts., N. W., Washington, D.C. 20005.

Statisticians and Opinion Pollsters.

Statisticians work with numbers and symbols. They may teach or do research at a large university; work in a government agency; or work in industry. Some work in well-known public-opinion research organizations to find out what people think about particular social issues. With the computer the work of the statistician has expanded. Future need for statisticians will be great, and starting salaries are good. For further information write to: American Statistical Association, 806 15th Street, N. W., Washington, D.C. 20006.

REFERENCES

Antonio, Robert J. and George Ritzer, eds.
    1975   Social Problems: Values and Interests in Conflict. Boston: Allyn & Bacon.

Becker, Howard
    1963   Outsiders: Studies in the Sociology of Deviance. New York: Free Press.

Bernstein, Arnold and Henry Lennard
    1973   "The American Way of Drugging." Society 10, 4 (May/June): 14–25.

Berry, David
    1975   Central Ideas in Sociology: An Introduction. Itasca, Ill.: Peacock.

Dolbeare, Kenneth and Patricia Dolbeare
    1971   American Ideologies. Chicago: Markham.

Downs, Anthony
    1973   "The Issue-Attention Cycle." The Futurist (June): 108–9.

"Economy and Crime Top Concerns; Most Voters Confused on Stands." Allentown Morning Call (June 3): 1, 1976.

Fuller, Richard
    1938   "The Problem of Teaching Social Problems." American Journal of Sociology 44 (November): 415–35.

Fuller, Richard and Richard Myers
    1941   "The Natural History of a Social Problem." American Sociological Review 6 (June): 320–28.

Lauderdale, Pat
    1976   "Deviance and Moral Boundaries." American Sociological Review 41 (August): 660–76.

McNall, Scott
    1975   Social Problems Today. Boston: Little, Brown.

Manis, Jerome
    1976   Analyzing Social Problems. New York: Praeger.
    1977   "Assessing the Seriousness of Social Problems." Pp. 10–17 in Anne Kilbride, ed. Readings in Social Problems 77/78. Annual Editions. Guilford, Conn.: Dushkin.

Mills, C. Wright
    1956   The Power Elite. New York: Oxford University Press.
    1958   "The Structure of Power in American Society." The British Journal of Sociology 9, 1 (March): 23–38.
    1959   The Sociological Imagination. New York: Oxford University Press.

Perrucci, Robert and Marc Pilisuk
    1971   The Triple Revolution Emerging: Social Problems in Depth. Boston: Little, Brown.

Quinney, Richard
    1970   The Social Reality of Crime. Boston: Little, Brown.

Reich, Charles
    1970   The Greening of America. New York: Random House.

Reissman, Leonard
    1972   "The Solution Cycle of Social Problems." The American Sociologist 7, 2 (February): 7–9.

Ryan, William
 1976 Blaming the Victim, rev., updated ed. New York: Random House.

Shostak, Arthur B.
 1976 "Looking into an Uncertain Future: Some Means, Problems and Possibilities." Paper delivered at 1975-76 Indiana-Michigan Conference of Danforth Associates (April 9).

Spector, Malcolm and John Kitsuse
 1976 "Social Problems: A Re-Formulation." Pp. 6-13 in Anne Kilbride, ed. Readings in Social Problems 76/77: Annual Editions. Guilford, Conn.: Dushkin.

Thomas, William I.
 1923 The Unadjusted Girl. Boston: Little, Brown.

Turner, Jonathan H.
 1972 American Society: Problems of Structure. New York: Harper & Row.

Wickman, Peter
 1976 "Perspectives: The Nature and Study of Social Problems." Pp. 2-5 in Anne Kilbride, ed. Readings in Social Problems 76/77: Annual Editions. Guilford, Conn.: Dushkin.

Williamson, John B., Jerry Boren, and Linda Evans, eds.
 1974 Social Problems: The Contemporary Debate. Boston: Little, Brown.

SUGGESTED READINGS

Antonio, Robert J. and George Ritzer, eds. Social Problems: Values and Interests in Conflict. Boston: Allyn & Bacon, Inc., 1975.
Views problems at individual, group, and institutional levels, analyzing each one on the basis of conflicting social values and interests.

Campbell, Angus, Philip E. Converse, and Willard L. Rodgers. The Quality of American Life: Perceptions, Evaluations and Satisfactions. New York: Russell Sage Foundation, 1976.
An empirical study that attempts to gauge how the American people view a large number of social issues affecting their lives. Good measurements are used in developing various social indicators of the quality of life and satisfaction among Americans.

Douglas, Jack D. Defining America's Social Problems. Englewood Cliffs, N.J.: Prentice-Hall, 1974.
Probes the social factors accounting for different definitions of and proposed solutions to social problems.

Gorham, William and Nathan Glazer, eds. The Urban Predicament. Washington, D.C.: The Urban Institute, 1976.
Some of sociology's best-known scholars synthesize insights about problems of crime, education, transportation, housing, and the economy. Definitions, causes, and analysis of social problems are presented, but few solutions are proposed.

Kinsley, Michael. Outer Space and Inner Sanctums: Government, Business and Satellite Communication. New York: Wiley, 1976.
Depicts the innovations and complexity involved in modern coordination and cooperation of major social institutions to link the world closer together by satellite communications. It also shows how groups may resist change when it is not to their advantage to accept it.

U.S. Bureau of the Census. Status: A Monthly Chartbook of Social and Economic Trends, 1976.
This new publication has a superb collection of charts and graphs, as well as up-to-date data on people, the community, economy, and trends for measuring most social problems.

Periodicals Worth Exploring
The Futurist
Journal of Social Issues
The Public Interest
Public Opinion Quarterly
Science and Society
Social Forces
Social Policy
Social Problems
Social Research
Society

PART ONE

One of the most important lessons a student can learn from a social-problems course is that there is a link between personal problems and his social environment. Certain environments compel individuals to adapt or react to their life situations in particular ways. This often leads to social issues, especially when millions of persons, because of their social situation, begin to act in similar ways.

In this part of the book we examine a number of social problems that appear to originate out of the "personal troubles" of individuals. We will concentrate on those limited areas of social life of which a person is directly and personally aware.

When young persons have their desires for money, prestige, or status blocked because of their environment and social structure, they turn to alternative ways of satisfying their personal needs. Some do it in socially unacceptable ways. Thus, personal problems may lead to social problems, such as crime and delinquency. Law-abiding citizens may also view crime as a personal problem, involving their own personal safety, security, and well-being.

Forming One's Biography: Personal Problems Leading to Social Issues

In our society drinking has been viewed as one readily available way of soothing and easing one's personal troubles. But when millions of individuals begin to drink or take drugs to excess, society labels them as alcoholics or drug addicts and a large-scale social issue comes to the fore. What starts out as a personal solution to a personal problem soon becomes a social issue.

The family is often considered the last sacred bastion of personal privacy and comfort, a haven for personal peace, contentment, and happiness. Too often, the family, the basic unit of every society, becomes a hell. It is usually within the family that most persons learn what it is to be a man or a woman. Yet individuals often seek to grow out of the family-imposed mold of what a man or woman should be. Individuals begin to look for and follow new patterns of sexual and social behavior outside the traditional family. This striving for personal development and fulfillment at the expense of the family soon becomes a social problem.

Thus, persons responding to their immediate problems and troubles in a similar way soon produce critical social issues.

Crime, Juvenile Delinquency, and Administering Justice

I. Crime and Juvenile Delinquency

DEFINITIONS OF THE PROBLEM
Relative definitions based on law and custom.
Three kinds of crime: (a) street crime, (b) "suite" crime—occupational (white-collar) crime, and (c) victimless crime (morals).

INCIDENCE AND PREVALENCE OF THE PROBLEM
Upswing in reported crime since early 1960s.
Stabilization of crime in 1976.
Unreported crime at least twice as high as reported crime.

CAUSES OF THE PROBLEM
Various theories from biological to sociological.
Sociological theories: anomie (Robert Merton), differential association (Edwin Sutherland), differential opportunities (Cloward and Ohlin), and labeling (Howard Becker).
Delinquency theories: subcultural theories and control theory (Travis Hirschi).

PROPOSED SOLUTIONS TO THE PROBLEM
More uniform laws.
Primary, secondary, and tertiary prevention of crime.
Outlawing handguns.
Improved police technology.
Social intervention and nonintervention.
Radical social change.

FUTURE OF THE PROBLEM
Fewer births may mean less crime.
Future values and beliefs about crime.

SUMMARY

II. Administration of Justice

DEFINITIONS OF THE PROBLEM
Liberal and radical definitions of injustice of police, courts, and prisons.
Conservative and public's definitions of system as too lax on law offenders.
Police discretion, discrimination, and corruption.
Courts backlogs, inadequate representation of poor, bail and plea bargaining, irrational sentencing.
Prisons: overcrowding, and social costs.

INCIDENCE AND PREVALENCE OF PROBLEM
Only 20 of 100 criminals are caught, and only three go to prison.
Reported abuse is limited, and public (except blacks and youth segment) has confidence in police.
Court cases have doubled in last 10 years but judges increased only 25 percent.
About 350,000 were in prisons in 1975.
Overcrowding, violence, and understaffing are crucial problems in most prisons.

CAUSES OF THE PROBLEMS
Changes in traditional values and norms.
System designed to affect the powerless and poor.
Courts protect and perpetuate existing economic, political, and social systems.
Immediate causes of problems of police, courts, and prisons.

PROPOSED SOLUTIONS TO THE PROBLEM
Improved community–police relations.
Legal changes to limit judges' powers; other judicial innovations.
Deinstitutionalizing the prison system and the revolution against it.
Community-based corrections; democratic participation in running prisons.

FUTURE OF THE PROBLEM
Decline in future crime due to decriminalization of acts.
More professionalized police force.
Not much change in court system.
Innovations in prisons, using social-science techniques.
"New breed" prison officials.
Abandonment of prisons.

SUMMARY

Adam, Eve and Cain committed the worst offenses possible, and after Abel was killed, all survivors — or 75 percent of the first four human beings — had criminal records.

From Kurt Weis and Michael Milakovitch, "Political Misuses of Crime Rates," **Society** 11, 5 (July/August 1974): 91.

I. DEFINING CRIME AND DELINQUENCY

Crime is as old as man himself. Technically "crime" did not arise until nation-states established formal rational laws, but some people have always violated generally accepted norms and rules. There has always been "too much" crime. A presidential commission has reported that "virtually every generation since the founding of the nation and before has felt itself threatened by the specter of rising crime and violence" (1967: 19).

Although society considers delinquency and crime a social issue, the person committing a crime considers it a short-term solution to a personal problem. He may need money to feed a drug habit. A person may find an "easy way" to make a good living. We may rig a contract or pad a bill to make ends meet, or may find an answer to our powerlessness and frustration.

Relative Definitions

Crime is defined as *any act that violates a law*. Hence, it is defined relative to laws, and varies

from society to society
from state to state
from time to time
from strict enforcement to none.

Conservatives, liberals, and radicals all have different notions as to what kinds of behavior should be considered a crime. Over time, the definition of criminal behavior changes due to conflicting values and social forces in our society. Until 1973, abortion was a crime; now most is legal. Sunday shopping used to be illegal; now it is accepted in some states and towns. Heroin and opium were legal in America until 1914 when steps were taken to control its distribution and tax it. Even Coca-Cola contained cocaine until 1903 (Stark, 1975: 158). During the 1920s, drinking or possessing alcohol was a crime. Now it is not, in most areas of the country.

Law enforcement defines the *real* limits of crime. For example, in an experiment with 15 students who had "Black Panther" bumper stickers on their cars, the law was strictly enforced. All the students had had "exemplary" driving records before the experiment. As reported:

> The first student received a ticket for making an "incorrect lane change" on the freeway less than two hours after heading home in the rush hour traffic. Five more tickets were received by others for "following too closely," failing to yield the right of way," "driving too slowly in the high-speed lane of the freeway," "failure to make a proper signal before turning right at an intersection," and "failure to observe proper safety of pedestrians using a crosswalk." On day three, students were cited for "excessive speed," "making unsafe lane changes" and "driving erratically." And so it went every day ... Altogether the participants received 33 citations in 17 days (Heussenstamm, 1971: 32).

So crime is defined relative to the society, state, time, or degree of enforcement.

Types of Crime

Besides defining the problem of crime, one must examine the different kinds of crime and criminals. Better known as "delinquency," errant juvenile behavior is often labeled as a kind of crime. Delinquency entails offenses by minors that may or may not be crimes if committed by an adult. In many states, juveniles can be arrested for smoking cigarettes, walking on railroad tracks, skipping school, and being "incorrigible" or sexually promiscuous. There are dozens of other vaguely defined acts that would not be punishable, or not as severely, if committed by an adult. For example, in the famous 1967 Supreme Court decision in the *Gault* case, Gerald Gault, age 15, was accused of making lewd phone calls to a woman. He was given a six-year sentence at the Arizona State "Industrial School" for "committing an offense for which an adult would have been fined five to 50 dollars or jailed not more than two months" (Zietz, 1969: 138). Because young people hold no positions of power or authority in our "corporate society," their rights are often ignored.

About 60 percent of all juvenile "crimes" are "status offenses"—that is, not a crime in the generally accepted sense. Yet the status offenders are treated as criminals. On the other hand, a majority of such crimes as stealing cars, larceny, and burglary are committed by persons under 18. So juvenile "crime" is defined to include both criminal and noncriminal acts.

But other kinds of crimes exist. When people define or perceive crime, they usually have a specific kind in mind. Three major kinds of crime are:

1. "Crime in the streets": direct acts against person or property. Such crime involves nonprofessional and professional criminals.
2. "Crime in the Suites": white-collar (occupational) and organized criminals from political "dirty tricks" to illegal wiretapping by the FBI or CIA; the category ranges from corporate culprits who fix prices to the Mafia.

3. Crimes without victims: policing people's morals for drinking or drugs, and for homosexuality or prostitution.

Those who engage in "street crime" are often the "losers" and the powerless in a social structure stacked against them. To get money, prestige, status, and recognition, persons who can get them no other way turn to street crime. The most successful are the professional criminals. They are dedicated to a life of crime; they earn their living by it, and take pride in their accomplishments. They include safecrackers, full-time shoplifters, truck hijackers, and fences for stolen goods.

Crime in the suites is (occupational) white-collar and organized crime. White-collar crimes are committed by businesspersons, politicians, and professionals. First studied by Edwin Sutherland, this behavior was defined as "crime committed by a person of respectability and high social status in the course of his occupation" (Sutherland, 1961: 9). The public usually does not define such acts as crime, and the occasional public outrage is muffled and stifled. Prosecution and conviction for them are rare, and frequently they are omitted from crime statistics. Yet most of the crime in our society occurs in the executive suites, not in the streets. Since executives are an important part of the "corporate state," serving the power elites, their crimes are often disregarded. The selection by Russell Baker humorously points out this social fact.

CLEARANCE   Russell Baker

One of the last great bargains in the age of 35-cent candy bars and 65-cent gasoline is crime.

The bargain-conscious gentleman who pointed this out to me is an executive in a large corporation, a man professionally quick at the science of holding down budgets while increasing profit. In today's market, he believes, crime is such a bargain that big companies ought to be setting up legitimate crime divisions to fulfill their obligation to stockholders to maximize profits.

His point is that while the cost of everything else from meat to men's socks has been rising like corn in Iowa, the cost of committing the most profitable crimes has not gone up in 20, 30, in some cases, 40 years.

Recently, for example, several big companies and their executives were caught in the highly profitable business of making illegal campaign contributions, and were convicted. Although the contributions ranged from $25,000 to $100,000, the maximum fine for each guilty company was only $5,000; for each executive, only $1,000.

At these prices, the companies and their bosses would have been failing their stockholders if they had not chosen crime over law and order. Crime was a great buy and the capital risks were negligible. . . .

Source: Russell Baker, "Clearance," *New York Times Magazine* (June 16, 1974): 6.

Giant aircraft firms and other corporations entertain top government officials at their "hunting and fishing lodges," where high-class prostitutes are provided—all this at the taxpayers' expense. Corporate contributions and bribes to government officials and political parties, even to foreign officials by major oil firms, are considered by many a normal expense of doing business. Since these crimes are committed by persons with power and prestige, their behavior is often rationalized or, if brought to trial, they are found not guilty because of the top legal talent they can afford to hire. The resignation of Bert Lance from the Carter administration illustrates how society may react to white-collar crime.

Not only "white-collar" crime but also "organized crime" is a major social issue. The most successful and wealthy criminals are those who run the rackets, the syndicate, the Mafia—organized crime. They are respectable because of their power, but they use violence when needed. Their crime is different from "street" crime, for it has a power hierarchy and a structure. It exercises monopolistic control and influence and depends on violence to stay in business. Since its tentacles touch police and courtroom alike, it has a high degree of immunity from the law.

It is very difficult to obtain convictions against leaders of organized crime because witnesses are both scarce and scared. Those who use the services of the "syndicate" seldom complain. Only the Feds are organized

Organized-crime leaders control various illegal activities and resort to violence to enforce discipline and loyalty to "the family."

credit: © 1972 by Paramount Pictures Corp. All rights reserved.

credit: Charles Gatewood

As sex roles change and society becomes more permissive, sex is bought and sold as a profitable commodity. Prostitution is defined as a crime and takes up much of the police's and court's time in trying to curb such victimless crime.

to tackle such crime, and when they get a family leader it is usually for income-tax evasion, lying under oath, or some other infraction of the law. If convicted such criminals get very light sentences.

"Victimless" crime is committed by those who violate society's morals and mores. The real problem of trying to enforce people's morals is that it diverts law-enforcement agencies from fighting major and more serious crimes. It also clogs the courts and jails with minor offenders who are not hardened or dangerous criminals. The seven "index" crimes—allegedly the most serious crimes, as reported by the FBI—are murder, forcible rape, robbery, aggravated assault, burglary, theft (larceny over $50), and auto theft. Yet Kurt Weis and Michael Milakovich observed that "less than 10 percent of those arrested are charged with any of these offenses" (1975: 4). Conservatives argue that most immoral behavior should be made a crime, while liberals feel a person's constitutional rights are more important. Radicals maintain that most personal behavior should never be controlled by law or society.

Defining a Subculture

The notion of a "subculture" is important in understanding some causal theories of delinquency and crime. As used by sociologists, a subculture is "a group within a culture that holds beliefs, norms or customs different from those of the larger culture" (Stark, 1975: 37). Most sociologists who view the commission of crime and delinquency as subcultural see such acts as conforming to the norms of subcultures that differ from the dominant middle-class culture of American society. They also explain the nature and distribution of such subcultures as due to the structure and power of the larger society and other social factors.

INCIDENCE AND PREVALENCE OF CRIME AND DELINQUENCY

The incidence and prevalence of crime and delinquency are severe and widespread. Every minute, 21 serious crimes are committed—about one every three seconds. Every year about 20,000 persons are murdered. Every 10 seconds someone breaks into a building to burglarize it. Every 32 seconds a car is stolen; every 38 minutes someone is robbed, raped, assaulted, or killed (*Uniform Crime Reports*, 1975: 9). Over two-and-a-half billion dollars' worth of goods is stolen every year ("Crime Rate, Teen Arrests Show a Sharp Increase," 1975: 2). Juvenile crime alone costs our society about $12 billion a year ("Children and the Law," 1975: 71). Yet we see in the *Uniform Crime Reports* only the tip of the iceberg. Since these are official measures of crime, they are often better indicators of police than of criminal behavior. We do not know how much "dark-side" (unreported) crime really exists.

Having issued our disclaimer about the dependability of the official figures, let us now look at what the reports of crime and delinquency reveal. (Unless stated otherwise, figures are from the FBI's *Uniform Crime Reports*.)

Recent Stabilization of Crime

During 1975, the number of major crimes (seven "index" crimes) in the United States increased by nearly 10 percent over the previous year. However, each quarter the rate of increase dropped slightly, reaching only 4 percent greater in the last quarter of 1975. In 1976 the only crime showing an increase was theft (larceny), up 5 percent. All other crimes decreased or remained steady. Overall there was no reported increase or decrease in crime during 1976. During the first quarter of 1977, reported crime dropped 9 percent, as compared with the same period in 1976.

Violent crimes, as a group, rose 5.3 percent in 1975 over 1974. In 1976 such crimes were down 3.9 percent. Table 2-1 shows the change in number and percentage of the seven major index crimes in 1976.

However it is measured, crime has become a serious social issue. In 1976 about one million violent crimes were reported. Since the early 1960s, the rate of all serious crimes has doubled. From 1973 to 1974, it

table 2-1 PERCENTAGE AND NUMERICAL INCREASES OF THE SEVEN MAJOR "INDEX" CRIMES IN 1975

	NUMBER	PERCENTAGE CHANGE OVER 1974
MURDER	18,780	−8.4
FORCIBLE RAPE	56,730	1.1
ROBBERY	420,210	−9.6
AGGRAVATED ASSAULT	490,850	1.3
BURGLARY	3,089,800	−5.0
THEFT — LARCENY	6,270,800	4.9
AUTO THEFT	957,600	−4.3
ALL VIOLENT CRIME	986,580	0.9
ALL PROPERTY CRIME	10,318,200	0.9
TOTAL PERCENTAGE INCREASE		0.4

Source: Uniform Crime Reports, 1976.

jumped 17 percent, the largest increase in the 44 years for which the FBI has been collecting crime figures. In 1975 it rose another 10 percent. Since 1976, reported crime figures showed crime somewhat under control. In 1976 preliminary figures show major crime increased 3 percent in large cities having over one million people but declined or stabilized in population areas of 50,000 to 1,000,000 (Uniform Crime Reports, Preliminary Annual Release, March 30, 1977: 1). Most reported crime declined in 1976 as compared with 1975. Only larceny increased (by about 5 percent), while the other crimes remained the same or dropped 5 to 10 percent. Crime in the Northeast jumped 5 percent, while it declined slightly in the Midwest. In early 1977 the figures on reported crime showed another downward trend.

Violent crimes since the early 1960s have risen faster and higher than the national average of all crimes. As Figure 2-1 shows, the four major violent crimes—murder, rape, robbery, and aggravated assault—have soared since 1961, until declining slightly in 1976.

Of all crime figures, those for murder are the most reliable. In 1976 over 20,000 Americans were murdered. A Chicago study showed that the risk of physical assault was one in 77 for a black slum dweller, one in 2,000 for members of the white middle class, and one in 10,000 for upper-middle-class suburbanites (Loftus, 1969: 79).

To the degree that arrest figures are any gauge of crime, then delinquency and youth crime represent a large and disproportionate part of the problem. Seventy-five percent of all arrests for major crimes in 1975 were of teenagers and young adults (under 25). Forty-five percent of all murders are committed by persons 25 or younger. If we do not count murder, then 75 percent of arrestees for street crimes are persons under 25, and 45 percent are under 18. Age 15 is the peak age for violent crimes ("The

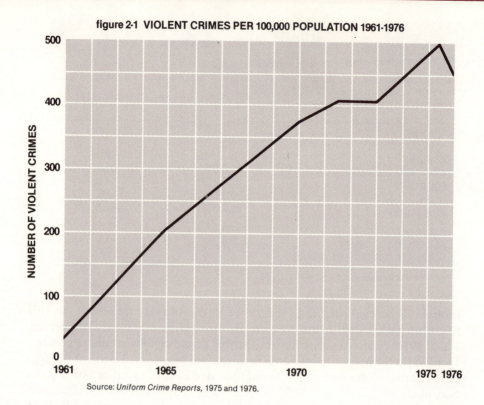

figure 2-1 VIOLENT CRIMES PER 100,000 POPULATION 1961-1976

Source: *Uniform Crime Reports*, 1975 and 1976.

Crime Wave," 1975: 11). A survey covering an eight-year period in Philadelphia, prepared by the well-known sociologist and criminologist Marvin Wolfgang, showed that out of 10,000 boys, 3,475 were delinquents; of those, 627 were "chronic" offenders. This small percentage of chronic offenders was responsible for two-thirds of the violent acts and over half of *all* offenses committed by the group (Loftus, 1969: 1, 79). Mayor Thomas Maloney of Wilmington, Delaware, pointed out in 1976 that 16 juvenile delinquents in that city were responsible for 384 serious crimes (an average of over 20 crimes per juvenile).

A study by the United States Law Enforcement Assistance Administration and the Census Bureau discovered that "half the crimes in the nation's five largest cities are not being reported to the police" (Weis and Milakovich, 1975: 91). The National Institute of Law Enforcement and Criminal Justice undertook a Pilot Cities Victimization Study in eight cities (Atlanta, Baltimore, Cleveland, Dallas, Denver, Newark, Portland, and St. Louis), surveying 200,000 persons in all. The findings confirmed that official police statistics reflect less than *half* the total number of serious crimes reported.

A 1974 National Crime Panel survey of 24,000 persons in 13 cities revealed a similar pattern—actual crime is *at least* twice as high as official statistics report. Table 2-2 shows the rates of victimization by crime and the ratio of unreported crime to actual crime, in the 13 cities surveyed.

CAUSES OF CRIME AND DELINQUENCY

Long lists of causes, varying from the biological to the sociological, are given for crime and delinquency.

table 2-2 — CRIME VICTIMIZATION IN 13 SELECTED CITIES

	CRIME VICTIMIZATION RATE PER 1,000 RESIDENTS 12 AND OVER				HOUSEHOLD VICTIMIZATION PER 1,000 HOUSEHOLDS			COMMERCIAL VICTIMIZATION PER 1,000 BUSINESS ESTABLISHMENTS		
	Crimes of Violence	Rape and Attempted Rape	Robbery	Assault	Burglary	Household Larceny	Auto Theft	Burglary	Robbery	RATIO OF UNREPORTED CRIME TO REPORTED CRIME
DETROIT	68	3	32	33	174	106	49	615	179	2.7 to 1
DENVER	67	3	17	46	158	168	44	443	54	2.9 to 1
PHILADELPHIA	63	1	28	34	109	87	42	390	116	5.1 to 1
PORTLAND, ORE.	59	3	17	40	151	149	34	355	39	2.6 to 1
BALTIMORE	56	1	26	28	116	100	35	578	135	2.2 to 1
CHICAGO	56	3	26	27	118	77	36	317	77	2.8 to 1
CLEVELAND	54	2	24	28	124	80	76	367	77	2.4 to 1
LOS ANGELES	53	2	16	35	148	131	42	311	47	2.9 to 1
ATLANTA	48	2	16	30	161	102	29	741	157	2.3 to 1
DALLAS	43	2	10	31	147	147	24	355	48	2.6 to 1
NEWARK	42	1	29	12	123	44	37	631	98	1.4 to 1
ST. LOUIS	42	1	16	25	125	81	47	531	94	1.5 to 1
NEW YORK	36	1	24	11	68	33	26	328	103	2.1 to 1

Information for five largest cities covers 1972. Information for eight others is based on surveys carried out in July-October 1972 covering previous 12 months.

Source: National Crime Panel Surveys. Law Enforcement Assistance Administration. Justice Department.

Biological Theories of Crime and Criminals

The most popular explanations of crime focus on the criminal as being different from the rest of society. This approach uses an ideology of "blaming the victim" and "the art of savage discovery," as William Ryan calls it (1976). In the nineteenth century the causes of crime were found in the biological characteristics of the criminals. The Italian criminologist Cesare Lombroso, early in his career in the 1880s, identified various "cranial types" to determine what criminal traits emerged. Later Lombroso changed his ideas about the likelihood of criminals' being a distinct species or subspecies of man. In the 1940s William Sheldon reported delinquents to be predominantly mesomorphic (sturdily built, muscular, athletic) rather than either endomorphic (fat and slow-moving) or ectomorphic (tall, thin, and fragile). He noted that mesomorphism and a complementary temperament (somatotomia) produced delinquents, as well as other achieving and aggressive types. A "double-Y" chromosome theory of crime has more recently emerged, although the extent of the genetic criminal explanation is still debatable.

Various psychologists theorize that unconscious drives and attempts to resolve psychic conflict are the underlying causes of crime. Juveniles "acting out" antisocial behavior to get attention is one psychological explanation. "Frustration-aggression" theory is another.

Sociological Theories of Crime

But the major explanations of crime and delinquency today are sociological. All sociological explanations assume that social variables and structures, not biological or psychological states of mind, cause crime. Shaw and McKay, in their study of "delinquent areas" in Chicago, were the first sociologists to correlate high crime rates with overcrowded central-city poverty neighborhoods. No matter what group or kind of persons lived in certain areas of the city, the crime rate continued to persist there. Thus, it was the social environment rather than the individual or group that lived in an area that caused crime and delinquency. Although individuals turned to crime to solve personal problems, the inequalities and injustices produced by our social structure, it was found, led to the crime.

Numerous sociological theories based on social environment are offered as an explanation of why crime occurs. The principal ones are:

- Robert Merton's theory of "Anomie"
- Edwin Sutherland's theory of "Differential Association"
- Cloward and Ohlin's theory of "Differential Opportunities"
- Howard Becker's theory of "Labeling."

For delinquency, in addition to the above causes, other subcultural and control-theory explanations are given. Some of these theories of delinquency also serve as causal explanations for some adult crime. Tied in with all these theories is the recognition that rapid social change in traditional values and norms, the social structure, and economic conditions (such as unemployment) often spawn crime and delinquency. A study by Isaac Ehrlich of the University of Chicago shows that where unemployment rates are low, so is crime. This suggests that if a person is part of the "corporate state" and has power, money, and recognition, he will not engage in street crime. Let us look briefly at each major sociological theory for the cause of crime.

Anomie. One of the oldest reasons given for crime is "anomie," linking deviance and social disorganization theory. The concept of anomie was first developed by Emile Durkheim. He saw a "normlessness," or confusion in norms, stemming from any sudden change in social structures. Robert Merton went one step further. For him, anomie arises from a situation in which there are seemingly insurmountable obstacles between cultural goals and the social means available to reach them. This is particularly true of success in our culture and society. Success is the biggest goal for most Americans, but some groups and individuals find that the means to reach it are blocked. Hence, they turn to crime. In Merton's terms, they become "deviant innovators"—criminals or delinquents. Our society worships material goods, but often denies people access to them. This encourages theft and other ripoffs. If male "success" is measured by sexual experience, this encourages rape and prostitution. If youth "success" means having good clothes, they may steal money to get them.

Differential Association. Edwin Sutherland used "differential association" as the main explanation for crime. Involvement in crime results from a "learning process" from others with whom a youth associates. He receives "an excess of definitions favorable to violation of the law." He gets specific instructions from his peers and friends for theft, burglary, or any other crime, even padding an expense account. He absorbs the "motives, drives, rationalizations, and attitudes" needed to commit crime (Sutherland, 1972: 81–83). This theory resembles the popular notion that "bad friends" can get a kid in trouble very easily. Of course, not everyone who has "bad friends" will commit a crime. Much depends on the frequency, duration, and intensity of the association, and the meaning of the relationship for a person. Association in and of itself does not explain all crime. Nonetheless, "differential association" is an important explanation for crime and delinquency.

Differential Opportunities. In Cloward and Ohlin's view, crime is the result of "differential opportunities." There are some groups that have a better chance of learning how to commit illegal acts than others (1960). A person may learn either conventional or criminal means of achieving success. In prison, for example, there are many opportunities to learn how to rob a bank, whereas in a middle-class suburban community the opportuni-

Robbery involving the use of handguns, such as bank holdups, is generally viewed as major crime, even though white-collar criminals and members of organized crime steal much more money from the public than armed robbers.

ties would be more toward how to drink or drive. So the kinds of illegal opportunities are not available to everyone in the same way. Embezzlers have opportunities to handle and manipulate money. Policemen have many opportunities to take bribes that most schoolteachers do not have. Cloward points out that some persons may be "double failures." They have neither legal nor illegal opportunities available to them. This theory explains the occurrence of certain "occupational" crime. It suggests why doctors may get involved with drugs, why computer programmers may embezzle millions, why some policemen accept bribes or burglarize, and why politicians are involved in collusive real-estate or road-contract deals. Opportunities in and of themselves may be a necessary but not a sufficient cause for certain kinds of crime.

Labeling Theory. Howard Becker sees the cause of crime as stemming from society's reaction to a person. "Labeling" a person as a criminal produces a self-fulfilling prophecy. The person begins to live up to the label and the reputation. In our society so many acts are labeled criminal that we literally create much of our crime problem. If taking marijuana were not a criminal offense, we would have less crime. If illegal drugs, drinking, and driving were handled differently, we would have fewer criminals and crimes. But once labeled, a person might be driven into a subculture or group that accepts his behavior. This acceptance reinforces patterns of criminal behavior. Labeling theory explains why so much repetition of criminal acts (recidivism) exists. The ex-con that no one will trust or hire is a product of such labeling. In addition, labeling theories point out the inconsistencies in how judges sentence blacks and whites for the same criminal act. This suggests that the essential difference between criminals and noncriminals lies not in what they do but in how and why society reacts to what they do. Labeling supplies an explanation for crime in the best tradition of C. Wright Mills. The powerful often label the powerless and their acts as criminal and crimes.

These are some of the major explanations of crime. There are other theories, especially subcultural, that specifically explain delinquency. Albert Cohen (1971) attributes delinquency to "status frustration." Cloward and Ohlin (1960) emphasize "differential opportunities." Walter Miller (1958) feels that delinquents identify with lower-class values and concerns. Delinquent behavior thus stems from one's socialization into a lower-class culture and subculture.

Control Theory

Control theory, as set forth by Travis Hirschi, is one of the most recent major explanations of delinquency and crime. It assumes that deviance is exhibited by persons who have little to lose from delinquent behavior. Society is organized so that those with power have much to lose, whereas the powerless and the lower classes have little to lose from crime or delinquency. The critical element is that the pressures for conformity, or noncriminal behavior, reside in the bonds between society and the individual. If the bonds are strong, persons will conform to society's norms and not commit crime. If the bonds are weak, the potential for crime or delinquency increases. The strength of the social bonds preventing crime depends upon a person's attachment and commitment to, and involvement with, society (Hirschi, 1969).

Control theory seems to fit the facts better than other theories, and it does not assume that persons in our society are inherently moral or bound by their consciences not to commit crime. Instead, it assumes that crime can be expected whenever people have little or nothing to lose, and something to gain, from criminal activity. It points to the fact that our society is so structured and organized, with power in the hands of a small elite, that many have little to lose by turning to crime.

The crucial part of control theory is that morality and conformity stem from the social bonds between the individual and society. When those bonds are strong, people will conform to society's norms; when the bonds are weak or almost nonexistent, norm violations become more likely. When cultural or racial minorities are loosely attached to the larger society, when they have not shared equally in its benefits, they may turn to crime.

Let us see what our society can do to deal effectively with crime and delinquency.

PROPOSED SOLUTIONS TO CRIME AND DELINQUENCY

More Uniform Laws

In a rapidly changing society, solutions to crime (and to what the law defines as a crime) are difficult to find. As values change, laws change; so what may once have been viewed as a serious crime becomes a misdemeanor. This has already happened in some states in respect to smoking marijuana. Other states have legalized gambling. In some areas prostitution can flourish because no law is being broken, whereas other areas strictly enforce laws against it.

Therefore, the first solution proposed by conservatives and liberals alike to curb the increasing crime problem is to adopt more uniform laws so that the meaning of crime does not vary from state to state or community to community. Since law-enforcement efforts focus on victimless crimes, perhaps another solution is to eliminate victimless crime from our laws. This liberals and radicals usually advocate.

Primary, Secondary, and Tertiary Prevention

The ultimate solution to crime and delinquency is to prevent them from happening in the first place. A conceptual model by Paul Brantingham and Frederic Faust is based on a public-health paradigm of primary prevention, secondary prevention, and tertiary prevention (July 1976: 284–96). According to this model, *primary* crime prevention identifies conditions of the physical and social environment that provide opportunities for or that precipitate crime. The object of intervention is to alter those conditions so that crime cannot occur, or to make it more difficult to engage in crime. Conservatives have called for primary prevention that would include increased police patrols; better lighting; environmental design of buildings; crime-prevention education; and "neighborhood watch" programs. Liberals call for programs to restrict handgun sales and to solve such social problems as poverty, drug addiction, and race relations.

Essential for preventing crime, according to the radicals, is the elimination of its root causes by changing the existing social structure, thereby alleviating the inequality of wealth, power, and resources. A first step in that direction would be to guarantee every American adequate food, clothing, and shelter. A guaranteed decent, secure, well-paying job also would be a step in that direction.

Secondary crime prevention requires early identification of potential offenders and seeks to intervene in their lives in such a way that they never commit a serious crime. Various programs that help school dropouts, truants, poor academic performers, and school vandals or troublemakers fall into this category. Recreational and athletic programs sponsored by police and community groups are also viewed as secondary crime preventatives.

According to Brantingham and Faust, tertiary (third-step) crime prevention deals with actual offenders who are caught and involves intervention in such a fashion that they will not commit further crimes. Liberal reforming of the prisons and rehabilitating the prisoners would be examples of the tertiary approach. These approaches are discussed in the next section, on the administration of justice.

Table 2–3 illustrates the primary, secondary, and tertiary prevention activities outside the criminal-justice system needed to solve the problem of crime and delinquency, according to Brantingham and Faust.

table 2-3 PREVENTION ACTIVITIES OUTSIDE THE CRIMINAL-JUSTICE SYSTEM

PERFORMED BY	PRIMARY	SECONDARY	TERTIARY
PRIVATE CITIZENS	Household and business security precautions; General charity	Big-brother programs; Delinquency-specific social activities	Correctional volunteers
SCHOOLS	General education	Predelinquent screening; Educational intervention programs	Prosecution of truants and delinquents; Institutional education programs
BUSINESS	Security provisions	Employee screening	Prosecution of offenders; Hiring of former offenders
PLANNERS	Modification of physical environment to reduce criminal opportunity; Modification of social environment to reduce impulses toward criminal behavior	Crime-location analysis for neighborhood-education and-modification programs; Criminal-residence study for neighborhood social work	Institutional design to discourage crime
RELIGIOUS AND SOCIAL AGENCIES	Moral training; Family education; General social work	Welfare Services: Child protection; programs for disadvantaged and predelinquent youth; crisis intervention	Aftercare services

Source: Paul J. Brantingham and Frederic L. Faust, "A Conceptual Model of Crime Prevention." **Crime and Delinquency** 22,3 (July 1976): 295. Reprinted by permission of the National Council on Crime and Delinquency.

Handguns are easy to get, and most violent crimes are committed with them.

Outlawing Handguns

Another primary-prevention solution advocated by some conservatives and liberals to curb crime is to outlaw small handguns, especially so-called Saturday-night specials. There are over 40 million handguns in the United States, and one is sold every 13 seconds. Some 23,000 children and adults are accidentally killed every year from firearms in the home (Wright and Marston, October 1975: 106). The advocates of handgun control argue that it will save lives and reduce crime. For example, in Great Britain, where a police certificate of need is required to own a handgun, there are fewer than 500 handguns per 100,000 persons. In the United States there are 12,000 per 100,000. The number of yearly handgun deaths in England and Wales, with over 50 million persons, is 50 or fewer. In one American city, Houston, Texas, there were 213 such deaths in 1974 (Jackson, July 1975: 2). Of the 20,000 murders in the United States in 1975, over half were with handguns. The pamphlet from the National Gun Control Center (see pp. 40–41) reveals some "myths and facts" about handgun control. Many view control of handguns as a partial solution to crime. Nevertheless, the debate over such legislation continues, and the issue is far from resolved ("Controversy," December 1975).

Improved Police Technology

Another proposed solution by conservatives to the crime problem is greater use of technological means to detect and keep track of crimes committed and of changes in the law to make apprehension of suspects and evidence easier for police. The computer has been employed effectively to trace stolen cars quickly. Since 1968, new communication systems, police equipment, armaments, and technical hardware have been added to local police departments through grants from the Law Enforcement Assistance Administration (LEAA). For example, use of sodium-vapor lighting and helicopter surveillance have been funded by the LEAA. For the last 10 years or more, this use of new hardware and technology has been viewed as an important remedy by police and politicians, and many police departments have been improved through LEAA funding. For example, "improved professionalism of personnel, better data collection, record-keeping and communications, and first-time efforts at comprehensive planning" have resulted (Holden, July 2, 1976: 37). Liberals and radicals have criticized the LEAA approach as ineffective, bureaucratic, wasteful of money, and not really dealing with the baisc causes of crime. They want to abolish LEAA. ("Kill LEAA," September 7, 1976: 1).

To combat white-collar crime more effectively, many liberals feel we should strengthen antitrust laws and make fines and imprisonment for white-collar crimes equivalent to those for other criminal acts. Funds and staffs for law-enforcement agencies responsible for combating white-collar crimes, such as the Justice Department, should be increased.

Dealing with Delinquency

Many solutions, usually of a secondary or tertiary prevention type, have been used against delinquency. A review of the literature by sociologists Lundman, McFarlane, and Scarpitti (1976) confirms the wide range of approaches social scientists suggest for dealing with delinquency and juvenile crime. The most frequently suggested remedy is some type of social intervention and interaction between the juvenile and an adult change agent. Most frequently groupworkers and caseworkers, counselors, psychotherapists, and "outreach" gang workers have also been employed to combat juvenile crime.

Another method for dealing with delinquency attempts to change the school environment of juveniles, since the schools often fail to meet the needs of the young. Such programs seek "smaller classes with diversified and expanded curricula; remedial writing, reading, and arithmetic..."(Lundman, McFarlane, and Scarpitti, 1976: 300). The theory behind such programs is that the teacher acts as a conforming role model for deviant teenagers.

Other preventive programs for delinquents include recreation and athletics, expanded job opportunities, neighborhood delinquency-control groups and projects, and diversion from the juvenile penal system. Diver-

MYTHS & FACTS

1

MYTH: Handguns are needed for self-protection.

FACT: A handgun in the home is much more likely to result in death or injury to family members than it is to burglars.

A mere 2% of burglars are shot every year on the average, and for every burglar who is stopped, six family members are shot in accidents. One fourth of those accidentally killed are less than 14 years of age.

Few intruders kill their victims. Nearly three-fourths of all murders occur between family members, friends or lovers, a situation which is encouraged by the easy access to handguns in the home.

Instead of protecting family members from intruders, a handgun in the home is like a firebomb.

2

MYTH: Saturday Night Specials are used in most handgun crimes.

FACT: The Saturday Night Special is generally described as a cheap, short-barreled, low calibar handgun.

The myth that Specials are used in most handgun crimes has encouraged the false belief that only these cheap handguns need be eliminated to reduce crime. Most proposed anti-Special laws would only stop their manufacture and have no provisions for taking care of the millions of Specials already in circulation.

The New York City Police Department has reported that only 30% of the handguns it confiscates are Saturday Night Specials. Both attempts on President Ford's life were with regular, standard-sized pistols.

Most of the 40 million handguns in this country are quality weapons, and elimination of the Saturday Night Special alone would have little effect on reducing handgun crimes, suicides or accidents.

3

MYTH: The Constitution guarantees the personal right to bear arms.

FACT: The Second Amendment to the U.S. Constitution states that "A well regulated militia being necessary to the security of a free State, the right of the people to keep and bear arms, shall not be infringed."

The United States Supreme Court has ruled four times that this does not guarantee the right to personal gun ownership. Instead, it establishes the right of the State Militias—now the National Guard—to bear arms. The Constitution protects the collective right to bear arms for military purposes in maintaining the security of the state. The right of an individual to possess handguns exists only in myth, not in the Constitution.

Source: National Gun Control Center (now the National Coalition to Ban Hand Guns), 120 Maryland Avenue, N.E. Washington D.C.

ABOUT HANDGUN CONTROL

4

MYTH: Guns don't kill people. People kill people.

FACT: Over half of all murders and suicides are committed with handguns, which are five times more likely to cause death than knives, the next most popular murder weapon.

Most murders are spontaneous acts, committed during the heat of violent passions. Without a handgun available, many murders would be turned into non-fatal assaults if the attacker were forced to use some less potent weapon. The 3,000 who die in gun accidents every year would live if no gun were around.

The South's murder rate is double the rate in the Northeast, where only half as many households have guns. Handguns make murder and suicide quick, convenient and sure.

Even granting for a moment that guns don't kill people, it is painfully clear that people with guns do kill people.

5

MYTH: Handgun control won't work.

FACT: In Great Britain, where handguns are strictly controlled, there are less than 500 handguns per 100,000 people. In the U.S. there are 12,000 handguns per 100,000 people. In 1974, Houston, Texas, alone had over four times as many handgun murders as all of England and Wales, with over 50 million people.

The gun murder rate in the U.S. is 200 times higher than in Japan, where private handgun ownership is totally prohibited. New York City, which has the toughest gun control law in the country, has the second lowest murder rate of the nation's ten largest cities.

Proper gun control laws do work and could save thousands of lives in America every year.

6

MYTH: The Natl. Rifle Assn. can block any attempt at handgun control.

FACT: Many people who favor handgun control have given up because they believe the N.R.A. is all-powerful.

While the N.R.A. does have the power to mount massive letter-writing campaigns which have frightened some legislators, its ability to sway elections on the issue of gun control is highly questionable. The N.R.A. has taken credit for defeating a few pro-control Senators and Congressmen, but these men actually lost for reasons other than gun control.

In the January 1975 issue of the *American Rifleman,* even the N.R.A. admits that 27 Congressmen who opposed gun control lost in the previous elections—while not one Congressman who favored control was defeated.

Obviously the N.R.A. is not all-powerful, and the more people who learn that, the more who will decide to take a positive stand for handgun control.

sion is sometimes referred to as "radical nonintervention"—simply to "leave the kids alone whenever possible" (Schur, 1973). Obviously, Schur admits, a few youths may have to be isolated from society, but most others would probably be much better off if courts and juvenile authorities intervened as little as possible. Most young people (especially males) commit some kind of misdemeanor or status offense, but the majority outgrow their "juvenile" behavior. They "mature out" of delinquency and crime, and this fact should be recognized.

Radicals maintain that major changes in our schools and our economic system are needed before delinquency can be effectively controlled. When teenagers are unemployed and have no alternative ways to earn a living or spend their time, they will continue to turn to crime and delinquency.

THE FUTURE OF CRIME AND DELINQUENCY

Fewer Births May Mean Less Crime

What is the outlook for crime and delinquency? The best predictor of future crime is the age makeup of our population. Our fertility rate (births) has been moving downward for about the last 20 years. Since violent crime and delinquency are especially a "youth business," we can expect sharp declines in violent crimes in the not-too-distant future. Let us see how this will happen. According to the FBI's *Uniform Crime Reports for 1975*, young people between the ages of 10 and 17, 16 percent of our population, accounted for almost half of all arrests for violent crimes and theft. An even larger group, those between 14 and 24, swept into society (and crime) during the 1960s and 1970s in overwhelming numbers. Here is how one study pictures the situation:

> America's post-World War II baby boom has swollen the traditional crime-prone age bracket (14 to 24) as never before—and possibly never again. In 1950 there were 24 million young Americans in this age group. A decade later [1960] it was 27 million and now [1975] it is 44 million; the bulge will not disappear until the 1980s (Time, June 30, 1975: 17).

The point is that by the 1980s the numbers and percentage in the crime-prone population (14 to 24) will decline and when it does, so should crime.

Albert Biderman of the Bureau of Social Science Research in Washington, D.C., thinks that we may already have seen the high point in property crimes. But, he stated in 1976, it may take "a few more years" for violent crimes to peak, because they tend to be committed by a slightly older age group than those who commit property crimes ("Next 25 Years . . .," March 22, 1976: 41). Leon Bouvier, former vice president of the Population Reference Bureau (a private population-research group in Washington, D.C.), says there should be a "dramatic drop" in the crime rate before the end of the 1970s (Ibid.).

But other scholars are not so certain that crime will decline in the future. Nonpopulation factors, such as geographical mobility, make it difficult to predict the future crime rate. For example, Larry Long, a Bureau of the Census official, notes that crime has leveled off in some cities, but has risen in the suburbs. He concludes that crime "is not likely to decrease any time soon" (Ibid.).

Since the nature of crime is defined by law, and since laws are often based on the values and beliefs of society, future crime will depend in part upon our future values. Criminologist Leslie T. Wilkins, speculating about crime at the turn of the twenty-first century, noted that "it is impossible to discuss the future of crime, how it is defined, and what may be done about it, without paying considerable attention to the probable change of moral standards and value systems" (1973: 18).

In addition, Professor Wilkins feels that in the immediate future, most research spending for crime-related topics will be influenced by short-term political considerations. As long as crime research continues to be attached to local or national government funding, it will be of limited value in curbing crime.

SUMMARY

There has always been too much crime in society. Today crime obsesses and concerns many citizens, and with good reason. Every minute, 21 serious crimes are committed. Theft of over $2.5 billion of goods occurs every year.

Crime is defined relative to laws and varies from society to society, state to state, and time to time; enforcement is sometimes strict, at other times nonexistent. Conservatives, liberals, and radicals have different notions of how much and what kinds of behavior should be considered crime. There are three major kinds of crime: Crime in the streets, crime in the "suites"—occupational (white-collar) and organized crime—and crimes without victims. Most citizens consider only the first kind as serious crime.

During 1975, major "index" crimes increased by 10 percent nationwide, and 12 percent in New York City. In 1976, reported major crimes began to stabilize, though theft and larceny increased. Studies, however, reveal that only about half the crimes committed are ever reported to the police.

Explanations of crime and delinquency include both biological and sociological theories. The major sociological theories are anomie, differential association, differential opportunities, and labeling. Delinquency is explained by many subcultural theories as well as by Travis Hirschi's theory of "control." The social structure and powerlessness of the young, poor, and minorities also account for crime and delinquency.

Solutions include primary, secondary, and tertiary prevention of crime. For example, changing laws to eliminate victimless crimes is considered by liberals and radicals as a solution to some of the problems. More funding of police departments, as well as better technical equipment and research methods, particularly as provided by LEAA, is looked upon by conservatives as a help in curbing crime. Programs of social intervention in the lives of delinquents and potential delinquents are also beneficial in limiting crime, but radicals see the need to radically change our basic social institutions before any sizable cut can be made in crime or delinquency.

The outlook is for less crime as crime-prone youth begin to shrink in numbers, but prediction of where declines will occur and to what extent is difficult. The future of crime depends a great deal on our values and beliefs and on how we define crime in the future. As Emile Durkheim observed, crime and the criminal are functional for society, by reminding people of the most important norms and mores. In this view, at least, crime will probably be with us for a long time to come.

II. DEFINING THE ADMINISTRATION OF JUSTICE

Our system for administering justice is viewed by some as a solution to the problems of crime and delinquency. But others feel that our system creates more problems than it solves.

What is wrong with our system of justice? Some sociologists, liberals and radicals, define the problem in terms of the police, courts, and prisons that practice and perpetuate injustice rather than justice. They argue that the great myth is that all persons are treated fairly and impartially; that persons are presumed innocent until proven guilty; that everyone is given a fair and speedy trial; that there is protection against "cruel and unusual punishment"; that there are legal guarantees against being put in jail for long periods of time without trial.

These are the myths. Here are some of the social realities:

1. Last month a police board of inquiry found Patrolman Joseph Stasnek guilty of beating a 16-year-old high school student without apparent provocation. He was suspended from the force for five days without pay. This week the Fraternal Order of Police (FOP) voted to make it a five-day paid vacation . . . from FOP funds (Moore, 1975: 1).

2. Two black men who spent 12 years in prison (eight of them on "death row") for the murders of two white men that another white man had confessed to nine years ago were finally set free in 1975. The men, Freddie Pitts and Wilbert Lee, had maintained their innocence, but they were twice convicted by all-white juries in Florida. On his release, Pitts said: "In our case, you are dealing with personal emotions.

When personal emotions and politics enter into the administration of justice, justice must take a back seat" ("8 Years on Death Row . . .," September 20, 1975: 11).
3. In the same year that Pitts and Lee were released, so were Herbert Kalmbach, Jeb Magruder, and John Dean, major Watergate conspirators, who served only from four to six months in jail for their crimes.
4. At Cummins Prison in Arkansas the bodies of three inmates were found in shallow graves in a mule pasture on the prison farm. Two had been decapitated, and the skull of the other was crushed. And there were others who died from their treatment at that prison. Willie Stewart, a fifteen-year-old, weighing about 115 pounds, was (according to prison records and verified by the *Washington Post*) "chased by a car as he entered the main gate, shot at, ordered to dunk his entire body in a pool of water, slapped, did 31 minutes of push-ups, made to jump up and down holding a hoe pressed to his head and had his hair clipped . . . and [was] dumped on a floor by two guards who decided he was faking an illness. . . ." On the way to the hospital, he died. His mother was told her son "had eaten something that disagreed with him and he died" (Wooden, 1976: 114).

So one reality of the problem may largely be defined as *injustice* on the part of the police, courts, and correctional institutions.

The Lax-and-Permissive Definition

There is another definition of the problem, however, recognized by scholars, conservatives, and a large segment of the public. This is the definition that the system is too lax and permissive on law offenders. Police are not given the respect (or pay) they deserve. During a five-year period, from 1971 through 1975, 631 policemen were killed in the line of duty (Uniform Crime Reports, 1975: 223), and the situation is becoming more dangerous as more people ignore the law and carry guns. People complain that criminals arrested one day are often back on the street the next day to commit new crimes. Indeed, many of those arrested never stand trial, for the case against them is simply dropped. When tried, few are convicted and even those who are usually do not go to jail. The system is ineffective and does not deter crime. Ours is more like a "revolving door" than a rational system.

The hands of the police are usually tied by Supreme Court decisions that often protect the criminal rather than the public (though innocent suspects are protected, too). If policemen do not warn a suspect of his right to a lawyer and to refuse to answer questions; if they arrest him without probable cause; or if they search beyond the immediate area of the suspect without a warrant, the case is usually thrown out of court. Even if a strong case is made against a criminal, judges are often "soft" and let him off with a warning or place him on probation (i.e., he must report to a law officer every so often), or impose a fine or light sentence. Even if a criminal should go to jail, the prison board may soon release him by parole (i.e., he is released early for good behavior). All this often just puts hardened criminals back on the streets to commit more crime.

In 1976, the police and federal agents in Washington, D.C., set a trap for local burglars and thieves. They posed as Mafia mobsters who bought the crooks' stolen goods (worth about $2.5 million). After secretly photographing all their transactions, they invited their "clients" to a party. Most of them showed up and were arrested on the spot. What did the records reveal about the 152 persons arrested? One hundred five (almost 70 percent) were on parole, probation, or some kind of pretrial release (like bail) on a pending criminal charge. And 114 of them had prior criminal records.

The boxed item below illustrates just one of many cases across the country in which criminals are turned loose to hurt society again. Such a system of administering justice is in truth *criminal*.

Any crime is a deviance from accepted social norms that must be punished if society is to maintain its important norms and values. Even when in prison, deviance occurs, and this must be controlled by society. Violence in prison comes from other inmates, not from the guards alone. Francis Marziani, a former inmate at Lewisburg Federal Prison, testified in court that "the going price for murder [is] two cartons of cigarettes." Furthermore, homosexuality, drug abuse, and other crimes persist in jails all over the country. Marziani testified at a government hearing: "I'm not exaggerating when I say that if they ever had a total shakedown at Lewis-

---

"REVOLVING DOOR" JUSTICE

One case ... illustrates how rapidly a criminal can go in and out of the "revolving door" of criminal justice. The man has been arrested at least seven times. Here is his record for just last year:

On May 25, 1975, he was arrested for robbery at gun point. While free on bond, he was arrested on July 22 for illegal possession of a gun. Again he was released, this time without bond. The next day he was arrested on a charge of petty larceny. The charge was reduced to attempted petty larceny, and he was released without bond.

On July 31, this man was rearrested for armed robbery. This time, bond of $2,000 was required. He made the bond and was released. On October 9, while still out on bond, he was arrested again—for armed robbery. On November 20, his gun-carrying charge was dropped by the prosecutor. On December 4, he was arrested for "unauthorized use" of an automobile. But that charge was also dropped. On January 26 of this year, the man finally pleaded guilty to the attempted-petty-larceny charge of last July 23, and was released to await his sentencing.

Source: "'Revolving Door' Justice: Why Criminals Go Free," *U.S. News & World Report* 80, 19 (May 10, 1976): 36.

burg, they'd find enough cash money to start a bank in any major city and enough drugs to keep every junkie in Philadelphia happy for years" (Inmate Who Complained . . .," June 3, 1976: 12). Inmates at the $35-million state penitentiary in Lucasville, Ohio, report that "it's a place where you might be stabbed simply for sitting in the wrong chair, a place where young men sometimes are sold into sexual slavery, and a place where more than a few persons regularly give up part of their income to avoid being beaten" (Douthal, June 1976: A-11). Clearly, rehabilitation programs for criminals have failed; we need tougher laws, stricter jails, and longer jail sentences, the conservatives argue.

So, the problem of administering justice can be defined in two ways: by liberals and radicals, who consider the system too tough and unjust on the poor and powerless accused of crimes; and by conservatives and others, who see the system as too lax and permissive, and define the problem in terms of deviant behavior involved.

Let us look further into the administration of justice and the three major institutions involved—the police, the courts (judges, prosecutors, and lawyers), and prisons or detention centers. We shall follow the "injustice" definition of the problem. This definition is accepted by many sociologists, especially those who adhere to the liberal or radical anaylsis of the social structure and power. Within this framework, police problems can be defined as too much discretion, discrimination, and corruption; problems of the courts as case overload (leading to delay, inefficiency, and injustice), plea bargaining, inadequate representation of the poor by lawyers, and improper, irrational sentencing by judges; and problems of the prisons and juvenile centers as emphasis on punishment and inadequate rehabilitation programs.

The Police

Discretion. The police have to exercise a great deal of discretion on what laws they will enforce or ignore, whom they will arrest, and whom they will harass and haze. Many police officers must make several such vital decisions every day. As Norval Morris wrote, "The policeman exercises a larger judicial discretion than the judge, and . . . if you are to understand police work you have to recognize the vast range of discretion he has to apply. . . . the police are deciding many more cases than are the judges" (1968: 13).

Often the immense discretion of the police is abused. Overreacting to danger, police officers reflect attitudes that are sometimes less than humane toward suspicious, suspected, or apprehended persons. For example, a research study of 125 inmates at the Mansfield, Ohio, State Reformatory found that their first arrests produce a seriously negative image of the police. Over half said the police were "mean" to them when they were arrested; 74 percent said the police lied to them at the time; 69 percent said they were not informed of their rights; 75 percent said the

Historically, blacks and other racial minorities have been abused and mistreated by the police.

police used more force than necessary; and 40 percent said they were beaten by the police (Kratcoski and Scheuerman, 1975: 313).

Discrimination. The same problem is made worse by police discrimination against minority groups and lower-income people. One out of five blacks in a post-riot survey in Detroit reported that police had in some way abused or harassed them. In New York City the situation against minority groups and others is similar (Chevigny, 1969). In Philadelphia in 1977, a special grand jury was busy investigating charges of police abuse of black citizens.

Police discrimination against the people they encounter also has a social-class bias, in addition to one of color. Edward Green found that arrest rates were highly related to one's social class, unemployment, migration, and attitudes connected with the lower socio-economic class (1970: 478–89). Bias and discrimination among police have traditionally been shown against women in rape cases. Too often the police do not believe the woman or imply that she must have done something to "ask for it." In Berkeley the police asked a rape victim to tell the story four different times "right out in the street" while her assailant was escaping (Griffin, 1975: 82). This male bias points up the need for more women on police forces, which for many years have discriminated against women in their system.

Corruption. In addition to abused discretion and discrimination is the problem of police corruption. A study issued by the Police Foundation depicted corruption as a "natural disease" of police. The Knapp Commission investigation into police corruption in New York City "found corruption to be widespread." Plainclothes police officers collected regular biweekly or monthly payoffs of up to $3,500 from each gambling house in their area. The monthly take per man ranged from $300 to $400 in downtown Manhattan to $1,500 in Harlem. When supervisors were involved, they received a little more (Knapp, August 3, 1972: 525–27). It is not just New York City where police corruption grows. In many major cities it is a problem.

The Courts

Police corruption is only a part of our problems in the administration of justice. The heart of the system is the courts, which are plagued with overloads that lead to an inefficient, unjust system. Also, some persons, especially the poor, are not properly represented by lawyers, and bail is hard to raise. Guilty pleas and plea bargaining have therefore become a substitute for a speedy and fair trial. In addition, sentencing by judges is often illogical, irrational, even, at times, incomprehensible.

The court system is a seventeenth-century anachronism used by those in the power structure to perpetuate inequality and inequity. The courts have hardly, then, kept pace with the realities of the twentieth century. Courts are overloaded with cases, and not only more judges but also more prosecutors, public defenders, clerks, and courtrooms are badly needed. A study in Chicago found that a Cook County judge's day involves about two and three-quarter hours in his chambers. A more productive, efficient system is needed. Some persons wait three or four years before their cases come up for trial. Others experience assembly-line justice, as the judge devotes a mere sixty seconds (or less) per case. How can anyone receive justice in such a system?

Treatment of the Poor and Minorities. Another social problem of the courts involves unjust treatment of the poor and minorities. The myth is that everyone is equal before the law and has the right to a lawyer to defend him in court. The reality is that if a person is poor or a minority-group member, this may not always happen. Most poor persons have no attorney in the lower courts. They are usually defenseless in matters involving eviction from their apartments and situations involving less than a year in jail (i.e., a misdemeanor). The added injustice is that lower-income persons are often forced to pay the court costs for the action brought against them by those in power. The lower courts in our "corporate state," dominated by powerful elites, often live off the fines and court costs paid by the poor, who can least afford to pay. As most state and county courts now operate, they cannot possibly handle the number of persons awaiting trial.

Because of calendar overloads and postponements, cases are often *lost* (literally). The problem is especially bad for the poor, who usually cannot afford to raise any money for bail. Thus, they sit in jail waiting for their trials.

A Justice Department study revealed only a token compliance with the 1972 Supreme Court decision requiring that a lawyer be made available to defend any poor person facing a possible jail term. This study, based on field work in nine major cities, showed:

> Judges often openly encourage defendants to give up their constitutional rights to have a lawyer.
>
> In lower criminal courts there is "limited concern" with fairness in procedures.
>
> Lawyers appointed to defend the poor are "often inexperienced or of limited competence." They often are not prepared to represent their clients' best interests.
>
> Most lawyers condone the mediocre judges in the lower courts.
>
> Law schools have done little to educate students about these problems in the courts (Oelsner, November 15, 1975: 1, 28).

Ethnic minorities and the poor are often victimized and frustrated by the court's legal procedures and processes. Here, an Indian woman waits to testify in her attempt to obtain custody of her children, who had been taken from her by the state.

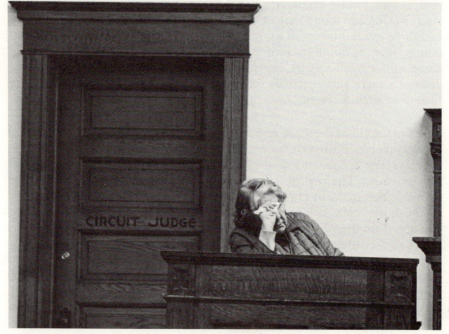

credit: Lawrence Frank/Critical Focus.

Bail and Bargaining. The bail system discriminates against the poor, for a poor person often does not have property or money to put up for bail or even to pay the bail bondsman's fee. If he cannot raise the money, he is forced to stay in jail until his court case comes up. One study points out the connection between bail and jail:

> If bail practices are inadequate and speedy trials cannot be provided, then those who get out, stay out; those who do not, stay in. The effect on sentencing is also enormous. A detained defendant is more than twice as likely to plead guilty and more than eight times as likely to be sentenced to jail than is his bailed counterpart (Alterman and Becker, 1976: 312).

The use of guilty pleas and plea bargaining is also problematic. The Perry Mason myth that everyone receives a fair, impartial trial—represented by capable lawyers and facing a jury that has rationally weighed the evidence—comes nowhere near the reality of the court system. Over 95 percent of those who appear in lower courts plead guilty (often without a lawyer) and are sentenced on the spot. Even in federal courts, where more severe matters are handled, only 10 percent of all cases actually go to trial; the rest plead guilty. Thus, the mode of operation of courts is not the trial but the guilty plea.

As a result of our social system, "a collusion among prosecutors, judges and defense counsel" emerges. It aims to dispose of the courts' cases with "a maximum of reward and a minimum of stress" to the lawyers and judges, even if it produces "a grossly inequitable distribution of justice" (Glaser, 1973: 60). In addition, lawyers are generally interested in getting their fee for representing a client. Most defense lawyers rely on the court judges to get their fees. For example, in Los Angeles one of the most regularly accepted grounds for delay in a case is informally called "Rule Number One": the defense attorney asks the judge to delay the case until the client pays his attorney's fees.

Sentencing. American judges have great power in handing down a sentence. Generally only a person's *conviction* can be appealed, not the imposed *sentence*. Because of this, a wide variety of sentences is possible for the same or similar offenses. A person's race and social class can often make a difference in the sentence received. In a study for the judges of the United States Court of Appeals (Second Circuit), 50 federal judges were given 20 identical files, drawn from actual cases. They were asked what sentence they would impose on each defendant. The results showed a "glaring disparity." In a case involving a middle-aged union official convicted on several counts of extortion, one judge imposed a sentence of 20 years in prison plus a $65,000 fine. Another judge gave him a three-year sentence with no fine. In another case, involving possession of barbiturates (a drug) with intent to sell them, one judge gave the defendant five years in jail, while another put him on probation (Dershowitz, 1976: 268).

At a school for judges in Reno, Nevada, Judge Philip Saeta gave 37 judges identical fact sheets on hypothetical cases and asked them to pass sentence. In each case the *maximum* penalty stipulated was one year in jail and a $500 fine. The maximum probation allowed was three years. Here is one of the sample cases:

> "Joe Cut," 27, pleaded guilty to battery. He slashed his common-law wife on the arms with a switchblade. His record showed convictions for disturbing the peace, drunkenness and hit-and-run driving. He told a probation offficer that he acted in self-defense after his wife attacked him with a broom handle. The prosecutor recommended not more than five days in jail or a $100 fine (Jackson, 1975: 187–88).

The judges' sentences ranged from a $50 fine and six months' probation to a $250 fine and six months in jail. When Joe was identified as white, probation was more likely and jail sentences varied from three to ten days. When he was black, Joe got a fine and five to 30 days in jail.

Such sentencing differences have been documented in many surveys. They show that judges are generally harder on

- the poor
- nonwhites
- those with no hired or court-appointed lawyers
- those who go to trial rather than plead guilty
- those who commit personal and property crimes rather than white-collar crimes.

Once in the hands of the police and court system, a person begins to see that he is within an impersonal, assembly-line system controlled by the powerful in society that has little to do with the abstract concept we call justice. As Professor Jonathan Casper has observed:

> The defendants also learn that, once they are arrested, they are on an assembly line. The people who tend the line (the police, the public defenders, the prosecutor, the judge) really aren't interested in **you** – you are an object (like the car on which the cop sticks a ticket) to be processed, dealt with, and gotten rid of. The outcome has little to do with **you** – with what you are like – but more with the production ethic, with what will get rid of your case most quickly. Lawyers, prosecutors, and judges are dealing not with people, but with files, and to them you are a file (1975: 317).

Prisons and Rehabilitation

The end of the assembly line is the prison. People are sent to prison for a variety of reasons—punishment, restraint, deterrence, and rehabilitation. Until society decides on which purpose we want them to serve, prisons will be a serious social issue.

Conservatives want prisons to emphasize punishment, restraint, and deterrence, so that the punishment fits the crime. Penology experts, such as Robert Martinson and Norval Morris, point to the high rate of prison repeaters (recidivists), about 70 percent, as proof that rehabilitation does not work. The National Committee for the Study of Incarceration, after a four-year study, concluded that rehabilitation should be abandoned as a goal because there is little evidence that it works ("Penal Rehabilitation," February 19, 1976: 2). According to criminologist Hans Mattick, prisons make good actors out of people—prisoners act as though they have been rehabilitated in order to get out of jail. But how prisoners act in jail is no indicator of their behavior in society.

Liberals suggest that rehabilitation has never really been tried in prisons. For example, psychiatrist Martin Groder argues that rehabilitation has not worked because "programs have been too limited, too short-term, and run by people who have merely administered them rather than become personally involved" (Holden, May 23, 1975: 817). According to Groder, policy makers and penal officials claim nothing works so that "they can get on with the grand old business of repression."

Dr. Jerome Miller, former Massachusetts Commissioner of Youth Services, who closed down all the state's reform and training schools, said:

> Reform schools are no damn good. They neither reform nor rehabilitate. The longer you lock up a kid in them, the less likely he is to make it when he gets out. They don't protect society. They're useless, they're futile, they're rotten (Ross and Kupferberg, September 17, 1972: 4).

In defining the social problem of prisons, we are questioning the whole notion of imprisonment itself, along with the purposes of incarceration and the social and economic costs involved.

Hence, in their efforts to administer justice, all three agencies—the police, courts, and prisons—suffer from and produce serious problems. According to radicals and some liberals they all reflect the power and indifference of the "corporate state" toward powerless individuals and their problems. Among the police, we have problems of abused discretion, racial and female discrimination, and corruption in the ranks. In the courts we have problems of case backlogs (leading to inefficiency and injustice), inadequate representation of the poor by lawyers, forced guilty pleas, plea bargaining, and irrational sentencing. In prisons and juvenile facilities, we have defined the problems of their purpose and social costs.

These problems are all familiar. They have long attended our system of justice and are a reflection of a social structure in which wealth, power, and prestige, according to radical analysis, are far out of kilter.

INCIDENCE AND PREVALENCE OF THE PROBLEMS OF ADMINISTERING JUSTICE

Perhaps the best way to measure the incidence and prevalence of the social issue of criminal justice, and how individuals who commit crimes to solve personal problems are affected by police, courts, and prisons, is to examine the relationship between reported crime and what happens thereafter. Table 2-4 compares the situation in 1967 with that in 1975. The figures suggest that, under our present system of crime detection and prosecution, crime *does pay*.

The most obvious fact is that most criminals (80 percent) are not caught by the police. Of the 20 percent arrested, only about 3 percent end up in prison. If the criminal-justice system is an "assembly line," it is a very inefficient and obsolete one. Every year it costs society some $15 billion in taxes to support our police, courts, and prisons ("The Wages of Sin," 1976: 7).

Another way to gauge the seriousness of the problem of injustice among our police, courts, and prison systems is to examine research studies and public-opinion polls on this question.

Incidence of Police Abuse

How often do the police abuse their discretion and use excessive force—especially with blacks? We do not know the answer because the occurrence of violence is hidden and usually not reported by the victim. The one definitive study by sociologist Albert Reiss, based on his eyewitness observation in three major cities, revealed the following:

> In only 37 of 3,826 contacts observed did the police use excessive force.

table 2-4 THE FACTS SAY CRIME DOES PAY

1967	1976
Of each 100 offenses known by police,[1] ...	
78 are never caught.	80 are never caught
22 are "cleared" by arrest.	20 are "cleared" by arrest.
Of 22, 16 are held for prosecution.	Of 20, 18 are held for prosecution.
Of 16, 7 are sent to juvenile court;	Of 18, 6 are sent to juvenile court;
5 are found guilty as charged;	6 are found guilty as charged;
3 are found not guilty; and	2 are found not guilty; and
1 is found guilty of a lesser charge.	1 is found guilty of a lesser charge.[2]

[1]Recent surveys show that 6 to 9 times more crimes occur than are known by the police. Figures for 1975 are based on a sample of 2,198 cities.
[2]Since the reported figures show the disposition of only 15 out of the 18 held for prosecution, we must assume that the other 3 are still pending in court.
Source: **Uniform Crime Reports**, 1967: 109; 1976: 216, 219.

Police often use excessive force in arresting suspects, especially if they are poor or from a minority group. Here, police subdue a Spanish-American demonstrating for Puerto Rican independence.

Of the 4,604 white citizens in these contacts, 27 experienced police abuse (5.9 per 1,000 citizens).

Of the 5,960 blacks involved, 17 were abused by police, a rate of 2.8 per 1,000.

Of 643 white "suspects," 27 were abused (41.9 per 1,000).

Of 751 black "suspects," 17 were abused (22.6 per 1,000).

For every 100 white policemen, 8.7 will abuse people (1975: 89–90).

In the same study, Reiss reported that those who were obviously poor were much more subject to abusive language and more likely to be hit and shoved by police. The worst part of the "excessive force" witnessed by Reiss was that much of it took place in police stations after the suspect was already under control. Of the 37 cases of "excessive force" used on the streets by the police, only one witness complained (Stewart, 1976: 323).

Public-opinion polls suggest, however, that most Americans have confidence in police discretion. A Harris Poll reports that 66⅔ percent say that state and local police are doing a good job. Only 11 percent regard police officers as "not too bright"; 9 percent consider them "corrupt"; and 6 percent believe that they are "violent." Only among blacks and youth is there widespread belief that the police use "excessive brutality" (Harris, 1973: 176).

Court Personnel and Case Load

Part of the severity of the problems with the courts can be measured in terms of the number of laws, legal personnel, and cases that make up the system. There are 30,000 local, state, and federal laws that must be interpreted by thousands of local, county, state, and federal courts. In 1970 over 350,000 lawyers were functioning, most in cities of more than 250,000 persons. Legal services, particularly for the poor, have grown in recent years. In 1972 over 144,000 legal-service organizations existed. Of these, 77,282 retained paid employees (*Statistical Abstract of the U.S.*, 1975: 163). A study commissioned by the American Bar Association revealed in 1974 that one-third of all families surveyed had never used a lawyer, while another third had taken only one problem to a lawyer.

To the question "Do most lawyers charge more for their services than they are worth?," 62 percent said "yes" and 29.5 percent "no" (Greene, August 10, 1975: 8). The 1974 median yearly income of attorneys was $40,100. A 1973 Harris Poll showed that the public had little confidence in law firms. Only 18 percent reported confidence in them, as compared with higher confidence in "garbage collectors, police, or business firms" (Ibid., 54). Most adults or delinquents in lower courts have no attorney to represent them, unless (in rare instances) appointed by the court.

Courts all over the country are faced with case backlogs. Case loads have doubled in the last 10 years, but the number of judges increased only 25 percent. Nationally there are 2,975 juvenile courts with 3,202 judges who hear about one million cases a year. In some areas these same judges must rule on family problems, such as support payments for children in cases of divorce. In addition, 40 percent of the young persons heard in court are status offenders, those who have commited no crime but may be runaways from home or truant from school.

Extent of Bail Problems. Bail presents problems, too. Many poor persons cannot afford bail. For example, the President's Commission on Law Enforcement and Administration of Justice reported that "25 percent of those arrested could not come up with the $25 in cash that would have enabled them to be set free on bail" (McKee and Robertson, 1975: 468). Today about 100 no-bail programs are in effect throughout the country, especially in New York, California, and Washington, D.C. In addition, a federal law compels pretrial release (for charges other than murder) as long as persons have community ties, good character, and it seems likely they will not flee (Landau, 1976: B-17).

A problem also attends release on bail (or release without bail). Too many persons who should be kept in jail are turned loose. An example of the incidence and prevalence of this problem comes from a study by the United States Attorney, which shows that "70 percent of persons indicted for robbery were rearrested while awaiting trial" (Ibid.). Six out of ten persons arrested for felonies (serious crimes) in Washington, D.C., have prior criminal records. Between 1971 and 1975, a mere 7 percent of those arrested for serious crimes accounted for 24 percent of all such arrests ("Revolving Door Justice," 1976: 36).

Prevalence of Prison Problems

Prisons have severe problems, too—especially overcrowding, violence, and understaffing. The proportion of the population imprisoned (including those in local jails and juvenile institutions) is about one-fifth of 1 percent (Wilkins, 1976: 156). Twice as many persons are living in the community under "correctional supervision" through probation or parole as are in prison (Stark, 1975: 196). Our society spent more than $1 billion in 1975 to confine nearly 250,000 people in state and federal prisons. Some 100,000 others are confined in 3,319 local and county jails (Ross and Kupferberg, November 4, 1973: 6). The nearly 225,000 persons in state prisons and the 25,000 in federal prisons in 1975 represented an 11 percent increase over 1974. The national prison population had declined for a decade after 1963, but it suddenly began to increase in 1973 as jobs became difficult to find. The United States Attorney General reported that as of 1976, the inmate population of 47 federal prisons and halfway houses exceeded their capacity by about 3,000 inmates.

Overcrowding. At Lucasville, Ohio, the following overcrowding was observed:

> Designed to hold some 600 men in single cells, the prison had slightly more than 1,200 in the spring of 1975, when the guards struck for two weeks. Today the population exceeds 2,000 and is climbing fast. A quarter of the prisoners are now double-bunked and many have nothing to keep them busy in a place where idle hands soon become fists (Douthal, June 6, 1976: A-11).

To make matters worse, more than half the prisoners are black, while almost all the guards are white. Most of the blacks are from large cities, while the white guards are from all-white rural areas. They have had little past contact with blacks, and this only adds to the tension and violence. A report by the Law Enforcement Assistance Administration showed that 47 percent of state prisoners are black, and more than 60 percent are high-school dropouts ("Blacks Found Composing . . .," June 2, 1976:3).

Juvenile prisons (called training schools or institutions) are also overcrowded and inadequate. In 1975, 100,000 young people (under 18) were committed to juvenile prisons. Some 600,000 more delinquent, or status, offenders and neglected children were put in jail pending their court hearings.

Violence. The overcrowding, among other reasons, leads to more tension and violence between guards and inmates and among inmates themselves. Violence has become a severe problem. During the Attica State Prison uprising in New York in 1971, nearly 40 inmates were killed by State police and guards. The Second Circuit Court of Appeals, in issuing a court order to stop reprisals and physical abuse, described what happened at the prison after it had been taken over by the authorities:

> Beginning immediately after the state's recapture of Attica on the morning of September 13, and continuing until at least September 16, guards, state troopers and correctional personnel had engaged in cruel and inhuman abuse of numerous inmates. Injured prisoners, some on stretchers, where struck, prodded, or beaten. Others were forced to strip and run naked through gauntlets of guards armed with clubs, . . . spat upon or burned with matches, . . . poked in the genitals or arms with sticks. According to the testimony of inmates, bloody or wounded inmates were not spared in this orgy of brutality (Mitford, 1974: 290).

A new kind of violence—behavior modification—has penetrated the prison walls; it is used to justify the most violent and brutal treatment of people imaginable. For example:

The 1971 uprising at Attica Prison in upstate New York was brutally put down by state police and guards. Nearly 40 inmates were killed, and many more were cruelly abused and beaten.

credit: Wide World Photos.

At the Wisconsin State Penitentiary, sex offenders are wired with electrodes, shown erotic pictures, and then shocked in the groin.

In California's maximum-security Vacaville Rehabilitation Center, intractable convicts are subjected to sensory deprivation. They are locked in solid white rooms and cut off from all communication or sensory stimulation for months.

At the Iowa Security Medical Facility, inmates who lie or swear are injected with ampomorphine, which causes them to vomit uncontrollably for up to an hour.

In other programs across the country, drugs, electroconvulsive shock treatments, brainwashing, psychosurgery, and other medical experiments are used (Sage, 1975: 191).

The violence perpetrated on inmates in some of our prisons may be more scientific, professional, and psychological, but it is just as brutal and inhumane as traditional physical violence.

Understaffing. Another basic problem of prisons is understaffing, particularly by professional staff. For example, staff in New York prisons is in a one-to-two ratio to prisoners (6,306 staff for 13,000 prisoners). Yet despite this relatively good staff ratio, over 70 percent of the staff are guards; only 7 percent are involved in counseling and education, and only 1 percent are professional medical personnel (Mitford, 1974: 187). In the California prison system (one of the best in the nation), "treatment" accounts for 13 percent of its annual budget. Academic and vocational education are allotted about $10 a month per inmate. Not too many teachers or educational staff can be hired on such an allotment. In the entire system there are only 32 full-time psychiatrists and 24 psychologists—most of whom are at the California Medical Facility at Vacaville.

CAUSES OF THE PROBLEMS OF ADMINISTERING JUSTICE

The principal underlying causes of all the problems discussed are these:

1. The crime rate has risen because of changes in traditional values and norms.
2. The system of administering justice is designed almost exclusively to affect the powerless and the poor. Those who have the time and money can benefit from the system. Those who do not, cannot.
3. The courts are established to "protect existing economic, political, and social relations" (Lefcourt, 1971: 253).

The priorities of the police, courts, and prisons are directed toward protecting the "corporate state" and power elites, say the radicals. The deck is stacked from the very start against powerless individuals who have little money or prestige. This has historically created a pattern of selective law enforcement that benefits white upper- and middle-class people. The bail requirements and plea bargaining often victimize propertyless defendants. They are, in effect, prejudged. The very roles of the judge, prosecuting attorney, and even the defense lawyer for the poor only reinforce the bias. They are all trained for and experienced in the administration of court bureaucracies, not social justice.

Immediate Causes of Police Problems

More immediate causes have also been given for police problems of abused discretion, discrimination, and corruption. Jonathan Turner, in his book *American Society: Problems of Structure* (1972), sees the following three causes of these problems, in addition to police professionalism and political power.

Police and Community Relations. Police are often forced to become peacekeepers instead of law enforcers. This puts their duties beyond the bounds of law and creates an overextension of authority (Baldwin, 1970: 2). They respond to public pressure to "keep the streets clear of crime," often resorting to abusive and discriminatory means to do so.

Internal Structure of the Police. Efficiency calls for an extensive bureaucracy that affects people's legal rights. A bureaucracy generates its own *internal* policies, procedures, and rules to get the job done—no matter what the means. Also, a large web of informal rules emerges among police as a subculture, which creates secrecy about what really goes on.

Police Ideology. This ideology directs the police to
1. maintain secrecy about practices from a hostile public
2. get respect from the public, even if it must be coerced
3. complete an important arrest by any means, legal or illegal (Turner, 1972: 148).

This ideology emerges because the dangers of police work make police officers suspicious of people. In addition, they may have to assert their authority against a hostile public and must always appear efficient and effective.

Immediate Causes of Court Problems

One reason for different sentences for similar crimes is often that different and conflicting laws could apply to the situation. For example, when Lynette "Squeaky" Fromme was arrested for pointing a loaded gun at President Ford in 1975, debate arose over whether to charge her under federal law or the laws of California (where the crime occurred). The federal law carries a sentence of "any terms of years," while the California law allows the judge to sentence the guilty person "to prison for six months to life, or in a county jail not exceeding one year, or by fine not exceeding five thousand dollars." The judge who finally sentenced Miss Fromme to life imprisonment had the widest possible choices in fixing her sentence. This situation is not unique and is really the major cause of wide disparities in sentencing by court judges.

Liberals contend that having so many laws that attempt to regulate moral behavior (drinking, gambling, sex, etc.) is another cause for court inefficiency, backlogs, and the need for guilty pleas and plea bargaining. If many social customs and practices were decriminalized, the backlogs would be alleviated overnight. As Alexander Smith and Harriet Pollack note:

> For every murderer arrested and prosecuted, literally dozens of gamblers, prostitutes, dope pushers and derelicts crowd our courts' dockets. If we took the numbers runners, the kids smoking pot, and the winos out of the criminal justice system, we would substantially reduce the burden on the courts and the police. If we permitted the sale of heroin on a controlled prescription basis (as the British do, and as we do with other dangerous drugs) we would probably eliminate well over half of the cases going through our criminal courts. . . . It has been estimated that as little as 10 per cent of the courtroom hours available in our criminal courts are now devoted to the processing of serious crime (1971: 98-100).

Immediate Causes of Prison Problems

This same cause operates to overcrowd our prisons, traditionally reserved for more serious crimes.

There are some more recent causes for prison problems. According to Norman Carlson, Director of the Federal Bureau of Prisons, overcrowding of prisons has three major causes:

1. rising crime rates in recent years
2. increases in the number of prosecutions and convictions
3. increases in the number and length of court-imposed prison sentences ("Federal Prisons Termed Crowded . . . ," March 15, 1976: 2).

These causes for prison problems must give us pause to consider what might happen if our courts became more efficient and effective in convicting people of crimes. Although we might eliminate one problem (of the courts) in the system, we would only create a larger one (our prisons) in the same system.

The basic cause of prison problems, however, is the public's attitudes and indifference toward persons in jail. The prevailing attitude in America is that prisoners are getting what they deserve. Just as Michael Harrington described the invisibility of the poor, so also prisons and prisoners are generally out of sight, out of mind. Since most Americans have not experienced life behind bars, they do not care what happens to prisoners once the gates are slammed shut. An Attica riot may make the television or headline news for a week or so, but it quickly fades from public view and concern. Most upper- or middle-class people with money and power are not concerned with the poor or minorities who break the law in order to survive in an unfair social structure.

PROPOSALS TO SOLVE THE PROBLEMS OF ADMINISTERING JUSTICE

There are about as many proposed solutions to problems of the criminal-justice system as there are writers on the subject, from acceptance of the system to revolution.

Improving the Police

For the police problems of abused discretion, discrimination, and corruption, the following liberal reform proposals are recommended by Donald Bouma in his book *Kids and Cops* (1969).

1. Develop strong departmental rules against the use of such words as "wop," "nigger," "polak," "boy," or "girl" (the last two when addressed to adults).
2. Assign police officers known to be strongly prejudiced to noncritical jobs.
3. Undertake honest and effective investigation of civilian complaints, together with appropriate correction.
4. Institute police cadet programs where high-school-age boys (especially minority youth) are apprenticed to police departments to develop future careers in police work.
5. Increase the pay of police officers so that one can expect to achieve a higher level of professionalization.
6. Plan much more intensive and professional in-service training programs, with heavy emphasis on human relations (1975: 128–29).

Commissions in the 1960s, among them President Johnson's Crime Commission in 1967 and the Kerner Commission's Report on Civil Disorders in 1968, recommended that the police take steps to improve their relations with the community they serve. Part of their suggestions involved employing more minority-group members as police officers. Arthur Waskow suggests three ways of doing this:

1. Restructure metropolitan police forces into neighborhood police forces, with local elections of commissioners.
2. Create countervailing power through organizations able to hear grievances, and to protest injustices.
3. Break down the barriers that separate the police from the citizens to avoid the social isolation of police. Getting police

officers out of the squad cars and back on the neighborhood beat would be a good beginning (December 1969: 4–7).

Along the lines of further professionalization of officers, the National Commission of Justice Standards and Goals recommends at least one year of college for all police department members. The Commission hopes by 1982 police officers will be required to have four years of college.

Educating police about the inherent inequities that our social structure produces—sometimes forcing people to commit what our society defines as crime—is a solution of liberals to discriminatory treatment of the poor and minorities. Changing the very function of police—from arresting to helping—would be revolutionary, but in the long run might be more successful in reducing crime in a society where police represent the power of the well-to-do and enforce the status quo.

Improving the Courts

Solutions to problems of the courts, such as case overloads, discrimination, plea bargaining, excessive guilty pleas, and disparate sentencing, center around liberal changes in the law regarding the treatment of delinquents and adults. The Joint Commission of the American Bar Association and the Institute of Judicial Administration recommended the following reforms in the juvenile-court system:

diversion of first offenders, whenever appropriate, from the court process to youth-service agencies; this is beginning to happen in some states today

upgrading family courts; providing lawyers for children in delinquency proceedings; giving notice and a hearing before school discipline; and helping children, not punishing them ("System of Juvenile Justice," May 23, 1976: A-11).

Help could be provided by remedial education to teach youngsters to read and write while detained or imprisoned. A four-year study by the Juvenile Justice Standards Project recommended similar changes ("Radical Changes Urged . . ."' November 30, 1975: A-2). The National Council on Crime and Delinquency, as well as juvenile advocate Kenneth Wooden, urges complete elimination of all status offenses from state juvenile codes. They call for diverting status offenders into rehabilitation activities, such as family counseling, employment programs, and educational plans. Many states are already beginning to move in this direction (Horn, August 1975: 32). Liberals point out that our society must build a better economic and educational system that provides real opportunities for the young to learn and earn.

The radicals maintain that since the social structure and inequality of power contribute significantly to this social problem, only revolutionary institutional changes, such as redistribution of wealth, can ever hope to resolve it. Although major institutional changes are long overdue in the court system, we are beginning to take the first few steps to remedy the most gross inequities in sentencing and in reducing caseload. But clearly more radical change is needed.

Judicial Innovations. In early 1976, the Committee for the Study of Incarceration—a privately funded group of liberal scholars, lawyers, and politicians—made several recommendations after a four-year study of court sentencing:

> Violent criminals should be jailed, but petty thieves and most first offenders should be released with only a warning from the judge.
>
> Sentencing an offender on the basis of the seriousness of the crime and his role in it, without a chance for probation or parole, "is the only fair basis for sentencing people."
>
> Courts, or a panel, should work out specific penalties to apply to each type of crime. Except in unusual cases, these penalties would apply to all.
>
> The parole system should be abandoned, and the prisoner should serve his full sentence.
>
> Jail sentences for serious crimes should run up to five years, but usually no more than three years ("Penal Rehabilitation," February 19, 1976: 2 and *Doing Justice,* 1976). At present, because of parole for good behavior, such sentences are usually indefinite, but are usually for over three years.

Another recent innovation aimed at solving problems of overcrowded courts and of sentencing differences is Accelerated Rehabilitative Disposition (ARD). Approved by the Pennsylvania Supreme Court in 1973 and designed for first-time offenders of minor, nonviolent crimes, ARD allows the defendant to confess his crime to the judge "off the record," and he is not judged guilty or innocent. For instance, a middle-class person arrested for smoking marijuana avoids having a criminal-court record if he completes a period of probation, pays the costs of prosecution, and meets all stipulated conditions of good behavior. If the defendant fails to meet all conditions, prosecution may start again.

Another judicial innovation is called "Shock Probation." Based on the theory that the first taste of prison may cure as fast as (or faster than) the whole dose, the program is used in borderline cases in which the judge had a problem deciding whether to commit a person at all. A first offender jailed for a crime may be granted probation by a judge after serving between 30 and 60 days.

For many first offenders, the worst part of prison comes when they first enter it. Stunned by the "strip search," rigid rules, and violent guards, an offender is quite awed. If he is suddenly rescued from such a situation, the chances are better that the offender will not want to return for several years of further ill treatment. Ohio, Indiana, and Kentucky have used Shock Probation quite successfully for several years. Ohio has released over 4,000 prisoners under this program since 1966. Of these only 9 percent have returned to jail, far better than the national recidivism rate of 80 percent ("Shock Probation," *Time*, May 7, 1973: 103).

While Chief Justice Burger and some conservatives see plea bargaining as a way to reduce the courts' backlogs, other conservatives call for its absolute end. The 1973 report of the National Advisory Commission on Criminal Justice Standards and Goals urged: "As soon as possible, but in no event later than 1978, negotiations between prosecutors and defendants . . . concerning concessions to be made in return for guilty pleas should be prohibited" (Casper, 1975: 318).

Clearly, many proposals for reforming court sentencing would also help to solve many of the problems of prisons, especially overcrowding.

Improving Rehabilitation Programs

The most startling, if not revolutionary, solution to the problems of prisons is to abolish them (at least most). This is not really so far-fetched, and it has actually been done for juveniles in Massachusetts. Within three years Dr. Jerome Miller, as Commissioner of the Department of Youth Services, closed down most of the juvenile jails and institutions. Of nearly 2,000 young men and woman who would otherwise be behind bars, only about 80 hard-core violent cases remained confined for treatment at special psychiatric-care facilities.

In addition, the National Advisory Commission on Criminal Justice Standards and Goals (made up of law-enforcement officials) recommends that only "hard-core" offenders should be imprisoned. It urges conjugal visits (so that normal sex can take place), coeducational facilities, and an end to prison uniforms for convicts and guards. The report reads in part:

> Incarceration is not an effective answer for most criminal offenders. The failure of major institutions to reduce crime is incontestable. Recidivism rates are notoriously high. Institutions do succeed in punishing but they do not deter ("Replace Most Prisons. . .," October 15, 1973: 1).

It goes on to recommend that states build no new prisons for juveniles "under any circumstances," and none for adults except in rare cases in which no alternative exists.

Radicals propose an end to prisons by revolution and violence if necessary. They argue that prisons are part of an oppressive economic and political system that must be changed. Most persons in prisons are the poor, minorities, and revolutionaries who violently oppose the system. These powerless victims are, in effect, political prisoners of a system designed to perpetuate inequality and injustice. If the Attica uprising and other prison disturbances can cause minor social changes in their operation, how much more change will come when millions of persons, in and out of the prisons, rebel against a system that is basically unjust and unfair?

> ## VIOLENCE AT ATTICA
>
> What took place in the Attica Correctional Facility, Attica, New York, is the most telling event of what is taking place. The Attica uprising by inmates on September 13, 1971, merely duplicates the domestic lesson America intends to impose. What commentators somehow overlook in regard to what happened on that fateful day is that there emerged another instance of a a race war upon American soil, another step among many toward the final solution. Seventy-three percent of the inmates in the rebellious D. Yard were nonwhite; no Black person, but rather a white governor and presently the Vice-President of the United States, Nelson Rockefeller, ordered the military assault; and there were no Blacks among the 600 state troopers who chanted "white power, white power" when surging into the yard. The insurrection, therefore, represents not an uprising within a penal institution but a racist massacre. In the words of I. F. Stone, "... the State troopers went in with murder in their hearts, like a lynch mob in the South 'to get them niggers.'" The intensity of hatred toward Blacks is so strong that White troopers willingly paid the price for killing not only scores of *unarmed* and *trapped* Blacks, but ten of their very own!
>
> Source: Sidney M. Willhelm, "Black Obsolescence in a White America." In James M. Henslin and Larry T. Reynolds, *Social Problems in American Society*. Boston: Holbrook Press, 1976: 113.

Community-Based Corrections. The major new trend and proposal for change in prisons, stemming from Attica and the President's Advisory Commission on Criminal Justice Standards and Goals, is the development of *community-based* corrections programs. Small community "prisons" help to make brief home visits, study and work-release programs, and halfway houses more feasible. In addition, community-based rehabilitation centers are much cheaper to operate than fortress-type prisons, although most states persist in having and filling the latter type. Most states also cling to outmoded juvenile institutions to imprison the young ("States Ignore Cheaper Methods," December 28, 1975: A-3).

Another possible solution to the problems of prisons is the approach used by the "Just Community" in Niantic, Connecticut. Parole is granted only after a predetermined sentence is served. Participation in the educational and rehabilitation programs is assumed, but will not help a prisoner get out any earlier. The main idea at Just Community is to have the prisoners—both men and women—participate in running the prison and learn responsibility for their own actions. All decisions are by majority rule, with guards and prisoners each having one vote. Director Joseph Hickey has noted about this method:

> They are learning that you have to confront a problem, that life is painful and that you have to deal with it. I don't do this to reform inmates. I do it to reform the system ("Crime Wave," *Time*, June 30, 1975: 22).

The secret to Just Community's success is small size (only 30 inmates). We do not know whether such democratic participation would work in a larger prison, but the idea of responsible participation in running an organization may in some ways better prepare offenders to take part as responsible citizens than totally controlling their lives in prison.

All of these proposals to solve the problems of our prisons, from abolition to reform, depend on what happens to the courts and police. Prisons are as good or as bad as the rest of the system requires them to be. So all proposals for solving the problems of the criminal-justice system must be given *equal* attention. Redistribution of wealth, power, and prestige must be given first priority if the system is to become truly a system of justice for all.

THE FUTURE OF THE ADMINISTRATION OF JUSTICE

The future functions and problems of our police, courts, and prisons depend on what happens to crime. As we pointed out in the first part of this chapter, the best predictor of future crime is the age makeup of our population. As our young population declines, so will crime.

Professor James Vorenberg of the Harvard University Law School sees the need for a "deliberate, long-term effort of perhaps ten years" if crime is to be cut and the criminal-justice system made right. With such a commitment, the problems of our justice system may be substantially improved. Criminologist James Q. Wilson estimates that a rational fixed-sentencing structure alone would quickly cut crime by 20 percent. The outlook for decriminalization of many acts (either by law or nonenforcement) appears relatively certain. If present norms, values, and beliefs about the rights of consenting adults to behave as they see fit continue, the future should bring decriminalization of gambling, prostitution, and use of certain illegal drugs. Some states have already passed laws permitting the use of marijuana in one's home. In other states the marijuana laws are virtually ignored by the police. Current changes in sexual mores may well be a harbinger of legalized prostitution. Gambling laws have already changed, as several states make use of a lottery as a way to raise money instead of raising taxes.

The Future of the Police

The future of the police clearly seems to be in the direction of more professionalization. This means a better-educated, better-trained police force. Whether it means a more humane one remains to be seen. Technology and weapons will dominate the thinking of law-enforcement people, from patrol officer to chief. Greater emphasis will be placed on discipline, professional pride, and impersonal relations with the public. Programs to train police in good community and human relations will continue to be needed. The move is clearly away from personal involvement with people in the neighborhood. That died when walking the beat was replaced by the two-man patrol car. What personal involvement can there be when local neighborhoods are monitored by closed-circuit television cameras and helicopters, all directed by a centralized computer?

Greater cooperation among and coordination of local law-enforcement activities will come from state and federal sources. The outlook is for more emphasis on equipment and technology, rather than positive interaction with the community. As local police become more dependent on state and federal funds, standardization and conformity with state and federal rules will increase. Can central direction and command of local police be far behind?.

The Future of the Courts

Not much change can be expected in our courts. Of all our institutions, they are one of the most rigid and will remain very difficult to change. But the potential is there. If judges, lawyers, and prosecutors become serious about wanting to reduce case loads and backlogs, they could modernize the handling of cases by employing technology and new social organization. They could employ the computer in scheduling cases and keeping track of the status of pending cases. They could also hire a full-time administrator to tell the judges how many cases they must hear. Perhaps even a system to motivate judges to hear more cases would be installed. The dangers here are obvious, such as quick, impersonal consideration of cases without due regard for special circumstances involved. A premium might be put on speed of the "assembly-line" instead of on deliberation and justice.

The Future of the Prisons

Most future innovations and changes will take place in our prison system. The public, scholars, politicians, and penal officials are all aware that the present system is simply not working. The most recent reforms are centered around social-science techniques to modify the inmate's behavior. This may well be the wave of the future in prisons. A dim outline of the prison of the future is beginning to emerge as one based on using up-to-date techniques of medicine and social science. These include mind-altering drugs, brain surgery designed to eliminate violent antisocial behavior, electric shocks, and pain-inducing drugs to "negatively condition" prisoners. These techniques are clothed in garments of psychiatry, sociology, and medicine, but they represent a basic drive to control the lives of prisoners. Prisons of the future may make guinea pigs out of human beings.

A New Breed of Prison Official. In this prison of the future, we will also see the rise of a new breed of correctional official: liberal, academically trained, and intelligent enough to understand the social dynamite they are handling. They will attempt to undercut the revolutionary spirit of blacks as they continue to make up a larger segment of the inmate population, and more of the officials will be black themselves. They will attempt to remove the boredom and frustration from daily prison life, and will give more attention to Maslow's "higher needs" for fulfillment. They will even talk about opening "lines of communication" and of "sharing power with responsible inmates" when the prisoners attempt to unionize or organize. Yet most of it will only be talk. All this time, they will be ready, willing, and able to use whatever force (physical, psychological, or medical) that is necessary to deal with prisoners who do not cooperate with the system. Their ultimate goal will be to maintain a prison system whose main aim will be to have prisoners passively conform to the rules. With new techniques of physical and social science to aid them, these new prison administrators will create a "liberal totalitarianism" in the prison of the future. It should arrive just about on schedule—1984 (Pallas and Barber, 1974: 355).

For nearly two centuries, reformers and government commissioners have repeated the same criticisms, recounted the same abuses, urged the same reforms, while the prison system continued virtually unchanged. Perhaps the future of the prison is that it has none (or very little). In utter rebellion and disgust with their failures and their costs, the public and political structure may decide to abandon them (with minor exceptions). Perhaps the future of prisons has been been expressed by James Doyle, a federal judge of the Western District of Wisconsin:

> I am persuaded that the institution of prison probably must end. In many respects it is as intolerable within the United States as was the institution of slavery, equally brutalizing to all involved, equally toxic to the social system, equally subversive of the brotherhood of man . . . (Morris and Jacobs, 1974: 2).

So the functions and operations of each part of the system, the police, courts, and prisons, will remain intertwined and related. Thus, a change in one institution could bring challenges and changes into the others.

SUMMARY

The system of administration of justice is defined by liberals and radicals as too harsh and unjust, and by conservatives as too lax and permissive. The "injustice" perspective was used in analyzing the problems. The three major law-enforcement agencies—police, courts, and prisons—are all found guilty of practicing and perpetuating injustices within our social system. Police abuse power and discriminate against certain groups of people. The courts are plagued with case backlogs and overloads. The poor are not properly represented, and their bail is hard to raise. Plea bargaining and forced guilty pleas rather than fair, impartial trials dominate the system. Sentencing by judges is often conflicting, prejudiced, and irrational.

Prisons are the end of the assembly line where prisoners face problems of overcrowding, understaffing, and violence (from guards and inmates alike). Putting young people, especially status offenders, in jail, reform schools, or detention centers has proved unnecessary and harmful. Even the best prisons suffer from serious understaffing of professional staff, especially psychiatrists, doctors, counselors, and educators.

The incidence and prevalence of the problems of administering justice are evident from the large percentage (about 80 percent) of offenders that are never caught. Of those 20 percent arrested, only about 15 percent end up in jail. In 1975 nearly 250,000 persons were in state and federal prisons, 11 percent more than in 1974. Federal prisons alone were 21 percent overcrowded in 1976.

The principal underlying causes of the problem of administering justice include these:

> The crime rate has risen because of changes in traditional values and norms.
>
> The system is designed to punish the poor and powerless and benefit the powerful. This, in turn, affects the operation of police, courts, and prisons.
>
> The courts perpetuate and protect existing economic, political, and social relationships.

Other immediate causes explain problems with police, courts, and prisons. Liberal proposals and recommendations for attempting to solve some of the police problems vary from improved community-police relations to better pay, more recruitment of minorities, neighborhood forces, countervailing power groups, and changing the basic function of the police from arresting powerless individuals to helping them. Conservatives recommend changes in laws, fixed rather than indeterminate sentences, and limitations on judges' power as solutions to court problems. Community-based prisons and halfway houses, as well as deinstitutionalizing juvenile offenders and shutting down the jails, were some of the solutions put forth by liberals for the prison system.

The outlook is for a decline in crime as the crime-prone ages, between 14 and 24, become fewer in number. The future should bring a more professionalized police force, but also one that is more militaristic, impersonal, and centralized. Courts, for the most part, will function much as they have in the past. Prisons may be (virtually) abolished, or they may become more scientific institutions for behavior modification and control. In all, the future holds a mixed picture—with much that pleases, but much also that alarms—and with much for us to do if the basic inequities and injustices are to be changed.

Criminologists.

Such a sociologist specializes in research on the relations between criminal law, the social order, and causes of crime. More are being employed by law-enforcement agencies, although most teach sociology, criminology, law enforcement, and administration of justice courses at colleges and universities. With continued federal financing of crime prevention, career outlook and opportunities are good. For further information write to: The American Society of Criminology, American University, Washington, D.C.

Counseling Occupations.

Professional counselors help delinquents and youth to better understand themselves and their opportunities so they can make and carry out decisions for a more satisfying life. Counseling may be personal, educational, or vocational. Counselors must be objective as well as genuinely concerned about all people. Members of professional occupations — sociologists, psychologists, social workers, college student personnel — do counseling as well as do people in teaching, health care, law, religion, personnel, and other fields related to sociology. Career planning and placement counselors who can direct potential delinquents (and others) into socially acceptable occupations will be in demand in the future.

Police and Private Security Guards (and Watchmen).

Over 800,000 public and private police and security personnel are employed. Demand is usually good for both. Basic entry levels call for varied skills, education, and training, though sociology helps one to understand where security fits into the organization and how crime can be prevented within the organization. Public police employment is generally determined by civil-service tests and political contacts. Standards for private security guards vary. Shift work is the norm, and part-time employment as a night guard (or watchman) may be available as an entry-level job. As public police officers become more professional, a college degree in social sciences or the administration of justice will become more important. Salaries vary by location and jurisdiction. For further information write to: American Federation of Police, 110 N. E. 125th St., North Miami, Fla.

Probation/Parole Officers.

Probation is a court disposition with no prison involved. To aid the judge to dispose of the case, the officer investigates the background, family experience, education, and underlying personal or emotional problems of the offender. He also supervises the activities of the person put on probation.

Parole is release from prison under guided supervision. The parole officer investigates the parolee's prospective job and talks to people with whom the parolee will live. After release from prison, the parole officer meets periodically with the parolee and counsels him about employment, educational, and vocational goals; about family, interpersonal, and community relations; and about general adjustment to release. According to the National Council on Crime and Delinquency, "at least 30,000 more full-time officers are needed in the . . . areas of adult and juvenile probation and parole." Many probation and parole departments now require a B.A. in social sciences, and some prefer a graduate degree in social work or one of the social sciences. Salaries range from $8,500 to $15,000 a year in the more professional systems. For further information write to: The American Correctional Association, 4321 Hartwick Rd., Suite L-208, College Park, Md. 20740.

Paralegal Aides.

Large law firms in metropolitan areas have launched programs employing paralegal aides, some of whom have backgrounds in sociology. Special courses are usually required after completion of college (or during summer months at some universities). The paralegal aide investigates cases for attorneys, does library research, helps lawyers in preparing court briefs, contacts witnesses to ensure their appearance in court, and handles other tasks and responsibilities assigned to them by members of the bar. Understanding human behavior as sociologists do can be an asset in this career. This can be a good stop-gap job for sociology majors if thinking about law school, or can branch out into other occupations in law and the administration of justice. For further information write to : The National Center for Paralegal Training, 1290 Avenue of the Americas, New York, New York 10019.

REFERENCES

I. Crime and Juvenile Delinquency

"ABA Falls 2 Votes Short in Bid to Ease Prostitution Penalties." The Allentown Morning Call (February 17): 3, 1976.

Baker, Russell
1974 "Clearance." New York Times Magazine (June 16): 6.

Bingham, Jonathan
1975 "Should Manufacture and Sale of Handguns for Private Use Be Prohibited in the United States?: Pro." Congressional Digest 54, 12 (December): 296–300.

Brace, Charles Loring
1880 The Dangerous Classes of New York, 3rd ed. (New York: Wynkoop & Hallenbeck), p. 27, as quoted by Edward Banfield, The Unheavenly City. Boston: Little, Brown, 1968.

Brantingham, Paul and Frederic Faust
1976 "A Conceptual Model of Crime Prevention." Crime and Delinquency 22, 3 (July): 284–96.

Burnett, Albert
    1976 "Citizens Crusade Against Crime, Neighborhood Watch Panel Workshop Report." Muhlenberg College Board of Associates Conference on Citizens Crusade Against Crime. March 27, Allentown, Pa.

Burnham, David
    1974 "New York Is Found Safest of 13 Cities in Crime Study." New York Times (April 15): 51.

"Children and the Law." Newsweek (September 8): 66–72, 1975.

Cloward, Richard A. and Lloyd Ohlin
    1960 Delinquency and Opportunity. New York: Free Press.

"Controversy over Proposed Federal Handgun Legislation: Pro and Con." Congressional Digest 54, 12 (December): entire issue, 1975.

Cordasco, Francesco, ed.
    1968 Jacob Riis Revisited: Poverty and the Slum in Another Era. Garden City, N.Y.: Anchor.

"Crime: A Case for More Punishment." Business Week (September 15): 92–97, 1975

"Crime Rate, Teen Arrests Show a Sharp Increase." Allentown Call Chronicle (November 18): 2, 1975

"The Crime Wave." Time 105, 27 (June 30): 10–24, 1975

"Fear of Crime, Victimization Now Common to Many Americans." The Gallop Opinion Index, Report No. 24 (October): 6–17, 1975

Ferdinand, Theodore
    1967 "The Criminal Patterns of Boston Since 1849." American Journal of Sociology 73 (July): 84–99.

Graham, Hugh D. and Ted R. Gurr, eds.
    1969 Violence in America: Historical and Comparative Perspectives. New York: Bantam.

Harris, Louis
    1973 The Anguish of Change. New York: Norton.

Heussenstamm, F. K.
    1971 "Bumper Stickers and Cops." Trans-Action 8 (February): 32–33.

Hirschi, Travis
    1969 Causes of Delinquency. Berkeley: University of California Press.

Hirschi, Travis and David Rudisill
    1976 "The Great American Search: Causes of Crime in 1876–1976." Annals of the American Academy of Political and Social Science 423 (January): 14–22.

Holden, Constance
    1976 "Law Enforcement Assistance Administration: Anticrime Agency Faces Criticism, Lowered Budget." Science 193, 4247 (July 2): 37.

Horn, Jack
    1975 "The Juvenile Status Offender: Neither Fish Nor Fowl." Psychology Today (August): 31.

Jackson, Maynard
  1975 Fund-Raising Letter on Behalf of the National Gun Control Center. Washington, D.C.

Jacobson, Alvin
  1975 "Crime Trends in Southern and Nonsouthern Cities: A 20-Year Perspective." Social Forces 54, 1 (September): 226–42.

Katzenbach, Nicholas
  1967 "The Chairman of the National Crime Commission Answers Some Tough Questions About Crime." Look (March 7): 101–6.

"Kill LEAA, Congress Is Urged." Allentown Morning Call (September 7): 1, 1976.

Lane, Roger
  1969 "Urbanization and Criminal Violence in the 19th Century: Massachusetts as a Test Case." Pp. 468–84 in Hugh D. Graham and Ted R. Gurr, eds. The History of Violence in America. New York: Bantam.
  1976 "Criminal Violence in America: The First Hundred Years." The Annals of the American Academy of Political and Social Science 423 (January): 1–13.

Loftus, Joseph
  1969 "Panel Says Crime by Youths Is Key to U.S. Violence." New York Times (January 30): 1, 79.

Lundman, Richard, Paul McFarlane, and Frank Scarpitti
  1976 "Delinquency Prevention: A Description and Assessment of Projects Reported in the Professional Literature." Crime and Delinquency 22, 3 (July): 296–308.

Matza, David
  1964 Delinquency and Drift. New York: Wiley.

Mauss, Armand
  1975 Social Problems as Social Movements. Philadelphia: Lippincott.

McVeigh, Frank
  1972 "The Use of Dogs by Police in Urban Areas." Paper presented at Pennsylvania Sociological Society Annual Meeting. October 21, Bethlehem, Pa.

Milakovich, M. E. and Kurt Weis
  1975 "Politics and Measures of Success in the War on Crime." Crime and Delinquency 21, 1 (January): 1–10.

Miller, Walter B.
  1958 "Lower Class Culture as a Generating Milieu of Gang Delinquency." Journal of Social Interest 14: 5–19.

Murray, Douglas
  1975 "Handguns, Gun Control Law and Firearm Violence." Social Problems 23, 1 (October): 81–92.

"Next 25 Years: How Your Life Will Change." U.S. News & World Report 80, 12 (March 22): 39–42, 1976.

Ogren, Robert W.
  1975 "The Ineffectiveness of the Criminal Sanction in Fraud and Corruption Cases: Losing the Battle against White-Collar Crime." American Criminal Law Review 11 (Summer): 959–88.

Pepinsky, Harold
  1976 "The Growth of Crime in the United States." The Annals of the American Academy of Political and Social Science 423 (January): 23–30.

President's Commission on Law Enforcement and Administration of Justice
  1967 Task Force Report: Crime and Its Impact – An Assessment. Washington, D.C.: U.S. Government Printing Office.

Raab, Selwyn
  1976 "Major Crime Up 11.8% Here in 1975." New York Times (February 10): 1, 12.

Ring, Robert W.
  1976 Letter from Crime Prevention Unit, Allentown Police Department, about "Neighborhood Watch" and "Operation I.D."

Ryan, William
  1976 Blaming the Victim, Rev. and updated ed. New York: Random House.

Schur, Edwin M.
  1973 Radical Non-Intervention: Rethinking the Delinquency Problem. Englewood Cliffs, N.J.: Prentice-Hall.

Smith, Alexander B. and Harriet Pollack
  1975 "Crimes Without Victims." Saturday Review (December 4, 1971). Pp. 98–101 in Peter Wickerman et al., eds. Annual Editions: Readings in Social Problems 75/76. Guilford, Conn.: Dushkin.

Stewart, Elbert W.
  1976 The Troubled Land, 2nd ed. New York: McGraw-Hill.

Sutherland, Edwin H.
  1961 White Collar Crime. New York: Holt, Rinehart and Winston.
  1972 "Theory of Differential Association." Pp. 81–83 in Rose Giallombardo, ed., Juvenile Delinquency. New York: Wiley.

Uniform Crime Report. Federal Bureau of Investigation. Washington, D.C.: U.S. Government Printing Office, 1976

Uniform Crime Reports: Preliminary Annual Release, March 30. Federal Bureau of Investigation. Washington, D.C.: U.S. Government Printing Office, 1977

Weis, Kurt and Michael Milakovich
  1975 "Political Misuses of Crime Rates." Society 11, 5 (July/August 1974): 89–95.

"White Collar Crime: Huge Economic and Moral Drain." Congressional Quarterly (May): 1047–49, 1971

Wilkins, Leslie T.
  1973 "Crime and Criminal Justice at the Turn of the Century." Annals of the American Academy of Political and Social Science 408 (July): 13–29.

Wright, James D. and Linda Marston
  1976 "The Ownership of the Means of Destruction: Weapons in the United States." Social Problems 23, 1 (October): 93–106.

Zietz, Dorothy
  1969 Child Welfare: Services and Perspectives, 2nd ed. New York: Wiley.

II. Administering Justice

Allison, Junius L.
- 1973 The Juvenile Court Comes of Age. Public Affairs Pamphlet No. 419. New York: Public Affairs Committee.

Alterman, Daniel and Theodore Becker
- 1976 "Bleak House Lives! The Brooklyn House of Detention Case." Intellect 104, 2371 (January): 311.

"ARD Participants." Allentown Morning Call (November 26): 4, 1976

Baldwin, Roger
- 1975 "Why Innovative Programs in Family Crisis Intervention Training Are Particularly Effective." Paper presented at the American Society of Criminology Annual Meeting, Toronto, Canada (November 2).

"The Consequences of the Overdistention of Authority and the Police Image." Criminologica 7, 4 (February): 36–47, 1970.

Billias, George A., ed.
- 1965 Law and Authority in Colonial America. New York: Dover.

"Blacks Found Composing 47% of States' Inmates." Allentown Morning Call (June 2): 13, 1976.

Bouma, Donald
- 1969 Kids and Cops. Grand Rapids, Mich.: Eerdmans.
- 1975 "Narrowing the Hostility Gap." Pp.120–29 In Paul B. Horton and Gerald R. Leslie, eds. Readings in the Sociology of Social Problems. 2nd ed. Englewood Cliffs, N.J.: Prentice-Hall.

Casper, Jonathan
- 1975 "Criminal Justice: View from the Bottom." Intellect 103, 2363 (February): 315–18.

Chevigny, Paul
- 1969 Police Power: Police Abuses in New York City. New York: Pantheon.

"Corruption Is Part of Policeman's Lot, Scholar Maintains." New York Times (March 31): 20, 1975.

"Cost of Juvenile Prisons Shows 40% Rise in Two Years." New York Times (September 2): 32, 1975.

"Cover-Up on Attica." Time (April 21): 58, 1975.

"The Crime Wave." Time (April 21): 58, 1975.

Dershowitz, Alan
- 1976 "Criminal Sentencing in the United States: An Historical and Conceptual Overview." The Annals of the American Academy of Political and Social Science 423 (January): 117–32.
- 1976 "Let the Punishment Fit the Crime." Pp. 268–71 in Anne Kilbride, ed. Readings in Sociology, 76/77: Annual Editions. Guilford, Conn.: Dushkin.

Douthal, Strat
- 1976 "Crowding Creating Violence in Nation's Prisons." Allentown Sunday Call-Chronicle (June 6): A-11.

"8 Years on Death Row End as Pair Leaves Jail." Allentown Morning Call (September 20): 11, 1975.

"Federal Prisons Termed Crowded Beyond Capacity." Allentown Morning Call (March 15): 2, 1976.

"15 on ARD." Allentown Morning Call (May 11): 17, 1976.

Fosdick, Raymond B.
1921 American Police Systems. New York: Century.
Friedman, Laurence M.
1973 A History of American Law. New York: Simon & Schuster.
Glaser, Daniel
1974 "From Revenge to Resocialization." Pp. 58–61 in Peter Wickman, ed. Annual Editions: Readings in Social Problems 73/74. Guilford, Conn.: Dushkin.
Green, Edward
1970 "Race, Social Class and Criminal Arrest." American Sociological Review 35 (June): 478–89.
Greene, Mark
1975 "The High Cost of Lawyers." New York Times Magazine (August 10): 8–62.
Griffin, Susan
1975 "Rape: The All-American Crime." Ramparts (September 1971). Pp. 78–85 in Susan Friedman, ed. Annual Editions: Readings in Social Problems, 75/76. Guilford, Conn.: Dushkin.
Harris, Louis
1973 The Anguish of Change. New York: Norton.
Haskins, George L.
1960 Law and Authority in Early Massachusetts. New York: Macmillan.
Hersey, John
1968 The Algiers Motel Incident. New York: Knopf.
Holden, Constance
1975 "Prisons: Faith in 'Rehabilitation' Is Suffering a Collapse." Science 188 (May 23): 815–17.
Horn, Jack
1975 "Kids in Jail." Psychology Today 9, 3 (August): 32.
Hoult, Thomas
1975 "Street Justice in Arizona." Pp. 401–5 in Thomas Hoult, ed. Social Justice and Its Enemies. New York: Wiley.
Hudson, James R.
1970 "Police-Citizen Encounters That Lead to Citizen Complaints." Social Problems 18,2 (Fall): 179–93.
"Inmate Who Complained about Violence Is Freed." Allentown Morning Call (June 3): 12, 1976.
Jackson, Donald
1975 "Justice for None." Pp. 186–90 in Susan Friedman, ed. Annual Editions: Readings in Social Problems, 75/76. Guilford, Conn.: Dushkin.
Knapp, Whitman
1972 "Report by the Commission to Investigate Allegations of Police Corruption in New York City." Pp. 525–34 in Jerome Skolnick and Elliott Currie, eds. Crisis in American Institutions. 3rd ed. Boston: Little, Brown, 1976.
Kratcoski, Peter and Kirk Scheuerman
1975 "Convicted Offenders' Perceptions of the Criminal Justice Process." Intellect 103, 2363 (February): 312–14.

Kress, Jack M.
1976 "Progress and Prosecution." Annals of the American Academy of Political and Social Science 423 (January): 99–116.

Landau, Jack
1976 "'Law' Practice of Releasing Suspect without Bail Being Closely Reviewed." Allentown Sunday Call-Chronicle (May 16): B-17.

Lefcourt, Robert, ed.
1971 Law against the People: Essays to Demystify Law, Order and the Courts. New York: Random House.

"Living In." Time (April 21): 33–34, 1975.

McKee, Michael and Ian Robertson
1975 Social Problems. New York: Random House.

Mitford, Jessica
1974 Kind and Usual Punishment: The Prison Business. New York: Vintage.

Moore, Acel
1975 "FOP Pays Officer Who Beat Youth, 16." Philadelphia Inquirer (March 13): 1.

Morris, Noval
1968 "Politics and Pragmatism in Crime Control." Federal Probation (June): 13.

Morris, Noval and James Jacobs
1974 Proposals for Prison Reform. Public Affairs Pamphlet No. 510. New York: Public Affairs Committee.

"Much Work Ahead on Prison Ship." Allentown Sunday Call-Chronicle (May 23): A-10, 1976.

Nelson, William
1974 "Emerging Notions of Modern Criminal Law in the Revolutionary Era: An Historical Perspective." Pp. 100–126 in Richard Quinney, ed. Criminal Justice in America. Boston: Little, Brown.

"Next 25 Years: How Your Life Will Change." U.S. News & World Report 80, 12 (March 22): 29–42, 1976.

Oelsner, Lesley
1975 "Study Finds Poor Unaided in Court." New York Times (November 15): 1, 28.

Pallas, John and Bob Barber
1974 "From Riot to Revolution." Pp. 340–55 in Richard Quinney, ed. Criminal Justice in America. Boston: Little, Brown.

"Penal Rehabilitation Seen Useless." Allentown Morning Call (February 19): 2, 1976.

Platt, Anthony
1974 "The Triumph of Benevolence: The Origins of the Juvenile Justice System in the United States." Pp. 356–89 in Richard Quinney, ed. Criminal Justice in America. Boston: Little, Brown.

"The Prisons Overflow." Time 106, 45 (November 10): 43, 1975.

Quinney, Richard, ed.
1974 Criminal Justice in America: A Critical Understanding. Boston: Little, Brown.

Reiss, Albert
    1975   "Police Brutality: Answers to Key Questions." Pp. 82–94 in Paul Horton and Gerald Leslie, eds. Readings in the Sociology of Social Problems. 2nd ed. Englewood Cliffs, N.J.: Prentice-Hall.

"Replace Most Prisons, Panel on Crime Urges." Allentown Morning Call (October 15): 2, 1973.

"Report Says Attica Probe Was 'Unfair' to Prisoners." Allentown Morning Call (December 22): 1, 1975.

"'Revolving Door' Justice: Why Criminals Go Free." U.S. News & World Report 80, 19 (May 10): 36–40, 1976.

Ross, Sid and Herbert Kupferberg
    1972   "Shut Down Reform Schools?" Parade Magazine (September 17): 5.
    1973   "The Shame of Our Country's Jails." Parade Magazine (November 4): 6–19.

Rothman, David J.
    1971   The Discovery of the Asylum. Boston: Little, Brown.

Sage, Wayne
    1975   "Crime and Clockwork Lemon." Pp. 191–96 in Susan Friedman, ed. Annual Editions: Readings in Social Problems, 75/76. Guilford, Conn.: Dushkin.

"Shock Probation." Time (May 7): 103, 1973.

Smith, Alexander and Harriet Pollock
    1975   "Crimes without Victims." Pp. 95–98 in Susan Friedman, ed. Annual Readings in Social Problems, 74/75. Guilford, Conn.: Dushkin.

Stark, Rodney
    1975   Social Problems. New York: Random House.

"States Ignore Cheaper Methods of Handling Juvenile Offenders." Allentown Sunday Call-Chronicle (December 28): A-3, 1975.

Steele, James and Donald Barlett
    1975   "The Courts Are Worse Than Anybody Thought: Justice in Philadelphia." Pp. 140–42, in Julia Cheever, ed. Your Community and Beyond. Palo Alto, Calif.: Page-Ficklin.

Stewart, Elbert
    1976   The Troubled Land: Social Problems in Modern America. New York: McGraw-Hill.

"System of Juvenile Justice Is Condemned as a Failure." Allentown Sunday Call-Chronicle (May 23): A-11, 1976.

Turner, Jonathan
    1972   American Society: Problems of Structure. New York: Harper & Row.

"2 on Death Row 8 Years about to Win Freedom." Allentown Morning Call (September 17); 16, 1975.

Uniform Crime Reports: 1976. Washington, D.C.: U.S. Government Printing Office, 1977.

Uniform Crime Reports: 1975. Washington, D.C.: U.S. Government Printing Office, 1976.

Uniform Crime Reports: 1967. Washington, D.C.: U.S. Government Printing Office, 1968.

Von Hirsch, Andrew
   1976 Doing Justice: The Choice of Punishment. New York: Hill & Wang. "The Wages of Sin." Good News (May): 7, 1976.

Waskow, Arthur
   1969 "Community Control of the Police." Trans-Action 7 (December): 4–7.

Wilkins, Leslie T.
   1976 "Equity and Republican Justice." The Annals of the American Academy of Political and Social Science 423 (January): 152–62.

Wooden, Kenneth
   1976 Weeping in the Playtime of Others. New York: McGraw-Hill.

SUGGESTED READINGS

I. Crime and Juvenile Delinquency

Albrecht, Mary Ellen with Barbara Lang Stern. The Making of a Woman Cop. New York: Morrow. 1976.
> A woman's view of what it takes to become a law-enforcement officer and the many hurdles to overcome in becoming a part of the police department.

Finestone, Harold. Victims of Change: Juvenile Delinquents in American Society. Westport, Conn.: Greenwood Press. 1976.
> Traces the historical causes and treatment of juvenile delinquency, together with the modern theories and programs for remedying this social problem.

Hendrickson, Robert. Ripoffs. New York: Viking. 1976.
> A complete survival guide to protect yourself against muggers, rapists, obscene phone callers, credit-card crooks, and con men.

McCaghy, Charles. Deviant Behavior: Crime, Conflict and Interest Groups. New York: Macmillan. 1976.
> Describes society's views of crime and how various groups retain a vested interest in crime.

Moquin, Wayne and Charles Van Doren. The American Way of Crime: A Documentary History. New York: Praeger. 1976.
> Readings from a variety of perspectives describe and analyze the local and international activities of organized crime.

Rubin, Arnold P. The Youngest Outlaws: Runaways in America. New York: Messner. 1976.
> A discussion of young runaways, including case studies and statistics, and how they are treated by the law and society.

Sanders, William B. Juvenile Delinquency. New York: Praeger. 1976.
> Gives the reader a basic understanding of the problem of delinquency and emphasizes the interactionist approach, often overlooked in this field, as well as viewing the legal aspects of delinquency.

Wooden, Kenneth. Weeping in the Playtime of Others: America's Incarcerated Children. New York: McGraw-Hill. 1976.

A national profile and exposé of legal child abuse as practiced by state juvenile institutions. A passionate plea to exempt "status offenders" from treatment as criminals. Also an interesting case history of murderer Charles Manson.

Periodicals Worth Exploring
Adolescence
Crime and Delinquency
Criminology
Journal of Criminal Law & Criminology
Law and Contemporary Problems

II. Administering Justice

Dodge, Calvert R., ed. A Nation without Prisons. Lexington, Mass.: Heath. 1975.

A broad overview of various schools of thought about effective rehabilitation of offenders. It aims to stimulate thought and action.

Rosett, Arthur and Donald Cressey. Justice by Consent: Plea Bargains in the American Court House. Philadelphia: Lippincott. 1976.

Traces one criminal case through court procedures, reveals how the system functions, and examines proposals for reforming the system.

Thomas, Wayne H. Bail Reform in America. Berkeley: University of California Press. 1976.

A study of national efforts, past and present, to provide the quickest and least restrictive form of release consistent with justice and public safety.

Toch, Hans. Peacekeeping: Police, Prisons and Violence. Lexington, Mass.: Lexington Books. 1976.

Deals with violence as encountered by criminals and criminal suspects with the police, prison inmates, and staff.

Vetter, Harold J. and Clifford D. Simonsen. Criminal Justice in America: The System, the Process, the People. Philadelphia: Saunders. 1976.

A good overview and analysis of the entire criminal justice system and the actors in it.

Periodicals Worth Exploring
Criminal Justice & Behavior
Criminology
Federal Probation
Journal of Criminal Law & Criminology
Journal of Police Science and Administration

Problems of Drug and Alcohol Abuse

I. Drugs *wed.*

INTRODUCTION

DEFINITIONS OF THE PROBLEM
Various drugs—stimulants, depressants, and hallucinogens.
Three definitions of the drug problem:
a) "Drug Fiend."
b) Subcultural deviance.
c) "Total culture."
Difficulties in defining drug abuse.

INCIDENCE AND PREVALENCE OF THE PROBLEM
By 1976, 33 million had tried marijuana; 12 million regular users.
Some 300,000 to 400,000 daily heroin users, and about one-and-a-half million youngsters (ages 12 to 18) used heroin at least once.
Polydrug use and abuse have grown as new drugs appear.

CAUSES OF THE PROBLEM
Personality theories (dependent, immature, addictive).
Poor environmental and subcultural conditions.
Peer pressure and influence.
Pleasure.

PROPOSED SOLUTIONS TO THE PROBLEM
Therapeutic communities and halfway houses.
Outpatient treatment programs.
Methadone maintenance.
Strict law enforcement v. liberalizing the laws.

FUTURE OF THE PROBLEM
Legal changes.
Redefining the problem.
Using the British system.

II. Alcohol

DEFINITIONS OF THE PROBLEM
Classification and types of drinkers.
Socialization to accept alcohol.
Definitions of alcoholism and intoxication.

INCIDENCE AND PREVALENCE OF THE PROBLEM
Some 90 million Americans drink—9 to 10 million are alcoholics, and millions more are problem drinkers.
Youth alcohol abuse is severe.
Socioeconomic factors affect alcohol abuse.
Problems from alcohol abuse:
a) Some crimes and auto accidents.
b) Admissions to mental hospitals.
c) Higher suicide rate among alcoholics.
d) Family violence.
e) Costs to business.

CAUSES OF THE PROBLEM
Environmental.
Subcultural.
Peer pressure.
Pleasure.

PROPOSED SOLUTIONS TO THE PROBLEM
Treatment programs for alcoholism.
Family's role in rehabilitation.
Alcoholics Anonymous.
Halfway houses and other treatment centers.
Educational efforts to change values.

FUTURE OF THE PROBLEM
Increased use and abuse of alcohol.
New uniform laws to treat alcoholism.
New medical approaches.
Change of basic attitudes through education.

SUMMARY

A taxi driver lights a cigarette. An accountant working late drinks a cup of coffee. A politician offers friends drinks in his office. An insomniac takes a prescribed sleeping pill. Lawyers and business people at a dinner party pass around marijuana cigarettes. A sixth-grader sniffs glue in her bedroom. A teenager uses money from a stolen purse to buy heroin and "shoots up." An electronics engineer consumes three Manhattans with dinner at a restaurant; on the way home he kills two people in an auto crash.

At about the same time, a professor at a cocktail party refuses a drink. A high-school student quietly leaves the room when his friends start passing a marijuana "joint." A truck driver turns down the cigarette his buddy offers. And a housewife decides to see whether her headache will go away without aspirin. Such is the American drugscape in the 1970s.

Joel Fort and Christopher Cory, **The American Drugstore.** Boston: Little, Brown, 1975: 3.

I. DEFINING THE DRUG PROBLEM

With these words Dr. Joel Fort and Christopher Cory open their widely known book *American Drugstore: A (Alcohol) to V (Valium)* (1975). The point they make is that what we usually define as "the drug problem" is much more than heroin addicts and pushers. The problem is a lot closer to home than we know or care to admit. It is in our bathroom medicine cabinet, or dining room liquor closet, or our kitchen cubby. We live in a drug-oriented culture and society.

Thus, the social issue of drugs begins with a personal problem, for which we pop a pill. Millions do it, so the instant solution to our personal problem itself becomes a social issue. But there are many definitions of the various types of drugs, and differences over what constitutes our society's "drug problem." What makes one drug socially acceptable and another illicit and illegal, and how have terms to describe drug use changed?

Types of Drugs and Terminology

Medically, a drug is any chemical substance that modifies a person's normal bodily processes or functions. According to the National Commission on Marijuana and Drug Abuse (hereafter referred to as the National Commission) a drug is "any substance other than food which by its chemical nature affects the structure or function of a living organism" (1973:9). A drug may be used as an aid to healing when one is sick, or it may be used to alter one's mood and perceptions. Some drugs satisfy both purposes. Most drugs are psychoactive—they are capable of altering a person's behavior by affecting consciousness, thinking, or emotions.

Psychoactive Drugs. Many common substances, such as coffee, tea, tobacco, and aspirin, are also drugs (and may be habit-forming). Psychoactive drugs are of three major types: stimulants, depressants (narcotics and sedatives), and hallucinogens.

Stimulants activate the user's central nervous system, increasing one's alertness and, depending on the dose, stimulating the user. Natural drug stimulants include caffeine (in coffee, tea, and cola), cocaine (from the coca leaf), and nicotine (in tobacco). Man-made stimulants are called amphetamines.

Depressants calm people by slowing the functioning of the central nervous system. Depressant drugs include the opiates, or narcotics—opium, heroin, morphine—and the sedatives (natural, artificial, and synthesized)—alcohol, barbiturates, and tranquilizers. Narcotics induce sleep or stupor and relieve pain.

Hallucinogens can disorganize thoughts, distort perceptions, and (as the term implies) cause hallucinations. They make users extremely sensitive to their emotional and physical environment although, again, much depends on the dose. LSD,* mescaline, peyote, and psilocybin are the common ones.

Marijuana is in a class by itself, and researchers disagree on how it should be classified. It comes from the female hemp plant, *cannabis sativa*, and is a relaxant that produces various degrees of euphoria. Table 3–1 shows the various classifications of the drugs just described.

Drugs and the drug problem are defined in three different ways: (1) the "drug fiend" or "dope fiend" concept, reinforced by a strict criminal approach; (2) the concept of youth subcultural or countercultural deviance; (3) the "total drug culture." The public and law-enforcement agencies usually endorse the first two approaches but reject the third.

The Drug-Fiend Definition. The oldest definition is that of the drug fiend. It was put forth in the 1920s and 1930s and publicized by the Bureau of Narcotics under the leadership of Harry J. Anslinger. In this conservative view, the drug addict is an "immoral, vicious social leper" who must be punished as a criminal. Marijuana was considered a "killer drug," which inspired crimes of "violence, acts of sexual excess, impotency, insanity and moral degeneracy" (Reasons, January 1975:21). However, actual scientific research into the real effects of drugs was restricted.

The Youth-Subculture Definition. The definition of youth-subculture or countercultural deviance grew out of youth's involvement with drugs during the 1960s. Social scientists, such as Howard Becker, stressed the social and subcultural "learning process" involved in youth's use of drugs. This drug counterculture was defined by the public as one of many rebellious acts aimed at destroying the traditional culture.

---

*lysergic acid diethylamide.

table 3-1   DRUG CLASSIFICATIONS

SEDATIVES	STIMULANTS	NARCOTICS	HALLUCINOGENS	MARIJUANA
Alcohol	Caffeine	Opium	LSD	Hashish
Barbiturates	Nicotine	Opium derivatives:		
Luminal	Cocaine	Morphine	Peyote	
Amytal		Heroin	Mescaline	
Nembutal	Amphetamines:	Codeine		
Seconal	Benzedrine	Hydomorphine	Psilocybin	
Pentathol	Dexadrine	Synthetic	DMT (Synthetic	
Tranquilizers:	Methedrine	narcotics:	derivatives	
Thorazine	Desoxyn	Methadone	DET of psilocybin)	
Compazene	Preludin	(Dolophine)	THC (chemical deriv-	
Stellazine	Dexamyl	Meperidine	ative of	
Reserpine	Anti-depressant	(Demerol)	marijuana)	
Barbituratelike	drugs:			
tranquilizers:	Tofranil			
Doriden	Elavil			
Miltown				
Librium	Amphetaminelike			
Quaalude	drugs:			
Somnes	Nardil			
Nectoe	Parnate			

Source: Frank Scarpitti. **Social Problems** (New York: Holt, Rinehart and Winston, 1974):343.

Drug addiction by the young is seen as linked to long hair, free love, sexual promiscuity (even homosexuality), and dropouts from the straight society. According to sociologist Joseph Gusfield (1975:9), the connections between drug use and cultural change became quite clear to the public. Many who accept this definition consider the drug counterculture as revolutionaries trying to overthrow our society by urging young people to "turn on" to drugs and to "turn off" self-control and obedience to authority. Some even view drug use as a Communist plot to weaken the youth of our nation. In this view "addiction happens automatically whenever someone takes sufficiently large and frequent doses of certain drugs, particularly the opiates" (Peele and Brodsky, 1975:29).

The Total-Drug-Culture Definition. A third definition of drugs and the drug problem has emerged. The first two views of the problem made a sharp distinction between illegal drugs (heroin, marijuana, LSD, etc.), which they condemned, and "legitimate" drugs, which are medicines. Most Americans still define drugs and the drug problem as heroin, cocaine, or marijuana. Table 3-2 shows the extent to which certain substances are considered to be drugs. A narrow group of "psychoactive" substances were viewed as drugs by the public in that study, while alcohol

table 3-2 SUBSTANCES CONSIDERED DRUGS BY ADULTS AND YOUTH

	ADULTS (N = 2,411)	YOUTH (N = 880)
	(percentage)	
HEROIN	95	96
COCAINE	88	86
BARBITURATES	83	91
MARIJUANA	80	80
AMPHETAMINES	79	86
ALCOHOL	39	34
TOBACCO	27	16
NO OPINION	1	1

Source: **National Commission on Marijuana and Drug Abuse,** Drug Use in America: Problem in Perspective" (1973): 9.

A vast arsenal of drugs is readily available to almost everyone at the local drugstore in our drug-oriented culture.

and tobacco were generally not. Drug abuse was viewed as taking a drug for a nonmedical purpose.

The third definition ignores this difference and points to the widespread use of many different drugs for medical and nonmedical reasons in our "drug culture" (as suggested in the opening quotation of this chapter). Since the early 1950s drug taking has become a way of life. Doctors write over 230 million prescriptions a year for various drugs. During 1970, "five billion doses of tranquilizers, three billion doses of amphetamines and five billion doses of barbiturates were produced in the United States" (Bernstein and Lennard, May/June 1973:14).

The behavior of white middle-class, well-educated youngsters is rationalized by liberals and radicals as not being as serious as we once thought. A whole new vocabulary is used to describe the situation. "Addicts" become "abusers"; "abusers" are "dependent" on drugs, or simply "users"; "users" become "experimenters"; and we now talk of "controlled substances" rather than even naming the drug involved. Advocates of this view seek legalization of marijuana and a lessening of criminal penalties for its possession or use (and have been successful in some places). As well, they propose eventual heroin-maintenance doses for addicts so that they would no longer have to engage in crime to meet the high cost of the drug habit.

This third definition, the total drug culture, is widely accepted by social scientists, while the first two are generally accepted by the public and law-enforcement officials. As we pointed out earlier, most people do not consider alcohol, caffeine, or tobacco as drugs. Nor do they equate prescription drugs with illegal drugs. They fail to appreciate how by law or custom we label certain drugs and behavior legal or socially acceptable and others illegal and deviant. Those who accept the first two definitions (drug fiend and youth subculture) fail to notice the difference between limited use of a drug, and abuse or addiction, or between occasional use and drug taking as a lifestyle. Excessive use or abuse leads to dependence—a recurrent, uncontrollable craving (physical or psychological) for drugs. The addicted user becomes physically dependent on a drug, and severe physical withdrawal symptoms may occur. Normal physical and social functioning is impaired.

As social researcher Daniel Yankelovich notes, "We recognize the degrees of drinking, the social context of drinking, and the line that divides the person who can stop from one who cannot. Yet, when it comes to drugs, suddenly we lose all sense of discrimination and fall back on stereotypes" (October 1975:39).

In his research, Yankelovich found three different kinds of students (who may be typical of adults in our society). At one extreme were conservative antidrug students who cling firmly to traditional moral and social values and lifestyles. (These are typical of advocates of the first definition.) At the other extreme was a far smaller liberal and radical group who make drug abuse an integral part of their life. (This group is typical of what

> ## DRUGS—A COMMENTARY ON SOCIETY
>
> Let's play guess-the-drug.
>
> 1. What widely used substance answers this description: "It's mechanism of action on the brain and other body organs is unknown; it accounts for thousands of deaths and illnesses each year, and it produces not only chromosomal breakage, but actual birth defects in lower animals"?
>
> 2. Which drug "strongly stimulates the central nervous system with excessive doses producing tremors, convulsions, and vomiting"?
>
> 3. What might you take to get "increased alertness and mental activity and a greater capacity for muscular work . . . a very potent mood-elevator or euphoriant and perhaps the strongest antifatigue agent"?
>
> Now the answers. How many said LSD for No. 1? Well, you're wrong. Heroin? Wrong again. It's aspirin. But don't worry; birth defects have been observed only in *lower* animals.
>
> No. 2 sounds rather gruesome, doesn't it? It's nicotine.
>
> No. 3 seems to be potentially valuable for combating fatigue and depression. But somehow American doctors haven't gotten around to prescribing cocaine. They probably will, though. It's not that they have anything in principle against dispensing addictive drugs.
>
> Source: From Linda Hess's review of Joel Fort, *The Pleasure Seekers: The Drug Crisis, Youth and Society* (Indianapolis: Bobbs-Merrill, 1970), in *Saturday Review* 53 (March 14, 1970): 34-35.

definition two describes.) Between the two extremes (nonusers and abusers) is the majority of young people, who fit neither definition. Some members of this group associate with drug users (not addicts) but do not take drugs themselves. Others take narcotic drugs or marijuana to a limited extent but function reasonably well. Still others in this middle group experiment with drugs on rare occasions.

Elements of Drug Abuse

Clearly part of the social issue of drug addiction is that no one can agree on what constitutes the "drug problem," "drug addiction," or "drug abuse." The National Commission on Marijuana and Drug Abuse found that the following statements were mentioned most often in connection with "drug abuse":

nonmedical purposes
prone to excess
habit forming
damaging to health
using for pleasure (to feel good, to get high, etc.) (1973:12).

Only four percent of those surveyed equated the *taking* of illegal drugs per se with the term "drug abuse."

The imprecision of the term "drug" has had serious social consequences. Because the referent of the word differs so widely between the therapeutic and social context, the public is conditioned to believe that "street" drugs act according to entirely different principles from "medical" drugs. The result is that "the risks of the former are exaggerated and the risks of the latter are overlooked" (1973:11). Nevertheless, all three definitions of the drug problem—drug fiend, youth subculture, and drug culture—enter into an understanding of drug addiction as a social problem.

INCIDENCE AND PREVALENCE OF DRUG USE

Ever since 1914, when the Harrison Act restricted and controlled through a tax the use of certain drugs, the incidence and prevalence of drug use and abuse have waxed and waned. Figure 3-1 illustrates the number of "addicts" officially counted by the Bureau of Narcotics through the early 1960s. During the mid- and late 1960s the reported incidence and prevalence of drug abuse increased, and the public became concerned.

In 1972 a nationwide survey on drug use for the National Commission revealed the extent to which both adults and young people use drugs for nonmedical purposes. Table 3-3 shows the results and the different drugs preferred by the young and adults.

Since 1972, drug abuse in the United States has been spreading. Official federal figures generally undercount the number of "hard-drug" addicts. In 1973, government officials thought that the rise in heroin use had ended. Later figures in 1976 showed that we are still in the midst of an increase in use of most drugs, although public concern about the problem has become less intense than in the late 1960s and early 1970s.

The National Commission's 1972 survey reported that over 25 million Americans had tried marijuana at least once and that 8.3 million were "current users" (1972:7). By May 1976, an estimated 33 million persons had tried the drug, and 12 million used it "with some regularity" ("Drugs . . . ," May 10, 1976:26). A 1976 national survey of high-school seniors showed that nearly 53 percent had tried marijuana and 20 percent had used it at least 20 times. Use was up five percent over 1975.

Hearings of the Senate Subcommittee on Internal Security in 1975 revealed that the total number of marijuana users had increased 35 percent since 1971. The number of persons who used it at least once a day, however, has grown from less than half a million in 1971 to "more than three million today" (Maugh, November 28, 1975:867). Estimates from various sources indicate that the total amount of marijuana flowing into the United States in 1975 "was enough to prepare 6.5 to eight billion cigarettes" (Ibid.). Even hashish oil, a more concentrated form of marijuana, has been coming into the country in larger quantities. All this suggests that "the average user is not only using a more potent form of cannabis but also is using more of it" (Ibid.).

3 PROBLEMS OF DRUG AND ALCOHOL ABUSE

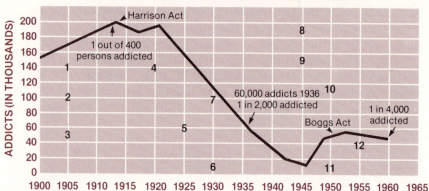

figure 3-1 HISTORY OF NARCOTIC ADDICTION IN THE U.S.

Source: Bureau of Narcotics, U.S. Treasury Department, "Prevention and Control of Narcotic Addiction" (Washington, D.C.: Government Printing Office, 1962): 5

1
- Cases of Addiction 1900—1915
  1. Chinese opium smoking
  2. Civil War opium eaters
  3. Invention and use of the hypodermic needle
  4. Opium, marijuana, and heroin freely available
  5. Heroin introduced as cure for morphine
  6. Opiates as cure for alcoholism
  7. Opium content of patent medicines
  8. Opiates were the only analgesic available
  9. Laudanum

2
- Traffic Supplied by, 1900—1915
  1. Free legal sale of manufactured drugs
  2. Chinese, Persian, and Indian smoking opium (small tax)

3
- Characteristics, 1900—1925
  1. Heavy habits: 2 to 10 grains per day, some 20 to 40 grains
  2. Many cocaine users
  3. Opium smoking common

4
- Traffic Supplies by, 1920
  1. Doctors
  2. Illegal purchase from pharmacies
  3. Official clinics
  4. Diversion from factories and wholesalers
  5. Far and Near East opium
  6. Persian, Bolivian, and Japanese cocaine

5
- Traffic Supplied by, 1920—1940
  1. Imports from manufacturers in Switzerland, Germany, France, etc. (smuggling)
  2. Production of Japanese heroin and morphine factories
  3. Rx forgeries and wholesalers diversion
  4. Small drug store larcenies
  5. India, China, and Near East opium
  6. Limiting of manufacture to world medical needs puts accent on clandestine factories in Europe and Near East

7
- Clandestine manufacture of heroin and morphine in Europe and Near East

6
- Characteristics, 1925—1940
  1. Light habits
  2. Cocaine disappers
  3. Five males to one female
  4. Opium smoking on wane

7
- Addiction, 1900—1945
  Predominantly Caucasian and Chinese

8
- Cause of Addiction, 1945—1960
  1. Italian heroin diversion
  2. Chinese Communist traffic
  3. Turkish, Lebanese, Syrian, and Italian heroin
  4. Light penalties (heavy penalties enacted 1956)
  5. Peruvian cocaine diversion 1946—1948
  6. Reduced enforcement (FBN Training School established 1956)
  7. Juvenile delinquents

9
- Traffic Supplied by, 1940—1960
  1. Turkish, Lebanese, Syrian, Chinese, italian, and French heroin
  2. Mexican heroin (California)
  3. Mexican opium
  4. Drug store robberies, thefts and Rx forgeries

10
- Characteristics
  1. 1946 to 1950, fairly heavy habits
  2. 1950 to 1960, very light habits
  3. 1946 to 1960, heroin addiction predominates

11
- Addiction, 1945—1960
  1. Mostly blacks and Puerto Ricans
  2. Chinese disappearing

12
- Narcotic Control Act (1956)
  Increased enforcement programs of local police in major cities

table 3-3 DRUG USE FOR NONMEDICAL PURPOSES BY AMERICAN YOUTH AND ADULTS, BASED ON 1972 SURVEY

	Youth (Ages 12-17)		Adults (18 and Over)	
	Percentage	Number of Persons	Percentage	Number of Persons
ALCOHOLIC BEVERAGES[1]	24	5,977,200	53	74,080,220
TOBACCO, CIGARETTES[1]	17	4,233,850	38	53,114,120
PROPRIETARY SEDATIVES, TRANQUILIZERS, STIMULANTS[2]	6	1,494,300	7	9,784,180
PRESCRIBED SEDATIVES[2]	3	747,150	4	5,590,960
PRESCRIBED TRANQUILIZERS[2]	3	747,150	6	8,386,440
PRESCRIBED STIMULANTS[2]	4	996,200	5	6,988,700
MARIJUANA	14	3,486,700	16	22,363,840
LSD, OTHER HALLUCINOGENS	4.8	1,195,440	4.6	6,429,604
GLUE, OTHER INHALANTS	6.4	1,593,920	2.1	2,935,254
COCAINE	1.5	373,575	3.2	4,472,768
HEROIN	.6	149,430	1.3	1,817,062

[1] Within the last 7 days.
[2] Nonmedical use only.
Source: National Commission on Marijuana and Drug Abuse.

Heroin Use

Heroin addiction is increasing steadily after an 18-month decline that began in 1972. Dr. Robert L. Dupont, Director of the National Institute on Drug Abuse, noted: "The epidemic is continuing. It had never ended. What we had was an interruption—a temporary downturn" ("Addiction to Heroin . . . ," March 17, 1976:11). Dr. Dupont estimated that in early 1976 there were 300,000 to 400,000 daily heroin users, compared with 200,000 to 300,000 during the brief downturn. But the number in 1976 had not yet reached the 1971 peak of 500,000 to 600,000 addicts. Sociologists Alfred Blumstein, Philip Sagi, and Marvin Wolfgang have indicated that estimates of heroin addicts in the United States "range from 100,000 to more than 10 times that number" (1973:205). According to the National Commission's nationwide survey, about one-and-a-half million Americans between the ages of 12 and 18 have used heroin at least once (Mushkin, January 1975:29). About nine percent of adults and 10 percent of youth have used heroin.

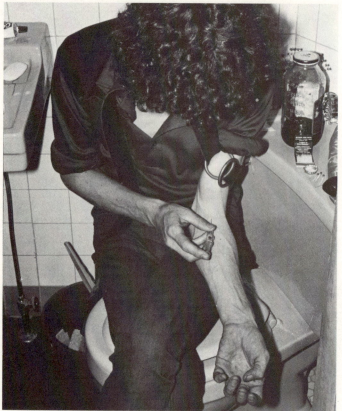

Shooting drugs, or "mainlining," can become a way of life.

Drug-Induced Illnesses and Deaths

Drug-caused illnesses are more prevalent from legal prescription drugs than from illegal use. A 1976 report from the National Institute on Drug Abuse shows that the tranquilizer Valium is the cause of more drug-abuse illnesses than heroin or any other drug. Alcohol mixed with drugs is second. Heroin and morphine are linked more often than other drugs to death from overdose ("Valium...," July 9, 1976:10; "Alcohol and Drugs," July 26, 1976:74). Over 12,000 deaths were connected with drug use in 1975. Table 3-4 shows the drugs (in rank order) leading to serious treated illness or death. Barbiturates alone cause 18 percent of all accidental deaths and an estimated 6 percent of all suicides. Women account for more than 3,000 suicides a year from barbiturate overdoses (Perry and Perry, 1976:361).

Each year we spend over one billion dollars on more than 225 million drug prescriptions for tranquilizers, stimulants, and sedatives. The exact extent of abuse of these legal drugs is practically impossible to assess. In a recent year, 10 billion doses of barbiturates, or 50 doses per person, were manufactured illegally. The legal output of tranquilizers is even higher.

table 3-4 DRUG-INDUCED ILLNESS OR DEATH

DRUGS CAUSING ILLNESS (IN RANK ORDER)	DRUGS CAUSING DEATH	
1. Valium (tranquilizer)	1. Morphine	15% of all deaths
2. Alcohol with other drugs	2. Heroin	
3. Heroin	3. Alcohol with other drugs	13% of all deaths
4. Marijuana		
5. Aspirin		
6. Seconal Elixir		
7. LSD		
8. Analgesics (e.g., Darvon)		
9. Librium (tranquilizer)		
10. Barbiturates (sedative)		

Source: National Institute on Drug Abuse, July 1976. The statistics are compiled by the Federal Drug Abuse Warning Network (DAWN) from more than 1200 hospital emergency rooms, medical examiners and drug-crisis centers in 23 metropolitan areas across the country.

Estimates of the number of persons addicted to these drugs range from 200,000 to over one million (Mauss, 1975:248). Dr. Joel Fort and Christopher Cory note that "estimates derived from the Report of the National Commission... indicate that perhaps 37 million people use sedatives such as barbiturates legally and illegally, and over 63 million smoke tobacco..." (1975:6).

Polydrug Use

A relatively new and potentially very destructive drug-abuse problem is "polydrug use," which seems to increase every year. Mixing drugs and mixing drugs with alcohol (as happened with Karen Quinlan) can produce personal and social problems beyond the scale and scope of the past. As new drugs (legal and illegal) come on the market, the boundaries for drug abuse expand in quantumlike jumps. For example, polydrug use was evident in the National Commission's survey. It found that 86 percent of the adults who smoke marijuana drink regularly, and 55 percent use prescription drugs; 33 percent of sedative users also take stimulants. People are wandering further and further into a chemical jungle, uncertain of where they will come out.

Costs of Drug Abuse

The Strategy Council on Drug Abuse reported that the measurable cost of drug abuse in the United States (excluding alcohol) is between $10 billion and $17 billion a year and will continue to rise. The report read: "The combined dollar costs of alcohol and drug abuse can be conservatively estimated at $35 billion a year." Calling the effects of drugs on individual, family, and community life "unmeasurable," the Council gave these measurable social costs:

> Annual property loss because of drug-related property crime, $6.3 billion
>
> Health-care costs, nearly $200 million
>
> Criminal-justice costs, $620 million, with more than half of state and local spending related to marijuana
>
> Direct drug-abuse program costs, $1.1 billion ("Drug Abuse...," May 31, 1975:2).

Personal problems leading to drug taking have now become a social issue.

A presidential message to Congress in 1976 stated that "in simple dollar terms, drug abuse costs us up to $17 billion" ("Drugs...," 1976:25). In that year, federal spending to combat the drug problem cost more than $750 million—up from $100 million in 1969. With this additional money, law-enforcement programs were enlarged, 100,000 addicts were treated over that seven-year period, and research conducted about the effects of drugs and their uses.

Clearly the social issue of drugs costs society and individuals more than just money. Why, then, do people use and abuse drugs?

CAUSES OF THE DRUG PROBLEM

It is impossible to offer a single answer to this question, for the reasons vary from drug to drug and person to person. We have already seen that cultural values (our "drug culture" and our pill-popping ethos) and definitions of the problem greatly influence drug use. Both personal and social reasons explain the causes behind drug abuse. "Dependent," "immature," and "addicted" personalities; the social structure; poor environmental conditions, from which minorities and others attempt to escape the power of the "corporate state"; peer pressure; and pure pleasure are all put forth as causes of the drug problem.

Personality Factors

Most Americans do not become drug addicts. To explain this fact, psychologists and sociologists have focused on finding distinctive personality traits connected with drug abuse. A major element in profiles of drug addicts is the "dependent personality." In general a drug abuser or a drug-dependent person—

> has difficulty handling frustration, anxiety, and depression (often caused by our demanding social structure and values);
>
> wants immediate gratification of desires;
>
> is lonely and unsuccessful in family and other human relationships;
>
> has low self-esteem;

is impulsive, takes risks, has little regard for health and safety; resents authority and flouts rules (Hill, 1974:9).

However, some persons who have all these characteristics do not turn to drugs; so personality theories do not explain all drug addiction.

Isidor Chein's findings, along with Richard Blum's research, show that drug abusers have likely been trained to accept and exploit a dependent, "sick" role. As Claude Brown, in his famous book about growing up in the black ghetto, *Manchild in the Promised Land*, says: "Nobody expected anything from you if you were a junkie. Nobody expected you to accomplish anything in school or any other areas. . . . You were suddenly relieved of any obligations. People just stopped expecting anything from you from then on. They just started praying for you" (1955:206).

Charles Winick has also found heroin addiction to be a detour from maturity—the addict wishes to remain dependent on drugs and on others. Winick speculates that drug addiction is a temporary reaction to the challenges of late adolescence and early adulthood. Chein also theorizes that rituals connected with heroin use have a powerful appeal for one who is not psychologically prepared to accept an adult role. Such rituals as making contacts, getting money, avoiding arrest, and preparing and administering the injection give addicts a feeling of really living—a feeling they have not gained through normal life.

Related to psychological and social causes is Stanton Peele's analysis of addicts' personality. According to his theory, there are certain types of personalities that can be "addicted" to anything—a lover, a role, or a drug or drugs. Peele's theory starts with the concept of the "weakened self": the person lacks a sense of power to deal effectively with the world and needs a dependency relationship with some external support or prop. The object of the addiction is used repeatedly and gives predictability and certainty to an uncertain life situation. The fear and insecurity produced by our economic and social structure lie behind this uncertainty (1975).

Social Factors

Another cause of the drug problem is our existing social structure. According to neo-Marxist social critic Herbert Marcuse and others, our power structure encourages the masses to indulge in a variety of drug experiences, including alcohol, to divert them from taking action against the oppressive social system in which they live. By encouraging people to concentrate on their personal pleasure and lives, the power elites need not worry about masses of people uniting to revolt against the existing power structure. Drugs keep people insensitive to existing social problems by anesthetizing them against the larger social issues and give them temporary relief from personal worries and troubles. Since millions of dollars are obtained by the sale of drugs, legal and illegal, it is very profitable for some to encourage use of those drugs. This is especially true of brand-name prescription drugs and alcohol.

Addictions of various kinds are serious problems in America; but some are more socially acceptable than others, and one's social class determines how society labels the person's behavior.

Environmental Conditions and Subcultures

Another social cause for drug abuse is escape from environmental conditions. Minority-group members—blacks, the Spanish-speaking, and American Indians—have historically been encouraged to use and abuse drugs to "escape" from social conditions created by the existing power structure in ghettos and slums. This ensured those in the dominant positions of power that minorities would remain powerless and under control. In addition, living within a social environment that encourages, or does not discourage, deviant behavior adds to the probability that drug abuse will occur.

Sociologist Daniel Glaser and associates, for example, have compared 37 New York City addicts with their nonaddicted siblings. The addicts were active in "street life" and the illegitimate-opportunity structure earlier and more seriously than their nonaddicted siblings. The addicts had been arrested and jailed, closing legitimate opportunities to them because of "labeling." At the same time, they gained status among their drug-abusing peers, because they were knowledgeable and experienced in using drugs and were successful in "hustling" for a buck to support their habit. In contrast, their nonaddicted siblings very early avoided involvement in the illegitimate world, played it straight, and sought regular employment (1971:510–21).

According to liberals, changing a drug abuser's social environment and giving him opportunities for a normal life and a decent job can undercut the environmental cause of drug addiction. For example, sociologist Lee Robins discovered in his follow-up study of Vietnam veterans who had gone through the Army's detoxification program that 90 percent had been off heroin after eight to ten months of civilian life (Fort and Cory, 1975:13). Only 8 percent said they used narcotic drugs regularly. New medical tests have verified the claims of these nonabusers. Further, Robins found that some former opium users not detected in the Army's medical-screening program had gotten off heroin without special treatment.

What were the reasons for this amazing success? First, most of the Vietnam addicts were emotionally stable and mentally alert, since preinduction screening eliminates mentally deficient, emotionally disturbed, or criminally oriented persons. Second, they had had a relatively short history of heroin or opium addiction, although most had drunk or smoked before. Since they had no stigma as drug addicts or criminals, they found jobs when they became civilians. No longer in a war situation thousands of miles from home, they found that the lure of drugs took last place to other more positive alternatives. Their social environment and opportunities had changed once they had returned to civilian life. Even alcohol use, which was higher than heroin use in Vietnam, dropped when the men returned to civilian routines; but 53 percent were still drinking heavily, compared with only eight percent continuing on regular use of heroin.

Various subcultures encourage people to use drugs. In studies of addicts who come from poor ghetto areas, the environment does much to cause the addiction and keep them on the drugs, since opportunities for legitimate, well-paying jobs are often not made available on a fair and equitable basis. College subcultures, particularly in large urban university settings, encourage experimentation with various drugs. Ghetto and certain minority-group subcultures foster drug abuse. Dr. Charles Hudson, a Chief of Psychiatric Services with the United States Public Health Service in Alaska, pointed out the cause for drug addiction among minority-group peoples, such as Indians, Eskimos, blacks, and poor whites. He writes: "The major problem is social disintegration. The original social structure in many places in rural Alaska has been blown apart, much as it has been in the central cities, the ghettos and Appalachia" (Fort and Cory, 1975:23). Until our social structure produces stable and prosperous communities, drug abuse will continue out of control, maintain liberals.

Peer Pressure

Another important social cause behind drug addiction is peer pressure and influence. Some drug experts consider this the dominant reason for drug abuse, at least among young people. The National Commission studying causes of marijuana use observed, "One of the most influential factors in determining behavior in contemporary America among adolescents and young adults is peer-group influence. Knowing other people who use marijuana predisposes the individual to use marijuana, and having marijuana-using friends provides the social opportunity for the curious" (1972:43).

A Columbia University study of 8,000 New York State high-school students found that most young users first became involved in drugs when among their friends. By smoking marijuana with their friends, they gain status and reinforce the drug-use behavior of their peers (Hill, 1974:10). Sociologist Richard Dembo and others, in studying young people's reasons for using marijuana, found that its use was "normative" in that it reflects "a commitment to a peer-oriented, adolescent lifestyle that values an openness to new experiences" (1976:177).

Pleasure from Drugs

An additional cause of drug use and abuse is often overlooked by overly grim and sober social scientists—the pursuit of pleasure and fun. We are a pleasure-oriented culture and society. Self-control, sacrifice, and abstinence may have been typical for some in the past, but today the emphasis is on gratification of one's immediate needs. In 1970 a Canadian government commission's explanation for marijuana use was "the simple pleasure of the experience." Edward Brecher and the editors of *Consumer Reports* note that persons who explained to them why they took drugs said: "We do it for fun. Do not try to find a complicated explanation for it. We do it for pleasure" (1972:456). In a hedonistic culture, do fun and pleasure need complicated explanations? Whenever drugs are readily available, and it seems that "everybody is doing it," young people find it easy and reasonable to try illegal drugs.

In review, therefore, causes involving "dependent," "immature," and "addictive" personalities; social structure; poor environmental and subcultural conditions; peer pressure; and pure pleasure underlie the problem of drugs in America.

PROPOSED SOLUTIONS TO THE DRUG PROBLEM

Attempts to treat illegal-drug abusers or addicts have a long and unsuccessful history in the United States. The oldest federal treatment programs were those of the U. S. Health Service in narcotics hospitals at Lexington, Kentucky, and Fort Worth, Texas. They were based on withdrawal from drugs and included only prisoners convicted of federal crimes. Follow-up studies of addicts treated under this program suggested a very high failure rate, well over 90 percent. The hospitals failed because nothing was done to change the social structure that caused or encouraged the problem. The effects of being labeled criminals also accounted for the program's failure.

A major study of 37 federally funded drug-treatment programs operating at 80 sites throughout the country analyzed three liberal treatment

PROPOSED SOLUTIONS TO THE DRUG PROBLEM

Synanon was one of the earliest and most successful therapeutic communities for treating drug abusers. Many other treatment approaches learned from its successes and failures.

approaches—residential therapeutic-community programs, outpatient abstinence programs, and methadone-maintenance programs. Let us look at each of these approaches as possible solutions.

Therapeutic Communities

Therapeutic communities grew out of the evident failure of the early federal treatment programs at Lexington and Fort Worth. Based on sociological concepts of group interaction and mutual support, they form a total and new subculture. In encounter-group fashion, addicts become part of a highly structured community. The model for the successful therapeutic communities is Synanon, which was established in California in 1958 and now has eight houses across the United States and in Puerto Rico. Other successful social communities of former addicts include Daytop Village, Odyssey House, Conquest House, and Phoenix House. The therapeutic-community approach seems to work as long as the members are in the "home." When they leave the "community" some revert to hard drugs. The same reasons for taking drugs in the first place often still persist, such as discrimination and inequality, and force persons back onto drugs.

Outpatient Treatment

Our society, as a matter of policy and practice, approaches the solution of drug abuse from a medical viewpoint. There are over 2,000 centers in the United States for treating addicts (to narcotics and alcohol) on an outpatient basis. The New York Temporary Commission to Evaluate Drug Laws found that addicts in treatment are becoming able to function and are available for training and jobs. Adequate jobs are an important aspect of rehabilitation, and one of the best predictors of successful treatment is prior employment. Yet only a beginning has been made to remove social barriers to hiring those who are addicts and have criminal records (Ferguson et al., 1974:4–6).

Follow-up and evaluation of clinical programs are needed to determine the effectiveness of each. Funding in recent years under the Mental Health Centers Act has included money for drug-abuse clinics, which should help us to grapple more effectively with the problem of drug abuse.

Methadone Maintenance

The third approach to the drug problem by liberals and radicals is methadone maintenance. This approach concedes that the addict is so

Methadone maintenance, though not without its problems, has made it possible for some former heroin addicts to function in the community.

Credit: Bettye Lane.

habituated to drugs that he cannot live without them. Methadone is legally used as a substitute for heroin because addiction to methadone is considered less serious, though some claim it is more addictive than heroin. It enables the addict to function and work as long as he receives his dosage of methadone.

The methadone-maintenance program was started in 1964 by Drs. Vincent Dole and Marie Nyswander at Rockefeller University. Since then thousands of addicts have been successfully treated at centers all over the country. It is estimated that 100,000 heroin addicts receive their treatment at methadone clinics each day ("Methadone . . . ," 1975:3). Even critics testify to the program's relative success. It has doubled the employment rate of its patients (some centers combine methadone treatment with job and personal counseling), gotten many off welfare rolls, reduced their crime rate, and ended their recidivism. Those who stay in the program rarely return to regular heroin use.

But many sociologists, conservatives and liberals have raised objections to the methadone approach as a solution. Selma Mushkin points to four pitfalls of methadone:

> increased use of other drugs
>
> spread of addiction to methadone of those who have not used heroin; many persons prefer addiction to a drug they can function with, so they buy methadone illegally
>
> uncertainties about methadone's long-term physical effects
>
> on-again, off-again use of heroin encouraged by ready access to methadone centers (1975:37).

Furthermore, some black and other minority-group leaders feel that it is a way to keep addicts "enslaved"—to the drug and those who dispense it—rather than to really free them of the addictive habit ("Methadone . . . ," 1975:6).

Antagonist Drugs

Another possible solution to the problem is the use of narcotic "antagonists"—drugs that can block the narcotic "high" that people get from heroin or other drugs. Two experimental drugs, naloxone and cyclazocine, have been tried as "antagonists." Unfortunately, such chemicals are not as practical as Antabuse, the "antagonist" that has been helpful in treating alcoholism. Cyclazocine has unpleasant side effects if the dosage is not carefully controlled. Naloxone has slight side effects, but must be given with a needle, not a good idea for addicts. Also, it must be taken in dangerously large doses. Some experimenters are trying to implant a supply of naloxone under the skin in a rubber pellet, which will slowly release a small but adequate amount. Thus, research for the perfect antagonist goes on (Saltman, 1972:27).

In addition to these three major approaches, many other suggestions for solving the illegal and legal drug addiction problem have been made.

Conservative state and national leaders from time to time advocate tougher drug laws. Strict laws have not worked too well, although they seem to have discouraged use of legal prescription drugs. The National Commission has made more than 100 recommendations on how to remedy the drug situation. Among the recommendations were:

> Establish mandatory treatment programs for those charged with possession of any narcotic except marijuana, but impose no punishment more severe than a $500 fine.
>
> Place a moratorium on all drug-education programs in the schools until they can be evaluated and made more realistic; repeal all state laws requiring drug-education courses.
>
> End advertising of "mood-altering drugs"—sedatives, tranquilizers, and stimulants—that promise to produce "pleasurable mood alteration" or halt "malaise caused by stress or anxiety."
>
> Retain existing legal controls on the availability of narcotics, placing the "highest possible restrictions" on heroin (Weaver, March 23, 1973:1).
>
> Possession of marijuana for personal use would no longer be an offense.
>
> Casual distribution of small amounts of marijuana for no, or insignificant, remuneration not involving profit would no longer be an offense ("First Report . . .," March 1972:152).

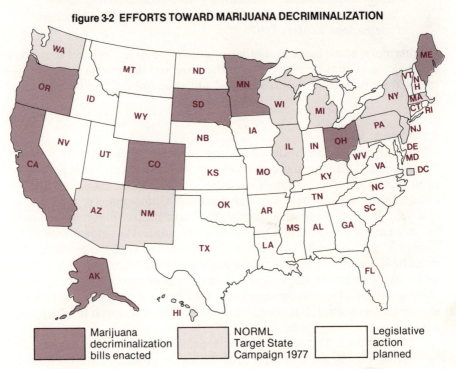

figure 3-2 EFFORTS TOWARD MARIJUANA DECRIMINALIZATION

Marijuana decriminalization bills enacted | NORML Target State Campaign 1977 | Legislative action planned

Source: NORML.

Liberalizing Marijuana Laws

As a result of these recommendations (particularly the last two), a debate has raged over whether or not to decriminalize private use of marijuana. By 1977 every state had reduced first-time marijuana possession or personal use of small quantities from a felony to a misdemeanor, cutting the former penalties of one to ten years in prison to probation, not more than a year in jail, or fines. Since October of 1973, Oregon has imposed a maximum $100 fine for possession of up to one ounce of marijuana. After the law was in effect for one year, a statewide evaluation found that 40 percent of those who had used "pot" before the law was changed reported they actually decreased their use (Fort and Cory, 1975:49). Six states now have minor civil fines for personal use of marijuana, and other states are considering it. Nevertheless, the public, according to opinion-survey polls, is still opposed to legalizing marijuana. Figure 3–2 illustrates the status of marijuana laws in 1977.

The Domestic Council Drug Abuse Task Force prepared a white paper for the President in late 1975. It noted that "a great deal of controversy exists about marijuana policy," and recommended that priority be given to enforcement efforts and treatment facilities for drugs *other than marijuana* ("Alcohol and Marijuana . . . ," November 24, 1975:118). In 1976 a report by the Strategy Council on Drug Abuse to the President urged the government to consider reducing penalties for marijuana smoking. It pointed to the "relatively high price" society pays to enforce such laws and to marijuana's "widespread recreational use" ("Panel Wants . . . ," December 13, 1976:2).

The National Organization for the Reform of Marijuana Laws (NORML) calls for the following changes in the law:

Make illegal the possession or use of marijuana by those under 18, with penalties similar to those for alcohol.

Impose government regulations on the sale and distribution of marijuana similar to those on alcohol.

Make penalties for selling without a license or to minors similar to those affecting such selling of alcohol.

Place a complete ban on the advertising or promotion of marijuana (Morland et al., 1975:338).

We know today that drug problems with many causes require a variety of solutions proposed by conservatives, liberals, and radicals applied wisely over a long period of time. Hence, the solutions we have discussed need to be coordinated and applied in a comprehensive way.

THE FUTURE OF THE DRUG PROBLEM

The future of the drug problem depends on two things: how we define abuse in the future and how we treat drug abusers.

If the future definition of drugs excludes marijuana, then a sizable portion of what our society now considers "the drug problem" will disappear by redefinition. Historically, use of opiates was not defined as a serious social problem until 1914. At one time smoking cigarettes was defined as a serious problem and, later, as not very serious at all. After our Prohibition era (1920–30) it took well over 40 years before per capita liquor consumption reached pre-Prohibition levels and was again considered a problem. By changes in legal definitions of what is or is not a drug, we can reduce the size and scope of our problem. Almost every indication points in the direction of excluding marijuana from our social definition of dangerous drugs.

Our future treatment of drug abusers could change. We could legally or socially decriminalize the heroin addict. If we as a society accept the medical notion of drug addiction as a sickness to be cured, rather than as a crime to be punished, then our treatment of addicts will be more intense. Most important of all, decriminalizing drug addiction will eliminate the stigma of being a criminal. Drug abusers have been suffering from a triple stigma—as social and legal deviants, as drug addicts, and as criminals. If these labels are removed in the future, treatment will have a better chance of success, as indicated in the government's treatment of Vietnam veterans who had taken drugs. Getting back into the community with a steady, well-paying job is a step in the right direction.

Another possible development would be to adopt the British system for treating heroin and morphine addicts: drug maintenance of addicts by the government. Addicts are registered with the government, and only these persons can receive free doses of addictive drugs whenever they need them. British law is extremely severe on the use of heroin by anyone other than a registered addict, and the penalties for selling or supplying hard drugs can be more harsh than penalties for murder. The British treat the registered addict as sick rather than as a criminal: they feel that the addiction is punishment enough. As a result of this registration system, Britain has fewer than 3,000 registered narcotics addicts (one for every 21,000 persons in 1960, compared with one for every 294 persons in the United States) (Whitten and Robertson, 1973:141–43).

Whatever the future holds, it is quite clear that much of our society and culture is so addicted to one kind of drug or another that the problem of drugs will persist.

II. DEFINING THE ALCOHOL PROBLEM

Much of what we have said about drugs is true about alcohol, since it, too, is a drug that anesthetizes and desensitizes people. When the National Commission was established by Congress and the President, it was instructed to study the drug-addiction problem and make recommendations for government policy. After studying and analyzing various aspects of the drug problem, the Commission in 1973 concluded: "Dependence on alcohol is without question the most serious drug problem in the country today" (1973:143). What was true in 1973 is even more true today. Although the use and abuse of alcohol have been spreading in recent years, particularly among teenagers, the public generally does not define alcohol as a serious problem—and does not even define it as a drug. Definitions of alcoholism (or alcoholics) are hard to agree upon because there is a thin line between someone with a "drinking problem" and being an alcoholic.

Classification of Alcohol Disorders

Psychiatrists often use the designation "alcohol disorders" to define alcoholism. These disorders are based on categories provided in the *Diagnostic and Statistical Manual of Mental Disorders* of the American Psychiatric Association. Following are the categories of alcohol disorders:

alcoholic psychoses—(including delirium tremens, Korsakov's psychosis, other alcoholic hallucinoses, paranoid states, acute alcoholic intoxication, alcoholic deterioration, pathological intoxication, and other and unspecified psychoses)

alcoholism (including episodic excessive drinking, habitual excessive drinking, alcohol addiction, and other and unspecified alcoholism)

nonpsychotic organic brain syndrome with alcohol (disorders caused by or associated with impairment of brain tissue, as well as impaired orientation, memory, intellectual functions and judgment) (1968:22).

In their reports of a classic study of factors influencing physicians' diagnoses of alcoholic men in the emergency ward of a general hospital, H. T. Blane and associates write that those given alcoholic diagnoses were more often men "whose social characteristics were little in keeping with a number of commonly adhered-to social forms" and who "fit previous descriptions of derelicts." Diagnosed alcoholics tended to be "socially more deteriorated but physically less ill" than their nondiagnosed counterparts (Blane, Overton, Chafetz, 1963:640–63). If alcoholism is a "disease" it is a social disease produced by society with repercussions on society as well as individuals. The National Council on Alcoholism generally defines alcoholism as "an illness resulting in problems that affect [the alcoholic's] family, his job and himself" ("What Everyone Should Know," 1974:2). Alcohol problems have been defined in reference to the degree of dependence (social drinker, heavy drinker, problem drinker, alcoholic), complications connected with the quantity of alcohol consumed, and nutritional deficiencies involved in drinking. A "drunk" may not be an "alcoholic" and not every "alcoholic" is a "drunk."

Classification of Drinkers

A five-fold classification system of alcohol drinkers analyzed by Carl Chambers and others is as follows:

1. Abstainers—usually do not drink at all, but may take one drink once a year.
2. Infrequent drinkers—drink at least once a year, but less than once a month.
3. Light drinkers—take one or two drinks on each occasion, at least once a month.
4. Moderate drinkers—drink several times a month, but never more than three or four drinks on each occasion.
5. Heavy drinkers—drink every day and often five or six drinks each time, or several drinks during the day (Chambers et al., 1975:105-6).

But no matter how we define "alcoholism" or "alcoholic," our society and culture generally do not define alcohol as a serious health or social issue. William Martin of the Connecticut Association of Alcohol Councils maintains that "many people don't realize that alcohol is a drug, because it's legal. But it's probably the most vicious drug of all" (Shearer, February 22, 1976:4).

Socialization to Accept Alcohol

Our culture has shaped public opinion in favor of alcohol. We are subtly (and sometimes not so subtly) socialized to accept alcohol as an important part of our social life. For example, to do an interesting experiment to see how we are socialized unconsciously to accept alcohol, just watch one evening's television shows and record how often the phrases "Have a drink?" or "Would you like a drink?" or "I need a drink!" (or words to that effect) are used.

But there is another, new reason why many people do not define alcohol as a serious social issue or as a drug. It is best illustrated by the following story:

> A teenager blacked out and fell to the hallway floor of a Queens [New York City] high school. He was examined by school officials, who concluded that his condition was due to heavy drinking.
> A school counselor phoned the young man's mother. "We have bad news," the counselor said; "your son passed out at school today." The mother asked: "Is it drugs?" No, it was liquor," the counselor replied. "Thank God," the mother said.

In recent years, as this story suggests, the public panic over drug addiction has downgraded alcohol abuse and alcoholism as a national concern. Drugs make heavy drinking seem frivolous and trivial in comparison. In addition, parents themselves drink and usually think nothing of it. Even the vocabulary describing the addictions to liquor and drugs is different. "Liquor is respectable; heroin is not. Drunk is funny; overdose is tragic. Hangover inspires amusement or sympathy; withdrawal terrifies. And so it goes—bartender versus pusher, tavern versus opium den" (Soltis, June 22, 1974:25).

Alcohol and sex usually go hand in hand.

In defining the problem, we must clearly distinguish between the person who uses alcohol in the home or socially but in moderation and those who abuse it to the point of alcoholism or who become "problem drinkers." As one educator noted: "There is a world of difference between a person who drinks responsibly and one who drinks in a manner that causes problems to himself, to his family, and to society" (Miles, 1974:3). Drinking can produce different worlds for those who drink, depending on how frequently and how much they indulge.

Alcohol is a depressant (not a stimulant) drug, in the same general psychoactive drug family as anesthetics, sedatives (such as barbiturates), and narcotics (such as morphine, opium, and heroin). Thus, the dangers inherent in abuse of any depressant apply to alcohol. Alcohol used in drinks is ethanol (ethyl alcohol: C_2H_5OH), made from fermenting grains or fruit. Alcoholic content is measured in terms of "proof,"* and is calculated as twice the percentage of ethanol (so an "86 proof" Scotch is 43 percent alcohol).

---

*The term "proof" originated centuries ago as a test of the true potency of a beverage. If gunpowder saturated with alcohol exploded upon ignition, this was taken as "proof" that the liquor was more than half pure alcohol (Chambers et al., 1975:96).

table 3-5 BLOOD-ALCOHOL LEVELS AND THEIR INTOXICATING EFFECTS

PERCENTAGE	DEGREE OF INTOXICATION
0.035%	One drink.
0.05	Two drinks: not legally drunk, but mild effects felt and driving ability impaired.
0.10	Legally "drunk" when involved in a driving accident. Some impairment of judgment, muscle coordination, and vision. Reaction time slowed.
0.25	Quite intoxicated. Coordination impaired.
0.3-4	Severe intoxication. Coma (or death) may occur in some individuals.
0.5-0.8	Breathing and heart action slowed. Death occurs.

Source: Joel Fort, **Alcohol: Our Biggest Drug Problem** (New York: McGraw-Hill, 1973): 28. © 1973 by McGraw-Hill. Used with permission of McGraw-Hill Book Company.

Legal Definitions of Alcoholism

The degree of intoxication from alcohol is legally defined by the percentage of alcohol (in milligrams) present in the bloodstream. Various "drunkometers" or "breath analyzers" are used by police to determine whether a person is legally drunk (usually 0.1 percent). Table 3–5 shows what one or two drinks do to the blood-alcohol levels and the effects drinking produces in the body. Even though objectively a person's reflexes are slowed after only one drink, he might think or feel that there is no impairment.

This is the real danger in driving a car after drinking—the person erroneously thinks he can handle the car with no trouble at all. It takes a long time for alcohol to leave the body completely. As Figure 3–3 indicates, it takes two hours for the alcohol in one drink to leave the body, and 10 hours for five drinks. Food and body weight both affect the rate at which alcohol is absorbed into the bloodstream.

INCIDENCE AND PREVALENCE OF ALCOHOL ABUSE

As we indicated earlier in the chapter, the National Commission found that only about 36 percent of the public (39 percent of adults and 34 percent of youth) classified alcohol as a drug. In 1973, 24 percent of youth (ages 12 to 17) and 53 percent of adults (18 and over) reported drinking alcohol "within the last seven days." Today the percentages are much higher, especially for young people. Some 90 million to 100 million Americans drink. In the years between 1947 and 1971, the per-person yearly drinking of alcohol among persons of drinking age rose from 27 to 31 gallons. More recently, drinking has increased even more. In 1974, the

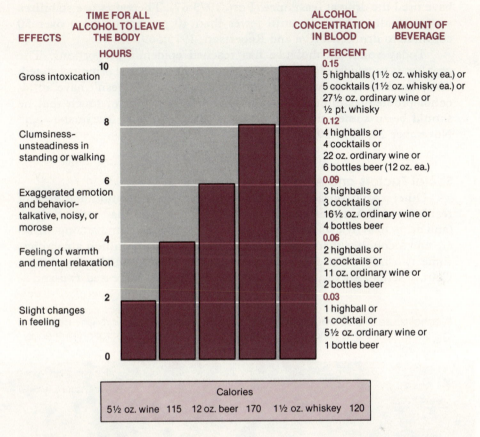

figure 3-3 ALCOHOL LEVELS IN THE BLOOD
After drinks taken on an empty stomach by a 150-lb. person

Source: Dr. Leon A. Greenberg

proportion of American adults who took an occasional drink reached 70 percent (95 million people), the highest it has been since Gallup Polls have been taken (Fort and Cory, 1975:8). Of these about one out of 11 is an alcoholic ("What Everyone Should Know," 1974:3).

There are between nine and 10 million alcoholics (depending upon how they are defined). Of persons who drink, 45 percent are "light" (up to five drinks a week) or "infrequent" drinkers, and 25 percent are "moderate" to "heavy" (more than six drinks a week). The other 30 percent do not drink at all.

Use and Abuse among Youth

The incidence of use rises rapidly from the middle teens to early adulthood (i.e., from 66 percent of teens to 80 percent of those between 22 and 25). Several national surveys of college students have found that nearly 90 percent use alcohol and 65 to 75 percent of high-school students have used the drug at least once (Fort, 1973:67). Thereafter use stabilizes and gradually tapers off, until fewer than 40 percent of those over 50 continue to drink (McKee and Robertson, 1975:569).

Today youth alcohol use has reached epidemic proportions. The problem is so widespread that a Washington, D.C., school principal stated: "Any headmaster or principal who says [his school] doesn't have an alcohol problem is either an out-and-out liar or so out of touch that he should be in some other line of work" ("Alcohol and Marijuana...," November 24, 1975:29).

Social Factors and Alcohol

Other social variables, such as sex, income, education and area of residence, affect use of alcohol. Although more men than women drink (and drink heavily), women today are more frequently found among drinkers and alcoholics than ever before. Of the nine to 10 million alcoholics, some two million or more (22 percent) are women. In the San Mateo County school survey, alcohol use among females increased two-and-a-

Alcohol is used, and abused, by members of all social classes. Many persons are subtly socialized (and pressured) into drinking as an expectation of friendly social behavior.

half times between 1970 and 1975 (DuPont, December 15, 1975:141). Since 1971, the percentage of women in Alcoholics Anonymous (AA) has increased from 25 percent to 40 percent (Shearer, 1976:54).

Another social factor affecting use of alcohol is socioeconomic status (i.e., income and education). Higher socioeconomic groups have *more* drinkers, but these are less likely to be *heavy* drinkers than those of lower-status groups. About 84 percent of adults with incomes over $15,000 drink, compared with only 44 percent of persons with incomes lower than $2,000 a year. Heavy drinking is most prevalent in the income groups under $4,000 a year. The largest number of alcohol users are professionals, semi professionals, and those in sales or managerial positions. Some 71 percent of college-educated persons drink, compared with only 38 percent with high-school education. Only about five percent of all alcoholics end up in "skid row"; thus, the popular image of drinkers and alcoholics as predominantly lower class is incorrect. A recent Gallup Poll survey showed that among the people who admit they sometimes drink more than they should, the largest category are those who "earn more than $25,000, have gone to college and are under 30 years old" (Soltis, June 22, 1974:23-24). Hence, though drinking per se is more frequent among higher social classes, problems of alcohol abuse are more severe and prevalent among lower social classes.

Urban residents are more likely to drink than rural residents. In a city, liquor is much more readily available. In addition, some conservative rural areas are traditionally "dry," and drinking (moderate or excessive) conflicts with their social norms and values.

Problems from Alcohol Abuse

Social deviance and social problems emerge from the use and abuse of alcohol. Approximately half of the five million annual arrests in the United States are for public drunkenness. Since there is a high rate of rearrests for drunkenness, it is estimated that the number of persons involved is only somewhere between 20 and 60 percent of the arrests for public intoxication (Fort, 1973:113). More than half of all persons arrested for murder, rape, burglary, and other crimes committed them while under the influence of alcohol. Alcohol is a major factor in up to 70 percent of the 55,000 annual highway deaths and 65,000 other deaths from drowning, fire, plane crashes, and so on. Alcohol contributes to thousands of deaths each year, but the prime cause is listed as something more socially acceptable. Table 3-6 shows the approximate number of alcohol-related deaths.

About 50 percent of all male admissions to mental hospitals are related to "alcoholic disorders" or a "drinking problem" (Bachrach, February 1976:1). As age and education increase (and the drinking problem becomes more severe), the percentage of drinkers diagnosed as mentally ill increases. For example, in one year 85 percent of all state and county mental-hospital admissions of males over age 55 who had completed high

table 3-6	ALCOHOL-RELATED DEATHS*
DISEASE	NUMBER OF DEATHS (PER YEAR)
HEART AND BLOOD-VESSEL DISORDERS	1,000,000+
CANCER	350,000
ALCOHOL ALONE	200,000 (approx.)
ACCIDENTS	120,000
INFLUENZA AND PNEUMONIA	60,000+
DIABETES MELLITUS	34,000
CIRRHOSIS OF LIVER	24,000

*All of these figures are approximations. It is impossible to assess the exact cause of death in many cases; in other cases, a combination of causes are implicated.

Source: Joel Fort, **Alcohol: Our Biggest Drug Problem** (New York: McGraw-Hill, 1973): 108. Used by permission.

school or attended college were diagnosed as "alcoholic" (Bachrach, January 1976:5).

Another socially deviant act related to alcohol is suicide. Statistics from the National Council on Alcoholism reveal that "the suicide rate is 58 times higher among alcoholics than nonalcoholics" (Gallagher, February 1976:47).

Since alcoholics directly affect four or five other persons (family, close friends, coworkers), the problem affects at least 40 or 50 million people. Families of the alcoholic or heavy drinker suffer most, and much family violence and unrest stem from alcohol. Dr. Fort argues that "up to 70 percent or more of our . . . annual divorces involve the use and abuse of alcohol" (1973:115).

Problem drinking on the job costs business and government an estimated $10 billion a year in absenteeism, low output, and poor judgment leading to work-related accidents. One report estimates that alcoholism and heavy drinking cost our economy $25 billion a year. More serious is the fact that fewer than 10 percent of all persons with drinking problems receive any treatment (Shearer, 1976:6). Only about a third of the major companies in New York City do anything about alcohol abuse among their employees. Of the two-thirds without programs, "more than half indicated lack of interest or denied that they had a problem" ("What Industry Is Doing," January 12, 1976:66–67).

CAUSES OF ALCOHOL ABUSE

The sociological reasons for taking alcohol are essentially the same as for taking drugs—those of environmental conditions, a dominant subculture, peer pressure, and pleasure. Psychologists use personality theories to explain the problem. And as with drugs, no one theory explains the cause of drinking or alcoholism.

However, two distinctions can be made about drinking alcohol and taking illicit drugs. Since liquor is much more socially acceptable than illegal drugs, an underlying cause of alcohol abuse and alcoholism is social drinking, which reduces a person's fears, worries, and anxieties. This kind of drinking is socially reinforced and rewarded, since it makes the person "sociable." The second distinction is that as a person becomes an alcoholic, he tends to alienate people around him and eventually takes to drinking alone. What starts out as a socially approved act ends up as social deviance. An attempt to deal with personal troubles becomes a social issue that needs a solution.

PROPOSED SOLUTIONS TO ALCOHOL ABUSE

Alcoholism is more treatable than heroin addiction. There have been many successful treatment programs. Since there is a continuum between use and abuse, there are various kinds of programs for different degrees of drinking. Both conservatives and liberals endorse the "treatment approach" in an attempt to remedy the problem. Radicals would view such an approach as manipulation of individuals to reprogram them so they serve the ends of the present social and economic system more efficiently. For some alcoholics various forms of psychotherapy may be useful, particularly group therapy for the alcoholic. Encounter groups or psychodrama are proving useful to some problem drinkers. The best kind of program, in short, is a comprehensive one that gives a person a choice. For example, Chit Chat Farms puts alcoholics through four weeks of group therapy. Schick-Shadel hospital in Seattle, like many hospitals and clinics, gives alcoholic patients the drug Antabuse, an inexpensive "antagonist" that produces nausea and illness when alcohol is consumed. After an Antabuse treatment, patients go to a special room called Duffy's Tavern, where they help themselves to a drink. The effects are so upsetting that participants are conditioned to think of alcohol as something unpleasant. Their resocialization is then reinforced by group therapy and counseling.

The Family's Role in Rehabilitation

But a variety of things must be done to ensure success of any alcoholic rehabilitation or treatment program. Nelson Bradly, M.D., medical director of the alcoholic-rehabilitation program at Lutheran General Hospital in Park Ridge, Illinois, notes that a "broad network of support" for the alcoholic is needed if rehabilitation is to succeed. He gives the rates of success for programs as follows:

> An alcoholic from a "drying out" program has a 6 to 10 percent chance of staying sober.
>
> With a followup program, chances of success rise to between 24 and 30 percent.

Well-organized, carefully structured followup counseling can bring success up to 50 percent.

When the alcoholic's family and employer are involved, the chances for success go up to at least 80 percent (Fort and Cory, 1975:55).

The family's involvement and understanding of the family are also essential to rehabilitation. The Public Television program "Drink, Drank, Drunk" (available from Indiana University Audio-Visual Center, Bloomington, Indiana) offered five tips to family members for helping a person with a drinking problem:

Don't overreact. Don't jump to conclusions about the seriousness of the problem.

Don't preach. Condemning or blaming abusers rarely helps. Listening helps.

Don't minimize. A heavy drinker is often convinced that he can control his drinking and can stop any time. Often he cannot.

Lead an independent but concerned life. Don't abandon the alcoholic, but refuse to let the person control your life. If a heavy drinker is constantly late for dinner, for example, don't wait to eat.

Don't give up. Much trial and error, progress and backsliding occur. One failure does not mean the situation is hopeless.

Detoxification

For those addicted to alcohol, a first vital step is "detoxification." Alcoholics need medical supervision, even though some general hospitals have been reluctant to accept them as patients. The American Medical Association's Committee on Alcoholism and Drug Dependence long ago asserted that an alcohol-dependent person is ill and needs medical care. It has been educating all hospitals to treat alcoholics. Tranquilizers are used for treating withdrawal symptoms and delirium tremens (dts). One of the most effective tranquilizers is haloperidol, which is still being used experimentally. If alcoholics are left unattended to suffer the convulsions and hallucinations that can occur after withdrawal from alcohol, as many as 20 to 25 percent may die. Besides tranquilizers, intensive nursing care, high-potency vitamins and fluid electrolyte balance are all used in physical rehabilitation of alcoholics.

Alcoholics Anonymous (AA)

One of the most effective social therapies, which uses group interaction, is Alcoholics Anonymous (AA). It is a grouping of men and women who share their experience, strength, and hope in an attempt to solve their common problem and to help others recover from alcoholism. The only

PROPOSED SOLUTIONS TO ALCOHOL ABUSE

Alcoholism usually leads to under-class status at the bottom of the social-class ladder.

requirement for membership is a desire to stop drinking. AA was founded in 1935 by two alcoholics who believed that alcoholics themselves could play a special role in helping each other remain sober. An organization for spouses of problem drinkers, Al-Anon, was formed in 1951 to offer help to the nonalcoholic husband or wife. Experiences are shared at meetings by others who live with alcoholics. These gatherings are therapeutic in that wives or husbands can unburden their problems to a very sympathetic audience, and they realize they are not alone in this situation. In 1957, Alateen developed from Al-Anon, to help teenagers deal with the problems that arise from living with an alcoholic parent. It strives to develop attitudes and supportive behavior patterns in the teenagers that will help make it easier for their parents to deal effectively with alcoholism.

Several thousand alcoholics are helped, and help others, through Alcoholics Anonymous. The first step, in the guiding principles of AA's "Twelve Steps," is "We admitted that we were powerless over alcohol—that our lives had become unmanageable." Until this fact is admitted, there is little expectation that the alcoholic can be helped or cured.

Halfway Houses and Treatment Centers

Halfway houses and treatment centers have been developed in a number of states to act as a transition from inpatient hospital care to entrance back into the community. The homes usually have about 20 or fewer residents. The anti-drinking rules of the house are therapeutic, and counseling takes place in a supportive environment. In addition, halfway houses encourage residents to become members of Alcoholics Anonymous.

Treatment centers, funded by the National Institute on Alcohol Abuse and Alcoholism, pay off in dollars and cents for the public. A study of the treatment of 4,777 persons in 41 centers for a six-month period showed that each dollar spent on the program will yield three dollars in benefits to society during the following 10 years.

Educational Efforts to Change Values

Another proposed solution, endorsed by conservatives and liberals alike, is the educational efforts of the National Institute on Alcohol Abuse and Alcoholism and the National Council on Alcoholism. Their information programs, which avoid scare tactics, are often aimed at young people to alert them to the dangers of excessive drinking. The principal points made in their preventive-education programs are:

> It is not always necessary to drink, and heavy drinking does not demonstrate adult status or virility.
> Encourage responsible drinking (sip and dilute drinks, and eat food while drinking).
> Learning to handle alcohol wisely is a part of education about living and coping with life.

Their educational approach is based on a rational, reasonable attitude toward alcohol.

Another solution to alcohol abuse lies in changing the prevailing social values and attitudes about drinking. Rupert Wilkinson, after a study for the Cooperative Commission on the Study of Alcoholism, recommended more emphasis on learning to drink at home; fixed limits to licenses to bars and liquor stores; and requirements that liquor stores display booklets on serving food with alcohol. The feeling here is that when family drinking is emphasized and drinking with food is encouraged, young people will grow up using but not abusing alcohol. Whether this will happen remains to be seen.

THE FUTURE OF ALCOHOL ABUSE

Radicals argue that as long as our social structure and economic system produce inequality, injustice, and role strains and tensions, alcoholism will persist. It appears evident that the age-old custom and tradition of drinking will continue in the future. If anything, the rate of drinking should accelerate along with social change. The attitudes and behavior patterns of today's young people will set the foundation for future generations of drinkers.

Ideally, education about the harm and hurt that alcohol can bring to a person's life and to society will help to control its future use. If society were structured and organized so as to produce people whose lives were meaningful, rewarding, and satisfying, the *need* for alcohol (or any other nonmedical drug) would either not exist or be very minimal. Today such a society does not exist, and there is little evidence that one will emerge in America in the foreseeable future.

All available evidence points to our continued use (and abuse) of alcohol. Dr. Wolfgang Schmidt of Canada's Addiction Research Foundation predicted at an international symposium on "Alcohol and the Liver" that by 1984 cirrhosis of the liver from alcoholic consumption will be the number-three cause of death among males aged 25 to 64. He also predicted that between 1972 and 1984 there will be a 72 percent rise in the use of alcohol in the United States and Canada ("Fastest Growing Disease . . . ," 1976:40).

Many of today's teenagers have learned the wrong lessons about use of alcohol in their own homes. But parents and the home will still provide the best place for education about living (and alcohol) in the future. Alcohol education in the schools should increase as the current problem becomes more obvious and abuse accelerates. Such educational efforts should be concerned with shaping attitudes and behavior conducive to responsible drinking and nondrinking, rather than use scare tactics about becoming an alcoholic and a derelict. Alcohol-education programs in public-health facilities will stress prevention, as well as help those who have already abused alcohol.

In the future, medical schools will educate doctors to know more about the psychological and sociological effects of alcohol and alcoholism, as well as the merely physical ones. Future education programs will provide teachers, clergy, public-health workers, social workers, nurses, lawyers, judges, police, and community leaders with a better understanding of the problem of alcohol abuse. There is no question that alcohol education in the future will involve many more people than it does now.

More states will adopt the Uniform Alcoholism and Intoxication Treatment Act, first drafted by the National Conference of Commissioners on Uniform State Laws in 1971. The objective of this model law is to facilitate treatment of heavy drinkers, rather than subject them to criminal prosecution and possible jail terms. As this objective is reached, the social problems connected with alcohol abuse and alcoholism will be treated as a health matter. This should open up new medical approaches for remedying the problem.

Two new medical approaches that may offer help for future alcoholics is electric shock combined with self-regulation, and the use of drugs to maintain alcoholics without adverse behavior effects. A new aversion therapy under experimentation involves the use of electric shocks on the

> # ELECTRIC SHOCK THERAPY AND SELF-DISCIPLINE
>
> A startling new therapy for alcoholics—involving electric shocks and self-discipline—offers new hope for an estimated 10 million Americans who have a serious drinking problem....
>
> "[T]he tests I carried out made it quite clear that an alcoholic doesn't have to give up drink altogether to be cured," [said] Dr. Glenn Caddy, who pioneered the treatment.
>
> "Results of the experiments were extremely good—with 76 percent of the patients cutting down considerably on their consumption," he added.
>
> He said 60 alcoholics took part in the year-long tests.... [These tests] were carried out once a week in a laboratory where the patients relaxed in armchairs. Attached to each patient's neck were two electrodes through which a painful electric shock could be delivered.
>
> "Other researchers and I served drinks," said Dr. Caddy. "Patients were given an alcohol limit—and as they proceeded with their drinking, breath-tests let them know when the limit was reached.
>
> "When it was [reached], they were told to continue drinking if they wished, but they had to expect intermittent electric shocks as a form of punishment. If they did keep drinking, they suddenly received shocks. This is extremely painful. This treatment was combined with the therapy of helping them to self-regulate their drinking by better understanding the problem—and themselves...."
>
> Source: "New Therapy Involving Electric Shocks...," *National Enquirer* (July 27, 1976):54.

neck, in combination with counseling, to encourage the person to regulate his own drinking. The boxed item describes this new behavior-modification technique. Another new experimental approach is use of the drug propranobol hydrochloride, normally used to control irregular heartbeat. Dr. Jerrold Bernstein of Harvard University used it on 24 alcoholic patients, who were all given equal amounts of alcohol to drink. Half were then given propranobol, the other half a placebo (a pill that has no effect). Those given propranobol showed no significant mood changes, but the patients who got the placebo showed "hostility, anxiety, and belligerence" from drinking. The study results suggest that propranobol tends to reduce adverse behavior responses to alcohol, but does not establish an immunity to or a cure for alcoholism. If it proves successful, such treatment might be used to maintain "confirmed alcoholics" without the adverse behavioral effects (just as methadone is used to maintain heroin addicts) ("Effects of Propranobol Studied," 1973:5).

The hope is that future generations will come to better understand and perceive the connection between our social structure, with the excess demands it places on people, and the injustices and inequities it perpetuates, and the abuse of alcohol as an escape from such conditions. The hope is that future generations will see what our society does to people and begin to remedy the situation.

SUMMARY

The social issue of drugs begins with a personal problem for which we pop a pill. There are three definitions of the drug problem—the drug fiend, subcultural deviance, and the total drug culture. The law has not stopped drug addiction. For example, by 1976 33 million people had tried marijuana, and 12 million use it regularly. In the same year, there were an estimated 300,000 to 400,00 daily heroin addicts. Drug abuse costs society $10 to $17 billion a year.

Causes of drug addiction include "dependent," "immature," and "addictive" personalities; poor environmental conditions; peer pressure; and simply pleasure. Proposed solutions to drug addiction include therapeutic communities and halfway houses, outpatient programs, methadone maintenance, strict law enforcement, legalizing marijuana for personal use, changes suggested by the National Organization for the Reform of Marijuana (NORML), use of antagonists such as naloxone, and second-chance communities.

The number-one drug problem, according to the National Commission, is abuse of alcohol. Although alcohol is a depressant, most Americans do not classify it as a drug. Some 90 to 100 million people drink, and of these, 10 million are alcoholics, and millions more are "problem" drinkers. Arrests, crime, mental illness, suicide, and family disorganization grow out of excessive use of alcohol.

The sociological reasons for taking alcohol are essentially the same as for taking drugs—those of a dominant subculture, role strain, and peer pressure and powerlessness. A variety of treatment programs may help if the family is involved in the process. One of the most effective social therapies is Alcoholics Anonymous (AA), as well as Al-Anon and Alateen to aid the alcoholic's family members. New medical approaches to the problem may help alcoholics in the future, although education and a change of basic attitudes toward alcohol and other drugs as well as changes in our social institutions are needed if the problems are to be solved.

CAREER OPPORTUNITIES

Rehabilitation Counselors.

They help persons with physical, mental, and social disabilities, such as drug addiction or alcoholism, to adjust their vocational plans and personal lives. Together the counselor and client develop a plan of rehabilitation, with the assistance of other specialists. They maintain close contact with families of clients and work closely with employers and agencies who hire former addicts. Caseload varies with experience and agency. Public and private rehabilitation agencies, as well as councils of drug and alcohol abuse, hire most counselors. Social-work and social-science courses and background are helpful and usually required. For further information write to: American Rehabilitation Counseling Association, 1607 New Hampshire Ave., N. W., Washington, D.C. 20009

Occupational Therapists.

They provide services to those whose abilities to cope with tasks of living are threatened or impaired by developmental deficits, the aging process, poverty, cultural differences, alcoholism, drug addiction, and physical injury or illness. An interdisciplinary curriculum of biological, physical, and social sciences is recommended. Eventual registration as an occupational therapist requires at least a college degree and passing a national certification examination. With emphasis on improved quality of life and increased professionalization of the field, the future career opportunities are good.

Health Educators.

They cover a wide variety of subject areas, agencies, and organizations. Essentially all health educators, including those in the field of drugs and alcohol, must have fluent knowledge of the basic biological operations and functions of the human body so facts may be explained to the public. Health educators, especially in the drug and alcohol fields, serve not only as educators but also as important public-relations representatives for their agencies or organizations. As more public funds are used to fund and finance health education, job opportunities for health educators will grow. A good background in sociology, education, and community organization is an excellent preparation for such careers. For further information write to: National Health Council, Inc., 1740 Broadway, New York, N.Y. 10019.

REFERENCES

I. Drugs

"Addiction to Heroin on Increase." Allentown Morning Call (March 17): 11, 1976.

"Alcohol and Drugs." U.S. News & World Report (July 26): 74, 1976.

"Alcohol and Marijuana: Spreading Menace among Teen-Agers." U.S. News & World Report 79, 21 (November 24): 28–30, 1975.

Bernstein, Arnold and Henry Lennard
1973 "The American Way of Drugging." Society 10, 4 (May/June): 14–25.

Blum, Richard et al.
1972 Horatio Alger's Children: The Role of the Family in the Origin and Prevention of Drug Risk. San Francisco: Jossey-Bass.

Blumstein, Alfred, Philip Sagi, and Marvin Wolfgang
1973 "Problem of Estimating the Number of Heroin Addicts," Second Report of the National Commission on Marijuana and Drug Abuse. Drug Use in America: Problems in Perspective, Appendix Vol. 2, Social Responses to Drug Use. Washington, D.C.: Government Printing Office.

Brecher, Edward M. and the editors of Consumer Reports
1972 Licit and Illicit Drugs: The Consumers Union Report on Narcotics, Stimulants, Depressants, Inhalants, Hallucinogens, and Marijuana — Including Caffeine, Nicotine, and Alcohol. Boston: Little, Brown.

1975 "Marijuana: The Health Questions." Consumer Reports (March/April). Pp. 280–86 in Anne Kilbride, ed. Readings in Sociology 76/77: Annual Editions. Guilford, Conn.: Dushkin.

Brown, Bertram S.
1975 "Drugs and Public Health: Issues and Answers." Annals AAPSS 417 (January): 110–19.

Brown, Claude
1965 Manchild in the Promised Land. New York: Signet.

Chein, Isidor
1969 "Psychological Functions of Drug Use." Pp. 13–30 in Hannah Steinberg, ed. Scientific Basis of Drug Dependence: A Symposium. London: Churchill.

Dembo, Richard, James Schmeidler, and Mary Koval
1976 "Demographic, Value, and Behavior Correlates of Marijuana Use among Middle-Class Youths." Journal of Health and Social Behavior 17, 2 (June): 177–87.

"Drug Abuse Cost Estimated at $10 Billion–$17 Billion." Allentown Morning Call (May 31): 2, 1975.

"Drugs: A $17 Billion-a-Year Habit that U.S. Can't Break." U.S. News & World Report 80, 19 (May 10): 25–26, 1976.

Ferguson, Patricia, Thomas Lennox, and Dan Lettieri
1974 Drugs and Employment: Nonmedical Use of Drugs in Occupational and Industrial Settings. Research Issues 1. Rockville, Md.: National Institute on Drug Abuse.

Ferguson, Robert
1975 Drug Abuse Control. Boston: Hollbrook.

First Report of the National Commission on Marijuana and Drug Abuse. Marijuana: A Signal of Misunderstanding. Washington, D.C.: U.S. Government Printing Office, 1972.

Fort, Joel, and Christopher Cory
1975 American Drugstore: A (Alcohol) to V (Valium). Boston: Little, Brown.

Glaser, Daniel, Bernard Lander, and William Abbott
1971 "Opiate Addicted and Non-Addicted Siblings in a Slum Area." Social Problems 18 (Spring): 510–21.

Gusfield, Joseph
1975 "The (F)Utility of Knowledge?: The Relation of Social Science to Public Policy toward Drugs." Annals AAPSS, 417 (January): 1–15.

Hill, Margaret
1974 Drugs—Use, Misuse, Abuse: Guidance for Families. Public Affairs Pamphlet No. 515. New York: Public Affairs Committee.

Lindesmith, Alfred R.
1940 "Dope Fiend Mythology." Journal of Criminal Law, Criminology and Police Science 31: 199–208.

McKee, Michael, and Ian Robertson
1975 Social Problems. New York: Random House.

"Methadone: An American Way of Dealing." A film by Julia Reichert and James Klein. Dayton, Ohio: Methadone Information Center, 1975.

Maugh, Thomas
 1975 "Marijuana: New Support for Immune and Reproductive Hazards." Science 4217 (November 28): 865-67.

Mauss, Armand L.
 1975 Social Problems as Social Movements. Philadelphia: Lippincott.

Morland, J. Kenneth, Jack O. Balswick, John Belcher, and Morton Rubin
 1975 Social Problems in the United States. New York: Ronald Press.

Mushkin, Selma
 1975 "Politics and Economics of Government Response to Drug Abuse." Annals AAPSS 417 (January): 27-40.

Musto, David F.
 1973 The American Disease. Cambridge, Mass.: Yale University Press.

National Commission on Marijuana and Drug Abuse
 1972 Marijuana: A Signal of Misunderstanding. New York: New American Library.
 1973 Drug Use in America: Problem in Perspective. Washington, D.C.: U.S. Government Printing Office.

Peele, Stanton and Archie Brodsky
 1975 Love and Addiction. New York: Taplinger.

Perry, John and Erna Perry
 1976 Face to Face: The Individual and Social Problems. Boston: Educational Associates.

Reasons, Charles
 1975 "The Addict As a Criminal: Perpetuation of a Legend." Crime and Delinquency 21, 1 (January): 19-27.

Saltman, Jules
 1972 Drug Abuse—What Can Be Done? Public Affairs Pamphlet No. 290A. New York: Public Affairs Committee.

Scarpitti, Frank
 1974 Social Problems. New York: Holt, Rinehart and Winston.

Stark, Rodney
 1975 Social Problems. New York: Random House.

Susman, Ralph
 1975 "Drug Abuse, Congress and the Fact-Finding Process." Annals AAPSS 417 (January): 16-26.

Swift, Pamela
 1975 "Marijuana's Future: Keeping Up . . . with Youth." Parade Magazine (November 2): 15.
 1975 "Pot Cities: Keeping Up . . . with Youth." Parade Magazine (December 28): 6.
 1975 "Pot Offenders: Keeping Up . . . with Youth." Parade Magazine (October 26): 12.

Tinklenberg, J. R., ed.
 1975 Marijuana and Health Hazards. New York: Academic Press.
 "Unusual Penalty Imposed on Student in Drug Case." Allentown Morning Call (June 6): 2, 1973.

"Valium Most Cited in Drug-Abuse Crises." Allentown Morning Call (July 9): 10, 1976.

Walton, Mary
    1975 "Heroin Rival: White Pill for White Addict." Philadelphia Inquirer (March 13): 1.

Weaver, Warren
    1973 "U.S. Drug Study Stresses Treatment, Not Penalties." New York Times (March 23): 1.

Weppner, Robert, Karen Wells, Duana McBride, and Robert Ladner
    1976 "Effects of Criminal Justice and Medical Definitions upon Delivery of Treatment: The Case of Drug Abuse." Journal of Health and Social Behavior 17,2 (June): 170–77.

Whitten, Philip and Ian Robertson
    1973 "A Way to Control Heroin Addiction." Pp. 141–43 in Peter Wickman, ed. Annual Editions: Readings in Social Problems 73/74. Guilford, Conn.: Dushkin.

Wilson, Morrow and Suzanne Wilson, eds.
    1975 Drugs in American Life. Reference Shelf 47, 1. New York: Wilson.

Yankelovich, Daniel
    1975 "Drug Users vs. Drug Abusers: How Students Control Their Drug Crises." Psychology Today 9,5 (October): 39–42.

II. Alcohol

"Alcohol and Drugs." U.S. News & World Report (July 26): 74, 1976.

"Alcohol and Marijuana: Spreading Menace among Teen-Agers." U.S. News & World Report 79,21 (November 24): 28–30, 1975.

Bachrach, Leona
    1976 "Characteristics of Diagnosed and Missed Alcoholic Male Admissions to State and County Mental Health Hospitals in 1972." Mental Health Statistical Notes, No. 124 (February): HEW 76-158.
    1976 "Educational Level of Male Admissions with Alcohol Disorders, State and County Mental Hospitals 1972." Mental Health Statistical Notes, No. 123 (January): HEW 76-158.

Blane, H. T., W. F. Overton, and M. E. Chafetz
    1963 "Social Factors in the Diagnosis of Alcoholism: Characteristics of the Patient." Quarterly Journal of the Study of Alcoholism 24: 640–63.

Chambers, Carl, James Inciardi, and Harvey Siegel
    1975 Chemical Coping: A Report on Legal Drug Use in the United States. New York: Wiley.

DuPont, Robert L.
    1975 "Drugs, Alcoholism and Women." Vital Speeches 42, 5 (December 15): 140–43.

"Effects of Propranobol Studied." Alcohol & Health Notes 1, 2 (January). Rockville, Md.: National Clearinghouse for Alcohol Information of the National Institute on Alcohol Abuse and Alcoholism, 1973.

"Fastest Growing Disease in Western World Is Cirrhosis of Liver from Alcohol Consumption." National Enquirer (July 27): 40, 1976.

Fort, Joel
　1973　Alcohol: Our Biggest Drug Problem. New York: McGraw-Hill.
Fort, Joel and Christopher Cory
　1975　American Drugstore: A (Alcohol) to V (Valium). Boston: Little, Brown.
Gallagher, Nora
　1976　"Why People Kill Themselves." Today's Health 54, 2 (February): 46–50.
Gaylin, Jody
　1976　"The Sacred and the Profane." Psychology Today 9, 10 (March): 101–2.
Lambert, Richard D. and Alan W. Heston, eds.
　1975　"Drugs and Social Policy." Annals AAPSS 417 (January): 1–119.
Lingeman, Richard
　1974　Drugs from A to Z: A Dictionary. 2nd ed. New York: McGraw-Hill.
McClelland, David, William Davis, Rudolf Kalin, and Eric Wanner
　1972　The Drinking Man: Alcohol and Human Motivation. New York: Free Press.
McKee, Michael and Ian Robertson
　1975　Social Problems. New York: Random House.
Miles, Samuel A., ed.
　1974　Learning about Alcohol: A Resource Book for Teachers. Washington, D.C.: American Association for Health, Physical Education and Recreation.
National Commission on Marijuana and Drug Abuse.
　1973　Drug Use in America: Problem in Perspective (second report, March). Washington, D.C.: U.S. Government Printing Office.
"New Therapy Involving Electric Shocks and Self-Discipline Offers Hope for America's 10 Million Alcoholics." National Enquirer (July 27): 54, 1976.
Shearer, Lloyd
　1976　"Women & Alcohol: Intelligence Report." Parade Magazine (February 22): 4.
Soltis, A.
　1975　"Alcoholism: Still the Prime Drug Problem." Pp. 104–10 in Morrow and Suzanne Wilson. Drugs in American Life. The Reference Shelf 47, 1 New York: Wilson.
"What Everyone Should Know about Alcoholism." Greenfield, Mass.: Channing L. Bete, 1974.
"What Industry Is Doing about 10 Million Alcoholic Workers." U.S. News & World Report 80, 2 (January 12): 66–67, 1976.
Wolf, I. et al.
　1965　"Social Factors in the Diagnosis of Alcoholism: Attitudes of Physicians." Quarterly Journal of the Study of Alcoholism 26: 72–79.

SUGGESTED READINGS

Coombs, Robert H., ed. Socialization in Drug Abuse. New Brunswick, N.J.: Transaction Books. 1976.
　Seeks to rebut the notion that drug abuse is an outgrowth of emo-

tional pathology. The model offered to explain drug abuse (from learning theory) is a "social career" within a functioning subsystem of American society.

Filstead, William J. and Jean J. Rossi, eds. Alcohol and Alcohol Problems: New Directions. Cambridge, Mass.: Ballinger. 1976
Internationally famous scientists and practitioners critically review major issues in alcohol abuse and treatment, offering strategies for new directions.

Hunt, Leon G. and Carl D. Chambers. The Heroin Epidemics: A Study of Heroin Use in the United States: 1965–1975. New York: Halsted Press.
Documents the incidence and prevalence of the heroin problem over a 10-year period, offering insights into reasons for its use and pointing out various treatment approaches.

Lee, Essie C. Alcohol, Proof of What? New York: Messner. 1976.
Discusses alcohol and alcoholism, including case studies of young people who have had to cope with alcoholism in a parent, friend, or themselves.

Nahas, Gabriel G., with Stanley L. Englebardt. Keep Off the Grass: A Scientist's Documented Account of Marijuana's Destructive Effects on Man. Pleasantville, N.Y.: Reader's Digest Press. 1976.
Based on laboratory research and scientific documentation, this study discusses marijuana's effects on brain functioning and other physiological dysfunctions.

Periodicals Worth Exploring

Adolescence
Annals AAPSS
Consumer Reports
Crime and Delinquency
Journal of Health and Social Behavior
Journal of Studies on Alcohol
Social Problems
Society
Today's Health

Changes in the Family and Sex Roles

INTRODUCTION

DEFINITIONS OF THE PROBLEM
Pessimistic "defenders" of the family.
Optimistic "challengers'" definitions of the family:
a) Contemporary marriages — O'Neills' "open marriage."
b) Motherhood — challengers' and defenders' views.
Changing sex roles:
a) Challengers' perspective of sex roles and socialization.
b) Unconscious ideology produced.
c) Defenders' perspective of female roles.
Homosexuality:
a) Defenders' perspective.
b) Challengers' perspective

INCIDENCE AND PREVALENCE OF THE PROBLEM
Trends in marriages (rate down).
Trends in divorce (rate up).
Size of families (getting smaller).
Illegitimacy (rate increasing, even with abortion).
Premarital and extramarital activities (increasing).
Working women — sexism in jobs and pay (slowly changing).

CAUSES OF THE PROBLEM
Industrialization.
Urbanization.
Conflicting values between the individual and the family:
a) Women's liberation.
b) Changing attitudes toward sex.
Affluence for a few but a social structure that forces
 women into work force.

PROPOSED SOLUTIONS TO THE PROBLEM
Retaining and reinforcing traditional sex roles, norms, and
 values.
Alternative family forms and sex roles.
Encouraging a national policy of equality for women.
Consciousness raising among women.

FUTURE OF THE PROBLEM
Future forms of marriage and the family — Herbert Otto's
 "new marriage."
Thomas McGinnis' "open family."
Future options and alternatives for marriage and sex roles.
Clare Booth Luce envisions little change in power.
Gagnon and Henderson's view of future sexuality.
The "sexual marginality" perspective.

SUMMARY

> The changes necessary to bring about equality were, and still are, very revolutionary indeed. They involve a sex-role revolution for men and women which will restructure all our institutions: child rearing, education, marriage, the family, medicine, work, politics, the economy, religion, psychological theory, human sexuality, morality and the very evolution of the race.
>
> Betty Friedan, **New York Times Magazine,** March 4, 1973.

The family is the basic social unit of every society. The groups we belong to, the town or city we live in, and the social milieu we find ourselves in are linked to our families. It is the group and social institution we know the best, and our deepest emotions and memories—positive or negative—are linked to it. Yet we know that within our lifetime, many changes have taken place that affect our relationships and feelings toward our families. What do these changes mean for the family? Is it likely to become stronger or weaker, more or less crucial for people? Will it be replaced, or have a new rebirth?

Other related questions come readily to mind: How much has the traditional family changed? How much does the family today differ from that of the past? What changes can be documented and how widespread are they? Why has the American family changed so drastically? What, if anything, can be done about the situation? Is there a family in our future, and is there a future for the family as we know it? These questions are appropriate if we are to look at the changing family and sex roles as a social problem.

DEFINING THE CHANGES IN THE FAMILY AND SEX ROLES

Everybody agrees that American society is in transition. But not many agree on where the change is or should be leading us. Among the social institutions riding the crest of this wave is the family (Toffler, 1970).

Sociologists have debated for years whether there has been a "withering away" of the American family; to what degree urbanization has separated the nuclear family from kin; whether the extended family has declined in importance; and whether changes in the family's structure and function are attributable to, or preceded, such political and economic variables as industrialization and urbanization.

On this last controversy, William Ogburn (in his *Technology and the Changing Family*, 1955), Talcott Parsons and Robert Bales (1955), and David and Vera Mace (1959) argue that industrialization and urbanization have destroyed or changed traditional family structures. William Goode (1963), Frank Furstenberg, Jr. (1966), and others argue that major changes in the structure and functions of the family took place *before* industrialization occurred. William Goode in particular describes the preindustrial American family as a stereotype and myth: "the classical family of Western nostalgia" (1963: 6). Nevertheless, the basic question for most sociologists remains what impacts have social change had on the family and what social problems have emerged from the change? Sociologists have reacted to these changes in optimistic or pessimistic ways. Optimists argue that the family is merely reorganizing, adapting, or adjusting to a new society, and becoming more individualistic. Pessimists argue that the family is decaying, disintegrating, or dying and losing its social solidarity. Sociologist Armand Mauss calls the pessimists the "defenders" of the traditional family who want to "conserve" the norms and values of the past; he calls the optimists the "challengers" who want to "liberalize or radicalize" the traditional norms and values (1975: 475).

The Defenders' Views of the Family

The defenders, such as George Gilder (*Sexual Suicide*) and Arlene Rossen Cardozo (*Woman at Home*), point out that women's roles are accepted, and even enjoyed, by the overwhelming majority of women—even by those who must work outside the home. A 1976 Gallup Poll reported that 76 percent of American women view marriage and children as one of the "important elements" that would provide the "most interesting and satisfying life for them." Participants were each handed a card with five alternative lifestyles, as indicated in Table 4-1. They were also given the following question. "Let's talk about the ideal life for you personally.

table 4-1 THE IDEAL LIFESTYLE, ACCORDING TO WOMEN

ANSWERS AMONG WOMEN (PERCENTAGE)

	Married, children, full-time job	Married, no children, full-time job	Married, children, no full-time job	Married, no children, no full-time job	Single, full-time job	Undecided	Totals
NATIONAL RESPONSE	32%	6%	44%	3%	9%	6%	100%
EDUCATION:							
COLLEGE	37	11	34	3	10	5	100%
HIGH SCHOOL	31	3	49	3	9	5	100%
GRADE SCHOOL	32	6	42	5	7	8	100%
AGE:							
18–24	45	8	31	1	15	*	100%
25–29	30	4	48	*	12	6	100%
30–49	36	4	48	2	4	6	100%
50 AND OLDER	24	6	46	6	10	8	100%

*Less than 1/2 of 1%.
Source: "Women in America." The **Gallup Opinion Index**, Report No. 123 (March 1976): 30.

Which one of the alternatives on this card do you feel would provide the most interesting and satisfying life? . . . ."

Michael Novak observes that intellectuals and college-educated persons, the top 10 percent of our population, often have distorted ideas of what is really occurring (or should occur) in family life, because of their own limited view of college-student behavior. He writes:

> Some 66 percent of all Americans remain married to the same man or woman throughout a lifetime. . . . Thus the image of America we gain through television and the movies, through **Time** and **Newsweek** and the "style" and "modern living" sections of our newspapers, gives a more accurate view of the culture of the top 10 percent than of the bottom 90 percent. . . . The point is that the public image of the nation is vastly out of tune with the public reality (1975: B–1).

Sociologist Urie Bronfenbrenner, one of the leading experts on children and family life, has concluded that "the system for making human beings human in this society is breaking down" (Horn, 1975: 32). Looking at trends in the first half of the 1970s, Bronfenbrenner found that factors pointing to the well-being of children were in a down trend. At the same time, factors of "risk, isolation, and danger" were up. He foresaw "impairment rather than improvement in the competence and character of the next generation of Americans" (Ibid.). Looking at factual evidence on marriages, divorces, births, deaths, household makeup, and education, Bronfenbrenner felt that the most important trend he uncovered was "the progressive fragmentation and disintegration of the family" (Ibid.). He admits the problem is more severe in poor and nonwhite groups, but the "family fracture" cuts across lines of income, race, and education. And it is not just a big-city problem. He notes that ". . . the high levels of family fragmentation which, six years ago, were found only in major metropolitan centers, are now occurring in smaller urban areas as well" (Ibid., 34).

In sum, then, the defenders draw upon what social scientists call "strain theories and social disorganization theory." That is, they define the problem around the disorganizing aspects of changes within the traditional family—changes, in this case, for the worse, they argue. The key question here is, "How far has the disintegration proceeded, and can more change be accommodated?" As sociologist Joseph Julian observes, "A social problem arises only when the pressure for change can no longer be accommodated within the limits of the existing structures, or when those who wish to maintain the structures fear that it cannot" (1973: 343).

The Challengers' Views of the Family

In defining the social issue of the family, the optimists, the "challengers" of the traditional family, argue that the family has actually changed for the better. It has adjusted and adapted its structure, functions, and roles to our individualistic, mobile, urbanized-industrialized, fast-changing society, and it continues to serve the most basic functions of any family: reproduction, socializing the young, and economic and emotional support of its members.

In a mobile society, some regard a small, nuclear family structure as imperative, an improvement on the obsolete and cumbersome extended family of the past. Today, no one questions our need for physical mobility. As one scholar has noted:

> We crossed an ocean, settled a continent, built a powerful nation. We move to find jobs, to take a better job, to enjoy the sun, to fulfill a dream. . . . At first we took the family with us when we moved, its traditions, obligations and permanence. Then, as we moved faster and faster, we began to drop off the excess baggage that slowed us down. The family grew smaller and the time spent together shorter. Now family is parents and children, and their years together have shrunk to less than two decades (Young, 1973: 11).

This modern "nuclear" family, according to sociologist Talcott Parsons, is "functionally differentiated"—it performs fewer but more specialized functions for its members than in the past. The emotional support—love, affection, and warmth—that it gives to its members is crucial, for the family is one of the few remaining social units in our mass, bureaucratized society in which one can expect to find such treatment. So, while the family today may perform fewer functions, the specialized ones it does perform are invaluable. It also does a better job in socializing the young to the values of "instrumental activism," as it better prepares the child to be efficient and rational, to achieve, and to be master of his own fate in our competitive and conflict-oriented society (Parsons and Bales, 1955; Hyman Rodman, 1965: 262-86). Some commentators go so far as to see the family changing from the old patriarchal, authoritarian form into more of a "companionship," "colleague," or "fringe" form—a change and adaptation generally considered by the challengers to be beneficial and functional for modern men, women, and children.

How are marriage, motherhood, sex, and men's dominance defined by the challengers and defenders? The challengers, who encourage individualism and equal rights, agree with Mervyn Cadwallader about traditional marriages:

> Marriage is a wretched institution. It spells the end of voluntary affection, of love freely given and joyously received. Beautiful romances are transmuted into dull marriages; eventually the relationship becomes constricting, corrosive, grinding and destructive. The beautiful love affair becomes a bitter contract (1967: 48).

Why ruin a beautiful friendship by marriage?

Contemporary Marriages

The most widely accepted definition of contemporary marriage by the challengers is Nena and George O'Neill's concept of "open marriage"

(1973). In their book they point out that couples can transcend "mere togetherness" and reach "the ultimate in cooperation ... that creates, through expanding feedback and growth, a *synergesic couple*." They can replace an "archaic, rigid, outmoded, oppressive, static, decaying, Victorian" marriage with one that is "free, dynamic, honest, spontaneous, creative" (1973: 267). They condemn traditional marriage for its "conditional and static trust, unequal status, limited love and a closed self-limiting energy system, bondage." Instead, they stress the autonomous, independent growth of the two partners, with emphasis on privacy, separate identities, and separate lives. A partner should be free to go out with other friends of both sexes whenever he or she wants to. If adultery occurs, we should understand that this happens; if there is enough trust between the couple, it should not ruin their marriage.

The O'Neills see the married couple as two equal, independent individuals who maintain a "dynamic growth partnership." They envision roles of the partners as flexible and reversible—sex-specific functions and responsibilities are obsolete. The defenders of traditional marriage, while seeing *some* functionality in this approach, argue that "open marriage" would weaken marriage, family roles, and society. According to George Gilder's analysis:

> Though they deny it, when one actually scrutinizes their concept, equality turns out to mean sameness. The man earns money; so must his wife. The man initiates sex; so must she. The woman decorates the house, cooks a meal, or makes a bed; the man must eventually reciprocate (1973: 49).

Open marriage, in this view, begins to assume a rather rigid and burdensome structure of its own, as it becomes governed by a tight calculus of reciprocity.

For example, the O'Neills cannot see women being equal in marriage unless they are making money. By this, they mean a challenging, meaningful career for the woman. The home only "programs her for mediocrity and dulls her brain." They admit that such "equal family support" will not be possible for everyone, "until major societal change is effected in terms of family and child-rearing arrangements" and women are given the same opportunities as men in training and jobs (1973: 197). This change is starting to occur because of the "ESE factor"—the woman's new Educational, Sexual, and Economic freedoms. Without any one of these ESE factors, the woman is a subordinate marriage partner. With all three she is free to find fulfillment, with or without marriage.

The defenders respond that by defining marriage this way—emphasizing solely *individual* development—the O'Neills ignore the essential *social* nature of marriage and the family.

Motherhood

The challengers have a much different definition and view of motherhood from that of the past. Although a woman can freely choose to be a mother, society should not insist she become one, since motherhood is *not* every woman's destiny. There is no innate biological drive for women to have children; if there were, cultural pressures for women to have children would not exist.

With technology in the kitchen and contraception in the bedroom, the modern mother can engage in "continuous mothering"—spending practically every waking hour with her child (Lopata, 1971: Chap. 4). But it is neither necessary nor good for the "healthy emotional development" of the child. What is important is the quality and kind of care the child receives, rather than who provides it and how much time per se is given over to it. A full-time mother not only is not needed for the growth of the child, but also may contribute to the child's problems—even to mental illness. In this way a mother may pass on problems from one generation to the next. Full-time motherhood does not sufficiently challenge or develop the woman, nor does it greatly benefit the child. As sociologist Alice Rossi argues, after being a mother for 15 or 20 years as her only occupation "women have to face the question of who they are besides their children's mother" (1964: 624).

The defenders, in contrast, support traditional notions of motherhood. At one time, sex and motherhood were inseparable: motherhood helped make sex respectable. The traditional role expectation was that every woman would some day be a mother, for this was first and foremost her destiny. Freud argued that "anatomy is destiny," and even in our folk sayings, everyone was "for motherhood and against sin." Motherhood was the pinnacle of achievement for a woman, a "rite of passage" into full womanhood. It is the ultimate creative act that any human being can perform, and, according to most traditionalists, the woman's most socially rewarding status.

Of course, the very survival of the human race and the prosperity and growth of a nation ultimately depend on motherhood. Without motherhood there would be "instability in marriage; . . . or worse still, . . . race-suicide" (Ibid., 282). Traditionally, not to bear children was a curse, and a woman could not opt to remain childless "without either the shriveling disapproval or the humiliating patronage . . . the wrath or the pity of the community in which she lived" (Decter, 1974: 151).

Yet even as the family becomes smaller, the motherly role of socializing the children has become more important. Society judges the parents by professional standards, and asks that they meet the child's physical, moral, and emotional needs. Ultimate responsibility here is placed on the mother, as the heart and center of the family. Despite a woman's wider range of choices, motherhood remains popular today: over 70 percent of married couples have children. And, in the view of the defenders, a majority of women will always continue to have children. The most precious possession of any human being is life—life from a woman who decided to become a mother. This, in sum, is the defenders' view of motherhood—basic, beneficial, and blessed.

Changing Sex Roles and the Family

The last difference between the challengers and defenders is the social problem of our changing sex roles, which centers around male dominance of society and women. The challengers feel that the issue of male dominance is "the 'gut' feminist question" (Luce, 1975: 156).

The biological basis for traditional male supremacy has weakened. Brute physical strength is not needed in a technological, white-collar economy as it was earlier in an agricultural world. Since cultural and social conditions such as these have changed so radically, the "cultural lag" of male dominance must be profoundly reduced and eventually eliminated altogether, the challengers argue.

In addition, the social-learning process by which sex-role identity is acquired must be changed. Scientific evidence shows that this is the nub of the problem. Males, as boys, are taught that they are superior, and females, as girls, are taught that they are inferior. An "unconscious ideology" is absorbed: girls and women are "passive, emotional, expressive, and delicate," boys and men are "active, logical, instrumental, and tough." This ideology begins at birth. Dressed in pink, the little girl is given special treatment: when mothers and babies are still in the hospital, mothers smile at, talk to, and touch their female infants more than their male babies.

As children begin to read, story-book characters are the images and models little boys and girls are supposed to act like and imitate. One survey (Fisher, May 24, 1970: 6) found five times as many males as females appear in children's book titles. In another survey of 134 books used by a public-school system, boy-centered stories outnumbered girl-centered ones five to two, and biographies of men exceeded those of women six to one. Girls are never doctors, but they are more likely to be nurses, librarians, or teachers (but never principals). Girls play house with dolls; boys play with cars and guns. Girls were most often depicted in books as "passive and dependent, lacking in initiative or ambition, domestic, and usually inferior to the opposite sex in any kind of competence. Girls were always helpers, never doers" (Doyle, 1974: 6).

As children grow up, more unconscious sex-role socialization occurs. Two Yale sociologists, Lever and Goodman, found that "very few" scientific toys are bought for girls. Three out of four chemistry sets picture only boys on the package. Although building-block sets show both girls and boys, more complex erector sets show only boys (Doyle, 1974: 7). Boys are encouraged to take more of an interest in mathematics and science. Even if the girls do well at math, after the second year in high school "they think it's unfeminine and will hamper their relationship with boys" (Swift, 1976: 19).

All this leads to stereotyping and to subhuman treatment of women in later life. Even women's perception of themselves becomes one-sided and distorted. For example, the assumed inferiority of women came out even

Women have become more politically active in recent years. Here a Pennsylvania state senate secretary wears a T-shirt whose double meaning reflects changing opinions about a woman's role.

among radical young people in 1968. During the student rebellion at Columbia University over equal rights for students, when militant students took over the administration building, the males immediately assigned the domestic tasks of preparing food and making coffee to the women students. While the men planned and decided the next move, the women were supposed to "stay in the kitchen." They refused. The women wanted to make revolution, not coffee. So, from then on the tasks were assigned without regard to sex (Duberman, 1977: 70–71). The challengers demand that traditional sex-role assignment of tasks cease.

Unconscious Ideology of Women's Inferiority. So strong is this "unconscious ideology" of women's inferiority that by the time girls reach college, many are prejudiced against women and their abilities to achieve. Sociologist Philip Goldberg gave college women sets of booklets containing six identical professional articles in traditional male, female, and neutral fields. An article in one set bore the name *John* T. McKay; in another set the same article bore the name *Joan* T. McKay. Each booklet contained three articles by "women" and three by "men." Questions at the end of each article asked the women students to rate the articles on "value, persuasiveness, profundity," and the authors' "style and competence." Articles with a male by-line fared better in every aspect, even in such "feminine" fields as art history, elementary education, and dietetics.

Goldberg concluded that "women are prejudiced against female professionals and, regardless of the actual accomplishments of these professionals, will firmly refuse to recognize them as the equals of their male colleagues" (Goldberg, 1968: 29).

What happens when women are conditioned *not* to compete with men in careers? Matina Horner's classic study of this issue shows that whereas a man must worry about failure in a career, the woman must worry about success. She asked undergraduate women to complete the following story: "After first-term finals, Anne finds herself at the top of her medical-school class and _____." An identical story was given to a control group of men, but with the name John in place of Anne. After reading the stories written by the women, Horner concluded that 65 percent of them wished to "avoid success," compared with only 10 percent of the men.

Such attitudes are the result of years of brainwashing that tells women they are inferior, cannot compete with men, and should stay in the home. The challengers maintain that such "male chauvinism" must be ended. Women (and men) should be encouraged to become androgynous (andro=male; gyne=female), a role mixture of attributes of both sexes. That is, we should be brought up to combine the best traits of both sexes and thereby to help reform our society (Bern, 1975: 58–62).

Defenders of Female Roles. The defenders' point of view is sharply different. Although the biological basis of assumed male dominance has been eliminated in modern society, the biological differences will always remain. As the French say, "Vive la différence." Certain women, for example, assert that "normal" women do *not* feel inferior to men—they are equal in their own way. They do not feel downtrodden, unliberated, or dominated. Phyllis Schlafly, who heads the movement to "Stop ERA" (Equal Rights Amendment for Women), claims that passage of ERA will destroy women's privileged position in our society. Her perspective, in turn, gains support from women defenders of the family who have succeeded in finding true fulfillment as women in the home. Changing traditional male-female arrangements threaten all the success they have earned.

Spirited organizations have formed around the defense of the traditional "feminine role." These groups include MOM (Men Our Masters), HOW (Happiness of Womanhood), and the Pussycats. The motto of this last group is "the lamb chop is mightier than the karate chop," which reflects the defenders' view that much more is to be gained by showing love and affection toward men than by pursuing an aggressive, combative stance for "liberation."

The defenders also assert that if any change in attitude is needed toward society's sex roles, we should assign more prestige and status to women's traditional roles, rather than try to get them to pursue some "grail-like quest" for a rewarding and fulfilling career outside the home. Most jobs for women and men in our elite-controlled economy are *not* challenging or rewarding. Many more rewards and challenges calling for professional know-how may lie within marriage and the home than is commonly recognized. It is especially within marriage and the family that a female can become a "total woman," as popular writer Marabel Morgan (1974) suggests.

Homosexuality. Another aspect of the problem of changing sex roles is homosexuality, along with bisexuality and transsexuality. Homosexuals (known as lesbians when they are female) have a sexual preference for members of their own sex. Bisexuals engage in sexual relations with members of both the opposite sex and their own. Transsexuals have a gender identity that is usually opposed to their biological makeup. Despite having the genes, hormones, and anatomy of one sex, they desire to be of the opposite sex, and wish to change their body, their social role, and the gender of their sex partners. Transsexuals undergo operations to change their sexual organs. Transsexuals should not be confused with transvestites, who express an opposite sexual self by dress, but do not have a change in genitalia. Transvestites are usually not considered homosexuals.

The defenders argue that homosexual behavior is a distortion of the social, cultural, and biological roles of men and women. As Margaret Mead observes in *Male and Female*, "The relationships between the sexes . . . have been essential to the preservation of human society" (1967: 188). Kingsley Davis, in his analysis of sexual behavior, points to "some examples of accepted but not esteemed homosexuality under restricted circum-

Transvestites dress as women, act effeminate, but are not necessarily homosexuals. In some communities, transvestism is illegal. Can you tell who in this picture is the transvestite?

stances" in primitive cultures; but homosexuality is disapproved of in "nearly all societies" because it is incompatible with the family and established sexual norms (1976: 252–53). Defenders of traditional sex roles maintain that encouraging or failing to censure such "abnormal" sexual behavior will undermine the institutions of marriage and the family, as well as society itself. They feel that known homosexuals should not be permitted to hold responsible jobs or come in contact with children in the classroom.

The challengers see homosexuality, bisexuality, and transsexuality as responses to the problems that traditional sex roles have given to individuals and society. In addition, sex roles are culturally learned rather than biologically determined, and therefore they can be changed. There is no *universal* prohibition against homesexuality or transsexuality.

As Gagnon and Henderson write:

> With the possible exception of incest (and even that was practiced by some early civilizations), there are no sexual behaviors that are universally prohibited. There is no unbending set of norms that govern sexual makeup or activity. Social structures of considerable variety have existed in the past, or exist today, that were (or are) capable of supporting, allowing, or requiring widely different forms of sexual behavior (1975: 11).

In addition, since sexual pleasure has now been separated from reproduction, no harm can come to society or the individuals as long as consenting adults are involved. The challengers argue that if the aim of sex is pleasure, what difference does it make from which sex one derives that enjoyment? Homosexuality gives people sexual alternatives and choices not often available in the past. Some persons, either because of hormonal imbalances or psychological preferences, consider themselves women trapped inside men's bodies (or vice versa) and correct "nature's error" through surgery. Widely known examples of transsexuals, such as Jan (formerly John) Morris and tennis player Dr. Renee Richards (formerly Dr. Richard Raskind), have dramatized the difference between original anatomical sex and a person's gender-role feelings.

Whether one accepts the definitions of the conservative defenders or of the liberal and radical challengers, it seems evident that homosexuality, bisexuality, and transsexuality are much more openly discussed and expressed in our changing society than in the past. Homosexuals and transsexuals have "come out of the closet," although they remain society's "skeleton in the closet" for many. The 1977 vote in Dade County, Florida, over whether homosexuals should be protected under local civil-rights ordinances is illustrative of the nationwide debate on this issue.

Within all this ambiguity and the conflicting views of defenders and challengers, a unified view of our changing sex roles is obviously difficult. Value conflicts among conservatives, liberals, and radicals over changing sex roles are evident. One point emerges from the evidence discussed earlier: sex roles are in a state of confusion, change, and anomie. Without

> ## MY LIFE OF LONELY AGONY
>
> "Only another transsexual could understand that lifetime of lonely, personal agony. But the nightmare is over now."
>
> With these words, spoken slowly and softly, Dr. Renee Richards summed up the mental torment she endured for more than 40 years, feeling and thinking like a female inescapably trapped inside the body of a male.
>
> "I am a woman," declared Dr. Richards, the famous tennis-playing transsexual, in an exclusive *Enquirer* interview. "And the relief of being able to say that with certainty is indescribable.
>
> "I have some female sexual organs now, the physical appearance of a woman and female blood hormone levels," she said with a hint of pride in her voice.
>
> "I think like a woman—I've done so for years. I like shopping with other women in the supermarket. I cook, I sew. In the eyes of the law I am female. But years of struggle for full acceptance lie ahead."
>
> The 42-year-old ophthalmologist, who created a tempest in the tennis world after top professional women players refused to compete against her, admitted she still has some masculine traits. She stands 6-foot-2 and her handshake is strong; her body is wiry and her voice is deep for a woman.
>
> "More than 40 years as a son, a husband and a father cannot be shed in a few weeks," shrugged Dr. Richards, toying with a gold earring.
>
> Source: Jan Goodwin, *National Enquirer*, September 28, 1976: 4.

taking sides, one could simply state that an important part of the social problem of changing sex roles is role confusion and personal troubles that emerge from it. Sociologist Frank Scarpitti notes:

> At the root of much of the discussion surrounding each of the non-conforming forms of sexual behavior lies the fact that the norms themselves are seriously under question. What is a "normal" male? A "normal" female? (1974: 465)

The basic term to be defined in this chapter is "sexism"—any unequal or discriminatory treatment of women (or men) on the basis of their sex. Sexism perpetuates inequality between women and men and often reflects the "alienating effects of powerlessness and oppression that affect our body politic" (Kilbride, 1976: 126). In this struggle for equality of treatment, the persons in power are usually men. Sexism is a personal problem experienced by so many women that today it is considered a social issue.

INCIDENCE AND PREVALENCE OF CHANGES IN THE FAMILY AND SEX ROLES

Since there are two conflicting views—those of the defenders and of the challengers—about the social problem of the family and changing sex roles, the incidence and prevalence of the problem will be measured by the various social indicators most agreed upon. What is not agreed upon is what the indicators means and in what direction they should be pointing. For the defenders, the incidence and prevalence of the problem is greater whenever certain indicators are larger (in absolute numbers or percentages) and others are smaller when compared with the past. The larger indicators are divorces, illegitimacy, premarital and extramarital sex, and working mothers. The smaller indices include marriage rates, size of family, birth rates, and sexism—all of which are smaller today. For the challengers the incidence and prevalence of the problem is less whenever these indicators show the opposite tendencies.

The meaning and significance of the indicators are quite clear to the defenders. They show that the family is being weakened and is disintegrating. The challengers, on the other hand, see the indicators merely as manifestations of an "adaptive" family and of changing sex roles in modern society.

Marriages

In early 1977 there were over 110 million females in the United States. Of these, over 14 million were ages 18 to 24. These are the critical years during which young women make decisions about marriages,

Traditionally, marriage in America has been viewed as a sacred institution and until now has always been between a man and a woman.

careers, or a combination of both. Often the 14 million young men of the same age group affect their decisions in some way.

In 1974 marriages declined by 2 percent compared with 1973. This was the first time marriages had dropped since 1958, and the decline continued during the first half of 1975, down 4 percent from the first half of 1974. The marriage rate was 9.3 per 1,000 population, the lowest rate in 10 years (*The World Almanac*, 1976: 959).

Today younger women are putting off marriage. For example, in 1960, 28 percent of women 20 to 24 years old were single; in 1976, this rose to over 40 percent ("Growing at a Slower Pace," May 16, 1977: 65). Even in the age group between 15 and 19, only 11 percent were married in 1974, compared with 15 percent in 1960 (Sklar and Berkov, 1975: 694). Census figures show that the increase in singleness during the 1960s was greatest among women who had *not* attended college. Today, of course, nearly three times as many women are in college as in 1960, and singleness affects mostly women in their twenties (Glick, 1975: 17).

Whether this trend in delaying marriage will continue is difficult to say, but one expert has noted that "just as cohorts of young women who have postponed childbearing for an unusually long time seldom make up for the child deficit as they grow older, so also young people who are delaying marriage may never make up for the marriage deficit later on" (Ibid., 18). This may mean fewer marriages and families in the future.

Divorce

The sharpest indication of what has been happening to the family in recent years is divorce. According to William Goode: "Divorce is a strain point within a kinship system that values marital stability highly" (1956: 6). If measured by the rate per 1,000 population, divorce is relatively low (5.0 per 1,000 in 1976) as compared with marriage (9.9 per 1,000) ("New Look at America Today," May 16, 1977: 65). In comparing first marriages per 1,000 single women 14 to 44 with divorces per 1,000 for married women between the same ages, the marriage rate is about 100, while the divorce rate is about 35 ("Domestic Life . . .," May 1977: 1). Nevertheless, both the number and the rate of divorces continued a 10-year upward trend during the 1970s. In 1974, 44 out of every 100 marriages ended in divorce. Next to Sweden, we had the world's highest divorce rate (Peterson, 1975: 4). If only *first* marriages are counted, about one out of every two marriages ends in divorce. If desertions and separations are added, the incidence of marriage dissolution becomes even greater. In California, one out of every two marriages end in divorce, and in the Los Angeles area there is one divorce for every marriage (See, 1975: 201). In 1976, over one million divorces were granted, double the number in 1965 (see Figure 4-1). As more persons turn to divorce (often in desperation) as a solution to their personal problems, it soon becomes a social issue that affects family life and sex roles.

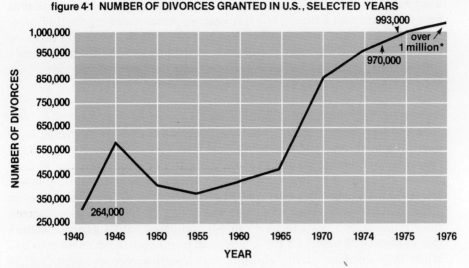

figure 4-1 NUMBER OF DIVORCES GRANTED IN U.S., SELECTED YEARS

* Twelve months ending June 30, 1976.

Source: Division of Vital Statistics, National Center for Health Statistics, reported in the *World Almanac and Book of Facts, 1976:* 959-60.

Most who divorce later remarry, as William Goode observes in his classic study, *After Divorce* (1956: 277); but overall it has a disruptive effect on stable family life. Remarrying is both stable and risky, too: those who remarry have a two-thirds chance of not divorcing again; if couples have had two divorces, the chances are 80 percent that they will have a third (Horton and Leslie, 1974: 202).

Even among Catholics, rates of divorce are increasing. Somewhere between three and five million Catholics are divorced, and at least half of them have remarried, according to Reverend Jim Young, a Paulist priest and author of *Questions Divorced Catholics Ask* (Allentown Morning Call, 1975: 3). Divorce has become so prevalent that companies have begun printing "divorce announcement" cards (Goldstein, 1975: E-2). Some of the cards read: "Marriage is like a crossword puzzle. Sometimes you just can't work it out"; or "A divorce is nature's way of telling you to get rid of the His and Her towels."

But for millions of children divorce is no joke. In the early 1950s the number of divorces was greater than the number of children affected; now the number of children is greater than the number of divorces (Horn, 1975: 32-33). In 1948 only one out of 14 children under six was living with one parent; by 1973, the number doubled to one out of seven children. In 1970, 30 percent (some 10 million) of all children under 18 were living with one or both parents who had been divorced, separated, or deserted (Glick, 1975: 21-22). Traditionally men deserted, for without money and a job, men lose much of their power over women; but women today are deserting in greater numbers. The Tracers Company of New

York reports: "Ten years ago we were looking for 300 runaway husbands for every wife that fled, . . . but last year we were searching for 147 *more* missing wives than husbands" (Cassady, 1975: 42). Wife beating takes on the dimensions of a serious social issue as men try to solve their economic and personal troubles by "taking it out" on their wives.

Declining Birth Rates and Family Size

Another social indicator that the American family is changing is its declining birthrates and shrinking size. The very essence of a traditional family was children. Today 30 percent of married women by age 30 have had no children. The crude birthrate in 1976 was near an all-time low—fewer than 15 babies for every 1,000 population, down from 25 babies in 1957. In 1976 only about 65 babies were born for every 1,000 women in their reproductive years (ages 15 to 44) compared with a general fertility rate of about 125 babies in 1957. The total number of children women had when they finished having children was less than two children (1.7) in 1976; in 1957 they had 3.7 children. In New York City and Washington, D.C. there have been more legal abortions than live births in recent years.

In early 1975 the Census Bureau said there were 71 million households in the United States. About two out of three were maintained by a married couple, but the other 34 were run by "a group of relatives but not by a married couple" (12 percent), or by a person living with nonrelatives or "entirely alone" (22 percent) (Shearer, 1976: 14). The Bureau noted that people are occupying more and more separate living quarters with fewer occupants per unit. This "separate living" is a sign of the deteriorating family and the division and "apartness" that tears at the American family, or so the defenders argue. This is evidence of the liberation, individualism, and freedom from traditional forms of the family, the challengers respond.

No matter what this smaller family size and "household separation" means, for the first time in our history the average household consists of fewer than three persons (*New York Times*, July 7, 1975: 36). The Census Bureau notes: "This is part of a basic change in how Americans live and how they relate to each other" (Ibid.).

Illegitimacy

Illegitimacy refers to children born to unmarried women. Reported illegitimacy underestimates, to an unknown degree, the extent of the problem. Reported illegitimate births in the United States have increased nearly fourfold in the past generation, as the number of young women in our society increased. In 1940 it was estimated that 89,500 children were born out of marriage; in 1968, the figure was over 339,000.

The rate of such births per 1,000 unmarried women (14 to 44) rose from about seven in 1940 to 24 in 1968 (Julian, 1973: 355). In 1973, out of

One out of 10 American teenage girls became pregnant during 1977. The public-television documentary **Guess Who's Pregnant?** tells the story behind this growing social problem.

every 100 live births, 13 were illegitimate. About 40 percent of illegitimate births occur to women under 20. By 1973, among young whites 20 out of 100 births were illegitimate; among blacks, 70 (Scanzoni and Scanzoni, 1976: 162).

In the early 1970s, New York and California reported drops in their illegitimacy rates as abortion became legal. But indications are that the teenage illegitimacy rate has begun to rise again. These renewed increases are occurring despite high rates of legal abortion for unmarried mothers (almost 50 per 1,000 in 1973–74 in California). Figures from 1965 to 1973 from New York, Hawaii, Washington State, and Oregon "suggest that California's experience is indicative of trends in the nation generally. . . . In each of the four states, teenage illegitimate-fertility rates were higher in 1973 than in 1965, a year when legal abortion was not an available option" (Sklar and Berkov, 1975: 697).

On the basis of these facts the present-day outlook for traditional marriage and family life is not good. Why is that? The defenders say because the incidence and prevalence of premarital and extramarital sex have increased so dramatically (especially among women) in recent years. To solve their personal worries and troubles and to find some power and satisfaction in a society that deprives them of such pleasures, millions of men and women turn to sex.

Premarital Sex

The so-called sexual revolution is nothing new. Some scholars trace an increase in premarital sex in the United States to World War I. Before that time, only about 7 percent of women engaged in sex before marriage; but Lewis Terman found that 67 percent of males and 49 percent of females had done so during the 1920s. Most had premarital sex relations with people they later married (1938: 134–37). Dr. Alfred Kinsey found that of women born after 1900, nearly 50 percent had engaged in premarital sex (1953: 286–87). For men it varied by education: 98 percent of males with a grade-school education, 85 percent with a high-school education, and 68 percent with some college education had sex before marriage.

But the real changes in premarital sex took place, especially among women, in the 1960s (the decade of the pill). A 10-year follow-up study by Bell and Chaskes at one university discovered that the rates of premarital sex had not only increased, but had nearly doubled for those "going steady" or "dating." In 1958, most believed that a girl had to be engaged before sexual intercourse took place. By 1968, 23 to 28 percent of the college females dating or going steady had engaged in sex, compared with only 10 to 15 percent in 1958 (Scanzoni and Scanzoni, 1976: 63). A similar 10-year follow-up study by Christensen and Gregg showed not only that premarital sex had more than tripled, but also that the age at which it was experienced was decreasing (Ibid., 64).

In 1971 two Johns Hopkins professors, John Kantner and Melvin Zelnik, drew a representative national sample of over 4,000 single young women. By age 19, 46 percent of them were no longer virgins. In contrast, Kinsey's 1953 sample showed that only 20 percent of the women had experienced sex by age 20. The rate had more than doubled in less than 20 years. The proportion of teenagers who have premarital intercourse is even higher, "since about 60 percent of *married* teenagers report having had intercourse prior to marriage" (1973: 21). Ira Reiss, however, believes that most people, based upon his national adult survey and a five-school student sample, feel that affection and love should be linked with sex (1971).

In 1975 new evidence appeared that young women were now engaging in premarital sex to a greater extent than ever before. A national survey of female sexuality, based on responses of 100,000 women, revealed that "nine out of 10 women under the age of 25 have had premarital intercourse, and the average age when it occurred was 17" (Shearer, 1975: 18).

Such changes as these strike at the very foundation of traditional family life and to some unknown degree explain the smaller number of marriages, later marriages, increased illegitimacy, reliance on abortion, and childless marriages. Today sex is often related to "having fun not children." Such a high incidence of premarital sex may lead in some instances to other alternatives to marriage and the family, such as cohabitation. This is generally defined as "having shared a . . . bed with someone of the opposite sex (to whom one was not married) for four or more nights a week for three or more consecutive months" (Macklin, 1974: 55). Cohabitation has become so widespread and so widely accepted on college campuses that dozens of researchers have measured the extent of this new "pseudofamily" form. Research suggests that anywhere from 10 to 33 percent of college students cohabit. A 1972 study at Cornell University reported that 31 percent of the students had at some time cohabited. Cornell, like many schools, gives students the option of living off campus, and allows 24-hour visiting privileges for those living on campus. Coed dorms are the rule in many universities. In 1968 a Barnard College sophomore became a national celebrity when she was disciplined for living off campus with a man. The incident made the front page of the *New York Times* and was a feature story in *Time* magazine. Today it is not news anymore. In 1976 a U.S. Census special survey reported that over one million "unmarrieds" were living with a person of the opposite sex ("Growing at a Slower Pace," May 16, 1977: 65).

Extramarital Affairs

Such rapid changes in sexual mores and behavior have struck at the very stability and strength of the traditional family and may even have encouraged another change in family life—extramarital affairs (adultery). Most studies show that people who engage in extramarital affairs have usually engaged in premarital sex—so as the latter increases, so should the former, though both could increase without one necessarily causing the other. Extramarital affairs, in the past, were usually engaged in by married men with single women or prostitutes and most people disapproved of them as wrong and detrimental to a marriage. But even that has changed today, as well as the incidence and prevalence of infidelity (Hunt, 1969: 457).

In the 1950s, Kinsey reported a cumulative incidence (past and present) of adultery for about half of the married men and a quarter of the married women surveyed. Recent surveys show that women are having more extramarital affairs than ever before. In addition, they are starting earlier, at about age 35, instead of age 40, as Kinsey reported. Although 25 percent of married women in the 1950s were unfaithful, today, according to sociologist Robert Bell, "the number of married women now having affairs may run as high as 40 percent" (Hoover, 1975: 25).

A 1972 Playboy Foundation study revealed that about 24 percent of young wives (under age 24) had had extramarital intercourse. In Kinsey's time in the 1950s, only 8 percent of young wives had done so. In 1974, nearly 50 percent of 2,372 married women surveyed in 28 states "approved of extra-marital affairs" and would "certainly" or "probably" become involved in the future. Robert Bell, who conducted the survey, said the women he interviewed were "well-educated working wives," but that "these liberal attitudes will eventually be adopted by women at all social levels" (Ibid.). If and when they are, the defenders maintain, it will be the death knell for the American family and marriage as we have known them.

Thus, extramarital affairs are becoming institutionalized and rationalized. But what will become of the family? Adultery (institutionalized or not) will shake the foundations of stability for family and children. Yet in our pressure-filled bureaucratic society, people sometimes need assurance that they are alive and vital, so they turn to sex for reassurance.

Working Mothers

One more social indicator that measures what has happened to the American family and traditional sex roles is the "working mother." Until recently, most mothers worked because they had to—the family needed the money, especially if it was poor or broken by divorce, desertion, or death of the husband. Since most people in our society are not wealthy, they had little choice. But a new breed of working mother has emerged, among upper- and middle-class women. They are placing more emphasis

Socialization into the male and female sex roles occurs early, though these roles can be changed (usually with some difficulty) later. Here men are socializing children in a day-care center.

on finding a career, fulfillment, and identity, as well as power and prestige. Personal choice for women is the key, and in the process, alternative forms of child care, such as day-care centers, are set up so that the woman need not worry about her own children while at work.

As of mid-1975, 37 million women worked, representing over 40 percent of all workers. They accounted for over half of all women 18 to 64 years old. The greatest increase has come in the number of working mothers. Women with children under 18 have increased *ninefold* in the work force since 1940 (U.S. Department of Labor, 1975:n.p.). Between 1961 and 1973 the labor-force participation rate of married women increased from 38 to 42 per 100 women in the population. Most of this rise came from a large increase in the percentage of young women with young children. The participation rate of childless young wives rose by 20 percent; that of young mothers with no children under three increased by 35 percent; but there was an 86 percent jump among mothers of prenursery-school children ("Married Women in the Labor Force," 1974: 9). This means that babies, at the most critical time of their human development, are cared for by others because their mothers either must or choose to work.

Some five million working mothers with children under six have over seven million children. Licensed child-care centers have room to care for only slightly over one million of them. What happens to the other six million children while the mother is working is anybody's guess. But the trend of working mothers continues unabated. Well over 14 million mothers with children under 18 now work. This represents an increase of about four-and-a-half million in the 10 years between 1965 and 1975. Thus, over 50 percent of school-age children (over 27 million) have working mothers, two-thirds of whom work full time (Horn, 1975: 34). This is the second generation in which young teenagers have been left alone in the home while mothers work. This ensures greater privacy for premarital sexual encounters and is a factor in the increase in premarital sex and illegitimacy among teenagers, according to a survey of 15- to 19-year-old unmarrieds by Drs. Melvin Zelnik and John F. Kantner (McCormack, 1977: A-12).

Occupational Sex-Typing

Just as institutional racism and discrimination operate to keep blacks in marginal, low-paying, menial jobs, so "sexism" does the same to women. In the past 20 years (1955–75), nearly 17 million women have gone to work for the first time. In spite of this, women are "clustered in the same industries and occupations as women 35 years ago" (Klein, 1975: 13). "Occupational sex-typing" places women in such routine and low-paying jobs. At the turn of the century, more than 70 percent of all employed women (about 18 percent of the work force) were semiskilled "operatives," servants, or farm laborers. By the late 1970s work had changed, but 70 percent of all employed women are still primarily in three low-prestige job categories—clerical, personal services, and "operatives" (Regan and Blaxall, 1976: 105).

The majority of the low-status white-collar jobs are held by women: keypunch and telephone operators, typists, and file clerks. Women are also overly represented on assembly-line jobs. Typists in particular have low status and low pay to match. Members of typing pools are considered interchangeable parts in a paper-flow system. The secretary symbolizes the employment status of females today. Secretaries account for nearly one-third of all female workers. Judy Klemesrud has observed that the secretary is stereotyped as a "gum-chewing sex kitten; husband hunter; mini-skirted ding-a-ling; slow-witted pencil pusher; office go-fer ('go-fer coffee,' etc.); reliable old shoe" (*New York Times*, March 7, 1972: 34).

Changes for Women at Work

On the other hand, the traditional placement of women in industry has slowly begun to change. For example, women since 1900 have about doubled their percentages among professional and technical workers (nurses and teachers account for two-thirds of these). Women have in-

table 4-2 WOMEN'S CHANGING JOB DISTRIBUTION 1900, 1930, 1976 (in thousands)

OCCUPATION	1976 NUMBER	1976 PERCENTAGE	1930 NUMBER	1930 PERCENTAGE	1900 NUMBER	1900 PERCENTAGE
TOTAL	34,606	100.0%	10,752	100.0%	5,319	100.0%
CLERICAL:	12,243	35.4	2,246	20.9	212	4.0
SECY., STENO, TYPISTS	4,395	12.7	1,031	9.6	96	1.8
SERVICE:	6,201	21.1	2,964	2u.5	1,886	35.4
PRIVATE HOUSEHOLD	1,095	3.2	1,910	17.6	1,526	28.7
PROFESSIONAL AND TECHNICAL:	5,551	16.0	1,482	13.8	434	8.2
BELOW COLLEGE TEACHERS	2,281	6.6	854	7.9	325	6.1
NURSES AND HEALTH WORKERS	1,511	4.3	289	2.7	11	0.2
OPERATIVES	4,179	12.0	1,870	17.4	1,264	23.7
SALES	2,224	6.4	736	6.8	228	4.3
MANAGERS AND ADMIN.	1,953	5.6	292	2.7	74	1.4
CRAFTSMEN	471	1.4	106	1.0	76	1.4
LABORERS	383	1.1	158	1.5	138	2.6
FARM WORKERS	307	0.9	907	8.4	1,008	18.9

Source: Figures for 1930 and 1900 are adapted and derived from Sar Levitan and William Johnston, **Work Is Here to Stay, Alas,** (Salt Lake City: Olympus, 1973): 52, and are based on Census data. Figures for 1976 are from **Employment and Earnings,** (March 1976): 32, 33, 58. The latter figures are based upon monthly surveys of 47,000 households and may not be exactly comparable with the Census data.

More and more women today are working in jobs that were traditionally male.

creased their percentage of managers and administrators fourfold between 1900 and 1976 (although they still represent only 5.6 percent of all women employed). Table 4-2 shows this long-term increased incidence of women holding certain jobs.

In more recent years, women's gains in the professions have been notable. In law and medical schools, women made up only about 5 percent of enrollment in 1960. But by 1974, they made up about 20 percent, and in 1976, about 25 percent. Today the percentage is even higher. As the prevalence of women working as professionals and being admitted to professional schools increases, institutional sexism and discrimination should decrease in the work place. The same should be true for black women. The Department of Labor reported that in 1974, compared with the situation since 1962, black women (and men) had shown "slight, but steady progress" in filling the more desirable, highly paid jobs (Garfinkle, 1975: 29). In professional jobs, black women did better than black men, raising their percentage of all women in professions from 7 percent in 1962 to 10 percent in 1974.

Women have not only been denied equal job and educational opportunities, but also usually make less money than men for the jobs they hold.

table 4-3 COMPARISON OF MEDIAN EARNINGS OF MEN AND WOMEN

	MEN'S EARNINGS	WOMEN'S EARNINGS	WOMEN'S EARNINGS AS PERCENTAGE OF MEN'S
1956	$ 4,462	$2,828	63%
1964	6,283	3,710	59
1975	13,144	7,719	59

Source: "Consumer Income." Current Population Reports. Series P.60, no. 105 (June 1977): 167–68.

Table 4-3, based on the median earnings of full-time year-round workers, illustrates this trend. Today women holding full-time jobs earn 41 percent less than men, compared with 37 percent less 20 years ago. Thus, the situation seems to be getting worse. "Equal pay for equal work" remains only a slogan for many women. Even today, female high-school graduates (with no college) who work full time average less income than full-time men who have not completed elementary school.

Despite their increased numbers in colleges and graduate schools, women often receive less money than men because of pervasive discrimination in the academic world (although government-ordered affirmative action programs are changing some of this). Two economists at the University of Wisconsin estimate that a college degree is worth $118,000 in additional lifetime income to a man, but only $65,000 to a woman. A Carnegie Commission report notes that female college professors receive nearly $200 million a year less than men because of discriminatory salaries (Doyle, June 1974: 10).

When one begins to put all the social indicators together, a composite picture of today's family life and changing sex roles emerges. For the defenders, these indicators spell disaster and disintegration. For the challengers, they spell change and adaptation. For the objective sociologist they show us something of both.

CAUSES OF THE CHANGES IN THE FAMILY AND SEX ROLES

Three major social causes stand out most clearly as causes of these problems of the family and changing sex roles:

1. industrialization and urbanization
2. conflict in values and norms (derived in some cases from the first cause); immediate causes are the women's liberation movement and separation of sex from reproduction.
3. a social structure and system designed to exploit and keep women (as well as men) subordinate and powerless in relation to the power elite.

The Move from Farm to City

Although some social historians, as well as such sociologists as Furstenberg (1966) and Goode (1963), argue that the American family experienced social problems before the Industrial Revolution, most nineteenth-century families were large, kin-oriented, and lived in rural areas. And although there were some stresses and strains, these were of a different kind and degree from those of an urban, industrialized society. It was not until 1920 that we had more people living in *urban* areas (over 2,500 population) than in *rural* areas. On many farms the extended family was the prime basis for social organization. In comparison with many families today, it was a relatively solid, stable unit of economic production, vocational training, education, religious socialization, and recreation. The community reinforced family ties; marriage was for life (a shorter one); divorce was virtually unthinkable; and roles of women and men were relatively fixed, certain, and accepted (by most people). Children were economic assets, and many were had. Social solidarity and family needs triumphed over individual desires and aims.

"The Waltons," then, were typical of American families before industrialization and urbanization made their inroads. Gradually these two social developments eroded the foundation of the extended family and produced a more mobile, independent nuclear family.

Traditionally, families were large and worked together as a unified social group, usually on a farm or in a factory.

In cities, families crowded into smaller quarters. Adults and children spent less time at home. Children became an economic drain on the pocketbook and either worked or looked to other institutions for education, income, direction, and recreation. The family in an industrial, urban society ("Gesellschaft") was no longer the center of one's life that it was in a rural society ("Gemeinschaft"). In a mobile society, family members, after a certain stage in the life cycle, became *separated, segmented,* and *segregated* from one another.

Conflict in Values and Norms

The most basic conflict in values and norms is not just over the modern role of women (although this causes plenty of anomie and confusion). The conflict concerns two central values in our society—those favoring the individual and those favoring the family. The basic unresolved issue is *whose* needs, desires, and wishes are to take precedence—the group's or the individual's? The winds of change now shaking the foundation of the family come from a relatively new emphasis and stress on the rights, needs, and desires of the individual. In such a situation some family members get isolated and hurt in the process, as the boxed item on the facing page suggests.

Far less is stressed about the responsibilities, promises, or the burdens to be borne as a family member. Instead, some Americans urge us to view the individual as supreme. His or her concept of happiness or fulfillment is to take precedence over family roles. Patrice Horn summarizes Urie Bronfenbrenner's ideas. She observes that "the crisis evolves from a crazy overemphasis on individualism so embedded in society that commitment and community have become suspect" (Horn, 1975: 34).

Bronfenbrenner states:

> A person cannot be committed to a child unless other people are committed to that person's commitment to children. In other words, you have to have family-support systems. . . . It is, I think, significant that this kind of crisis is coming at our second 100 years.
>
> The Constitution . . . says you can keep your individual identity and your community commitment and you don't have to sacrifice the one for the other. Well we've taken the first part of that, and really written it up as "Do your own thing," don't commit me to anything, not even a child (Ibid.).

So the conflict in norms and values comes down to commitment: how much? by whom? to what? Commitment to a permanent family as a social unit seems to be waning.

Women's Liberation. The structural cause behind changes in sex roles and the family stems from the oppressive inequality and injustice

> ## PUTTING TOGETHER A FRACTURED FAMILY
> ### Leontine Young
>
> Young people spoke with deep feeling of the need of old people for their children. One girl not yet twenty talked indignantly of an old man taken ill in a summer hotel where she was working. His only child lived two thousand miles away. She called the son and told him about his father. After questioning her about the details, the son suggested, "Call me tomorrow and let me know how he is."
>
> "What do you want me to do? Call and tell you he's dead?"
>
> There was a startled silence. Then the son said, "You mean you think I should come now?"
>
> "I certainly do," the girl answered.
>
> The son was talking about his father's medical condition. The young woman was talking about his human need. As she explained indignantly, "What was wrong with that old man was loneliness. He could have died of it. When his son came he got better. I told him he should take his father home to live with him. And he did."
>
> Source: Leontine Young, *The Fractured Family* (New York: McGraw-Hill, 1973): 35.

that a male-dominated power structure created and has controlled for centuries. Women are now beginning to respond to their powerlessness by organizing in an attempt to equalize power. This effort has produced two of the most important *immediate* causes contributing to our changing family and sex roles: the women's liberation movement and the separation of sex from reproduction—a move from propagation to pleasure as the primary motive for sex.

The tremendous concern about contemporary sex roles is largely a result of the women's liberation movement. Although not new historically, the movement got a fresh start in the 1960s with the writings of Betty Friedan and especially with the formation of the National Organization of Women (NOW) in 1966. This movement succeeded in launching a drive for social change that has altered, and will continue to alter, some of the basic norms, values, and beliefs by which we live. As William Chafe points out:

> Although feminism is not new in America, the present movement is distinctive in at least three ways: it is grounded in and moving in the same direction as [the] underlying social trends; it has an organizational base that is diverse and decentralized; it seeks objectives that strike at some of the root causes of sex inequality (1976: 137).

The collective behavior and ideology of the women's movement converged quite well with budding social changes, which reinforced the aims of the movement. For example, over the past three decades women have entered the work force in greater numbers; the size of the average family has been cut in half since the 1950s; and cultural values about reproduction and sex have never been the same since "the Pill" was first marketed in 1960. Although none of these social changes produced equality of the sexes, they helped to lay the social foundation for building a strong women's movement for equal rights. Women's lib, because of these and other cultural and social changes that had taken place by the mid-1960s, had a large audience who, though not active members of the social movement, were partisans who identified with its aims (Gusfield, 1968: 445).

A panel of women's-club leaders came to the conclusion that after a decade or so of feminist activity, the American woman will have experienced permanent changes. The women, from 30 groups joined under the banner of the Associated Women for a Better Community, noted that the opening up of job opportunities for women has brought about "fundamental changes in both lifestyle and thought processes, especially in young women." The panel felt there had been a decisive, beneficial break with the homemaker tradition for a whole generation of women (Kupferberg, January 11, 1976: 20).

Changing Attitudes toward Sex. The second immediate cause of problems behind changing sex roles and family life is the change in attitudes toward sex and reproduction. With the increasing social acceptance of contraceptives, especially the Pill, it became possible to separate sexual intercourse—inside or outside of marriage—from the fear of pregnancy. Once this occurred, the primary reason for sex could become pleasure rather than propagation. This opened up new alternatives and options for men and women, who could with impunity find pleasure in heterosexual, bisexual, homosexual, or transsexual encounters.

Along with this separation of sex from reproduction, a strong theme of women's liberation centered around the "importance of women knowing their own bodies and having the freedom to use them as they see fit" (Chafe, 1976: 128). This led to new norms encouraging (or at least not discouraging) a greater tolerance toward a diversity of sexual experiences and a lessening of guilt over such behavior. Although such newly found sexual freedom can victimize women, the women's liberation movement's support for abortion, lesbian and homosexual rights, and free bodily expression did much to create new attitudes and values toward homosexual patterns of behavior.

Social Structure

The third underlying cause of these changes in sex roles and family behavior is our social structure, whose maldistribution of wealth and power has forced millions of housewives out of the home and into the factory or office. The majority of American families depend on the earnings from at least two jobs in order to maintain a modest standard of living. Thus, most women work because they have to work. Louise Kapp Howe writes: "Of the 33 million women now in the labor force, more than 20 percent are single; another 20 percent are widowed, divorced, or separated; and about 15 percent more have husbands who are earning less than $5,000 a year" (1976: 133). In other words, 55 percent of the women who work must do so to survive economically. Some 13 million American women maintain their own households and are responsible for the welfare of about 10 million children (Ibid.).

Consequently, when one seeks to explain the changing roles of women (especially outside the home), we must look not only in "women's liberation," but also in economic and social necessity (i.e., the husband has died or deserted, or the two have been divorced). Added to the millions of women who have always worked out of necessity are a growing number of married middle-class women who have been forced by inflation in the last 10 years or so to seek paid employment. As Louise Howe noted: "The rapid surge in the number of working mothers had *not* been primarily due to the Women's Movement. Inflation, taxes, and the rising cost of living have been far greater factors" (1976: 134).

PROPOSED SOLUTIONS TO THE CHANGES IN THE FAMILY AND SEX ROLES

At the root of any solution to the present problems are various definitions of the situation.* A basic ambiguity exists over exactly what the

---

*Much of the research and drafting of the "solution" and "future" sections of this problem were done by Robert Goodman, a youth social worker for the Youth Development Association, East Northport, N.Y. He was formerly an advanced sociology student at Muhlenberg College.

Although there is still some opposition, men are more readily accepting women at work on an equal basis.

Credit: Christian Simonpietri/Sygma.

problem is and how to deal with it. Does one see the problem as an erosion of the traditional family and male supremacy and as society's acceptance of new forms, norms, and values about the family and sexual equality? On the other hand, if one favors those new forms, norms, and values of the family and of sexual equality, the problems are the vestiges of the traditional family, male supremacy, and sexual inequality. Faced with these conflicting and confusing alternatives, which direction does society choose? Conservatives, liberals, radicals, and other groups in society see the question from a different angle; hence any one solution will fail to satisfy all.

Three possible directions seem feasible. The first is to retain and reinforce the traditional nuclear family and sex-role norms and values. The second is to move toward alternative family forms and sex roles. The third direction is to encourage, as a matter of national policy, sexual equality and justice for women.

Retain Traditional Norms and Values

On the surface, the idea of retaining and reinforcing the traditional norms and values may seem a bit ridiculous and old-fashioned—if not totally impossible. Yet evidence from Gallup polls and other scientific surveys indicates that there is strong support for many traditional values, such as marriage, having children, and the woman's rearing them at home. George Gilder, in *Sexual Suicide*, asserts that while such an idea may seem ridiculous in view of the *seemingly* legitimate rights of women, it is in fact imperative that we retain the sex roles and stereotypes that up to now have operated quite well. Gilder maintains that sexual differences are "perhaps the most important condition of our lives" (July 1973: 42). "The man must be made equal to the culture; he must be given a way to make himself equal," according to Gilder, in order to solve his problems. Man is only what he makes of himself within the social parameters allowed him. With little to fall back on in the realm of sexuality, man's social identity is of maximum importance. Strip him of this—as equality and women's liberation would do—and man would be left with virtually no superiority. Furthermore, if we tamper with the structure of the family and marriage, we risk losing the bonds that presently tie men down.

Manhood, according to Gilder, can be validated and expressed only in action. Man is full of undefined energies, which need the guidelines of culture. Society must be the architect of man, for he is entirely dependent on it for the definition of his social role and position. Hence men need the extra support and special treatment that they receive from society.

Following this theory, men have the right to better jobs and more pay than women—for these are the affirmation of a man's masculinity and his importance as a provider. Money and position will greatly determine whether a man will be able to court a woman and enter into marriage and thereby become integrated into the community. If this does not happen, men will seek recognition and meet their biological needs through antisocial methods—thereby harming society and women.

Often viewed as a solution to the problem of traditional sex roles in the home, the increasingly popular use of day care for children is really another danger to the social order, according to the defenders. If women use day care to enable them to work, they will increasingly occupy the role of provider, transforming ours into a matriarchal society. This danger becomes more real when one considers that social pressure on young, well-educated women is more toward career advancement than toward the traditional marriage and family. Women with the best brains and genetic backgrounds will opt not to reproduce, while those with less education and fewer genetic strengths will reproduce. Eugenically, it may be argued, this will be dysfunctional for, and detrimental to, society. Thus, the availability of child care and the pressures on women are conducive to their entering and succeeding in "male territory." If this happens, men would lose their functional place in society and also their chief socializing agent (Gilder, 1973). The cost would also be high for women, who are already suffering under the physical, psychological, and social stresses from the competitive work world and from trying to be like men. Over the past 30 years the male-female ratio of ulcers has dropped from 20 to 1 to 2 to 1. Some five million women now have ulcers. Such ailments are due to stress and tension, as well as smoking and drinking. If women are to compete with men, they must run the same risks.

The ideal of the successful career woman that the feminists are striving to establish would be unobtainable for some women. These women would then face the disenchanting news that they are inferior to the men to whom they were supposedly superior. Furthermore, many women are content within their roles as housewives and mothers, as evidenced by the number of women's groups formed in defense of the status quo. Midge Decter, in *The New Chastity and Other Arguments against Women's Liberation*, takes exception to Betty Friedan's *The Feminine Mystique* by asserting that women have a great deal of value in their present social positions and good reason to be proud of their efforts as housewives, mothers, sex partners, and wives (1972). Decter also feels that the modern American woman has a great deal of freedom and choice within the role society has assigned her. What is often overlooked are the many traditional marriages that produced very happy, well-adjusted people who found fulfillment and happiness in a marriage based on a lasting love. The boxed item on page 162 describes such a traditional marriage.

One proposed solution for reinforcing and retaining the traditional roles of women in the home is for society and the government to give women more social and economic recognition and prestige for rearing children and for making a "house" a "home." Recently formed, the Martha Movement hopes to "improve society's concept of the homemaker." The group's founder, Jinx Melia, states: "We believe homemakers are essential to solving such social problems as the increase in divorce, child abuse, racism, juvenile delinquency, inflation, drug abuse and alcoholism" (Rosenfeld, July 11, 1976: E-3). Although she may be exaggerating the impact mothers as homemakers may have on social problems, her point is that society has overlooked and often demeaned a helpful ally in coping with its ills. Even the more prestigious National Wo-

---

THE LAST OF A VANISHING SPECIES (A LOVE STORY)
Anonymous

In a time when divorce has become nearly as frequent as marriage, and "alternative marriage styles" are offered as the solution, it is appropriate to preserve a record of a real-life couple's "Great Love" marriage. I fear they are a vanishing species.

Henry and Chris were just real, down-to-earth people. But they experienced a relationship so precious and beautiful that everyone who knew them was touched by the quality of their love.

Henry's greatest joy lay in Chris' happiness, and he idolized her. He delighted in her wearing lovely things (she still cherishes her "see-through" nightie that went on all their travels). When they grew older, his gallantry and devotion still grew, and romance never wavered. When Chris was disabled by a stroke, he tenderly dressed her every day for the rest of his life. When she limped to the altar on his arm for communion, others in the church felt God's presence in them.

Chris, of course, responded with total adoration, putting Henry's needs and happiness above all else in her world. When he was on a restricted diet, she readily accepted the same limitations, and was content.

They entertained graciously; and when they danced, Chris was the envy of every woman on the floor. They shared a life that today's individualistic young "marrieds" could not comprehend or even imagine.

This giving and pleasing each other never left either feeling martyred or "put down." They rose to the heights by giving, freely and lovingly; and that kind of giving can never be a sacrifice; the rewards are too great.

When Henry died, truly a part of Chris was torn away, and her greatest hope is to resume their union as soon as she can be released from this world. She feels that this "marriage made in Heaven" surely must continue there, and still feels Henry's nearness.

Such "Great Love" marriages do exist today; but, sadly, many more live only in fond memory. Based not on a battle for individuality, but on a joy in being one, they prove the biblical quotation, "... the two shall become one." Marriage can be a truly great life experience of faith and trust, in which each partner's greatest joy lies in that of the other. Each is entitled to all rights as a person, but like the "right-of-way" on the road, these rights are to be freely given—not demanded—if a head-on collision is to be avoided. Couples who have shared a "Great Love" have been so busy pleasing each other that the thought of demanding anything would appall them! It's not necessary.

We go to great lengths to preserve beautiful artifacts and vanishing species of animals. Should we not give as great a value to the memory of human relationships as they were before modern individualism destroyed them?

men's Agenda includes an item that "economic and legal recognition" be given to "homemakers' work." Along the same line, Margaret Mead proposed in 1976 that work women do in the home should be covered under the Social Security system. Even liberated feminists point to the social and economic contribution wives have made to the success of their husbands. So the proposed solution for preserving traditional sex roles is that our culture and society give more prestige, status, and recognition to women who socialize future generations in the home.

Alternative Forms of the Family and Sex Roles

A second solution to problems of the changing family and sex roles is to move toward new alternative family forms and sex-roles. A great deal of media attention has recently been devoted to the various "new" forms of marriage and the family. Many of these forms have discarded even the appearance of the old in favor of something that is more adapted to individual needs.

The fact that these new forms are receiving a great deal of attention does not mean that they are totally a recent development. Lucile Duberman, in *Marriage and Other Alternatives*, discusses the many and varied forms of marriage and family. When she comes to the so-called new forms of the family, Duberman notes:

> There are and always have been many forms of the family other than the traditional nuclear family. What is new is that their existence is being discussed more often by social scientists today and is now being recognized, albeit not necessarily approved, by more members of our society (1977: 12).

These changes in the form of the family are seen by many as attempts to bring the old notion more into line with one's own goals and needs. Consequently, while the goal remains self-fulfillment, the means to that end has been changed. The challengers maintain that as society and individuals change, the family—which acts as an intermediary between the two—must also change. The many different forms that the family now takes are nothing more than attempts by individuals to cope with the stresses and strains of our social structure. As a result, some see the nuclear family as giving way to more innovative and fulfilling approaches for individuals (Ibid., Chap. 1).

Group Marriage. Among the many "new" approaches is group marriage. In this approach several men and women are married to one another and are involved in many group relationships. Distinctions between personal husbands and wives are reduced, as are the distinctions between mothers and fathers for children. There is a sharing of all—from income and tasks to sexual relationships—on a basis of reciprocal exchange and the interests of the group (Ibid.). Although group marriage may appeal to a small segment of society, it does have its shortcomings. It is difficult to find a group of adults who can live in harmony with each other. Even normally well-adjusted adults usually find it difficult living together with a number of other persons in the same social setting. Personal problems of sex and love are often a source of friction between the individuals. Often, too, fewer females than males are interested in group marriage. Consequently, it presently has a very limited appeal (Otto, 1970: Chap. 8).

Communal Families. Communal families became popular in the 1960s and early 1970s, at least in the eyes of the media. In fact, such families have existed extensively throughout history. A grouping of several monogamous couples and their children—who share everything except sexual relationships—performs in much the same way as an extended family. A big problem for this type of familial relationship is developing enough trust in the other couples to surrender one's possessions and income. Its greatest appeal is to those who feel a need to share and who desire a sense of belonging to a community.

Polygamous Marriages. Others advocate polygamous marriages for certain segments of the population. In a segment of the population where women outnumber the men (as with the aged) a relationship between two or more women and one man is a realistic alternative to the loneliness due to the unavailability of mates. Relationships of this sort would fill the void that is left when the elderly are excluded from the nuclear family. This type of relationship does not fit the pattern of moral norms or values presently accepted by our society at large, let alone by the typically more conservative elderly. In addition to that obstacle, the legal complications are often a problem.

Single-Parent Families. Another recently popular form of family organization is the single-parent family. Although such families are sometimes created by accident (through divorce, death of a spouse, illegitimacy, or desertion), they are increasingly being created intentionally. Some persons are not suited for marriage, and yet feel very comfortable in the role of parent. Increasingly, single parenthood has become a state of permanence rather than simply a transitory state between marriages. In recent years, there has been an increase in the number of single people choosing to adopt children (Scarpitti, 1977: 145). Despite the current popularity and increasing prevalence of single-parent adoption, there are several obstacles. The first is the prevailing notion that a child needs two parents for a healthy development. Another is the high financial and emotional cost to the single parent.

Cohabitation. An alternative to marriage popular among the upper middle class and intellectuals, especially during the college and postcollege years, is cohabitation, mentioned earlier. In this arrangement, two persons of the opposite sex live together conjugally while remaining legally single. Often, financial arrangements are shared. Most couples who assume this type of relationship are committed to each other, and many legally marry when they decide that they are ready. If this type of relationship occurs when the individuals are past the childbearing years, legal marriage usually does not follow (Duberman 1977: Chap. 1).

Alternative Marriage Forms. Marriage should be changed, and better alternatives added. If they would review 14 such alternatives to marriage by Herbert Otto, the challengers might suggest the following:

"pairings" at any time at the mutual consent of the partners

"polygamy, polyandry, homosexual marriages, and permanent and temporary associations"

"marriage as a nonlegal voluntary association" with "state registration" eliminated

"a periodically renewable legal bond"

"progressive monogamy" (the practice of taking several partners, one at a time)

"group marriage" and "polygamy"

"intimate networks of families" . . . with "a trained, professional third parent" (1970: 6–7).

Margaret Mead had proposed marriage in two steps: "individual" and "parental." The individual marriage license would unite two individuals who would be committed to each other as long as they wished to remain together. The parental license would be issued to those specifically interested in forming a family.

There are, of course, many other forms of marriage and family that are unique in form and functions, such as the Israeli kibbutz. The number could be infinite. One thing they all have in common is their abandonment of the "norm" of the nuclear family in favor of a form that is more compatible with the individual's perceived needs and goals as well as sexual equality. In Duberman's review of the literature, she found that a majority considered it irrational to expect that one form of marriage will be right for everyone. In the vastness of the United States there are many different, coexisting value systems, attitudes, and behavior patterns. Duberman further suggests that it is time to accept the different alternatives to marriage and family that exist within our society. Regardless of this infinite variety, however, a majority of Americans still opt for the more conventional form of marriage.

Sexual Equality and Justice for Women

The social and economic recognition of the goal of equality for women and of new egalitarian norms and values for society has been taking place for quite some time. Equal rights and justice should now be accorded all women, as a matter of national policy. The proposed final

Massive demonstrations for the Equal Rights Amendment (ERA) for women have not yet convinced enough states to vote for it. If 38 states do not ratify the ERA by March 1979, it will fail to become part of the Constitution.

legal step would be the ratification of the Equal Rights Amendment (ERA). Thirty-eight states must ratify the amendment for it to become a part of the Constitution. By early 1977, approval by only four more state legislatures was needed to pass it; ratification must occur by March 1979. The ERA Amendment provides, in Section One, that "Equality of rights under the law shall not be denied or abridged by the United States or by any State on account of sex." The amendment will have far-reaching effects on the everyday lives of all Americans. It will mean, essentially, that federal, state, and local governments must treat each person, regardless of sex, as an individual, not as a man or woman. The significant phrase "under the law" signals that the amendment will affect many laws, but will not interfere in personal relationships or private activities ("Equal Rights Amendment," n.d.: 2).

The enforcement of affirmative-action programs (which govern the hiring and promotion practices of most firms), along with executive orders and the Civil Rights Act of 1964, is the means by which the government attempts to contest sex discrimination against women. By committing itself to supporting equality between the sexes, government can remove vestiges of prejudice and inequality that linger within the economic and legal sectors of society. Proposals have been made to strengthen the enforcement and legal power of the Equal Employment Opportunities Commission (EEOC), to ensure quick compliance with the law.

The National Women's Agenda, which is supported by over 90 nationally based women's organizations, has outlined 75 demands for the government and society to adopt. The agenda aims to eliminate all barriers to women's full participation in our society. The areas covered range from political representation to economic equality and justice, and from adequate housing to respect for the individual woman ("National Women's Agenda," June 1975).

The courts also have played a vital part in striking down unfair laws and practices with regard to sex. They are an essential part in the move to assure women and men equal status and justice under the law, although in criminal law many problems still remain (as discussed in Chapter 2).

As we mentioned while defining this social problem, education perpetuates traditional and unfair sex-role stereotypes. A concerted effort to reduce such discriminatory stereotypes requires the revision of educational textbooks, policies, and practices. Most women's groups are committed to such action and change.

Similarly, mass media can and should do much more to elevate the status of women and promote equality of the sexes—just as it has until recently perpetuated the inequality. Television commercials still depict women as "decorative sex objects," as well as "hare-brained, dumb, detergent- or diaper-crazy housefraus," who, like Edith Bunker, are considered stupid "ding-bats" or "ding-a-lings." To overcome these demeaning images of women, the Image Committee of the National Organization of Women (NOW) monitors television and radio ads and protests such sexist stereotyping to both broadcasters and advertisers. The committee also compiles lists of the 40 worst television ads for distorting the image of women and presents annual booby prizes to the advertisers (Doyle, 1974: 21). Other actions are taken against billboard and magazine ads which exploit women and their sexual image for commercial purposes.

must have before June 30, 1982.

Consciousness Raising among Women

Any new legislation or mass-media attitudes affecting sexual equality must filter down to the interpersonal level to really effect change. Attempts toward sexual equity and equality have made some inroads on the interpersonal level, and this has helped to raise the consciousness of many women and men concerning how they speak about and treat women.

Consciousness raising among women is considered another solution to the social problem of our changing sex roles. Local chapters of the National Organization for Women (NOW) have contributed to the formation of consciousness-raising groups all over America, and have educated a small number of women to assume leadership roles in their communities. Although a majority of women have not joined such groups, the activities of the women's liberation movement have helped to unite many women in an effort to achieve a common goal.

Once equality between the sexes is obtained as matter of national policy, a social environment will exist in which women will have greater freedom to choose sexual lifestyles according to their personal preferences. Although such freedom of choices will not be a panacea for the social problems discussed, it will produce a social climate conducive to

MICK JAGGER IS LOOKING BLACK AND BLUE

The Rolling Stones must be feeling a little black and blue themselves from the reception to their latest album, Black and Blue. The Stones' distributors came up with an ad campaign that featured a scantily clad woman, bound and bruised, straddling the album cover, with the caption: "I'm 'Black and Blue' from the Rolling Stones—and I love it." When the first billboard went up on Los Angeles' Sunset Strip, it was defaced in a matter of days by an outraged women's group, Women Against Violence Against Women.

Late one night, armed with buckets of fire-engine-red paint, five women scaled the "Black and Blue" billboard, painted over Jagger's face and scrawled "This is a crime against women." The team finished their protest by plastering the women's movement symbol next to the infamous Stones' logo . . .

Mother Jones (Sept./Oct. 1976): 8. By permission.

more thoughtful consideration of how best to solve the problems that arise. By retaining *the best* of our family and sex roles and traditions, while experimenting with new family and marriage forms and ensuring sexual equality and justice, more positive solutions to our family and sex role problems will be worked out.

THE FUTURE OF THE CHANGING FAMILY AND SEX ROLES

Since no one has come up with an alternative to the family that is both effective and efficient in transmitting culture, raising children, and providing an emotional center for our lives, it would appear that the family, in some form, will be with us for some time to come. As we mentioned earlier, there are many ongoing attempts to revitalize the family. Duberman found that many professionals see the institution as becoming more flexible and permissive (Duberman, 1977: Chap. 5). Consequently, we may see a greater variety of marriage and family options, and persons may feel freer to explore and choose the one most suited to their personal needs.

But what of recent trends that have alarmed us? Sociologists believe that the trend toward later marriages and later childbearing will continue. They also foresee a further decrease in the number of families with four or more children. The number of divorces will continue to increase (and approach two million by the year 2000), while the number of marriages will increase for a while and then decrease as the post-World War II baby boom works its way through the marriage years ("Family Trends...," October 27, 1975: 32).

Divorce laws will undoubtedly continue to be revised to make divorce easier and less painful to the persons involved. "No-fault" divorce laws will likely gain acceptance in an increasing number of states. Futurist Alvin Toffler believes that serial marriage, a string of successive, temporary unions, will become more the norm, with divorce rates remaining high. Because of the high number of divorcees who remarry, this is much the case already (Ibid., 76).

Parallel Changes

Future changes in marriage and family will largely parallel changes in society. As women achieve their goal of equality, family roles will become more democratic and sex roles will become more individualistic and flexible. As day-care centers gain wider acceptance, society will participate more directly in the socialization process from an earlier age. Occupational roles will become less rigid, and people will be able to pursue more than one career in a lifetime. If women continue to supplement the family income, men will feel less pressure to confine themselves to a job they do not like. This would provide greater fulfillment for working couples and families. Parents will be able to spend more nonworking hours with their children, instead of simply maintaining them.

Marriage will no longer be a secure refuge for men and women. Instead of marrying for security, escape, domestic comfort, and sex, individuals will marry for emotional satisfaction and base their interaction on mutually satisfying emotional rewards. Marital relations will become more expressive than instrumental; some persons will move from relationship to relationship, while others will find permanence. Marriage will become more a private than a public matter, and will rely more on ethics than legality (McCary, 1975: 380–81).

Discussing the family's future, Herbert Otto describes what he calls the "new marriage." Its distinguishing characteristics include these:

1. We realize that both partners are functioning at a fraction of their potential.
2. Love and understanding are a means of actualizing those potentials.
3. Both partners desire to participate in groups that will help self-actualization.
4. Both partners realize that personality and potential are affected by social institutions, and sometimes these institutions must be changed.
5. It is clear that a couple's interpersonal relationships, along with their physical environment, affect the actualization of potential.
6. The new marriage is involved in the here and now and not bound by the past.
7. Partners think of their marriage as an evolving, developing, and flexible union.
8. The partners have an interest in exploring the spiritual dimensions—values and beliefs—of their marriage.
9. The new marriage provides a commitment to and planned action for the realization of marriage potential (Otto, 1970: 113–17).

Implicit within these characteristics is respect and love for one's spouse. The new marriage also incorporates consideration for the individual's goals and needs, with support and assistance from other family members when necessary. It places more emphasis on the parents' goals and needs within the family setting than the present child-centered environment.

Dr. Thomas McGinnis, a psychotherapist and marriage counselor, suggests an open-family approach. He maintains that many families today are locked together in a kind of imprisonment: "Nobody is quite free to have his own friends and interests. In the open style, people keep in touch but do not intrude." A "closed family" demands obedience, courtesy, and neatness of the child, whereas an open-style parent encourages candor, questions, and open expressions of feeling. "Even the smallest child is regarded as a person." His hope and expectation is that the open family will dominate our future (Moorehouse, July 27, 1976: 16).

Future Changes in Sex Roles and Choices

Sociologist Joan Huber is also optimistic about the future of changing sex roles. She feels that past norms, values, and attitudes regarding working married women with children have changed. With more women forced to make their own living today because of our economic system, social changes will inevitably follow—much as they already have in recent decades. She predicts that the number of childless marriages will increase so that the government will need to step in to make having children more desirable—perhaps through increased tax benefits and more day-care centers to lessen the burden. She further envisions no role reversal, but rather sees men and women sharing more responsibility within the home, much as they are now beginning to share it outside the home. Lastly, she believes that institutional changes will keep pace with individual changes, and thereby make the burden less for those who wish to change their sex roles ("Liberated Woman," 1976: 46–48).

Clare Booth Luce, playwright, congresswoman, and ambassador, envisions only limited change in the power and position of women. After reviewing what she considers very little progress for women in filling top-power posts in society, she looks ahead about 50 years:

> I now reach, somewhat reluctantly, for my crystal ball.
>
> I am sorry to say that the picture I see there is **not** one of Woman sitting in the Oval Room of the White House in 2024. I see her playing many more roles that were once considered masculine. I see her making a little more money than she is making now. But I see her still trying to make her way up—in a man's world—and not having very much more success than she is having now. There may be, and probably will be, great political and technological changes in the world in the next half century. But I venture to suggest that none of them will greatly affect the relative inferior status of the American woman (1975: 159).

She makes three points to reinforce her prediction about the future:

1. Feminists are trying to overturn a worldwide culture system—a pretty large task for any group.
2. The durability and persistence of the "superior male-inferior female" relationship is strong evidence that it has *so far* served the best interests of society.
3. The endurance of male superiority is not in itself proof that it will survive another century—although the odds are it will.

John Gagnon and Bruce Henderson envision liberation in sex-role choices and sexuality. They foresee an increase in the erotic level of the environment, less censorship, more sexually interested and experienced women (along with men), celibacy as a viable option for individuals, enhanced sex in marriage, more sexual activity among the young, a greater demand for sex therapy, more sex research, gradual legal reform of existing prohibitions against various forms of sexual encounter, a continuing

Changes in norms and values about sex and marriage have led to homosexual marriages. What does this mean for the future of marriage and the family?

erosion of gender differences, and finally, a view of sexuality from the individualistic perspective (1975: 60–62).

The idea that the future will be a mere extension and exaggeration of some present tendencies is perhaps erroneous. Although experts forecast seemingly extreme predictions, we should seriously consider the possibility of "sexual marginality" as the wave of the future. This concept asserts that although there are distinct and separate major camps with respect to sexual ideology, identity, and ways of life, many people in the future may not neatly fall within the confines of such camps, but instead fit better into the margins between them. This change will occur at different stages of the life cycle.

For example, young persons may have homosexual experiences, later to be changed to heterosexual ones (inside or outside of marriage). As middle age approaches, an episodic drift back to homosexuality may occur, perhaps between marriages. As persons begin to experience the elderly stage of life, celibacy, voluntary or involuntary, may best describe their sexual lives. In this sense, "sexual marginality" may be the situation millions will experience in the future. As a result, although we may fear the extremes that the "defenders" and the "challengers" forecast, we must recall that many people will continue to fall somewhere in between those margins.

Whether we have disintegrating or more stable family life and marriage in the future depends upon the decisions of millions of couples. The options and alternatives are many, ranging from the traditional stable, permanent family to a loosely fragmented, impermanent arrangement. As Richard Farson observed several years ago:

> Given the total family unit, there is now social technology available to help each family invent its own future — gaming techniques, simulation techniques, group process techniques, and so on. The family can become a learning unit that can plan, discuss, debate, and revise its own small society in ways never before possible (Farson et al., 1969: 112).

SUMMARY

In defining the family as a social problem the interpretation one gives to the effects of social change is crucial. Some interpreters, the "challengers," are optimistic. They see the family as merely "adapting" and "adjusting" to the demands of modern society, especially for mobility and individualism. Others are pessimistic "defenders" of the family, who see the family as disorganized, disintegrating, and declining as a viable unified social unit. Opinions vary on the degree to which change should occur in norms and values governing marriage, motherhood, sex, working mothers, and sexism. The challengers argue for even more change in the traditional family structure, functions, and roles. The defenders opt for retaining and maintaining traditional ways, for they believe less change is needed to preserve the family.

Major indicators show the problematic and changing features of America's families. Marriages have declined for the first time in years, and many persons are delaying marriage and childbearing. While families are shrinking in size, divorces (over one million in 1976) are reaching unprecedented numbers. Illegitimacy is a growing problem, even where liberal abortion laws operate. Premarital and extramarital affairs have reached all-time highs, weakening and disorganizing marriage and family life as never before. To add to the family's problems, women are now working outside the home in ever larger numbers, though they still face sexist discrimination in jobs and pay.

Underlying causes for the plight and problems of the family stem from our long process of industrialization and urbanization, as well as our conflicting values between the individual and the family. An exploitive social structure that keeps most women (and men) subordinate and powerless is also a major cause of family problems, conflicts, and dissension.

Solutions to the problem take three possible directions:

1. Retain and reinforce traditional sex roles, norms, and values.

2. Permit new family forms, sex roles, norms, and values.
3. Encourage, as a matter of national policy, equality and justice for women.

Whatever solutions are adopted, the future clearly holds new forms of both marriage and family structure, as suggested by Herbert Otto and others. In addition, couples will have many more options and alternatives, as well as social tools and aids to forge their own kind of family.

CAREER OPPORTUNITIES

Family Counselors.

They are usually counseling psychologists, psychiatrists, or social workers. All work with persons facing family problems. Such clients are not usually mentally ill but are often emotionally upset, anxious, or struggling to resolve some problem that affects the behavior of other family members. Family counselors may work in a university setting, for a marriage-counseling agency, community health center, or with a state or federal agency. A degree in sociology, social work, psychology, or medicine is needed. For further information write to: National Council on Family Relations, 1219 University Avenue, S.E., Minneapolis, Minnesota, 55414; or to: Family Services Association of America, 44 E. 23rd Street, New York, N.Y. 10010.

Recreation Workers.

As families continue to lose their role as providers of most recreational acitvities, the need for various types of recreation workers and services will grow. Participation in organized recreational activities will become an important part of life outside the family. Recreation workers organize and lead social, cultural, and physical-education programs for all age groups, particularly the young and old, at camps, playgrounds, community centers, hospitals, and workplaces. Activity specialists, usually with a college degree in sociology for better positions, often have specialized training in a particular subject, such as art, music, drama, or athletics and physical education. Working as a camp counselor is good preparation for those seeking career opportunities in recreation or other types of counseling, or in working with young people. For further information write to: National Recreation and Parks Association, 8 West 8th St., New York, N.Y. 10011.

Child-Care Workers.

They care for children housed in city, county, or other government or private institutions. Such workers interact with children on a one-to-one and group basis; give instruction and guidance to children, as well as personal counseling; lead and direct recreational activities; and must sometimes be required to deal with emotionally disturbed children. Background and education in sociology (as well as some psychology) would be quite useful. For further information write to: Child Welfare League of America, 67 Irving Place, New York, New York 10003.

REFERENCES

"Affirmative Action and Equal Employment." A Guidebook for Employers 1 (January). Washington, D.C.: U.S. Equal Employment Opportunity Commission, 1974.

"American Families: Trends and Pressures." Hearings before the Subcommittee on Children and Youth of the Committee on Labor and Public Welfare. U.S. Senate, September 24, 25, 26, 1973. Washington, D.C.: U.S. Government Printing Office, 1974.

"The American Family: Can It Survive Today's Shocks?" U.S. News & World Report 79 (October 27):30, 1975.

"The American Family: Image and Reality." Westwood, Mass.: Paper Book, 1976.

"Average U.S. Household Drops Below 3 Persons for First Time." New York Times (July 7):36, 1975.

Ball, Donald W.
1972 "The 'Family' as a Sociological Problem." Social Problems 19, 3 (Winter):295–307.

Bell, Robert R.
1971 Marriage and Family Interaction. Rev. ed. Homewood, Ill.: Dorsey.
1971 Social Deviance: A Substantive Analysis. Homewood, Ill.: Dorsey.

Bell, Robert and Michael Gordon, eds.
1972 The Social Dimension of Human Sexuality. Boston: Little, Brown.

Bern, Sandra
1975 "Androgyny vs. the Tight Little Lives of Fluffy Women and Chesty Men." Psychology Today 9, 4 (September):58–62.

Berger, David and Morton Wenger
1973 "The Ideology of Virginity." Journal of Marriage and the Family 35, 4 (November):666–76.

"Black Working Wives Hike Family Income." Allentown Morning Call (April 21):3, 1976.

Bowman, Elizabeth
1975 "Child Care Programs: Federal Role Debated." Congressional Quarterly Weekly Report 33, 49 (December 6):2635–40.

Bucher, Glenn R.
1974 "Liberation, Male and White: Initial Reflections." The Christian Century 71, 11 (March 20):312–16.

Cadwallader, Mervyn
1967 "Changing Social Mores." Current (February):48.

Campbell, Angus
1975 "The American Way of Mating: Marriage Si, Children Only Maybe." Psychology Today 8, 12 (May):37–43.

Cassady, Margie
1975 "Runaway Wives: Husbands Don't Pick Up the Danger Signals Their Wives Send Out." Psychology Today 8, 12 (May):42.

Chafe, William
1976 "Feminism in the 1970s." Pp. 126–31 in Anne Kilbride, ed. Readings in Social Problems 76/77: Annual Editions. Guilford, Conn.: Dushkin.

"Child Care Programs—Federal Role Debated." Congressional Quarterly 33, 49 (December 6):2635–40, 1975.

Chilman, Catherine S.
    1973 "Public Social Policy and the Family in the 1970s." Social Casework (December):575–79.

Citizens Advisory Council on the Status of Women
    1975 "Women in 1974." Washington, D.C.: U.S. Government Printing Office.

Cogswell, Betty
    1975 "Variant Family Forms and Life Styles: Rejection of the Traditional Nuclear Family." The Family Coordinator 24, 4 (October):391–406.

Davis, Kingsley
    1976 "Sexual Behavior." Pp. 291–63 in Robert K. Merton and Robert Nisbet, eds. Contemporary Social Problems. 4th ed. New York: Harcourt Brace Jovanovich.

Decter, Midge
    1972 The New Chastity and Other Arguments against Women's Liberation. New York: Capricorn.

Denfeld, Duane and Michael Gordon
    1970 "The Sociology of Mate Swapping: The Family That Swings Together Clings Together." Journal of Sex Research 7, 2 (May):85–99.

"Divorce Is Called Marital Safety Valve." Allentown Morning Call (November 16):3, 1975.

Dixon, Marlene
    1975 "Public Ideology and the Class Composition of Women's Liberation (1966–1969)." Pp. 254–65 in Susan Friedman, ed. Readings in Social Problems 75/76: Annual Editions. Guilford, Conn.: Dushkin.

"Do Children Need Sex Roles?" Newsweek 83, 23 (June 10): 79–80, 1974.

"The Domestic Life of Americans." Interchange 6, 3 (May):1–3, 1977.

Doyle, Nancy
    1974 "Women's Changing Place: A Look at Sexism." Pamphlet No. 509. New York: Public Affairs Committee, Inc.

Duberman, Lucile
    1975 Gender and Sex in Society. New York: Praeger.
    1977 Marriage and Other Alternatives. 2nd ed. New York: Praeger.

Dvorkin, David
    1976 "On Manhood." Pp. 145–47 in Susan Friedman, ed. Readings in Social Problems 75/76: Annual Editions. Guilford, Conn.: Dushkin.

"The Equal Rights Amendment: What Does It Mean to You?" Washington, D.C.: National Organization for Women, n.d..

"Excerpts from Action Plan of Women's Meeting." New York Times (July3):8, 1975.

"Family Sickness." Time 106, 21 (November 24): 73, 1975.

"Family Trends Now Taking Shape." U.S. News & World Report (October 27): 32, 1975.

Farson, Richard D., Philip Hauser, Herbert Stroud, and Anthony J. Wiener
    1969 The Future of the Family. New York: Family Service Association of America.

Fern, Duane William
    1974 "Can Modern Marriage Work?" Parents' Magazine 49 (February):52–53.

Fisher, E.
    1970 "The Second Sex, Junior Division." The New York Times Book Review 7 (May 24):6.

Flexner, Eleanor
    1973 "Women's Rights—Unfinished Business." Pamphlet No. 469. New York: Public Affairs Committee.

Freeman, Jo.
    1973 "The Social Construction of the Second Sex." Pp. 104–11 in Helena Lopata, ed. Marriages and Families. New York: Van Nostrand.

Friedan, Betty
    1963 The Feminine Mystique. New York: Norton.

Furstenberg, Frank J.
    1966 "Industrialization and the American Family: A Look Backward." American Sociological Review 31 (June):326–37.

Gagnon, John H. and Bruce Henderson
    1975 Human Sexuality: An Age of Ambiguity. Boston: Little, Brown.

Gans, Herbert J.
    1967 The Levittowners. New York: Pantheon.

Garfinkle, Stuart
    1975 "Occupations of Women and Black Workers, 1962–74." Monthly Labor Review 98, 11 (November):28–31.

Gilder, George
    1973 "The Suicide of the Sexes." Harper's 247, 1478 (July):42–54.

Gilmartin, Brian G.
    1975 "Suburban Mate-Swapping." Psychology Today 8, 9 (February):55–58.

Glass, Joel B.
    1974 Family Therapy: An Overview. Intellect, 103, 2360 (October):106–8.

Glick, Paul
    1975 "A Demographer Looks at American Families." Journal of Marriage and the Family 37, 1 (February):15–26.

Goldberg, Philip
    1968 "Are Women Prejudiced against Women?" Transaction 5 (April):28–30.

Goldberg, S. and M. Lewis
    1969 "Play Behavior in the Year-Old Infant: Early Sex Differences." Child Development 40 (1969):21–31.

Goldstein, Fred J.
    1970 "Sex Identity Deviation and Inversion." Pp. 93–106 in Georgene H. Seward and Robert C. Williamson, eds. Sex Roles in a Changing Society. New York: Random House.

Goldstein, Lee B.
    1975 "Divorce Cards a Profitable Market." Allentown Sunday Call-Chronicle (August 24):E-2.

Goode, William
  1956   After Divorce. Glencoe, Ill.: Free Press.
  1963   World Revolution and Family Patterns. New York: Free Press.
Gordon, Suzanne
  1976   "What's Come over the Women's Movement? The New Denial of Sexuality." Mother Jones (June):23–27.
"Growing at a Slower Pace." U.S. News & World Report 82, 19 (May 16): 64–65, 1977.
Gusfield, Joseph
  1968   "The Study of Social Movements." Pp. 445–50 in David Sills, ed. International Encyclopedia of the Social Sciences 14. New York: Macmillan and the Free Press.
Hedge, Janice N.
  1970   "Women at Work: Women Workers and Manpower Demands in the 1970s." Monthly Labor Review (June): 19.
Hoover, Eleanor
  1975   "There's No Recession of Extramarital Affairs." Allentown Morning Call (September 9):25.
Horn, Patrice, ed.
  1975   "Newsline: A Look at the Disintegrating World of Childhood." Psychology Today 9, 1 (June):32–36.
Horner, Matina
  1969   "Fail: Bright Women." Psychology Today 3, 5 (November):36–41.
Horton, Paul B. and Gerald R. Leslie
  1974   The Sociology of Social Problems. 5th ed. Englewood Cliffs, N.J.: Prentice-Hall.
Howe, Louise Kapp
  1976 "Women in the Workplace." Pp. 132–55 in Anne Kilbride, ed. Readings in Social Problems 76/77: Annual Editions. Guilford, Conn.: Dushkin.
Hunt, Morton
  1969   "The Affair." Pp. 457–63 in Arlene Skolnick and Jerome Skolnick, eds. Family in Transition. Boston: Little, Brown, 1971.

SUGGESTED READINGS

The Family

Carter, Hugh and Paul Glick. Marriage and Divorce: A Social and Economic Study, rev. ed. Cambridge, Mass.: Harvard University Press. 1976.
Contains a storehouse of facts and information about the changing patterns, social classes, work experience, and incomes of the married and divorced in the United States.

Hunt, Morton. Sexual Behavior in the 1970s. Chicago: Playboy Press. 1974.
Documents the recent changes in sexual mores, attitudes, and behavior.

Koch, Joanne and Lew Koch. The Marriage Savers. New York: Coward, McCann & Geoghegan. 1976.

All about marriage counseling, family therapy, sex clinics, and other agencies to improve marriages.

Libby, Roger W. and Robert N. Whitehurst. Marriage and Alternatives: Exploring Intimate Relationships. Glenview, Ill.: Scott, Foresman. 1977.

Readings on the pros and cons of traditional monogamous marriage and alternative intimate lifestyles, drawing upon observations and research in a variety of fields.

Otto, Herbert, ed. Marriage and Family Enrichment: New Perspectives and Programs. Nashville, Tenn. Abingdon Press. 1976.

A complete resource handbook describing 19 marriage-enrichment programs. It contains a list of available resource materials for those interested in such programs.

Periodicals Worth Exploring

Family Coordinator
Journal of Family Counseling
Journal of Marriage and the Family
Social Casework
Social Work

Changing Sex Roles

Chapman, Jane Roberts, ed. Economic Independence for Women: The Foundation for Equal Rights. Vol. 1 of Sage Yearbooks in Women's Policy Studies. Beverly Hills, Calif.: Sage. 1976.

Articles on economic worth of women to society, family, and industry. Covers a variety of social problems faced by women in our economy.

Friedan, Betty. It Changed My Life: Writings on the Women's Movement. New York: Random House. 1976.

A description of the attitudes, life experiences, preparations, and tribulations involved in starting and strengthening the Women's Liberation movement.

Gagnon, John H. Human Sexualities. Glenview, Ill.: Scott, Foresman. 1977.

Explores the sociological, psychological, and physical factors shaping human sexual behavior, from developmental, life-cycle, and learning perspectives.

Hyde, Janet and B. F. Rosenberg. Half the Human Experience: The Psychology of Women. Lexington, Mass.:Heath. 1976.

Presents major emerging trends in women's achievement, motivation, sexuality, and sex roles.

Kaplan, Alexandra and Joan Bean, eds. Beyond Sex Role Stereotypes. Boston: Little, Brown. 1976.

Readings develop a psychology of sex roles that moves from traditional female/male polarities to a model of androgyny.

Periodicals Worth Exploring

Ms.
Quest — A Feminist Quarterly
Signs — Journal of Women in Culture and Society

"Inside Title VII: CLGW Staff Has Two-Day Workshop on Law." Voice of Cement, Lime & Gypsum Workers International Union 39, 8 (August):16–19, 1976.

"Is the American Family in Danger?" U.S. News & World Report 74, 16 (April):76, 1973.

Julian, Joseph
1973 Social Problems. New York: Appleton-Century-Crofts.

Kamerman, Shelia B. and Alfred Kahn
1976 "Explorations in Family Policy." Social Work 21, 3 (1976): 181–86.

Kantner, John and Melvin Zelnik
1973 "Contraception and Pregnancy: Experience of Young Unmarried Women in the United States." Family Planning Perspectives, 5, 1 (Winter):21–35.

Kilbride, Anne, ed.
1976 Readings in Social Problems 76/77: Annual Editions. Guilford, Conn.: Dushkin.

Kinsey, Alfred C., Wardell B. Pomeroy, Clyde E. Martin, and Paul H. Gebhard
1953 Sexual Behavior in the Human Female. Philadelphia: Saunders.

Klein, Deborah P.
1975 "Women in the Labor Force: The Middle Years." Monthly Labor Review 98, 11 (November):10–16.

Klemesrud, Judy
1972 "Secretary Image: A Tempest in a Typewriter." New York Times (March 7):34.

Kohlberg, Laurence
1966 "A Cognitive-Developmental Analysis of Children's Sex-role Concepts and Attitudes." Pp. 82–98 in Eleanor E. Maccoby, ed. The Development of Sex Differences. Stanford, Calif.: Stanford University Press.

Kupferberg, Herbert
1976 "Women Discuss Their Changing Role." Parade Magazine (January 11):20.

Lawrenson, Helen
1975 "The Feminine Mistake." Pp. 274–82 in Robert Antonio and George Ritzer, eds. Social Problems: Values and Interests in Conflict. Boston: Allyn & Bacon.

Le Masters, E. E.
1970 Parents in Modern America: A Sociological Analysis. Homewood, Ill.: Dorsey Press.

Levitan, Sar and William B. Johnston
1973 Work Is Here to Stay, Alas. Salt Lake City: Olympus.

"Liberated Women: How They're Changing American Life." U.S. News & World Report 80, 23 (June 7):46–49, 1976.

Lindberg, P.
1972 "What's Happening to the American Family?" Better Homes and Gardens 50 (October): 52–53; 128–29.

Lopata, Helena Z.
1971 Occupation Housewife. New York: Oxford University Press.

Luce, Clare Boothe
    1975   "The 21st-Century Woman—Free at Last?" Pp. 156–69 in Susan Friedman, ed. Readings in Social Problems 75/76: Annual Editions. Guilford, Conn.: Dushkin.

McCary, James L.
    1975   Freedom and Growth in Marriage. Santa Barbara, Calif.: Hamilton.

McCormack, Patricia
    1977   "Working Mothers Linked to Teen Trysting." Allentown Call-Chronicle (April 8):A-12.

Mace, David and Vera Mace
    1959   Marriage East and West. Garden City, N.Y.: Doubleday.

Macklin, Eleanor D.
    1974   "Cohabitation in College: Going Very Steady." Psychology Today 8, 6 (November):53–58.

"Married Women in the Labor Force." Statistical Bulletin, Metropolitan Life Insurance Co. (August):9–10, 1974.

Mauss, Armand L.
    1975   Social Problems as Social Movements. Philadelphia: Lippincott.

Mead, Margaret
    1967   Male and Female: A Study of the Sexes in a Changing World: New York: Morrow.

Meyerson, Bess
    1975   "A Call to Action: The National Women's Agenda." Redbook (November):71–75.

"Military Gays Fight Back." Mother Jones (June):5–6, 1976.

Montagu, Ashley
    1970   The Natural Superiority of Women. London: Collier.

Moorehouse, Rebecca
    1976   "The 'Open Family' Is Open to Life." Allentown Morning Call (July 27):16.

Morgan, Marabel
    1974   The Total Woman. Old Tappan, N.J.: Revell.

National NOW Action Center
    n.d.   "The American Way: Ratify the ERA." Washington, D.C.: National Organization of Women.

Novak, Michael
    1975   "Opinion Makers Appear Out of Touch with Most Americans." Sunday Call-Chronicle (October 26):F-1.

O'Neill, Nena and George O'Neil
    1973   Open Marriage: A New Life Style for Couples. New York: Avon.

Otto, Herbert A.
    1970   The Family in Search of a Future: Alternative Models for Moderns. New York: Appleton-Century-Crofts.

Parsons, Talcott and Robert Bales
    1955   Family, Socialization and Interaction Process. Glencoe, Ill.: Free Press.

Peterson, Charles
    1975   "The Divorce Boom Keeps Booming." Parade Magazine (October 26):4.

Regan, Barbara and Martha Blaxall
   1976 "Occupational Segregation in International Women's Year." Signs: Journal of Women in Culture and Society 1, 3 (Spring), part 2:1–5.

Reiss, Ira L.
   1971 The Family System in America. New York: Holt, Rinehart and Winston.

Rodman, Hyman
   1966 "Talcott Parsons: View of the Changing American Family." Pp. 262–86 in Hyman Rodman, ed. Marriage, Family and Society: A Reader. New York: Random House.

Rollin, Betty
   1970 "Motherhood: Who Needs It?" Look 34, 19 (September):15–17. Pp. 346–56 in Arlene S. Skolnick and Jerome H. Skolnick. Family in Transition.

Rosenfeld, Megan
   1976 "Homemaker's Job Essential, Martha Movement Contends." Allentown Sunday Call-Chronicle (July 11):E-3.

Rossi, Alice S.
   1964 "Equality between the Sexes: An Immodest Proposal." Daedalus 93 (Spring):607–52.
   1972 "Sex Equality: The Beginnings of Ideology." In Constantina Safilios-Rothschild, ed. Toward a Sociology of Women. Lexington, Mass.: Xerox College Publishing.

Scanzoni, Letha and John Scanzoni
   1976 Men, Women and Change: A Sociology of Marriage and Family. New York: McGraw-Hill.

Scarpitti, Frank R.
   1974 Social Problems. Holt, Rinehart and Winston.
   1977 Social Problems. 2nd ed. Hinsdale, Ill.: Dryden Press.

See, Carolyn
   1975 "California Children." New Times (January 10). Pp. 201-4 in Peter Wickman, ed. Readings in Social Problems 75/76: Annual Editions. Guilford, Conn.: Dushkin.

Shearer, Lloyd
   1976 "The American Scene: Intelligence Report." Parade (January 11):14.

Simmons, Adele, et al.
   1975 Exploitation from 9 to 5: Report of the Twentieth Century Fund Task Force on Women and Employment. Lexington, Mass.: Lexington Books.

Sklar, June and Beth Berkov
   1975 "The American Birth Rate: Evidences of a Coming Rise." Science 189, 4204 (August 29):693–700.

Slocum, Walter
   1974 Occupational Careers: A Sociological Perspective. 2nd ed. Chicago: Aldine.

Sorenson, Robert C.
   1973 Adolescent Sexuality in Contemporary America. New York: World.

Staines, Graham, Carol Tavris, and Toby Epstein Jayaratne
   1974 "The Queen Bee Syndrome." Psychology Today 7 (January 4):19.

Stewart, Elbert W.
    1976   The Troubled Land: Social Problems in Modern America. 2nd ed. New York: McGraw-Hill.

Swift, Pamela
    1976   "Girls Do As Well: Keeping Up with Youth." Parade (January 4):19.

Terman, Lewis
    1938   Psychological Factors in Marital Happiness. New York: McGraw-Hill.

"37 Million Women in U.S. Workforce." AFL-CIO News (December 6):6, 1975.

Thoman, E. B., P. H. Leiderman, and J. P. Olson
    1972   "Neonate-Mother Interaction during Breast Feeding." Developmental Psychology 6 (June):110–18.

"Throwaway Marriages — Threat to the American Family." U.S. News & World Report 78 (January 13):43–46, 1975.

Tinker, Irene
    1975   "International Women's Year." Science 190. 4221 (December 26):1249.

"Today's Marriages: Wrenching Experience or Key to Happiness?" U.S. News & World Report (October 27):36, 1975.

Toffler, Alvin
    1970   Future Shock. New York: Bantam.

U.S. Department of Labor
    1975   "Twenty Facts on Women Workers." Employment Standards Administration, Women's Bureau (June). Washington, D.C.: U.S. Government Printing Office.

U.S. Population Commission on Population Growth and the American Future. New York: Bantam, 1972.

"View of Women through the Ages." Task Force on Women, United Church of Christ, n.d..

Weitzman, Lenore J., Deborah Eifler, Elizabeth Hokada, and Catherine Ross
    1972   "Sex-Role Socialization in Picture Books for Preschool Children." American Journal of Sociology 77 (May):1125–50.

"Why Marriages Turn Sour — And How to Get Help." U.S. News & World Report 79 (October 27):44–46, 1975.

"Woman Charges White House Bias." Allentown Morning Call (December 15):10, 1975.

World Almanac and Book of Facts, 1976. New York: Newspaper Enterprise Association, 1975.

Young, Leontine
    1973   The Fractured Family. New York: McGraw-Hill.

PART TWO

As a person grows up, he moves out into an immediate social environment (or social milieu) beyond the family. For the first time, he encounters social groups and organizations that affect behavior and precipitate social problems.

As a person is exposed to our social structure he begins to recognize how his neighborhood and physical surroundings can impinge on his life. Crowded into a rundown apartment in a neighborhood where social services are limited because of the city's financial problems, a person begins to recognize how urban problems and issues are reflected in his life's troubles and worries. Often people are treated impersonally, as neighborhoods deteriorate because millions of working- and middle-class persons, along with industries, desert the central city for life in the suburbs.

More and more of those trapped in the central city are poor, members of racial minorities, or old. They are left to face their problems as best they can—until the whole situation itself becomes a pressing social issue.

Within the city, masses of persons are forced by their immediate social milieu and environment to live in poverty. In such a social environment and human group, life becomes difficult and often unbearable for over 25 million Americans. This is the "Other America" about which Michael Harrington wrote in the early 1960s. But by the late 1970s the poor are still very much among us, especially in urban enclaves. A result of unequal advantages and opportunities among our social classes, poverty soon becomes a social issue on America's conscience, if not on its national agenda.

Groups, Immediate Social Environment, and Social Issues

Equally damaging to the "life chances" of millions of Americans is the systematic institutional discrimination against minority-group members—blacks, the Spanish-speaking, and American Indians. Such groups are usually quite powerless against the overwhelming odds of a society dominated and controlled by white groups and social structures. Most minorities cluster together in urban ghettos, in barrios, or on reservations, and about one-third suffer from poverty.

Persons black and white, poor and rich, urban and suburban all eventually find themselves permanently assigned to a new group—the elderly and aged. Few meaningful social roles are left for the elderly to perform when they are forced to retire. This leads to many personal troubles and social issues, from finances to health, that an elderly person must face. Some "disengage" themselves from social activity; others cling more tenaciously to members of their own age group and social milieu in the hope of solving their troubles and problems. Groups such as the Gray Panthers are formed in response to the social issues confronting the aged.

Members of our bureaucratic, highly structured society attempt to deal with personal troubles and social issues that affect their lives. The inequality and vast differences in power and wealth emerging from the social structure often cause and aggravate our many social problems for various groups, such as the poor, the minorities, and the elderly. Also our social structure often makes a meaningful or permanent solution to these problems difficult.

Urban and Suburban Problems

INTRODUCTION
DEFINITIONS OF THE PROBLEM
Definitions of European sociologists.
Antiurban bias.
Urban types.
INCIDENCE AND PREVALENCE OF THE PROBLEM
Housing and physical blight.
Overcrowding and depersonalization (bystander apathy).
Financial problems.
Transportation and traffic problems.
CAUSES OF THE PROBLEM
Rapid migration out of the city.
Technological changes in transportation and decline of rapid transit.
Fragmentation of government.
Special-interest structural forces.
PROPOSED SOLUTIONS TO THE PROBLEM
Preserving green space.
Housing allowances.
HUD programs and policies.
Urban homesteading and renewal.
Private efforts to save the cities (downtown and new towns).
Metropolitanization; structural decentralization of government.
Transportation and traffic.
Radical proposals.
FUTURE OF THE PROBLEM
Regionalization.
Balance between urban and rural areas.
Housing still a problem.
New towns and futuristic cities.
Improved transportation.
A bright outlook except for the Northeast.
SUMMARY

> Why are the mayors all quitting?
> Why are the cities all broke?
> Why are the people all angry?
> Why are we dying of smoke?
> Why are the streets unprotected?
> Why are the schools in distress?
> Why is the trash uncollected?
> How did we make such a mess?
>
> Anonymous— Arno Press ad for **The Rise of Urban America,** 57 books edited by Richard C. Wade, Distinguished Professor of History, Graduate Center, City University of New York.

A recent study of man and urban life began by observing. "The modern world is one for which society has made no preparation. It is a jigsaw puzzle that we must—at this late date—learn to assemble from pieces we know too little about" (Smith, 1972:1). We frequently hear or read about the urban crisis, for it is in the city that "many problems are shown in sharpest silhouette, including poverty against a background of affluence, and rats, filth, and squalor in little alleys overshadowed by the great structures of modern engineering" (Stewart, 1976:16). The modern city is a place of tension and strain: tension generated by traffic, noise, and congestion; strain stemming from crowded housing, slums, and the financial worries of citizen and government alike.

But the city is more. It is also the center of "civilization"—art, music, literature, and "culture." It is diverse and heterogeneous; active, innovative, and alive. It contains constructive forces. It helps newcomers become Americanized and assimilated into middle-class life. And it urbanizes rural blacks, Puerto Ricans, and Southern whites, just as it did Europeans. As Charles Silberman put it: "the principal business and the principal glory of the American city is to bring people from society's backwaters into the mainstream of American life" (Silberman, 1964:19).

Metropolitan areas are home for over 70 percent of us, and by 1980 nearly 90 percent of all Americans may be urban dwellers. By the year 2000, 60 percent may live in metropolitan areas of one million or more (*Population and the American Future*, 1972:34). The future of the United States appears to be an urban one, even if the central city is the focus and locus of numerous social problems, as well as being a social problem itself.

What is the nature of the city? How is the city defined as a social problem, and what social problems are connected with it? How do people experience these problems in their daily lives? How extensive and serious are our urban problems? What are the major causes behind our urban problems? Can the city be salvaged or saved? If so, how? And will tomorrow's cities be much different from today's?

DEFINING THE URBAN AND SUBURBAN PROBLEMS

All these questions begin and end with how a city or an urban area is defined.* Writing in 1887, the German sociologist Ferdinand Tonnies, using the city as a typical example, contrasted the social relationships and values of rural with urban settings. The rural "Gemeinschaft" community had close personal relationships; members shared traditional values and sentiments, and each was valued as a full person. The urban "Gesellschaft" association of people was impersonal, "rationally calculated," and distant. Most people were strangers, values varied, and the main basis for social interaction was dependent upon the special function, or service, someone else performed (Holland, 1974:197–201). His definitions of rural and urban areas in terms of "Gemeinschaft" and "Gesellschaft" help us to understand such urban social problems as depersonalization, alienation, and bystander apathy.

Other European sociologists, such as Max Weber and Georg Simmel, stressed the rapidity of change, dense living conditions, and constant, impersonal interaction endured by urban man. They emphasized how an urban social structure itself often produced or caused social problems. Most European sociologists had a latent antiurban bias, which was later diffused to American scholars.

Robert Park, Ernest Burgess, and Louis Wirth, all sociologists at the University of Chicago, viewed the city as a problem to be studied. Park, in his 1916 essay "The City," pioneered an ecological approach to analyzing city problems. This approach asks us to look at urban areas as a social and physical environment: such "natural areas" as neighborhoods and small census areas, called "tracts," were studied and behavior patterns were linked to them. This approach led to an exploration of such social problems as land use, segregation, housing, crime, mental illness, and other "social pathologies" often considered the primary urban problems.

The classic statement of the "Chicago School" about the city was Louis Wirth's essay "Urbanism as a Way of Life." In it, Wirth distinguished between "the city," "urbanism" and "urbanization." He wrote: "For sociological purposes a city may be defined as a relatively large, dense, and permanent settlement of socially heterogeneous individuals" [different] (Wirth, 1938:8). Wirth stressed the "mass" nature of the city, the breakdown of social bonds, and the tendency of city institutions to organize their services for "the average person" rather than for unique individuals. Since Wirth's 1938 essay, this description and depiction of city life has served as the prime basis of analyzing city problems.

Wirth viewed "urbanization" as the process whereby "urbanism" spreads beyond the boundaries of the city itself. Today, many urban, sub-

---

*Besides the many definitions that sociologists have given to "the city," "urbanism," and "the slum," others have defined these terms using cultural, economic, political, or demographic criteria.

urban, and metropolitan areas are affected by such growth. Although the most dysfunctional or negative aspects of the central city are severely scaled down in outlying surburban communities, most suburbs *are* socially and economically integrated with (and dependent upon) the central city. Even "satellite" or "new towns" depend on older central cities.

A more recent characterization of urbanism that tries to account for our suburbs is that of the well-known urban sociologist Herbert J. Gans. He points out that Wirth's description of the city "ignores the fact that this population consists mainly of relatively homogeneous groups, with social and cultural moorings that shield it fairly effectively from the suggested consequences of number, density, and heterogeneity" (Gans, 1972:34). In his study of urban renewal in the Italian-American community of Boston's West End, Gans focused on a socially unified ethnic community. He described the residents as "urban villagers," rather than as the isolated, depersonalized people Wirth had earlier depicted (1962).

Urban Types

Gans sees five distinct urban types: the cosmopolites, the unmarried or childless, the "ethnic villagers," the deprived, and the trapped or downwardly mobile.

The cosmopolites include professionals, intellectuals, and the rich and powerful. They often live in high-rise apartments convenient to the center city, so as to avoid such urban problems as transportation and traffic. These are the people urban planners try to draw back into the city by building luxury apartments.

The unmarried or childless may live in the inner city for a limited time. When the singles marry, they move to a transient city neighborhood of young apartment dwellers, then to the suburbs. The permanently single stay in the city and live in housing commensurate with their income. Many childless couples are cosmopolites. The urban problems of mobility, housing, and isolation sometimes affect this group.

The ethnic villagers are found in certain old, inner-city neighborhoods, like New York's Lower East Side, living within their own subcultures. In this lifestyle, the family and neighborhood remain crucial. Overcrowding and high density are sometimes linked to this group.

The deprived are the very poor, the emotionally disturbed, broken families, and generally the nonwhite. This urban group is the one usually associated with the urban crisis—issues and social problems like housing, poverty, crime and delinquency, and mental illness. Its members live in rundown, substandard housing and make up the bulk of those left behind in the slums.

The trapped or downwardly mobile stay behind when a neighborhood changes because they cannot afford to move. They are mostly the elderly, living out their existence on a meager pension. Social problems of alienation, isolation, depersonalization, poverty, and inadequate health care are associated with these urban dwellers.

Hence, how we define the city and its residents profoundly affects the social problems we see or do not see. For example, some sociologists associate the city and its social problems with its slums. Kirson Weinberg defines the slum as "a physical, social and psychological amalgam characterized by low income, overcrowded substandard housing, mixed land use, racial and ethnic concentrations, broken homes, working mothers, low levels of education, and high rates of tuberculosis, mental disorders, and victims of crime" (1970:85). Such a definition reflects the traditional view of sociologists about the "social pathology" and deviance that is a part of every large city. Quite different is a recent reinterpretation of the slum, which finds considerably more social organization and functioning of neighborhood and peer groups than the "social pathology" view expected, all as a sign of the normal operations of the city (Suttles, 1968). The deviance approach to defining problems of the city suffered from an "anti-urban" bias that has only recently been recognized by sociologists.

The Conservative Antiurban Bias

An antiurban bias has traditionally pervaded conservative thinking and definitions of city life. Thomas Jefferson asserted that cities were "pestilential to the morals, the health, and the liberties of man.... Our governments will remain virtuous for centuries, as long as they are chiefly agricultural" (Stedman, 1972:21). Other Americans, such as Ralph Waldo Emerson, Henry Thoreau, Edgar Allan Poe, Henry Adams, Henry James, Frank Lloyd Wright, and John Dewey also felt that the city corrupted man and was evil (White and White, 1961: 166–78). Even sociologists Charles Cooley and Robert Park, to mention only two, had an antiurban bias. They nostalgically yearned for the day when life was simpler, pastoral, and peaceful. They shared a distorted, often idealized view of the rural past (McVeigh, 1962). A student's view, expressed in "Why I Stick to the City" (page 192) reflects this antiurban bias.

As a reaction against this antiurban bias, another definition of urban life has emerged. This view rejects the liberals' or radicals' notion of urban decline or crisis and dismisses it as myth. The leading spokesman for this conservative definition of urban "problems" is Edward Banfield, in his books *The Unheavenly City* (1968) and *The Unheavenly City Revisited* (1974). He notes:

> Most of the "problems" that are generally supposed to constitute "urban crisis" could not conceivably lead to disaster. They are — some of them — important, in the sense that a bad cold is important, but they are not serious in the sense that a cancer is serious. They have to do with comfort, convenience, amenity, and business advantage, all of which are important, but they do not affect

either the essential welfare of individuals or what may be called the good health of the society (1968:6).

Thus Banfield considers urban problems as minor and conditions as very much improved in recent years. Furthermore, when serious social problems do exist, they are not unique to cities. He writes:

> The serious problems of these places, it should be stressed, are in most instances not caused by the conditions of urban life as such and are less characteristic of the city than of small-town and farm areas. Poverty, ignorance, and racial injustice are more widespread outside the cities than inside them (Ibid., 12).

Banfield's interpretation of urban problems has sparked sharp debates and rebuttals, and the issue remains unsettled (Lockard, 1971: 69–72).

WHY I STICK TO THE CITY

"Why do I stick to the city?" You might as well ask a rat why he sticks to the garbage dump.

When I walk along a crowded city street, I give the same little snicker that a rat gives when he dives into a load of freshly dumped garbage. The city is an interesting place, an exciting place, a place to have fun in. On this point the rat and I completely agree.

I think every "kid" should have a chance to be brought up in the city. Even living in the city is an education in itself. The city has several advantages for a "kid" trying to grow up. In a city there are plenty of ice cream cones, comic books and Frankenstein movies. When a boy reaches his adolescence, he has a larger choice of women to go out with than has his contemporary on the farm! And also, being a "sharp character" with more experience, he can "hand" his "doll" a better "line" than the average farmer can.

You can't slow down a city. Things have got to go on, and, unless there is a power cut-off, things never stop. If you try to slow down in the city, you just get pushed down and run over. Have you ever watched an old lady cross a busy intersection? She moves or else. This all adds to the interest and excitement that a city can offer.

From J. R. Seeley, R. A. Sim, and E. W. Loosley, *Crestwood Heights* (New York: Wiley, 1963): 432–33.

INCIDENCE AND PREVALENCE OF URBAN AND SUBURBAN PROBLEMS

Though urban problems from alcoholism to zoning are endless, let us analyze the incidence and prevalence of four crucial ones that are not covered in other chapters of this book. They are:

housing and physical blight
crowding and depersonalization (bystander apathy)
financial problems
transportation and traffic.

Housing and Physical Blight

Housing people in the city is a persistent problem. Over the years very little has been done by private developers or government to keep pace with the housing needs of the center-city poor—those who need decent homes the most. A Harvard University-MIT study reports that at least 20 percent of the nation's families were "housing-deprived." Of some 13 million inadequate houses, nearly seven million had poor plumbing or heating, five-and-a-half million required "excessive" rent, and over half a million were "overcrowded." In the New York City area, 28 percent of the houses were inadequate, as were 25 percent in the Newark area (Birch, 1973).

Since the first Housing Act was passed in 1937, our society has built fewer units of public housing than needed (National Commission on Urban Problems, 1969:13). Slightly over one million units of public housing for the urban poor have been built since 1937, compared with over five million Federal Housing Administration insured homes for middle-class, suburban Americans. Nearly two-thirds of all new private housing, and less than 20 percent of all public housing, are built in the suburbs. In our profit-oriented economy, private developers find little profit in building housing for the poor, except with direct government financing. The pri-

Urban-renewal projects often destroy more homes than they build.

vate developers find much greater profit in meeting the housing needs of the rich and upper middle class than the poor or working class in cities.

Even urban renewal which was supposed to help provide housing has exacerbated the situation for the center-city poor. Under urban renewal since 1949 over 400,000 housing units were destroyed, but fewer than 40,000 replacement dwellings were built by the mid-1960s. The result has been higher rents for the fewer available houses. Almost half of center-city people are either ill housed or pay more than 20 percent of their incomes for rent. Blacks pay 35 percent of their income, more than some white suburbanites (Horton and Leslie, 1974:449).

But in the early 1970s, the government tried to remedy the inner-city housing problem by having the Federal Housing Administration (FHA) offer special high-risk loans, subsidies, and low down-payment, long-term mortgages in the inner city. But vested financial interests and speculators, not those who needed the houses, profited from the effort. Here is how the housing and real estate system continues to operate. A builder or speculator buys a rundown house for, say, $12,000 and spends $2,000 for "cosmetic" surface repairs. He then finds a low-income buyer for the FHA's low down payment of $200 and bribes or "cons" an FHA appraiser to value the house at $19,000. With the FHA certifying the home and guaranteeing the mortgage, the speculator ends up with $19,000 in his pocket for a $14,000 outlay.

The new buyer, however, soon finds he has bought a lemon. The furnace breaks down, and the plumbing or roof starts leaking. Few of the low-income city dwellers have money for repairs. As a result, some simply move out and abandon the house. Others stop paying on the mortgage, and the FHA ends up owning the house. FHA now owns or has insured mortgages in default on over 215,000 homes. Entire blocks of homes in Philadelphia are owned by FHA. Two federal funds to back up the FHA program were $1.5 billion in the red in 1975, with possibly heavier losses in the future. All costs for subsidized housing, mostly in cities, could "run as high as $7 billion by 1978" (Grimes, 1974:22). In spite of all the money being spent, the urban housing problem is still serious. Thousands of homes and apartments in our center cities are abandoned—the result of higher costs (for owners and tenants alike) and increased neighborhood deterioration.

The practice of "red-lining" adds to the problem of housing. Red-lining is a policy and procedure of banks and insurance firms not to lend money to persons or insure buildings in certain urban areas. The area is "red-lined" on a map by the money interests as unworthy of investment. Only in 1976 did the federal government finally recognize the dangers of such practices (*New York Times*, January 26, 1976:40). Congressional hearings have been held to further expose this practice, and tougher legislation to control it has been proposed and passed by the Senate.

Crowding and Depersonalization

Another major social problem growing out of the city and its housing is crowding (density of population) and bystander apathy. Some homes are overcrowded (more than 1.1 persons per room), especially among poor center-city blacks and the Spanish-speaking. Nationally, eight percent of housing is officially "overcrowded"; in cities the percentage is much higher. Some city neighborhoods are extremely overcrowded; yet if urban planners in Chicago have their way, 100,000 people would be housed in six blocks (Monahan, 1973:6). Although density in American cities has declined in recent years, it is still much higher than in suburban or rural areas.

Studies of deer, rats, lemmings, and other animals show that crowding has very deleterious effects. It encourages increased competition, excessive sexual activity, lowered birth rates, high infant mortality, and even cannibalism. John B. Calhoun called these results of overcrowding a "behavioral sink" (1962:139–48). But does crowding affect people in the same way? Some sociologists and city planners believe that crowding in cities has a profound impact on people's lives. As reported, "they blame crowding for disease, mental illness, crime, riots, drug addiction, divorce and, in one often-cited study, war" (Ford, 1975:29). In a recent study, however, New York social scientist Jonathan Freedman doubts whether urban social problems can be traced entirely to crowding or overcrowding. Freedman believes that "the real source of our urban ills . . . lies not in crowding but in discrimination, poverty, inadequate housing, drug abuse, alcoholism and other conditions" (Ibid., 30).

Bystander Apathy

One well-documented effect of dense urban living is bystander apathy and indifference. City dwellers do not want to "get involved." Persons are murdered in cold blood while others merely stand by and watch.

As many whites flee the center city, parts of the city deteriorate, physically and socially. The anonymity of a large city may foster vandalism and destruction of property, especially in areas where homes are officially destroyed by government action.

Credit: Charles Gatewood.

Experiments suggest that when others are around, individuals usually do not come to another's aid, for they would rather have someone else do it. When persons are rushed and pressed for time (as urbanites usually are), they will not stop to help anyone. The boxed item reports on research about bystander apathy so typical of large cities.

Anonymity may be another factor in apathy and antisocial behavior. Philip Zimbardo undertook an experiment to test the difference between city and small-town behavior. He left a car unattended for about two-and-a-half days in New York City and in the small town of Palo Alto, California. Both cars were made to look abandoned; they had no license plates and the hoods were raised. Both cars were observed during the entire time of the experiment. In New York the car was vandalized within 10 minutes. Twenty-four separate acts of theft and vandalism were committed, leaving the car completely stripped. In Palo Alto, the car was not touched, with one exception—when it started to rain, someone passing by closed the hood so the engine would not get wet. Zimbardo concluded that the anonymity engendered within New York City may have contributed to the vandalism behavior there (1969:237–307).

Financial Problems

A third urban problem is money. Large cities all over the United States are running out of money and into severe financial troubles. When they raise taxes, people and businesses are driven out of the city. When they cut services, the poor and the aged suffer. When they cut the budget,

---

BYSTANDER APATHY: A LADY IN DISTRESS

An experiment by Latane and Rodin clearly illustrates the way in which people will accept more interpersonal responsibility if they are on their own. Three separate experimental situations were used. In the first, subject was shown into a waiting room by a young woman and requested to complete a questionnaire. The woman then left and went into an adjoining room. A few moments later, the subject heard the sound of furniture falling over, and the woman screaming that she was hurt and trapped beneath the furniture. The incident lasted for a full two minutes. Of the subjects who were waiting alone in the room, some 70 percent came to her aid. In the second experimental situation, the conditions were the same but subjects were shown into the room two at a time. In these circumstances, only 40 percent of the subjects came to her aid. In the third experimental situation, an associate of the experimenters was shown into the room with the subject, and when the incident took place, the associate displayed no concern or reaction whatever. Under these conditions, only 7 percent of the subjects responded and went to the aid of the woman.

Source: Bibbe Latane and Judith Rodin, "Bystander Apathy: A Lady in Distress." *Journal of Experimental Social Psychology* 5 (April 1969): 191–92.

Financially troubled big cities often cannot meet wage demands of their employees, leading to strikes by sanitation and other workers. The people in such cities suffer and must live among the litter and stench of uncollected garbage.

the city's economy is affected. Financial power elites today are investing more and more money in suburban communities rather than cities because that is where higher profits can be earned, no matter what the social or economic impact their actions may have on the cities. Investors and powerful financial interests find more lucrative opportunities in the South and Southwest than in cities of the East. Profits take precedence over people or their problems. A spokesman for the Brookings Institution revealed at the 1975 National League of Cities meeting that Gary, Indiana, and "nine other major cities had social and economic problems even more serious than those in New York." Bond-rating companies have reduced the "ratings" on bonds that cities sell to raise money. The lower rating, in turn, increases the amount of interest cities must pay to banks to get money ("Bond Rating," January 28, 1976:3).

These financial problems of the cities make it more difficult for them to handle social problems. Homes are not built. Programs and services for the aged are cut. Neighborhoods are not rehabilitated; garbage is not collected as often; pollution of water and air continue. Without enough money, the city runs down and is left to deteriorate. As the mayor of Benton Harbor, Michigan, put it: "We're running short and running down" (Forestell, 1976:13).

Transportation and Traffic

The chief culprit of the problem of urban transportation and traffic is the automobile. As autos continue to multiply, they make the problem still worse. At present there are over 110 million cars on the road (plus trucks, buses, etc.). In 1970, 26 percent of city households and 45 percent of suburban families owned two or more cars (Gist and Fava, 1974:131). At present over 85 percent of all commuters use cars, while only 10 percent use buses and four percent use rail and rapid-transit systems. Each day, almost 700,000 vehicles clog New York City's "narrow downtown business center," and 200,000 crawl through Washington, D.C.—most having only one occupant. The story is the same in other cities (Anderson, December 28, 1975:10).

Highway Destruction of Neighborhoods

To convey cars to and from center cities, huge expressways have cut wide paths through the hearts of urban neighborhoods, destroying homes, displacing people, polluting the air with soot and noise, degrading and downgrading the city. Even *proposing* to build a highway through a neighborhood seems to lead to deterioration of housing and the landlords' refusal to fix their buildings (Koch, February 1, 1976:B-1).

Businessmen thought highways would restore downtown shopping areas and raise property values. Mayors thought they would reduce traffic congestion, curb the flight out of the city, and provide some construction jobs in the city. In most cases the highways were paid for primarily (90 percent) by federal funds. It was a good deal for the city—or so we thought.

Now it is obvious that in cities from Boston to San Diego, expressways have destroyed old neighborhoods, reduced available housing, and reduced tax revenue as displaced persons moved out of the city. Instead of drawing people downtown to shop, the expressway has made it easier for city residents to drive out to suburban shopping centers, with their ample parking and lack of congestion. Just as in early cities—when development, people, and jobs followed the trolley lines and elevated trains from the city—today the expressway and federal highways are the major lines of exodus from the city. Because of these factors, more people are opposing the building of new highways through cities, and some political leaders are touting the value of public rapid transit instead of highways and autos.

As center cities continue to lose people and suburban communities continue to grow, urban problems of housing, depersonalization (bystander apathy), government financial problems, and transportation are likely to plague city and suburb alike.

CAUSES OF URBAN AND SUBURBAN PROBLEMS

The problems of urban life can be traced back to four major and overarching causes:

1. migration in and out of the city
2. technological change, especially in modes of transportation

3. fragmentation of government
4. structural forces working against people and for private commercial interests and profit.

Migration into and out of the City

The single most important cause of urban decay and decline appears to be the flight of middle-class homeowners and business to the suburbs. At the same time, entrance of poor rural blacks and the Spanish-speaking into the city (along with inflation) has depleted sources of revenue. Between 1970 and 1974 alone, about 7.7 million whites left central cities. By 1978 the population of most major cities was predominantly black and Spanish-speaking, often far poorer than the whites who left. However, the urban power structure, private and public, continued to be controlled by well-to-do whites.

Today most people live in "metropolitan urban areas," but not in cities. Just as 1920 was the tipping point in the move from farms to cities, so 1970 was the tipping point from city to suburbs, as shown in Figure 5-1.

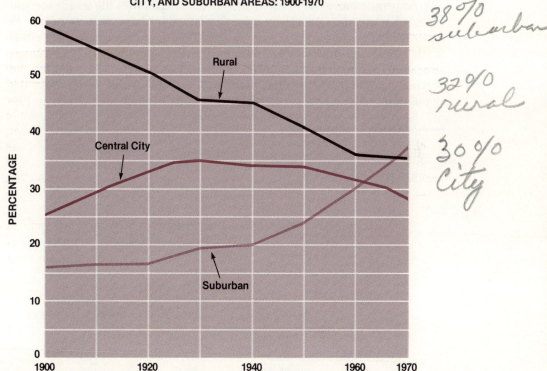

figure 5-1 PERCENTAGE OF U.S. POPULATION IN RURAL, CENTRAL CITY, AND SUBURBAN AREAS: 1900-1970

Note: 1960 boundaries are used throughout to permit comparability.

Source: David Birch, "From Suburb to Urban Place." *Annals,* AAPSS 422 (November 1975): 27. Reprinted by permission of the author and the publisher.

By 1974 over 150 million people lived in metropolitan areas. Suburbs accounted for over 75 million people, and are still growing. But central cities, especially the large ones, are losing people. Between 1970 and 1975 cities have lost about five million people to the suburbs (Lent, 1975:19).

During the last 15 years we have become a suburban nation. Most people (more than 38 percent) live in suburbs; 32 percent live in rural areas, while less than 30 percent live in our central cities ("New Look at America Today," 1977:64). Table 5-1 shows where people lived in 1976 as compared with 1960 and 1970. Just between early 1975 and early 1976, all cities had almost two million people (net) move out while suburbs gained over 1.5 million from those who moved in (Ibid.)

Most urban growth has occurred in the Southwest, Midwest, and Far West, while the sharpest declines have taken place in the East. In fact, a recent Census report suggests that some rural areas are growing faster than either cities or suburbs, the first time in the twentieth century that this has happened. Dorothy Whitson of the Census Bureau notes, "In Pennsylvania and pretty much all over the country you can see the same pattern. People are moving out, way out. They're leaving both the suburbs and the cities. We first noticed this in the 1970 census. That was just a shimmering of what is to come" (Baldwin, 1976:B-15).

As people move out of metropolitan areas and cities the incidence and prevalence of urban problems increase. Clearly this movement causes or exacerbates the financial plight of the city: whites flee the center cities while blacks still make up only about 5 percent of suburban populations (Shearer, 1975:8). Thus, fewer homeowners and taxpayers help to fund the services supplied by the city.* Industry and jobs leave faster than the population, leading to greater urban unemployment and poverty. The

---

*Some of the first people to leave the city are doctors. This hurts the quality of health care city people receive. Urbanologist Pierre de Vise uses "doctor-exodus" statistics as major measures of neighborhood decline (Monahan, 1973:7).

---

table 5-1 MOVEMENT OUT OF CENTER CITIES TO SUBURBS 1960, 1970, 1976

	Percentage of Total Population		
	CENTER CITIES	**SUBURBS**	**RURAL & ELSEWHERE**
1960	33.5%	33.2%	33.3%
1970	31.5	37.1	31.4
1976	28.9	38.9	32.2

Source: U.S. Census Bureau, "Population Profile of the U.S.: 1976." Current Population Reports, Series P-20, No. 307 (April 1977): 26.

CAUSES OF URBAN AND SUBURBAN PROBLEMS

figure 5-2   THE MAJOR MEGALOPOLISES IN THE UNITED STATES

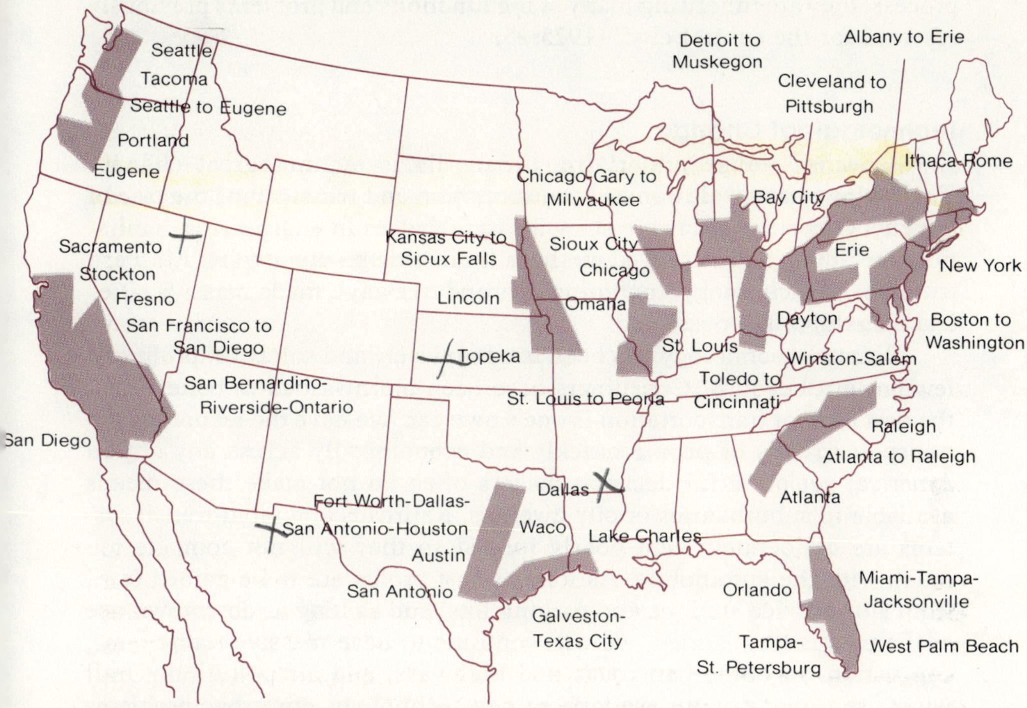

201

Seattle
Tacoma
Seattle to Eugene
Portland
Eugene
Sacramento
Stockton
Fresno
San Francisco to San Diego
San Bernardino-Riverside-Ontario
San Diego
Detroit to Muskegon
Cleveland to Pittsburgh
Chicago-Gary to Milwaukee
Kansas City to Sioux Falls
Sioux City
Chicago
Lincoln
Omaha
Topeka
St. Louis to Peoria
Bay City
Erie
Dayton
St. Louis
Toledo to Cincinnati
Albany to Erie
Ithaca-Rome
New York
Boston to Washington
Winston-Salem
Raleigh
Atlanta to Raleigh
Fort Worth-Dallas-San Antonio-Houston
Austin
San Antonio
Dallas
Waco
Lake Charles
Galveston-Texas City
Atlanta
Orlando
Tampa-St. Petersburg
Miami-Tampa-Jacksonville
West Palm Beach

Source: Department of Commerce, Bureau of the Census.

outmigration from the city aggravates problems of transportation and traffic, as millions who still work in the city must commute daily from their suburban or rural homes.

The prevalence of other urban problems, such as overcrowding and inadequate housing, are somewhat reduced as population thins out in the city. More and better housing opens up to city dwellers as millions seek a new home in suburbia, but thousands of homes are also abandoned as they deteriorate. Density and concentration of population have been cut in half in most large cities since 1900. At the same time, however, greater concentrations of population are taking place in the "megalopolis," a series of metropolitan areas made up of cities and intervening suburbs. The largest megalopolis is the great chain of cities and suburbs along the East Coast, stretching from Boston to Virginia. It is home for 40 million persons in an almost continuous urban tract, or sprawl. Other great megalopolises dot our Great Lakes, Pacific Ocean, and Gulf of Mexico areas.

Figure 5-2 shows our 13 major megalopolises. Some day soon, most Americans will live in one of these areas. Such geographical clustering of people merely transfers some of the social problems of the inner city to the neighboring suburbs. People are finding out that they cannot simply escape from urban problems. As David Birch observes, "Suburbs are gradually gaining full urban status as nodes in a series of networks. In the process, they are inheriting many of the functions and problems previously reserved for the central city" (1975:25).

Technological Change

A second cause underlying urban ills is technological change. Technology has revolutionized transportation and transformed the face of the city. Our cities today are spawned by advances in engineering, sanitation, medicine, and improved methods for raising plenty of food. All these triumphs of technology, including cars and freeways, made massive cities and megalopolises possible.

Yet such technology has been used unwisely and solely for profit of a few powerful groups. Consumers have been brainwashed to believe that the best form of transportation is one's own car. We have the technology to transport masses of people quickly and economically across any city in America; yet powerful decision makers often do not make these means available to suburbanites or city dwellers. Railroads and rapid-transit systems are deliberately kept poorly funded so they will not compete too much with the automobile. As long as vast profits are to be gained (e.g., from auto service stations and parking lots) and as long as downtown use of the cars is not banned, we will continue to have massive traffic jams, congestion on our urban roads and highways, and air pollution. Until wiser use is made of our available or new technology, our urban problems of transportation will persist.

The present urban problem of traffic and transportation stems from the 1956 law authorizing the financing and building of 41,000 miles of interstate highways, built over a 16-year period at an original cost of $41 billion. Passage of the law was greatly aided by a highway lobby, a nationwide group of tire, oil, and trucking firms, together with highway department officials and the American Automobile Association. A trust fund was set up from taxes on gas, tires, and other transportations items, and could be used only to build highways. Until about 1975, due to strong opposition from highway and road-construction groups, no money from this Highway Trust Fund was used for public transit systems. Today some of it is used for cities to buy transit cars and buses and maintain equipment.

In the early twentieth century, our urban public-transportation system was quite adequate. But with our growth in urban population and the coming of cars, public transit has gotten worse. In 1930 there were 15.2 billion riders of public transport, compared with 7.3 billion in 1970 (Palen, 1975:315). Most of the decline in mass transit is due to a rise in costs and indirect subsidization of cars by government building of highways rather than rail lines. This made building cars more profitable and popular than if roads had not been government-financed. Between 1956 and 1971, over

CAUSES OF URBAN AND SUBURBAN PROBLEMS

Overcrowding in a central city often leads to indifference to the plight of other human beings. Nevertheless, rapid transit may still be the best solution to traffic congestion in such areas.

Bradford Snell: AMERICAN GROUND TRANSPORT

Ground transport is dominated by a single, diversified firm to an extent possibly without parallel in the American economy. General Motors, the world's largest producer of cars and trucks, has also achieved monopoly control of buses and locomotives which compete with motor vehicles for passengers and freight. Its dominance of the bus and locomotive industries, moreover, would seem to constitute a classic monopoly. Although GM technically accounts for 75 percent of current city-bus production, its only remaining competitor, the Flxible Company, relies on it for diesel propulsion systems, major engine components, technical assistance, and financing. In short, Flxible is more a distributor for GM than a viable competitor; virtually its sole function is the assembly of General Motors' bus parts for sale under the Flxible trade name. Likewise, in the production of intercity buses, its only remaining competitor, Motor Coach Industries, is wholly dependent upon GM for diesel propulsion systems and major mechanical components. In addition, General Motors accounts for 100 percent of passenger and 80 percent of freight locomotives manufactured in the United States. Such concentration in a single firm of control over three rival transportation-equipment industries all but precludes the existence of competitive conduct and performance.

Source: Jerome H. Skolnick and Elliott Currie, *Crisis in American Institutions*, 3rd ed. (Boston: Little, Brown, 1976): 304.

200 bus companies went out of business. By 1970, mass transit had 357 fewer companies, 25,500 fewer vehicles, and far fewer passengers than in 1950 (Tass, 1971).

Fragmentation of Government — are separated

Another cause of urban problems, especially financial, has been fragmentation of government. There are over 3,000 counties in the United States, along with millions of small municipalities and townships. In 1969, 228 metropolitan areas each had an average of 90 local governments (National Commission on Urban Problems, 1969:8). New York City and outlying areas are served by 1,400 governmental and administrative districts. The same is true in San Francisco, Chicago, and most large cities. In addition, thousands of independent "authorities" or "districts" exist to raise money or deal with a particular urban problem, from waste disposal to transportation. All are separate and autonomous governmental units.

Most cities and towns are creatures of state governments and are separate from the counties in which they exist. We might think that states would be concerned enough about cities to provide clear organizational laws and a flow of authority and money. In that way, states "might produce a well-woven governmental blanket rather than a torn and fragmented cloth" (Lugar, 1975:88). Yet outmoded and divided jurisdictions persist, along with "elaborate rhetoric and protective legislation."

As Melvin Webber notes: "We cannot hope to invent local treatments for conditions whose origins are not local in character, nor can we expect territorially defined governments to deal effectively with problems whose causes are unrelated to territory or geography" (1968:1093). Yet states do not allow cities much leeway in how they can raise taxes for vital services. No logical boundary of responsibility exists for rendering certain services. On the other hand, local governments rarely cooperate in dividing the labor to meet human needs.

In the last 15 years, a few small and middle-size cities have merged with their counties. Five recent combinations are Nashville-Davidson County, Tenn.; Jacksonville-Duval County, Fla.; Indianapolis-Marion County, Ind.; Columbus-Muskogee County, Ga.; and Lexington-Fayette County, Ky. Whether such consolidations will solve urban problems remains to be seen. Even within such arrangements there are fragmented special districts and authorities, as well as duplication of services and efforts. Such "boundary-tinkering" may not be as important as "economic resources and their distribution within the metropolis" (Lineberry, 1975:9).

Special-Interest Structural Forces

The fourth cause of urban problems is the special-interest structural forces that work against people but enhance private commercial interests and profit. C. Wright Mills, in his analysis of cities, pointed out that cities and metropolitan areas were not communities in any real sense, but "unplanned monstrosities" in which people are segregated into "limited milieux." This, accordingly, leads to a "blasé manner," accounting for the impersonal treatment of people. Inner-city residents are confined to their own rather narrow neighborhoods and are usually powerless to affect decisions that elites make on a city-wide basis. As Mills puts it:

> Men are not equal in power. The private in an army has no chance to view the whole structure of the army, much less to direct it. But the general does. His means of information, of vision, of decision are much greater. In like manner with the owner of a development tract, as against an individual householder. In short, are we not coming to see that the chaos of our cities is first of all part of an irresponsible economic and political system? (Horowitz, 1967:400–401)

Thus the city and its problems are the result of the deliberate (though partial) plans of those with the power and prestige to enhance private commercial interests and profit. The main social forces that consciously shape the city's structure and land use are private commercial interests, together with local government, which is "more or less beholden to them." Through both government urban-renewal programs and private development schemes, our major cities have experienced "the private expropriation and the profitable misuse of the very landscape on which the men, the women, the children of these cities are now trying to live." Mills concludes by observing about city governments that "often they seem most readily understandable as committees for a complex of real estate interests" (Ibid.).

The urban social problems of housing, depersonalization, finances, and transportation can be attributed to those structural forces built on pursuing the vested interests of business and the buck. When such powerful elites can make more money in the suburbs, they abandon the city—no matter how many people are hurt in the process.

PROPOSED SOLUTIONS TO URBAN AND SUBURBAN PROBLEMS

In 1959 C. Wright Mills pointed out that something had to be done with our cities if we were ever going to remedy its problems. He wrote:

> Consider the metropolis—the horrible, beautiful, ugly, magnificent sprawl of the great city. What should be done with this wonderful monstrosity? Break it all up into scattered units, combining residence and work? Refurbish it as it stands? Or, **after evacuation, dynamite it,** and build new cities according to new plans in new places? (1959:9–10)

Yet many social scientists today argue that we have made a commitment to city life and simply cannot destroy or abandon our cities. For better or worse cities have been and remain the center of our civilization. But can the city be salvaged or saved? We are just starting to understand what is needed to make a city more habitable and humane.

Preserving Green Space

Conservative urban planners, for example, have begun to appreciate the function of green space in the city, and greater efforts are now being made to create, preserve, and more effectively use open space in the city. Cities such as New York and Philadelphia have experimented with converting some city streets into malls, for bicycles and buses only—or even solely for pedestrians. Spokane, continuing a development started for Expo '74, has built a system of second-story walkways so that people can walk among six city blocks without ever going outside. Minneapolis has a similar "skywalk" as well as a pedestrian mall ("Downtown Is Looking Up," July 5, 1976:54). These and similar schemes are the conservative and power structure's attempts to solve our urban problems.

Much more is needed, however, to really remedy our urban ills. The crucial urban problem that desperately needs solution is housing.

Housing Allowances

Happily, a liberal national housing policy to help the cities is beginning to take shape at last. The major shift is from direct subsidies to builders for constructing new housing (for the poor or nonpoor), to giving more money directly to families to find their own housing. If this new policy succeeds, fewer urban poor will live in government-owned housing. This proposed policy gives people a better choice of where to live, and it costs "about 40 percent of what it takes to subsidize a new public housing unit each year" (Peabody, March 9, 1974:22). The originators of "housing allowances" admit, however, that these cannot be used when housing is scarce. Vacancy rates should be five to six percent before the system can work effectively. Otherwise, government subsidies for new-housing construction will be needed.

Some liberal advocates of this program see it as *the* answer to problems of housing for low- and moderate-income families. Others feel it will work well in some cities but fail in others, depending upon the price and supply of housing in each city. Still others say it will "keep low-income families from clustering, and . . . will give families genuinely free choice in housing" (Neuman, May 1973:8). Another contention is that housing allowances will only drive up the cost of housing for everyone without improving the quality of housing for urban low-income families. The federal government might even end up subsidizing slum landlords.

Public-housing projects for the poor have traditionally been clustered together in center cities, often segregating the poor and minorities from the rest of society. Recent court decisions and HUD policies hope to open suburban communities to housing for the poor.

HUD Programs and Policies

Other programs administered by the Department of Housing and Urban Development (HUD) offer some liberals hope of solving the cities' housing problems. A rent-subsidies program, for which 27 million families could possibly qualify, would replace almost all other housing subsidies for low- and moderate-income families in the city. Called Section 8 "Lower-Income Housing Assistance" (under the Federal Housing and Community Development Act of 1974), the program gives rent subsidies to persons with annual incomes (by family size) not exceeding 80 percent of their area's median income. Families pay anywhere from 15 to 25 percent of their gross income toward the rent, and the government makes up the difference (up to a certain price). This program encourages landlords to mix subsidized and unsubsidized tenants, so that middle- and lower-income people would be living in the same building and neighborhood. During 1976 HUD had enough money to help 400,000 families, but it did not aid nearly that number. Most of the help had gone to the elderly.

To make possible these HUD programs just mentioned, Congress passed a $4 billion bill for spending in 1977 on housing ("Congress Reinvents...," August 19, 1976:16). Most of this money will be spent to help remedy the housing problem in cities and urban areas.

Other HUD programs enable families in high-crime areas to purchase homeowner's insurance at reasonable rates. This helps to overcome some of the problem of red-lining in center cities. HUD is also encouraging "urban homesteading" in 23 cities, by making 1,000 government-owned homes available for use by working- and middle-class families.

Urban Homesteading and Renewal

Under urban homesteading, these families buy abandoned homes from the city at a very small cost (usually $1) and promise to repair them and live there for at least five years. Homesteaders often receive financial aid to bring the houses up to standard condition within two years. Cities such as Philadelphia, Baltimore, and St. Louis have adopted the homesteading program or similar ones to rehabilitate abandoned homes. In a little over a year, more than 400 abandoned homes were rehabilitated in Philadelphia ("Philadelphia's Urban Homesteading Program," September 23, 1975, and Gillespie, February 25, 1976:5). Although the program is not as extensive as the need, it is an attempt by cities to lure white middle-class people back into the city. In those cities that have tried it, the homesteading program seems to be working.

Another proposed solution by a coalition of liberals and conservatives has been urban renewal and redevelopment. In some respects, urban renewal caused more problems than it solved. Established under the Housing Act of 1949, urban "redevelopment" was supposed to provide "a decent home and a suitable living environment for every American family." In fact, it destroyed more homes in the central city than it built or planned.

Urban-renewal projects used federal money to buy, clear, and improve land in the central city, after which the ownership of the land reverted to the private sector. The private developer then agreed to build and use the land in accordance with a government-approved development plan. Urban-renewal programs were funded by HUD grants on a project-by-project basis, and administered through a local redevelopment agency.

In 1974 all this was changed by passage of the Federal Housing and Community Development Act. Now, after an application for funds is approved by HUD, the city itself receives block grants that can be used for a variety of purposes throughout the city (rather than within a designated project area). A total of $8.4 billion was available under this program between 1975 and 1977. Such community-development activities include acquisition of property, construction of public works, enforcement of housing codes, demolition or rehabilitation of buildings, relocation payments to persons displaced by demolition, and comprehensive planning ("New Act to Aid...," December 1974:1). The Act requires the involvement of citizens in determining needs and in setting goals for community-development planning efforts. The conservative and liberal proponents of Community Development aid argue that the program cuts federal bureaucratic red tape and that local communities have more of a say in how the money should be spent.

Private Efforts to Reconstruct the Cities

Encouraged by programs such as federal revenue sharing and the Community Development Act of 1974, large private corporations and developers have started to reconstruct the downtown areas of many cities. They feel a profit can be created by using tax dollars to refurbish the city. This has been done through construction of new high-rise buildings and rehabilitation ("recycling") of buildings. There is hardly a major city in the United States whose downtown is not getting a facelifting ("Downtown Is Looking Up," 1976:54–62).

An Urban Land Institute survey shows that recycling of old buildings and houses, based largely on a combination of private-public funding, is going on in almost half of the 260 American cities with more than 50,000 population ("Recycling Slums . . .," April 5, 1976:60). Even the Haight-Ashbury section of San Francisco (once a haven for the "hippie" subculture during the late 1960s) is returning to middle-class status through renovation. All this new construction activity and renovation suggests a possible rebirth and revitalization of our cities for big business. As one article put it: "The American City, far from being down and out, is clearly growing up (and up)" ("Downtown Is Looking Up," 1976:54).

Can buildings— new or recycled—help to restore the social health of the city and solve its social problems? If great architects and grandiose buildings could help the housing, crowding, financial, and transportation problems of the cities, these would all have been solved by now. But obviously more is needed.

New Towns

Another approach to urban problems (especially overcrowding) is to decentralize population in "new towns" outside the city limits, while making the towns economically dependent on the central city. Such well-known new towns as Columbia, Maryland; Reston, Virginia; and Jonathan, Minnesota, are having their own financial and social problems and are hardly a panacea for urban ills. In 1975, some 15 new towns, with HUD loan guarantees for private developers of $441 million, were cut off from further federal aid and as a result the developers are suffering financially (Shostak, 1975:2). These totally planned communities offer a model for how suburban communities might be built and operated, but offer little hope for revitalizing massive urban centers. In view of recent court decisions involving zoning (such as the Mt. Laurel, New Jersey, case) that would encourage low-income housing in suburbs, together with rent supplements and allowances for the poor to find their own housing, the new-

New towns or large planned communities in rural or suburban areas are sometimes viewed as a solution to urban problems. In many cases, however, they develop financial problems of their own.

town concept might eventually be able to absorb a few former city residents. For the most part, however, higher housing costs and limited job opportunities in new towns restrict most central-city residents from settling there.

Proposed Solutions for Finances and Fragmentation

Other proposals by liberals (and some conservatives) include:

1. a revised tax structure to draw in tax revenues from suburbanites who work in the city, or use city roads or other services, and continuation of federal revenue-sharing funds to major cities
2. metropolitanization—combining the city with the surrounding county and suburban communities as one governmental unit and taxing body, thus creating a regional approach to urban problems of housing, density, finances, and transportation
3. a structural decentralization of city government to give neighborhoods more power; direct funneling of federal and state monies to individual neighborhoods instead of through city hall (McVeigh, November 1973:29–31).

Let us briefly discuss each of these three proposals.

Revised Tax Structure

Income at the city level comes mainly from property and sales taxes. About 72 cents out of every dollar that cities and states raise come from these two sources ("The Only Thing . . .," July, 1976:28). Yet many city services are provided to persons who do not live there. Consequently, we need a better and more "progressive" tax system through which cities can raise money. ("Progressive" taxes increase as a person's income increases, as opposed to a "regressive" tax, which remains the same regardless of income.)

One such tax we could use is a city wage tax based on the amount of money *anyone* earns in the city. This forces suburbanites who earn their living in the city to contribute something to maintaining the city. Another recent method of raising tax revenue is to insist that suburbanites who are employed by the city government move to the city. Chicago and other major cities, backed by a favorable court decision, have now enforced the rule that city government workers must live in the city or lose their jobs.

The American Federation of State, County, and Municipal Employees, which has a vested interest in keeping city and county workers employed, has proposed changes in the tax and federal system that would help cities:

1. Have the federal government pay for all health, welfare, and other human-service programs. Welfare is a big cost for some cities.
2. Close tax loopholes in our federal tax system so that more money would be available for cities.
3. Change federal spending policies and priorities so that more money goes to building schools than to building bombers
4. Make sales taxes fairer by allowing exemptions for food, clothing, and medicine and by adopting "progressive" sales taxes, as done in Hawaii, New Mexico, and Vermont (Ibid.).

Cities in the United States, particularly in the Northeast, are in serious financial straits. To try to remedy this situation, Congress in 1972 passed a federal revenue-sharing program. For a five-year period, this program returned $30 billion of federal tax money to states, counties, and local governments, although much of this in the past had been sent in direct federal grants, some of which were eliminated in 1972. During the five years between 1972 and 1976, many cities and counties were rescued from crucial money problems. The proposal now is to continue such funding to major cities that need it the most, especially those losing population.

Metropolitanization

Another liberal solution offered for all the problems mentioned, as well as for environmental pollution, is to metropolitanize; that is, extend the city's taxing and servicing jurisdiction to match the boundaries of the metropolitan area itself. Early in their history, such cities as San Francisco, Denver, Philadelphia, and New York consolidated with their counties to achieve this match. Recently, Nashville, Baton Rouge, Jacksonville, Miami and its suburbs, Indianapolis, and other cities have done so. At the same time, voters in Cleveland, St. Louis, Richmond, and elsewhere have turned down this approach.

Other cities have used various social structures and forms to deal realistically with regional problems. These have usually taken the form of a regional planning authority, so-called Councils of Governments (COGs), and other boards (Scott, November 1975:43). There is a plan now on the back burner in Congress to give regional planning boards authority over zoning and selection of sites in a region for multi-unit housing. Recent court decisions on "restrictive zoning" against housing for the poor in suburban areas, as well as busing decisions involving area-wide school districts, are moves in this direction.

Structural Decentralization

The third proposal, by innovative planners and some radicals, envisions a structural decentralization of city government itself. This could entail creation of neighborhood-action groups consisting of residents and city officials. These groups could act as "community cabinets" to identify and act upon neighborhood needs. Experiments by way of setting up "little city halls" have been conducted in various neighborhoods of Atlanta and Boston. Similarly, pioneer community organizations like the one in East Columbus, Ohio, have called on the federal government for money to be channeled directly to them, bypassing city hall and the state house. These community organizations would direct the affairs of the neighborhood without reference to the rest of the city. The argument for this kind of decentralized structure within the city is that "the same system that allows 20,000 people in a suburb substantial control over their civic destiny—allows them to create their own exclusive environment...—denies 20,000 people in an urban neighborhood any effective role in shaping the institutions that shape their lives" (Canty, 1969:156).

Urbanologist Milton Kotler, Director of the Institute for Neighborhood Studies and author of *Neighborhood Government*, states that "we are seeing across the country a formalization of citizen participation, at the neighborhood levels by ordinances." He feels that city problems cannot be solved entirely by professionals, better management, or more money. Municipal governments also cannot solve all our social problems, nor can they afford to pay for all social services. The idea behind decentralized neighborhood government is to transfer to the neighborhoods functions that are run inefficiently on a city-wide basis. Washington, D.C.'s 37 neighborhood commissions—with a total of 330 commissioners—review and approve all city bills. The zoning board must also explain its decisions to the satisfaction of the commissioners ("Decentralized Government . . .," January 29, 1976:21). If this proposal were seriously adopted in all our cities, it might revolutionize city government.

Transportation and Traffic

Solutions to the problems of transportation and traffic congestion are social, technological, and financial. The major emphasis of most solutions is to find alternatives to the use of autos in downtown areas. One of the best alternatives seems to be rapid transit—express trains, subways, and buses. Under the 1974 Mass Transportation Assistance Act, $11.3 billion is provided until 1980 to support urban mass-transit systems. Money may be used for new equipment (train cars) or for operation and maintenance of existing equipment in urban areas. Of this sum, one-third (nearly $4 billion) will be distributed to cities based equally on total population and on population density. So the larger the city and the more densely populated, the more money it will get.

In addition to the Act for mass transportation, the 1973 Federal-Aid Highway Act (amended in 1976) for the first time permits use of money for mass-transit projects in cities. Before 1973, money could be used only for highways. Now, too, highway funds may be used for bicycle pathways or lanes on non-Interstate highway projects (LVTS Annual Report, 1974:3).

Despite opposition over the years from the highway and road-construction lobby, and rural Congressmen, there is growing social pressure from liberal urban Congressmen to develop, with government help,

The Bay Area Rapid Transit (BART) system, completed in the early 1970s, was the first major rapid-transit system built in the United States since 1907. Washington, D.C. opened a new rapid-transit system in 1977.

rapid-transportation systems in our major cities. A single rapid-transit track can carry 60,000 persons an hour—the equivalent of 20 expressway lanes (Palen, 1975:314). San Francisco's Bay Area Rapid Transit (BART) system can carry up to 200,000 riders a day. Although BART is experiencing equipment and financial problems, the system has the potential for eliminating traffic congestion ("New Cures...," April 1976:16). Even experimental flywheels added to transit cars in New York City could reduce electric operating costs by 20 percent ("Mass Transit...," February 16, 1976:32).

Some liberal critics of present rapid-transit systems argue that if the cities' transportation problems are ever to be solved, we must have a free-fare system whose costs are paid for by the government, not the riders. The theory here is that people will be willing to abandon their autos if the economic advantages of riding public transit exceed the comfort and convenience of their present method of commuting.

Of course car pools, special lanes for cars with three or more passengers, and bridge-toll discounts have been used in some areas to make more efficient use of the automobile itself. One answer to the problem of too many cars downtown is a balanced mix of programs that recognize the need for some automobile traffic in the central city.

Radical Proposals

Radical proponents, adhering to concepts of C. Wright Mills, argue that the problems of the cities can never be solved until the profit motive behind city development and urban planning is modified. Use of the land to benefit most people should be the criterion for reshaping the city. Use of technology that would benefit the people, not a few powerful interest groups, should form the basis of an urban transportation system.

Changes are needed in the power structure of our federal and state legislatures that would directly benefit our cities, rather than the rural and suburban interests. Much legislation intended to benefit cities is written by rural and affluent suburban representatives so as to funnel money away from major cities and into other areas. With a new power structure controlling our legislatures, the needs of the cities would be better met.

In C. Wright Mills's essay "The Big City," he recommends that we "transcend local milieux in order to consider publicly, imaginatively, planfully the city as a structure: to see it, in brief, as a public issue and to see ourselves as a public... We must realize, in a word, that we *need* not drift blindly, that we can take matters into our own hands" (Horowitz, 1967:398). When Mills speaks of "we," he is talking about city dwellers. They must become politically active to change the existing economic and social system. Specifically, he advocates that urbanites "organize and agitate against the sources of decision and lack of decision that fail to consider properly the human landscape in which we must live" (1967:400). Mills calls for a movement to hold the political and economic elites responsible for what they have done. In conclusion, Mills also advocates a discussion of the quality and meaning of human life itself, particularly in cities. The environmental movement in some respects has begun to do this. The hope is that environmental concerns will encompass the urban problems discussed. These solutions taken together should help to improve the quality of our cities and to reduce and control the problems that the urban social structure produces.

THE FUTURE OF OUR CITIES AND SUBURBS

Do our cities have a future? Some say "No"; most say "Yes." The positive or optimistic school of thought sees our cities as a part of a larger metropolitan area, which in the future will be planned and used on a coordinated basis. Regional attention to social problems and possibilities will be the most significant trend.

The costs of maintaining suburban governments often encourage formal and informal agreements with other nearby suburbs and with cities in the area. They may share a health inspector, or a county and city may jointly maintain a street on a common boundary. These unpublicized, ad hoc arrangements have already provided a major form of metropolitan governmental coordination "without requiring structural reform; clearly they will continue to do so in the foreseeable future" (Scott, 1975:42).

In the late 1960s the Congress began providing grants for areawide and regional planning. Then the federal government instituted the so-called A-95 process, which requires a regional planning agency to review and comment upon local applications for most federal grants. The Housing and Community Development Act of 1974 required ongoing, areawide comprehensive planning with citizen participation for proposals to meet housing needs and for other land use (Ibid.).

Regionalization will become inevitable, for the population in metropolitan areas by the year 2000 will number between 225 and 273 million ("Population and the American Future," 1972:36). Much of this metropolitan growth will be in areas of one million or more persons living in a megalopolis. By the year 2000 it is estimated that over 80 percent of the American people will be living in 25 large urban megalopolises. When this happens, government function will follow its form.

A Balance between Urban and Rural Areas

Dr. Peter Goldmark has a vision of a new rural society for the future. He anticipates the future outmigration of 70 million city dwellers to the countryside by the year 2000, a shift that would balance the rural and urban population. Such a shift would lay to rest one myth about the city's future, namely that masses of people will be "piled on top of one another." City density has been decreasing since 1900, and density of population and overcrowding in the central cities will actually become less severe than it is today (Gist and Fava, 1974:94–95).

To achieve this future society, Goldmark is conducting a $400,000 experiment (with HUD funds) to draw people into a 10-town rural area of 65,000 persons in northeastern Connecticut, known as the Windham region (about 25 miles from Hartford). Dr. Goldmark feels that future use of telecommunications will increase rural labor opportunities and improve education, job training, and medical and health services so that the countryside will be "an attractive place to live and work" ("Inventor-Physicist Tries to Lure 70 Million . . .," December 26, 1974:19). Dr. Goldmark aims not at creating "new towns" or rural communities but at building gradually on some 5,000 existing towns with populations of 5,000 to 100,000. Ideally, they would be at least 25 or 30 miles from cities of one million or more and at least 10 miles from cities of 250,000 to 500,000. The future movement from city to small towns and rural communities has already begun and public-opinion polls consistently show that 60 to 70 percent of those living in cities would prefer to work and live in rural areas or small towns.

The Continuing Housing Problem

For the near future the housing problem will persist and may get worse. The National Housing Conference (NHC) sees the need, by 1980, for 2.6 million new homes a year, with 1.2 million of them being government-assisted units. Leon Weiner, President of NHC, sees better coordination between housing and national economic policies, as well as increased regular funding of government-assisted housing ("Housing Leaders Urge . . .," April 1976:36). Something will also have to be done to bring the average new home into the price range of most Americans. If direct government funding is not used, compact, smaller homes with fewer frills will probably enter the market to make it possible for families to buy a home. Quite clearly, mobile homes will account for a larger share of the private home market.

New Towns and Cities of the Future

The future of new towns is dim unless they receive funds from public or private sources. In addition, these towns must effectively demonstrate that they offer more than other planned suburban communities or "planned residential developments." Unless they can do so (and at a reasonable cost for all involved), they will not survive.

The widely known architect Paolo Soleri has some unique ideas for the city of the future. Instead of contructing a city that sprawls over 200 square miles, he would confine cities to a few square miles but make the buildings 300 stories high. His high-density vertical cities are based on what he calls "arcology"—architecture plus ecology. Everything—

THE FUTURE OF OUR CITIES AND SUBURBS

Credit: Peter Vandermark/Stock, Boston.

Any city of the future will include enclosed areas for all activities from factories to schools. Shopping malls, such as the one shown here, are contemporary models of certain future cities, which, like Paolo Soleri's hexahedron city, will be completely enclosed.

factories, stores, apartments, schools, cultural centers—would be jammed into such a high-rise city. His hexahedron city would hold 170,000 people, have a density of 1,200 people per acre, and be 3,600 feet high ("Paolo Soleri's Visionary Cities," June 1970:26). He is now building a futuristic city in Arcosanti, Arizona, 70 miles north of Phoenix. Planned as a small city of 3,000, it will be only 25 stories high and could be completed toward the end of the century ("City of the Future," March/April 1976:5).

Of course an adequate system of transportation will be needed to link small cities together and to connect them to the larger cities. Federal Highway Administrator Norbert Tieman predicts what urban transportation will look like in the year 2000:

1. Cars, in some form, will still be the major form of transportation, but they will be much more energy efficient and come in more varieties. They will range from small "mopeds" to multipassenger vans with diesel or rotary engines, or accelerated by a flywheel under the car. Electric or solar power cars, with speeds below 30 miles an hour, will be used in cities. High-speed vehicles will race between cities linked by interstate highways.
2. Trucks will operate only in designated lanes, and "trains" of three to 12 semitrailer units will be pulled by a single truck.
3. Carpooling will be an established way of life. During rush

hours in cities, more than 75 percent of private vehicles will carry more than one person.
4. Exclusive bus lanes will be in use in all large cities, and there will be several automobile-restricted zones.
5. Buses will continue to play a major role in urban mass transit. Few *new* subways will be built, unless there are major breakthroughs that greatly reduce the required capital investment. Increased use will be made of "light" fixed-rail cars (a version of the old trolley car) ("Highway and Transit Predictions . . .," June 1976:96).
6. Monorail and tube trains (which operate in a vacuum) will be capable of high speeds, but their use will be rather limited. Hydrofoil boats that skim the water at high speeds are an alternative to highways for commuter traffic. The use of flying belts that jet people short distances across a city would probably be the most efficient mode of transportation in the future. But vested money interests in cars and highways would not permit widespread use, since it would cut into their profits from gasoline, cars, and roads (Leinwand, 1969:141–48).

On balance, urbanologists see signs of hope for the future of the cities. Cities not in the Northeast, such as Dallas, Houston, Denver, and Indianapolis, are in good financial health. These cities will experience a modest flow of upper- and middle-income people and business back into the city. Yet the most knowledgeable urban sociologists see no quick comeback for the old big cities, especially in the Northeast. For example, Professor George Sternlieb, Director of the Center for Urban Policy Research at Rutgers University, is pessimistic about the future of the cities. He states: "The decline has gone too far. Jobs, housing, even restaurants and cultural institutions increasingly are in the suburbs. Our society has decided it's cheaper to turn our old cities over to the poor and buy them off with welfare" ("Cities in Peril," 1976:175). Thus, for most cities the near future is bleak. Most sociologists see no sweeping or spectacular attempts to solve our urban problems. Rather they see at best a "slow and painful recovery," to make cities a better place in which to work and live.

SUMMARY

The city is the focus of numerous social problems, as well as being a social problem itself. An antiurban bias pervades America, even in definitions of the city.

Our cities face four major problems (among others) that affect millions of people in their daily lives: housing, overcrowding and depersonalization, lack of money, transportation and traffic.

Three major causes of urban problems stem from rapid migration of people into and especially out of the city, technological change in modes of transportation that make urban sprawl and suburban living possible, and fragmentation of government services and revenue sources. Decisions by power elites and special interest groups to abandon the city for more profitable opportunities in suburbia are also a cause.

Housing allowances, urban homesteading, new HUD programs, and outlawing both discriminatory housing patterns in the suburbs and "redlining" in central cities have been tried or proposed as answers to our urban housing problem. Private developers and recycling old buildings to attract business and residents back into the city, as well as New Towns, have been used to try to save the cities. Other proposed solutions to our urban ills include:

> a tax structure to draw in revenues from suburbanites who work in cities or use city services and better allocation of federal funds to cities that need help the most
>
> metropolitanization—combining the city with surrounding communities
>
> decentralization of city government and power to local neighborhoods
>
> improved systems of mass transportation, car pools, park-ride plans, and staggered working hours to alleviate traffic
>
> revising the power structure in our state and federal legislatures to benefit the cities and encouraging citizen participation in urban politics, as suggested by C. Wright Mills.

In the future, cities will be more regionalized and rural development encouraged as mass outmigration from central cities continues. Improved transportation is also inevitable. The hope is that a slow step-by-step rehabilitation of cities will eventually make cities a better place in which to live and work than at present.

CAREER OPPORTUNITIES

Urban Planners.

Students with a good grounding in sociology, social groups, and community organization may find opportunities in the field of urban planning. Working part-time during the summer for your town's planning agency or redevelopment authority might give you an edge over others in getting an entry-level job in the planning field. Courses in urban sociology, demography (population), and community development or organization are good preparations. Future opportunities should expand as more federal funds come into our cities. For further information write to: American Institute of Planners, 917 15th Street, N. W., Washington, D.C. 20005.

Marketing-Research Workers.

This is a field for students with a good background in sociological research methods and interviewing, as well as marketing research. Researchers interview the public about its opinions and consumer preferences. Analysis of such data helps companies make decisions on where to locate a store or business—in the city, suburbs, or rural areas. For further information write to: American Marketing Association, 230 N. Michigan Ave., Chicago, Ill. 60601.

City Managers and Assistants.

Duties vary by size of city, but generally the job requires administering organizations and coordinating day-to-day operations of the city. A background in sociology is useful. City managers study current problems, including financial and budget matters, and many cities employ assistants to aid managers. Under the manager's direction, they administer programs, prepare reports, receive visitors, answer letters, and help to keep the city running smoothly. They compile operating statistics or review and analyze work procedures. A good knowledge of social organization and bureaucracy is an asset for these jobs. For further information write to: American Society for Public Administration, 1225 Connecticut Ave., N. W., Washington, D.C. 20036.

REFERENCES

"America's Housing Needs: 1970–1980." Joint Center for Urban Studies of Harvard University and Massachusetts Institute of Technology, 1973.

Anderson, Jack
    1975 "Can We Conquer Parking Space?" Parade Magazine (December 28):10.

Baldwin, Tom
    1976 "Population Spurts in Rural Counties." Allentown Sunday Call-Chronicle (January 4):B-15.

Banfield, Edward
    1968 The Unheavenly City: The Nature and Future of Our Urban Crisis. Boston: Little, Brown.
    1974 The Unheavenly City Revisited. Boston: Little, Brown.

"Banks and State Near Plan to Save Housing Agency." Allentown Morning Call (January 7): 3, 1976.

"Being Bold with the Old." Time 108, 1 (July 5): 61, 1976.

"Billions for Housing: Something for All." U.S. News & World Report 80, 18 (May 3): 70–71, 1976.

Birch, David
    1975 "From Suburb to Urban Place." The Annals of the American Academy of Political and Social Science 422 (November): 25–35.

"Bond Rating Dips for Philadelphia." Allentown Morning Call (January 28): 3, 1976.

Bryan, Jack
    1972 "Philadelphia Is Turning Old Town into New Town." Journal of Housing 29, 5 (June), reprint.

Calhoun, John B.
   1962   "Population Density and Social Pathology." Scientific American 206, 2 (February): 139–48.

Canty, Donald
   1969   A Single Society. New York: Praeger.

"Cars and Cities on a Collision Course." Fortune (February): 125, 1970.

Carter, Curtis
   1976   "Habitat: A Festive Air, Serious Business." Science 193, 4252 (August 6): 475, 512.

Chudacoff, Howard P.
   1975   The Evolution of American Urban Society. Englewood Cliffs, N.J.: Prentice-Hall.

"Cities Are Becoming Dumping Grounds for Poor People." U.S. News & World Report 80, 14 (April 5): 54–56, 1976.

"Cities in Peril." Pp. 175–76 in Peter Wickman, ed. Readings in Social Problems 76/77: Annual Editions. Guilford, Conn.: Dushkin, 1976.

"City of the Future." NRTA Journal 27, 130 (March/April): 5, 1976.

Cole, Richard
   1975   "Revenue Sharing: Citizen Participation and Social Service Aspects." Annals AAPSS 419 (May): 63–74.

"Congress Reinvents the Housing Subsidy." Business Week 2444 (August 9): 16, 1976.

Conlon, Michael
   1976   "Rising Costs Plague Capital Subway." Allentown Sunday Call-Chronicle (March 14): 19.

Cook, Joe
   1976   "Kicking the HABITAT Habit, or Rainy Days at Jericho Beach." Intercom 4, 7 (July) 1, 6. Washington, D.C.: Population Reference Bureau.

"'Cracking' Suburbs for Blacks." U.S. New & World Report 80, 18 (May 3): 69, 1976.

Davis, Allen, and Mark Haller, eds.
   1973   The Peoples of Philadelphia: A History of Ethnic Groups and Lower Class Life, 1790–1940. Philadelphia: Temple University Press

"Decentralized Government Described for City Group." Allentown Morning Call (January 29): 21, 1976.

"Detroit's Downtown Gets a Tonic." Business Week 2444 (August 9): 52, 1976.

Doughton, Morgan
   1976   People Power: An Alternative to 1984. Bethlehem, Pa.: Media America, Inc.

"Downtown Is Looking Up." Time 108, 1 (July 5): 54–62, 1976.

Farrell, William E.
   1976   "'Redlining' Gains U.S. Legal Status." New York Times (January 26): 40.

Fava, Sylvia
   1975   "Beyond Suburbia." The Annals AAPSS 422 (November): 10–24.

Ferdinand, Theodore
 1967 "Criminal Patterns of Boston Since 1849." American Journal of Sociology 73 (July): 84–90.

Ford, Barbara
 1975 "New Evidence on Crowding." Science Digest 78, 3 (September): 28–36.

Forestell, Bill
 1976 "City Cutbacks Deepen as They Prepare to Go It Alone." The American City & County 91,1 (January): 13.

Fuerst, J. S.
 1974 "Class, Family and Housing." Society 12, 1 (November/December): 48–53.

Gans, Herbert J.
 1962 The Urban Villagers. New York: Free Press.
 1972 "Urbanism and Suburbanism as Ways of Life: A Reevaluation of Definitions." Pp. 31–50 in John Kramer, ed. North American Suburbs. Berkeley: Glendessary Press.

Gillespie, John T.
 1976 "City Selling Abandoned Houses for $1." Philadelphia Evening Bulletin (February 25): 5.

Gist, Noel P. and Sylvia F. Fava
 1974 Urban Society. 6th ed. New York: Crowell.

Grimes, John A.
 1974 "How to Build a Housing Scandal." The American Federationist (July): 20–24.

Gutman, Robert and David Popenoe, eds.
 1970 Neighborhood, City and Metropolis: An Integrated Reader in Urban Sociology. New York: Random House.

"Hartford's Suburban Crunch." Business Week 2431 (May 10): 75, 1976.

"Highway and Transit Predictions for 2001." The American City & County 91, 6 (June): 96, 1976.

Hill, Gladwin
 1976 "U.N. Meeting Urges Curb on Private Land Holding." New York Times (June 12): 1, 5.
 1976 "U.N. Opening a Parley on Communities Ills." New York Times (May 31): 3.

"Hitting at Redlining." Business Week 2430 (May 3): 107, 1976.

Holland, John
 1974 "Contrasting Types of Group Relationships." Pp. 197–201 in Edgar A. Schuler et al. Readings in Sociology. 5th ed. New York: Crowell.

Horowitz, Irving Louis, ed.
 1967 Power, Politics and People: The Collected Essays of C. Wright Mills. New York: Oxford University Press.

"Housing Leaders Urge Crash Program to Speed Up New Home Construction." The American City & County 91, 4 (April): 36, 1976.

"In America's Big Cities: The Clampdown Is On." U.S. News & World Report 79, 17 (October 27): 15–16, 1975.

"Inventor-Physicist Tries to Lure 70 Million City Folk to Rural Life." Philadelphia Evening Bulletin (December 26): 19, 1974.

Jordan, Vernon
    1976 "Courts Desegregating Suburbia." Allentown Morning Call (May 7): 14.

Koch, John H.
    1976 "1st Ward Acts to Halt Blight." Allentown Sunday Call-Chronicle (February 1): B-1 and B-3.

Leinwand, Gerald
    1969 The Traffic Jam. New York: Washington Square Press.

Lent, Norman
    1975 "Another Opinion: Revenue Sharing and Suburbia." Long Island Press (December 15): 19.

Lineberry, Robert L.
    1975 "Suburbia and the Metropolitan Turf." The Annals of the American Academy of Political and Social Science 422 (November): 1-9.

Lockard, Duane
    1971 "Banfield's Unheavenly City: A Symposium and Response. Patent Racism." Transaction 8, 5 & 6 (March/April): 69-72.

Lugar, Richard G.
    1975 "Modernizing Local Government." The American City & Country 90, 4 (April): 88-90.

LVTS Annual Report: Lehigh Valley Transportation Study. Commonwealth of Pennsylvania, 1974.

McGee, Reece
    1973 Points of Departure: Basic Concepts in Sociology. Hinsdale, Ill.: Dryden Press.

McIntosh, James R.
    1973 "The Urban Fringe: Social Life, Social Change, and the Urban Voyeur." Pp. 303-13 in John Walton and Donald Carns, eds. Cities in Change: Studies on the Urban Condition. Boston: Allyn & Bacon.

McKee, Michael and Ian Robertson
    1975 Social Problems. New York: Random House.

McVeigh, Frank J.
    1962 "The Good Old Days." Voice of the Cement, Lime & Gypsum Workers International Union 26, 10 (October): 29-31.
    1973 "Solutions to Our Urban Problems." Paper presented at the 24th Annual Meeting of the Pennsylvania Sociological Society, November 3, Elizabethtown, Pa.

Masotti, Louis H.
    1975 "The Suburban Seventies: Preface." The Annals AAPSS 422 (November): vii.

"Mass Transit: The Flywheel Goes Underground." Business Week 2419 (February 16): 32, 1976.

Monahan, Anthony
    1973 "How to Predict Chicago's Future." Chicago Sun-Times (June 17): 6-9.

National Commission on Urban Problems
　1969　Building the American City. New York: Praeger.

Neuman, Nancy
　1973　"Experimental Housing Program." Focus (May): 7–8.

"New Act to Aid Community Development." JPC Newsletter 4, 6 (December): 1–10, 1974.

"New Cures Prescribed For Ailing BART." The American City & County 91,4 (April): 16, 1976.

"New Look at America Today: Evidence of Major Change." U.S. News & World Report 82, 19 (May 16): 64–65, 1977.

"New York Bill Clears; Funds Measure Coming." Congressional Quarterly Weekly Report 50 (December 13): 2699, 1975.

"New York Escapes by Skin of Its Teeth — For Now." U.S. News & World Report 79, 17 (October 27): 14, 1975.

Olson, Philip
　1970　The Study of Modern Society. New York: Random House.

"The Only Thing Local Government Doesn't Get from the Average Taxpayer." Allentown Morning Call (July): 28, 1976.

Palen, J. John
　1975　The Urban World. New York: McGraw-Hill.

"Paolo Soleri's Visionary Cities." HUD Challenge (May/June): 26, 1970.

Peabody, Malcolm E.
　1974　"Housing Allowances: A New Way to House the Poor." The New Republic 170, 10 (March 9): 20–23.

"Philadelphia's Urban Homesteading Program" (September 23): 1–24. City of Philadelphia, 1975.

Pierce, Neal
　1976　"Cities: Mayor's No-Nonsense Policies Give Wilmington a New Life." Allentown Sunday Call-Chronicle (April 18): B-15.

Population and the American Future. Report of the Commission on Population Growth and the American Future. New York: Signet Special, New American Library, 1972.

"Recycling Slums — A Spark for Revival in Decaying Areas." U.S. News & World Report 80, 14 (April 5): 60–61, 1976.

Riis, Jacob
　1890　How the Other Half Lives. In Francesco Cordasco, ed. Jacob Riis Revisited. New York: Anchor Books, 1968.

Scott Thomas
　1975　"Implications of Suburbanization for Metropolitan Political Organization." Annals of the American Academy of Political and Social Science 422 (November): 36–44.

Sena, Peter J.
　1971　"Leading Corporations Unveil Dual Plan for $400 Million 'New Town' and Community-Aid Programs in Center City." News Release (June 3): 1–12.

Shearer, Lloyd
　1975　"What's Happening to America: Intelligence Report." Parade Magazine (November 16): 8.

Shostak, Arthur
 1975 "America's New Towns: In Trouble Despite a First-Rate Record." Working Paper for Revision. (April): 104.

Silberman, Charles
 1964 Crisis in Black and White. New York: Random House.

Smith, Fred
 1972 Man and His Urban Environment: A Manual of Specific Considerations for the Seventies and Beyond. New York: Man and His Urban Environment Project.

"Staggered Work Relieves 'Rush-Hour' Crush." The American City & Country (June): 152, 1972.

Stedman, Murray
 1972 Urban Politics. Cambridge, Mass.: Winthrop.

Steinlieb, George and Robert W. Burchell
 1973 Residential Abandonment: The Tenement Landlord Revisited. New Brunswick, N.J.: Center for Urban Policy Research, Rutgers University.

Stewart, Elbert W.
 1976 The Troubled Land. New York: McGraw-Hill.

Stewart, Maxwell
 1971 "Money for Our Cities: Is Revenue Sharing the Answer?" Public Affairs Pamphlet No. 461 (April). New York: Public Affairs Committee, Inc.

Stoloff, David
 1971 The National Survey of Housing Abandonment. New York: National Urban League. Pp. 624–25 in Gist and Fava. Urban Society. 6th ed. New York: Crowell, 1974.

Suttles, Gerald D.
 1968 The Social Order of the Slum. Chicago: University of Chicago Press.

Tass, Leslie
 1971 Modern Rapid Transit. New York: Carlton Press.

Taylor, Robert
 1976 "We're Giving More and Getting Less." The Philadelphia Sunday Bulletin (June 13): 14.

U.S. Census Bureau
 1975 Current Population Report, Series P-23, No. 55, "Social and Economic Characteristics of the Metropolitan and Nonmetropolitan Population: 1974–1970" (September), Washington, D.C.: U.S. Government Printing Office.

"A Victory over the Suburbs." Business Week 2419 (February 16): 83, 1976.

Warren, Donald and Rachelle Warren
 1975 "Six Kinds of Neighborhoods." Psychology Today 9, 1(June): 74–80.

Webber, Melvin
 1968 "The Post-City Age." Daedalus 97, 4 (Fall): 1091–1110.

Weinberg, S. Kirson
 1970 Social Problems in Modern Urban Society. 2nd ed. Englewood Cliffs, N.J.: Prentice-Hall.

"What Happens if GRS Is Killed?" The American City & County 91, 6 (June): 26, 1976.

White, Morton and Lucia White
    1961 "The American Intellectual versus the American City." Daedalus (Winter): 166–78.

Wirth, Louis
    1938 "Urbanism as a Way of Life." American Journal of Sociology 44 (July): 1–24.

Zikmund, Joseph
    1975 "A Theoretical Structure for the Study of Suburban Politics." The Annals AAPSS 422 (November): 45–60.

Zimbardo, Philip G.
    1969 "The Human Choice: Individuation, Reason and Order, Versus Deindividuation, Impulse, and Chaos." In W. Arnold and D. Levine, eds. Nebraska Symposium on Motivation. Lincoln: University of Nebraska Press.

SUGGESTED READINGS

Hughes, James W. and Kenneth Bleakly, Jr. Urban Homesteading. New Brunswick, N.J.: Transaction Books. 1976

    Analyzes the possibilities and promises of this innovative way to restore housing in our major cities. Success stories are combined with realistic analysis of urban homesteading.

Kaplan, Samuel. The Dream Deferred: People, Politics and Planning in Suburbia. New York: Seabury Press. 1976.

    An inquiry into the reasons why social problems of ecology, housing, schooling, and discrimination have not been solved in suburbs. The need for better large-scale planning is viewed as one answer.

Lottman, Herbert. How Cities Are Saved. New York: Universe Books. 1976.

    Cities from Bologna to Venice are used as models to show how cities can be made more livable and humane, as well as urbane.

Schwartz, Barry, ed. The Changing Face of the Suburbs. Chicago: University of Chicago Press. 1976.

    Articles consider how the switch from cities to suburbs came about, the institutional and behavioral effects, and the ultimate limits of such a change.

Siegan, Bernard H. Other People's Property. Lexington, Mass.: D. C. Heath. 1976.

    Articles focus on land use, housing, environment, business, city growth, and individual freedom.

Walton, John and Donald Carns. Cities in Change: Studies on the Urban Condition. 2nd ed. Boston: Allyn & Bacon. 1977.

    A reader that explores urban processes, lifestyles, change, and the future of ecology, busing, education, and city finances.

Periodicals Worth Exploring

American City & County
Journal of Housing
Journal of Urban History
Real Estate Review
Sage Urban Studies Abstracts
Urban Affairs Quarterly
Urban Life
Urban Research News

Poverty and Inequality

INTRODUCTION
DEFINITIONS OF THE PROBLEM
Jack Douglas's four aspects of poverty:
   a) Absolute poverty.
   b) Nutrition-adequacy poverty.
   c) Absolute social standard of poverty.
   d) Relative poverty (50 percent of median family income).
Income definitions of poverty:
   a) Bureau of Labor Statistics (high, moderate, and low levels).
   b) Social Security Administration.
Inequality and "life situation" definitions of poverty.
S. M. Miller's typology of the poor.

INCIDENCE AND PREVALENCE OF THE PROBLEM
Recent growth in numbers of the poor.
   a) 26 million in 1975 by Social Security Administration definition.
   b) Lowest 20 percent of families receive only 5 percent of income, same as in 1950.
Social characteristics of poor families:
   a) Black or Spanish-speaking minorities.
   b) Nonhigh-school graduates.
   c) Headed by female.
   d) Many children under 18.
   e) Headed by elderly.
   f) Unemployed or underemployed.

CAUSES OF THE PROBLEM
The individual; "blaming the victim."
The culture or subculture of poverty.
The social structure.

PROPOSED SOLUTIONS TO THE PROBLEM
Welfare system does not work to reduce poverty.
Guaranteed annual income or negative income tax.
Steady, well-paying jobs (Humphrey-Hawkins Bill).
Public-service employment (CETA).
A demogrant program financed by a value-added tax (VAT).
Other liberal and conservative proposals, from federalization of welfare to tax incentives for business.

FUTURE OF THE PROBLEM
Increased gap between those in poverty and the mainstream.
Gap between white and black family income.

SUMMARY

The **lack** of money is the root of all evil.

Reverend Ike, New York City black minister, who preaches about the positive value of material success and money.

The poor have always been with us, but we have not always welcomed them with open arms or hearts. For many years in America during the nineteenth and twentieth centuries poverty was so common that we simply assumed that not much could be done to alleviate it. Society did not feel responsible for an individual's tough luck or laziness.

Nevertheless, our interest and concern have vacillated greatly. During the Progressive Era of the early twentieth century, we worried about the poor; in the 1920s there would be a chicken in every pot; in the 1930s most people worried about poverty in a very personal way; the 1940s found us at war or work; in the 1950s we achieved our "affluent society"; in the 1960s we rediscovered poverty (thanks, in part, to Michael Harrington's *The Other America,* 1962) and launched a war (or was it a skirmish?) on it. Now, in the 1970s, we have no time to worry about the poor—we are too busy trying to make ends meet in our inflated, job-scarce economy.

But how do we know that someone is poor? Is poverty just a lack of money? Is it an absolute or relative situation? What are the real causes of poverty? Is it the individual's fault? Is it his subculture? Could it be our social structure and economy?

Can we do anything *effective* about the situation? Will things get better or worse for the poor? These and a host of other questions need to be asked and answered about the social problem of poverty.

DEFINING POVERTY AND INEQUALITY

How do we know when someone is poor? Does he lack money alone? There are many conflicting ideas of how to define poverty. As Jack Douglas put it, "we find great conflicts over the use of the term and over its definition as a social problem" (1974: 133).

The difference in definitions of poverty is more than academic. Different definitions produce different counts on the incidence and prevalence of the problem. Depending on how we define poverty, anywhere from 7 to 28 percent of Americans are poor (Williamson and Hyer, 1975: 656). Opposing definitions can affect our perception, analysis, and solutions.

In England precise attempts to define poverty date back to Roundtree's scale of 1899. To be considered poor, "a family must never purchase a halfpenny newspaper, or write letters, the children must have no pocket money and the father must not smoke tobacco" (A. B. Atkinson, 1973:

466). Roundtree's poverty line was 20 percent or less of *average* earnings for a single person. Since that time, sociologists have used many ways to classify and define poverty. Let us look at some of these approaches.

Douglas's Four Aspects of Poverty

According to sociologist Jack Douglas, there are four aspects or meanings of poverty. The first is "lacking in material goods to the point of physical suffering from hunger, weather or disease." Here the emphasis is on absolute or objective criteria, such as hunger, and an absolute amount of material goods to meet the human needs of survival. This was probably the aspect that Harvard economist John Kenneth Galbraith had in mind in the 1950s when he wrote that poverty had virtually disappeared in our "affluent society."

The second meaning of poverty is "lacking the material goods necessary to meet [agreed-upon] human needs of health." The criterion is any diet that medically produces less than adequate physical development. Housing adequate to maintain physical health is sometimes included, but the attention is on nutrition. This is sometimes called the "nutrition-adequacy" definition, which led Rose Friedman in 1965 to conclude that fewer than five million American families were poor (Douglas, 1974: 134). The United States Chamber of Commerce, using such a definition, concluded that poverty was not a serious social issue.

The third aspect or meaning of poverty is "lacking the material goods necessary to enjoy a decent standard of living." This is the meaning behind the official poverty line of the Social Security Administration. It was used as the basis of legislating for and operating the war-on-poverty programs in the 1960s and early 1970s, and it attempts to tie the meaning of poverty to an *absolute* physical or social standard.

A fourth aspect of poverty is the relative approach. The poor often think of their social situation relative to that of everyone else in society. This tendency has led to the concept of "relative deprivation" popularized many years ago by sociologists Samuel Stouffer and Robert Merton. Relative deprivation "sharpens resentment and stirs revolt" (Broom and Selznick, 1973: 597). A New York City welfare family is probably much better off than most people in nineteenth-century England; but they compare themselves only with others in their society today.

In a relative definition, poverty is "any condition that falls at the lower end of the socioeconomic scale." Ben Seligman uses such a definition in pointing out that poverty did not decrease during the prosperous 1950s, and may actually have increased (1968: 35). S. M. Miller and Pamela Roby likewise classify poverty in terms of absolutes, relativity, and inequality (1970: 21–22, 34–37). They hold that poverty *should be* defined according to what share of the total national income is received by those at the bottom. They note that "in this approach poverty is sharply regarded as inequality." This approach, in turn, has led two researchers on black poverty to conclude that "the magnitude of black economic gains in the decade of the Sixties has been slight. The walls of economic discrimination have weathered the trumpeting of 'affirmative action'" (Villemez and Rowe, 1975: 191).

The Income Definition

Income seems to be the common denominator of most definitions of poverty, be it the absolute, relative, or inequality approach. Those who define poverty in terms of absolute low income, or minimum subsistence, use an income line based on "family budget" needs or a "poverty line." The Bureau of Labor Statistics uses the "family budget" approach—low, moderate, and high. In 1977 the family budgets for a particular standard of living for an urban family of four were:

high—$23,759
moderate—$16,236
low—$10,041 ("For a Family of Four...," 1977: 1).

Today the almost unanimously applied absolute-poverty and near-poverty line is the one designed by the Social Security Administration. It has been used since 1964, and has been changed yearly to compensate for some cost of living increases. For an urban family of four, the poverty line stood at $5,038 in 1974, $5,500 in 1976, and $5,850 in 1977. The level increases or decreases according to the number of persons in a family, sex of the household head, and residence—urban or rural areas. But the SSA figure, as an absolute yardstick, has serious drawbacks. As we can see, it is well below the lowest family-budget figure ($10,041). In addition, it assumes incorrectly that only one-third of a family's income is spent on food. It also does not take into account the percentage of money most poor persons pay for housing. Many scholars find fault with the SSA approach (see Williamson and Hyer, 1975: 65), but the government continues to use it.

The Relative Definition

Most *absolute* measures of poverty do not reflect increases in the standard of living or wages, but do take inflation into account. Therefore, we require a *relative* measure of the poor in order to grasp poverty as a social issue. The most frequently used relative measure is 50 percent of the median family income, which in 1976 was $7,430.

Absolute and relative definitions of poverty *do* make a difference, as we will see shortly. In addition, there are many different kinds of absolute and relative measures of poverty. Williamson and Hyer alone analyzed 16 (1975: 662–63).

The Inequality and "Life Situation" Definitions

The inequality or share approach shows even less progress for the poor than the absolute and relative standards. Of course, absolute poverty can be reduced or eliminated by putting money into the hands of the poor; even relative poverty can be greatly alleviated by giving people more cash. But inequality cannot be solved by moving people above a certain fixed or relative line. As long as there are people at the bottom of the income scale, they are in some way poor. As long as we have social stratification (and radicals would want to abolish that if possible), the issue becomes how well or poorly those at the bottom are doing in comparison with all others. The liberal solution in this approach is reducing inequality itself. In a society that gives liberty, freedom, and opportunities to some, conservatives remind us, it is doubtful whether inequality can ever be abolished. We can only hope to redistribute income more fairly than in the past.

Besides defining poverty economically, we can define it socially, in terms of the impact such inequality of income has on the life situation and life chances of the poor.

The poor are caught up in what sociologist Thomas Gladwin identifies as vicious circles. Being poor means "living in a poor neighborhood, which means going to a second-rate school, which means having an inadequate education, which means having a low-paying job or no job at all, and thus being poor" (1967: 76–77). Or being poor means eating poor food

Children in rural areas are often unseen victims of poverty. Their life situation is often determined early, and they are caught up in a series of vicious circles before they realize it.

Credit: Diane Koos Gentry/Black Star

and living in rundown housing, which means having poor health, which means missing a lot of work or school; it means being handicapped or too weak to handle the heavy manual work which is often the only kind available, and thus being unemployed much of the time.

Each circle begins and ends with being poor. Each circle of events feeds on itself, reinforcing and perpetuating poverty in the lives of the victims. Gladwin, in his book *Poverty USA*, has unique chapter headings that summarize what poverty means. To many, poverty is being poor, being despised, being incompetent, and being powerless. Edward Banfield suggests four degrees of poverty that reflect a person's life situation. These are destitution, want, hardships, and relative deprivation (1970: 116).

Another life-situation definition of the poor is Georg Simmel's famous one. The "poor" are labeled as those who receive financial help or assistance from society. As Simmel put it in the early 1900s, "It is not personal need which makes for poverty; rather the sociological category of poverty emerges only when those who suffer from want are receiving assistance" (Coser, 1971: 108). On that basis only about *half* the people officially defined as poor by the SSA poverty line could be labeled poor. Most poor people do not like to be on welfare or to receive help from others. In addition, a bureaucratic welfare system, controlled by the power structure and middle-class technicians, seeks to exclude or cut off as many recipients as possible; thus, only about half of the poor in America ever receive welfare. To be denied economic or other help, and to be powerless to do anything about it, is part of the social problem of poverty. The boxed item (p. 236) illustrates the tragedy that results from such powerlessness.

The reason the stigma of poor is placed on those receiving welfare is the expectation that they cannot contribute to society. In turn this degrades them to "unilateral receivers." Therefore, one answer to poverty, according to sociologist Lewis Coser, is to give the poor themselves a chance to make a positive contribution to society. Put them to work as paraprofessionals helping others, and the stigma of poverty will disappear (1971: 144).

S. M. Miller's Typology of the Poor

Sociologist S. M. Miller offers another life-situation definition of poverty. He describes the lower class in terms of a typology based on the degree of economic and family stability (Miller, 1964). According to their situation the following four types of poor are possible:

	FAMILY STABILITY	FAMILY INSTABILITY
ECONOMIC SECURITY	The stable poor	The strained
ECONOMIC INSECURITY	The copers	The unstable

FALLING THROUGH BUREAUCRATIC CRACKS

By all accounts it was the happiest day in the unhappy life of Joanne Bashold; not in all her 24 years had her family ever heard her so exuberant.

"I had a baby girl yesterday," Joanne announced on September 2 from a pay telephone somewhere in New York's Bellevue Hospital. Her younger sister Barbara, receiving the call at the Bashold residence in Kirtland, Ohio, was astonished. The family hadn't known Joanne was pregnant and wasn't even sure where she was.

...Joanne wanted only to talk about her baby girl, Cara. "She had tons of black hair. She's so little and so cute."

Four days after that conversation... the baby was dead. It was devoured and killed by a starving German shepherd, Joanne's own pet and sole companion in the East Harlem slum she called home.

Unable to work after six months of pregnancy, she had gone on welfare. She got $270 a month and rented a sixth floor, two-room, walk-up apartment for $120. It had no furniture, except a folding chair, and no cooking utensils. There was no bed, so she slept on the floor.

Her story is that of a woman who fell through the cracks of a complicated bureaucratic welfare and medical system that is supposed to help people in need—but often does not.

The baby's savage death occurred while Joanne went to Bellevue Hospital in an unsuccessful attempt to retrieve $120 from the personal-property room there. It was money she had left there when she entered. But the property room was closed when she was discharged on Sunday night. She needed the money to feed herself and her baby, but when she returned early the next day (Labor Day), to get it, the room was still closed. So she went back home, where she found her baby, eaten alive by her dog. The dog had not eaten for five days.

The extraordinary unanswered question about Joanne's three months' existence in her apartment is how she survived under such conditions. Perhaps even more important is how her needs went unmet, first by welfare workers and later at Bellevue Hospital.

Source: Adapted from Richard Severo, "The Tragedy of Joanne," *New York Times* (October 15, 1976): B-1, D-15.

The "stable" poor are stable economically and in their family situation. They are working regularly, but do not earn enough to escape the poverty level. Rural Southerners and the aged make up most of this group.

The "strained" have a secure job situation but an unstable family life. This might stem from a lifecycle problem—"wild" young workers who married too soon, or alcoholic older workers who disrupt family stability. This group is usually a transitional one: it could lead to a "generational" deterioration to even worse poverty, or families could persist with a low but steady income.

The "copers" experience such job problems as severe layoffs or prolonged unemployment. A large number of blacks (because of discrimination) and downwardly mobile persons are in this category. Their children are likely to move eventually into either the "stable" or "unstable" situation.

The "unstable" have neither economic nor family stability. These persons are unskilled, irregular workers; they come from broken and large families, and are aged, physically handicapped, and suffer from mental illness. They are often blacks recently arrived from the South, ethnic-group slum residents who did not make it, or traditionally poor whites (Miller, 1964).

Regardless of how we define the poor, however, they are still with us. They may often be invisible to us, as Harrington points out, but they suffer from both absolute and relative deprivation. They lack proper medical care, decent housing, and food. They often cannot support or help their own children, and as a result they lose their self-respect and dignity as human beings. They are poor in spirit as well as in body, for society stigmatizes them as stupid, retarded, and less than human. They often cannot help themselves and they have no future. They are too old to work or too young to die.

Such is the case with "many of the aged and sick, the blind, and those crippled in body and mind" (Stewart, 1976:190). Many more of the poor are children, and unless our social structure and system change to ensure a minimum standard of living for all people, radicals maintain, poverty will continue indefinitely.

INCIDENCE AND PREVALENCE OF POVERTY AND INEQUALITY

How widespread is poverty and who are the poor? As we pointed out earlier, the incidence and prevalence of poverty varies greatly, depending on which definition is used. If we rely upon the SSA's definition, then poverty has dropped dramatically in 15 years. In 1959, 22 percent of the population would have been poor, compared with only 12 percent in 1975 (U.S. Bureau of the Census, September 1976:2). Of course, one must keep in mind that in 1959 the standard used to measure poverty represented 54 percent of the median income in the United States then; in 1975 it represented only about 40 percent of the median income (Procopio and Perella, 1976:14). Nevertheless, there were nearly 25 million poor people in 1976. The number of poor persons increased by two-and-a-half million between 1974 and 1975, the "largest rise in a single year since the government began keeping poverty statistics in 1959" (Shanahan, September 26, 1976:1).

If we use a relative measure of poverty, such as those below 50 percent of the median income, then the percentage living in poverty has held steady for almost 30 years. On that basis, about 30 percent of our citizens are poor.

If we adopt an inequality or shares-of-income measuring stick, then poverty is widespread and we have made no progress in the last 25 years.

table 6-1 — INEQUALITY OF INCOME DISTRIBUTION, 1950–1975*
(in percentages)

YEAR	LOWEST FIFTH	SECOND FIFTH	MIDDLE FIFTH	FOURTH FIFTH	HIGHEST FIFTH
1950	5%	12%	17%	24%	43%
1955	5	12	18	23	42
1960	5	12	18	23	42
1965	5	12	18	24	41
1970	6	12	17	24	42
1975	5	12	18	24	41
1974	5	12	18	24	41

Source: **Current Population Reports**, "Consumer Income" Bureau of Census, Series P-60, No. 80, October 1971: 28; No. 99, July 1975: 8; and No. 103, September 1976: 17.

*Income is **before** taxes. Capital gains are not included. This grossly **overestimates** the percentage of the lowest fifth and **underestimates** the percentage of the **highest** fifth. This is due to our tax structure and tax loopholes for the rich. Percentages are rounded.

Table 6-1 illustrates the imbalance in income between the lowest and highest groups. Taking gross income (before taxes), the lowest 20 percent of families get only 5.5 percent of the nation's income, while the upper 20 percent get over 40 percent. Indeed, the richest 10 percent hold almost 30 percent of the income and 56 percent of the wealth. Stocks, bonds, savings, and insurance are all concentrated in the hands of a wealthy few (Jordon, 1973:10). What was said of the poor in the 1960s remains true today: "If the American economy can be compared to a 20-story luxury apartment house where even the ground floor tenants share the comforts, then one-fifth of our population inhabits a subbasement out of sight and almost out of mind" (Kephart, 1966:496).

In addition, a study of poverty in the United States found that 26 percent of the population live *below* a "minimum level of adequacy," while 40 percent live below a "minimum level of *comfort*." The study concluded that "the position of groups on the bottom level of the income hierarchy has deteriorated dramatically since the Depression of the 1930s when compared with the societal average income" (Rydell and Rydell, 1973:397).

Senator Hubert Humphrey of Minnesota pointed out that if our economy grows and jobs open up for the unemployed and the underemployed, we could make a substantial dent in the prevalence of poverty. It was no mere coincidence that the poverty roll was reduced by 14 million persons in the 1960s, when unemployment dropped from 6.7 percent of the workforce in 1961 to 3.6 percent in 1968 ("Senator Hubert H. Humphrey Speech," Summer, 1976:47).

Sar Levitan went one step further and argued that "for about $11 billion a year we could raise every poor American *above* the poverty level"

(1973:243). In fact, we are moving in that direction now, although we still have a long way to go. Our present Social Security system keeps about 13 million elderly persons near but *just above* the official poverty line.

Social Characteristics of the Poor

Who are the poor, and what are their social characteristics? Poor people tend to come from families that

> are black or Spanish-speaking minorities
> are headed by nonhigh-school graduates
> are headed by females
> have many children under 18
> are headed by the elderly
> are unemployed and underemployed.

Let us look at each of these characteristics.

Racial Minorities. Nearly a third of all blacks (8,106,000) are poor, compared with only about 8 percent of all whites (17,770,000). But since whites are the majority group, they still account for the majority of the poor. In 1975 whites below the poverty line rose by 13 percent over the previous year, while black poverty increased by five percent. Part of the white poor are of Spanish-speaking origin. Some 23 percent of all Spanish-Americans (2,900,000) live in poverty, about 11 percent of the poor. About two-thirds of poor Spanish-Americans are Chicanos who live in five Southwestern states.

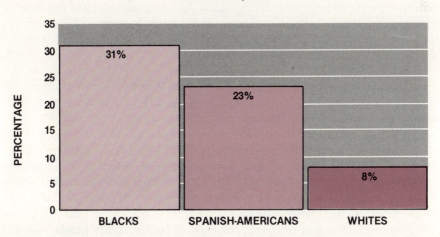

figure 6-1 PERCENTAGE OF POOR BLACKS, SPANISH-AMERICANS, AND WHITES, 1975

Source: Bureau of Census, CPR, Series P-60 No. 99, July 1975: 18-19; and "Money Income and Poverty Status of Families and Persons in the United States 1974-1975," September 1976.

Education and Females. Two-thirds of the poor never finished high school, and their median education is 10 years. Among heads of poor white families, 64 percent did not get their diplomas; among blacks heading a family, 77 percent did not make it through high school; and for Spanish-American family heads, 86 percent had no high-school degree (U.S. Bureau of the Census, CPR, Series P-60, No. 98, 1975:5).

Of all the poor, 38 percent live in families headed by a female. This compares with only 18 percent in 1959. About 55 percent of all poor black families are headed by a female, compared with 27 percent of all poor white families. When a female heads a household, she earns much less money than a male-headed home or a husband-wife family, even if she works full time. The median income of a household in which both husband and wife work is $17,237; but it is less than $10,000 for a female-headed household (Shanahan, 1976:36).

Nearly three-fourths of all low-income families have children under 18, whereas only 55 percent of all nonpoor families have children. Over 90 percent of female-headed poor families have children living at home. Of the nearly 26 million poor, over 11 million are children under 18 ("How Many Live in Real Want?" November 8, 1976:58).

The Elderly. The elderly account for about 15 percent of all the poor, or nearly three-and-a-half million of those 65 and older. Elderly blacks are disproportionately poverty-stricken; 36 percent of all blacks 65 and older are poor (U.S. Bureau of Census, CPR No. 99, 1975:19).

The percentage of the elderly poor has fallen slightly below its level of 1959. Since 1970, progress has been made in moving the elderly at least barely above poverty. Increases in Social Security payments have been made since 1970, and in 1972 a cost-of-living escalator clause was added to the Social Security system. Benefits to the elderly are now increased each year to try to keep pace with living costs. Additionally, in 1974 the federal government, through the Supplemental Security Income (SSI) program, took over the state-run Old Age Assistance welfare program, thus increasing benefits to millions of elderly poor.

Unemployment and Underemployment. The last social characteristic of the poor is their frequent lack of work. In 1975, 62 percent of the men who headed low-income families worked at least part of the year. Of those who worked, about 35 percent had a year-round, full-time job. Even those who earned the federal minimum wage of $2.30 an hour and worked 40 hours a week, 52 weeks a year, grossed only $4,784. But this was not enough to get them out of poverty. The Census Bureau reported that about 42 percent of the increase in poor families between 1974 and 1975 was due to the head's being "unable to find work during the entire year" or being "unemployed 15 weeks or more" (Shevis, 1976:7). Family heads who did not work were mostly women with children, or the elderly.

The poor, in short, are composed of persons who tend to be from a

Many families in poverty are headed by a woman (with a limited formal education), are members of a racial or ethnic minority, and have children under 18. The family head is usually unemployed or underemployed.

minority group, have less than a high-school education, are children who live in families headed by females, or are elderly and retired. Even working does not help everyone to escape poverty.

The poor should not be considered synonymous with those on welfare. Less than half of the poor receive welfare, and most who do are children. Only about 63 percent of female family heads of poor families go on welfare ("Food Stamps," S.P. 23, no. 61, July 1976:6). Only about 40 percent of all poor families get food stamps. Thus, welfare does not help to curb poverty, since most poor do not depend on it or do not need it for long. A University of Michigan study reported that "40 percent of the American population, some 85 million persons, were eligible for welfare benefits at some time during the last six years" ("On the Brink," July 1974:back cover). The researchers followed a sample of 5,000 families since 1968. Of those living in poverty, only 20 to 30 percent actually had below-poverty income all six years of the study. Of these, most were black. A follow-up study in 1976 reported "only 38.4% of the black children were able to avoid poverty . . . while 86.5% of the white youngsters never were poor in that time" ("How Many Live . . . ," November 8, 1976:58).

CAUSES OF POVERTY AND INEQUALITY

People hold two basically different views of the causes of poverty. It is due to "circumstances beyond an individual's control," or to "lack of individual effort." On this issue the American conservatives and liberals are hopelessly divided (Gallup, 1964:45). In recent years, however, more positive attitudes toward the poor and welfare recipients have emerged (Carter et al., 1973:10–11).

We can offer three main causes of poverty: the individual; the culture or subculture of poverty; and the social structure (Elesh, 1973:359–73). Let us examine each one in turn.

The Individual

In America, we have a conservative ideology of individualism, which expresses itself through an extreme self-concern, along with competition and the drive for success. It fosters an attitude of every man for himself and produces a feeling that the losers of the race for success are not our responsibility. Hence, both success and failure become individual matters. If one ends up in poverty it is his own fault. Why? He is poor because of "playing the ponies, drink, laziness, or shiftlessness" (Lane, 1962:331).

This conservative ideology of exaggerated individualism even maintained that poverty was good for the individual and for society. It would help to motivate a person to succeed so that he would not starve. And if he did starve, it would be the best thing for society, for the fittest will survive (Carnegie, 1901; Spencer, 1850, in Will and Vatter, 1970:27, 36). This was part of the ideology of individualism and of finding the cause of poverty within the individual.

Another aspect of this ideology is the Protestant ethic, described by Max Weber, which emphasizes salvation through individual effort, virtue, and honest work. It dovetails into the economic beliefs in the individual's power to win success through his own exertion, honesty, frugality, and hard work. If he fails, he has no one but himself to blame. Behind his failure are the human weaknesses of intemperance, vice, idleness, and other bad habits (Meissner, 1973:2).

As William Ryan reminds us, every ideology—in this case, blaming the victim of poverty—has four aspects:

> the belief system itself—the way of looking at the world
> the systematic distortion of reality reflected in those beliefs
> the unconscious or unintentional nature of the distortion
> the ideas that serve a specific function—keeping the status quo in the interest of a specific group (1976:11).

The typical "victim blamer" of the poor is a middle-class person who is enjoying reasonably good material success. He has "a fairly good job, a steady income, a good house and car." Such a person argues: "Basically the system is pretty good the way it is. I had to struggle to make it—why can't the poor? There must be something wrong *with them!*"

But there is another reason the middle-class person can find the cause of poverty within the individual. He desires to keep the poor where they are—below him. As Adam Walinsky explains it:

> Virtually everyone who has reached his final life-station must and does believe and say that choice, or more commonly "the breaks" or "the system" **prevented** him from rising higher. But this same man must and does believe and say that his own abilities are primarily responsible for how far he has risen above others. People above oneself are regarded as no better than equal. People below oneself are regarded as inferior (1975:90).

Even occasional liberal tinkering with the opportunity structure, leading to tokenism, serves as further proof that those below us need special help because they are deficient and inferior.

The emphasis on the individual and on blaming the victim spawns stereotypes about the poor and welfare recipients. Yet as Michael Harrington says in *The Other America,* people are poor because they made a big mistake. "They made the mistake of being born to the wrong parents, in the wrong section of the country, in the wrong industry, or in the wrong racial or ethnic group" (1962:21).

The Culture or Subculture of Poverty

The second cause of poverty is the culture (or subculture) of poverty. Instead of focusing on the individual, this ideology focuses on the way of life of the poor. Such a culture system blocks any attempts of society to change the values, norms, beliefs, and lifestyle of the poor. The "culture of poverty" concept suggests that despite economic changes in this century, and particularly in the last few decades, the poor have remained so because of their culture or subculture. "The culture of the poor has continued to foster the typically disparaging behaviors and values associated with poverty; it has kept them out of the mainstream of industrial society" (Massey, 1975:597).

Oscar Lewis popularized the notion of a culture of poverty (1959, 1961, 1966, 1970). His studies in Mexico, Puerto Rico, and among Spanish-Americans viewed the poor as members of a culture different in kind from the "dominant" one. As Lewis put it, it was a special culture that passes on poverty from generation to generation.

> The culture of poverty, however, is not only an adaptation to a set of objective conditions of the larger society. Once it comes into existence, it tends to perpetuate itself from one generation to another... the elimination of physical poverty per se may not be enough to eliminate the culture of poverty which is a whole way of life (1970:69, 78).

This conservative concept, often shared by politicians and the public, gave our society a reason for doing little or nothing about poverty and the poor as a social problem; it shifted the nation's attention away from our institutions and social structures as a cause of poverty.

Advocates of this ideology identify lower-class culture and assumed lifestyles as themselves *causes* of continued poverty (Ryan, 1976:119). They tend to confuse the *effects* of poverty with its causes. To illustrate this, one "culture of poverty" advocate writes:

> The subcultural adaptation to poverty would seem to interact with the poverty situation to perpetuate lower-lower class status. For the welfare of many of the very poor, as well as for the welfare of the rest of society, it seems to be necessary to help a large group re-adapt its life styles to more effective patterns (Chilman, 1966:116).

Such an approach to explaining the causes of poverty eventually stereotypes the poor. For example, the poor are thought to share certain social and mental traits that make them different from the rest of us. They are considered fatalistic, authoritarian, promiscuous, male chauvinistic (males), matriarchal, and physically and emotionally isolated from the community and one another (Sweet, 1967:6).

The "culture of poverty" approach argues that if we give the poor an easy way to get money, they will lose the incentive to work. Studies from the Institute for Research on Poverty at the University of Wisconsin prove that this is not the case at all. Steady work is an important value, though a

Children born into the subculture of poverty are assumed to be the **causes** of their continued poverty, rather than the **victims** of a social structure that causes and perpetuates poverty.

scarce commodity, for the poor. For example, in a real-life experiment the federal government gave $5 million to 650 working poor families (some on welfare) to see whether they would lose their incentive to work. Most of them did not. In addition, 31 percent of families in the experimental group actually increased their job income more than $25 during the first year of the study. About 25 percent did show a decline in earnings, but so did 23 percent within the control group of similar socioeconomic status.

When asked what the poor recipients did with the money given to them, the investigators replied: "We found very few cases of squandering. Most people were glad to get the money and use it for the things they really needed—food, clothing and shelter" ("Most Families . . .," 1973:2). This willingness of the poor to work is verified by other studies. Yet the cultural or subcultural explanation as a cause of poverty persists (Kaplan and Tausky, 1974:185–98).

The Social Structure

The first two causes—the individual and the culture of poverty—are widely accepted by conservatives, large segments of the public, and many politicians (Ramsey and Braito, 1973:65–80). But a third cause of poverty is more commonly accepted by liberals, radicals, and sociologists—the social structure itself. Our social institutions, especially our economy, stack the deck against the poor. It is not accidental that poverty is most frequently linked to "low educational attainment, lack of employable skills, long-term unemployment or underemployment, . . . racism, and rural residence" (Chilman, 1975:54). Our social institutions themselves,

---

POVERTY IS . . .

Poverty is taking your children to the hospital and spending the whole day waiting with no one even taking your name, and then coming back the next, and the next, until they finally get around to you. . . . Poverty is having a child with glaucoma and watching that eye condition grow worse every day, while the welfare officials send you to the private agencies and the private agencies send you back to the welfare, and when you ask the welfare officials to refer you to this special hospital they say they can't—and then when you say it is prejudice because you are a Negro, they deny it flatly and they shout at you: "Name one white child we have referred there." When you name twenty-five, they sit down, and they shut up, and they finally refer you, but it is too late then, because your child has permanently lost 80 percent of his vision, and you are told that if only they had caught it a month earlier, when you first made inquiry, they could have preserved his vision.

Mrs. Janice Bradshaw, Pueblo, Colo., in William H. Jennings, *Poor People and Churchgoers* (New York: Seabury Press, 1972):10.

even the welfare system, are designed to cause and perpetuate poverty. Piven and Cloward argue that our welfare system pays the poor so little (while stigmatizing them at the same time), in order to have a cheap labor supply ready, willing, and able to work for marginal employers and to do society's heavy labor.

When we as a society structure our social institutions to preserve poverty, there are important advantages that come to us, especially to the rich. For example, Harry Caudill documents how the vested interests profited from the economic aid sent in to help the poor in Appalachia. Appalachia "One" (power and wealth) prospered, while Appalachia "Two" (the poor) starved and the area became a "welfare reservation" (1973:31–34).

Sociologist Herbert Gans, in a similar vein, has pointed out 13 functional gains—economic, political, and social—that the middle class derive from having a poverty group in society. These range from getting society's "dirty work" done to helping society uphold conventional norms; and from acting as domestics for the affluent to stabilizing the political process by voting for the Democrats (1971:166–69).

In truth, we tolerate poverty because we do not want to change the social structure, values, and norms that encourage or perpetuate it. For example, if the elderly lived with their married sons or daughters instead of alone, we would achieve a sizable reduction of poverty among the elderly. But our values and family structure do not encourage this (Lebergott, 1975:61).

Our educational institutions are not structured or designed to encourage poor children to learn or stay in school. If a poor child misses a few days of school and is found to be truant, he is suspended from school for a few days. Studies have documented the desire of the poor for education. Parents of poor blacks locked into segregated central-city schools protest that their children are not getting quality education. Nevertheless, the social structure denies them adequate opportunities and avenues to become educated; hence they become or remain poor (Ryan, 1976:31–62). Inadequate health care adds to the problems of the poor as the boxed item "Poverty Is" illustrates.

When corporate institutions mandate retirement at age 65, they help create a situation of instant poverty. When automated machines and new computers reduce the need for human labor or unskilled workers, more poor are added to the welfare rolls. We must also realize that as our industry becomes more automated, a smaller proportion of our population will be involved in "productive" work. The days when our society needed millions of unskilled or semiskilled workers are past. Henceforth, the poor will find it increasingly difficult to find a job.

Society also exacerbates the social problem of poverty when it hardens its attitudes against hiring persons with a police record, or a school dropout. It perpetuates an inequity whereby over half of poor families cannot afford a car, while 30 percent of our families own two or more.

> ## BEING POOR
>
> The late Fanny Brice may have demonstrated greater insight into this problem than most of the learned psychiatrists when she said, "I've been rich and I've been poor; and, believe me, rich is better!" Being poor is stressful. Being poor is worrisome; one is anxious about the next meal, the next dollar, the next day. Being poor is nerve-wracking, upsetting. When you're poor, it's easy to despair and it's easy to lose your temper. And all of this is because you're poor. Not because your mother let you go around with your diapers full of bowel movement until you were four; or shackled you to the potty chair before you could walk. Not because she broke your bottle on your first birthday or breast-fed you until you could cut your own steak. But because you don't have any *money*.
>
> Source: William Ryan, *Blaming the Victim* (New York: Vintage Books, 1976, rev. ed.):157.

Government regulations encourage a man to desert his family so it can get money for food and rent.

Hardly any public housing is built for the poor in suburbs, whereas 150,000 second homes are built each year for the rich (Soderlind, 1971:15). Elected officials blame poverty on the "inherent inferiority" of the poor (Ramsey and Braito, 1973:65–80)

We feed our cats and dogs the best, while children go without proper food and thus become brain damaged (Lewin, 1975:29–34).

PROPOSED SOLUTIONS TO POVERTY AND INEQUALITY

One reason that many solutions have been offered to remedy poverty is that the present system of welfare simply does not work effectively to reduce the problem. For example, only about 7 percent of the population is on public welfare—Supplemental Security Income, Aid to Families of Dependent Children (AFDC), and General Assistance (GA) programs among others—though nearly 13 percent of the population is poor. As of January, 1977, the AFDC and GA systems (what the public considers "welfare") in the United States had the following numbers of recipients and money paid out, as shown in Table 6-2. These figures indicate that less than 50 percent of the 26 million poor (as defined by the SSA) receive welfare. It is also clear that the annual welfare benefits (between $1,790 and $2,828) paid to the average poor family are less than 50 percent of the federal government's own definition of poverty ($5,850 in 1977).

Other problems plague the existing welfare system; for example: excessive paperwork, differing state benefits and eligibility requirements, poor control over and checking of welfare fraud, invasion of personal privacy, excessive over- and under-payments to persons, spiraling costs, a

table 6-2 WELFARE RECIPIENTS AND MONEY PAID OUT
(Jan. 1977)

AFDC WELFARE		GA WELFARE	
No. of Families	3,584,919	No. of Cases	698,624
No. of Persons	11,215,463	No. of Persons	921,240
No. of Children	7,896,041		
Avg. Monthly Payment:		Avg. Monthly Payment:	
Per Family	$235.65	Per Case	$149.13
Per Person	75.32	Per Person	113.09
Avg. Annual Amt. Paid		Avg. Annual Amt. Paid	
Per Family	$2,828	Per Case:	$1,790

Source: "Public Assistance," Table M-34, Social Security Bulletin, 40, 7 (July, 1977) 77.

tendency to discourage work, and lack of coordination between different welfare programs.

Guaranteed-Income Plans and Negative Income Taxes

Although the present system, with prodding and guidelines from the federal government, is trying to improve its efficiency and performance (which usually means cutting poor people off the rolls), many liberal plans for a guaranteed annual income or a negative income tax have been proposed (Weinberger, Summer 1976:1–27). After a one-and-half-year study of the inadequacies of the existing welfare systems by the Department of Health, Education and Welfare, Casper Weinberger, HEW Secretary from early 1973 to late 1975, proposed a solution to help the poor and eliminate welfare as we have known it. His plan is similar to, though not identical with, many other proposals. He would eliminate immediately the three largest federal welfare programs—AFDC, SSI, and food stamps—and substitute a simple cash grant based on need (measured by income and assets), payable only to those who meet a strong work requirement (if they are able to work). The Carter administration is considering a similar plan calling for a grant of up to $4,200 for a poor family of four. This new plan would be coordinated and administered by the Internal Revenue Service.

Persons or families with incomes above a certain figure set by Congress would pay taxes; those with incomes below that level would receive a federal cash grant, which would decline as the income of the family increased. The plan would also increase the existing income-tax exemptions ($750 per dependent in 1976) and the standard deductions (between $1,700 and $2,800 in 1976). This would provide a tax cut for low- and middle-income families before the program even starts (Ibid.).

This plan advocated by Weinberger is a variation of the so-called negative income-tax plan. But he feels there are two essential features of this proposal which, if ignored, would actually make the situation worse than the present welfare system.

> The three programs for which the new plan would be substituted, AFDC, SSI, and food stamps, must be abolished.
>
> It is "absolutely essential" that work be required of all able-bodied participants before any person or family receives a federal cash grant.

According to Weinberger, experience under the present system shows that without a strong work requirement, there will not only be "no incentive for welfare families to leave public assistance," but also every inducement to stay.

Sociologist Nathan Glazer cites the case of a mother and six children in Massachusetts who receive money from welfare, along with free health and educational services at an alternative school and day-care center. All these services cost $5,000 a year. As Glazer notes, "the family pays no taxes ... and a working head of a family would have to earn at least $20,000 to match this standard of living" ("Reform Work...," 1975:4). He points out, too, that although Massachusetts welfare benefits are "generous," New York provides cash grants that are 16.5 percent higher.

Weinberger documents a potential savings of about $20.2 billion by cutting out the present programs, along with subsidized housing and school-lunch programs, and estimates costs of $3.8 billion for the first year of the new plan (1976:19).

Although such a negative income-tax proposal has certain merits, we must analyze certain potential shortcomings.

> The Congress considered and vetoed a similar plan (the Family Assistance Plan) in 1973 and 1974 because the liberals and conservatives could not agree on the level of benefits or the kind of work requirement that would be demanded.
>
> The crucial point is the amount of the federal grant and the total income poor people would receive under such a plan. The guaranteed income level must be at least equal to the federal government's own definition of how much money a family should have in order not to be considered poor. Too often, plans such as this one have not provided for a minimum level of subsistence. Even the Carter administration proposal of 1977 to guarantee the poor an annual income of up to $4,200 is $1,650 below the official poverty line (Rosenbaum, May 17, 1977:1)
>
> When we look at the people on the existing welfare rolls, it is clear that the overwhelming majority of welfare recipients are children, the elderly, and female heads of households. Hence, a "strong work provision" would apply to only a small and insignificant number of welfare recipients.
>
> Even if Carter insists that people work to receive benefits under his plan, where will the jobs come from when unemployment is high (as it has been for the past few years)? If there

were more well-paying jobs, some recipients would not be on welfare in the first place.

Steady, Well-Paying Jobs

This leads to a second major liberal proposal for solving the problem of poverty—providing steady, well-paying jobs. Study after study done by the Institute for Research on Poverty and by other organizations (as well as congressional hearings) consistently shows that most people would rather work than draw welfare (Wright and Wright, September/October 1975:24–32).

One of many proposals to create new jobs is the Full Employment and Balanced Growth Act of 1976. The level of near-full employment envisioned by the proposed legislation is three percent unemployment out of the adult labor force (as opposed to the seven to eight percent level in the late 1970s). The proposal establishes the right of all persons 16 and older to opportunities for paid employment at "fair rates." To back up that right, the act commits the federal government to "fundamental reform in the management of the economy so that full employment and balanced economic growth are achieved and sustained" ("Provisions . . .," June/July

Severe unemployment among minority-group adults and youth in the ghetto must be ended if we intend to solve the social problem of poverty. Although not a cure-all, steady, well-paying jobs are a giant step in halting the spread of poverty.

Credit: Charles Gatewood.

1976:167). It would create a permanent institutional framework through which Congress, the Federal Reserve Board (which controls the flow of money), and the President can develop and establish economic goals and policies needed to provide full employment. It also requires specific employment programs to achieve the three percent unemployment goal within four years after the bill becomes law. Specific programs would focus on "reducing cyclical, structural, regional, youth unemployment, and unemployment due to discrimination" (Ibid., 168). It would set up a full-employment office within the Department of Labor that would use special means for training, assisting, and providing jobs for persons unable to find them.

This act, also known as the Humphrey-Hawkins Bill, calls for the President, within 90 days after it becomes law, to develop and submit a "coherent and flexible . . . program to reduce high unemployment coming from cyclical swings in the economy." This program would include government jobs, standby public works, antirecession grants for state and local governments, skill training in both the public and private parts of the economy, and other programs. At this writing, it is not clear whether Congress will fully support such a bill calling for massive federal government economic planning (Leckachman, September 20, 1976:194).

Public-Service Employment

Public-service employment is designed to benefit the poor (i.e., any person unemployed, underemployed, or with income less than the federal poverty standard). Since 1973 such a program of government jobs has been carried out by federal funding under the Comprehensive Employment and Training Act (CETA). During 1975, its first full year of operation, about 300,000 persons received jobs under the CETA program ("Present Federal Jobs . . .," June/July 1976:164–65).

In early 1977 a new emergency public-works program began, with a congressional appropriation of nearly $4 billion. Sponsors believe that the emergency program will provide up to 300,000 jobs, many of them in the construction industry (which has been hard hit by chronic unemployment). A problem with this program is that just over $1 billion goes to local governments for "countercyclical" aid (to overcome high unemployment in the economy), and can be used to grant pay raises to local government employees instead of for jobs for the poor (Eccles, September 18, 1976:2515).

The Demogrant Proposal and VAT

A rather conservative proposed solution is the "demogrant," financed through the value-added tax (VAT). Similar in intent to the negative income tax or the guaranteed annual income, the demogrant is essentially different insofar as it will be paid to all, rich and poor alike.

Leonard Greene, President of the Institute for Socioeconomic Studies, advocates such a plan to solve our problems of poverty and income maldistribution. According to Greene's study, "a demogrant is a transfer payment made without regard to income or wealth; it is paid to all persons, the amount depending on family structure or other demographic criteria" (1976:1). Adults, especially the elderly, would receive about nine dollars for every four dollars received by a child. A demogrant is similar to the children's allowances used by Canada and some European countries. A value-added tax (VAT) is a tax on consumption of goods and services; it is like a sales tax, but it would be paid on *all* business transactions. Under Greene's proposal, however, corporations would not pay a tax on total sales, but on "sales less the cost of goods and materials: on its value added" (Ibid.). It would be paid at each stage of production where any value is added. The VAT is already being used by some European countries, including England.

In specific terms, the plan makes these provisions:

> A 10 percent national value-added tax (VAT) would be levied, with the proceeds used to pay the demogrants.
>
> Adults would receive an average of $522 a year, children $232. This money would in turn be taxed by the government.
>
> About 31 percent of poor families would be raised out of poverty, and 53 percent of the population would have a net gain in disposable income.
>
> The demogrant, combined with the value-added tax (VAT), could be an effective part of an income-maintenance program.

The hope of such a plan is that it would not adversely affect the economy, would be easy to administer, and would be politically acceptable.

There are some clear problems with such a proposal:

> If corporations pay a VAT on sales *minus* the cost of goods and materials, there would be little if any incentive to hold down costs in industry. Business might feel encouraged to inflate their costs; this might even produce a kind of "cost-plus" contract situation in which businesses know that the higher the costs of producing goods, the *less* tax they would have to pay. This would be counter-productive, causing even greater inflation than we have now, and would hurt the poor the most.
>
> Ultimately any VAT will be passed on to the consumer who buys the goods or uses the services. Just like state sales taxes, the poor would be hurt the most, since the price of all goods would be raised. Since there would be no exemptions for food or other necessities (as most state sales taxes provide), the VAT would harm the poor even more than present taxes.
>
> Since any demogrant would in turn be taxed by the federal government, most people would receive far less (about 21 percent less) than they might at first think. The demogrant might even be enough to put them in a higher income-tax bracket.

Other Proposals

Other proposals have been put forth to remedy the problem of poverty. These include the following.

Federalize existing welfare programs, with eligibility and benefits to be set by Congress. This would eliminate the incentive for the poor to move from Mississippi, where the average AFDC participant receives $14.39 a month, to Wisconsin, where he would get over $102 a month.

Improve Social Security benefits so that millions of elderly people just below the poverty level would no longer (technically) be poor.

Close tax loopholes for the rich so that income may be more adequately redistributed, through the federal tax system, to benefit the low- and moderate-income families.

Improve unemployment-compensation benefits, making them available for a longer period of time so that working-class people will not have to resort to welfare when hit by long-term unemployment.

Improve the economy by giving more tax breaks to business to encourage plant and job expansion. The Tax Reduction Act of 1975 especially provides that employers who hire welfare recipients can claim an income-tax credit of 20 percent of the wages paid to them. More legislation of this type is needed (Social and Rehabilitation Service, 1976:8).

Strengthen and finance community programs for the poor, and maintain a "central advocate" office within the federal government to ensure that poverty programs are carried out effectively. The executive branch of the government should retain a focal point, such as the former Office of Economic Opportunity, for problems of the poor.

Radicals argue that nothing short of a massive redistribution of wealth and power will in any way eliminate poverty. Until everyone is assured of a modest, but adequate, standard of living by society, poverty will persist in the future.

Liberals and conservatives maintain that if their solutions are adopted, in whole or in part (especially those that are complementary), poverty may gradually be further alleviated, as it has been over the last 50 years.

THE FUTURE OF POVERTY AND INEQUALITY

The future of poverty is linked to the future of the economy. Barring a major economic depression, most indications are that the economy will grow steadily through the rest of the 1970s and the 1980s. The median income for families is expected to grow from around $10,000 in the early 1970s to over $16,000 in 1985.

Nevertheless, according to Lee Rainwater, "there are no indications to suggest that this income will be distributed more equitably in the future than it is at present" (1976:213). All classes will increase their real incomes by 1985, but those at the bottom will *not* increase as fast as others (Ibid.). Table 6-3 shows the percentage of family incomes expected by various income levels in 1985, as compared with family incomes in 1968. The result of these increases will be that by 1985 half of our society will have a standard of living that only 3 percent of the population enjoyed in 1947 or the top 15 percent had in 1970 (Ibid.).

table 6-3 FAMILY INCOME IN THE UNITED STATES: ACTUAL 1968 INCOME WITH PREDICTED INCOME IN 1985

INCOME LEVELS	1968	BY PERCENTAGE (1970 DOLLARS) 1985
Families	50,500,000	66,700,000
UNDER $3,000	10%	4%
$3,000 to $4,999	12	6
$5,000 to $9,999	38	18
$10,000 to $14,999	25	23
$15,000 to $24,999	12	16
$25,000 and over	3	16
Mean income	$9,600	$16,100
Median Income	$8,600	$14,700

Source: Adapted from Lee Rainwater, "Post-1984 America," p. 213 in Anne Kilbride, ed. **Readings in Sociology 76/77: Annual Editions.** Guilford, Conn.: Dushkin, 1976.

The gap will grow, however, between the poor- and the average-income earner between now and 1985. As Rainwater notes: "The constant dollar gap between the underclass income and that of the man in the mainstream also grows—from $2,800 in 1947 to $5,600 in 1971 to $8,400 in 1985" (1976:218). The gap is widening with every passing year. Hence, people we called poor in 1970 on the basis of their way of life we will probably call poor in 1985, for their way of life will be much the same even though they will probably have slightly more in the way of material goods. The issue of relative poverty and the apparent progress in reducing it during the past few decades have long concealed economic inequality and the fact that we have done very little to redistribute income.

At current unemployment rates and with the six percent or higher rate predicted for 1980 by the Labor Department, it is highly unlikely that differences between black and white income will close much in the future. Blacks and other minority groups will continue to have a higher percentage of their population living in poverty. Harold W. Guthrie has projected comparative incomes of white and non-white families and suggests that at

In the future the rich will grow richer, and the poor will grow poorer.

1972 unemployment rates, equality of income between black and white families would take "well over 100 years to achieve" (Rainwater, 1976:219).

Barring unforeseen radical changes in national priorities, political policies, or social norms and values, the poor will continue to be with us in the future. And the gap between the affluent and indigent will be even greater than today. The lack of money will still be the root of all evil, and of many social problems.

SUMMARY

Three definitions of poverty are "absolute" poverty (measured by the Social Security Administration), "relative" poverty, and "inequality" or "life-situation" poverty. The bottom 20 percent of families in the United States have only about five percent of all income, while the upper 20 percent get over 40 percent—a distribution figure that has not changed much since 1950. Poverty affects a person's life chances and the degree of economic and family stability.

About one-third of all blacks are poor, compared with only about 8.5 percent of all whites, yet whites still account for over 60 percent of the poor. The poor have certain socioeconomic characteristics, such as belonging to a minority group or to a family headed by a female, having less than a high-school education, being retired or elderly, and unemployed or underemployed.

Three main causes of poverty are offered: the failure of the individual, the culture or subculture of poverty, and the social structure. "Blaming the victim," according to William Ryan, seems to be our society's main focus in explaining poverty, whereas what we really need is a major change in our social structure so that income will be more fairly distributed.

Since the present welfare system is deficient and inadequate for helping people out of poverty, other solutions have been proposed by liberals, conservatives, and radicals. These include—

> a guaranteed annual income or negative income tax, such as the one proposed by Casper Weinberger, and would eliminate our present welfare systems of AFDC, SSI, and GA: the plan has merits and limitations, as does a similar plan proposed by the Carter administration.
>
> guaranteed jobs so people can get off and remain off the welfare rolls: the Full Employment and Balanced Growth Act of 1976 is a step by the government in that direction;
>
> a demogrant program for everyone, financed by a value-added tax (VAT), that would lift about 31 percent of all below-poverty families out of poverty: this plan has serious drawbacks, especially for the poor and for all consumers;
>
> other liberal and conservative proposals, from federalization of welfare to tax incentives for businessmen;
>
> radicals call for massive redistribution of wealth and power.

The outlook for the poor is not good. Although by 1985 the poor will have more real income, the gap between them and those in the mainstream may increase to $8,400. Income inequality will change very little, and the gap between white and black family income will persist.

The root of all evil, and of many social problems, will still be the *lack* of money for millions of Americans, unless political priorities or cultural norms and values change radically.

CAREER OPPORTUNITIES

Family Counselors.

They are usually counseling psychologists, social workers, or psychiatrists. All work with those who are having difficulties facing family problems. Such clients are usually not mentally ill, but are often emotionally upset, anxious, or struggling to resolve some problem that affects behavior of family members. Family counselors may work in a university setting, for a marriage-counseling agency, community health center, or with a state or federal agency. A degree in sociology, social work, psychology, or medicine is needed. As family problems continue to grow, so will the need for family counselors. For further information write to: The National Council of Family Relations, 1219 University Ave., S.E., Minneapolis, Minn. 55414

Social-Service Aides (Caseworker Assistants).

Most social-service aides work under the supervision of other professional staff workers, such as a social worker or rehabilitation counselor. Because of the wide variety of social services, they work in many different job settings and perform a variety of different jobs. They usually work directly with clients, helping them to locate adequate housing or jobs, or counseling parents about their children. They may act as advocates for the poor by seeing that clients receive needed medical care and helping them to communicate their needs to other agencies. Usually a state or federal civil-service test must be taken. For further information write to: National Commission for Social Work Careers, 600 Southern Building, 15th & H Sts., N.W., Washington, D.C. 20005.

Employment Counselors.

Helping the poor to train for and find suitable employment is the principal task of employment counselors. Usually employed by the state employment office, some nevertheless work for private or community agencies, particularly in large cities. Others work in prisons, training schools for delinquents, mental hospitals, or for the Veterans Administration. Students with a background in sociology, plus some graduate courses in counseling, would be qualified for this job. For further information write to your State Civil Service Commission or U.S. Civil Service Commission, 1900 E St., N.W., Washington, D.C. 20415.

REFERENCES

Associated Press
1973 "Most Families on Guaranteed Wage Didn't Lose Urge to Work." Allentown Morning Call (March 26):2.

Atkinson, A.B.
1973 "Who Are the Poorest?" New Society 23, 543 (March 1):466–68.

Banfield, Edwin
1970 The Unheavenly City. Boston: Little, Brown.

Broom, Leonard and Phillip Selznick
1973 Sociology: A Text with Adapted Readings. 5th ed. New York: Harper & Row.

Carnegie, Andrew
1901 The Gospel of Wealth and Other Essays. P. 27 in Robert E. Will and Harold G. Vatter, eds. Poverty in Affluence, 2nd ed. New York: Harcourt, Brace & World. 1970.

Carter, Genevieve, Lillene H. Fifield, and Hannah Shields
1973 Public Attitudes Toward Welfare—An Opinion Poll. Regional Research Institute in Social Welfare, School of Social Work, University of Southern California, December.

Caudill, Harry
1973 "O Appalachia!" Intellectual Digest (April). Pp. 31-34 in Peter Wickman, ed. Annual Editions: Readings in Social Problems 75/76. Guilford, Conn.: Dushkin.

Chilman, Catherine
1966 "Growing up Poor." Welfare Administration, No. 13, U.S. Department of Health, Education and Welfare. Washington, D.C.: U.S. Government Printing Office.

1975 "Families in Poverty in the Early 1970's: Rates, Associated Factors, Some Implications." Journal of Marriage and the Family, 37, 1 (February):49–60.

Cohen, Wilbur
1973 "Toward the Elimination of Poverty." Current History 64, 382 (June):268–96.

Cornell, George
1974 "Partner of Poor: Yule Joy Clouded by Mass Starvation." Allentown Evening Call-Chronicle (December 17):1-2.

Coser, Lewis
1971 "The Sociology of Poverty." Social Problems 13 (Fall). In Esther Penchef, ed. The Four Horsemen: Pollution, Poverty, Famine, Violence. San Francisco: Canfield Press. 1965.

"Current Operating Statistics." Social Security Bulletin 40, 7 (July):77. U.S. Department of Health, Education and Welfare, Social Security Administration. Washington, D.C.: U.S. Government Printing Office, 1977.

Davis, Allen F. and Mark H. Haller, eds.
1973 The Peoples of Philadelphia: A History of Ethnic Groups and Lower-Class Life, 1790-1940. Philadelphia: Temple University Press.

de Schweinitz, Karl
1943 England's Road to Social Security. New York: A. S. Barnes.

Douglas, Jack
    1974 Defining America's Social Problems. Englewood, N.J.: Prentice-Hall.

Eccles, Mary E.
    1976 "Public Works Jobs Funds." Congressional Quarterly Weekly Report 34, 38 (September 18):2515.

Elesh, David
    1973 "Poverty Theories and Income Maintenance: Validity and Policy Relevance." Social Science Quarterly 54, 2 (September):359–73.

"For a Family of Four, Just Living Costs More." Allentown Morning Call (April 27):1, 1977.

Gallup, George
    1964 "Two Basically Different Views Held on Causes of Poverty." Pp. 45–46 in Robert E. Will and Harold G. Vatter, eds. Poverty in Affluence, 2nd ed. New York: Harcourt, Brace & World, 1970.

Gans, Herbert
    1968 "The 'Equality' Revolution." Pp. 80–88 in Rose Giallombardo, ed. Contemporary Social Issues. Santa Barbara, Calif.: Hamilton.
    1971 "The Uses of Poverty: The Poor Pay All." Social Policy (July/August). Pp. 166–69 in Peter Wickman, ed. Annual Editions: Readings in Social Problems 75/76. Guilford, Conn.: Dushkin.

Geldart, C. B.
    1966 Personal correspondence about the history of The Western Association of Ladies for the Relief and Employment of the Poor (December 7) Philadelphia.

Gillin, John L.
    1937 Poverty and Dependency: Their Relief and Prevention. 3rd ed. New York: D. Appleton-Century.

Gladwin, Thomas
    1967 Poverty, U.S.A. Boston: Little, Brown.

Glazer, Nathan
    1975 "Reform Work, Not Welfare." Public Interest 40 (Summer):4–12.

Greene, Leonard M.
    1976 A Plan for a National Demogrant Financed by a Value-Added Tax. White Plains, N.Y.: The Institute for Socioeconomic Studies.

Harrington, Michael
    1962 The Other America. New York: Macmillan.

"How Many Live in Real Want? Profile of America's Poor." U.S. News & World Report 81 (November 8):55–58, 1976.

Hunter, Robert
    1904 Poverty. New York: Macmillan. In Hanna H. Meissner, ed. Poverty in the Affluent Society. Rev. ed. New York: Harper & Row. 1973.

"Inflation." Voice of the Cement, Lime & Gypsum Workers International Union (July):7–8, 1974.

Jennings, William H.
    1972 Poor People and Churchgoers. New York: Seabury Press.

Jordon, Vernon E.
    1973 "Missing Tax Reform Proposals." Allentown Morning Call (June 1):10.

Kaplan, Roy and Curt Tausky
   1974 "The Meaning of Work among the Hard-Core Unemployed." Pacific Sociological Review 17, 2 (April):185–98.

Kelso, Robert W.
   1929 Poverty. New York: Longmans, Green and Co.

Kephart, William
   1966 The Family, Society and the Individual. Boston: Houghton Mifflin.

Kihss, Peter
   1976 "Creation of Jobs Is Held by Study to Be Way of Reducing Welfare." New York Times (September 19):52.

Lane, Robert E.
   1962 Political Ideology: Why the American Common Man Believes What He Does. Glencoe, Ill.: Free Press. In Robert E. Will and Harold G. Vatter, eds. Poverty in Affluence. 2nd ed. New York: Harcourt, Brace & World, 1970.

Lebergott, Stanley
   1975 "How to Increase Poverty." Commentary 60, 4 (October):59–63.

Lekachman, Robert
   1976 "Full Employment." Christianity and Crisis 36, 11 (September 20):194–97.

Levitan, Sar
   1973 "The Poor: Dimensions and Strategies." Current History 64, 382 (June):243–67.

Lewin, Roger
   1975 "Starved Brains." Psychology Today 9, 4 (September):29–34.

Lewis, Oscar
   1959 Five Families: Mexican Case Studies in the Culture of Poverty. New York: Basic Books.
   1961 The Children of Sanchez. New York: Random House.
   1966 La Vida: A Puerto Rican Family in the Culture of Poverty—San Juan and New York. New York: Random House.
   1970 Anthropological Essays. New York: Random House.

McVeigh, Frank
   1962 "The Good Old Days." Voice of Cement, Lime & Gypsum Workers International Union (October):29–31.

Massey, Garth M.
   1975 "Studying Social Class: The Case of Embourgeoisment and the Culture of Poverty." Social Problems 22, 5 (June):595–600.

Meissner, Hanna H., ed.
   1973 Poverty in the Affluent Society. Rev. ed. New York: Harper & Row.

Miller, S. M.
   1964 "The American Lower Class: A Typological Approach." Social Research 31, 1 (Spring):1–22.

Miller, S. M. and Pamela Roby
   1970 The Future of Inequality. New York: Basic Books.

"Most Families on Guaranteed Wage Didn't Lose Urge to Work." Allentown Morning Call (March 26):2, 1973.

Moynihan, Daniel P., ed.
    1968 On Understanding Poverty: Perspectives from the Social Sciences. New York: Basic Books.

"On the Brink." Voice of the Cement, Lime & Gypsum Workers International Union (July): back cover, 1974.

"Present Federal Jobs Programs." Congressional Digest 55, 6 & 7 (June/July):164–65, 1975.

Procopio, Mariellen and Frederick J. Perella, Jr.
    1976 Poverty Profile USA. New York: Paulist Press.

"Provisions of the Proposed Humphrey-Hawkins Bill." Congressional Digest 55, 6 & 7 (June/July):167–69, 1976.

"Public Assistance." Social Security Bulletin 40, 5 (May):58, 1977.

Rainwater, Lee
    1976 "Post-1984 America." Pp. 213–19 in Anne Kilbride, ed., Readings in Social Problems 76/77: Annual Editions. Guilford, Conn.: Dushkin.

Ramsey, Charles and Rita Braito
    1973 "Public Concepts of Poverty: The County Commissioners' Views." Journal of Sociology and Social Welfare 1, 2 (Winter):65–80.

Riis, Jacob
    1890 How the Other Half Lives: Studies among the Tenements of New York. New York: Scribner's. In Francesco Cordasco, ed., Jacob Riis Revisited. New York: Anchor, 1968.

Rosenbaum, David E.
    1977 "High-Level Officials Agree on Welfare Plan." Allentown Morning Call (May 17):1.

Ryan, William
    1976 Blaming the Victim. Revised ed. New York: Vintage.

Rydell, Lars and Charlene Rydell
    1973 "Poverty: Waning or Waxing?" Social Praxis 1, 4 (Winter):389–97.

Seligman, Ben B.
    1968 Permanent Poverty. Chicago: Quadrangle.

"Senator Hubert H. Humphrey Speech." The Journal of the Institute for Socioeconomic Studies, 1, 1 (Summer):35–52, 1976.

Shanahan, Eileen
    1976 "Poor in U.S. Rose by 2.5 Million in 1975, Most in Recent Decades." New York Times (September 26):1, 36.

Shevis, James M.
    1976 "Poverty Up Record 10.7% Under Ford." AFL-CIO News 21, 40 (October 2):1, 7.

Shostak, Arthur B.
    1974 Modern Social Reforms: Solving Today's Social Problems. New York: Macmillan.

Social and Rehabilitation Service
    1976 Annual Report of Welfare Programs in Fiscal Year 1975. U.S. Department of Health, Education and Welfare. Washington, D.C.: U.S. Government Printing Office.

Soderlind, Sterling
    1971 "From TVs to Houses, Families Find that One Is Not Enough." The National Observer (March 29):40.

Spencer, Herbert
    1850 Social Statics. Pp. 36–38 in Robert E. Will and Harold G. Vatter, eds. Poverty in Affluence. 2nd ed. New York: Harcourt, Brace & World. 1970

Stewart, Elbert W.
    1976 The Troubled Land. New York: McGraw-Hill.

Sumner, William Graham
    1900 What Social Classes Owe to Each Other. New York: Harper & Brothers.

Sweet, J. Stouder
    1967 Poverty in the U.S.A. Public Affairs Pamphlet No. 398. New York: Public Affairs Committee.

Trattner, Walter I.
    1974 From Poor Law to Welfare State. New York: Free Press.

U.S. Bureau of the Census
    1975 "Characteristics of the Low-Income Population: 1973." Current Population Reports. Series P-60, No. 98 (January). Washington, D.C.: U.S. Government Printing Office.
    1975 "Money Income in 1973 of Families and Persons in the United States." Current Population Reports, Series P-60, No. 97 (January). Washington, D.C.: U.S. Government Printing Office.
    1975 "Money Income and Poverty Status of Families and Persons in the United States: 1974." Current Population Reports. Series P-60, No. 99 (July). Washington, D.C.: U.S. Government Printing Office.
    1976 "Money Income and Poverty Status of Families and Persons in the United States: 1975." Current Population Reports. Series P-60, No. 103 (September). Washington, D.C.: U.S. Government Printing Office.

Villemez, Wayne and Alan Rowe
    1975 "Black Economic Gains in the Sixties: A Methodological Critique and Reassessment." Social Forces 54, 1 (September):181–93.

Walinsky, Adam
    1975 "Keeping the Poor in Their Place." Pp. 89–95 in Rose Giallombardo, ed. Contemporary Social Issues. Santa Barbara, Calif.: Hamilton.

Weinberger, Casper
    1976 "The Reform of Welfare: A National Necessity." The Journal of the Institute for Socioeconomic Studies 1, 1 (Summer):1–27.

Will, Robert E. and Harold H. Vatter, eds.
    1970 Poverty in Affluence. 2nd ed. New York: Harcourt, Brace & World.

Williamson, John B. and Kathryn Hyer
    1975 "The Measurement and Meaning of Poverty." Social Problems 22, 5 (June):652–63.

Wright, Sonia and James Wright
    1975 "Income Maintenance and Work Behavior." Social Policy 6, 2 (September/October):25–32.

SUGGESTED READINGS

Caudill, Harry M. The Watches of the Night. Boston: Little, Brown. 1976.
    A look back at attempts by the war on poverty (and other federal antipoverty programs) to solve the problem of poverty in Appalachia.

It describes the social and economic forces that blocked the changes.

Levitan, Sar A. and Robert Taggart. The Promise of Greatness. Cambridge, Mass.: Harvard University Press. 1976.

The social and economic policies that dominate thinking about poverty and the administration of welfare. Suggestions are made for improvements in the present system.

Pechman, Joseph and P. Michael Timpane, eds. Work Incentives and Income Guarantees: The New Jersey Negative Income Tax Experiment. Washington, D.C.: The Brookings Institution. 1975.

Result of a two-day conference reviewing and appraising the results of the Office of Economic Opportunity's experiment of granting money to poor persons to see whether it would affect their incentive to work.

Plotnick, Robert D. and Felicity Skidmore. Progress against Poverty: A Review of 1964–1974 Decade. New York: Academic Press, 1975.

The Wisconsin University Institute for Research on Poverty reviews the progress, problems, and promises in the war-on poverty program during parts of the 1960s and 1970s.

Siegal, Harvey A. Outposts of the Forgotten: New York City's Welfare Hotels and Single Occupancy Tenements. New Brunswick, N.J.: Transaction Books. 1977.

A poignant description of the old, nonwhite, unemployed, disabled poor who live amidst the affluence on the Upper West Side of Manhattan, yet are ignored by their neighbors.

Periodicals Worth Exploring

Human Resources
Human Resources Abstracts
Social Casework
Social Service Review
Social Work
Social Problems
Social Security Bulletin

Problems of Minorities in America

INTRODUCTION

DEFINITIONS OF THE PROBLEM
Cultural deprivation.
Inadequate family life.
Reverse discrimination.
Prejudice, discrimination.
Racism (symbolic or institutional).

INCIDENCE AND PREVALENCE OF THE PROBLEM
Blacks:
a) In-migration of blacks to cities; white flight to the suburbs.
b) Deficient health care.
c) Economic conditions; lower income, high unemployment and low-status employment.
d) Separate and unequal education.
e) Segregated housing patterns.
f) Political progress.
Spanish-Americans (Chicanos):
a) Growing numbers and dispersion.
b) Life conditions.
c) Plight of Puerto Ricans.
American Indians:
a) The Navajo nation.
b) Apaches on the reservation.

CAUSES OF THE PROBLEM
Prejudice.
Discrimination, segregation.
Institutional racism (class differences).

PROPOSED SOLUTIONS TO THE PROBLEM
Change of physical conditions.
Providing good jobs.
Changing white attitudes and norms.
Busing (a controversial proposal).
The Civil Rights Commission's report.
The new Coleman report.
Metropolitan-wide busing.
Desegregation and integration of schools.
Affirmative-action programs.
A hierarchy of priorities.

FUTURE OF THE PROBLEM
Larger numbers of minorities.
Four possible future approaches:
a) "Present policies."
b) "Enrichment."
c) Integration.
d) Separatism.

SUMMARY

The issue of equal rights for American Negroes is ... an important issue. And should we defeat every enemy, and should we double our wealth and conquer the stars and still be unequal to this issue, then we will have failed as a people and as a nation. For with a country as with a person, "What is a man profited, if he shall gain the whole world, and lose his own soul?"

President Lyndon Johnson's message to Congress urging passage of a voting-rights bill, March 15, 1965, as quoted by Robert Bellah, **Religion in America,** 1968:16.

Although the open conflict of the 1960s has passed, blacks and whites remain in a clear and open conflict situation.

Richard Ashmore, "The Today and Likely Tomorrow of American Race Relations," **The Journal of Social Issues** (Spring 1976):3.

"Our nation is moving toward two societies, one black, one white, separate and unequal." With these words a presidential commission in 1968 began to describe race relations as a social problem in America. It warned society that "within two decades the [black-white] division could be so deep it would be almost impossible to unite" (Report of the National Advisory Commission on Civil Disorder, 1968:407). About one decade has passed; yet much still remains to be done to understand and solve this critical social issue.

DEFINING THE MINORITY PROBLEM

Some conservatives view the racial problem as one of cultural deprivation. Blacks, Spanish-Americans (sometimes referred to as Chicanos*),

---

*William Madsen, professor of anthropology at the University of California, Santa Barbara, reports that "the origin and meaning of the word 'Chicano' are still being debated.... The prevailing opinion seems to be that 'Chicano' is short for 'Mexicano' but the two words are not synonymous and many Mexican-Americans who refer to themselves as 'Mexicanos' do not wish to be called 'Chicanos.'... Originally used as an epithet, the term has recently acquired new meanings, including the idea that a Chicano is a person of Mexican ancestry who will fight to defend himself and improve his position... A recent survey conducted by the University of Texas Center for Communications Research showed that most Mexican-Americans in the Southwest prefer to be called Mexicanos or Mexican-Americans rather than Chicanos. Of the persons interviewed in Texas, Arizona, and California, only 6 percent preferred to be called Chicanos" (1973:2, fn. 1).

and American Indians have not yet been acculturated into white, middle-class ways. As soon as these groups become better acculturated and assimilated into the dominant culture, they will be fully accepted, according to this definition of the problem. Their laziness, irresponsibility, and immorality are all considered part of this cultural deprivation. As Charles Silberman put it, a black tenant farmer working in the fields can drink a can of beer and toss the empty into a cotton patch—and no harm is done. But if this same black moves to the big city in the North, he cannot just toss his empty beer can out the window. If he does, there is trouble (1964:36–47).

Another conservative view of the problem is to see the "Negro family" as the principal problem in race relations. Daniel Moynihan's famous report, *The Negro Family: The Case for National Action* (1965), best illustrates this definition of the issue. Moynihan points out the absence in many black homes of male-role models, especially for young males. He sees widespread illegitimacy and a prevalence of matriarchy, or dominance of women, in rearing the children. Often, too, job opportunities are greater for black women than for men.

Both of these definitions of the problem are in line with the ideology of blaming the victim (Ryan, 1976:6). Nevertheless, research has shown that a large percentage of Americans accept these two definitions of the problem (Pettigrew, 1975:92–126).

Sociologists Horton and Leslie have pointed out some "myths, evasions, and rationalizations" used to define the racial problem. These include:

> It's their own fault.
> They like it that way.
> They prefer to be with their own people.
> Why don't Negroes work their way up like other immigrant groups did?
> Blacks are better off in America than in Africa.
> Whites have troubles, too (1974:391–96).

Reverse Discrimination

More recent definitions of the problem have emerged, including reverse discrimination and "they're taking over now." As government involvement, such as affirmative action and court decisions, opens up more equal job opportunities for minorities, members of the white dominant group consider such steps reverse discrimination. As social changes of the last decade or so begin to make blacks and other minorities more visible in education, housing, jobs, and politics, and as people encounter nonwhites in positions of power and authority for the first time, whites begin to assert, "They're taking over now."

The DeFunis case illustrates these definitions of the problem. Marco DeFunis, a white student, argued reverse discrimination when he was not accepted into the University of Washington's Law School, whereas black students with lower grades were admitted. A lower court decision upheld his case and he was admitted in 1971. The state supreme court ruled against him, but he appealed and was allowed to remain at school until a decision was reached. By the time the case came to the Supreme Court, DeFunis had graduated; so the high court neither accepted nor rejected his arguments—the case was "moot." This case, however, illustrates the emergence of the two new interpretations of the racial problem in America (Hamilton, 1974:24–25).

A similar case in California involved Glen DeRonde, a white student with higher test scores than 74 other applicants (mostly minority-group members) who were admitted to law school while DeRonde was rejected. The lower court ruled that DeRonde had not proven his case; but the judge did forbid further use of procedures that admitted those with lower test scores, calling such procedures reverse discrimination ("Reverse Discrimination," March 29, 1976:26). The Allen Bakke case at the University of California's Davis Medical School, involving reverse discrimination, has been appealed to the U.S. Supreme Court ("Reverse Bias Ruling," December 31, 1976:995). Sociologist Nathan Glazer maintains that the United States has adopted a policy of "affirmative discrimination" under the 1964 Civil Rights Act, favoring blacks in jobs, housing, and education ("Equal Opportunity," January 22, 1976:151–53).

Most sociologists define the racial problem in terms of prejudice, discrimination, and institutional racism of the dominant group (white) against various minorities. The largest minority groups in the United States are blacks, the Spanish-speaking (or Chicanos), American Indians, Asians (Japanese, Chinese, etc.), and Jews. Together they make up over 18 percent of the population and number over 37 million. (Women, although a minority group in respect to roles, status, position, and treatment, are discussed in Chapter 4.)

Although American Indians and Spanish-Americans have emerged as dynamic minority groups in recent years, our concern about race relations usually focuses on the blacks when we wish to analyze and understand the issue. They are our largest racial minority, and are easily differentiated from and by the dominant group because of their skin color. Historically and geographically, most of the country has been directly or indirectly affected by the black situation (Pettigrew, 1975:xiv). Spanish-Americans, Puerto Ricans, and American Indians have not spread as widely across our society as blacks. Also, it was the black civil-rights movement of the 1960s that called our society's attention to the plight of other minority groups (Himes, 1974:8–10). Hence we will here emphasize the black-white issue, although also giving attention to Spanish-Americans and American Indians.

7 PROBLEMS OF MINORITIES IN AMERICA

Key Concepts

The three key concepts in examining the social problem of race relations are prejudice, discrimination, and institutional racism.

Prejudice. Prejudice means literally to prejudge. A predisposition or attitude exists among many dominant-group members to judge a minority person or group on limited or incorrect information. The same holds true for the minority-group member who is prejudiced against the dominant group. (Of course, one predisposition may be the cause and the other the effect.) Prejudice exists and persists only if it cannot be changed by new knowledge or experience.

The important point about racial prejudice is that it is often unconscious. Gordon Allport pointed this out in his classic work *The Nature of Prejudice* (1954). The most prejudiced persons are often the last to know it. This unconscious nature of prejudice makes it possible for otherwise-concerned persons to be indifferent or hostile to members of minority groups. Allport observes that different "levels of action" may emerge from prejudice. The first would be verbal, a racial slur; second, avoidance; third, overt discrimination—an act against the minority group; fourth, physical abuse and attack; fifth, extermination (1954:14–15). The inherent danger of prejudice is that it can escalate and explode into racial conflict. As the boxed item reports, prejudice may lead to violence.

Discrimination. Discrimination is the "unfavorable treatment of individuals or groups based on purely arbitrary grounds—such as race, religion, or sex" (Freeman and Jones, 1973:138). Discrimination ignores in-

Prejudice, discrimination, and racism—whether symbolic or institutional—may lead to conflict and violence between blacks and whites.

> **ANTIBIAS PLANNER SLAIN IN OHIO**
>
> A desegregation planner, Dr. Charles A. Glatt, was fatally shot ... in the building in which he was writing an integration proposal for the city's schools, a hospital reported.
>
> Hours after the incident, Neal Bradley Long, 48, a white Dayton service station attendant, was arraigned before a U.S. magistrate in the same building.
>
> Long was charged with murder. No plea was entered and a preliminary hearing was set ...
>
> After the shooting—about 3 p.m.—Glatt, 47, was operated on at a local hospital for four bullet wounds. He died on the operating table.
>
> Source: *Allentown Morning Call*, September 20, 1975:2.

dividual attributes or characteristics and acts on the basis of real or imagined group categories. It is often the outgrowth of the society's social structure and value system, rather than the personality of people (Kitano, 1966:23–31). It becomes a social problem when enough people become aware of it, view it as undesirable, and feel that something can and should be changed.

It was once thought that discrimination always resulted when individual or group prejudice was present. Several studies, including those of Merton (1949), Rabb and Lipset (1972), Grimshaw (1961), Linn (1965), Warner and Dennis (1970), and Watson (1973), suggest this is not always so. Prejudice can exist with or without discrimination resulting; and discrimination can occur with or without prejudice. In addition, social scientists know that prejudice and discrimination can reinforce one another (Simpson and Yinger, 1972:29). Prejudice is learned, usually early in childhood from parents and peers. Negative racial attitudes are formed more often by contact with prejudiced persons than by contact with a minority group (Linn, 1965).

Institutional Racism. To analyze race relations as a social problem, we must understand a third concept, institutional racism. In this situation, people with the best intentions may produce the worst results. As Jonathan Brower put it, "... the disturbing aspect of institutional racism is that many racist consequences are entirely unintentional" (1975:50). According to Robert Friedman, institutional racism is "any action, policy, ideology, or structure of an institution which works to the relative disadvantage of blacks as compared to whites" (1975:386). This institutional racism is so critical to our understanding of the racial problem. The issue of race relations emanates mainly from the normal, daily operations of white-controlled groups, organizations, and social systems. Often no overt racial malice or hatred is involved, and in this respect the nature of our racial problem has changed.

Hence, an employer who requires a high-school diploma for unskilled or semiskilled jobs wittingly or unwittingly screens out many otherwise qualified minority-group applicants. A bank that lends money only to those with a stable work history excludes millions of minority-group members who have taken jobs where and when they could get them. An insurance firm that issues no policies in high-risk neighborhoods makes money in, but alienates residents of, such areas. A college or university that automatically does not accept high-school students below a certain grade average keeps out minority-group students who come from schools that may not have motivated them to do well. A community whose zoning laws forbid certain kinds of housing produces a racially apartheid society.

Sometimes a feeling of innate superiority, conscious or unconscious, is a part of racism (Daniels and Kitano, 1970). At other times, strong negative feelings toward the poor—blacks, Spanish-Americans, and whites—are all part of institutional racism.

The Equal Employment Opportunity Commission (EEOC) recognizes the existence of institutional racism in business; for example, that the most pervasive discrimination in industry today results from normal, often unintentional, and seemingly neutral practices throughout the employment process (EEOC, 1974:4–5). A company's personnel department often perpetuates the racial discrimination of the past by hiring minorities only for traditional unskilled, low-status occupations. It is such "systemic" discrimination that affirmative-action programs are designed to eliminate. Similarly, the courts have consistently ruled that it is the effects of employment practices—not "their intent" or the motivation of the employer—that determine their legality.

Symbolic Racism

In addition to the three key concepts of prejudice, discrimination, and institutional racism, the social problem has become a bit more complex with the appearance of symbolic racism. Social scientists point out that *direct expression* of racial prejudice is less socially acceptable than it was 10 or 20 years ago. Now prejudicial feelings and beliefs are symbolically masked in issues that "appear at face value to be independent of racial bias but which reflect racial concerns" (Hamilton and Bishop, Spring 1976:53). For example, support of law-and-order policies, criticism of welfare programs, and advocacy of freedom-of-choice policies in housing or in school busing symbolically and really reflect antiblack attitudes and fears (McConahay and Hough, Spring 1976:23–46).

INCIDENCE AND PREVALENCE OF THE MINORITY PROBLEM
Black Americans

Since the more than 23 million blacks make up only 11½ percent of our population, we might be tempted to say that the racial problem is not very prevalent. Yet if we include other minority groups (other than women) who experience prejudice, discrimination, segregation, and institutional racism, the number grows to nearly 40 million, or 18 percent of our population. Chicanos and other Spanish-speaking Americans, according to one source, now number about 22 million, and possibly in the 1980s will outnumber blacks as our largest minority group (Halsell, May 13, 1977:1). Table 7-1 shows the number and percentage of minority-group persons in the United States.

Another way to interpret the problem is to see how the numbers and percentages of blacks have diffused throughout our society. In doing so, we will examine the movement of the people (and by imputation the problem) into urban areas. After that, we shall look at some of the ways our social institutions have affected the environmental conditions and life chances of blacks as a group.

Movement in Cities. Every ethnic group coming to America has moved into neighborhoods originally dominated by some other group. This social and ecological process is called "invasion." When the new ethnic group comes to dominate that area by numbers, "succession" has taken place. It is this process of invasion and succession that often makes the larger society sensitive to and aware of race relations as a social problem.

The rapid influx of new people into an area is sometimes viewed as a social problem in itself. When the newcomers are of a minority group, the problem is compounded; for it brings minority- and majority-group members into contact with one another, frequently for the first time.

table 7-1   MINORITY GROUPS IN THE UNITED STATES — 1970–1976
(in rank order)

RACIAL OR ETHNIC GROUP	1976 POPULATION	1970 POPULATION	PERCENTAGE OF U.S. POPULATION 1970
BLACKS	23,785,000	22,933,000	11.25
JEWS	6,653,725*	5,634,000	2.75
MEXICAN-AMERICANS (CHICANOS)	6,590,000	5,073,000	2.48
OTHER SPANISH ORIGIN	2,774,000		
PUERTO RICANS	1,753,000	1,454,000	.71
AMERICAN INDIANS	N.A.	827,000	.40
JAPANESE	N.A.	539,000	.26
ASIATIC (EXCEPT JAPANESE & CHINESE)	N.A.	284,000	.14
CHINESE	N.A.	269,000	.13
TOTAL		37,013,000	18.12

*Includes Canada.
Source: Adapted from U.S. Bureau of the Census, **Current Population Reports,** Series P-20 and P-25 (February/March 1970). 1976 figures from U.S. Bureau of the Census, **Current Population Reports,** Series P-20, No. 307 (April 1977):42. Figures on 1976 Jewish population from Ann Golenpaul, ed. **Information Please Almanac,** 1977:411.

As long as the black population was clustered in the rural South, racial problems tended to be analyzed as rather limited and regional. In 1900, 90 percent of blacks lived in the South. In 1915, because of World War I, an exodus of about 250,000 blacks occurred. The exodus has continued ever since, although the rate of outmigration is beginning to slow down. The result of the long-term migration has been startling, as Pettigrew reported.

> Today more Negroes live in the New York metropolitan area than in any single southern state, about as many Negroes live in metropolitan Chicago as in the entire state of Mississippi, and more Negroes live in metropolitan Philadelphia than in the entire states of Arkansas and Kentucky combined (1969:47–48).

That was in 1960. Between 1960 and 1970, according to the Census figures, nearly a million-and-a-half more black people left the South, more than three-fourths went to five large industrial states—New York, California, New Jersey, Illinois, and Michigan (Rosenthal, 1971:1).

But something else happened, too. As Southern blacks moved North and West, Northern and Western whites moved to the South in record numbers. Between 1970 and 1974, there were 1,800,000 more immigrants to the South than outmigrants (U.S. Bureau of the Census, Current Population Reports, Series P-20, No. 292, 1976:24). The result of this dual flow is the continuing long-term trend toward the gradual dispersion of the black population throughout the country. The South in 1975 contained only about 53 percent of the black population (compared with 77 percent in 1940). The Northeast and Midwest had about 39 percent of the black population and about 8 percent resided in the West.

The outmigration signaled a shift from a rural population to an urban one. Today, about three-fourths of all blacks live in metropolitan areas and many large cities are over 50 percent black. While the population of central-city blacks (and other races) increased by over 1.5 million (+11.5 percent) between 1970 and 1976, the white population decreased by over three-and-a-half million (−8.2 percent). In suburbs close to metropolitan areas, the white population increased almost five times faster than minorities. In suburbs and towns outside of metropolitan areas, the black population held steady, while white population increased by nearly 5 million.

White people and businesses by the millions have fled the central cities for the suburbs. Table 7-2 shows how unmistakable this trend has been since 1960. (Of course, Chicanos are classified as white. If they were added to the category of blacks and other races, the change would be even more dramatic.)

Our social structure itself has added to the inequality and improper treatment of minority-group people. Sometimes unintentionally, other times deliberately, our social structure has had a dramatic and negative impact on the immediate social milieux, life conditions, and life chances

table 7-2   POPULATION DISTRIBUTION AND CHANGE, INSIDE AND OUTSIDE METROPOLITAN AREAS (1960, 1970, 1975, and 1976) (numbers in millions)

AREA	BLACKS AND OTHER MINORITY RACES				WHITES			
	1960	1970	1975	1976	1960	1970	1975	1976
UNITED STATES	18.9	24.5	27.1	27.7	158.8	175.2	181.6	182.6
METROPOLITAN AREAS[1]	12.8	18.1	20.7	21.2	106.4	118.9	121.3	121.4
CENTRAL CITIES[2]	9.9	13.9	15.3	15.5	49.5	48.9	45.5	45.2
OUTSIDE CENTRAL CITIES	2.9	4.1	5.3	5.6	56.9	70.0	75.7	76.1
OUTSIDE METROPOLITAN AREAS	6.1	6.4	6.3	6.5	52.4	56.3	60.3	61.2

CHANGE, 1970–1976

	BLACKS AND OTHER MINORITY RACES		WHITES	
	Number	Percentage	Number	Percentage
UNITED STATES	3.2	13.0	7.4	4.2
METROPOLITAN AREAS[1]	3.1	17.1	2.5	2.1
CENTRAL CITIES[2]	1.6	11.5	−3.7	−8.2
OUTSIDE CENTRAL CITIES	1.5	36.5	6.1	8.7
OUTSIDE METROPOLITAN AREAS	0.1	1.5	4.9	8.7

Source: U.S. Bureau of the Census, **Current Population Reports**, Series P-23, (July 1972): 18; Series P-20, No. 279 (March 1975): 21; Series P-20, No. 292 (March 1976): 23; and Series P-20, No. 307, (April 1977): 26.
[1] Population of the 243 SMSAs as defined in the 1970 Census publication.
[2] Data for 1975 refer to their January 1, 1970 boundaries and exclude areas annexed since 1970.

of minority groups. Our white-dominated social institutions—medical care, corporations, unions, schools, real estate and political systems—have often done little to reduce the inequality and discrimination against minorities.

Health Care. Proper health care traditionally has not been made available on an equal basis to blacks or other minorities. As a rule minorities do not visit a doctor or dentist as often as whites, and when they do, it is more likely in a hospital clinic or emergency room than an office (Hill, 1973:5). Often, because of discrimination, they cannot afford good care. In addition, hospital care in black communities is worsening. Of the some 50 black hospitals that were operating when medical care was more segregated, only about 30 remain, and they are having a hard time surviving financially.

All these inequities in delivery of health care to minorities are reflected in the higher rates of adult, infant, and maternal mortality among blacks. The life expectancy of blacks has always been lower, too. Blacks (both male and female) can expect to live six years fewer than whites of the same sex. These differences actually became wider during the 1960s (McVeigh, 1970:46). The infant mortality rates of nonwhites also have always been greater than for whites, and are about 65 percent greater today (Kotelchuck, 1976:6). The same holds true for women dying in childbirth. No matter what aspects of health care we measure, the result is usually worse for blacks, American Indians, and Chicanos than for whites.

Income. The economic outlook has improved somewhat for blacks in recent years through higher incomes and better employment opportunities in corporations. But they are still far behind whites, as we can see from Figure 7-1.

Black families in 1976 earned only 62 percent of white families' median income ($9,240 compared with $15,540). The percentage of poverty-level persons among blacks (and other minorities) in 1975 was much greater than for whites (31.3 percent for blacks and 27 percent for Spanish-Americans compared with only 9.7 percent for whites) (U.S. Bureau of the Census, CPR, P-20, No. 307, 1977:42). Since 1947, in constant dollars, the increase in income for white families has been greater by $1,351 than for black families. It cannot be assumed, as Banfield

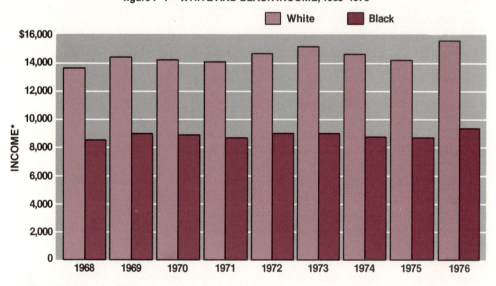

figure 7-1 WHITE AND BLACK INCOME, 1968–1976

*The figures are for median family income, adjusted to eliminate the effects of inflation.

Source: Bureau of the Census.

table 7-3	BLACK AMERICA'S ECONOMIC STATUS			
UNEMPLOYMENT		BLACK	WHITE	YEARS
OVERALL		12.9%	7.1%	1976*
		13.4	7.5	1975†
		9.8	4.8	1974
		8.2	4.5	1970
TEENAGERS (16 to 19)		33.6	15.6	1976
		31.7	15.1	1971
		29.1	13.5	1970
EMPLOYMENT (BY OCCUPATIONS)				
WHITE-COLLAR WORKERS		33.5%	50.0%	1976
BLUE-COLLAR WORKERS		39.0	33.5	1976
SERVICE WORKERS		24.4	12.8	1976
FARM WORKERS		3.1	3.7	1976
		100.0%	100.0%	
PROFESSIONALS		1,072,720	11,659,000	1976
		+40%	+12%	1970–76
MANAGERIAL		399,800	8,864,000	1976
		+34%	+11%	1970–76
INCOME				
BELOW POVERTY LEVEL ($5,500)		31.4%	9.0%	1975
MEDIAN FAMILY INCOME		$9,240	$15,540	1976

Sources: Employment & Earnings August 1976: 5, 26, 35; Current Population Reports, "Consumer Income" Series P-60, No. 100 (August 1975) and No. 102 (January 1976).
*All 1976 dates are through July.
†Unemployment in 1975 was at the highest level since the 1930s, with nonwhites hit hardest.

(1974:135) and Wattenberg and Scammon (1973:35–44) do, that most blacks have made it: the economic and corporate social structure still does not operate as well for blacks.

Unemployment and Employment. Part of the reason for the lower family income among blacks is unemployment. Over the years, the *reported* unemployment rate of nonwhites has been consistently about twice as high as for whites (McVeigh, 1970:47–48), as we can see from Table 7-3. Among black teenagers the problem is even worse.

The effects of the long and persistent history of institutional racism and discrimination in some of the building-trades unions can be seen in Table 7-4. But unions are not the only institution to put barriers in the way of blacks and other minorities who are qualified to hold good jobs.

Occupations. Although some progress has been made in the percentage and number of white-collar jobs opening up for blacks, much still

table 7-4 UNION MEMBERSHIP

(IN UNIONS WITH HIRING-HALL OR REFERRAL PRACTICES)

UNIONS	BLACK	SPANISH SURNAME	ORIENTAL	AM. IND.	WHITE
PLUMBERS	0.8%	1.4%	0.5%	0.5%	96.8%
CARPENTERS	2.9	4.9	0.2	0.4	91.6
RETAIL CLERKS	5.6	8.8	4.1	0.2	81.3
TEAMSTERS	8.3	6.1	0.5	0.2	84.9
HOTEL–RESTAURANT	12.8	8.7	4.4	0.2	73.9
LABORERS	24.1	10.7	0.3	1.3	63.6

Source: 1969 Equal Employment Opportunity Commission Survey.

remains to be achieved by corporations. Between 1970 and 1976, the number of blacks hired as professionals and managers increased about 37 percent. But in that period, as well as from 1960 to 1972, black women made more progress than black men. Furthermore, these recorded gains were in the lower-paying professional jobs, such as technicians, rather than the higher-paying professions, such as doctors or lawyers. Even in public education, where some 450,000 blacks are employed, most are concentrated in the lower job classes (see Table 7-5).

The data also reveal that about 40 percent of the jobs all blacks hold are as household and service workers (females) and as service and nonfarm laborers (males). This represents only a slight change over the situation in 1965 (McVeigh, 1970:47). Because of lack of equal opportunities blacks

table 7-5 BLACK PERCENTAGE OF TOTAL EMPLOYMENT BY OCCUPATION IN PUBLIC EDUCATION 1975

OCCUPATIONAL CATEGORY	BLACK PERCENTAGE OF TOTAL
PROFESSIONAL TECHNICAL	8.2%
MANAGERS/ADMINISTRATORS	7.0
SALES WORKERS	5.4
CLERICAL WORKERS	9.8
CRAFTSMEN	8.2
OPERATIVES	14.5
LABORERS	12.7
SERVICE WORKERS	18.3
NOT ACCOUNTED FOR IN OTHER CATEGORIES	15.9
	100.0%
PERCENTAGE OF ALL WORKERS IN PUBLIC EDUCATION	9.9

Source: Adapted from "Industries," *Black Enterprise* (March 1976): 46.

are often forced to join the army as the only realistic alternative to unemployment. As the boxed item indicates, blacks make up a higher percentage of the army than their numbers would merit. Thus, our economic structure is still not color blind and must continue to change if black-white occupational distribution is to reach parity and equality.

Education. It is often said that if blacks want to earn as much as whites, they should be just as well educated; that they have lower income and poorer jobs because they have less education. There is some validity to such statements—but not much.

In 1969, figures showed that white males with only a high-school education earned $9,462 while black males with a college degree made only $8,652. Here was economic discrimination at its worst. The latest figures still show about a 40 percent gap in overall income between blacks and whites. Recent studies also suggest that blacks with "some college" often end up with jobs of the same quality and pay as white high-school graduates.

Despite this disparity, blacks are continuing to get more education. In 1960, 192,344 blacks enrolled in college; in 1970, 522,000 enrolled—16 percent of the black college-age group (Thompson, 1974:18). By 1976, their numbers increased to 1,062,000 (U.S. Bureau of Census, CPR, No. 307, 1977:18). Also, blacks are attending more white colleges and universities than previously.

Nevertheless, education as a social structure is a segregated one. Even though the 1954 Supreme Court decision outlawed "separate but equal" schools, and called on school districts to desegregate "with all deliberate speed," the schools have remained separate (and by no means equal). Nearly 25 years later, our educational institutions remain as segregated as ever, sometimes more so in the North than in the South.

ARMY GROWING BLACK

There is a higher percentage of blacks in the U.S. Army than ever before in the history of the nation.

Constituting 11 percent of the population, blacks account for 30 percent of the army's personnel. The jobless rate for young blacks ranges from 32 to 42 percent, which is the basic reason so many young black men and women join the Army. Pentagon officials say no attempt will be made to proportion enlistments racially.

When the all-volunteer Army replaced the draft, many legislators predicted that the U.S. Army would become predominantly black unless the economy boomed or held steady. Their predictions may yet come to pass.

Source: Pamela Swift, "Keeping Up with Youth," *Parade Magazine* (November 20, 1976):4.

In the South the situation has changed somewhat since 1954. In 1968, 78.8 percent of all black students in the South were in schools between 80 and 100 percent black. Some 68 percent were in all-black schools. By 1971, only 32.2 percent of black Southerners were in schools between 80 to 100 percent black, and only 9.2 percent were in all-black schools (Thompson, 1974:177). Although the South began to make progress desegregating its schools, whites fleeing the city public schools have been a problem. Many Southern city schools have lost white pupils, either to the suburbs or to the 3,000 or so private, all-white academies that sprang up when desegregation began. Major Southern cities, such as Atlanta, Birmingham, Jackson, Memphis, New Orleans, Norfolk, Richmond, and Savannah all have black majorities in their schools (Ravitch, 1976:167).

It will be several more years before we are sure whether we will have racially integrated schools or "separate but equal" schools in "two separate societies, one black, one white." Judging from the ecological patterns of "invasion and succession" over the past 30 years (and barring a dynamic, liberal administration in Washington), it appears we are headed toward a racially apartheid school system and society.

Housing. Perhaps no other institution has done so much to increase the incidence and prevalence of racial problems as our real estate and housing system. For example, school busing to achieve integration would be relatively unnecessary if we had integrated housing patterns.

In 1965, Karl and Alma Taeuber discovered that American cities had become almost incurably segregated. A normal distribution of the population, without respect to race, would require 88 percent of the black population to move from their present blocks to all-white blocks (1965:34). In 1966, the black population in central cities numbered 12 million; by 1975, it was over 15 million, and is projected to be nearly 21 million by 1985 (Report of the National Advisory Commission, 1968:390). In 1960, about 4.5 percent of our suburban population was black; in 1975 the figure was still the same and by 1985 the percentage of suburban blacks will be much the same, according to the National Commission on Urban Problems. Even then, most blacks who will live in the suburbs will live chiefly in all-black communities. If we do not begin to do something about segregated neighborhood housing patterns now, it will be too late to achieve an integrated society in 1980, 1990, or 2000.

The quality of housing that blacks must live in is worse than for whites. Approximately 20 percent of black housing units are overcrowded (more than one and one-tenth persons per room), compared with only seven percent of white housing units.

About 42 percent of blacks own their own homes, compared with almost 67 percent of whites. Some two million white Americans own two or more homes, whereas one-sixth of our population, mostly poor and minority-group persons, do not have decent housing.

In spite of gains the civil-rights movement brought to minority groups in the 1960s and 1970s, the predominant attitude is clearly to discourage a change in our segregated housing patterns (Pettigrew, 1975:21–84).

Political Progress. One social structure that has changed for blacks in recent years is the political one. Political activity was begun by the civil-rights movement in the 1960s, encouraged by the Voting Rights Act of 1965, and sustained by black activism in the 1970s. Extension of the Voting Rights Act in 1975 to include American Indians, Chicanos, and other minorities should encourage even more political participation. In 1975 there were 3,503 black elected officials nationwide (Golenpaul, 1976:29). These dramatic gains in elective offices are overshadowed by the total number of elective offices in our country. Blacks in 1972 held only one-half of one percent of all elective offices in the United States (Hamilton, 1974:13).

Nonetheless, black gains reflect their numbers in large urban centers and in parts of the South where they are clustered together. The number of blacks elected to office increased significantly between 1970 and 1975. See Table 7-6 for selected totals.

Voter registration in the 11 Southern states has increased markedly, and represents a historical change; yet in the 1976 presidential election only 46 percent of eligible Southern blacks voted.

By the 1970s, a new way of understanding race relations had emerged. The social issue of race is basically institutional, not personal, and the incidence and prevalence of the problem are increased by the structural arrangements we have established in health care, our economy, education, housing, and politics.

Spanish-Americans (Chicanos)

Spanish-Americans are officially defined by the Census as "persons of Spanish origin." These include Mexican-Americans (Chicanos), Puerto Ricans, Cubans, persons from Central or South America, and those of "other Spanish origin." About 60 percent of Spanish-Americans are Chicanos and about 16 percent are Puerto Ricans. In all, over 11 million

table 7-6 BLACK ELECTED OFFICIALS

	1970	1975
U.S. SENATORS	10	17
STATE REPS., LEGISLATORS, EXECUTIVES	178	299
MAYORS AND OTHER LOCAL OFFICIALS	599	1,878
JUDGES, MAGISTRATES, POLICE CHIEFS, LAW-ENFORCEMENT OFFICIALS	161	387
MEMBERS OF LOCAL SCHOOL BOARDS	362	939*

*Includes local school boards, college boards, and others.
Source: Joint Center for Political Studies, Washington, D.C. 1974 and Ann Golenpaul, ed., *Information Please Almanac*, 1977:29.

persons of Spanish origin were estimated by the Census Bureau in 1976 (CPR, No. 302, 1976:3–7). Of course, there are millions more who may not have been counted, and many are illegal aliens who have avoided detection. This had led some to estimate the Spanish-American population at about 22 million in 1977 (Halsell, May 13, 1977:1). The Spanish-Americans are the nation's youngest and fastest growing group and should no longer be ignored by our society. The United States now is the fifth largest Spanish-speaking nation in the world, and Spanish now ranks as one of the world's main languages.

Growing Numbers and Dispersion. We tend to think of this minority group as clustered in certain regions of the country: Chicanos in the Southwest and California; Puerto Ricans in the Northeast, particularly the New York City area; and Cubans in the Southeast. Although this is generally true, New Jersey has more Spanish-Americans than Arizona; and the State of Illinois (with about one million) has more Spanish-Americans than Arizona and New Mexico combined. Their sheer numbers will expose the problem of discrimination so that the prevalence of this social problem will grow as their numbers grow and they begin to spread across the nation. Some 84 percent of all Spanish-American families live in metropolitan areas, with the majority residing in the central cities areas, usually segregated in "barrios" (virtual ghettos).

Mexican-Americans (Chicanos) as an ethnic and cultural group were the creation of the imperial conquest of one nation by another through military force. Before 1836 and the Mexican-American War of 1845, Texas and most of the Southwestern United States were owned by Mexico. With the signing of the Treaty of Guadalupe Hidalgo, the Mexican-Americans "were created *as a people;* Mexican by birth, language and culture; United States citizens by the might of arms" (Alvarez, 1973:920, 923). Yet many Anglos still think that all Spanish-speaking persons have recently come across the border to pick crops.

Life Conditions. Today, because of discrimination and lack of equal opportunities in education and employment, over 25 percent of Mexican-American families live in poverty. Chicanos in 1975 had a median family income of $9,546, about two-thirds that of Anglo families (U.S. Census Bureau, CPR, No. 307, 1977:42). In some sections of Texas, poverty-stricken Mexican-Americans live in unbelievably primitive conditions (Madsen, 1973:33). Countrywide, the unemployment rate among Chicanos is usually twice as high as the unemployment rate among Anglos. Also, the vast majority of employed Mexican-Americans work at unskilled or low-skilled, low-paying jobs. Only about 8 percent are officially employed as farm workers.

Mexican-Americans average four years less schooling than Anglos, and two years less than blacks. Only about one-third of Chicanos have had a real opportunity to complete high school. There is also a traditional lack of institutions of higher learning "of, for and by Chicanos," as compared with over 100 black institutions of higher learning. Chicanos are just beginning to develop such schools (Alvarez, 1973:938).

Health conditions among Chicanos are generally poor, but accurate statistics are hard to find because Mexican-Americans are usually lumped together with whites. In Colorado, a survey showed that persons with Spanish surnames had a life expectancy of only 56.7 years—10 years less than the life expectancy of Colorado Anglos. According to José Angel Gutierrez, a respected Chicano leader, "This kind of thing is found all over the Southwest" ("Tio-Taco Is Dead," 1970:23).

But poverty and poor health are only part of the story. Mexican-Americans have long been subjected to violence by the authorities. For years, law-enforcement agencies in the Southwest have acted as if it were "open season" on Chicanos. Overall, the insensitivity of Anglos—whether in government, in education, or simply on a person-to-person basis—has amounted to social oppression of wide dimensions. The social structure of a predominantly Anglo society is stacked against a people who wants to succeed and enjoy the same rights as all other Americans. "Why do they persecute us?" asks Bob Castro, a Chicano activist in Los Angeles. "Why do they beat us and throw us into prison? Why do they insult our language and our culture and our history? Why do they call us names? Why do they deny us jobs?" And he adds: "Why do they hate us?" (Ibid.)

The Plight of Puerto Ricans

Puerto Ricans, though smaller in numbers than Mexican-Americans, suffer from essentially the same pervasive prejudice and institutional discrimination. Puerto Ricans as a group have lower income, higher unemployment, lower high-school completion rates, and greater concentration in central cities than Mexican-Americans or other groups of Spanish origin.

A recent report of the U.S. Commission on Civil Rights says that living conditions for second- and third-generation Puerto Ricans in Northern cities are worsening. The Commission reports that "mainland Puerto Ricans generally continue mired in the poverty facing first generations of all immigrants or migrant groups" ("Puerto Ricans . . . ," June 22, 1977:19).

Unemployment and underemployment in the Chicago Puerto Rican community is at least two to three times that of white Chicagoans, and unemployment among Puerto Rican teenagers may be 40 percent or greater.

The Commission termed as "grave" the educational problems of Chicago Puerto Ricans and said the high absenteeism, school dropout rate, and the low reading scores of Puerto Rican youths reflect the failure of the school system to provide for their needs.

A study by Northwestern University found that Puerto Ricans complain of "daily harassment and insults" from the police and that they "continue to be short-changed in important government services" (Ibid.).

It also cited the poor and decaying housing conditions in which large numbers of Puerto Ricans are forced to live.

American Indians

According to the 1970 Census, there were 827,091 American Indians, nearly .05 percent of our total population. Because of undercounting in the census, some "unofficial estimates place the Indian population as high as 1.5 million" (Faherty, 1976:165). Discrimination and hatred against Indians are nothing new, and notions about Indians as savages to be eradicated were long part of official United States government policy. In 1830 the Indian Removal Act was signed into law, justifying the forceable removal of Indians from lands the white man wanted. After the Civil War, government reservations were set up to impound Indian tribes. In 1871, Congress ended the making of treaties with Indian tribes because "it was degrading for Congress to give equal status to nations of primitive people" (Ibid.). From then until 1924, all Indians became "property" (wards) of the federal government without any rights as citizens.

In 1890 (a year after the Sioux Indians were put onto reservations), thinking that Indian "Ghost Dances," a religious revival ritual, were a preparation for warfare, the Army massacred 200 Indian women and children and 98 disarmed Indians at Wounded Knee, South Dakota. It was not until 1973 that the Indians "recaptured" that town as a real and symbolic reminder of how white society has mistreated them.

The structural basis of institutional racism against Indians can be seen in the life conditions produced among the Navajo Indians, and among the Apaches on the San Carlos, Arizona, reservation.

The Navajo Nation. The Civil Rights Commission in 1975 issued a report entitled "The Navajo Nation: An American Colony." In its report the Commission called the conditions on the reservation "shocking and disgraceful" ("U.S. Panel . . . ," September 17, 1975:63). The Navajo reservation, the largest in the nation, covers parts of Arizona, New Mexico, and Utah. There, unemployment among about 137,000 Indians was extremely high, and per capita income was about 25 percent of the national average. Education on the reservation was inadequate and uncoordinated by the states and agencies responsible for it. According to the Commission, health care is "not only inadequate, it is unsafe. . . . The hospitals are understaffed and the staff is overworked—and mistakes, serious mistakes, are common" (Ibid.).

Apaches on the Reservation. On the San Carlos, Arizona, reservation Apache Indians experience similar life conditions. Unemployment fluctuates between 25 and 40 percent; almost 2,000 of the 5,000 Indians are on some kind of welfare; over 80 percent of the reservation's homes were found unfit to live in; and about 20 percent of the population had a serious alcohol problem. A rising suicide rate was also reported (Nilsson, August 5, 1973:D-7).

These life conditions are typical of the social environment produced by a white-dominated social structure that prefers to ignore or discriminate against "native Americans" rather than produce a society that would give them the means to live in dignity and with equality.

Innocent women and children and unarmed Indian men were killed by the Army at Wounded Knee, South Dakota, in 1890. The occurrence became a symbol of white brutality and hatred toward the American Indian, though the whites labeled the incident a "battle."

About 82 years after the massacre of Sioux Indians at Wounded Knee, over 200 armed supporters of the American Indian Movement seized the town and demanded that the Senate investigate Indian grievances. They held the town for about 70 days. Since then, Congress has shown only sporadic interest in Indian problems.

CAUSES OF THE MINORITY PROBLEM

What causes the behavior patterns between the dominant and minority groups that make race relations a social problem? Many things. A rough consensus among sociologists suggests the following major causes of our racial problems: racial prejudice, overt and covert discrimination, racial segregation, institutional racism (as previously defined), and subcultural and social-class differences. As we discuss these points, we will be examining the attitudes, actions, and values of blacks and whites.

Racial Prejudice

Racial prejudice has many different causes, often acting in combination with one another. Theories to explain the causes of prejudice include economic competition or exploitation, frustration and aggression, scapegoating, the authoritarian personality, power or status motivation, ideological clash, and historical factors (Simpson and Yinger, 1972: Chaps. 3, 4, 5).

According to Rose and Rose, all intergroup prejudice and discrimination are based upon power conflict, racism, social structure, individual psychology, and ideological conflict (1972:350). This chapter follows essentially the theories of social structure and institutional racism to analyze this social problem.

Prejudice is learned from early childhood. As the song from *South Pacific* proclaims, "You've Got to Be Taught." Mary Ellen Goodman's study of four-year-old nursery-school children (57 black and 46 white) revealed that children absorb racial prejudice from parents very early in life. As she reported:

> The high degree of race awareness we have seen in so many of these children is startling, and not only because it does not fit our adult expectations. . . . It is shocking to find that four-year-olds, particularly white ones, show unmistakable signs of the onset of racial bigotry (1964:245).

Race prejudice also occurs consciously as part of the socialization process. It is just one more thing we learn to help us function in society. It teaches children to compartmentalize their thoughts and feelings so that, despite being prejudiced, they can still think of themselves as good persons.

For instance, the novelist Lillian Smith, writing about her childhood experiences in the South, described how she was taught to separate her "good" self from her "prejudiced" self.

> The mother who taught me what I know of tenderness and love and compassion taught me also the bleak rituals of keeping Negroes in their place. The father who rebuked me for an air of superiority toward schoolmates from the mill, and rounded out his rebuke by gravely reminding me that "all men are brothers,"

Racial prejudice is still very much a part of white society. If this social disease is to be eradicated, we must begin to change attitudes and social structures that develop it in the young.

> trained me in the steel-rigid decorums I must demand of every colored male. They who so gravely taught me to split my body from my mind, and both from my "soul," taught me also to split my conscience from my acts and Christianity from southern tradition (1949:17–18).

This transmission of prejudice to the young can occur so subtly and indirectly that we are often unaware of having learned and absorbed it.

In 1956 Hyman and Sheatsley compared white attitudes toward blacks with those in studies done in 1942 and 1944. They found great improvements in attitudes, including positive changes in the racial opinions reported by white Southerners. Two later studies (Hyman and Sheatsley, 1964; and Greeley and Sheatsley, 1971) found even further improvement in white racial attitudes. But the rate of improvement in attitudes slowed down in the late 1960s and early 1970s, as compared with the gains made during the 1950s and early 1960s (Angus Campbell, 1968 and 1971; Pettigrew, 1975).

Prejudice is still very much with us. What has changed significantly is public reaction to those who make prejudiced or bigoted remarks. Such expressions are no longer socially acceptable.

Discrimination

Overt and covert discrimination still persists in America. We need only look at the housing patterns anywhere in the United States. Discriminatory barriers, which may be covert and even unintended, also persist in the recruitment and hiring policies of many companies. For instance, "word-of-mouth" recruitment is discriminatory insofar as it tends to perpetuate the racial status quo. Most whites do not know many blacks who are looking for jobs.

Segregation

Discrimination, overt and covert, leads to and is reenforced by segregation. Discrimination in housing results in segregated schools, neighborhoods, churches, and so on. Segregation plays an important causal role in the social problem of race relations. It makes normal social interaction between the races difficult, if not impossible. Furthermore, it reinforces any prejudice that may exist by keeping whites generally ignorant of and oblivious to the serious difficulties that minority groups face.

Institutional Racism

No matter what the causes of our racial social problem, they usually have an institutional base. Prejudice is learned, starting in "the basic institution"—the family. It is sometimes reenforced in the educational institution. Textbooks used in schools have been found to be slanted and biased (by their silence and omissions) in respect to most minority groups—blacks, Chicanos, American Indians, women and girls (Sloan, 1966; Cavender, 1972; Weitzman et al., 1972). Overt and covert discrimi-

---

FORD ACCEPTS BUTZ'S RESIGNATION

President Ford accepted the resignation of his misty-eyed secretary of agriculture Monday and said parting with Earl L. Butz was "one of the saddest decisions of my presidency."

The resignation followed a weekend of rapidly escalating controversy over an obscene racial slur uttered last August following the Republican National Convention and traced to Butz last week. . . .

Both Butz and the President said the resignation was occasioned solely by the off-color story about blacks and did not mean any change of farm policy on the part of the Ford administration.

"This is the price I pay for a gross indiscretion in a private conversation," Butz told reporters in the White House press room following a private meeting with Ford. . . .

Ford said Butz had been "wise enough and courageous enough to recognize that no single individual, no matter how distinguished his past public service, should cast a shadow over the integrity and good will of American government by his comments. . . ."

Source: *Allentown Morning Call*, October 5, 1976:1.

nation has an institutional basis too. It is harbored and hides in a wide variety of institutional settings—from business to unions, and from churches to sports teams. Segregation has an institutional foundation. Housing patterns are the direct result of community and real estate practices and procedures. Local governments and planning boards, by institutionalizing its land use, via zoning, often exclude low-income minority groups from the community. Institutional racism by definition implicates all our social organizations—from art museums to our zoos.

Subcultural and social-class differences find expression in, and are either accepted or rejected by, institutions such as the family, mass media, the legal system, and government itself.

Subcultural and Social-Class Differences

Prejudice, discrimination, segregation, and institutional racism, it is argued, are due to social-class differences, not race. If only blacks were more like middle-class whites, they would be accepted. If only blacks did not have subcultural norms and values different from the dominant culture, they would not be rejected. This is the causal explanation of problematic race relations accepted by many whites (Banfield, 1974:94–95; Freeman and Jones, 1973:156).

Although it has some validity, this factor as a cause fails to explain why blacks have so often been denied the right to vote in the South; access to expensive housing in the suburbs, even though they could afford it and were middle class; and equal employment opportunities, even when qualified. It fails to explain why blacks so often have been the victims of white violence, no matter what their social class or values. Surely Dr. Martin Luther King was killed because he was black and outspoken, not because he embodied lower-class norms.

Much of the past IQ controversy, resurrected by Arthur Jensen's 1969 article in the *Harvard Educational Review*, even transcends the subcultural or social-class factor to focus upon genetic differences between blacks and whites. Jensen hypothesizes, but does not prove, that an average IQ difference of 15 points between them is due mostly (80 percent) to heredity. He ignores the fact that a segment of the black community (10 percent or more) has IQs higher than *half* of the white group. His study failed to point out that IQ differences are greater *within* groups, both black and white, then *between* groups. Perfect "subculture-free" IQ tests have not been constructed, and it is highly unlikely that they ever can be.

In one of the most exhaustive and definitive reviews of the literature about IQs, *The Science and Politics of IQ*, Leon Kamin of Princeton University states at the outset:

> There exist no data which should lead a prudent man to accept the hypothesis that IQ test scores are in any degree heritable (1974:1).

At the end of his book, he writes:

> There is no adequate evidence for the heritability of IQ within the white population. To attribute racial differences to genetic factors, granted the overwhelming cultural-environmental differences between races, is to compound folly with malice (1974:177).

PROPOSED SOLUTIONS TO THE MINORITY PROBLEM

About one hundred years ago (1877), a political decision was made to end "reconstruction" in the South (Turner, 1972:121). The solution to the racial problem in America does not seem as easy today as it did in the 1860s or the 1960s. Clearly, improvements must be made in the health, housing, employment, educational and life conditions of black Americans if equality is to be a reality. The question is how do we accomplish all this?

Change of Physical Conditions

Some liberals and conservatives say the solution to the racial problem in America is to improve the *physical* conditions under which minority groups live. Install better health and hospital facilities within their immediate social milieu. Build better houses and schools so that their ghetto existence will not be so hard. If their physical environment is improved, if the ghetto is gilded or enriched, then the racial problem, for the most part, will be solved. There will be separate but equal conditions of life for blacks and whites alike, each in their separate society (Ibid., 22).

Providing Good Jobs

Liberals say the answer to the problems of race relations rests in providing blacks with stable, well-paying jobs that will enable them to "buy into" the dominant white society—better housing, better schools, better medical care, and better neighborhoods (Schiller, Spring 1976:111–20). Eventually this economic approach will lead to a racially integrated society.

Changing Attitudes and Norms

Many black scholars, such as Thomas Pettigrew, contend that these approaches are not long-term solutions. They maintain that symbolic and institutional racism must be cured, discrimination must be controlled, and prejudice must be curbed.

Many proposals made a decade ago by the Presidential National Advisory Commission on Civil Disorders are still relevant today. The Commission, among other things, recommended:

opening opportunities to those who are restricted by racial segregation and discrimination, and eliminating all barriers to their choice of jobs, education, and housing

removing the frustration of powerlessness among the disadvantaged by providing the means for them to deal with the problems that affect their lives and by increasing the capacity of our public and private institutions to respond to these problems

increasing communication across racial lines to destroy stereotypes, to halt polarization, and to end distrust and hostility (1968:23).

Busing – A Controversial Proposal

One of the most controversial proposals to the problems of inequality and the inaccessibility of quality education is busing. The use of busing has been advocated by liberals, who see it as an opportunity for young people to get to know each other as persons, regardless of their race. It stems indirectly from the 1954 Supreme Court decision *Brown* v. *Board of Education*. The Court held that the "separate but equal" doctrine permitting racially segregated schools was unconstitutional, since separate schools were inherently unequal. In 1968 (in the *Green* case) and again in 1971 (in the *Swann* case), the High Court specifically approved busing as a

Busing is one possible solution to the problem of educational inequality. Yet many whites bitterly oppose having their children bused to black schools or to having blacks bused into their neighborhoods.

remedy by the Charlotte-Mecklenburg, North Carolina, schools to redistribute black and white pupils throughout the district. Because busing has been used to achieve racial balance, much opposition to it has developed, including that of former Presidents Nixon and Ford (Shabecoff, May 28, 1976:A-11). Public-opinion polls have consistently shown that the overwhelming majority of whites (and some blacks) are opposed to busing for purposes of achieving racial balance in the schools.

Since real school integration is seldom possible without busing, whites can oppose busing while claiming to favor integration (as most whites do) without much danger of achieving it in the schools. Busing of schoolchildren for purposes other than racial integration has been on the increase for years, without much public objection. The so-called neighborhood school often turns out to be on the other side of town, as school districts centralize education and close down schools (because of the declining birthrates and enrollments) and consolidate with others further from home.

The Civil Rights Commission's Report. A 1976 report by the U.S. Civil Rights Commission pointed out that "only seven percent of all public school children and only 3.6 percent of all schoolchildren were carried by bus for desegregation purposes . . . even though about half of the nation's schoolchildren take buses to school" (Hicks, August 25, 1976:21). The report was based on four Commission hearings, four state hearings, a mail survey to 1,300 school districts, and a thorough study of 29 school districts, 27 of which (it said) desegregated peacefully. The report maintained that antibusing legislation proposed by former President Ford and supported by Congress was counterproductive to peaceful school desegregation.

More than any other factor, the Commission report emphasized, local leadership achieved school desegregation. In 411 districts that had had no serious disturbances, at least two-thirds of the business and political leaders and nine out of 10 religious leaders either supported desegregation or took no public stand against it. In communities where violence erupted, less than one-third of the political and business leaders and only two-thirds of the religious leaders did the same.

The Commission's 1976 report also noted that there had not been a massive exodus of whites from neighborhoods in which schools were being desegregated. However, this was not true in schools that were 40 percent or more black when desegregation began. Between 1968 and 1972, all districts surveyed had a six percent decline in white student enrollment; but in districts that were more than 40 percent black, the drop in white enrollment was 15 percent (Hicks, 1976:21).

In several cities, the Commission has been told of inner-city schools that have been improved "magically and almost overnight" when the district began a busing program. A black parent from North Carolina gave the following written testimony:

> Within one month, the parents of the white children who were bused managed to get the black school painted, repairs made, new electric typewriters and sewing machines, and the shelves filled with books....
>
> I contend that busing for one year will upgrade all our schools quicker than anything the President or Congress can do (1975:518).

Busing has usually worked well in small cities and countywide school districts. But in large central cities, critics of busing offer evidence that desegregating schools only causes (or speeds up) white flight to the suburbs. In many big-city school districts, the majority of students are black. For example, in 1973 14 of the 20 largest cities had a black majority in their public-school systems. According to the Department of Health, Education and Welfare, more than 70 percent of black students in all-black schools are concentrated in 19 cities.

The New Coleman Report. University of Chicago sociologist James Coleman, whose famous report in 1966 was used as the basis of desegregating schools to give black students equality of educational opportunities, reported in 1975 that busing, at least in Southern cities, had hampered more than helped to integrate the schools. According to Coleman, "the findings ... were that the loss of whites did increase when there was a reduction of segregation" (1976:164). This loss is greater

1. as the size of the city is greater;
2. as the central-city school district has a higher proportion of black students;
3. as the racial disparity between city and suburbs is greater, with a distinct segregation between districts (blacks in central-city district and whites in the suburban districts).

He reported the following data to show the impact of school desegregation on white outmigration from the city to the suburbs:

> Eleven cities out of the first 19 [surveyed] experienced little or no desegregation at all between 1968 and 1973. Based on the white loss that occurred in these cities in 1968–69, they would have been expected to lose 15 percent of white students between 1969 and 1973; their actual loss was 18 percent.....
>
> Those eight cities [that did experience some degree of desegregation], based on their losses in 1968–69 — before desegregation occurred — would have been expected to lose only 7 percent of white students between 1969 and 1973; they actually lost 26 percent (Goodman, November 1975:3).

Although Coleman was criticized for analyzing only Southern cities, and because part of the sample was irrelevant to school busing, other data from Boston and other cities suggest that the number of whites leaving the cities might well be directly related to busing to desegregate the schools.

Thus it is clear that desegregation in large cities is not solving the problem of school segregation; it (along with other factors) seems to be continuing or fostering more segregation between central cities and suburbs.

Metropolitan-Wide Busing between Cities and Suburbs

To overcome the segregation between black schools (in the central-city school districts) and white schools (in suburban districts around the cities), the courts have begun to order metropolitan-wide busing across city and suburban school-district lines. The Supreme Court has ruled this is legal in the Louisville, Kentucky, and Wilmington, Delaware, areas. Along similar lines, a bill has been introduced in Congress by Representative Richardson Preyer (a conservative from North Carolina) requiring states to write their own plans to lessen racial isolation. States would establish cross-district sharing of school facilities and a metropolitan "majority-minority transfer plan." This would permit a pupil to transfer to any city or suburban school in which his own race was not a majority.

If such a modified scheme of busing across school district lines becomes a commonplace, the problem may well be on its way toward a solution. Once whites are convinced that fleeing the city will not guarantee an all-white school, they might decide to stay in the city. In addition, an integrated school would probably be in line for more state money than a segregated one.

School Desegregation and Integration

In attempting to solve the problems of racial inequality in our schools, we must remember the distinction, made by Harvard social-psychologist Thomas Pettigrew, between desegregation and integration. Desegregation is achieved by simply ending complete segregation and bringing some blacks and whites together. It implies nothing about the quality of interracial interaction. (Some school districts may have one or two blacks in otherwise all-white schools, and are thus counted as desegregated.) Integration requires far more, including positive intergroup contact, interracial acceptance, equal dignity, and equal access to resources.

To alleviate the problem of race relations and unequal educational opportunities, according to Pettigrew, we must achieve integration out of desegregation. Pettigrew suggests eight conditions that enhance the probability for integration within our schools.

1. There must be equal racial access to school activities and resources.
2. Classroom (not merely school) desegregation is essential.
3. Strict and rigid ability groupings should be avoided.
4. School services and remedial training must be maintained or increased.

5. Desegregation should start in the early grades.
6. The need for interracial staffs is critical.
7. Substantial, rather than token, minority percentages are necessary.
8. We must also desegregate by social class (1975:234–39).

Affirmative-Action Programs

Other proposals advocated by liberals include affirmative-action programs to achieve better job opportunities for minority groups. Such programs resulted from court decisions under Title VII of the Civil Rights Act of 1964 and the Equal Employment Opportunity Act of 1972. As we mentioned earlier, the courts look not at the intent of the employer in his hiring or promotion procedures, but at the effect these factors have on minority-group employment and positions. A policy or practice that has a "disproportionate" impact on the employment opportunities of minorities is often interpreted as illegal. The courts have found evidence of racial discrimination on the basis of statistical disparity. For example, if only one percent of a firm's workforce is black but 25 percent of the community's workforce is black, a statistical disparity exists, serving as evidence of racial discrimination. All companies with large government contracts are expected to have an affirmative-action program, lest they lose future contracts. Large back-pay awards have been made to minority persons discriminated against in being hired or promoted. For example, AT&T (the Bell System) has agreed, by consent decrees, to pay out over $100 million to 50,000 minority employees (including females) for discrimination in promotion and pay. Nine major steel corporations, by consent decrees, agreed to provide "prompt and full utilization of blacks, Spanish-surnamed Americans, females and long-time service, production and maintenance employees . . . by increasing their promotional transfer opportunities" ("A Decade of Equal Employment Opportunity," 1977:5). The decree in the steel industry provides for $931 million in back pay to minority employees discriminated against in the past.

In the past several years, the Department of Health, Education and Welfare has begun to apply affirmative-action plans and goals—already approved for industry by the Equal Employment Opportunity Commission—to colleges and universities (under Title IX), to legal and medical organizations, labor unions, civil-service jobs, and other organizations having at least 25 employees (Ornstein, January/February 1976:10–17). If these organizations do not comply with the affirmative-action goals of hiring and promoting minorities, federal money may be withheld.

Some blacks and other minorities argue that not enough progress has been made under affirmative-action programs (Churchill and Shank, March/April 1976:111–16). New laws and tougher enforcement of existing laws (especially withholding government funds) are offered as ways to speed progress. Conservatives feel that more harm than good has resulted from affirmative action and that the bureaucrats who regulate the program have benefited most (Sowell, Winter 1976:47–65).

A Hierarchy of Priorities

In addition to passage of laws aimed at changing the racial situation, liberals and radicals argue we must give some serious thought and action to a hierarchy of priorities in developing innovative plans and changing our social structures. These priorities all entail major institutional changes and a change of power and wealth in our society. If there is any preference for a hierarchy of priorities for trying to solve the racial problem in America, it would be as follows:

1. Provide steady, well-paying jobs for minorities.
2. Integrate housing in both cities and suburbs.
3. Integrate schools throughout the nation.
4. Educate whites about their role in institutional racism, segregation, and discrimination.

A change in our economic institutions could open up more jobs to more people. With steady, well-paying jobs, more blacks (and other minority groups) could afford to buy a home in a suburban neighborhood. Once this is done, schools (of necessity), since they are based on existing housing patterns, would become integrated; then the minority group child would be more likely to receive a better education than in an almost all-black or Chicano school in the central city. There are, of course, some excellent black central-city schools, but they are exceptions to the rule (Sowell, Spring 1976:26–58). Hence, with or without busing, it is quite doubtful whether schools will improve for blacks until and unless we eliminate the crucial problem of segregated housing. A major reform in government policies and structural changes in the real estate industry will be needed to achieve this and encourage integrated housing.

In addition, we must educate white Americans about the dangers of the racially apartheid society we are continuing to develop. High unemployment, stemming from an inequitable economic system and social structure that fosters racial discrimination in employment, together with a massive concentration of blacks in central cities can only lead to more of the racial conflict and riots that we witnessed in the 1960s. Although all whites should be better educated about the racial situation, this is particularly important for the young in school and police officers on the beat. Both groups often know little or nothing about the real grievances, life experiences, and history of black people.

Young people will determine the future of race relations in America. Yet elementary and secondary schools have done little to encourage black-studies courses; and where they have been established, they are usually looked upon by white students and administrators as courses for blacks only. This attitude should be changed since the racial *problem* basically is one of *white* norms, values, beliefs, and practices, such as institutional racism.

As the National Advisory Commission on Civil Disorders long ago observed, we must face a fact:

> What white Americans have never fully understood — but what the Negro can never forget — is that white society is deeply implicated in the ghetto. White institutions created it, white institutions maintain it, and white society condones it (Report of the National Advisory Commission, 1968:2).

The sooner our schools recognize the racial problem for what it is—essentially a *white* problem—the sooner education of the young can be useful in solving the problem. However, education of the young is not found solely in the classroom. Young people are educated about race relations when they witness how school districts strive to avoid integration of the schools, when they see how their parents preach prejudice against minorities, and when schools refuse to hire no (or very few) black teachers and counselors. If the young are to be fully educated about racial matters, adults must teach by example in their handling of racial matters involving the school.

THE FUTURE OF THE MINORITY PROBLEM

At the moment, the outlook for the racial situation in America is not bright. Much will depend upon when and how racial conflict in South Africa is resolved. If it is resolved peacefully and blacks are accorded the independence and freedom that we obtained for whites in 1776, this could have a positive influence on race relations in America. If a bloody civil war between whites and blacks ensues, the role of the United States in such a "bloodbath" would become crucial for race relations at home. Such international events will influence and affect our racial problems for years to come. We should begin to recognize that fact.

One thing about the racial future of our society is certain. There will be more blacks, Chicanos, and Indians in the future, and they will make up an increasingly larger percentage of our population, as their birthrates far outrun the declining birthrates of whites. By 2000, the U.S. Bureau of the Census estimates, blacks will make up about 13 percent of our population, as compared with only 11 percent today (*Current Population Reports*, Series P-25, No. 601, 1975:11). About 10 years ago it was predicted that "by 1985, the 12.1 million Negroes segregated within central cities today will have grown to approximately 20.8 million, an increase of 72 percent. Prospects for domestic peace and for the quality of American life are linked directly to the future of these cities" (Report of the National Advisory Commission, 1968:390).

The battle for civil rights for blacks, American Indians, and other minority groups continued during the 1970s, though it has not received the media coverage given to the civil-rights conflicts of the 1960s. The outlook for minorities is grim, even though their numbers will grow.

The point here is that if we were unable to resolve racial strife when we had about 12 million blacks in the cities, how will we remedy the problem when there are nearly 21 million urban blacks in 1985? The remedy, by default, will be racist separatism. The problem, by sheer numbers, will have grown out of control. If cities are having financial problems today, how much greater will those problems be by 1985? If schools are racial tinderboxes, and frustrated, unemployed urban youths are like "social dynamite," how can a racial conflict be avoided tomorrow? The future is grim indeed for the racial problem in our cities.

We have several paths we may either purposely choose or drift onto because of inertia. As the Report of the National Advisory Commission on Civil Disorders saw it, our society has three basic choices for the future.

First, we can continue our present policies and devote the same small share of our resources and concerns to the poor, unemployed, and disadvantaged. But this approach would not be enough to stop, let alone reverse, the decline in the quality of life in central-city ghettos. This approach carries the highest ultimate price—racial conflict and possible revolution or racial genocide. As technology displaces more blacks from jobs (or makes fewer available for growing numbers of younger blacks), trouble can be expected. Professor Samuel Yette of Howard University, writing about this situation, contends:

> Black Americans have outlived their usefulness.... Once an economic asset, they are now considered an economic drag....
> Thanks to old Black backs and newfangled machines, the sweat chores of the nation are done. Now some 25 million Blacks face a society that is brutally pragmatic, technologically accomplished, deeply racist, increasingly overcrowded and surly (1971:18).

Second, we can also make the "enrichment choice." This approach would seek to create dramatic improvements in the quality of life in disadvantaged central-city neighborhoods, both white and black. It would require greatly increased spending for education, employment, job training, housing, and social services. If it is done on a large enough scale, it could improve ghetto life; but it would do little to alleviate the concentration of blacks and Spanish-Americans in central cities or in segregated suburbs. Yet it would make an intolerable situation at least tolerable.

Third, we can also pursue integration (combined with some enrichment) as our principal policy. Specifically, our society and government would encourage integration of "substantial numbers" of blacks and Chicanos outside of our central cities. Enrichment would be only an interim policy to prepare all whites for eventual integration (Report of the National Advisory Commission, 1968:22-23).

On the other hand, a fourth alternative is possible. Blacks and other minorities could follow another deliberate path—toward two separate societies. A few black and other minority groups feel that separatism is needed to create social unity and political power among themselves.

For some, it is advanced as a temporary phase, during which the racial group will concentrate on itself and attain a sense of racial security. Then, some time in the future, blacks will have attained enough confidence and strength to hold their own, on a basis of equality, with the dominant group. Racial integration will then take place between equals.

The real "hard liners" on separatism, however, visualize a total and permanent division, with separate states or portions of states given to blacks. Thus, the Republic of New Africa envisages the slicing off of several states to be turned over to black populations as the territorial base for a black nation.

The overwhelming majority of black Americans still feel that their future lies in their American citizenship and in more, rather than less, integration into the mainstream. They fully favor instilling a sense of racial pride in themselves and their young; they would agree that what has been done along these lines in recent years is generally worthwhile. For most, this newly found racial identity does not carry separatist overtones; equality, not superiority, is the watchword. Perhaps they have unconsciously drawn a lesson from the Jews, who have maintained their belief in themselves as the chosen people without mistreating their neighbors.

Those who embrace separatism despair of genuine movement toward an integrated society; they simply do not believe that the majority's professed dedication to a single society is sincere. They see the prediction of the Kerner Commission—that this nation is moving toward becoming two societies, separate and unequal—destined for fulfillment. Thus, they draw the logical lesson that all energy should be devoted to exploiting separateness as a source of strength. Complete integration of blacks, Chicanos, and American Indians in a predominantly white society could mean cultural genocide. We cannot stress too strongly that this sentiment for separatism is likely to grow in the future, given a continuation of the present national policies (Morsell, July 1973:87–88).

This choice of black separation is built on despair and anger. For other minorities, such as the Spanish-Americans, it is based upon a desire to preserve their unique culture and traditions.

If we travel the high road toward racial integration, the dream of Dr. Martin Luther King will come true: "I have a dream that my four little children will one day live in a nation where they will not be judged by the color of their skin but by the content of their character" (1974:51).

If whites or blacks choose instead to travel the low road of present policies, or of separation, then the words chiseled on the tomb of Dr. King will be the only fitting epitaph for all black Americans: "Free at last! Free at last. Thank God Almighty I'm free at last." What we as a society decide to do in the future will help to determine which of the four alternatives comes true.

SUMMARY

Almost 10 years ago a presidential commission reported that "our nation is moving toward two societies, one black, one white, separate and unequal." Today we are further down that road toward two separate societies.

The racial problem is defined in different ways. Conservatives blame the victims by pointing to their cultural deprivation or weak family life. Others see the problem as "reverse discrimination," or (as held by most sociologists and liberals) problems stemming from the prejudice, discrimination, and racism (symbolic or institutional) that are a part of our social structure. Minority groups encountering such problems include blacks, Spanish-Americans, and American Indians; however, we have primarily examined blacks in our effort to understand and analyze the social problem of race relations.

The severity of the racial situation can be seen by looking at the patterns of the immigration of blacks into cities and the flight of whites to the suburbs. Life conditions and life chances of blacks are affected by deficient and deplorable health care, economic conditions (low income, high unemployment, and low-status employment), education, housing, and limited political power.

A consensus among sociologists suggests that the major causes of the racial problem are prejudice, discrimination, segregation, racism (institutional and symbolic), and subcultural and social-class differences. These causes all involve an inequitable economic and social system that shapes the attitudes, actions, and values of whites and blacks toward one another.

Proposals for improving the health, housing, income, employment, and education of blacks were offered by the National Commission on Civil Disorders in 1968. These proposed solutions are just as valid today as when they were made 10 years ago. Other solutions to some of the racial problems include stronger and more widely used affirmative-action programs, busing and other integration plans, and a "hierarchy of priorities" involving steady, well-paying jobs, integrated housing, and educational approaches stressing positive white relationships with blacks.

The future depends in part upon the international black-white situation, as in South Africa, which can have beneficial or detrimental effects on racial matters in America. Blacks will become larger in numbers and as a proportion of our population. Approaches of continuing present policies, "enrichment," or "integration" (combined with enrichment) are three paths available to the white power structure in the future. Separatism rather than integration is a fourth road some blacks and other minority groups may choose to walk in the future.

Whatever road our society finally chooses, it is evident that something must be done today to deal more effectively with this crucial social problem. Charles Silberman, writing about "our crisis in black and white," observed:

> The time is short, the hour is late, the matter is urgent. It is not incumbent upon us to complete the task; but neither are we free to desist from doing all we possibly can (1964:356).

CAREER OPPORTUNITIES

Affirmative-Action Specialists.

Corporations, as well as large universities, must meet federal requirements for hiring minorities and women. They must set up affirmative-action programs to ensure equal opportunities within the organization. Specialists in affirmative action help to recruit minorities, as well as coordinate and administer established programs. They must keep abreast of rules and regulations governing such programs, and must be able to resolve any problems of racial discrimination. This is a relatively new career with great potential for sociology majors. For further information write to: Equal Employment Opportunity Commission, 2041 E St., N. W., Washington, D.C. 20506.

Community Organizer.

His task related to those of some sociologists and social workers, a community organizer must be able to communicate with people in urban neighborhoods and help blacks and whites alike to resolve their problems. Usually a community organizer trains and helps people to develop as neighborhood leaders so that the needs of the community are met. The community organizer must act as a spokesman for the group until it is adequately organized and local leadership emerges. Such work often helps minority-group people to recognize the importance of community unity and power. For further information write to: The National Association of Neighborhoods, 1901 Q St., N. W., Washington, D.C. 20009.

Human-Relations Specialist.

Most states and local communities have human-relations commissions. These agencies investigate complaints of discrimination. Knowledge of federal and state civil-rights laws are important, as is an interest in investigating cases of human relations and interaction. Reports and cases must be thoroughly researched since they often serve as the basis of litigation when the case is not resolved or conciliated. For further information write to your state and local Human Relations Commissions.

REFERENCES

Allport, Gordon W.
1954 The Nature of Prejudice. Cambridge, Mass.: Addison-Wesley.

Alvarez, Rodolfo
1975 "The Psycho-Historical and Socioeconomic Development of the Chicano Community in the United States." Social Science Quarterly 53 (March): 920–42.

Banfield, Edward C.
1974 The Unheavenly City Revisited. Boston: Little, Brown.

Barbour, Russell B.
1967 Black and White Together: Plain Talk for White Christians. Philadelphia: United Church Press.

Blackwell, James E.
1975 The Black Community: Diversity and Unity. New York: Dodd, Mead.

Brower, Jonathan
1975 "Whitey's Sport." Pp. 50–55 in Annual Editions: Readings in Social Problems 74/75: Annual Editions. Guilford, Conn.: Dushkin.

Brown, W. Aggrey
1971 "Theories of Racism and Strategies of New World African Liberation." Pp. 111–27 in Vernon Dixon and Badi Foster, eds. Beyond Black or White: An Alternate America. Boston: Little, Brown.

Campbell, Angus
1971 White Attitudes Toward Black People. Ann Arbor, Mich.: Institute for Social Research.

Campbell, Angus and Howard Schuman
1968 "Racial Attitudes in Fifteen American Cities." In the National Advisory Commission on Civil Disorders, Supplemental Studies. Washington, D.C.: U.S. Government Printing Office.

Campbell, Ernest
1961 "Moral Discomfort and Racial Segregation: An Examination of the Myrdal Hypothesis." Social Forces (March): 228-34.

Campbell, Ernest and Thomas F. Pettigrew
1959 "Racial and Moral Crisis: The Role of Little Rock Ministers." American Journal of Sociology (March): 509-16.

Cavender, Chris C.
1972 "A Critical Examination of Textbooks on Indians." Pp. 421-27 in Arnold M. Rose and Caroline B. Rose, eds. Minority Problems. 2nd ed. New York: Harper & Row.

Churchill, Neil and John Shank
1976 "Affirmative Action and Guilt-Edged Goals." Harvard Business Reviews 54, 2 (March/April): 111-16.

Coleman, James S.
1976 "Racial Segregation in the Schools: New Research with New Policy Implications." Pp. 163-66 in Anne Kilbride, ed. Readings in Sociology 76/77: Annual Editions. Guilford, Conn.: Dushkin.

Cortese, Charles, Frank Falk, and Jack Cohen
1976 "Further Considerations on the Methodological Analysis of Segregation Indices." American Sociological Review 41,4 (August):630-37.

Coser, Lewis
1956 The Functions of Social Conflict. Glencoe, Ill.: Free Press.

Daniels, Roger and Harry H. L. Kitano
1970 American Racism: Exploration of the Nature of Prejudice. Englewood Cliffs, N.J.: Prentice-Hall.

Davidson, Basil
1961 The African Slave Trade: Precolonial History 1450-1850. Boston: Little, Brown.

"A Decade of Equal Employment Opportunity 1965-1975." Tenth Annual Report, United States Equal Employment Opportunity Commission. Washington, D.C.: U.S. Government Printing Office, 1977.

Dixon, Vernon J. and Badi Foster, eds.
1971 Beyond Black or White: An Alternate America. Boston: Little, Brown.

Faherty, Robert L.
1976 "The American Indian: An Overview." Pp. 163-68 in Ian Robertson, ed. Readings in Sociology: Contemporary Perspectives. New York: Harper & Row.

Freeman, Howard and Wyatt C. Jones
1973 Social Problems Causes and Controls. 2nd ed. New York: Rand McNally.

Friedman, Robert
1975 "Institutional Racism: How to Discriminate without Really Trying." Pp. 384-407 in Thomas F. Pettigrew, ed. Racial Discrimination in the United States. New York: Harper & Row.

Gist, Noel P. and Sylvia F. Fava
1974 Urban Society. 6th ed., New York: Crowell.

Glazer, Nathan
1976 "Equal Opportunity Gone Wrong." New Society 35, 694 (January 22): 151–53.

Goldaber, Irving and Holly Porter
1974 "The 'Laboratory Confrontation': An Approach to Conflict Management and Social Change." Pp. 122–33 in Arthur Shostak, ed. Putting Sociology to Work. New York: McKay.

Golenpaul, Ann, ed.
1976 Information Please Almanac, 1977. New York: Simon & Schuster.

Goodman, Mary Ellen
1964 Race Awareness in Young Children. New York: Collier Books.

Goodman, Walter (interviews James S. Coleman)
1975 "Integration, Yes; Busing, No." Education Digest 41, 3 (November): 2–6.

Greeley, Andrew M. and Paul B. Sheatsley
1971 Attitudes Toward Racial Integration. Scientific American 225, 6: 13–19.

Grier, George and Eunice Grier
1966 Equality and Beyond: Housing Segregation and the Goals of the Great Society. Chicago: Quadrangle.

Grimshaw, Allen
1961 "Relationships among Prejudice, Discrimination, Social Tension, and Social Violence." Journal of Intergroup Relations (Autumn): 302–10.

Halsell, Grace.
1977 "Hispanics: A Minority Report." National Catholic Reporter 13, 29 (May 13): 1, 4.

Hamilton, Charles V.
1974 The Fight for Racial Justice: From Court to Street to Politics. Public Affairs Pamphlet No. 516. New York: Public Affairs Committee.

Hamilton, David and George Bishop
1976 "Attitudinal and Behavioral Effects of Initial Integration of White Suburban Neighborhoods." Journal of Social Issues 32, 2 (Spring): 47–68.

Hicks, Nancy
1976 "Rights Panel Finds That 'Desegregation Works' But Chides Ford on Busing Stance." New York Times (August 25): 21.

Hill, Robert
1973 "Health Conditions of Black Americans." Urban League News 3, 5: 5.

Himes, Joseph S.
1974 Racial and Ethnic Relations. Dubuque, Iowa: Brown.

Horton, Paul B. and Gerald Leslie
1974 The Sociology of Social Problems. 5th ed. Englewood Cliffs, N.J.: Prentice-Hall.

Howard, John R.
1974 The Cutting Edge: Social Movements and Social Change in America. Philadelphia: Lippincott.

Hyman, Herbert and Paul Sheatsley
1956 Attitudes Toward Desegregation. Scientific American 195: 35–39.
1964 Attitudes Toward Desegregation. Scientific American 211: 16–23.

"Inside Title VII." Voice of the Cement, Lime & Gypsum Workers International Union 39, 8 (August): 16–19, 1976.

Johnson, Daniel A., Richard Porter, and Patricia L. Mateljan
1971 "Racial Discrimination in Apartment Rentals." Journal of Applied Social Psychology 1: 364–77.

Kamin, Leon
1974 The Science and Politics of IQ. Potomac, Md.: Laurence Erlbaum Associates.

Kitano, Harry H. L.
1966 "Passive Discrimination in the Normal Person." The Journal of Social Psychology 70: 23–31.

Kotelchuck, David, ed.
1976 Prognosis Negative: Crisis in the Health Care System. New York: Vintage.

Linn, Laurence S.
1965 Verbal Attitudes and Overt Behavior: A Study of Racial Discrimination. Social Forces 43 (March): 353–64.

Lipset, Seymour Martin
1976 "The Wavering Polls." The Public Interest 43 (Spring): 70–89.

Liszkowski, R. J.
1969 Let's Talk Sense about Black Americans. Chicago: Claretian.

Long, Elton, James Long, Wilmer Leon, and Paul Weston
1975 American Minorities: The Justice Issue. Englewood Cliffs, N.J.: Prentice-Hall.

Lyman, Stanford M.
1972 The Black American in Sociological Thought. New York: Capricorn.

McAllister, Ronald et al.
1971 "Residential Mobility of Blacks and Whites: A National Longitudinal Study." American Journal of Sociology 77 (November): 448–53.

McConahay, John B. and Joseph Hough
1976 "Symbolic Racism." The Journal of Social Issues 32, 2 (Spring): 23–46.

McVeigh, Frank J.
1970 "The Life Conditions of Afro-Americans." Afro-American Studies 1: 45–49.
1972 "Black 'Ghetto Mentality' and the 'Peasant Mentality.'" Paper presented at the Fifth Annual Meeting of the Pennsylvania Historical Society, Bloomsburg, Pa., March 24.

Madsen, William
1973 The Mexican-Americans of South Texas. 2nd ed. New York: Holt, Rinehart and Winston.

Merton, Robert K.
 1949 "Discrimination and the American Creed." Pp. 100–110 in Robert M. MacIver, ed. Discrimination and National Welfare. New York: Harper & Row.

Morsell, John A.
 1973 "Ethnic Relations of the Future." Annals of the American Academy of Political and Social Science 408 (July): 83–93.

Moynihan, Daniel P.
 1965 The Negro Family: The Case for National Action. Washington, D.C.: U.S. Government Printing Office.

Nilsson, Joel
 1973 "Apache Reservation No Country Club." Allentown Sunday Call-Chronicle (August 5): D-7.

Ornstein, Allan
 1976 "Quality Not Quotas." Society 13, 2 (January/February): 10–17.

Pettigrew, Thomas F.
 1969 "Issues in Urban America." Pp. 47–94 in Bernard F. Frieden and William W. Nash, Jr., eds. Shaping an Urban Future: Essays in Honor of Catherine Bayer Wurster. Cambridge, Mass.: M.I.T. Press.
 1975 Racial Discrimination in the United States. New York: Harper & Row.

"Puerto Ricans' Lot Worsening Report Claims." Allentown Morning Call (June 22): 19, 1977.

Quinn, Olive W.
 1954 "The Transmission of Racial Attitudes among White Southerners." Social Forces 33: 41–47.

Rabb, Earl, and Seymour Lipset
 1972 "Prejudice and Society." Pp. 297–406 in Arnold Rose and Caroline Rose, eds. Minority Problems. 2nd ed. New York: Harper & Row.

Ravitch, Diane
 1976 "Busing, the Solution That Has Failed to Solve." Pp. 167–70 in Anne Kilbride, ed., Readings in Sociology 76/77: Annual Editions. Guilford, Conn.: Dushkin.

Report of the National Advisory Commission on Civil Disorders. New York: Bantam, 1968.

Report of the National Advisory Commission on Civil Disorders: Summary of Report. New York: Bantam, 1968.

"Reverse Bias Ruling to Be Appealed." Facts on File (December 31): 995, 1976.

"Reverse Discrimination: Has It Gone Too Far?" U.S. News & World Report 80, 13 (March 29): 26–29, 1976.

Rose, Arnold and Caroline Rose, eds.
 1972 Minority Problems. 2nd ed. New York: Harper & Row.

Rosenthal, Jack
 1971 "Blacks Streaming North at Same Rate." New York Times News Service (March 4): 1.

Ryan, William
 1976 Blaming the Victim. Revised ed. New York: Vintage.

St. John, Nancy
 1975 School Desegregation. New York: Wiley.

Schiller, Bradley
    1976   "Equality, Opportunity and the 'Good Job.'" Public Interest 43 (Spring): 111–20.

Shabecoff, Philip
    1976   "White House Says Ford Erred in Remark on '54 School Case." New York Times (May 28): A-11.

Silberman, Charles
    1964   Crisis in Black and White. New York: Random House.

Simpson, George E. and J. Milton Yinger
    1972   Racial and Cultural Minorities: An Analysis of Prejudice and Discrimination. 4th ed. New York: Harper & Row.

Sloan, Irving J.
    1966   The Negro in Modern American History Textbooks. Chicago: American Federation of Teachers.

Smith, Lillian
    1949   Killers of the Dream. New York: Norton.

Smith, Sam
    1977   "Bias Still Ails State after 20 Years." Allentown Morning Call (April 22): 9.

Sowell, Thomas
    1976   "Affirmative Action Reconsidered." Public Interest 42 (Winter): 47–65.

"Supreme Court Refuses to Hear School Bias Cases." Allentown Morning Call (April 22): 9, 1975.

Taeuber, Karl E. and Alma F. Taeuber
    1965   Negroes in Cities: Residential Segregation and Neighborhood Change. Chicago: Aldine.

Thompson, Daniel C.
    1974   Sociology of the Black Experience. Westport, Conn.: Greenwood Press.

"Tio Taco Is Dead." Newsweek 75, 26 (June 29): 22–28, 1970.

Turner, Jonathan H.
    1972   American Society Problems of Structure. New York: Harper & Row.

U.S. Bureau of the Census
    1972   "The Social and Economic Status of the Black Population in the United States, 1971." Current Population Reports, Series P-23, No. 42. Washington, D.C.: U.S. Government Printing Office.
    1973   "Characteristics of Negro Immigrants to Selected Metropolitan Areas: 1970." 1970 Census of Population: Supplementary Report, PC (S1): 47. Washington, D.C.: U.S. Government Printing Office.
    1973   "Negro Population." Census of Population: 1960 Subject Reports, Final Report PC (2) - 1B. Washington, D.C.: U.S. Government Printing Office.
    1975   "Money Income in 1973 of Families and Persons in the United States." Current Population Reports, Series P-60, No. 97. Washington, D.C.: U.S. Government Printing Office.

1975 "Population Estimates and Projections: 1975 to 2050." Current Population Reports, Series P-25, No. 601. Washington, D.C.: U.S. Government Printing Office.

1975 "Population Profile of the United States: 1974." Current Population Reports, Series P-20, No. 279. Washington, D.C.: U.S. Government Printing Office.

1976 "Population Characteristics, Persons of Spanish Origin in the United States: March 1976." Series P-20, No. 302. Washington, D.C.: U.S. Government Printing Office.

1976 "Population Profile of the United States: 1975." Current Population Reports, Series P-20, No. 292. Washington, D.C.: U.S. Government Printing Office.

1977 "Population Profile of the United States: 1976." Current Population Reports, Series P-20, No. 307. Washington, D.C.: U.S. Government Printing Office.

U.S. Commission on Civil Rights

1975 "Your Child and Busing." (May 1972). Clearinghouse Publications No. 36. Pp. 509–21 in Norman Yetman and C. Hoy Steele, eds. Majority and Minority: The Dynamics of Racial and Ethnic Relations, 2nd ed. Boston: Allyn & Bacon.

U.S. Equal Employment Opportunity Commission

1974 Affirmative Action and Equal Employment: A Guidebook for Employers. Vols. 1 & 2 (January). Washington, D.C.: U.S. Government Printing Office.

"U.S. Panel Boosts Cause of Navajos." Allentown Morning Call (September 17): 63, 1975.

Vander Zanden, James W.

1966 American Minority Relations: The Sociology of Race and Ethnic Groups. 2nd ed. New York: Ronald Press.

Warner, Lyle G. and Rugledge M. Dennis

1970 "Prejudice Versus Discrimination: An Empirical Example and Theoretical Extensions." Social Forces (June): 473–84.

Washington, Booker T.

1959 Up from Slavery. New York: Bantam.

Watson, Peter, ed.

1973 Psychology and Race. Chicago: Aldine.

Wattenberg, Ben, and Richard Scammon

1973 "Black Progress and Liberal Rhetoric." Commentary 55 (April): 35–44.

Weitzman, Lenore J., et al.

1972 "Sex-Role Socialization in Picture Books for Pre-School Children." American Journal of Sociology 77 (May): 1125–50.

Westie, Frank

1965 "The American Dilemma: An Empirical Test." American Sociological Review (August): 527–38.

Woodward, C. Vann

1966 The Strange Career of Jim Crow. New York: Oxford University Press.

Yette, Samuel

1971 The Choice: The Issue of Black Survival in America. New York: Putnam.

SUGGESTED READINGS

Austin, B. William. Population Policy and the Black Community. New Brunswick, N.J.: Transaction Books. 1977.

An in-depth study by the National Urban League examines population policy in America, its impact on black people, and how blacks view its impact.

Levin, Betsy and Willis Hawley, eds. The Courts, Social Science and School Desegregation. New Brunswick, N.J.: Transaction Books. 1976.

An excellent summary of the history, problems, and future of the school-desegregation issue and busing.

Lipsky, Michael and David Olson. Commission Politics: The Processing of Racial Crisis in America. New Brunswick, N.J.: Transaction Books. 1976.

Examines how the federal government and society "cool down" racial unrest by setting up study commissions. It explores the political and organizational behavior of riot commissions (especially in the 1960s) and the development of public policy toward blacks.

Scott, Joseph. The Black Revolts: Racial Stratification in the USA. New Brunswick, N.J.: Transaction Books. 1976.

Discusses and analyzes the social and economic forces systematically used by white power elites to subjugate blacks.

Steiner, Stan. The Vanishing White Man. New York: Harper & Row. 1976.

Analyzes the underlying white attitudes toward the American Indian and notes that little has changed in the past decade in the positions or power of Indians.

Willie, Charles, ed. Black/Brown/White Relations: Race Relations in the 1970s. New Brunswick, N.J.: Transaction Books. 1976.

Analyzes the effects of institutional racism on all races and the variety of adjustments racial minorities make to their situation.

Periodicals Worth Exploring

Black Enterprise
Black Scholar
Civil Rights Digest
Crisis
Ebony
Journal of Black Studies
Journal of Social & Behavioral Science
Negro History Bulletin
Phylon
Race and Class
Race Relations Abstracts
Review of Black Political Economy
Urban League Review

Problems of Aging and the Elderly

INTRODUCTION

DEFINITIONS OF THE PROBLEM
Myths and realities:
a) They are all the same.
b) They are "old fogies" and senile.
c) They are tranquil and serene.
d) They are not productive or creative.
e) They are conservative.
f) They are useless and worthless.

Comparison of public's and elderly's perspectives.
Social issues of the aged as a group:
a) Ageism.
b) Social conditions of elderly — income, housing, health care, nursing homes, and transportation.

Growing numbers as a group.

INCIDENCE AND PREVALENCE OF THE PROBLEM
Growth in numbers of elderly — 3 million in 1900 to 23 million in 1977.
Economic plight of the elderly.
Need and quality of nursing care.

CAUSES OF THE PROBLEM
Society's norms and values about youth and age.
Society's attitudes toward aging and the elderly.
Growing numbers of elderly because of increases in life expectancy and longevity.

PROPOSED SOLUTIONS TO THE PROBLEM
A change in norms, values, beliefs, and attitudes about the elderly.
Outlawing forced retirement.
Adjustments in Social Security payments.
A congressional investigation of nursing homes.
Meals on Wheels and LIFE programs.
Better provisions for housing.
Improved transportation for elderly.
Other programs and proposals.

FUTURE OF THE PROBLEM
Decreased death rates, increased longevity and life expectancy.
Economic dependency of elderly on nonelderly.
Population down, economic burdens up.
Problems in Social Security system.
Private-sector adaptations to the elderly.

SUMMARY

> A 1966 Rand Corporation study concluded that if the U.S. survived a nuclear war it would be "better off without old and feeble" citizens, and suggested that no provisions be made to care for the surviving elderly.
>
> "New Outlook for the Aged," **Time** (June 2, 1975): 44.

We have all wondered how long we will live. Chances are good in our society that we will live to a ripe old age. We will experience being old. College students today will be "old" in 2025, or at least over 65. The problems elderly people face today (as a group) are not just aging, a biological process. Instead, many of the problems that accompany old age stem from our society's reaction to older people rather than from age itself. Society itself, because of practices such as forced retirement at age 65, has created the "aged problem." It is not pleasant to grow old in our culture and society, whereas in most nonindustrialized societies being old ensured greater status and respect. But something new has happened. As a group, the problems of the elderly are no longer private matters. The care, treatment, and troubles of the elderly are now a social issue.

Let us look at some of the definitions by society and by the elderly as a group, to see the various myths, realities, and problems involved.

DEFINING THE PROBLEMS OF AGING AND THE ELDERLY

Like many other social problems, the process of aging and the conditions of the aged entail both myths and realities. Folklore and limited personal experience create myths about growing old and being old. In the United States, the designation of being old or elderly generally applies to those who have reached age 65. Although retirement from work can occur much earlier and although people are physically well past age 65, our Social Security system, established in 1935, fixed the retirement age at 65. Since then, 65 was institutionalized as the point between old and young. Six distinct myths have persisted in the public's definition of the elderly persons and their problems.

1. They are all the same.
2. They are "old fogies" and senile.
3. They are tranquil and serene.
4. They are not productive or creative.
5. They are conservative and hate to change.
6. They are useless and worthless (McVeigh, May 7, 1975: 1–11).

Opposed to these six myths are the realities about the aged, as verified by scientific study and analysis, especially a survey done for the National Council on the Aging called "The Myth and Reality of Aging in America"

(1975). Let us examine these definitions—both myths and realities—to get a better picture of the social situation.

The great myth is that elderly people are all the same. This myth persists because we have lumped them all into some kind of statistical age category—usually 65 years of age or more. Yet the differences among the aged are as striking and significant as their similarities. If we were discussing "the adult" rather than "the elderly," we would consider whether we were talking about a 21-year-old or a 50-year-old adult. We should also distinguish in some respects between a person who is 65 and one who is 95.

Furthermore, are we talking about someone in the lower socioeconomic class or the upper class? Someone with a college degree or someone who never finished high school? Are we talking about men or women? Are we considering persons after 65 who continue to work, or about retired persons? Are we talking about persons who are physically well or about the chronically ill? In reality, we cannot pigeon-hole the elderly into any one convenient category.

Let us consider five other myths to see what kind of picture of the elderly they portray. Some people say: "They're old fogies" or "senile." This myth implies that chronological age dominates a person's life. A more realistic measure of actual age might be that old maxim: "You're as young (or as old) as you feel." On that basis many of us on any particular day may be "old fogies." "Young" 80-year-olds can look and feel very

You're as young as you feel.

different from "old" 80-year-olds. It is a well-established reality that large disparities often exist between physiological, psychological, chronological, and social ages. People age at such different rates that physical factors show a much greater range in old age than in any other age group. And people may become more diverse rather than similar as they age.

As a person ages, some limitations on activities may be necessary. But only one out of every 20 persons 65 or older is so ill as to be homebound ("New Outlook...," June 2, 1975:45). This "old fogies" myth sees the elderly as old and decrepit—a rocking chair generation. It sees the elderly in a nursing home, in a home for the aged, or in the hospital. The reality is that only five percent of the aged are in nursing homes. Most of the aged, about 90 percent according to University of California gerontologist James Peterson, are in fairly good health. With planned exercise and good nutrition, they can "add years to their lives and life to their years" (1974:1). We should add that if the elderly are a "rocking chair" generation, the fault might lie with inadequate public transportation.

A related myth is that all elderly people are senile. Senility is excessively used by doctors and laymen alike to explain the behavior and condition of the elderly. Many of the emotional responses of old people, such as depression, grief, and anxiety, are attributed to senility, and are thus considered chronic, untreatable states. Polly Francis, a 91-year-old woman writing in the *Washington Post-Outlook*, said: "I've been called senile. Senility is a convenient peg upon which to hang our nonconformity" ("Old Age...," April 20, 1975:E-1). Senility too often is a label used by doctors who do not wish to spend the time and effort necessary to diagnose and treat the complaints of the elderly.

According to Butler and Lewis, the popular medical-school term for old people is "crocks" (1973:22). Thus, this myth forms attitudes that affect treatment of the elderly. Even where senile brain damage has occurred, there can be overlays of depression, anxiety, and psychosomatic disorders that can be remedied by proper medical, social, and psychological intervention. The Congressional Special Committee on Aging noted: "What appears to be senility...may often be a temporary physical or emotional condition caused by problems which may intensify in the later years of life: malnutrition caused by poor eating habits or poverty; overuse of pain relieving or tranquilizing drugs, some forms of kidney trouble...traumatic events, adverse environment..." (Perry, 1976:135). All these conditions can be treated. So-called senility may not be that at all, and is not a necessary part of aging.

Another myth is much more positive than the first two, but no less spurious; namely, that aged people are tranquil and serene. This is a rather contradictory position when one considers the general public apathy toward and neglect of the elderly. This myth sets forth the sugar-coated "Grandma-with-the-goodies" vision of old age as a time of idyllic serenity and tranquility when old persons enjoy the fruits of their labors. It is closely related to the old cliché that poor blacks are really rather happy and serene in their oppressed condition, and probably would not want it otherwise.

A combination of wishful thinking about their own old age and a denial of the present realities is evident in the younger generation's image of the happy-go-lucky elderly. Simone de Beauvoir, in her classic work *The Coming of Age*, summarized the third myth this way:

> If old people show the same desires, the same feelings and the same requirements of the young, the world looks upon them with disgust; in them love and jealousy seem revolting or absurd; sexuality repulsive, and violence ludicrous. They are required to be a standing example of all virtues. Above all they are called upon to display serenity. The world asserts that they possess it, and this assertion allows the world to ignore them (1972:3).

The counterpart of this myth of serenity and tranquility is that of the old fool in his dotage, the "dirty old man" if he is interested in sex. In any case, either by their virtues or by their degradation, they stand outside of humanity, according to de Beauvoir. Our society, or its leaders, therefore, need feel no guilt in refusing them the minimum of support—social, psychological, and economic—considered necessary for living like a human being. Facing the reality of being ignored or rejected by society produces neither tranquility nor serenity among the elderly.

Another prevalent myth is that old people are not productive or creative. Studies reported by Bernice Neugarten, Wayne Dennis, and others have documented when the creative works of scholars in the sciences, humanities, and arts were created and published. The studies reveal that the overwhelming majority of works, with a few notable exceptions, were not produced or created until the author was in his 50s, 60s, or 70s; this held for botanists as well as mathematicians; for geologists as well as novelists; historians as well as inventors (Dennis, 1968:106–14).

Such well-known persons as Voltaire, Cervantes, Picasso, Casals, and Winston Churchill all made their greatest contributions to the world and their fields when they were in their 70s and 80s. Many people become creative for the first time when they reach their later years; retirement can be a very productive and rewarding experience because of newly available leisure time, particularly in the absence of severe medical or personal problems.

Another myth is that the aged are conservative and resist change. Maggie Kuhn and her Gray Panthers see it differently. Studies by Norval Glenn and Ted Hefner (1972:31–47), Neal Cutler (1969–70:583–88), and others cast serious doubt on even the political conservatism of the elderly. Dr. Robert Butler, director of the government's National Institute on Aging, points out that "Gallup polls from 1964 on showed that a greater proportion of people over 55 than any other age group opposed U.S. intervention in the Vietnam War" (Holden, June 11, 1976:1083).

Although the adult character structure is often more stable than that of the young, the ability to change or resist change depends more on previous values and on personality traits than on anything inherent in old age. Conservatism is often the result of socioeconomic pressures, not of aging. For example, the decision of older people to vote against a school-bond issue often has a strictly economic basis.

The sixth and last myth is that the elderly feel useless and worthless. Whether this myth partly reflects reality depends upon the person's state of mind. Some are forced by society's prevailing attitudes and practices, such as retirement at age 65, to feel useless and worthless. As sociologist James Henslin put it:

> In spite of all the hoopla in our society about the joys of retirement, it is essentially a functionless position in a function-oriented society, a society in which positive approval and consequent self- and social identities are given for **doing** something. To be retired in our society, however, is taken to mean **not** doing something and, ultimately, to be useless . . . to **not** be (1976:153).

One 90-year old woman reflects the resilience of many elderly who act as foster grandparents and are involved in very useful and worthwhile community and church activities. She observes:

> Old age is not all pain and limitations. It holds its own joys and satisfactions. I want to cry out that the invisible part of me is not old. I still thrill to the beauties of this world—the dew upon the rose at dawn, the glow reflected by the sun, or a passing cloud when day is done . . . and now I have the time to enjoy them. I feel that old age sharpens our awareness (Francis, April 20, 1975:E-1, E-10).

It may be in the later years of life that the simple, elemental things assume greater significance as people sort out the more important from the less important.

The reality is that old age can provide an increased feeling of emotional and sensory awareness, and usefulness, and happiness. Many elderly people possess a great untapped resource: they have the *time* to structure as they see fit. Whether or not the last myth will come true depends on society's attitudes toward the elderly, on the elderly's attitude toward themselves, and on what they do to make their lives worthwhile.

Perspectives of the Elderly and the Public

As a basis for defining the social problems of the aged, Louis Harris studied public attitudes about the elderly for the National Council on Aging. He found that the public's concepts of "very serious" problems of old age were not those of the elderly. For example, half of those interviewed considered "poor health" and "fear of crime" to be "very serious" problems for older people. When the elderly were asked, only about 22 percent reported such concerns. Two-thirds of the public expect old people to sit around and watch television; only 36 percent of the elderly reported doing so regularly. The public (62 percent) believes that they "sit and think a lot"; only 31 percent of the elderly say they do so ("Myth and Reality of Aging," 1975:31, 59). Figure 8-1 shows the contrast between the public's expectation of serious problems the elderly face, compared with the elderly's experience of such problems.

However, the public and the elderly *defined* certain aspects of the problems alike. They agreed on the following:

The federal government should use "general tax revenues" to help support the elderly.

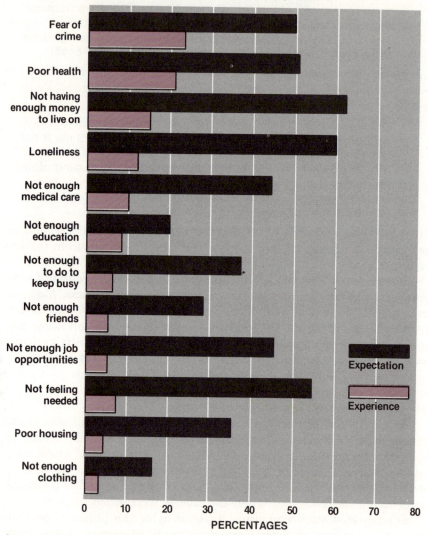

figure 8-1 "VERY SERIOUS" PROBLEMS OF OLDER PEOPLE
Public Expectations vs. Personal Experience

Source: Reprinted from *The Myth and Reality of Aging*, a study prepared by Louis Harris and Associates, Inc., for the National Council on the Aging, Inc., Washington, D.C. © 1975.

Social Security payments to the elderly should automatically increase to keep pace with living costs.

Forced retirement at age 65 should be ended.

The Harris Poll report concluded:

> The elderly do indeed have problems—not enough money, fear of crime, poor health, loneliness, inadequate medical care. But the biggest problem may be the public's attitude toward them (Moore, August 1975:30).

The myths and public opinion about the aged maintain and reinforce the shabby treatment of the elderly. Some sociologists, such as Palmore and Whittington, have concluded that our society often treats the aged as a minority group. They experience prejudice, discrimination, segregation, and isolation. Also, the aged many times *react* as a minority group (Palmore and Whittington, 1971:84–91).

The social problems of growing old and the elderly as a group in our society can be reduced to three basic ones:

"ageism"—prejudice and discrimination against people who are old

poor social conditions—particularly, low income, meager housing, inadequate health care and treatment, and almost nonexistent transportation

rapid growth in the number of the elderly.

We will now discuss each of these problems in turn.

Ageism

Ageism is prejudice and discrimination against people on the basis of their age. In recent years we have become more aware of ageism in our society. In literature and on television the elderly are often described and depicted as weak, sickly, irascible, and uncooperative. Just as schoolbooks have given a false image of blacks and women, they often do the same to the elderly. Ageism is reinforced by our industrial society's use of "throw aways" and functionality (every person and thing must perform a function). We are all socialized to use something and then discard it when it is used up. So it is with the elderly. They serve society and perform a worthwhile function—until age 65. Then they are shelved or forgotten.

Ageism works in diverse ways. A company may refuse to hire a person because he is 45, or not extend him credit because he is retired. The only decent place many elderly persons can afford and find to live is in a community or village segregated by age (even though they might prefer to be with others not their age). The older a person gets the harder it is to get a bank loan, home mortgage, auto insurance, or a driver's license.

Within our youth-oriented society, older citizens are being cheated of their fair share of material and social benefits. Ageism encourages institutional segregation. More and more there is a geriatric separation, as the elderly choose or are forced to play the roles of consumers, residents, relatives, victims, and others. Attitudes toward the old are negative and damaging to an older person's feelings about himself, unlike the positive attitudes toward the elderly in most other societies. As ageism spreads in our society, "we are losing some of our most basic human values in our rejection of the elderly" (Huyck, 1974:vii).

The ultimate impact of ageism is that we ignore the old. We do not bother with them at all. Mrs. Jean Rosenstein of Los Angeles, an elderly widow, lived in a cramped, inexpensive apartment near a freeway. She wrote a letter to the *Los Angeles Times,* explaining that she was "so lonely that I could die." Her letter said:

> I see no human beings. My phone never rings. I feel sure the world has ended. I'm the only one on earth. How else can I feel? All alone. The people here won't talk to you. They say, "Pay your rent and go back to your room." I'm so lonely, very, very much. I don't know what to do . . . (Percy, 1974:1).

Mrs. Rosenstein enclosed one dollar and six stamps. The dollar was for anyone who would phone her, the stamps for anyone who would write to her. The *Los Angeles Times* noted that in a city of nearly three million, 84-year-old Mrs. Rosenstein had no one to talk to, to see, or to care about her (Ibid., 2).

Social Conditions of the Elderly

The social conditions under which many elderly live are scandalous. Low income, substandard housing, expensive and inadequate medical care and treatment, and meager transportation are the outgrowth of ageism in the United States. Within the total group are subgroups that suffer in misery: the extremely old, the inner-city poor, and the institutionalized (Brody and Brody, 1974:545).

Low Income. Not everyone who is old is poor. Most scrimp by on savings, pensions, and Social Security. About one-third do not quite make it. For elderly couples, retirement payments are about half the income of the majority of couples. For individuals, pension benefits provide nearly two-thirds of total income (Bouvier et al., 1975:13). The low-income problem for the elderly is directly related to forced retirement. When people cannot work, their income suffers. Forced retirement brings both financial and emotional distress. Men and women at high levels of income and education tend to work longer, since they are often in jobs not covered by forced retirement. Consequently, those who can least afford to save for retirement are forced to retire sooner.

Elderly people living in poverty are often socially isolated, rejected, lonely, and useless, because other forms of social activity are not available to the poor. The middle-class elderly who have saved some money for retirement are forced to live on relatively fixed incomes while the cost of living rises.

Housing. Housing is another problem for the elderly. In our industrialized and urbanized society the trend is toward mobility and *nuclear families* and away from extended families. Therefore, the elderly increasingly live away from their children (McVeigh, 1975a:6–8). About 28 percent live alone or with nonrelatives. This is especially true for widowed women.

About 60 percent of the elderly live in their own homes, but they are increasingly burdened by escalating property taxes. This tax burden consumes close to 10 percent of their income, almost double that for any other group. Relocation can be beneficial if it improves living conditions and satisfaction. However, much relocation results in direct financial loss and increased costs of housing, transportation, food, and other essentials.

Most of the elderly (60 percent) live in central cities, 35 percent in small towns and five percent on farms. Urban housing is generally inadequate and harder to maintain, because of the structural weakness of buildings in slum areas. Nevertheless, many elderly wish to remain where they are because they have lived there for years and are familiar with the area, or because their only relatives and friends are there. The urban elderly are less likely to be employed, and their wages are often very low.

Separation from family and friends in one's declining years may lead to alienation, social isolation, and segregation.

Credit: Newspaper Enterprise Association.

Since the extended family and filial responsibility are more common in rural areas, the transition to retirement is easier there. However, the rural elderly often have lower earnings, less insurance, fewer benefits, and lower pensions. In addition many suffer from poorer health, greater isolation, and lack of transportation. The plight of those who are not cared for by families is increased by the lag in public-housing projects, which has affected the rural elderly most.

Health Care. Health care is another concern of most elderly Americans. Their medical expenditures exceed those of the total population by about 350 percent. They are more vulnerable to disease and suffer from more chronic diseases. The aged are hospitalized at two-and-a-half times the rate of persons under 65, and their average stay is twice that of younger persons. Of funds spent on health care by government programs, two-thirds is spent on the elderly (Mueller and Gibson, June 1976:18). But health-care costs have increased twice as fast as the Consumer Price Index. The average health-care bill for the elderly in 1976 was $1,521 but only $547 for those between 19 and 64. The elderly had to pay $404 directly for health care, as compared with $153 for those under 65. The elderly spend most of their income on such basic necessities as food and housing, and cannot afford this expensive medical care. The Medicare program requires the elderly to pay the first $124 for the first 60 days in the hospital from their own pockets and $31 a day up through the 90th day for each covered hospitalized illness. After that the elderly pay even more. As can be seen from Figure 8-2, even though government spending has increased for the elderly (since Medicare started in fiscal 1966) the elderly still had to pay $422 *more* in 1976 for their health care than before Medicare started. Elderly under Medicare who choose to have insurance for doctor fees pay $92.40 in premiums a year. So Medicare pays less than half the medical expenses of the elderly.

The elderly poor often forgo needed medical care which the average middle- or upper-class person would receive. Also many elderly cannot gain access to medical facilities because of a lack of transportation and numerous other factors. When unable to afford private physicians, they may spend hours or days waiting for treatment in hospital emergency rooms. In such instances the care received is often inferior.

Nutrition is another major concern of the aged since it is linked to both health and morale. Proper diets, particularly for the large number of elderly who require special diets, are very important. Yet many cannot afford good food or are unable to acquire it for various reasons. In 1976 the federal government was sued for not spending money authorized for community feeding programs that ensure the elderly decent food.

Nursing Homes. Nursing homes and personal-care homes sometimes make matters worse for elderly people. Although some homes provide good (though very expensive) care, most do not meet the needs of their

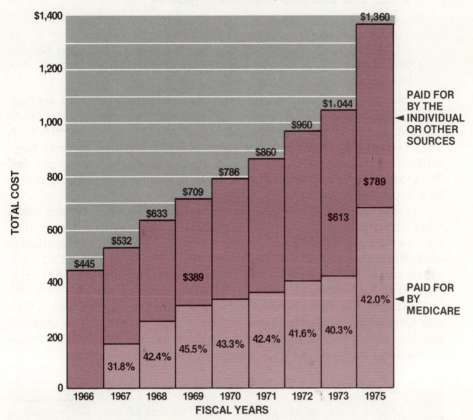

figure 8-2 MEDICAL-CARE COST PER AGED PERSON AND PROPORTION COVERED BY MEDICARE, 1966–1975

Source: Social Security Administration and *Social Security Bulletin*, June 1976

residents. Ralph Nader's Study Group Report on Nursing Homes pointed out that criticisms of nursing homes "ranged from callous and incompetent staff to shocking drug abuse, from lack of rehabilitative programs to neglect of patients by physicians" (Townsend, 1971:18). Other investigations have verified many such complaints. Chuck Waller, Director of the Nursing Home Ombudsman Program of the National Council of Senior Citizens, tells of some of the 2,300 complaints about nursing homes that his group investigated.

> While a resident was getting a permanent wave in the home's beauty shop, she was dropped by a nurse's aide. She suffered a concussion and died. The nursing home sent a bill to the family of the deceased for the cost of the permanent.
> An elderly woman considered "troublesome" by the staff of another home was tied by the ankles to keep her confined to a chair all day.

At one nursing home, the only member of the staff on duty was an aide who was "high" on drugs.

Patients in another home were being fed canned baby food.

All the rooms in one home were infested by roaches.

The residents in another nursing home were found to be badly bruised from rough treatment by aides (Cathcart, December 17, 1974:9).

Abuse, neglect, rough treatment, and poor living conditions are typical of many homes, even though most receive federal money under Medicare, Medicaid, or other government programs (Burger, 1973:207-9). A 1971 General Accounting Office audit of nursing homes in three large states found that more than half were violating basic government rules. For example, over half completely ignored the rule that patients be visited by a doctor every 30 days.

In nursing homes the elderly are viewed as an expense, and since most nursing homes in our society are in business to make money, they cut down on the patient's food, bedding supplies, and care. A Department of Health, Education and Welfare surprise inspection of 295 skilled nursing homes in 1975 revealed basically the same problems as the GAO study in 1971. The findings of HEW and GAO closely parallel the problems publicized by the Subcommittee on Long-Term Care of the Senate Special Committee on Aging ("Laxity Found...," 1975:10). The inherent problem here is that when federal guidelines, such as requiring dietitians in nursing homes, improve the situation, costs of care increase.

WAITING FOR THE END

A federal government investigation of nursing homes in three large states revealed the case of Mrs. Annie T. Bond. A disability recipient, she had resided for over two years at the Carver Convalescent Home in Springfield, Illinois, before being transferred to another home.

Mrs. Bond was covered with decubiti [bedsores] from the waist down;... the decubiti on hips were the size of grapefruits and bones could be seen;...[parts of the skin] were stuck together with mucous and filth so that tincture of green soap had to be used before a Foley catheter could be inserted;... her toes were a solid mass of dirt, stuck together, and not until they had been soaped... for three days did the toes come apart.

That letter from a nurse was sent to the Illinois Department of Public Aid. An investigation was ordered, but state records do not show whether one was ever made. The Carver Convalescent Home was destroyed by fire in 1972, and 10 patients died. The home was still licensed by the state at the time of the fire. Repeated calls by citizens for investigations into conditions at the home were ignored.

Source: Susan Jacoby, "Waiting for the End: On Nursing Homes," *New York Times Magazine* (March 31, 1974):82.

Inadequate Transportation. Another life condition of the elderly is inadequate transportation. Almost 45 percent of household heads over 65 do not own a car. Many aged reside in urban areas, where living costs are high; and most of them live in the inner city, where transit services may be poor or nonexistent. Mass transit is strongly oriented toward journeys to and from work and runs most frequently at hours unsuitable for the elderly. It often provides no access to hospitals, museums, libraries, senior-citizen centers, and shopping areas. For the rural elderly, the situation is even worse, for there is frequently no public transit at all. Health care, church attendance, shopping for a proper diet, and cultural, recreational, and social activities all depend upon transportation. When the elderly are denied mobility, health problems may worsen, loneliness increases, and the quality of life declines.

In urban and rural areas, the private automobile transports most people. As age increases, driving by the elderly decreases, not only because of lowered income but also because of fear of fast traffic and complex highways and their declining sensory-motor capacity. Some states require the aged to have a physical examination, which some elderly persons cannot afford. These former drivers must now learn to use public-transit vehicles whose steps are high, whose doors shut quickly, and which start and stop suddenly. The lessened ability of the elderly to make this adjustment probably explains their frequent use of taxis, despite the cost.

The third problem society faces with the elderly is their growing numbers as a group and as a proportion of our population. We will discuss this problem in the following section.

INCIDENCE AND PREVALENCE OF THE PROBLEMS OF AGING AND THE ELDERLY

The incidence and prevalence of social problems for the elderly grow as their numbers grow. The trend is clearly toward more aged persons in our society. In the future, many of our efforts will be directed to problems of the elderly rather than to those of youth. As sociologist Meyer Nimkoff stated: "If Ellen Key was right in calling the first half of the twentieth century the Children's Century, it may turn out to be appropriate to call the second half the Century of the Aged" (1969:451). As we begin our third century as a nation, this trend is unmistakable. In 1870, slightly over one million persons lived to the ripe old age of 65. In 1900 this number reached about three million (four percent of the population), and by 1940 it had tripled to nine million. By 1977, there were over 23 million persons 65 and over and they accounted for over 10 percent of our population.

Rapid Growth of the Elderly Population

The 1970 Census showed that, for the first time in our history, there were more persons 65 and older than children under five (20 million v.

17.2 million). By 1976 the difference had widened (22.9 million v. 15.3 million) (U.S. Bureau of Census, "Population Profile," 1977:12). The decline in population at the base of the population pyramid affects what happens at the top of the population "skyscraper." Dr. Robert Butler, first Director of the federal government's National Institute on Aging, summed up the situation well:

> We were caught by surprise in this twentieth century by an incredible explosion of older people. Our health-care system, our economic system, were not geared to meet this problem (Butler, July 12, 1976:29).

The elderly have not only grown in comparison with the past, but also will make up a larger percentage of our future population.

Current projections anticipate a population of nearly 30 million elderly by the year 2000 ("Population and the American Future," 1972:97). And only 20 years after that, there should be over 40 million (Bouvier, 1974:40).

In addition, persons over 65 are living longer. Out of the present 23 million persons 65 or older, 10 million are over 73 years of age; one million are 85 or over; and more than 106,000 are centenarians (Butler and Lewis, 1973:5). The old are getting older and will continue to do so.

There are more elderly females than males, although most studies concentrate on males (Beeson, 1975:52–59). In 1976 one out of every eight females (13.2 million) was 65 or more, compared with one of 11 males (9.1 million). More than one-third of elderly women have passed their seventy-fifth birthday.

Economic Plight of the Elderly

Not all elderly, of course, are poor. Nevertheless, anywhere from 15 to 30 percent of the elderly are counted as poor, and many are very close to the government's poverty line.

The basic economic problem of the elderly is that they live on relatively fixed incomes. Even though Social Security benefits automatically increase once a year, the elderly are always a year or more behind rising living costs. A 1976 study reported in the National Retired Teachers Association Journal shows that most retirees have only a constant income. The report estimated expenses for a retired urban couple maintaining a "lower," "intermediate," and "higher" standard of living. Most elderly come nearest to the intermediate level. Table 8-1 shows how much money is needed for each level for selected years.

Need for and Quality of Nursing Care

In early 1976 there were about 23,000 nursing and "personal-care" homes in the United States. These were home to over one million elderly people (5 percent of all elderly). But studies by Robert Kastenbaum and

table 8-1   AMOUNT OF MONEY NEEDED TO MAINTAIN THREE LIVING STANDARDS

LEVEL OF LIVING	1972	1973	SELECTED YEARS 1974	1975	1980 (est.)
LOWER	$3,442	$3,764	$4,178	$4,512	$5,491
INTERMEDIATE	4,967	5,416	6,011	6,492	7,901
HIGHER	7,689	8,044	8,928	9,642	11,734

Source: The U.S. News Washington Letter, 1977. Reprinted by permission.

Sandra Candy in Detroit suggest that the total of all elderly who are placed in a home (even temporarily) or who die in an "extended-care facility" is closer to 25 percent (Kart and Manard, 1976:173). There are 722,200 employees in nursing homes, or about 66 for every 100 residents ("Nursing Homes . . .," September 5, 1974:2). However, not all employees directly serve or assist the elderly.

The need for such services is often greater than those provided. A report by the Subcommittee on Long-term Care of the Senate Special Committee on Aging estimated that over two-and-a-half million persons over 65 need "in-home" services—only 300,000 of whom are now in institutions. Sociologist Ethel Shanas arrived at a figure of four million who need home health care, by adding the bedfast, homebound, institutionalized, and those who walk with difficulty. By this count, one out of five older Americans could use home care (Miller, 1976:134).

Inadequate, improper, and inhumane treatment of the elderly seems to be more prevalent in nursing homes than the public can imagine. A Health, Education and Welfare spot check of 295 skilled nursing homes (selected by computer to be representative of 16,000 such homes) revealed the following problems:

> 64 percent had from five to more than 20 fire-safety violations.
>
> 44.8 percent of the patients were given tranquilizers.
>
> 15.8 percent of the patients needed dental care.
>
> 9.5 percent of the patients had bed sores, an indication of inadequate nursing care.
>
> 18.6 percent of patients did not have prescribed diets; and, among those patients who did, half lacked plans containing pertinent information about special dietary needs and problems.
>
> 48 percent of patients had not been examined by a doctor within 48 hours of admission, and 25 percent had not been visited by a physician every 30 days during their first three months in a home—both required by federal regulations.
>
> 74 percent of the patients did not receive desirable bladder and bowel training, although government reimbursement is available for such services ("Laxity Found in Rest Home," April 3, 1975:10).

These are just some of the conditions the elderly live under and the government pays for in nursing homes across the country. Chuck Waller reports:

> We have uncovered instances where patients have died from neglect. We have found cases of maltreatment that are almost inhuman. Many of the so-called nursing homes where hundreds of thousands of old people are forced to spend their last years do not have the comforts and facilities of many prisons in the United States (Cathcart, 1974:9).

Waller blames the lack of tight government supervision of nursing homes, noting that anyone can open a nursing home without proper qualifications. He proved his point by filing an application in Michigan to turn a building into a nursing home. The application was approved; the building was his garage (Ibid., 9).

CAUSES OF THE PROBLEMS OF AGING AND THE ELDERLY

If we are to remedy the problems of low income, poor housing, improper treatment in nursing homes, and inadequate transportation, we must explore the underlying causes. There are three causes behind problems of the elderly.

1. society's present norms and values about youth and age
2. society's attitudes toward aging and the elderly
3. growing numbers because of increased life expectancy (at birth) and life span.

We are a youth-oriented culture. We place great stress on attributes of youth—speed, strength, sexual prowess. We emphasize what is new and make obsolete what is old—from autos to zoos. As part of our culture's norms and values, we often deprive older people of roles that are important to self-identity and continuity in their lives.

As Maria Hartmann, a social worker, notes in writing about the loss of roles and status by the aged: "Just as roles are established by society or social groups, so too, many of the consequences of role loss are created by societal or group norms and values" (1974:258). One of the most crucial roles of which we deprive older men and women is work. The elderly are forced into an inferior social position that results from the loss of prestige, status, and income from unemployment. As the old person is removed (or withdrawn) from meaningful social groups and activities, he is "devalued." As old roles are removed—earner, parent, spouse, friend—few if any new positive roles are assigned by our society or social structure. In our capitalistic, technological society once people can no longer work fast and produce wealth for elites who control the system, they are thrown on the social scrap heap and forced to retire. Since they do not produce anything for sale to make a profit, they are considered useless and of no value.

Because of age-stratification norms, cultural expectations require the elderly to restrict their interpersonal relationships to their own age group. So as work relations are broken and friends die, social contacts diminish. As Hartmann writes:

> Because of social and cultural factors the aged, as a group, suffer status loss. Compulsory retirement, our youth-centered and youth-valued emphasis, our system of age stratification — all serve to increase the isolation of the aged and make their position in society one of increasing unimportance (1974:259).

To make matters worse, our cultural norms and values have done little to prepare the elderly for such a drastic change. They have been socialized (before age 65) to value and seek independence, work, and social activity. Society has only recently begun to help the elderly to resocialize (to learn new values, norms, and beliefs). It has even encouraged early retirement instead of retirement at 70 or 75.

Attitudes of Society

Because of our usual social norms, values, and social structure, the attitudes of the nonelderly are shaped and formed in such a way that ageism is encouraged. Myths and stereotypes about the aged (discussed earlier) are fostered, and aging becomes an ordeal rather than an achievement.

Assertion of self among the elderly is important in a society that often holds myths about the aged.

Credit: Michael D. Sullivan

Negative attitudes toward the elderly are rare in preindustrial societies, according to research conducted by sociologist Eleanor Maxwell. In such societies the elderly play a "starring role" in cultural rituals. They play their most important roles in rituals that take place at various stages of the life cycle. Maxwell writes, "Old Apaches, for instance, bless babies, while elders of the Bankongo tribe of Africa train youngsters for adult life" ("Aging," March 1976:17). The elderly also play vital roles in work rituals and spiritual ceremonies. More than any other age group, the elders are believed to possess special powers.

But we are taught to respect new ideas and innovation, not the experience or insights that the old possess. Our attitudes are shaped in what Margaret Mead calls a "prefigurative" culture, in which the young begin to transmit new norms, values, and beliefs to the rest of society (including the old). Ours is a prefigurative culture. Most preindustrial cultures, including our own in the recent past, depend on older adults for guidance. But in a culture and society that changes so rapidly, pushed by the massive technology, power, authority and the drive for economic profit and wealth in our social structure, attitudes are shaped by the young. As long as innovations are valued and experience devalued, our negative attitudes toward the old will persist.

Life Expectancy

Another cause underlying the problems of the elderly is their growing numbers, stemming from longer life expectancy and life span. What happens to mortality, life expectancy, and life span will ultimately determine the degree and kinds of social repercussions our society must prepare for. The death rate in the United States has been cut in half since 1900. The average life expectancy today is about 71, compared with about 40 in 1900. Research during the 1950s, according to demographer Clyde Kiser, verified that *past* increases in the proportion of the elderly were the result "almost entirely of declines in the fertility rate and virtually not at all of declines in the mortality rate." But, Kiser added, "in the future, declines in the death rate may well emerge as the dominant factor in the further aging of the population in this country" (1968:361). And such indeed is the case.

The Presidential Commission on Population Growth and the American Future saw the significance of a drop in the death rate or an increase in life expectancy and longevity. It pointed out that mortality during the early years of life is ". . . already so low that any substantial further improvements in life expectancy will have to come primarily among persons over the age of 50" (Population and the American Future, 1972:12). The Commission, in somewhat of a glib understatement, concluded: "Consequently, further additions to the duration of life in this country would simply result in somewhat larger numbers of people at the older ages . . ." (1972:12). We cannot assume that mortality will remain at present rates or that decline in future death rates will affect only the newborn or the young.

PROPOSED SOLUTIONS TO THE PROBLEMS OF AGING AND THE ELDERLY

We are so intimately tied to our present norms, values, attitudes, and social structure that there can be no quick solutions to problems of the elderly. Ageism, like racism and sexism, must be recognized and dealt with by our society.

End Forced Retirement

One popular step, especially among the elderly, is to end forced retirement.

> "The present system of compulsory retirement from faithful employment solely on the basis of chronological age is completely unrealistic and should be abandoned," says Dr. Irving Wright, clinical professor of medicine at Cornell University's Medical College. "We must provide older people with an opportunity for work commensurate with their abilities rather than their years" (Percy, 1974:29).

Most people want to work as long as they are able, and most 65-year-olds are quite able to continue working, at least until 70 or 80. If our economic system and power structure were modified to produce jobs for everyone who wanted one, there would be no need to force people to retire. Radicals argue that our exploitive corporate system often finds it much cheaper to hire younger workers rather than retain those who have worked for them for years. In 1977 the Congress passed legislation to eliminate forced retirement at age 65. The 1971 White House Conference on Aging recommended a change in the Age Discrimination Employment Act to include persons 65 and older but conservatives have opposed such proposals.

It may well be argued that when our population was growing at a rate of two percent each year, forced retirement made sense to make room for the millions of youngsters who needed jobs. Now that our population is growing at less than one percent each year, voluntary retirement makes more sense. However, until our social structure is changed to provide jobs for all those who want them, the aged will be used as the powerless scapegoats to make jobs available for the young (whose wages are lower than long-term employees'). A voluntary-retirement law might also save the solvency of the Social Security Fund, for those over 65 would continue to pay into it but would not draw benefits until they (not the company or society) decided that they should retire.

Outlawing forced retirement is a rational solution to the problems of low income and poor housing. This would restore to many of the elderly

Elderly persons who are forced to live on fixed income are hurt most by inflation. Social action by the elderly may be necessary to make the public aware of their plight.

those social roles and functions, as well as status and prestige, that they lost the day they were forced to quit working for a living. The Senior Citizens Community Employment Program, financed nationally by the federal government, should be encouraged as a means of providing part-time work for those already retired.

As another solution to problems of the low-income elderly, the liberals on the Senate's Special Committee on Aging have recommended that Social Security payments be adjusted for cost-of-living changes twice a year, instead of annually ("6-Month Social Security . . .," July 9, 1976:10). This would give those on fixed incomes at least a fighting chance to keep up with inflation. At present they are always a year or more behind living costs.

Reform the Nursing-Home Industry

A congressional investigation of the nursing-home industry throughout the country has been advocated as a step toward alleviating the improper treatment of elderly patients. Similarly, federal, state, and local laws should more strictly provide and oversee better standards of nursing-home care. To be effective, such laws must be enforced by rigid, unannounced inspections. Any home that did not correct its shortcomings would lose its license to operate. As long as the profit motive undergirds the operation of nursing homes they will either be inadequate or too expensive for most elderly to afford.

We rely too much in our society on setting up institutions (prisons, mental hospitals, nursing homes) that segregate people from the mainstream of the community. We should, as a matter of national policy, deemphasize institutional care of the elderly. Two already-existing noninstitutional programs come to mind—Meals-on-Wheels and Live-In-For-Elderly (LIFE).

"Meals on Wheels" and the LIFE Program

The National Council of Senior Citizens has urged Congress to expand and directly fund the Meals-on-Wheels programs, which provide home-delivered meals to elderly and frail persons in many communities. Executive Director William R. Hutton has said that a national program would substantially reduce the number of elderly persons who are forced to enter costly nursing homes because of their difficulty in caring for themselves. He termed it a "tragedy" that huge sums are spent on hospitalization and nursing-home services when less costly programs "might enable an elderly person to remain in his home and active in the community."

The Live-In-For-Elderly program is specifically intended to avert putting the elderly into nursing homes. Instead, the elderly person moves into another family's home. The family is paid by the government for providing "room and board" for the oldster. According to Deborah German, a director of one such program, it is always "seeking homes that will provide the warmth and attention that add meaning to life." The added advantage of a LIFE program is "returning some of our elderly from institutions to family situations" ("LIFE Program . . .," 1974:25). Sometimes there are problems of matching the elderly person's background with that of the foster family, but the program is still a step away from institutions.

Programs like "Meals-on-Wheels" and "LIFE" are solutions to the elderly's social isolation and mistreatment in nursing homes. If these and similar programs are properly funded and staffed, they can go a long way toward solving many of the elderly person's problems. Churches and synagogues could cooperate with public agencies (as some have) to make these and similar programs a success. This, combined with visiting nurses and homemaker services, will help to reduce reliance upon institutional care for the elderly.

Solutions for Housing

Solutions offered for the housing problem include these:

> Provide tax exemptions for the elderly so they can continue to live in their homes without having to pay taxes.

Increase construction of more public housing for the elderly, with planning for their special needs, such as shopping, nearby centralized health-care and public transportation facilities, homemaker services, and such safety features as a baseboard cord they could pull for help if they fall.

Provide rent supplements and grants for those whose income is too high for public housing and too low for private housing.

Use local retirees to maintain, winterize, and repair homes of elderly people unable to repair their own.

Proposals for Better Transportation

Problems of transportation for the elderly could be alleviated in some of the following ways:

Reduce fares (provide free rides) for senior citizens in off-peak hours, as is done now in hundreds of towns across the country.

Coordinate use of government-agency vehicles and school and church buses, so that free transportation could be provided to the elderly.

Use mobile units to take services—grocery stores, medical facilities, and libraries—to the elderly in rural areas.

Introduce reduced-fare Dial-a-Ride taxi service, as New York City has done.

Use minibuses to help the elderly and handicapped to reach essential places without charge, as was done in a few New Jersey areas.

Form reduced-fare transportation cooperatives, as was done in 17 Missouri counties (Percy, 1974:51).

Other Programs and Proposals

Other programs, plans, and proposals to alleviate some of the social problems of the elderly include:

Promote continuing education (such as the Late Start program), recreation, and volunteer-service programs through ACTION (the Federal Volunteer Agency). This includes expansion of programs such as Retired Senior Volunteer Program (RSVP) (65,000 participants in 1974) and the National Older Workers Program (15,500 part-time jobs since 1974). With more funding these programs could reach millions who have never heard of these programs.

Increase funding of the Title VII Nutrition Program under the Older Americans Act. Used to feed elderly people at senior-citizen centers and other locations, the program received allocations of $200 million in 1976 and $250 million in 1977. It presently provides for only about 250,000 meals a week to elderly citizens. More money is needed to expand this worthwhile program (Bouvier et al., 1975:24).

Encourage electric and gas utility companies to adopt a "lifeline" rate for the poor and elderly, as Maine has done. For example, a person would pay less for the first 400 kilowatt hours of electricity. Anything above that necessary for life would cost more. The present system of utility rates generally does just the opposite—the more we use, the cheaper the rate. One study showed that the elderly poor pay 6 percent of their income on electricity, compared with 1 percent of the income for those who are "well off" (Rollins, January 31, 1975:3).

Establish a guaranteed annual income program to replace or supplement the Supplemental Security Income (SSI) for the elderly poor.

As we continue to change our norms, values, and attitudes about the elderly, through education and the mass media, many or all of these proposals can be applied to the plight of the elderly. Behind all these proposals is the assumption that major structural changes should be made in our economy and society to get to the root causes of all the problems discussed. If wealth and power were better distributed many of the problems of the elderly would be remedied. As long as we have people who hold inordinate power and wealth in our society the problems of the elderly, and other social problems, such as crime and poverty, will persist.

THE FUTURE OF THE PROBLEMS OF AGING AND THE ELDERLY

Increased Longevity

Lowered death rates, increased longevity among the aged, and extended life expectancy at birth are factors that will continue to affect the elderly's social problems. Realistically, we can anticipate substantial in-

---

PUC ACTS TO CONTROL SHUTOFFS

The Public Utility Commission issued an order . . . blocking utilities from shutting off service to their customers without prior PUC approval. . . .

The PUC acted after the death of an elderly woman in suburban Pittsburgh was blamed on a service cutoff by Equitable Gas Company.

Sophie Easer, 70, of Munhall was found frozen to death in her home where Equitable had turned off the gas January 5 for nonpayment of bills.

Another woman, Florence Benson, 82, of McKees Rocks, Allegheny County, was found . . . wrapped in blankets and crouched near a small electric heater in her home. Her gas had been turned off 10 days before for the same reason. She was hospitalized in fair condition.

Source: *Allentown Morning Call* (January 28, 1976):14.

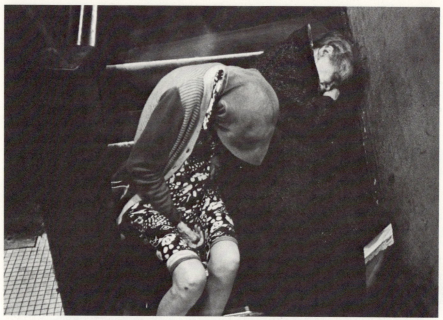

Resignation, apathy, and hopelessness may be spawned by the poverty suffered by some elderly persons. As the life span of the elderly increases, society may find it easier to eliminate some of the aged rather than eliminate their poverty.

creases in life expectancy by the early decades of the twenty-first century (Endres, 1975:123). Dr. Harvey Wheeler, in his report entitled "The Pursuit of Well-Being," speculates that the life expectancy of babies born *before* this century has ended will be about 110 years.

Increases in the length of life will raise social and ethical questions about whether medical knowledge should be applied to help older persons live another five or ten years. New norms and values about life and death will continue to be formed. Euthanasia, "death with dignity," and "living wills"—are these solutions to problems or new social problems? Are these a convenience for the dying or for the living? Are these kind and compassionate acts to help the elderly, or convenient ways of doing away with human beings who cost society too much to treat and keep alive, especially if they perform no productive function? These and other questions will be posed as the elderly's life span increases.

Dependency of the Elderly on the Nonelderly

Forced retirement of the elderly from the workforce will have economic repercussions. As larger proportions of the population reach 65, or retire early, the economic costs of providing proper physical, medical, and social services will put a financial strain on a shrinking workforce. When the children of the baby boom become old, between 2020 and 2030, "life for older people is likely to become much tougher financially" ("How Your Life Will Change . . .," March 1976:42). This situation will be particularly acute if reproduction rates remain at the replacement level (or below) for the next 25 years. The aged-dependency ratio (the number of persons 65 or older per 100 persons aged 18 to 64) has increased sharply in the last few decades and it will continue to do so in the future. The dependency ratio assumes that the elderly are dependent upon those in the workforce who generate income and pay taxes which, in turn, are used to support the elderly. In 1930 the ratio was 10:100; by 1970 it had reached 20:100; by the year 2000 it should reach almost 30:100 (Thompson and Lewis, 1965:96; *Population and the American Future*, 1972:20).

The active labor force will be economically squeezed in two ways. First, the decline in the retirement age before age 65 means people will live a longer period while in retirement. Second, if medical advances increase the life span of the elderly by five to 10 more years by the year 2000, new economic burdens will be added to the active workforce.

Population Down, Economic Burdens Up

Since the aged population is not spread evenly throughout the country, certain areas of the United States are experiencing an even greater economic impact than the national figures suggest. For example, in Nassau County, New York, the number of persons over 65 has increased by 65 percent in just the period between 1970 and 1975. At the same time, it is estimated that between 1970 and 1980 the school-age population in Nassau County will decrease by 49 percent. By 1990 this decrease in young people will be felt in the workforce. According to Owen Moritz, this situation raises "the specter of empty classrooms . . . [and creates] a new center of gravity—the senior citizens center" (1975:37).

The Regional Plan Association, a nonprofit research and civic organization that has worked for regional planning since the 1920s, recently reported that for the first time in over 300 years the New York City urban region (New York City and the surrounding 26 counties in New York, New Jersey, and Connecticut) has stopped growing. Between 1970 and 1975, the fertility rate declined by 27 percent in the area. Abortion has played a significant role in the fertility decline there. In New York City alone, one possible birth was aborted for every two recorded. In the area, both the working population—ages 20 through 64—and children under 14 have decreased (Morris, 1975:9). Unless future birthrates rise or more people move into the area than move out, the workers and taxpayers will decline as the elderly increase.

The Social Security System

The economic impact of a higher aged-dependency ratio is most poignantly seen in what has happened, and will continue to happen, to the Social Security System.

Because of our growing aging population, the number of people drawing Social Security in the next three or four decades will rise substantially, while the number of persons in their working years (ages 15-64) will not increase much above today's total.

A few salient facts show the impact of our aging population. In 1955, seven workers paid Social Security taxes for each person collecting benefits. In 1975 there were about three workers for each recipient. By early in the next century, only two workers will pay into the system for each recipient.

In 1947, the Social Security system had sufficient cash reserves to pay benefits for more than 15 years. In 1974, these would pay benefits for only about nine months.

In addition, the Advisory Council to the Social Security Fund recently recommended that Medicare benefits be financed solely from general government revenues, not from the Social Security Fund. Whatever the source of these benefits, the same small number of persons in the labor force will also pay for the medical benefits of an increasing number of the elderly.

Adaptations of Social Institutions

In the future the private sector—libraries, schools, churches, business, and industry—will have to adapt its social system to account for the larger number of elderly persons. For libraries this may mean whole sections of books with larger type; for schools it means programs and policies to attract and benefit elderly students; for churches, innovative approaches to accommodate the social and spiritual needs of the elderly faithful. This may be done by investing more money to build adequate housing for the elderly congregation and retirement communities for its elderly clergy. For business and industry it means more flexibility in retiring people, and in giving long-term employees at age 65 other options besides forced retirement. Industry and unions will become more active in conducting pre-retirement programs to assist their employees and members to live fuller and more active lives.

The field of gerontology (study of aging and the aged) will become more academically established. In 1975 the University of Southern California became the first professional school to offer undergraduate and graduate degrees in educational and administrative fields dealing with the elderly ("First School of Aging," April 1976:10). Today more colleges and universities have established such programs, and even more will soon exist to prepare students to assist the elderly in areas of health services, recreation, adult education, social services, public administration, and long-term care.

We hope that our future society will develop more positive attitudes toward aging and the elderly. Perhaps we will appreciate the wisdom and insights that some elderly persons develop through living. The hope is that we will accord more prestige and status to the elderly. This will call for radical changes in our attitudes and in our social institutions. Together, persons of all ages can share in this aim and make it a reality.

SUMMARY

It is not pleasant to grow old in our society and culture. The aged have many personal problems that have become social issues. Six myths shape our attitudes about the elderly:

They are all the same.
They are "old fogies" and senile.
They are tranquil and serene.
They are not productive or creative.
They are conservative and hate to change.
They are useless and worthless.

The realities show these ideas to be exaggerated or untrue. The basic social issues involving the aged or aging are prejudice and discrimination against the old—"ageism"; poor living conditions, especially problems of income, housing, medical treatment, and transportation; and rapid growth in numbers of those 65 and older.

The elderly have grown from about 3 million in 1900 (4 percent of the population) to 20 million in 1970 (10 percent). In 1977 they numbered over 23 million and by the year 2000 will reach 30 million, and probably 40 million by 2020.

Studies verify that the elderly have income problems after retirement, since their former income is cut in half. Over one million elderly (5 percent of them) exist in one of our 23,000 nursing or personal-care homes. But the need for such services is often greater than those provided. Federal government inspections reveal that over half the homes violate fire-safety regulations and do not have doctors available as required by law. Patients too often have died from neglect in nursing homes. Lack of strict government supervision, and desire to make a profit no matter what, are blamed, especially in homes that receive Medicare or Medicaid payments.

Three causes behind problems of the elderly include our society's present norms and values about youth and age, society's attitudes toward the elderly, and growing numbers of the elderly as life expectancy and the length of life increase. Eleanor Maxwell's research shows, by contrast, that negative attitudes toward the elderly are rare in preindustrial societies. In our capitalistic society if people are no longer productive and make no goods for profit they are often considered useless and worthless.

Solutions to the problems of the aged include:

a change in society's norms, values, beliefs, and attitudes about the old an end to force retirement

adjustment of Social Security payments twice a year

a congressional investigation of nursing homes

a deemphasis on institutional care of the elderly and an emphasis on programs like Meals-on-Wheels and Live-In-For-Elderly (LIFE)

better housing through tax exemptions, increased construction of public housing, rent supplements and grants, and use of retired persons to repair homes

expansion of volunteer programs, such as foster grandparents and others, to reach millions more

increased funding of nutrition programs to feed more elderly at centers

encouraging electric and gas utilities to adopt a lifeline rate that would benefit the poor and elderly

establishment of a guaranteed annual income program.

As we continue to change our values and attitudes about the elderly, as well as our social structure, through education of the young, these solutions can be applied.

CAREER OPPORTUNITIES

Nursing-Home Administrators.

As the need for nursing-home care grows, we will need more persons trained in gerontology (knowledge of the elderly) and sociology. Administrators and assistants will be needed in nursing homes to set up programs of recreation, acitvities, and care — since many nursing-home residents are ambulatory and active. Knowledge of social interaction and social organization, as well as government regulations about Medicaid, Medicare and nursing homes, would be helpful. For further information write to: American Association of Homes for the Aging, 1050 17th St., N.W., Washington, D.C. 20036.

Gerontologists.

Many careers and positions are beginning to open up in this relatively new field. At the postgraduate level, sociology with a concentration in gerontology should assure one of a good career in research, teaching, administration, or consulting. Courses in demography (population) would also be helpful. Graduate schools are just starting to offer advanced degrees in various aspects of gerontology, and persons with such degrees should be in great demand in the future. For further information write to: U.S. Department of Health, Education and Welfare, Office of Human Development, National Clearinghouse on Aging, Washington, D.C. 20201.

Social Security Administration Employee.

The Social Security Administration handles a wide variety of programs involving the elderly. Social Security offices are located all over America, and students with a degree in sociology who like to interact with the elderly will find such employment fulfilling. A federal civil-service test generally must be taken to fill positions with the Social Security Administration. For further information write to: U.S. Social Security Administration, 330 Independence Ave., S.W., Washington, D.C. 20201; or to the Federal Job Information Center in your state.

REFERENCES

"Aging: Primitives Handle It Better." Science Digest 79, 3 (March): 17–18, 1976.

Beeson, Diane
   1975 "Women in Studies of Aging: A Critique and Suggestion." Social Problems 23, 1 (October): 52–59.

"Boston Globe Wins Pulitzer for School Crisis Coverage." Allentown Morning Call (May 6): 1, 1975.

Botwinick, Jack
   1973 Aging and Behavior. New York: Springer.

Bouvier, Leon F.
   1974 "The Demography of Aging." Pp. 37–46 in William C. Bier, ed. Aging. New York: Fordham University Press.

Bouvier, Leon, Elinore Atlee, and Frank McVeigh
   1975 "The Elderly in America." Population Bulletin 30, 3 (August). Washington, D.C.: Population Reference Bureau.

Brickfield, Cyril F.
   1975 "Why Not Go Home?" Modern Maturity (February/March): 30.

Brody, Elaine and Stanley J. Brody
   1974 "Decade of Decision for the Elderly." Social Work 19 (September): 544–54.

Burger, Robert
   1973 "Commercializing the Aged." Pp. 207–9 in Peter Wickman, ed.: Readings in Social Problems 73/74: Annual Editions. Guilford, Conn.: Dushkin.

Butler, Robert
   1976 "How to Have a Longer Life and Enjoy It More: An Interview." U.S. News & World Report 81, 2 (July 12): 29–32.

Butler, Robert and Myrna Lewis
   1973 Aging and Mental Health. St. Louis: Mosby.

Calhoun, Arthur
   1945 A Social History of the American Family. Vols. 1, 2, 3. New York: Barnes & Noble.

Cathcart, John
   1974 "America's Nursing Homes Are Worse Than Prisons." National Enquirer (December 17): 9.

"Cold-Facts for Preretirees." National Retired Teachers Association Journal (March/April): 31, 1976.

"Commissioner Flemming Stresses Support for Home Winterization Programs." Aging 256–257 (February/March):4, 1976.

Cutter, Neal E.
  1969–70 "Generation, Maturation and Party Affiliation: A Cohort Analysis." Public Opinion Quarterly 33, 4: 583–88.

de Beauvoir, Simone
  1972 The Coming of Age. New York: Putnam.

Dennis, Wayne
  1968 "Creative Productivity between the Ages of 20 and 80 Years." Pp. 106–14 in Bernice Neugarten, ed. Middle Age and Aging. Chicago: University of Chicago Press.

Ehrlich, George E.
  1973 "Health Challenges of the Future." The Annals of the American Academy of Political and Social Sciences 408 (July): 70–82.

Endres, Michael C.
  1975 On Defusing the Population Bomb. New York: Wiley.

"First School of Aging Dedicated at University of Southern California." Aging 258 (April): 10, 1975.

"Flemming Urges Action in Crime Against Elderly." Aging 250 (August): 5, 1975.

Flieger, Howard
  1976 "We're Showing Our Age." U.S. News & World Report 80, 8 (February 23): 80.

Folsom, Joseph
  1943 The Family and Democratic Society. New York: Wiley.

Francis, Polly
  1975 "Old Age Increases Frustration." Allentown Sunday Call-Chronicle (April 20): E-1.

"Funds Sought to Provide Meals for Aged." AFL-CIO News 21, 27 (July 3): 6, 1976.

Furstenberg, Frank
  1969 "Industrialization and the American Family: A Look Backward." Pp. 50–69 in John Edwards, ed. The Family and Change. New York: Random House.

Glenn, Norval and Ted Hefner
  1972 "Further Evidence on Aging and Party Identification." Public Opinion Quarterly 36, 1: 31–47.

Gubrium, Jaber F., ed.
  1976 Time, Roles, and Self in Old Age. New York: Human Sciences Press.

Hartmann, Maria Mercedes
  1974 "Successful Aging: A Sociological View." Pp. 257–64 in William C. Bier, ed. Aging: Its Challenge to the Individual and to Society. New York: Fordham University Press.

Henslin, James M.
  1976 "Growing Old in the Land of the Young." Pp. 147–64 in James Henslin and Larry Reynolds, eds. Social Problems in American Society. 2nd ed. Boston: Holbrook Press.

Hicks, Nancy
  1975 "The Organized Elderly: A New Political Power." New York Times (June 22): 3.

Holden, Constance
  1976 "National Institute on Aging: New Focus on Growing Old." Science

192, 4244 (June 11): 1081–84.

"How Your Life Will Change: The Next 25 Years." U.S. News & World Report (March 22): 40–44, 1976.

Huyck, Margaret Hellie
1974 Growing Older: What You Need to Know about Aging. Englewood Cliffs, N.J.: Prentice-Hall.

Jacoby, Susan
1974 "Waiting for the End: On Nursing Homes." The New York Times Magazine (March 31): 13, 15, 76, 80, 82, 84, 86, 90, 92, and 93.

Kart, Cary S. and Barbara B. Manard, eds.
1976 Aging in America: Readings in Social Gerontology. New York: Alfred.

Kastenbaum, Robert and Sandra E. Candy
1976 "The 4% Fallacy: A Methodological and Empirical Critique of Extended Care Facility Population Statistics." Pp. 166–74 in Cary Kart and Barbara Manard, eds. Aging in America: Readings in Social Gerontology. New York: Alfred.

Kiser, Clyde V.
1968 "The Aging of Human Populations: Mechanisms of Change." Pp. 361–72 in Charles B. Nam, ed. Population and Society. Boston: Houghton Mifflin.

"Laxity Found in Rest Home Fire Safety and Health Care." Allentown Morning Call (April 3): 10, 1975.

"LIFE Program: Elderly May Live in Family Setting." Allentown Morning Call (July 2): 25, 1974.

McVeigh, Frank
1975a "The Impact of an Aging Population on the Family." Paper presented at the Second Annual World Population Society Meeting, November 22, Washington, D.C.
1975b "Myths and Realities about the Aged." Paper presented at the Aging Minicourse, sponsored by the Muhlenberg College Council for Continuing Education, May 17, Allentown, Pa.

Miller, Harriet
1976 "Darlings, We Are Growing Old." Pp. 131–41 in The Social Welfare Forum, 1975. Proceedings of the 102nd Annual Forum, National Conference on Social Welfare, May 11–15, 1975, San Francisco, Calif. New York: Columbia University Press.

Moore, Pam
1975 "What We Expect and What It's Like." Psychology Today 9, 3 (August): 29–30.

Moritz, Owen
1975 "A Point of View: Sub-Zero Population Growth." Long Island Sunday News (January 26): 37.

Morris, Tom
1975 "Report of Zero Growth Has Warning for Area." Newsday (January 8): 9.

Mueller, Marjorie, and Robert Gibson
1976 "Age Differences in Health Care Spending, Fiscal Year 1975." Social Security Bulletin 39, 6 (June): 18–31.

"The Myth and Reality of Aging in America." Conducted by Louis Harris and Associates, Inc. Washington, D.C.: The National Council on the Aging, 1975.

"New Outlook for the Aged." Time (June 2): 44–48, 1975.

Nimkoff, Meyer
1969 "Biological Discoveries and the Future of the Family." Pp. 445–54 in John N. Edwards, ed. The Family and Change. New York: Knopf.

"Nursing Homes: An Overview of National Characteristics for 1973–74." Monthly Vital Statistics Report 236 (September 5), Rockville, Md.: National Center for Health Statistics, 1974.

O'Donnell, Charles F.
1974 "Aging in Preindustrial and Contemporary Industrial Societies." Pp. 3–13 in William C. Bier, ed. Aging: Its Challenges to the Individual and to Society. New York: Fordham University Press.

Palmore, Erdman and Frank Whittington
1971 "Trends in the Relative Status of the Aged." Social Forces 50 (September): 84–91.

Percy, Charles H.
1974 Growing Old in the Country of the Young. New York: McGraw-Hill.

Perry, P. Wingfield
1976 "The Night of Ageism." Pp. 135–38 in Anne Kilbride, ed. Readings in Sociology 76/77: Annual Editions. Guilford, Conn.: Dushkin.

Peterson, James
1974 "Church Gets Low Marks on Attention to Older Persons." Interchange (June): 1–2.

Population and the American Future: Report of the U.S. Commission on Population Growth and the American Future. New York: Signet, 1972.

Porter, Sylvia
1973 "Your Money's Worth." Washington Star-News (April 2): 21.

"A Profile of Older Americans." U.S. News & World Report 80, 8 (February 23): 71, 1976.

Rollins, Hazel R.
1975 "The Lifeline Rate Concept." Memo to Frank Zarb, Administrator, Federal Energy Administration, from Director, Office of Consumer Affairs/ Special Impact.

"6-Month Social Security Adjustments Sought." Allentown Morning Call (January 31): 1, 34, 1976.

Smith, Russell, and Dorothy Zietz
1970 American Social Welfare Institutions. New York: Wiley.

Sontag, Susan
1975 "The Double Standard of Aging." Pp. 148–55 in Peter Wickman, ed. Readings in Social Problems. Annual Editions. Guilford, Conn.: Dushkin.

Spengler, Joseph I.
1968 "The Economic Effects of Changes in Age Composition." Pp. 589–603 in Charles B. Nam, ed. Population and Society. Boston: Houghton Mifflin.

Thomlinson, Ralph
1965 Population Dynamics. New York: Random House.

Thompson, Warren and David L. Lewis
1965 Population Problems. 5th ed. New York: McGraw-Hill.

Townsend, Claire
1971 Old Age: The Last Segregation. Ralph Nader's Study Group Report on Nursing Homes. New York: Grossman.

U.S. Bureau of the Census
1975 Statistical Abstract of the United States: 1975. U.S. Commerce Department. Washington, D.C.: U.S. Government Printing Office.
1977 "Population Profile of the United States: 1976." Current Population Reports, Series P-20, No. 307. Washington, D.C.: U.S. Government Printing Office.

SUGGESTED READINGS

Butler, Robert N. Why Survive? Being Old in America. New York: Harper & Row. 1975.
   A comprehensive and realistic portrayal of old age, and an examination of public policy toward the elderly.

Harris, Louis, and Associates. The Myth and Reality of Aging in America. Washington, D.C.: The National Council on the Aging. 1975.
   An in-depth survey of the elderly's attitudes and social situation that changed America's attitudes about aging and the elderly. Interpretation and analysis of the survey's data, with commentaries, are also included.

Hess, Beth B., ed. Growing Old in America. New Brunswick, N.J.: Transaction Books. 1976.
   This introduction to social gerontology analyzes aging and the elderly from physical, cultural, historical, structural, social, and economic perspectives. It will broaden the reader's view of how and when personal problems of the elderly become public issues.

Kart, Cary S. and Barbara Manard. Aging in America; Readings in Social Gerontology. New York: Alfred. 1976.
   Deals with theoretical, methodological, sociological, biological, and psychological issues involved with aging and the elderly.

Spencer, Marian G. and Caroline J. Dorr. Understanding Aging: A Multidisciplinary Approach. Englewood Cliffs, N.J.: Prentice-Hall. 1975.
   An overview of aging and the elderly, including biological, sociological, and psychological aspects, as well as the social welfare, nutrition, physical and mental health, and religious faith of the aged.

Periodicals Worth Exploring

Aging
American Geriatrics Society (Journal of)
Geriatrics
The Gerontologist
Human Development
Journal of Gerontology
Modern Maturity
Social Security Bulletin

PART THREE

Out of a society's groups and human needs grow social institutions. Social institutions involve aspects of life that are so important that a whole set of norms and roles is organized around their activities into an "interrelated system of expectations" (Bensman and Rosenberg, 1976:2). Institutions are the building blocks of social structure. Although they were originally set up to meet human needs and solve social ills, modern institutions often create social problems and issues rather than solve them.

After the family, the institution most persons encounter is education. The system of schools—from elementary to universities—attempts to prepare a person for the world in which he will live. But we must face the problems of how best to educate a person. What and how to teach (as well as who will control the schools and how they will be financed) are problems the schools and our society must resolve. Every year millions of young persons are the unwitting victims of the social problems generated by our educational institutions. Although schools benefit many, especially those with wealth and power, they often act as a mechanism of social control and conformity to ensure that masses of the young do not change the existing social structure. Conformity to society's existing norms, values, and beliefs is eventually rewarded by the lure of a well-paying job.

When a person leaves or completes school, he encounters the corporate social institution and work. In our society, one soon discovers that private corporations are closely linked to the military and government in a system controlled by power elites. One can see a higher degree of power and wealth concentrated in just a few hundred large multinational corporations. At work, instead of fulfillment, the worker may find dissatisfaction in a repetitive, insecure job. His life may be in jeopardy because of dangerous conditions at work—from mine cave-ins to chemical contamination.

Institutions and Social Issues

Technology is experienced, by workers and nonworkers alike, not as the servant of modern man but as his master. Goods are made by large bureaucratic corporations for the sake of production and for the profit of the wealthy and corporate elites, instead of meeting real human needs. Technology benefits the powerful but displaces workers, and sets up work routines that are geared to the machines' tempo rather than the workers' needs.

From time to time everyone needs proper medical and health care. Our medical institutions are supposed to meet people's health needs, but too often they serve the vested interests of doctors, hospital administrators, and drug companies. Rising costs add to the social problems of inadequate and inequitable delivery of medical services. As a rule the rich and powerful receive excellent medical care (and usually, as a class, live longer than others), while the powerless (minorities and the poor) often suffer from a lack of adequate health care and facilities. The medical system is stacked against them, so that they (literally) cannot afford to get sick.

Mental-health problems emerge from the existing social structure, which produces tension and anxiety and labels people, usually from the lower class, as neurotic and psychotic. Too often the institutions designed to handle mental-health problems make them worse. The tools of social science, from behavior modification to psychosurgery, violate people's rights. Frequently, mental-health treatment makes people overly dependent on drugs and on the system that is supposed to help them. Recent court decisions, as well as new laws and programs, have begun to reform our mental-health institution.

Social institutions of education, the economy, medical care and mental health all contribute to serious social issues. Our society must change its institutions to make them more responsive to human needs.

Problems in Education

INTRODUCTION

DEFINITIONS OF THE PROBLEM
Conflicting purposes; Conservation of status quo v. social change
What should schools teach?
West Virginia textbook controversy.
Sorting and socializing.
Power and control.

INCIDENCE AND PREVALENCE OF THE PROBLEM
Enrollment in schools:
a) Elementary — 34 million.
b) High school — 15 million (89,000 schools in nearly 17,000 school districts).
c) College and universities — 7 million.
Educational attainment.
Extent of illiteracy.
Costs of education($130 billion).

CAUSES OF THE PROBLEM
Conflicting values.
Rising expectations.
Discrimination and prejudice because of color or class.
A highly structured, bureaucratized society.
Inadequate and inequitable funding.

PROPOSED SOLUTIONS TO THE PROBLEM
A "voucher," or "free-market," system.
"Back-to-the-basics" movement, with three R's (Results, Realism, and Retrenchment).
Suggestions of Jonathan Turner to reduce formality and bureaucracy.
Local control of the schools.
Alternative goals for higher education.
Raising funds from government, tuition increases, cutting expenses.

FUTURE OF THE PROBLEM
A life-long process, but fewer young students.
Small-college decline.
Home education through technology.
Community-linked education.
New goals and techniques for education.
Racially "separate but equal" schools will persist.

SUMMARY

> The best index of a school's success or failure may not be reading scores but the number of rocks thrown through its windows in an average month.
>
> Christopher Jencks, **New York Times Magazine** (August 10, 1969):44.

Education as a social institution is both a problem and a solution to social problems. Some of the basic issues of education are questions of why educate (purposes), what are the functions of a school, what to teach (curriculum), how to finance and fund education, how to control the schools (locally or centrally)? Also, how much equal access do we allow (desegregation)? Are people overeducated, and does education result in well-paying jobs (outcome)?

In spite of such questions and issues, America has faith in our educational institution as a way—if not *the* way—of solving social problems. As Ivar Berg has put it: "Education has become the most popular solution to America's social and economic ills" (1975:186). But if education is to help us solve our social ills, we must first resolve the questions and issues about our mode of education itself.

Elementary education is generally defined as grades kindergarten through eighth grade. Secondary education encompasses grades nine through twelve, generally called high school. Higher education is any academic education past the twelfth grade. Public education is defined as any education directly funded from taxes. Private education is funded primarily from nontax sources.

DEFINING THE PROBLEMS OF EDUCATION

In discussing problems of education, sociologists (and students themselves) generally refer to such major problems as:

1. conflicting purposes
2. what schools should teach
3. socializing and sorting functions of education
4. power and control

Purposes of Education

What are the purposes of education and what should be taught in our schools? The two major different answers to these questions represent the ideologies of the liberal and the conservative points of view. One emphasizes change; the other stresses stability and the status quo.

The liberal stance holds that the primary purposes of education "must be rooted in the experiences of the child; it must take seriously the interests, purposes, and involvements of each student" (Morshead, 1975:16). Because the students' interests and concerns are continually changing, John Dewey, the famous liberal educator, argued that "the educational process has no end beyond itself" (Ibid.). Learning for learning's sake, and knowledge for knowledge's sake, are the ends and goals of a liberal education.

For the conservative, school ought not to be an institution or social system that reforms society or changes things. Instead, its prime purpose is to conserve and transmit the values and knowledge that make up the essential intellectual and moral basis of our society. Schooling, according to this view, should be focused on the mind and heart. The mind is shaped through hard, demanding tasks requiring discipline. The scholar-teacher directs the child to master the discipline being studied, and serves as an ideal of an educated person. Knowledge mastered should primarily be helpful in getting a job later. Mastering the moral values should make one an acceptable citizen and employee in the near future.

According to the conservative purposes, our society's schools should operate much like its industries and factories. The teacher conveys "inputs" to the student so that he can "work on them" and "put out" on a test or exam. This knowledge "output" and "production" are counted and weighted by a system of grading. When the student has produced (or reproduced) the proper output after a given number of years, he "graduates" to a higher level of educational output. This kind of education lends itself well to measurement of effectiveness—test scores for reading, math, science or anything else can be compared and contrasted with those of other students and schools.

What Should Schools Teach?

Sometimes the liberal and conservative views of education lead directly to serious social questions of what schools should teach. Consider the "book controversy" in the Charleston, West Virginia, area (Kanawha County School District) schools in 1974. The community conflict lasted about three months. Shootings, bombings, picketing, and demonstrations took place over the issue of certain assigned reading. Conservatives opposed to "the books" called them filth, the work of the devil, and defamers of "religion, morality and patriotism." Such books, with their passages on "prostitution, bombmaking, marijuana, and extremist politics," were un-American (New York Times, September 14, 1974:27).

Several high-school books had selections from such black leaders as Malcolm X, Eldridge Cleaver, and George Jackson. One anthology, called "Letters," included selections from the published prison letters of George Jackson, in which he called whites "the arch-foes of my kind" and urged blacks to form "a revolutionary group" with guns to "help the war effort" (Franklin, 1974:31). A ninth-grade reprint of *Catcher in the Rye* (with *some* obscene words deleted by the editors) was condemned as obscene. The

"War and Peace" series included poems against the Vietnam War and a vivid description of the My Lai massacre of Vietnamese women and children by American soldiers. These were labeled "unpatriotic."

After parents protested and boycotted the school by keeping their children home (while the men picketed coal mines in the area) the school board removed the books from the classrooms for 30 days so they could be reviewed by a special citizens committee. Superintendent Kenneth Underwood argued that the books were provided by reputable publishing companies and simply described life in America in modern times and language. He pledged that no child would be required to read the books if his parents objected. Doubleday's editor, Kenneth McCormick, speaking for the Freedom-to-Read Committee of the American Publishers Association, backed the right of qualified educators to select their own teaching materials. The citizens panel chosen to review the books voted 11 to 6 to approve the books for classroom use. The schoolboard, by a 4 to 1 vote, reaffirmed the decision. Nevertheless, demonstrations and protests continued.

Carl Marburger, an official of the National Committee for Citizens in Education, felt that the school board showed an "astonishing insensitivity to local cultural values" of the community in approving the books in the first place. White, rural, working-class West Virginia parents, he noted, were convinced that the new textbooks would teach their children values contrary to those learned at home. He concluded that even though we must guard against censorship in our institutions, we must also guard against "arrogance and insularity of power" (Marburger, October 24, 1974:41).

Parents of students formed a coalition and headquarters (pictured here) to oppose certain new books in the Kanawha County school district, near Charleston, West Virginia. Violence and strikes occurred because of the strong oppositon to use of the books, described as "revolutionary" and "dirty."

Credit: U.P.I. Photo.

Today parents in Kanawha County have a hand in evaluating books used in local classrooms. According to the chairman of the English Department at a Charleston high school, the guidelines used border on censorship and "are subject to such varied interpretations that they could effectively halt education in Kanawha County" (Wood, March/April 1976:52). According to the guidelines, texts "shall recognize the sanctity of the home . . . [and] must not contain profanity." They are mandated to "encourage loyalty to the United States . . . [and not to] defame our nation's founders or misrepresent the ideals and causes for which they struggled and sacrificed"; nor may they "encourage or promote racial hatred" (Ibid.).

Schools as Sorters and Socializers

There is also conflict over the functions education should serve. One of education's primary functions is to socialize the young and prepare them for jobs. It provides manpower for industry and reinforces our existing social-class system. Our schools carry out a latent stratification function, much like an elevator carrying many persons from the basement (kindergarten) to the top floor (PhD or professional degree) of a high rise.

This educational elevator stratifies society, dropping off men and women at different occupational levels. Even though education is not often connected with actual job performance, it is used as a screening sieve for the job market. We are still very much a "credential" society. Often this system discourages poor and minority-group students from finishing high school. Working-class students move on to vocational

School vandalism results when curricula or teachers do not respond to the felt needs of their students. Vandalism is one way some youngsters strike back at a bureaucratic, rigid school system.

Credit: U.P.I. Photo.

schools or community colleges. Middle- and upper-class youth surge on to colleges and universities, if they can afford them. As the White House Conference on Children put it, "The schools have become great sorting machines, labeling and certifying those who presumably will be winners and losers as adults. The winners are disproportionately white and affluent. The losers, too often, are poor, and brown, or black, or red" (Report to the President 1970:76).

Schools do more than stratify society. They also seek to socialize children for society. The family starts the job, but the school finishes it. With compulsory education, masses of the young are socialized to live in our society. The schools stress obedience, conformity, and adherence to rules, and they are bureaucratic organizations that socialize the young to accept a bureaucratic, stratified society.

Radicals argue that our schools are too bureaucratic and structured. With less bureaucratic structure, students could be socialized to develop their minds and spirits in a more open and critical manner. The schools do not have to function only to preserve the status quo but should be used to critically examine our social structure which stratifies our society to the detriment of the powerless and to the benefit of the powerful. Whatever inhumanity and inhumaneness exists in our schools stems from the stratification and socialization functions of education as a social institution.

Power and Control

Education is often used as a social means to reinforce the ideas and norms of the powerful. Elementary and secondary schools socialize the young to accept the notions of capitalism as the best economic system, and often ignore its serious shortcomings. Young students are generally educated to accept the past and present policies of corporate, military, and government elites. If teachers or students seriously criticize our system of economics or government, they are labeled "radical" or "socialist."

Social critic James Ridgeway has documented the ways in which higher education does the work and bidding of big business, big government, and the military. The boards of regents and local boards of education are often packed with spokesmen for the rich and for big business. Many researchers in education follow the government's green path of dollars, no matter where it leads them academically. The Pentagon remains a pot of gold for some universities. If the government wants an educator to study germ warfare or develop a poison gas, someone will do it for a price. If there is secret research to be done on psychological warfare, or on how to prevent revolution in underdeveloped countries, a school and its scholars will analyze it if the grant is large enough. For years the connection between cigarette smoking and lung cancer was denied by some scholars. Why? "Because the tobacco companies were paying for the research work in some of the universities. Columbia University even became involved in promoting a filter-tip cigarette," according to Ridgeway (Stewart, 1976:89).

Consider, too, how land-grant agricultural colleges have hurt the small farmer and helped the corporate giants. These schools have consistently followed curricula and research that make the big farms bigger and that benefit the large food processors, while ignoring the plight of the small family farm.

In large cities, a centralized school board usually controls the educational policies and procedures to be applied to every local school. The neighborhood parents usually have little say in how the school should be run. Some centrally appointed or elected school officials, together with a school board more interested in saving money than developing a critical or dynamic educational system, have the power and control over the schools.

INCIDENCE AND PREVALENCE OF THE PROBLEMS OF EDUCATION

Four indicators are used to measure the incidence and prevalence of our problems of education: (1) figures for enrollment (overall and at all levels) and school staff, (2) the extent of educational attainment for all groups, (3) the degree of illiteracy, (4) the costs of running our school systems. Let us look at each of the indices in turn.

Size of Enrollment and Staff

Education is big business today. It is a highly structured and organized system that provides a position in society for over 62 million persons. Most are students (about 59 million), while about 3 million are teachers, along with about 300,000 superintendents, principals, supervisors and other staff. All together nearly 3 out of 10 persons are *directly* involved with education (Grant and Lind, 1975:1).

Enrollment. Enrollments have increased in education for the last 30 years. Starting in 1971, however, slight decreases have occurred in elementary schools, reflecting our sharply declining birthrates. According to estimates from the National Center for Educational Statistics, there will be small yearly drops in elementary-school enrollments within the foreseeable future. High-school rolls reached a high point in 1975, held steady in 1976, and are now expected to shown annual declines. A 1976 report on the condition of education projects that enrollments in elementary and secondary schools will drop from 50.4 million in 1975 to less than 45 million in 1985. College enrollments are predicted to peak about 1980, after which a decline in the college-age population will become evident. However, the extent of the drop will depend on the trends in college attendance rates; in the fall of 1974, only 25 percent of 18-to-24 year-olds were enrolled in college (Ibid.,1).

Not much can be done about the decline in elementary- or high-school rolls, unless the birthrate increases and the high-school dropout rate is checked. But neither is likely to happen. On the other hand, colleges have a new group of potential students to draw from. Adult students—men and women over 22—now account for about *half* of the total college enrollment (degree and nondegree) of 10.6 million, and this number "includes more than 600,000 women over age 35" ("Mature Women . . .," 1976:E-7). Such part-time adult students will become more prevalent on college campuses as enrollment among the traditional age group declines. About one-third of the students enrolled in higher education in 1975 were part timers. They simply could not afford the luxury of full-time attendance at college.

The combined elementary and secondary system has some 89,000 schools located in almost 17,000 school districts across the country. According to the U.S. Department of Education, "it is believed that a system should serve at least 500 students in order to offer what is now regarded as a full program" (National Center for Education Statistics, 1975:55). Yet, 4,723 school systems in the country (about 29 percent) have enrollments of fewer than 300 students. Some states have dealt with this situation by consolidating school districts or closing down smaller schools. Other states have done nothing. Between 1969 and 1973, the number of school districts declined by 18 percent, and further consolidation and closings will continue.

Staffing. Staffing in the public schools follows traditional sex-role stereotypes. This perpetuates the status quo and traditional roles of women. Though 66 percent of public-school teachers are women, they account for only 14 percent of school principals. Women are overly represented, however, in staff positions, such as school librarians and nurses. Figure 9-1 depicts this imbalance in staffing by sex. Through such staffing patterns the younger generation is educated to believe that this is the way it should be for women. In elementary schools, 83 percent of teachers are women; in secondary schools women account for 46 percent of the teachers. As enrollments decline in future years, there will be fewer openings for teaching positions; thus it is doubtful whether such sexual imbalance will change (Grambs, 1977:39–42).

Extent of Educational Attainment

The extent of education is important if a society is going to change. Those with little education tend to accept and not question or criticize the status quo. The amount of education Americans have is usually affected by their age. The older people are, the less education they tend to have as a group. For example, the Bureau of the Census reported that the median number of school years completed by persons 20 and 21 years of age was 12.8 years; persons 45 to 54 completed 12.3 years; and persons 75 and over, 8.6 years (1975:2).

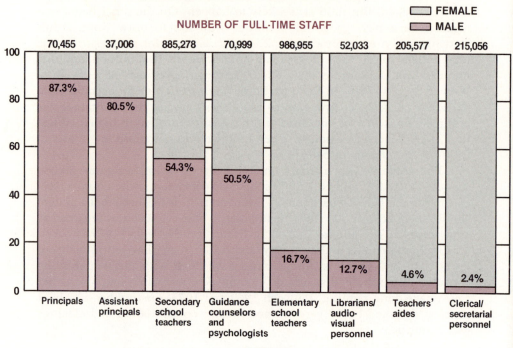

figure 9-1 PATTERN BY SEX AMONG ELEMENTARY AND SECONDARY SCHOOL STAFF
(Percentage distribution of full-time staff in 1974)

Source of Data: U.S. Equal Employment Opportunity Commission. In "The Condition of Education." U.S. Department of Health, Education and Welfare, National Center for Education Statistics (Washington, D.C.: U.S. Government Printing Office, 1977): 35.

To account for such variations in age, educational attainment is usually reported both for persons 25 years old and over and (more narrowly) for persons ages 25 to 29. The first grouping assumes that most persons will have completed their education by age 25. It combines past generations that had less education with those who have had more opportunities in recent years. Grouping only the 25- to 29-year-olds gives a clearer picture of more recent attainments by the younger generation. For those 25 years and older, the *median* educational attainment is 12.3 years—just slightly more than a high-school diploma. The 1930 figure was 8.4 years of school. Thus, in less than 50 years we have moved from being a society with a grammar-school education to one with a high-school education. Indeed, some scholars contend that we are now an "over-educated" society. Figure 9-2 shows the percentage of students remaining in school from fifth grade to the college degree.

Because of economic inequalities and past institutionalized discrimination, schooling completed remains less for minority groups than for whites. The median attainment for whites in 1975 was 12.3 years; for

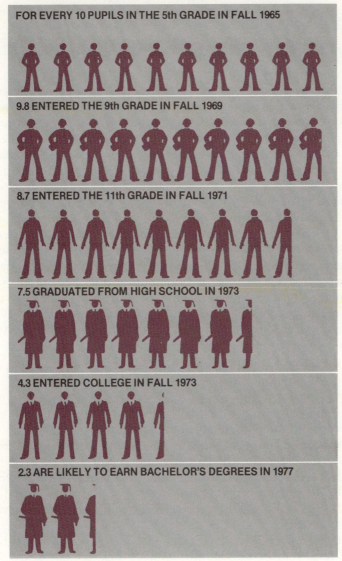

figure 9-2 ESTIMATED RETENTION RATES, FIFTH GRADE THROUGH COLLEGE GRADUATION: U.S., 1965–1977

Source: *Digest of Education Statistics,* 1977.

nonwhites, 11.3 years (U.S. Census Bureau June 1976:10–11). In 1940, there was a three-year gap between white and nonwhite attainment; today the gap is about one year. Of whites 25 and older, 64 percent finished high school by 1976, compared with only 44 percent of the blacks; over 15 percent of the whites and almost 7 percent of blacks had achieved college degrees (U.S. Bureau of Census, April 1977:20–21). By color, a gap persists. The same low participation rate prevails among Chicanos and American Indians. Too often, minority-group students are directed by white school counselors into vocational education rather than toward college.

Degree of Illiteracy

A third measure of the seriousness of our education problem is the degree of illiteracy in society. The less illiteracy in society, the less severe should be the problem of education. On the surface, there seems to be no problem of illiteracy. Comparative figures have been kept by the Census Bureau since 1870. At that time, 20 percent of our population was illiterate. During the 1960s our illiteracy rate was cut in half, from two down to about one percent.

Despite this progress, however, two points stand out. First, because of a lack of equal opportunities, illiteracy is still a problem among minority groups. In 1900, 6.2 percent of whites could not read or write, compared with 44 percent of blacks. By 1969 the rate was seven-tenths of one percent for whites and three-and-a-half percent for blacks. In a society based very much on reading and writing, illiteracy puts all such persons at an extreme disadvantage. The second point is that "functional" illiteracy is a very grave problem. A 1975 Office of Education study revealed that 20 percent of adult Americans are "functionally" illiterate. Testing of 10,000 adults between 18 and 65 found:

> 20 percent cannot read the daily newspaper. Projected to the entire population, this would be about 23 million persons.
>
> 58 percent could not read a simple paragraph explaining the law and tell why it would be illegal to be held in jail for two weeks without being charged with a crime.
>
> 30 percent could not select an airline flight at the right time to make a meeting in a distant city.
>
> 26 percent could not determine the best unit price for three different sizes of cereal boxes.
>
> 20 percent could not correctly explain "equal-opportunity employer."
>
> 13 percent could not properly address an envelope for mailing ("One Out of Five," October 30, 1975:21).

The 1976 study on "The Condition of Education" observes that writing skills of 13- and 17-year-olds have actually declined slightly since 1969. Fewer than half the 17-year-olds studied were able to follow directions on a traffic ticket.

These studies demonstrate that merely because people go to school or graduate from it does not mean they are educated, even in the most basic ways. They suggest that the median level of educational attainment may mislead us as to how well the schools are doing their jobs. For example, recent freshman-placement tests at Ohio State University (which has open admissions) show that "26 percent have not mastered high-school mathematics and 30 percent cannot write on an acceptable college level" ("Education: Colleges Offer More Remedial Courses . . .," 1976:A-13). As jobs for college graduates become more competitive, inadequate education at lower levels of the system ensures less competition, especially from minorities. The system seems content to keep them uneducated so their labor may be exploited.

There has been a recent nationwide trend of lower scores on tests of the College Entrance Examination Board, the American College Testing Program, and the National Assessment of Education Progress. A drop of eight to 10 points on the College Entrance Examination Board's SAT scores occurred in 1975. Between 1963 and 1975, average SAT "Verbal" scores dropped 44 points, while "Math" scores dropped 30 points ("Those Dropping Test Scores," 1976:171). As a result many colleges and universities, such as Johns Hopkins, Case Western Reserve, Stanford, Simmons, Columbia, and City University of New York, are considering or have launched various kinds of remedial courses in writing and reading.

Costs

The last measure of the incidence and prevalence of education as a social problem is the costs involved. Providing education for millions is *very* costly. Not providing it is even more costly to society because of the social problems that grow out of a limited or inadequate education for the young. Spending for education (private and public) has risen dramatically in the last few years. In 1960 we spent under $25 billion; by 1972 we spent almost $85 billion; by 1977 we spent over $130 billion (Mathews, May 1976:65).

Much of the increased spending is due to inflation. When adjusted for inflation by using constant dollars (1972), educational spending between 1972 and 1975 increased only slightly—from nearly $85 billion to $89 billion. This is only $4 billion in a real-spending increase, as opposed to the $25 billion inflated figure (National Center for Educational Statistics, 1975:4).

As measured by a portion of the Gross National Product (the value of all goods and services), spending on education has changed less than one percentage point. In 1968 it was 7.2 percent of the GNP; by 1976 it was 7.8 percent (Grant, May 1976: back cover). Nevertheless, few countries spend that proportion of their GNP on education.

CAUSES OF THE PROBLEMS OF EDUCATION

The underlying causes for several of our problems of education can be found in

1. conflicting societal values

2. rising expectations
3. discrimination and prejudice based on color and class
4. a highly structured, bureaucratic social structure
5. inadequate and inequitable funding

Conflicting Values

Conflicting purposes of education come from conflicting societal values. Some segments of our society value abstract thinking and ideas; others emphasize the pragmatic and practical. Some of us are concerned with the present; others contemplate and shape the future. Some value making a living as an end in itself; others value "making a life." Most of all, those who hold top positions of power in society, and control a large portion of the wealth, want the schools only to "train the young" to fill their work and career roles, not to consider the kind of society we have. The powerful do not want the masses to be educated to change the system in a significant way. Some liberal and radical educators, on the other hand, see the role of education as being more creative, innovative, and change-oriented.

With such conflicting values, it is amazing that we have reached somewhat of a consensus of what constitutes a basic education. A related cause, which explains many problems of education, is "mindlessness." According to Charles Silberman, this is "the failure to think seriously about purpose or consequence—the failure of people at every level to ask why they are doing what they are doing or to inquire into the consequences" (1970:36).

Rising Expectations

We have always had rising expectations about what education could do. We feel that education will solve all our social and personal ills, from inequality to ignorance. Although many more Americans have formal schooling (at every level) than members of any other nation in history, we are still dissatisfied with our performance. Part of our problem is that we always expect too much from it. The Coleman Report in the 1960s, Christopher Jencks' research in the 1970s, and Johnston and Bachman's study of high schools all point out that many other factors must also be at work before a person can achieve success. They are all pointing out the limitations of education as a panacea for our social ills.

Inequality

Schools are assumed to be ladders to success, yet many turn out to be high hurdles to failure. Higher education is proclaimed as the escape route from poverty and deprivation: success in school means success in life;

> ## MAKING IT DESPITE THE SYSTEM
> ### Charles Silberman
>
> A black student does poorly in a Northern high school for three years. When he expresses interest in college, his guidance counselor assures him that he is not "college material."
>
> Through the intercession of some white friends, and over the objection of the guidance counselor, he is admitted into the federally financed Upward Bound program at a nearby college, which provides an intensive remedial program during the summer, and special tutoring during his senior year. His grades shoot up so rapidly that the Upward Bound officials recommend him for a special Transitional Year program at Yale University, designed to give "underachieving students" with high potential the academic skills and the self-confidence they need to realize their potential. The counselor begrudgingly supplies the necessary transcripts, after remarking to the boy, "What, you at Yale? Don't make me laugh."
>
> But when the student is admitted—one of 60 selected, out of 500 applicants—the school system's public relations apparatus springs into action. The boy's picture appears in the local newspaper in an article reporting the high school's success story; the superintendent of schools introduces him to the public in an open meeting of the board of education; and when a group of local black leaders meet with school officials to press some of their complaints about the system, they are told that the boy's admission to the Yale program shows how well the school is serving black students.
>
> Source: Charles Silberman, *Crisis in the Classroom* (New York: Vintage Books, 1970): 80-81.

more school means more income. This is the message and the myth. But inequality pervades our schools. Despite reports and studies demonstrating that schooling does not make much of a difference for success, the public's attitude is that education does pay—if not in dollars and cents, then in many other important ways. According to a Gallup poll, well over 75 percent of the respondents considered education "extremely important" for future success. Table 9-1 reflects the public's view of the relationship between school and success.

Discrimination by Color and Class

A third important cause behind our educational problems—whether of unequal access, bureaucracy, or funding—is discrimination and prejudice based on color and class. We have already discussed the social impact and effects of racial discrimination and prejudice (especially institutional racism). Coleman's 737-page report, *Equality of Educational Opportunity*, documented in 1966 that "there is evident, even in the short run, an effect [positive] of school integration on the reading and mathematics

table 9-1　　THE IMPORTANCE OF EDUCATION TO SUCCESS

RESPONSES	NATIONAL TOTALS N=1,672	NO CHILDREN IN SCHOOL 928	PUBLIC-SCHOOL PARENTS 620	PRIVATE-SCHOOL PARENTS 124
EXTREMELY IMPORTANT	76%	71%	81%	84%
FAIRLY IMPORTANT	19	22	16	13
NOT TOO IMPORTANT	4	5	2	2
NO OPINION	1	2	0*	1

*This column totals 99 percent because of rounding.
SOURCE: Gallup International, Phi Delta Kappa, September 1973.

achievement of Negro pupils," even after differences in the socioeconomic background of the students are taken into account (1966:29). Coleman also showed that facilities, programs, and money spent were unequal, with less spent in the black segregated schools.

A series of exposés of the inadequacy of our schools—especially for the economically and socially deprived—came from James Conant (*Slums and Suburbs,* 1961), Jonathan Kozol (*Death at an Early Age,* 1968), John Holt (*Why Children Fail,* 1967), Herbert Kohl (*Thirty-Six Children,* 1968), James Herndon (*The Way it spozed to be,* 1968), and Charles Silberman (*Crisis in the Classroom,* 1970). These were just a few of the books that pointed out how the system's purposes, structures, procedures, teachers, and administrators worked against a black or low-income person's succeeding in school. When they did do well, it was in spite of the system, not because of it. For example, Charles Silberman, in the boxed item on page 363, illustrates how the system often operates against blacks and how, when they succeed in spite of the system, the school exploits the student's success as evidence of how good a job it is doing.

Nevertheless, the difference in educational achievement between social classes is evident and will affect success. Children from wealthy families stay in school longer than poor children. Lower-class white children have about a year and a half less schooling than middle-class whites. A study by Samuel Bowles shows that the child from the top 10 percent income level can expect to receive four-and-a-half more years of education than a child from the lowest 10 percent income grouping (1972:42-49). The richest one-fifth of all families place their children in schools that spend about 20 percent more than the schools of the poorest one-fifth (Jencks, 1972:27). The results are predictable. Only 20 percent of high-school graduates from low-income ($3,000) families go to college, whereas 87 percent of those from high-income ($15,000+) families attend. Inequality triumphs over need or ability.

Center-city schools for blacks are often overcrowded, underfunded, and run-down. All this adds up to inadequate and unequal educational opportunities for many Americans.

Affluent suburban schools provide better facilities and educational opportunities than most center-city schools. This situation gives white, upper- and middle-class students a competitive edge in going on to college and becoming professionals.

To ensure the failure of blacks and other minority groups, the school system frequently uses a method of "tracking" in the elementary and secondary schools. As the testing movement grew, so did tracking. It is no accident that the most prominent tracking plan in the 1920s was Detroit's XYZ plan. Placement in tracks was determined by intelligence and achievement tests. The X group contained the top 20 percent of the students, Z the lowest 20 percent, and Y the middle 60 percent (Lederer, 1968:178–79). The tracking system creates a kind of "Brave New World," in which students become alphas, betas, or epsilon-minuses depending on their alleged intelligence or abilities. Thus, the tracking system perpetuates a negative image of some students. The school, the teacher, and eventually the student himself come to expect and accept low performance from those assigned to the lower tracks. Is it any wonder that, under such conditions of "programmed failure," blacks drop out or are pushed out of high school at almost twice the rate of whites?

A widely known experiment by Robert Rosenthal and Lenore Jacobson shows the impact of such labeling on students' performance and learning (1969). The experiment was conducted at the "Oak School," an elementary school on the West Coast that was already divided into fast, medium, and slow tracks. The researchers administered what they called the "Harvard Test of Inflected Acquisition." They told the teachers that the test "will allow us to predict which youngsters are most likely to show an academic spurt," which would come "within the near future" (Coles, 1971:188). Picking children's names at random (without any connection to IQ or to the test performance), the researchers presented the teachers with the names and told them of the "spurters." They were asked not to reveal this "fact" to either the students or their parents. Hence, the only experimental variable between these students and the others was the teachers' expectation that their school work would improve greatly.

The children were presumably given no special help or attention by the teachers; yet the results were astonishing. A large number of the identified "spurters" displayed significant academic improvement. First- and second-graders showed the greatest growth. When tested for IQ, 50 percent of the "spurters" gained 20 points or more, compared with only 20 percent of the other children. The lesson was clear. Children of all backgrounds did better because their teachers expected them to. The greatest gains of all were by Chicanos, who were supposedly suffering from cultural deprivation. Too often, studies of disadvantaged or culturally deprived schoolchildren blame the child for his failure. More attention must be given to the educational institution and society itself, rather than being content with "blaming the victim" (Ryan, 1976).

Our Bureaucratic Society

Another cause behind the problems of our schools is our bureaucratic, highly structured society. According to Theodore Roszak, "when a society begins to fear that its culture is not interesting or important to the young—that indeed its culture violates nature—then it concludes that education must be *made* to happen; must be organized strenuously into existence and enforced by professionals" (1971:68).

This bureaucratic structure reinforces conformity, obedience, and adherence to rules and regulations. Thus school prepares the student to take his place in some other kind of bureaucracy—the corporation, armed services, or higher education. Students find themselves in a subordinate role in the bureaucracy, and of course they are compelled to attend classes.

Too often, though, the bureaucratic rules and regulations inhibit teaching and learning. In a suburban school, a sixth-grade biology teacher obtains the heart and lungs of a cow to show the class. He removes his coat, rolls up his sleeves, and demonstrates how the respiratory system works. Later in the day, he receives a note from the school superintendent, who had looked in on his class that morning: "Teachers are not supposed to remove their jackets in class. If the jacket must be removed, the shirt sleeves certainly should not be rolled up" (Silberman, 1970:145).

Let us analyze another important cause of our problems of education—the funding of education.

Funding

To ensure equality of opportunity, education must be reasonably priced. The cost of education is driving some schools out of business and some students out of school. In a society where wealth is unequally distributed, the rich benefit while the poor and middle class suffer. Expenses are causing other schools to trim budgets and cut back on programs and staff.

The past and present spending on education is summarized in Table 9-2. The total public and nonpublic expenditures for 1976 were about $120 billion. About $75 billion went to "lower" education, and nearly $45

table 9-2   SCHOOL EXPENDITURES FOR SELECTED YEARS

	1960*	1973*	1975†
SCHOOL SPENDING (in billions)	$24.7	$89.5	$110.4
ELEMENTARY AND SECONDARY (in billions)	18.1	57.5	70.9
PUBLIC (in billions)	15.7	52.1	64.0
AVG. SPENT PER PUBLIC-SCHOOL PUPIL	354.0	1,047	1,250
AVG. SALARY— PUBLIC-SCHOOL TEACHER	5,000	10,900	11,500

*Source: U.S.A. Statistics in Brief, Bureau of the Census: 3.
†Source: Statistical Abstract of the U.S. 1975: 112; figures are estimates.

billion to "higher." In 1977, total spending rose to about $130 billion. About 10 percent of the money came from the federal government, 34 percent from the state, 31 percent from local governmental sources, and 25 percent from other (mostly private) sources (Golladay, March 1976:189).

The crisis today is to meet rising costs. A recent survey by Citicorp in New York City revealed that an "overwhelming majority of Americans," about 80 percent, still regard a college education as essential and desirable for their children. But more than a third who plan to send their daughter or son to college say they will face an "extreme financial hardship." Perhaps that is why 63 percent, in the same survey, said that government should help in some way with the cost (Swift, 1976:15). The Commission on Non-Traditional Studies reported that "the cost of education was the highest-ranked obstacle to participation in postsecondary education" (Bergquist, 1974:15).

State Spending. The President's Commission on School Finance also noted the serious financial plight of schooling. In its final report, the Commission stated that "the financial problems of education derive largely from the evolving inabilities of the States to create and maintain systems that provide equal educational opportunities and quality education to all their children" ("Schools, People and Money," 1972:207). Public needs for education, at all levels, have simply outrun the ability or willingness of the states to pay for it. This has also caused serious disparities in what states can spend on education. In one year Alabama, a relatively poor state, spent only $489 per pupil, while Alaska spent $1,429. In addition, money raised for education can vary widely *within* a state. Wyoming has one school district that spends $14,554 per pupil (highest in the nation), but also one that spends only $617. In neighboring South Dakota, one district spends a mere $175 per student (lowest in the nation), while another spends $6,012.

These disparities in funding education do not stem from states and local communities alone. The federal government has in some cases added to the problem. A Syracuse University study, "Federal Aid to Education: Who Benefits?," found that most federal educational programs give more help per student to affluent school districts (Ibid., 208).

Private Colleges. Small liberal arts colleges, dependent on private funding, are also being pinched by rising costs. As Astin and Lee pointed out in 1972, "the [small] colleges are in a dismal position. They receive far less money from virtually all sources of revenue.... Without major infusion of new money the outlook for many [small] colleges is bleak" (1972:47). Since that time, a 1976 Special Report on the Financial State of Education states that "the condition of most private colleges and universities has dramatically worsened" (Lupton et al., 1976:25).

Unlike large universities, small private colleges receive less income from tuition and are less able to attract students through financial aid. Of the more than 2,000 colleges founded during the nineteenth century, only 20 percent have survived. Since 1970, 72 private colleges either have closed, merged, or turned over their operation to public control (McGrath, 1975:3).

Some formerly private universities, such as the University of Pittsburgh and Temple University, have become public to survive. During the 1980s it is estimated that some 200 small colleges will go out of business, unless they receive financial help ("Those Missing Babies," September 16, 1974:62).

Around 1950, 53 percent of students in higher education were at private colleges or universities. However, Professor Michael Kirst of Stanford University predicts that 80 percent of future college enrollment will be in tax-supported institutions ("Educational Predictions," 1975:12).

Let us turn now to some proposed solutions to problems of the functions of education, inequality of access to learning, bureaucratic structures and power, and financing education.

PROPOSED SOLUTIONS TO THE PROBLEMS OF EDUCATION

The Voucher System

A major proposal for improving the goals, functions and performance of the public-school system is the "voucher system." It is supported by persons who believe a monetary incentive system can do a better job at education than an unmotivated public system. Parents would receive a voucher from the local government specifying how much they paid in taxes for education. The voucher could then be applied toward tuition at any school the parents chose for their children. Andrew Lupton, staff director of New Jersey's Commission on Financing Post-secondary Education, supports the voucher, or "free-market," system for higher education. The Chairman of the Commission considers it "the best way, perhaps the only way, to promote both equity and quality while enhancing the independence of public institutions" (Braun, August 1976:19). Even if the plan to use the voucher system is defeated in New Jersey, the Commission feels that its recommendations will provide a model for other states. As yet, New Jersey has not adopted the voucher system.

The idea behind the voucher system is to create a more competitive educational system, in place of the monopoly held by the present public-school system. Instead of one public-school system to which they would send their children, parents could be selective; even the private schools would have to compete for students. To compete effectively, each school would have to offer good educational opportunities. Under the present system, only the affluent have effective control over the type of education their children will receive, by moving to districts with good public schools or sending their children to private schools. Education vouchers support

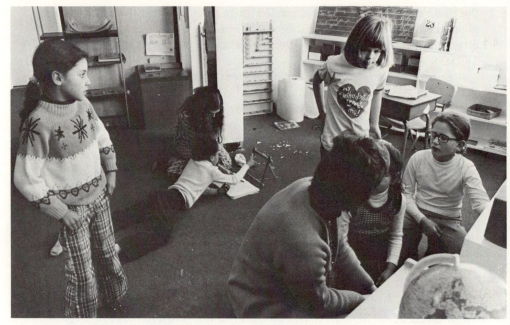

Private tutoring and schooling and small class size, as in this Montessori classroom, give upper- and middle-class children a competitive edge over those who must attend inadequate or overcrowded schools. A voucher system, if adopted, would benefit schools such as this one.

alternatives for all parents. According to a study of the voucher system by the Center for the Study of Public Policy, "educators with new ideas—or old ideas that are now out of fashion in the public schools—also will be able to set up their own schools. Entrepreneurs who think they can teach children better and cheaper than the public schools also will have an opportunity to do so" ("Voucher System," December 16, 1975:6).

By contrast, some liberal critics maintain that the voucher system will only exacerbate problems of equal access to education. A free-market system would result in more, not less, segregation by race, income, and ability. Educational resources would be further redistributed from disadvantaged to advantaged children. However, conservative advocates of vouchers respond that government would still be able to regulate the new competitive system to ensure an integrated system of education. One study notes: "It would be perfectly possible to create a competitive market and then regulate it in such a way as to prevent segregation, ensure an equitable allocation of resources, and give every family a truly equal chance of getting what it wants from the system" (Ibid.). The critics maintain that as long as the voucher system is administered within the confines of existing school districts, vouchers will have little, if any, effect on predominantly black urban school districts. To work, a voucher system would have to cross existing school-district lines. Although the proposed voucher system clearly has some drawbacks, it may well alleviate some of the problems of education if administered impartially.

Back-to-Basics Movement

Another proposed solution to the goals and functional problems of education is beginning to take shape. We call it the "back-to-basics" movement. Schools are putting into effect a new version of the three R's—results, realism, and retrenchment. This movement has received its impetus from parents and school administrators, as well as from "tight" market conditions, increased competition for jobs, lower test scores, and a recent Office of Education study. The study, which surveyed 30,000 students from the first through the ninth grades, reported that innovative, individualized programs made little difference in student achievement. Spending more time on basic reading and language skills in the early grades, however, did make a difference ("Education Briefs," November 1976:66). Hence, the emphasis is now on developing the students' abilities to read, write, and do arithmetic. Minimum competency standards are now being set at many elementary and secondary schools. These standards must be met before a student can graduate or be promoted to a higher grade. Remedial courses for slower students are becoming more widely available. Curriculum changes are also stressing subjects that will be more related to developing usable job skills.

In the San Francisco school district, a student who went through the public-school system sued the district for $1 million, claiming that he was not taught to read and write (Rosenberg, May 1976: back cover). As a result of the suit, the system is being overhauled at all levels. Specialized high schools are proposed that would offer concentrated courses in science, the performing arts, business, and college-preparatory studies. Minimum competency requirements will be established at elementary schools, and some schools will operate year-round to make better use of facilities.

In Houston, Texas, the school day has been extended by 55 minutes to devote extra time to reading, writing, and math. Teachers are also participating in a new after-school tutoring program. A Philadelphia program called "Academics Plus" concentrates on a back-to-basics approach, together with discipline, progress evaluation, and competence standards. The program, originally planned for only one school, was extended to others when some 5,000 parents requested it.

Other indications also suggest that some schools are beginning to recognize the decline in achievement-test scores and are trying to do something about it.

Overcoming Bureaucracy

To overcome bureaucratic rigidity in our schools, sociologist Jonathan Turner suggests that unnecessary formality be eliminated, following several principles put forth by the General Advisory Council for Education in England. He cautions that a trend toward informality should not be a mere educational fad or be considered a panacea; in addition, we should not simply replace "mindless formality" with "mindless informality" (1972:195). However, informality should permeate every aspect of the school structure—instruction, curriculum, relations between teachers and students, and between faculty and administrators—according to the following principles:

1. Childhood is a unique experience that must be nurtured by the school structure.
2. Children are innately curious. This curiosity can be used more fully in the educational process.
3. Children make much less of a distinction between work and play than adults. Schools must not impose the false dichotomy between work and play, for learning should be fun.
4. Children can learn much on their own and with other children in small groups.
5. Drill and instruction are necessary aspects of learning, but they can take place in more informal ways and settings.
6. School must make children less docile and more curious, flexible, intimate, and, most of all, more human (Turner, 1972:194).

In the overall administration of a school, Turner advocates the elimination of emphasis on measuring efficiency in terms of order and control. The administration, instead, must seek ways to promote contact, discussion, and freedom of movement among students. Age stratification, "one of the most destructive forces in education" according to Turner, must be minimized or eliminated. The physical plant itself must become more open. Most of all, the mania of the clock and lock-step routines for conducting activities must be abandoned.

"Deschooling" Society

In the 1960s, radicals saw education and schools as far too bureaucratic, structured, and organized. Social institutions, especially our schools, were charged with programming and brainwashing our children into accepting society's values, instead of socializing the young to think for themselves.

Ivan Illich argued that all reality had become "schooled." Therefore, to build a new social structure and upgrade education we had to "disestablish" school—to "deschool" society. He maintained that schools are meant to serve a kind of society that does not exist; so why build "bridges to nowhere"? We should change not only the schools, but also the educational, political, and economic systems (1970:73). One way to radically reshape our educational system, according to Illich, is to break up the

PROPOSED SOLUTIONS TO THE PROBLEMS OF EDUCATION

monopoly of the school. He writes: "The first article of a bill of rights for a modern, humanist society would correspond to the First Amendment ... 'The State shall make no law with respect to the establishment of education'" (1970:11). In this way, highly structured and bureaucratic schools would give way to educational learning experiences in a relatively unstructured, nonbureaucratic setting. Our problem is how to make a transition to such relatively unstructured learning experiences in such a way as to provide equal access to education for all persons.

Decentralizing Power and Control

Some radicals and liberals propose decentralized community control over education. This issue, among others, was behind the picketing and conflict in the Oceanhill–Brownsville area of New York City several years ago. Many educational problems would be resolved, it is argued, if the local neighborhood had power to hire and fire school principals and teachers and to determine curricula and school policy. This approach would eliminate whatever institutional racism existed in the school, restore local pride in the school, and do much to improve the quality of education. Although not a panacea, local control of the schools is considered a way to begin to restore the imbalance of power and authority be-

Decentralized community control of neighborhood schools is considered a solution to problems of centralized bureaucracy.

Credit: Charles Gatewood.

tween centralized school boards and directors and the neighborhood residents. As long as power elites control educational policy making and procedures, the inequities and deficiencies in education will continue.

Proposals for Colleges and Universities

The proposals offered thus far apply essentially to primary and secondary schools. Colleges and universities, especially small liberal arts colleges, have more peculiar problems of purposes, governance, and finances. Of all the proposals for solving the problems of our colleges' goals and purposes, three are especially prominent:

1. Concentrate on preserving traditional values.
2. Maximize growth by developing new markets for students.
3. Seek a new educational synthesis of the old and the new (Yarmolinsky, April 1976:23).

The first proposal, by traditionalists, is to maintain and improve the established liberal arts fields. In a rapidly changing society, perhaps a well-rounded, liberally educated person is more valuable than the narrow specialist. In such an option, the curriculum will be shaped by the faculty, with relatively little student participation.

The second proposal, by specialists, is predominantly student-oriented. Colleges and universities that choose it will offer a great deal of career-oriented instruction, with special emphasis on new careers. Schools will become as much concerned about their credentials for students as with teaching. Much of the instruction will be clinical or practical rather than restricted to the classroom, and much learning will take place in offices and workshops rather than on campus.

The third proposal, by pragmatists, is a compromise, combining aspects of the traditional liberal arts subjects with more professional and career-oriented courses. Faculty and students will have to make hard decisions about which subjects and majors are worth preserving and which will be replaced by new, more popular, career-oriented courses.

The problems of purposes and goals for some colleges might be solved by focusing on one of these three proposals. In that way, particular colleges and universities will have special appeal to certain groups of students.

The only solution to the financial problems faced by private colleges and universities seems to reside in government financing. Dr. Earl McGrath, in one of his many studies of private colleges and liberal education, points out three reasons for this conclusion:

1. Government assistance is the only remaining visible device to preserve our dual system [public and private] of higher education. Even the public institutions would be adversely affected by the disappearance of the private colleges and universities.

2. Without public help the religious influence in higher education will be gone, because some of the colleges with a religious connection or commitment are in the gravest financial danger.
3. To spend millions in state funds to build new facilities and increase offerings in public institutions while the same resources stand idle in the private sector is "an uneconomical and an unwise public policy" (McGrath, 1975:54).

Financing Higher Education. To overcome the problems of financing, many colleges and universities are beginning to trim budgets and cut back on expensive programs. According to Clark Kerr, Chairman of the Carnegie Council on Policy Studies in Higher Education, many college presidents have now become "a kind of super-accountant" (Morgenthaler, May 18, 1976:1). Raising money has also become an important part of a university or college president's job. Alexander Heard, Chancellor of Vanderbilt University, says that fund raising is hampered by the public's skepticism about the value and social usefulness of higher education. But presidents and other administrators in higher education continue to seek funds wherever they can be found.

Another possible solution to the financial crunch of colleges and universities offered by educators and administrators is to develop or expand continuing-education programs for adults and professionals. Many schools are also stepping up their efforts to win more research contracts. Presidents and the admissions staff of struggling private colleges are becoming more actively involved in recruiting students. College enrollments overall increased (by 250,000) in Fall 1976 for the first time in several years (U.S. Bureau of the Census, April 1977:18). Students are an important (though not the chief) source of revenue for most colleges. Every student represents $3,000 to $4,000 in tuition and fees, and if a college is 100 students short in its freshman class, it can be in serious financial trouble.

Evidence of increased enrollment efforts comes from a recent survey of 1,227 colleges and universities by the Carnegie Council on Policy Studies in Higher Education. It found that almost half the colleges expect their enrollments to continue rising by more than 10 percent through 1980. Only six percent of the schools predicted a decline in enrollments, while the rest expected them to remain about the same ("Now It's Soaring Tuition," March 1, 1976:26).

THE FUTURE OF THE PROBLEMS OF EDUCATION

We are a society that craves education, and we will continue to insist upon education for all. More people will be better educated as educational attainment continues to grow. The median number of years of school completed by persons 25 and older was 8.6 in 1940, rose to 12.2 in 1970, and should reach 12.4 by 1980. Table 9-3 shows the record of improved education between 1970 and 1980.

The most important factor affecting the future of education is the demographic one. Although the years 1980 and 2000 will have quite similar age distributions in the 18- to 21-year-old group, the years between will manifest sharp fluctuations, with serious implications for education at all levels. For example, between 1980 and 1994 there will be a 25 percent drop in the size of the traditional college-age group. Unless the slack is taken up by persons from other age groups, college enrollments could drop by about 1.8 million. This could result in a reduction in faculty size of about 100,000.

Future Enrollments

Undergraduate enrollments should continue to increase modestly through the early 1980s, as earlier studies indicated; thereafter a 10 percent decline should occur between 1984 and 1995. In the mid-1990s, enrollment should rise a bit, but the number of undergraduates enrolled in degree programs in 1995 is not likely to be higher than it was in 1975. Although enrollments in the next two decades should be fairly steady, the ups and downs within that period will be uncertain.

The future of college enrollment will depend largely upon two factors: first, the economy's ability to provide college graduates with well-paying jobs; second, the costs of getting a college degree. Schools could price themselves out of the market, so that only a smaller and smaller segment of high-school graduates will be able to afford a college education. If the costs of four-year colleges and universities rise, as they are predicted to do, more and more college-bound students will go to a

table 9-3 EDUCATIONAL ACHIEVEMENT BY PERSONS AGE 25 AND OVER, 1970–80 (in percentage)

	1970	1980
TOTAL	100.0%	100.0%
LESS THAN 1 YEAR OF HIGH SCHOOL	27.7	18.4
1–3 YEARS OF HIGH SCHOOL	17.1	16.4
4 YEARS OF HIGH SCHOOL	34.0	38.3
1–3 YEARS OF COLLEGE	10.2	12.4
4 OR MORE YEARS OF COLLEGE	11.0	14.5

Source: Bureau of the Census, reported in *Metropolitan Life Statistical Bulletin*, August 1972: 11.

cheaper community college for the first two years, and then transfer to a four-year school for the last two years.

If this occurs, community colleges throughout the United States will take on an important function as "feeder colleges" for some academic four-year schools. It is conceivable that some colleges and universities will eliminate the first two years of the traditional curriculum and concentrate on the last two and on graduate studies.

Financing Higher Education

The financial outlook for colleges and universities is not good, especially for small, private colleges. The Carnegie Commission predicts that if the funding and spending trends of the early 1970s continue, higher education will face a $26 billion gap in 1980 between income and expenditures. The money will have to be raised either from taxpayers and distributed through government funding or from students, through higher tuition and fees (or some combination of the two). Gazing into the future of higher education, sometimes with tongue in cheek, John R. Silber, President of Boston University, wrote the following:

> Politicians in general persisted in believing the superstition that independent colleges and universities were private, and they allocated comparatively little aid to the independent sector. By the end of the century the independent sector consisted of about 30 heavily endowed institutions and a handful of religious foundations. The state sector was not immune to the effects of declining enrollment, but most of its institutions—the largest ones—survived. (The average institution of higher learning in 1990 enrolled 17,500 students, while the largest single campus enrolled 100,000. Only three campuses remained in the United States with student bodies under 1,500.) (September 1976:41)

Prospects for Equal Access

The future for equality of educational opportunities for all races and classes is not too bright. We have still not legally recognized education as a constitutional right for all our citizens. A racially apartheid system of education has developed in our elementary and secondary schools, despite whatever efforts have been made to prevent it. If racial housing patterns are any indication, there is reason to believe we will witness more racially segregated schools and classrooms in the future. Only a major revolution in our social structure will change the situation. As the costs of higher education keep more students out of higher education, lower- and working-class students (as well as racial minorities) will have even fewer opportunities to obtain a college degree. What kinds of goals and curriculum will dominate education in the future? A number of alternatives can be envisioned.

In some schools individual attention and compensatory-education programs are given to children formerly deprived by society of equal economic, social, and educational opportunities.

Substitutes for and Supplements to School. With the move toward knowledge-based industries and an increase in leisure time, we can expect a small but significant number of highly educated persons to offer their children home instruction rather than depend solely on the schools. This possibility will be enhanced by improvements in computer-assisted education, electronic videotapes, holography, and other technical advances. Parents and students could sign short-term "contracts to learn" with the school. Students might continue to attend school for social and recreational activities or for subjects that cannot be electronically transmitted into the home. According to Alvin Toffler's vision, "pressures in this direction will mount as the schools grow more anachronistic, and the courts will find themselves deluged with cases attacking the present obsolete compulsory attendance laws. We may witness, in short, a limited dialectical swing back toward education in the home" (1970:406).

Like banks and brokerage houses, libraries will benefit from new techniques of storing, retrieving, reproducing, and transmitting information. As the number of periodicals and monographs multiplies (especially from translated sources), interschool and interlibrary transmission of information will occur. Small schools will depend on regional information and data by cathode-ray tube, teletype, computer, photo-facsimile by telephone, or other futuristic means (perhaps by laser beams). As one writer notes: "The long-range plan for the Library of Congress ... for the year 2000 [envisions] the storage in machine-recoverable form of the entire deposits, and the accessibility of any item, without queuing, to readers at electronically-linked metropolitan and university sub-stations" (Orlans, 1968:197).

Stanford Professor Frederick McDonald has proposed a kind of "mobile education" that takes students out of the classroom, not only to observe, but also to participate in significant community activity. Education, business, and government will move closer together as social institutions. In future secondary- and higher-education programs, adult mentors would demonstrate and transmit skills to students to show how textbook abstractions are applied. Accountants, doctors, engineers, urban planners, and businessmen might all become part of a community faculty, a function that part-time lecturers presently serve in some colleges and universities. Companies will establish closer and more meaningful relationships and a greater interchange of personnel with education.

A closer correspondence should occur between the secondary and elementary curricula and college-course offerings (and required admission tests). Learning will be stretched out over a lifetime, and continuing education for adults will become a larger feature of future educational

Cooperative programs between schools and industry often provide opportunities for students to apply what they learn and to give adults a chance to complete their education.

institutions and organizations. Education, therefore, will not always occur on a continuous track from beginning to end without interruption.

Innovations in Teaching

Such changes in education will call for innovations in teaching techniques. Today, lectures still dominate the classroom; tomorrow, they will not be as significant. New teaching methods will range from role playing and gaming to computer-mediated seminars. They will entail techniques that directly involve the students in learning games and simulated experiments, such as congressional hearings or other experiences that directly involve the students (McVeigh, October 1973:13-24). Of course, much future education will be audiovisual rather than predominantly written. Learning may also be stimulated through the use of controlled nutrition or drugs to raise awareness and memory, to raise IQ levels, and to accelerate reading speed.

Breaking Down the Bureaucracy

In the future, the rigid bureaucratic organization of the classroom and of school itself will slowly evolve toward what Toffler calls "ad-hocracy." This implies small-group leaders, project teams, task forces, and other temporary social structures to gather information or solve a problem. A team approach to evaluating students, similar to social-work team conferences in evaluating clients, will be a hallmark of future primary and secondary schools.

Although not certain they will be established, Toffler advocates that "councils of the future" be set up in every school and community. These councils would consist of teams of men and women devoted to probing the future in the interests of the present. By projecting alternative or assumed futures, by defining coherent educational responses to them, and by opening such alternatives to public debate, these councils "could have a powerful impact on education" (1970:404). Whether or not such councils are established, it is quite clear that our future educational system will be designed, in its purposes, curriculum, and teaching techniques, to prepare students more for the future than for the present. Such an education would encourage mastering three major "transferable" skills—learning how to learn, learning how best to interact with and relate to others, and learning how to choose from among alternatives (Ibid., 414).

Another trend that will shape our schools in the future will be emphasis on educating people for life in an international society—a global village. Education will no longer be able to afford the luxury of an ethnocentric education. All courses, of necessity, will be permeated with ideas and concepts from and about other cultures and societies. This should mean that such disciplines as anthropology and international relations will draw more students' interest than at present. Study of oceanography, geology, and astronomy should grow as we turn our attention to the sea and outer space in search of new resources and possible life.

SUMMARY

Education means different things to liberals, radicals, and conservatives. This leads to conflicting purposes, functions, and curricula, and to conflicts over which textbooks to use and what courses to teach. Some groups emphasize conservation of the status quo, while others opt for goals that will reform or radically change society. Issues are defined differently about how much bureaucratic structure is needed in our schools and how and by whom power and control over schools should be used.

In spite of conflicts (and sometimes because of them), we have achieved a higher level of learning than any other society in history. Our combined elementary- and secondary-school systems boast 89,000 schools, located in almost 17,000 school districts, although school districts and school enrollments are beginning to decline. Most persons have at least a high-school diploma. However, unequal access to quality education, bureaucracy in the schools, power and control over the schools, and higher costs of education are problems we have not resolved.

The underlying causes of the various problems of education can be found in conflicting societal values, rising expectations, discrimination and prejudice based on color or class, inadequate and inequitable funding, and a highly structured, bureaucratic society.

One proposed solution to our educational problems is a voucher or free-market system, enabling schools to compete for students and to ensure more nearly equal access for all students. Another solution is the "back-to-basics" movement, stressing reading, writing, and arithmetic, as well as three other Rs—results, realism, and retrenchment. We have also made suggestions for reducing bureaucracy and formality in our schools, including Ivan Illich's suggestion for "de-schooling society."

To cope with the centralized power and control over some schools, we have advocated decentralization of policy making to the neighborhoods. Although not a panacea for educational problems, such local control of the schools would be a step toward restoring the imbalance in power between centralized school boards and residents in the neighborhoods where the schools are located.

Various proposals for our colleges included concentrating on traditional values, increasing growth from new student markets, and seeking a new educational synthesis of the old and the new. To solve their financial problems, colleges have attempted to raise money from government or through tuition increases. Increasing enrollment and expanding adult "continuing education" have also been used.

The future of education in America is uncertain. More of us will be better educated in the future, and education will become more of a life-long process; yet future decades (starting in the 1980s) will see fewer young students enrolled at every level of education. Some small private colleges will have a particularly hard time, as they face eventual decline and death. Home education may expand, as sophisticated technology facilitates the transmission, storage, and retrieval of information. Racially separate but equal schools will persist, and races and social classes will still be apart in their schools. Future education will be more closely linked with the community, and changes in educational techniques to directly involve students will occur. Courses will emphasize how to "learn," "relate," and "choose." An international perspective will be introduced into the curriculum, and anthropology and international relations should grow as disciplines.

CAREER OPPORTUNITIES

Special-Education Teachers.

Since job opportunities for elementary and secondary teachers are not as available as in the past, teaching jobs at these levels are usually found by those trained and certified to teach mentally retarded or socially disadvantaged students. If more emphasis is placed on preschool education, those trained in early-childhood education will have greater opportunities for getting a teaching position. For further information write to: National Education Association, 1201 16th St., N. W., Washington, D.C. 20036.

School Counselors.

Counselors are concerned with the career, educational, and social development of students. They work directly with students, as well as with teachers, school administrators, parents, and community groups. They use various tests and records to help students evaluate their interests and abilities. Most states require counseling and teaching certificates, although a growing number of states no longer require the latter. For further information write to: American School Counselor Association, 1607 New Hampshire Ave., N. W., Washington, D.C. 20009.

Community College Teachers.

For majors in sociology and social science who are interested in teaching, community colleges offer some of the best opportunities. A Master's degree, or course work well beyond the bachelor's level, is usually required. Although classes are sometimes large, innovative teaching and new programs or courses often are encouraged. Competition for positions can be expected, but those willing to locate in nonurban areas have better chances for employment and career advancement. For further information write to: National Education Association, 1201 16th St., N. W., Washington, D.C. 20036.

REFERENCES

Astin, Alexander and Calvin B. T. Lee
1972 The Invisible College. New York: McGraw-Hill.

Berg, Ivar
1975 "Rich Man's Qualifications for Poor Man's Jobs." Pp. 186–94 in Paul H. Horton and Gerald Leslie, eds. Readings in the Sociology of Social Problems. 2nd ed. Englewood Cliffs, N.J.: Prentice-Hall.

Bergquist, William H.
1974 The Small, Private College in American Higher Education. Washington, D.C.: Council for the Advancement of Small Colleges.

Berman, Ronald
1974 "An Unquiet Quiet on Campus." New York Times Magazine (February 10): 14.

Bowles, Samuel
1972 "Getting Nowhere: Programmed Class Stagnation." Society 9 (June): 42–49.

Bowles, Samuel and Henry Levin
1969 "The Determinants of Scholastic Achievement—An Appraisal of Some Recent Evidence." Journal of Human Resources (Winter). Pp. 80–102 in Patricia Cayo Sexton, ed. School Policy and Issues in a Changing Society. Boston: Allyn & Bacon.

Braun, Robert
1976 "New Jersey's Free Market Plan." Change 8, 7 (August): 18–21.

Buder, Leonard
1975 "City Schools Plan to Charge Tuition for Foreign Pupils." New York Times (December 5): 1, 40.

Cartter, Allan M. and Lewis C. Solmon
1976 "Implications for Faculty." Change 8, 8 (September): 37–38.

Coleman, James S.
1966 Equality of Educational Opportunity. U.S. Department of Health, Education and Welfare, Office of Education. Washington, D.C.: U.S. Government Printing Office.

Coles, Robert
1971 "What Can You Expect?" Pp. 185–93 in Patricia Cayo Sexton, ed. School Policy and Issues in a Changing Society. Boston: Allyn & Bacon.

"Combat 'Alarming Trends,' President Urges Educators." Allentown Morning Call (February 17): 13, 1976.

Conlan, John
1975 "The Macos Controversy." Social Education 29, 6 (October): 388–90.

Cummings, Judith
1976 "Furlough at City University Is Postponed." New York Times (March 16): 59.

Curti, Merle
1959 The Social Ideas of American Educators. Totowa, N.J.: Littlefield, Adams.

Dow, Peter
1975 "Macos Revisited: A Commentary on the Most Frequently Asked

Questions about Man: A Course of Study." Social Education 39, 6 (October): 388–96.

"Driver Shot in Violence over Textbooks." New York Times (September 14): 27, 1974.

"Educational Predictions." Parade Magazine (October 26): 12, 1975.

"Education Briefs: Reading Improves." Education Digest 42, 3 (November): 66, 1976.

"Education: Colleges Offer More Remedial Courses in Basic Skills." Allentown Sunday Call Chronicle (March 7): A-13, 1976.

"Education Trends." The Education Digest 41, 8 (April): 68, 1976.

"18 Arrested in West Virginia as Textbook Protest Goes On." New York Times (October 8): 20, 1974.

Franklin, Ben
1974 "Textbook Dispute Has Many Causes." New York Times (October 14): 31.

Gibson, Robert, Marjorie S. Mueller, and Charles Fisher
1977 "Age Difference in Health Care Spending, Fiscal Year 1976." Social Security Bulletin 40, 8 (August): 3–14.

Gleazer, Edmund J.
1975 "The Emergence of the Community College as a Center for Service Learning." Synergist 4, 1 (Spring): 10–14.

Goldwin, Robert A., ed.
1966 Higher Education and Modern Democracy. Chicago: Rand McNally.

Golladay, Mary A.
1976 The Condition of Education. National Center for Education Statistics, Education Division, U.S. Department of Health, Education and Welfare. Washington, D.C.: U.S. Government Printing Office.

Grambs, Jean D'resdes
1977 "Women and Administration: Confrontation or Accommodation?" Education Digest 42, 7 (March;) 39–42.

Grant, W. Vance
1976 "Educational Expenditures as a Percentage of GNP." American Education 12 (May): back cover.

Grant, W. Vance and C. George Lind
1975 Digest of Educational Statistics. 1974 ed. U.S. Department of Health, Education and Welfare. Washington, D.C.: U.S. Government Printing Office.

Greeley, Andrew M.
1973 "Catholic Schools Are Committing Suicide." New York Times Magazine (October 21): 40–65.

Greer, Colin
1969 "The Myth of the Melting Pot." Saturday Review (November 15): 84.

Gross, Ronald and Paul Osterman, eds.
1971 High School. New York: Simon and Schuster.

Guzzardi, Walter
    1976   "The Uncertain Passage from College to Job." Fortune 93, 1 (January): 126–29; 168–72.

"Head of State University at Albany Accepts Cut in Programs." New York Times (March 16): 22, 1976.

Hofstadter, Richard and Wilson Smith
    1961   American Higher Education: A Documentary History. Vol. 1. Chicago: University of Chicago Press.

Illich, Ivan
    1970   Deschooling Society. New York: Harper & Row.

Jencks, Christopher
    1972   Inequality: A Reassessment of the Effect of Family and Schooling in America. New York: Basic Books.

Katz, Michael B.
    1971   Class, Bureaucracy and Schools: The Illusion of Educational Change in America. New York: Praeger.

Leacock, Eleanor Burke
    1969   Teaching and Learning in City Schools. New York: Basic Books.

Lederer, Joseph
    1968   "The Scope of the Practice." The Urban Review 3, 1 (September). Pp. 178–85 in Patricia Cayo Sexton, ed. School Policy and Issues in a Changing Society. Boston: Allyn & Bacon.

Lupton, Andrew, John Auigenblick and Joseph Heyison
    1976   "A Special Report: The Financial State of Higher Education." Change 8, 8 (September): 21–26.

Marburger, Carl
    1974   "The West Virginia Textbooks." New York Times (October 24:) 41.

McGrath, Earl J.
    1975   Values, Liberal Education, and National Destiny. Indianapolis, Ind.: Lilly Endowment.

Mathews, John
    1976   "With Education in Washington, Data." The Education Digest 41, 9 (May): 62–65.

"Mature Women Returning to College." Allentown Sunday Call Chronicle (February 1): E-7, 1976.

Morgenthaler, Eric.
    1976   "College Presidents Shift Focus to Bookkeeping from Peace-Keeping." Wall Street Journal (May 18): 1, 41.

Morse, Joseph L. and William Hendelson, eds.
    1973   "Land Grant Colleges." Funk & Wagnalls New Encyclopedia. Vol. 15. New York: Funk & Wagnalls.

Morshead, Richard W.
    1975   "The Clash of Hidden Ideologies in Contemporary Education." Education Digest 41 (November): 16–19.

National Center for Education Statistics, Education Division
    1975   The Condition of Education. Washington, D.C.: U.S. Government Printing Office.

National Education Association
    1893 Report of the Committee of Ten on Secondary School Studies. New York: American Book.

"Now It's Soaring Tuition That's Causing Campus Unrest." U.S. News & World Report (March 1): 25–26, 1976.

"One of Five Found Functionally Illiterate." Allentown Morning Call (October 30): 21, 1975.

Orlans, Harold
    1968 "Educational and Scientific Institutions." Pp. 191–99 in Daniel Bell, ed. Toward the Year 2000: Work in Progress. Boston: Beacon Press.

"Pittenger Makes Plan Schools' Top Priority." Allentown Morning Call. (March 1): 2, 1976.

"Poor Blacks Indicated Getting More Education." Allentown Morning Call (March 15): 2, 1976.

Pounds, Ralph L. and James Bryner
    1973 The School in American Society. 3rd ed. New York: Macmillan.

President's Commission on School Finance.
    1972 "Schools, People and Money." Congressional Digest 51, 8 & 9 (August/September): 203–9.

"A Profile of the U.S. Public Education System." Congressional Digest 51, 8 & 9 (August/September): 194–95, 1972.

"Protesters Assail 'Filthy' Textbooks in West Virginia." New York Times (September 6): 11, 1974.

Pucinski, Roman C.
    1971 Speech. "Should Congress Establish a Major Federal Role in General Financing of U.S. Education?": Pro. Congressional Digest 51, 8 & 9 August/September): 202–8.

Reischauer, Robert D. and Robert W. Hartman
    1973 Reforming School Finance. Washington, D.C.: The Brookings Institution.

Report to the President
    1970 White House Conference on Children. Washington, D.C.: U.S. Government Printing Office.

Reston, James.
    1975 "On Learning and Earning." New York Times (December 7): IV, 15.

Rosenberg, Max.
    1976 "Educator's Quiz." Education Digest 41, 9 (May): back cover.

Rosenfeld, Gerry
    1971 Shut Those Thick Lips. New York: Holt, Rinehart and Winston.

Rosenthal, Robert and Lenore Jacobson
    1969 Pygmalion in the Classroom. New York: Harper & Row.

Roszak, Theodore, ed.
    1967 The Dissenting Academy. New York: Pantheon.
    1971 "Educating Contra Naturam." Pp. 63–81 in Ronald Gross and Paul Osterman, eds. High School. New York: Clarion.

Rudolph, Frederick
  1962 The American College and University. New York: Vintage.

Ryan, William
  1976 Blaming the Victim. 2nd ed. New York: Vintage.

Silber, John R.
  1976 "The Rest Was History." Change 8, 8 (September): 40–41.

Silberman, Charles
  1970 Crisis in the Classroom: The Remaking of American Education. New York: Vintage.

Stewart, Elbert
  1976 The Troubled Land. New York: McGraw-Hill.

Swift, Pamela
  1976 "Keeping Up with Youth: College Still Necessary." Parade Magazine (February 22): 15.

"Those Dropping Test Scores — Experts Grope for the Reasons." Pp. 171–72 in Anne Kilbride, ed. Readings in Sociology 76/77: Annual Editions. Guilford, Conn.: Dushkin, 1976.

"Those Missing Babies." Time 104, 12 (September 16): 54–63, 1974.

Toffler, Alvin
  1970 Future Shock. New York: Bantam Books.

Turner, Jonathan H.
  1972 American Society: Problems of Structure. New York: Harper & Row.

U.S. Bureau of the Census
  1974 U.S.A. Statistics in Brief 1974. Washington, D.C.: U.S. Government Printing Office.
  1975 Statistical Abstract of the United States: 1975. U.S. Commerce Department. Washington, D.C.: U.S. Government Printing Office.
  1976 "Educational Attainment in the United States: March 1975." Current Population Reports. Series P-20, No. 295 (June). Washington, D.C.: U.S. Government Printing Office.
  1977 "Population Profile of the United States: 1976." Current Population Reports. Series P-20, No. 307 (April). Washington, D.C.: U.S. Government Printing Office.

"Voucher System Allows Parents a Choice of School." Allentown Morning Call (December 16): 6, 1975.

Warner, W. Lloyd, Robert J. Havighurst, and M. B. Loeb
  1944 Who Shall Be Educated? New York: Harper & Row.

Wolfe, Gary K. and Carol Traynor Williams
  1974 "All Education is 'Adult Education': Some Observations on Curriculum and Profession in the Seventies." American Association of University Professors Bulletin (Autumn): 291–95.

Wood, Nell
  1976 "Censorship: The Malady Lingers On." Today's Educator 65, 2 (March/April): 48–52.

Yarmolinsky, Adam
1976 "Challenges to Legitimacy: Dilemmas and Directions." Change 8, 3 (April): 18–25.

Yarrington, Roger
1975 "The Two-Year College Student: An Investor in the Future." Synergist 4, 1 (Spring): 15–17.

SUGGESTED READINGS

Goodlad, John I. The Dynamics of Educational Change: Toward Responsive Schools. New York: McGraw-Hill. 1975.

> Develops the idea that each school must be viewed as a separate entity, but must draw on ideas and resources from other schools in its geographical area. At the same time, each school must create for itself a climate that encourages change and is responsive to the needs of its students.

Goodman, Steven E. and Reference Development Corporation, ed. Handbook on Contemporary Education. New York: Bowker. 1976.

> A definitive and exhaustive handbook on most questions about the functions, operations, and planning of modern education.

Rosenbaum, James E. Making Inequality: The Hidden Curriculum in High School Tracking. New York: Wiley. 1976

> Provides new perspectives for understanding how schools subtly affect social selection and foster inequality.

Ross, Murray G. The University: The Anatomy of Academe. New York: McGraw-Hill. 1976.

> An analysis of the structure, functions, and problems of higher education.

Sandeen, Arthur. Undergraduate Education: Conflict and Change. Lexington, Mass.: Heath. 1976.

> A useful discussion of the key social problems facing higher education and what can be done about them.

Periodicals Worth Exploring

Change
Education and Urban Society
Harvard Educational Review

Higher Education
Human Resources
Journal of Physical Education & Recreation
Journal of Teacher Education
Liberal Education
Media and Methods
Phi Delta Kappan
Review of Educational Research
Social Education
Sociology of Education
Today's Education
Urban Education

Problems of Corporate Power and Work

Read for Fri.

DEFINITION OF PROBLEMS
Radical definitions — C. Wright Mills's analysis:
a) Corporate concentration and power.
b) Military-industrial complex.
c) Defense contracts and industry.
Liberal definitions:
a) The technostructure.
b) Ideas of John Kenneth Galbraith.
Conservative definitions:
a) Free enterprise and free markets.
b) Restricted government role.
Problems of work and the workplace.

INCIDENCE AND PREVALENCE OF THE PROBLEMS
Degree of economic concentration and power.
Degree of business power in government.
Immediate problems of work and the workplace:
a) The nature of work — alienation, job dissatisfaction, decline of the work ethic.
b) Automation and technological change.
c) Dangerous physical conditions of work.
d) Job equality.
e) Unemployment and underemployment.

CAUSES OF THE PROBLEMS
Value conflicts between culture and technoeconomic work system (Daniel Bell).
New cultural attitudes toward success, security, sex roles, social rights, and work (Daniel Yankelovitch).

Social change; cultural lag between changing expectations of workers and the demands of work.
Our economic structure and organization.
Profit motive of corporations.

PROPOSED SOLUTIONS TO THE PROBLEMS
Radical solutions.
Liberal and conservative proposals (Mintz and Cohen and others):
a) Legislate federal chartering of private corporations.
b) Maintain government-owned and -operated corporations, such as TVA.
c) Provide strong antitrust enforcement.
d) Strengthen federal regulatory agencies.
e) Establish a consumers' agency.
f) Break up or divest major corporations, such as oil firms.

Conservative and liberal proposals:
a) Job enrichment and enlargement.
b) Flexible work schedules and shorter work week.
c) Worker "codetermination" (sharing in corporate decision making).
d) Profit sharing.
e) Creation of new "people work" jobs.
f) Encourage and finance work-satisfaction experiments.

Safety, employment, and equality:
a) Effective laws needed.
b) Government-guaranteed jobs for all.

FUTURE OF THE PROBLEMS
Radical perspective: economic collapse inevitable.
Liberal and conservative perspectives:
a) Daniel Bell's postindustrial society.
b) More choice, autonomy, and diversity in jobs.
c) Need to create more jobs in future (72,000 new jobs each week by 1985).

Future job opportunities for women, racial minorities, and youth.
New careers and new jobs.

SUMMARY

> In the business community ... the natural history of competition in established industries in the United States has been a concentration of more and more power in fewer and larger corporations....
>
> Senator Robert W. Packwood, "Should Congress Approve Legislation to Break Up Major U.S. Oil Companies?: Pro." **Congressional Digest** 55, 5 (May 1976): 38.

DEFINING CORPORATE INSTITUTIONS AND POWER

C. Wright Mills pointed out that in large, highly structured societies such as ours, power and wealth are controlled by elites and concentrated in large institutions—the economic, political, and military. He wrote:

> The power to make decisions of national and international consequence is now so clearly seated in political, military, and economic institutions that other areas of society seem off to the side and, on occasion, readily subordinated to these. The scattered institutions of religion, education, and family are increasingly shaped by the big three, in which history-making decisions now regularly occur. Behind this fact there is all of the push and drive of a fabulous technology; for these three institutional orders have incorporated this technology and now guide it, even as it shapes and paces their development (1958: 27).

Such a technology and social structure, according to the Millsian analysis, produce an inequality in wealth and power that causes and exacerbates most of our social problems. In this chapter we examine the concentration of economic power and wealth in the large private corporations that operate our economy. Problems of work within the corporate setting are also explored.

Radical Definitions of the Problem

Radicals, liberals, and conservatives define the problem of corporate institutions and power differently. Radicals and neo-Marxists define the problem as the concentration and abuse of power by elites to the detriment of the rest of society. They believe that the corporate and economic structure of society basically shapes society.

They see our capitalist economy creating and fostering an imbalanced "class structure in which wealthy owners constitute a ruling class that uses the power of the state, both at home and abroad, in exploitative and selfish ways" (Dolbeare and Dolbeare, 1971:185). Further, they believe that such an economic and corporate system is "unjust, unnecessary, inconsistent with man's nature, and should be eliminated—peacefully or, if necessary, by force" (Ibid.). Great economic concentration of wealth, power, and technology has led to economic exploitation reflected in mass unemployment and inequality in work, especially for women. It has also led to a great economic surplus of goods. This surplus must be absorbed through greater advertising to spur on consumption of goods that people do not really need. Such an economic system, according to the radical definition, is irrational since it wastes so much production on artificially created wants and trinkets, while neglecting basic human needs for food, clothing, and shelter.

In addition, the radicals argue that the federal government, for the most part, caters to and is controlled by vested corporate interests. Social-welfare needs, which do not produce profit for business corporations, are often neglected by government. On the other hand, defense spending creates high profits for corporations; for this reason (among others) much tax money is spent for so-called defense. We are annually spending ourselves into greater and greater debt, with defense budgets well over $100 billion. We devote more resources to oiling the war machine than to health, hospitals, education, the elderly, housing, and community needs.

The Military-Industrial Complex. We are confronted with the prospect of a military welfare state in which the bulk of the nation's taxes support a vast institution that may exist independently of its original need, and that has a life of its own not necessarily consistent with the traditions it was set up to protect ("Toward a Military Welfare State," 1973:26).

The Pentagon now has a vested interest in our tax dollars, say some radicals, and has gained vast power over the federal government never intended by the Constitution. For example, only once in the past 30 years has Congress vetoed a major weapons system requested by the military. The defense budget increases every year and is always larger than all other federally funded programs combined. Yet Congress spends less time analyzing the Defense Department's spending than that of any other domestic agency. Voting down the B-1 bomber made history.

Along with increased money in the defense budget comes increased power for a military-industrial complex in society. Its power extends into major groups and institutions; as one author put it, "Pentagon power is institutionalized and built into the structure of American society" (Turner, 1972:176). The Department of Defense—located in the Pentagon, the largest office building in the world—employs over one million civilians, about one-third of all federal employees. It also owns more property than any other organization in the world, and has assets well over $200 billion. The military controls an industrial empire that produces as much as 30 percent of the gross national product each year. It draws on seemingly unlimited capital from the American taxpayers.

Defense Contracts and Industry. Through its defense contracts, the military controls corporations and major research in institutions of higher education, which often depend on money from the military.

Money is poured into the treasuries of large defense contractors. The 100 largest American corporations receive 75 percent of government defense contracts. More than 80 percent of all such contracts are awarded to corporations *without* competitive bidding. Thus, the large defense corporations set their own price and get it, no matter how high. Almost four million workers in industry owe their jobs to defense contracts, and one out of nine jobs is related to the military or defense. About 63 percent of all research-and-development workers (mostly scientists and technicians) work in war-related jobs. Lucrative contracts also go to university professors whose research programs benefit military needs. Top managers and executives of major defense contractors also sit on the boards of trustees of large universities. ROTC programs on college and university campuses, and even in high schools, show the extent to which the military has penetrated education. Labor unions, seeking high-paying jobs in defense work, support Pentagon policies and priorities.

Again, radicals attribute the problems of corporate power to three major social institutions—the military, the government, and the economy—operating for the benefit of power elites that dominate them. A radical change in social structure—by revolution and force, if necessary—is needed before the problem can be remedied.

There is a strong link between the government, the military, and the economy. Usually planes, such as this CA5 transport, are financed by the government for military purposes. This, in turn, keeps the aerospace industry profitable.

Liberal Definitions of Problem

The liberal definition of the problem of corporate institutions recognizes the many changes that have taken place in our society. Business has grown to meet the needs of millions of consumers, and more government regulation is needed to control whatever corporate abuse of power and wealth may exist. Liberals see the economy as consisting of a system of "countervailing powers"—business, consumers, government, military—all working out a compromise for the common good. Power is distributed and fragmented on particular issues so that no one sector of the economy or government can completely control or dominate the other. The overall economic and political systems are accepted for the most part, with reforms needed at times.

Liberal economist John Kenneth Galbraith admits that basic industry today is controlled by a few major producers—an oligopoly. Thus, price competition is limited, and the "free-market" forces often do not dictate supply or demand. Instead, Galbraith and other liberals see industry as controlled by a corporate "technostructure." This technostructure includes the top management of large corporations and "embraces all who bring specialized knowledge, talent or experience to group decision making. This . . . is the guiding intelligence—the brain of the enterprise" (1971:84).

According to this liberal analysis, decisions are made not by corporate elites but by groups of specialists, experts, and top corporate managers. The decision, it is assumed, has economic implications but does not fully take into account the social or political ramifications of decisions that affect so many people.

Liberal analyses include the need for a more equitable sharing of income and wealth in the United States. They view the closing of tax loopholes for big business and the wealthy as one way of achieving such a goal. Liberals see some short-term dangers in the power of large corporations, especially as that power affects consumers. This is the case whenever corporations severely limit competition to unfairly increase prices and profits; whenever they make large or illegal election-campaign contributions to support their own vested interests; and whenever they lobby against cleaning up environmental pollution or oppose legislation designed to protect the consumer (Williamson, Boren, and Evans, 1974: 13). Liberals generally maintain that consumers need government support if they are to be effective in counterbalancing the power of some large corporations. Whether they recognize it or not, most liberals follow a structural-functional approach to corporate power—the whole system is essentially sound; only minor dysfunctions must be changed and reformed so that the system will operate more efficiently for all.

Conservative Definitions of Problem

The conservative definition of the problem of corporations and the economy is that there is too much outside interference with the free-market and free-enterprise system. Such outside interference comes from big government, big unions, and "do-gooders." Conservatives feel that government overregulation is hurting business, destroying competition, and pushing up prices.

The individual and economic self-interest of corporations, especially for profit, must be encouraged by society. If this is done, the greatest number of persons will benefit and prosper economically. The free-market forces, which are based on supply and demand, should set prices and profits for firms. Government must encourage free enterprise, because the large corporations provide jobs and money for the masses of people. Without the economic prosperity of the corporation we would all suffer.

Another problem, according to conservatives, is that people are now less willing to work hard for a living. Too many persons feel the government and the corporation owe them a living. The notion of a fair day's work must be reinstilled in the American worker, especially the young.

Problems of Work and the Workplace

In addition to problems of power and wealth, more immediate social problems stemming from our economic institution center around problems of work and the workplace. Most sociologists see five issues facing workers and work groups today:

1. the nature of work, often leading to alienation, dissatisfaction, and decline of the work ethic
2. automation and technological change
3. dangerous physical conditions of work
4. job inequality, especially for minorities
5. unemployment and underemployment

We will now analyze each of these work-related problems, as well as the problem of corporate power and wealth.

INCIDENCE AND PREVALENCE OF PROBLEMS OF CORPORATE POWER AND WORK

Economic Concentration and Power

Morton Mintz and Jerry Cohen, in *America, Inc.*, suggest that a high degree of economic concentration exists in our society:

> In 1948, the nation's 200 largest industrial corporations controlled 48 percent of the manufacturing assets. By 1969 these firms controlled 58 percent, and the top 500 firms controlled 75 percent of these assets. Today, economic power is even more greatly concentrated (1971:38).
>
> In 20 years, the 200 largest corporations bought out more than 3,900 corporations with combined assets of over $50 billion (Ibid., 61).

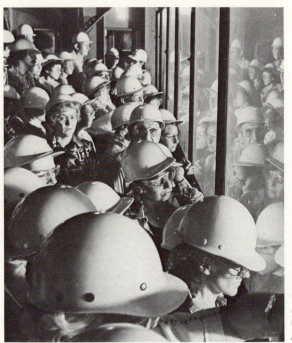

Although not all workers wear hardhats, work shapes most of our lives.

> International Telephone and Telegraph Corporation (ITT) is a sprawling international conglomerate of 433 separate boards of directors. The size of its workforce is the ninth largest in the world. Half of its domestic income stems from government defense and space contracts. But it is also in the business of finance, life insurance, investment funds, small loans, car rentals (Avis), and book publishing (Ibid., 49).
>
> General Motors is the world's largest industrial corpration. Its annual revenue is greater than any foreign government's, and greater than the gross national product of Brazil or Sweden (Ibid., 27).

Galbraith also pointed out that these privately controlled corporate organizations are wealthier than any state government: the revenues of General Motors alone are 50 times those of the State of Nevada and eight times those of New York State (1971:87).

At the turn of the century, there were about 2,200 automakers; today four large corporations control the market. The chemical industry is dominated by three major corporations; telephones, by two. In 1975, 65 percent of all corporate stock was held by only 1.5 percent of the population; and the economic control by large corporations increases each year through mergers and acquisitions (McCord and McCord, 1977:27).

Today large corporations have expanded beyond national boundaries to exert their enormous wealth and power. They have become multinational corporations. According to a 1973 United Nations study, "The United States accounts for more than half of multinational corporations having total annual sales of manufacturers of more than $1 billion" ("Multinational Corporations . . .," 1973:24). Eight of the 10 largest multinationals are American-owned; they account for more than half of direct foreign investment, an estimated $165 billion by 1973. Some 70 percent of such firms are in Latin America. The production (value-added) by *each* of the top 10 multinational corporations in 1971 was greater than the gross national product of over 80 countries ("U.N. Department of Economic and Social Affairs . . .," August 20, 1973:757, 759).

Business Power in Government

The power elite's control of big government is derived from the money and wealth it holds in industry. G. William Domhoff, in *The Higher Circles* (1971), refers to the Council on Foreign Relations. It started in 1921 with members of the New York Social Register (a listing of wealthy families) and limits its membership to 1,400 (half of whom must live in New York City). Since its existence, it has supplied the foreign-policy agencies of the federal government with many leaders. In the early 1960s, the Kennedy Administration appointees for secretaries of state, four senior members of the Defense Department, and two White House staff members were all members of the Council. Former secretaries of state and other cabinet posts also have been members of the elite Council (Fernandez, 1975:137-38). Most held important corporate posts in business before their government appointments.

A longitudinal study from 1897 to 1973 by sociologist Peter Freitag shows that there is an "interlock" between cabinet secretaries and major American corporations. The term interlock was used when the same person served in the cabinet and was a top officer, director, or lawyer in a major corporation before or after serving in his government post. Freitag's figures revealed that 62 percent of cabinet heads were corporate directors and/or officers, 14.1 percent were "corporate lawyers," and 11.7 percent were "unknown lawyers" with possible connections with business corporations. In all, only 12.2 percent of the top cabinet officials were not connected with major corporations (December 1975:141).

There were no significant difference in the percentage of "interlocks" between Republican and Democratic administrations. Freitag concludes that "this study casts heavy doubt upon the pluralist perspective and provides evidence which makes the elitist position more tenable" (Ibid., 151). Wealth and power go together in big industry and government. This is true not only in the executive branch, but also in the legislative. A report released in 1976 showed that at least 22 millionaires serve in the Senate of the United States and possibly more than that in the House of Representatives. This means that the corporate interests of the rich and wealthy will be well represented in the Congress (Lyons, January 4, 1976:A-10).

Large corporations recognize the economic value of having a power base in the federal government. For example, under the National Security Act of 1947, National Security Resources and Research and Development Boards were established. The National Resources Board has designated certain "essential materials" (such as aluminum, nickel, and rubber) as critical and strategic for the defense of the United States. To ensure their availability, the government pays private firms to keep it supplied with these essential materials. Stockpiled materials have been bought up by the government, which keeps them off the market, thereby driving up the price. This strategy also increases the profits made by these private corporations. The federal government has loaned millions of dollars to Lockheed Aircraft, has financed sophisticated space-communications systems for such private firms as ITT, and has paid large corporate farms billions of dollars for *not* growing crops.

Problems of Work and Alienation

When workers are alienated, dissatisfied, or are not productive, society suffers. Such problems stemming from work may produce social strife, strikes, and slowdowns, making it more difficult for our society to compete

Some workers, such as this skilled tool-and-dye maker, enjoy jobs that are intrisically challenging and rewarding.

effectively with others. So sociologists must explore the depths and extent of work-related problems so their effects on our economy and society can be better understood and analyzed.

Work, whether in the office, store, or plant, includes rigid, monotonous, meaningless tasks. The National Planning Association reports that 80 percent of all jobs are routine and require no specialized skills. The other 20 percent are looked upon as elite jobs (Berger, 1976:26). Most workers realize that they will not hold such a job.

Whether they wear a white collar or a blue one, they will spend most of their waking hours at a rather uninspiring job. This fact alone leads to such social issues as alienation, job dissatisfaction, and a decline of the "work ethic."

Alienation from Work. Modern man is alienated from many things—his community, his church, himself—but most of all from his work. Neo-Marxists argue that this is because the worker does not own the means of production. Whatever the reason, work has become instrumental—solely a means to an end. Modern man works for money so that he can "enjoy life" and find meaning *off* the job. The extent of alienation depends on a person's job. A popular conception of the nature of work among some intellectuals is that a college professor and factory worker both experience alienation because of the demands of their jobs. A professor is often forced to publish and is equally a victim of bureaucracy and specialization.

A young worker once suggested that a professor would begin to understand how factory workers often feel about their work if he were forced to type and retype a single paragraph from 9 to 5, every day of the week. Instead of setting his own pace, the professor's typewriter carriage would begin to move automatically at 9 and continue at a steady pace until 5. The professor's job would be at stake if his typing of the same paragraph didn't keep pace with the machine (Levison, 1975: 35).

The nature and organization of work itself adds to the alienation of workers. One female worker in a Vega auto plant put it this way:

> I work with a twelve-pound air gun tightening bolts, but the guns don't always work. Sometimes I have to drop mine on the floor to make it work. Now every job has been time-studied—so having to drop the gun makes me more work (Rothschild, 1976: 334).

At the widely known Lordstown, Ohio, assembly plant, workers face a new car assembly every 36 seconds—800 in eight hours. Every job and factory arrangement is designed for a 36-second rhythm of production.

White-collar workers often feel a similar frustration, as C. Wright Mills pointed out in *White Collar* (1951). Many modern offices actually resemble an assembly line. Computer keypunch operators and typists in a pool work on material or correspondence as it flows by on a systematic belt from station to station. Use of machines in the office adds to alienation when the human element is secondary. A telephone receptionist explains:

> You come in at nine, you open the door, you look at the piece of machinery, you plug in the headpiece. That's how my day begins. You tremble when you hear the first ring. After that, it's sort of downhill, unless there's somebody on the phone who is either kind or nasty. The rest of the people . . . just . . . don't exist. They're just voices. You answer calls, you connect them to others, and that's it. . . . You're there just to handle the equipment. You're treated like a piece of equipment, like the telephone (Terkel, 1974: 29–30).

Job Dissatisfaction. The influential study *Work in America*, issued by the Department of Health, Education and Welfare, documented the job dissatisfaction of many workers during the 1970s. It reported that a changing American workforce (young, educated, with new values and ideas about work) was becoming dissatisfied with "dull, repetitive, seemingly meaningless tasks, offering little challenge or autonomy" (1973: xv).

The study pointed to the familiar "blue-collar blues" and to serious job dissatisfaction at all occupational levels, though not as great among the better-paid jobs. Discontent often leads to low productivity, "absenteeism, turnover, wildcat strikes, sabotage, poor-quality products, and a reluctance by workers to commit themselves to their work tasks" (Ibid., xvi). The report also traced the connection between job dissatisfaction and other social problems. As a worker's problems increase, they adversely affect his physical and mental health, family stability, community participation, and political attitudes. Dissatisfaction on the job produces more alcohol and drug addiction, along with aggression and delinquency in the workplace and in society.

Dr. Herbert Greenberg, a social scientist and president of Marketing Survey and Research Corporation, reports that "four out of every five working Americans today are misemployed. . . . They are doing jobs they are not suited for and are thus miserable" (Cassidy, 1973: 7). Greenberg bases his conclusion on interviews he and his associates have conducted since 1957 with 250,000 employees of 4,000 firms "representing every job category and educational group from every part of the country." Job frustration, he adds, is as high at the managerial level as at lower levels. Both blue-collar workers and their bosses are caught in jobs they dislike, and both are digging themselves into deeper, more frustrating ruts. This misemployment affects workers and industry alike: "Among sales forces, for instance, 20 percent of the salesmen sell more than 80 percent of the products and services. The rest of the salesmen are obviously in the wrong job" (Ibid.).

Other studies, by the University of Michigan, the Upjohn Institute for Employment Research, and by HEW, all confirm that job dissatisfaction varies widely, depending on a number of key variables, including age, sex, race, education, wages, kind and nature of job, industry, and work group (Sheppard and Herrick, 1972:193; Braude, 1975:182–83). Generally the younger the worker the greater the dissatisfaction. Females tend to be

> ## "NO PRIDE IN THIS DUST"
> ### Bennet Kremen
>
> ... We bump along past dozens of roads, ore docks, rail lines, and shops, some a block long and hissing and clanging with the sounds of hammers, alarm bells, and deadly molten metal that rears from the furnaces like harsh sunshine. Awe—and a touch of uneasiness—shows on the young faces of those sharing the bus with me, their feelings surely paralleling my own. For to the uninitiated, it seems impossible that all these steaming slag piles and ore boats, blast furnaces and cranes that travel on tracks far above us can be managed by 8,200 mere workers, though they labor around the clock in three swing shifts every day of the year.
>
> "If they ain't got a lot of machines to do all this goddamn work," I announce in a fool-around tone, "we're all gonna have a sore back!"
>
> "I'm hip—better they use a dynamo than Little Joe. They ain't got no spare parts for men, man!"
>
> The laughter is heavy, though only the driver and a few new workers are left in the bus—Little Joe among them. And now, smack on the shore of the lake, where the wind hits like a razor, the driver calls out his last stop—our stop.
>
> "This is #2 Electric Furnace—only a half-hour walking time to the gate."
>
> He is smiling when he says it, but none of us stepping out into the damp cold shares his amusement.
>
> "You gotta be jivin', man—you mean from now on we gotta hoof it!"
>
> "That's it, Little Joe—coming in and going out."
>
> A low, angry grumbling at the thought of this cold, payless walk each day fades only gradually as we follow the driver through this noisy, dirty building to the foreman's office. When we enter, the grumbling is over, but a sullen silence remains.
>
> "OK—each of you have a number on the card they gave you. Memorize it, because that's what you're going to be called around here."
>
> 31-445, then, is who I am to the pair of foremen in blue hard hats who've just given each of us a bright yellow helmet worn by production workers on labor gangs. For $3.19 an hour, then, with a bit extra for late shifts and weekends, we now conclude these sterile preliminaries and don our hard hats, joining tens of thousands of other young workers thus initiated into the lowest ranks of the steel industry.
>
> Source: Bennet Kremen, "No Pride in This Dust." In Irving Howe, ed., *The World of the Blue-Collar Worker* (Newark: Quadrangle Books, 1972): 15.

more dissatisfied with their jobs, usually because of the low pay, and blacks are more dissatisfied than whites. In one survey, 37 percent of black workers under 30 expressed negative feelings about their jobs. A National Institute of Education analysis of 16 job-satisfaction studies reported that "no relationship was found between educational level and job satisfaction among workers who had not gone to college, but those who had obtained college degrees were consistently more satisfied with their jobs than were others" (Quinn and Baldi de Mandilovitch, March 1977: v).

table 10-1 PERCENTAGE OF WORKERS, BY OCCUPATIONS, WHO WOULD CHOOSE SIMILAR WORK AGAIN

PROFESSIONAL AND LOWER WHITE-COLLAR		WORKING-CLASS OCCUPATIONS	
Occupations	Percentage	Occupations	Percentage
Urban University Professor	93%	Skilled Printer	52%
Mathematician	91	Paper Worker	42
Physicist	90	Skilled Auto Worker	41
Chemist	86	Textile Worker	31
School Superintendent	85	Blue-collar Worker	24
Lawyer	83		
Church University Professor	77	Unskilled Steelworker	21
White-Collar Worker	43	Unskilled Auto Worker	16

Source: Adapted from Robert L. Kahn, "The Meaning of Work." In Angus C. Campbell and Philip E. Converse, eds., *The Human Meaning of Social Change*. (New York: Russell Sage Foundation, 1972): 182. © 1972 by Russell Sage Foundation.

The extent of dissatisfaction among blue-collar and white-collar occupations can be seen from Table 10-1. The table shows the percentage of workers in each occupation that would prefer the same kind of work if they could choose again. As we can see, 43 percent of the white-collar workers would choose the same job, as compared with only 24 percent of the

Many jobs in industry are dull, monotonous, and routine. This sometimes leads to job dissatisfaction.

Credit: Daniel Simon/Gamma.

blue-collar workers. This kind of study gives a clearer picture of the extent of job dissatisfaction than most studies that have merely asked workers whether they are satisfied with their jobs. In the latter type, 80 to 90 percent of the workers reply that they are satisfied, which may just be another way of saying they are glad they have a job so they can make a living.

Decline of the Work Ethic. The nature of industrial tasks weakens the work ethic and cuts down individual productivity. The Protestant work ethic, based on the notion that hard work leads to success both in this world and in the next, has shaped American character, groups, and society. But the nature of capitalism, work and bureaucracy has changed all that. The machine or an engineered system of workflow controls the pace of work, the output, and often the quality of the product. Little judgment is left for the worker, who must simply keep up with the machine or system. Workers look outside the workplace to leisure time for real satisfaction in life.

In his book *Blue Collar Life,* Arthur Shostak observed that "satisfaction at the job has apparently become less significant (for being less obtainable) than satisfaction from consumption; and success at one's job has become less important than success in one's after-work style of life" (1969: 60).

Although work is (and will probably continue to be) a very important value, workers find it increasingly difficult to accept the idea that their hard work can make a difference or be rewarding. As one writer observed:

> Corporation executives seem no less puzzled than many other Americans as to why young people entering the labor force — even in a time of job scarcity — are less enchanted with the so-called Protestant ethic of hard work and upward striving than their parents and grandparents.... University graduates entering business typically profess to abhor aspects of technology that tend to reduce man to a machine-like function (Deans, 1973: 8–9).

Some businessmen, unions and conservatives, however, do not view the incidence and prevalence of alienation, job dissatisfaction or rejection of the work ethic, as crucial social problems. To support their contention, they point out that most surveys show that job satisfaction is usually very *high* (80 to 90 percent, as just mentioned). Furthermore, this reported satisfaction has not changed much between the late 1950s and the late 1970s ("Job Satisfaction,..." 1974:51).

Samuel Florman, vice president of a construction company, defined the issue of work and alienation this way:

> I think that the problem of worker alienation has been overstated by social scientists who simplistically saw in the workplace a major cause of — and potential cure for — the ills of our society (1976:18, 22).

Although some blue-collar workers are dissatisfied with and alienated from work, they often do socially useful and constructive jobs.

Florman points to a recent study of a group of skilled construction workmen who do interesting, varied work. They are not closely supervised. They take pride in their work and can see immediate results from their efforts. Their unions help to control the pace of their work. They should not be alienated or discontent.

Yet E. E. LeMasters, in his study of these men—*Blue Collar Aristocrats*—found them alienated from their families, religion, politics, and society itself. They are bigoted, full of hate and suspicion, and confused. They spend much of their off-work hours at the local bar (1975:193–202). No improvement in the nature or conditions of their work can change all that. According to Florman, we see in the workplace only the symptoms of man's problems, not the "diseases of the soul" themselves. "Healthy people do not become heartless bosses or cruel foremen. Healthy people do not feel debased or dehumanized by menial work, or intimidated by blustering superiors. Sick people—alienated people—are not made whole by an interesting job" (Ibid., 22). Thus, the issue is *not* the nature of work or the workplace itself. Rather such a definition assumes that the individual is alienated *before* he encounters the social structure and system in the workplace.

Today with increased concern about getting a job, the perspectives of liberals and conservatives about work and "blue-collar blues" seem to have faded temporarily into the background, while society gives more attention to how best to generate jobs in our economy for those who need work.

Automation and Technological Change

Automation implies that machines will replace man and do work automatically. The computer, modern farms, continuous-flow oil refineries, and cement plants are prime examples of automation. It touches the office, farm, and factory, and has been called the second Industrial Revolution. Whether it is or not, technological change is very rapid. Almost overnight, new industries come into being, and old ones, like railroads, drop by the wayside. Products have a short life span; most of the goods on the market today were not produced 20 years ago. Today's skills will be obsolete for tomorrow's workers.

In 1966 a Presidential Commission on Technology, Automation and Economic Progress warned of the problems automation could bring in the 1970s. Although some of the fears may have been exaggerated (e.g., 20,000 workers displaced each week by automation), such basic industries as steel, automobile, glass, and cement hire and use fewer workers. At automated Ford Motor plants, nine men at three machines do the work formerly done by 34 men at 39 machines. An insurance company that now uses the computer reduced its staff from 198 to 85 (Perruci and Pilisuk, 1971: 180–81). Some 100,000 telephone operators were displaced when direct long-distance dialing became available, and elevator operators were replaced by push buttons. The capitalist often finds it cheaper in the long run to employ modern machines rather than men. As a result, millions have a hard time finding a job today.

Workers 45 or 50 years old often find themselves out of a job because of new technology. Such workers frequently must retrain for new jobs; but sometimes their work experience and education do not qualify them for what they seek to do. Automation causes special social, psychological, and organization problems for workers, while the owners of industry get richer. It often means a change in job content; less physical effort and strain are required, but isolation and boredom often increase. In a large plant or company, no matter how repetitive the task, primary groups of workers develop to encourage interaction. But as the automated plant's workforce shrinks in size and as machines separate workers from one another, alienation and discontent will increase.

These new kinds of technology have relieved some workers of monotonous and routine operations, but they have also made others mere

Automation and technological change bring both problems and promises to workers.

dial watchers or babysitters for machines. In chemical industries, for example, automation reportedly gives the workers greater autonomy, freedom, and control over the job; it reduces worker alienation. Other industries, such as automaking, still retain a high degree of worker alienation despite modern technology (Rothschild, 1976:329–41).

Computer-operated drills, lathes, and presses can be set for close tolerances (within millionths of an inch), correct their own settings, and work automatically. In basic industries, such as steel, cement, glass, and brewing, heavy physical labor has been reduced or eliminated. The product now "flows in a continuous process" without human handling. Light bulbs, tin cans, roller bearings, spark plugs, piston rods, and engine blocks can be made entirely by automated machines (Levitan and Johnston, 1973:106). Complex electronic machines dwarf the worker, who waits for the printouts, the cathode-ray tube, the closed-circuit TV, or the red blinking light to tell him what is happening.

Automation and technologically oriented industries become major social problems by the way they exploit workers and organize work. It has become increasingly profitable for American corporations to invest in automation abroad and then import foreign-made goods under their own label. Most electronic and TV firms do this, even though it means less money for investment in automation in the United States and fewer jobs for workers here. Scott McNall has suggested five ways in which industries affect the work situation:

1. They require an increase in role specialization and division of labor, leading to a fragmentation of work roles.
2. They are inherently dehumanizing since people are separated from one another. The work setting is dehumanizing because it alienates the worker from his product.
3. They destroy a sense of skill and craftsmanship, so important to the well-being of workers.
4. Machines grind out "ersatz, synthetic, and planned-obsolescence products to the point where many people have lost the ability to create qualitatively and consumers have abandoned their esthetic tastes for artisanship and artistry." Pride in what a worker produces is lost.
5. They contribute to environmental problems, on and off the job (1975:71–72).

We shall now examine the physical environment of work and in a later chapter explore environmental problems caused by modern industry.

Dangerous Physical Conditions of Work

Another major social issue, faced by workers and their families alike, is the dangerous physical conditions under which many labor. Corporations have usually found it cheaper to have a dangerous work environment than to make it safe. As a result, dangerous health and safety conditions are a way of life for far too many workers. Each year, on-the-job accidents kill 14,000 persons and disable 2.2 million others (Mintz and Cohen, 1971:48). Environmental pollution is real to those who work in a polluted place every day. Dr. Nicholas Ashford of MIT, a lawyer with a Ph.D. in chemistry, reported after a two-year study of industries that "a significant proportion of heart disease, cancer and respiratory disease may stem from the industrial process" (Dembart, March 17, 1976:23). This threat affects both white-collar and blue-collar workers. Job-related diseases and deaths (perhaps as many as 100,000 annually) have only recently become a social issue, but workers have suffered their effects for years.

Workers have long risked their lives in coal mining. In 1976, 15 miners were killed in a methane-gas explosion at the Scotia Coal Mine in Owen Fork, Kentucky. Two days later, a second explosion took the lives of eight more miners and of three federal safety inspectors who were in the mine making repairs and investigating the cause of the first blast. The U.S. Mining Enforcement and Safety Administration had cited the Scotia mine 855 times for safety violations. The mine had received 110 orders to close down temporarily and had paid nearly $80,000 in fines since 1970. Four safety violations were found the day before the first explosion ("Hearing Airs . . .," March 25, 1976:18).

In 1972, Pittsburgh Corning Corporation shut down its asbestos insulation plant in Tyler, Texas. A government survey showed that ventilation was poor and that workers were inhaling asbestos fibers. Nearly half of the long-time workers had symptoms of asbestosis (scarring of the lungs from inhaling asbestos fibers). This is a "significant illness by almost any standard, in that it is irreversible, untreatable, often disabling, and frequently fatal" (Brodeur, 1974:5). No medical follow-up has been done on the 832 men who worked at the plant over the years. A class-action law suit for $100 million was brought against the company for exposing employees to asbestos fibers "in extremely dangerous concentrations," causing them to suffer from asbestosis, lung cancer, and other diseases.

Because of the deaths of three workers at the B.F. Goodrich plant in Louisville, Kentucky, we now know that vinyl chloride (used in the plastics and chemicals industries) causes liver cancer. We learned that toxic chemicals used in making kepone, an ingredient in ant poison, can also poison workers. Acting on worker complaints, state health officials shut down the kepone plant at Hopewell, Virginia, when it became evident that workers' lives were at stake. The real danger here, however, is often hidden. It may take 10 or 20 years for a chemical to cause the death of a worker. The *Annual Report* of the President's Council on Environmental

Workers, such as this glass blower, often work in dangerous conditions without proper safety or protective equipment. The government, through the Occupational, Safety and Health Administration, is trying to change this situation.

Credit: Richard Bellak/Black Star.

Quality emphasized that exposure to cancer-causing substances at work was one of our greatest environmental threats ("Environment . . .," February 27, 1976:7).

Recent studies reveal that exposure to chemicals, lead, x-rays, and other work-related materials are especially harmful to pregnant women. Women who work in beauty parlors, factories, and hospitals run a special risk of losing their babies or having babies with birth defects. In addition, women and their babies may be contaminated by the materials her husband works with on his job. For example, a continuing study of the families of 354 asbestos workers in Paterson, New Jersey, reveals that 35 percent of the wives and children show lung problems similar to those of the men who work with asbestos (Sullivan, January 25, 1976:D-8).

Another study by five government scientists of a Pottstown, Pennsylvania, plant in 1976 showed that the wives of workers who came in contact with vinyl choride had twice as many miscarriages and stillbirths as wives of workers who did not work around the material (Burnham, 1976:42).

Workers run hidden health hazards even in an office. Researchers at New York's Mt. Sinai School of Medicine recently found high levels of asbestos fibers (from fireproofing materials) in office buildings in New York, Boston, San Francisco, Berkeley, and Chicago. Dr. William Nicholson, who directed the research study, said the levels of asbestos are "dangerously high" in some cases (Sullivan, January 25, 1976:D-8). Sheldon Samuels, health director for labor's Industrial Union Department in Washington, D.C., charges that the chemical DMCC (diemethylcarbamyl chloride) was suspected of being a powerful cancer-causing agent four years before the National Cancer Institute and the Ashland Oil Company told the public about it. Ashland denied the charge but stopped producing the chemical when questions were raised about its safety. Samuels used the case of DMCC as only one example of 150 industrial chemicals that are suspected of causing cancer. Reports on these were also not being released by the National Cancer Institute.

In addition to chemicals, noise and other unsafe physical conditions affect the health of millions of workers. Many Americans work in places noisy enough to impair their hearing. For protection of public health, the Environmental Protection Agency's "Levels Document" of goals in industry calls for a daily average sound level of 70 decibels. Yet many people work every day in noise well above that level (Weaver, 1976:160).

Job Inequality

Another current issue, as defined by government and millions of citizens, is inequality in the workplace for women and racial minorities. The problem is not only the lack of an intrinsically satisfying job but also a well-paying, steady job equal to one held by many white males.

Discrimination against black men in certain skilled jobs, such as carpenters, electricians, and plumbers, is still evident. Overall, black men

table 10-2 PARTICIPATION RATES OF BLACK MEN AND WOMEN, IN CERTAIN JOBS, 1974

JOBS — BLACK MALES	PERCENTAGE OF ALL MALES	JOBS — BLACK FEMALES	PERCENTAGE OF ALL FEMALES
Total Employed:	9.9	Total Employed:	12.4
Longshore Workers	30.4	Housekeepers, private home	37.8
Cement Finishers	30.4	Chamber Cleaners	35.1
Bus Drivers	27.1	Postal Clerks	28.0
Nursing Aides	25.2	Nursing Aides	26.3
Lumber Workers	24.5	Practical Nurses	24.3
Waiters	23.7	Farm Laborers	23.6
Taxicab Drivers	23.2	Social Workers	21.7
Furnace Workers & Smelters	22.7	Cooks	20.8
Cooks	22.2	Office-Machine Operators	15.0

Source: Stuart Garfinkle, "Occupations of Women and Black Workers, 1962–76," U. S. Dept. of Labor, Monthly Labor Review 98,11 (November 1975): 30–31.

increased their participation in skilled trades from 4.7 percent of all craft workers in 1962 to nearly 7.5 percent by 1974; yet their lowest rate of participation is still in the skilled trades, such as electricians (4.4 percent). Table 10-2 illustrates those jobs in which black males and females are overly represented. Those jobs listed tend to be lower-status and low-paying. Many women are forced to work standing and by waiting on men, as the boxed item on "Bars, Women and Culture" illustrates.

Not only have blacks been denied equal job opportunities, but they are usually in low-paying jobs. In addition, a U.S. Department of Commerce study shows that the pay situation for women, as compared with men, has gotten worse, not better. Women on the average earn less than 60 percent of the pay of men (December 8, 1975: 57), as pointed out in an earlier chapter.

Unemployment and Underemployment

The last important work-related social problem is the continuing issue of unemployment and underemployment. Since the war in Vietnam drew to a close in the early 1970s, America has experienced a recession-inflation trend (sometimes called stagflation). It has caused unemployment for millions, along with increases in the cost of living. It is a bad combination for workers and consumers alike. Unemployment hit the highest point in the mid-1970s, when more persons were out of work than at any time since the Great Depression of the 1930s.

Unemployment has been prevalent throughout the history of capitalism in our society. It gives employers another opportunity to exploit labor and keep wage rates low. The incidence and prevalence of joblessness is measured not only in absolute numbers of workers out of work, but also as a percentage of the total workforce. Furthermore, the officially reported figures seriously undercount the number and percentage of the unemployed. By early 1977, reported unemployment still hovered around 8 percent of the workforce. The Bureau of Labor Statistics projects that by 1979 unemployment will be around 6 percent. In other words, nearly 6 million persons will still be out of work (Kutscher, 1976:4).

True Prevalence of Unemployment. Of course different people in different industries experience sporadic unemployment throughout the year. Since official figures are reported on a monthly basis, the true prevalence of unemployment is not known until the end of the year. When

---

BARS, WOMEN AND CULTURE

Four men pick up their drinks and move away from the commotion at the bar to an empty table nearby. The cocktail waitress brushes against a shoulder as she places clean ashtrays and napkins in front of them. "Would you care to order another drink here?" Her smile is pleasant, yet detached. Her miniskirt and knee-high boots add silently to the image that her smile conveys.

"Scotch and water."
"Same."
"Manhattan."
"Gin and Tonic."

She remembers the orders easily and on her way back to the bar stops to empty dirty ash trays and retrieve the used glasses and bottles. Two customers at the next table are on their third round, and as the waitress passes their table, one reaches out, touching her waist: "What are you doin' after work, honey?" The other man at the table laughs, she steps out of reach, ignoring the question, and continues on her way. Seconds later, she gives the bartender her order, bantering with him about the customers. In a few minutes she is back, effortlessly balancing a tray of drinks, collecting money, making change, and always smiling.

Ritually, this scene is repeated millions of times each night in bars and cocktail lounges throughout the country. Here one finds a wide range of behavior to observe: lonely individuals seeking human companionship for a few hours, people hustling for a little action, businessmen conducting interviews and closing deals, others gambling, dancing, holding wedding celebrations, and even attending birthday parties—those individual rites of passage by which our culture marks off the transition from child to adult. From corporation executive to college student to skid-row bum, nearly every kind of person can be found in one or another type of bar. Bars are places where work and play overlap, and where many people find a home away from home. Scattered in great numbers throughout every city, town and village, bars represent an important aspect of American life.

Source: James P. Spradley and Brenda Mann, *The Cocktail Waitress: Woman's Work in a Man's World* (New York: Wiley, 1975):1-2.

unemployment is measured on this cumulative yearly basis, a more accurate picture emerges. In 1975 when *an average* of 7.8 million (8.5 percent of the workforce) were unemployed, over 20 million workers actually experienced unemployment at some time during the year.

An above-average incidence of unemployment exists among blue-collar workers, young people, blacks, and women. In 1974, on the average, 33 percent of all construction workers and 20 percent of all factory workers were unemployed. Although blue-collar workers account for only a third of the workforce, they made up over half of the unemployed in March 1976 ("Employed Persons . . .," April 1976:31).

For years black unemployment has been about twice as great as white. Unemployment rates are usually one or two percentage points higher among women than men. For example, in April 1976, the jobless rate for adult men was 5.5 percent of the workforce, while the rate for women was 7.3 percent ("Jobless Rate Remains . . .," May 8, 1976: 3).

Geographically, unemployment was quite widespread in 1975 and 1976. In 1976, the government reported that "substantial unemployment" blanketed most of the country, meaning 6 percent or greater unemployment (discounting seasonal factors) that is likely to continue. On this basis, 130 out of 150 *major* labor areas in the United States experienced "substantial unemployment," as well as 1,122 smaller labor areas. Thus,

Unemployment lines in recent years have touched all social classes, but joblessness disproportionately hits lower-income people, minorities, women, and youth.

Credit: J. P. Laffont/Sygma.

about 80 percent of all industrial areas had a high incidence of unemployment ("Severe Joblessness Persists, ..." May 8, 1976:1).

Social Repercussions of Unemployment. Unemployment is a serious social problem. Nearly 10 million persons could not find work in 1976. If we add to that those who earn so little that they are living in poverty, those who are underemployed, and those who have dropped out of the workforce (but would like to work), we end up with a social problem affecting millions of breadwinners and their families. This unemployment produces a "reserve army" for employers to exploit by paying less than adequate wages. In some industries, such as textiles, large firms are subsidized, in effect, by low wage rates of people who desperately need work.

The social repercussions of unemployment are vast. Society loses valuable production of goods and services. We lost almost 4 percent in total national output between 1974 and 1976 because of unemployment (Economic Policy Committee, AFL-CIO, 1976: 15). The President's National Commission for Manpower Policy estimates that $40 billion was spent in 1976 on "... unemployment insurance and other emergency payments to the idle and [the Commission] puts the annual toll in lost output at five times that sum" ($200 billion) (*New York Times,* December 23, 1975:24). While unemployment grew, the profits of most large corporations were increasing. Profits of 470 major corporations surveyed by the *Wall Street Journal* increased an average of 19 percent during the last quarter of 1976 ("Survey Shows 19% Gain," February 12, 1977:1).

Apathy and anxiety become a part of the unemployed worker's life. The unemployed often lose contact with the community. In some instances, when all resources are exhausted, they turn to crime. The jobless are under great stress and are often condemned by others. The home life of the unemployed is more often chaotic and filled with conflict. Family break-up becomes more likely if unemployment persists; divorce, alcoholism, suicide, and child beating all increase.

Unemployment causes other social problems, as Professor James Comer of Yale University notes in the accompanying boxed item.

CAUSES OF THE PROBLEMS OF CORPORATE POWER AND WORK

Major causes of the problems discussed are: value conflicts between our culture and our work system; social change; our economic structure; and the profit motive.

Daniel Bell, in *The Cultural Contradictions of Capitalism* (1976), points to the underlying causes of problems in the workplace. He cites basic value conflicts between our culture and the technoeconomic system of work. The most basic conflict is between a firm belief in individual satisfaction and self-realization in our culture and organizational efficiency and productivity in our work system.

> ## THE HIDDEN COSTS OF UNEMPLOYMENT
> ### James P. Comer, M.D.
>
> Unemployed people are more likely to have social and psychological problems and are often unable to rear their children in a way which promotes healthy development. Thus we will lose too many of two more generations of black people to drugs, crime, undereducation and underachievement....
>
> Communities of yesterday's unemployed and marginally employed are the places where many of the children of today's unemployed parents will grow up and prepare for adulthood. These communities, schools, decaying buildings and street gangs are often seething with hopelessness and despair, anger and alienation, apathy and disruptive behavior....
>
> It has always amazed me that we ask why young people who grew up in such homes and communities often can't go out and have a successful college career, learn a trade, hold a job, care for a family, find joy and happiness in leisure time and be all-around good citizens.
>
> Yet we know very well that preparation to do these things begins with the stability and security of their parents in the home—a security made possible by a job and a living wage....
>
> A 9-year-old black youngster from a poverty-stricken home was asked to say the Pledge of Allegiance at the start of school on Monday morning. He refused and ran out of the class, hotly pursued by his teacher, determined to make him respect his country. He ran into the arms of a school aide and said: "That old teacher is trying to make me say the Pledge, and I haven't had anything to eat all weekend!"
>
> At some level, he understood that "somebody up there" was responsible for his plight.... Whatever the solution [to unemployment] it is not just that blacks continue to bear the greatest burden of unemployment and pay the highest social and psychological price.
>
> Source: James P. Comer, M.D., "The Hidden Costs of Unemployment," *New York Times* (June 9, 1975): 31. Reprinted by permission.

New Cultural Trends

Sociologist Daniel Yankelovich uncovered five new trends that reflect these value conflicts between our culture and our work system. These cultural trends include:

1. the changing definition of success
2. reduced fears of economic insecurity
3. a new division of labor between the sexes
4. a spreading psychology of "entitlement," leading to the creation of new social rights
5. a spreading disillusionment with the notion of efficiency (1974:23–31).

The changing definition of success means that people are no longer willing to sacrifice everything for money or to live vicariously through the future success of their children. Emphasis is placed on present enjoyment rather than sacrificing for the future. The shift is to self-fulfillment and development rather than mere material gain. Institutional loyalty is being questioned, particularly if it does not benefit the individual.

Economic security is still important but, according to Yankelovich, most people now take it for granted. Many would rather see the environment cleaned up, even if a plant must be shut down in the process. This causes demands for change in the conditions of work. People are more willing to risk change and insecurity than ever before in the past. Whether this new cultural trend will persist in the face of large-scale unemployment remains to be seen.

The traditional sexual roles at home and at work have changed. No longer is the man looked upon as the sole breadwinner; no longer is the woman seen only as a wife and mother who stays at home. A greater flexibility now marks the relationship between the sexes as they both share the economic role of making a living and as more women remain single.

The fourth trend causing changes in work attitudes is "entitlement." A worker's wants or desires are converted into a set of rights. People now feel they have a *right* to a well-paying, secure, interesting job, as well as to medical care, education, and clean air. This trend dominated the thinking of social movements in the 1960s and 1970s for civil rights, ecology, women's liberation; and it continues to do so in the newer social movements.

The last trend is disillusionment with efficiency. People are recoiling from large bureaucratic organizations, which are structured and operated to obtain efficiency. Human values and personal existence are considered more important in many ways than mere efficiency. The outdoors, spontaneity, pleasure, and romance are considered equally or more desirable.

Social Change

Another cause is ongoing social change, which does not occur at an even pace in our workplaces, our society, and in the individual worker. Each changes at different rates of speed and with different degrees of responsiveness. There is a serious "cultural lag" (as sociologist William Ogburn called it) between our work institutions, on the one hand, and our society and the individual worker, on the other.

For example, alienation, dissatisfaction, and decline in the work ethic are all reflections of increasing education (formal and informal) and rising expectations and aspirations among the workers. The employer is motivated to maintain an efficient, productive, and profitable workplace; and this requires rules, regulations, and routine technical jobs. Workers strive for freedom, autonomy, variety, challenge, and opportunities for self-development. Instead, jobs are too often simplified and overspecialized. Workers want a voice in decisions that directly affect their lives, but or-

These Japanese workers relieve some of their pent-up job frustrations by banging on a dummy that looks like their boss.

ganizations stress impersonality and lower needs (Final Report of the Forty-Third American Assembly, 1973:4). As Brigitte Berger put it:

> For many it is no longer sufficient to obtain work that is regularly remunerated, safe, and clearly limited in terms of hours. It is now expected additionally to be nonmanual, nonroutine, and nonmonotonous; interesting, creative, challenging, and capable of providing personal meaning and self-fulfillment (1976:28).

Value conflicts (reflected in new cultural trends) and rapid social change are all underlying causes behind worker alienation, dissatisfaction, and decline of the work ethic. But what about automation, the poor physical conditions of work, inequality, and unemployment? What are the fundamental causes of these problems?

Economic Structure and Organization

These problems are often caused by the very structure and organization of our economic and industrial institutions. Economic power, capital, and wealth are concentrated in the hands of increasingly larger corporations. This economic concentration was well documented earlier. It is no accident that General Motors has been a pioneer in automating its auto plants in the United States and abroad. It has the capital needed for expensive and sophisticated technology. Without this high degree of economic concentration, it is doubtful whether many firms could afford to spend billions on automated equipment and machines. Instead they might employ labor as long as it was profitable. In addition, federal financing of research and development for large corporations stimulates automation. According to facts uncovered by the Joint Economic Committee of the Congress, the federal government in the early 1970s had helped finance business through subsidies exceeding $63 billion (Rodgers, 1973:xii). The free-enterprise system is not as free as we may have been taught. Taxpayers contribute indirectly to help subsidize big business' new technology.

A last important cause of work problems is the corporations' desire (and necessity in a capitalistic system) for profit. It is cheaper for companies to have workers handle dangerous chemicals than to protect them from this threat to their lives. It is cheaper to tolerate a high noise level, even if it means eventual deafness for millions of industrial workers. It is cheaper to pay lower wages to women and to keep them in low-paying positions. It is cheaper to discriminate against blacks and chicanos, so that if and when they are hired they will be satisfied with low wages. It is cheaper to lay people off when business is slack (even if overtime is paid to the remaining employees). The basic cause of all this lies in the economic and industrial system based on private profit and capitalism rather than on social or human needs.

PROPOSED SOLUTIONS TO PROBLEMS OF CORPORATE POWER AND WORK

Radical Solutions

Radicals advocate a major change in our basic economy so that capitalism will eventually be replaced by socialism. Under such a system, the central government would control, plan, and operate the entire economy for the good of the masses instead of the elites. Power would be derived from workers and people. Goods would be produced to meet essential individual and social needs, instead of for profit and privilege. Frivolous goods and services would be abolished, and the basic needs of all would be met. All citizens would have an adequate, though not luxurious, standard of living, with food, clothing and shelter, and a steady job guaranteed by the government. Economic security would be assured, but at the price of some individual liberty and freedom.

Thomas Ford Hoult opts for Democratic Socialism, which preserves democracy within the concentrated corporate political system while carefully controlling the large corporations for the public good. He advocates that such socialism be restricted "only to those aspects of the economic order that are so pervasive that they have become the tail wagging the dog:

the automobile industry, chemistry, steel, pharmaceuticals, banking, petroleum, and the like.... If we don't make it such, then it will surely become a Stalinized system where a new elite, with the ultimate power given it by modern technology, will achieve near-permanent dominance" (1975: 560). Thus, some radicals see the need for a limited application of socialism only to the major sectors of our economy, rather than covering our entire economic and political system.

Some alternatives advocated by radicals (and some liberals) are buyer, service, and production-distribution cooperatives (co-ops). Some food co-ops have been started in neighborhoods of such cities as Philadelphia, Minneapolis, Ann Arbor, Washington, D.C., and Berkeley. City-wide coordination and alliances of co-ops are still experimental. Although service and production co-ops have had limited success, they serve as models for an alternative type of economic system (Beitz and Washburn, 1974: 288–92). This is particularly true in the growing and selling of food, which is at present controlled by large agribusiness farms and supermarket chains.

Liberal Proposals

Mintz and Cohen advocate strict federal control and regulation of large corporations. Among their liberal reform proposals are federal chartering of private corporations and establishment of government-owned businesses.

Federal, instead of state, chartering of corporations would limit the activities in which a business could engage. For example, GM could be sharply restricted as to the auto parts it could produce and the cars and trucks it could market. ITT would be restricted to the telecommunications equipment field; they would be required to abandon baking Wonder Bread and Hostess Cakes, owning Sheraton Hotels, leasing Avis cars, and making consumer loans through Aetna Finance Company. Federal charters would narrow and define a corporation's field of interest and eliminate conglomerate mergers (whereby a large corporation in one field of business buys a company in another).

Federal chartering of corporations would allow the government to regain its proper role as "quarterback of the economy," without massive new bureaucracy and unnecessary meddling. The government would do this by using its powers to grant, modify, implement, or revoke charters to achieve national social goals that would benefit all (1971: 439, 441).

Government-owned and -operated enterprises are needed to provide essential services to society and to compete effectively with private corporations. For example, G.I. Government Life Insurance offers veterans life-insurance coverage at premiums well below those that private industry can offer. It has met an essential need of millions at a very low price; yet it has not driven private insurance firms out of business.

The largest and most successful of the few government-owned corporations is the Tennessee Valley Authority (TVA). It has made low-cost power available to an entire region of the country and has enabled that region to be competitive with others for new industry. The TVA's costs and procedures are open for all to see and provide a yardstick for private corporations to imitate in pricing and in meeting people's needs. Mintz and Cohen wish to make large private corporations more competitive (in price) and more responsible (in meeting human needs) by having the federal government set up its own publicly owned and operated corporations.

If these two proposals are to succeed, safeguards must be set up to ensure that private corporations, with their enormous wealth and power, do not direct or influence the government's actions.

Other proposals offered by Mintz and Cohen for curbing the power of corporation giants are:

1. Enforce the antitrust laws so that industrial power can be controlled and decentralized. This calls for a strong government commitment to prosecute violators of the law. At hearings of the Senate Antitrust and Monopoly Subcommittee, economist John M. Blair testified that "deconcentration of a mere eight industries would reduce the share of the [highly concentrated] industrial economy . . . from one-third to one-sixth" (1971: 448).
2. Strengthen the functions of federal regulatory agencies, so they really control business instead of being controlled.
3. Establish an independent consumer agency, which would represent consumers before such federal regulatory agencies as the Federal Trade Commission, the Federal Communications Commission, and the Food and Drug Administration.

Combined with federal chartering and government-owned corporations, these proposals could effectively curb and control the power and wealth of private corporate elites.

Some liberals have advocated breaking up or divesting large corporations into smaller company units with new owners. Recently, legislation has been introduced to break up or divest major "integrated" oil corporations of their monopolistic control over every aspect of the oil market. It would prohibit producers of crude oil from owning refineries or transmission pipelines ("Proposals to Break Up . . .," May 1976: 131). Such "vertical divestiture" would stimulate the domestic development of oil, make the industry more competitive, and reduce consumer costs. At the same time, a bill has been proposed to prohibit "horizontal" ownership of other energy resources by oil firms. This proposal would forbid corporations who produce or refine oil or natural gas from "owning any interest in the coal, oil shale, uranium, nuclear reactor, geothermal steam [produced by natural hot springs under the ground] or solar energy business" ("Proposed 'Horizontal Divestiture' . . .," May 1976: 135). Because of a massive advertising campaign and the political power of major oil corporations, neither of these proposed bills has been passed by Congress.

Conservative and Liberal Proposals to Remedy Problems of Work

In addition to changing our economy and controlling corporate wealth and power, what can be done to alleviate the problems of work and technology? Here are some of the proposals liberals and conservatives recommend for overcoming these problems:

1. job enrichment and job enlargement, as well as work teams and job rotation
2. more flexible work schedules (i.e., flexitime or "gliding" working time)
3. worker codetermination (i.e., sharing in decision making)
4. profit sharing
5. creation of new "people work" jobs
6. encouragement and financing of work experiments by the federal government

The following discussion will look further at each of these proposals.

Job Enrichment and Enlargement. Job enrichment and enlargement has received the greatest publicity, and has been tried at a number of leading corporations in the United States and Europe. Companies such as Volvo, Saab, Chrysler, Texas Instruments, Maytag, General Foods, General Motors, General Electric, Sears, Avis, Corning Glass, Chase Manhattan Bank, and a few others have engaged in job-enrichment programs. Such schemes allow an employee to work on an entire project from beginning to end. Although it does not entirely eliminate division of labor, it lets the worker do a much larger share of the work. Some workers feel greater satisfaction, autonomy, and responsibility. Close supervision and inspection are often eliminated, and workers are given more of a voice in determining their pace of work.

Dr. Richard Walton, Professor of Business at Harvard, notes three tendencies of all job-enrichment programs: work teams, whole tasks, and flexible assignment patterns (1974: 151). Arthur Shostak gives three good examples of how job enrichment and enlargement works:

1. At a California mountaineering-sports equipment company, the seamstresses are now asked to sew their own labels into their work. Each employee is a minority stockholder and is paid at piecework rates (none average less than $10,000 per annum). So free and trusting is the atmosphere that in an industry in which quality rejections sometimes run to 50 percent, there are no inspectors.
2. A new, well-publicized General Foods plant operates without supervisors, a personnel manager, or a maintenance or quality-control department. Instead, self-governing teams of

workers take care of everything by themselves. What is more, the men are paid on the basis of the work they are doing at any one time. As a result, the young worker continues to have something to gain and somewhere to grow as he becomes older.

3. Donnelly Mirrors, which makes automobile mirrors, not only divides its workforce into teams with decision-making powers, but also shares productivity gains and guarantees that its workers will not be unemployed because of technological change (Shostak, 1974: 192).

In Europe, Britain's Imperial Chemical Industries program involves some 55,000 workers in 75 plants. In many cases, men plan their own work day and check the quality of their own work. Time clocks are abolished, and workers take tea and lunch breaks on their own schedules. Productivity and wages are both up.

At the Saab auto company in Sweden, the assembly line is being replaced with assembly teams. Groups of only three or four are responsible for an assembly process from start to finish. Each team makes its own decisions about who does what and when. However, after working four weeks at a Saab plant near Stockholm, five of six American auto workers

Team production of an entire engine or car, as in this Swedish auto plant, is used to overcome routine and repetitive job situations. Such job enlargement is favored by Swedish workers, but American auto workers have reservations about such an approach.

said they preferred Detroit's assembly lines. They said the new job-enrichment and team approach produced "a work situation demanding greater concentration and a faster pace" ("Swedish Style..." January 7, 1975: 23). At the end of the visit, sponsored by the Ford Foundation and Cornell University, all six American auto workers were impressed by "the cleanliness, lighting, safety precautions and general attractiveness of the Saab plant. They also found the noise level there considerably below that back home" (Ibid.).

Clearly, job enrichment and enlargement are not always successful or completely accepted by the workers or their unions. Some prefer the rhythm of routine work so that they do not have to concentrate and can think their own thoughts. Some unions see job enrichment as just another management gimmick to get more out of the workers and to undercut the union. Unions feel that the best way to enrich a job and the worker is to improve existing wages, hours, and working conditions (Winpisinger, 1973: 5). However, although job enrichment and enlargement is not perfect, it seems to be a step toward humanizing work.

More Flexible Work Schedules. Another proposal to ease alienation from work is to make work schedules more flexible. This may be extremely helpful and appealing to female workers. The basic idea behind "flexitime" is to have most workers present during traditional hours (usually 10 AM to 4 PM) but to leave the remaining hours, and days per week worked, up to the employee. American workers seem to prefer the four-day week (10 hours each day), whereas Europeans prefer the five-day week with individual hours. Although this proposal has been widely discussed, industry has done little to initiate the four-day week (Shaffer, 1973: 21–40).

Another ingenious idea for flexible working schedules is the "cubic day." Two persons share a job that is done seven days a week; each works exactly half the time, but they decide who works when. One could work mornings, the other afternoons; or they could alternate days, weeks, or other blocks of time.

Shared Decision Making. Each worker could be given more of a voice in decision making, whether by having a say on how he will do his routine job or by setting policy as a member of the board of directors. This latter proposal is called "codetermination" (*Mitbestimmung* in German), which has been practiced in some European industries for over 25 years. As of July 1, 1978, every West German company employing more than 2,000 persons will have a supervisory board (roughly equivalent to a board of directors) divided equally between representatives of workers and stockholders. Sweden has passed a similar law giving unions policy-making power. This idea has not yet gained acceptance in America. If it did, it might have positive results in solving some of our job-related social problems. It would bring democracy to the workplace in a fashion not envisioned by most union or management leaders. Ralph Nader's insistence

Swedish workers' councils seem to give employees a more direct voice in industry decisions. In America workers usually use unions to gain some veto power over management decisions.

that corporations become more socially responsible and more concerned about consumers might open the door to codetermination.

Since the 1950s the German coal and steel companies have had equal representation of labor and management on their boards. As one labor expert put it, "codetermination has not prevented Germany from becoming Europe's leading industrial power and the wealthiest nation in Europe" ("When Workers Help . . . ," May 10, 1976: 83). Eberhard Mueller, a German economist, points out some beneficial results:

> Employers and workers began to share in a common thought process. The workers realized, as they did not always before, that the economy is not a cow that can be foddered in heaven and milked on earth. . . . Both sides are coerced into making cooperative decisions, and, at the same time, both benefit from a gradual learning process (April 1973: 40).

The human-relations school, as well as most of the great motivation theorists of industry—Elton Mayo, Kurt Lewin, Abraham Maslow, Frederick Herzberg, Douglas MacGregor, and others—stress the value of worker participation in the decision-making process. Usually fear, insecurity, and traditional, bureaucratic managerial systems have prevented these ideas from being put into practice. If they were, many job-related social issues would disappear.

Profit Sharing. Profit-sharing plans are based on the assumption that economic incentives directly related to output and efficiency will alleviate much work-related discontent and disssatisfaction. The *Work in America* study, among others, seems to confirm that as salaries increase, workers become more pleased with their jobs. The Scanlon Plan and the Kaiser Steel and Sears & Roebuck profit-sharing plans have laid the groundwork for many other successful plans. Thousands of companies already have some form of profit-sharing plan, and thousands of additional firms have the ability to work out similar arrangements with their employees and unions. If workers have a solid economic stake in the firm, there is no telling how many work-related problems will be remedied.

"People Work" Jobs. Meaning and satisfaction in work is increasingly linked to the public sector—to meeting people's needs directly. According to sociologist Brigitte Berger's proposal, "people work" serves "the more subtle—but nonetheless real—interpersonal and psychological needs of individuals as well as groups" (1976: 29). It would create vast new services for special groups and purposes. People work would serve the young, the old, cities and rural areas. Jobs would be created dealing with intergroup conflict resolution, community development, and political education. They would go beyond in purpose and function what is done today by government agencies. These jobs would help to decrease the alienating impact of bureaucratic and technological structures.

Such a liberal proposal would require a change in national priorities and purposes, as well as federal funding, but it could be done. As Gerald Piel, in his book *Consumers of Abundance*, wrote many years ago (1961: 16):

> The liberation of people from tasks unworthy of human capacity should free that capacity for a host of activities now neglected in our civilization: teaching and learning, fundamental scientific investigation, the performing arts and the graphic arts, letters, the crafts, politics, and social service.
>
> Characteristically these activities involve the interaction of people with people rather than with things. They are admittedly not productive activities; nor are they profitable in the strict sense. But they are highly rewarding to the individuals involved and add greatly to the wealth of the nation (1961: 16).

Federal Funding for Making Work Satisfying. "People-work" jobs, as well as many other proposals, could get off the ground if the federal government gave them an initial financial boost. Since tax money subsidizes business anyway, it seems fitting that some of it should be used to improve the lot of those who spend much of their time working. This may be just the spark needed to ignite innovative work procedures, which would free workers to use their latent talents and abilities to benefit themselves, their firms, and society. Congress is considering a research- and technical-assistance bill, which would study worker alienation and test methods for making jobs more satisfying. It is a potentially fruitful plan, but more such steps are needed.

Effective Laws for Health, Employment, and Equality. Most of the solutions proposed for problems of job safety and health, unemployment, and inequality lie in more effective laws and enforcement. For example, history was made in 1970 when the first Federal Occupational Safety and Health Act was passed; however, more money is needed to help finance the administration (OSHA) that inspects businesses and sets work safety standards. The government wants to emphasize consulting services for business (especially small business). But labor fears that this will drain needed funds and help from enforcement and compliance efforts, especially against big business, which employs thousands of workers. Full White House support of OSHA efforts to enforce the law is still needed to ensure the health and safety of millions of workers (Oravec, May 22, 1976: 9).

Proposals for curbing unemployment center around a federal job guarantee for all citizens who need work. Starting with the Emergency Employment Act of 1971, laws have been passed to create new public-service jobs with federal funding. But up to 1976 only about 320,000 jobs had been created, and millions more are needed to put a dent into unemployment ("Jobs Plan . . .," 1976: 8). People must work, and if private corporations cannot supply the jobs, then government must become the employer of last resort. It would cost an estimated $4 billion to provide 550,000 government jobs. Yet if the unemployment rate were cut from over 7 percent to 4 percent, the government would get $17 billion in taxes from the new workers, and would pay out $2.5 billion less in unemployment compensation. Government and society would both benefit from the creation of new jobs ("How to Find Jobs for All," March 22, 1976: 64–65).

A similar proposal is to expand the present Youth Conservation Corps, begun in 1971. At the start of 1976, only 60,000 youths, ages 15 to 18, were employed by YCC, improving the environment; yet we know that many more young people need employment (Swift, 1975: 6). Arthur Burns, Chairman of the Federal Reserve Board, has suggested that young people be given jobs but that their wages be *below* the national minimum wage ($2.65 an hour in 1978). This, conservatives argue, would make employers more willing to hire them.

A conservative proposal is to give business more tax incentives. By, in effect, cutting the taxes of businessmen, investment and business expansion will be encouraged. Then businesses, in addition, can hire more workers.

To solve the problems of inequality, we need strong, enforceable legislation. Prejudices and discrimination, particularly against women and minorities, are so strong that only an equally strong law with penalties for violations will convince people to treat minorities fairly.

THE FUTURE OF OUR CORPORATE INSTITUTIONS AND WORK

428

Based upon the present concentration of power and wealth in large corporations, there is every reason to believe that the future will be one of massive concentration.

The Radical Perspective

From the radical perspective, the picture looks bleak. The future economy, because of a top-heavy concentration of power and wealth, will be maintained by constant government propping. Eventually, as has historically occurred in our capitalist system, a severe economic depression will shake the system, and it will have to change radically to survive. Further, short-term government programs or policies do not offer a viable alternative to basically restructuring the economy in the future (Dolbeare and Dolbeare, 1971: 199). Our future corporate institutions will be profitable only if based upon continued military spending, maintenance of an imperialistic overseas empire, and (as a last resort) war. Thus, we can expect new political and economic crises. As Marxist scholars Paul Baran and Paul Sweezy note in *Monopoly Capital*: "The Great Depression is not the Great Exception but is the normal outcome of the workings of the American economic system . . ." (1968: 24).

According to such analysis, as capitalism matures in the form of a greater concentration of corporate power and wealth, the system "tends toward stagnation, depression, and therefore, crises; military spending, imperialism, and war can counter this tendency, but ultimately produce crises of the same dimensions" (Dolbeare and Dolbeare, 1971: 200). Hence, the outlook for the continuation of our corporate institutions as we know them is doubtful.

Liberal and Conservative Perspectives

To liberals, such massive concentration will mean steady economic growth and greater affluence for most persons. This will be due to greater efficiency of scale, as smaller and less efficient firms are absorbed by larger and more efficient ones. Improvements in managerial techniques and know-how will ensure a prosperous future for elites and masses alike, they argue. The federal government will, when necessary, stabilize the economy or, in the public interest, help large firms to survive financially, as it did with Lockheed Aircraft.

Conservative sociologist Daniel Bell sees the emergence, in the next 30 to 50 years, of a postindustrial society in America, Western Europe, Japan, and Russia. Just as industrial society was a significant departure from an agricultural one, so is our emerging postindustrial society from industrialism. Bell believes that production technology will be displaced by knowledge as the basis of our economy and society. Human services will replace manufacturing of goods; information will replace energy; and the "codification" (structuring and analyzing) of theoretical knowledge will replace economic growth based on production of goods. As knowledge grows exponentially and becomes organized and specialized, we will have the equivalent of our past technological revolution. In such a society, knowledge will become power. Whereas the industrial structure separated property owners with wealth from nonowners without it (creating a class structure), the new postindustrial society will be built on differences in access to information or decision-making power. Such access will be derived from one's educational achievements and position in a bureaucratic hierarchy. Scientists, professionals, and managerial elites will rule the corporate structure and society. Although Bell admits that these changes "pose management problems for the political system that arbitrates the society," he does not envision any revolutionary change coming from conflicts between "power elites" and masses (1973: x).

Whatever future conflicts ensue, they will probably be between centralized planners and experts, on one hand, and local communities, on the other. The postindustrial society will also bring major changes in the nature of work and the composition of the workforce. We will now examine the likelihood of these changes.

The Future of Work and the Workforce

Just 80 years ago, 60 percent of all workers raised food on a farm. This was the major form of work. Today less than 5 percent of workers are employed directly raising food. Manufacturing, once the hallmark of our industrial society, has declined over the years, as we move into a postindustrial situation. In less than 50 years, we moved from a blue-collar to a white-collar workforce. A service economy will be the destiny of work in the future. Automatic machines, even robots, will take over much of the dull and routine work, although men and women will still perform such tasks. There are two conflicting views of the future in respect to work, one optimistic, the other pessimistic.

Predictions of the future of specific occupations are quite unreliable because of the rapid rate at which our society changes and the unpredictable character of society's response to technological change. Despite these limitations the Bureau of Labor Statistics makes short-term predictions of general occupational categories. Based on persons presently in the workforce, it has projected changes for 1980 and 1985 (as compared with 1970), as shown in Table 10-3 on page 430.

According to the optimists, the greatest increases in future demand will take place in the higher-status occupations. Between now and 1985, workers will be available for higher-status jobs (mostly white-collar), but "we can expect substantial reductions in the proportion of workers who will be available for the lower-level" jobs (Wool, 1976: 27). This shortage stems from the slow-down in the birthrate during the 1960s and 1970s and the increase in the percentage of young people attending college. Hence,

table 10-3   PROJECTIONS OF EXPERIENCED CIVILIAN LABOR FORCE

Occupational-Status Groups		Number (millions)			Percentage Distribution			Percentage of change		
		1970	1980	1985	1970	1980	1985	1970-85	1970-80	1980-85
	Total:	75.1	91.5	97.5	100%	100%	100%	29.8%	21.8%	6.6%
GROUP 1	Professional and Technical	10.6	15.1	17.6	14.2	16.5	18.1	65.8	41.4	17.2
GROUP 2	Other White Collar, except low-level jobs; includes police, firefighters, and "protective-service" workers	24.8	32.0	34.8	33.0	35.0	35.7	40.1	28.9	8.7
GROUP 3	Skilled crafts and skilled services. High wage operatives in basic industries and foremen	15.9	18.4	19.2	21.1	20.1	19.7	21.1	16.2	4.2
GROUP 4	Operatives and low-level clerical and medium service jobs, except laundry workers and those in Group 3	15.6	17.3	17.4	20.9	18.9	17.9	11.9	11.2	0.2
GROUP 5	Laborers, low service jobs, and laundry and dry-cleaning operatives	8.2	8.7	8.5	10.9	9.5	8.7	2.9	5.9	−2.8

Source: U.S. Dept. of Labor, **Monthly Labor Review** (March 1976): 27.

the 1980s will see a sharp drop in the number and proportion of youth in the labor force, according to this projection.

The National Planning Association and the *Occupational Outlook Handbook* envision about 105 million employees will have jobs in 1985. Of these only about one-third of new job openings will be the result of economic growth or the creation of new jobs. Most future job openings will result from the need to replace workers who retire or die. However, according to this pessimistic view, to keep pace with population and automation and to check unemployment, we must create 72,000 new jobs *each week* between 1976 and 1985 ("Challenge to U.S. . . .," June 28, 1976: 20). This will be extremely difficult unless our economy begins to grow again. We will need them at a faster rate than between 1965 and 1975. During that period, "the economy created only an average of 35,770 jobs a week. New jobs between now and 1985, therefore, will need to be

The modern, automated factory often isolates workers from one another. But physical conditions of work in such plants are often ideal, and many dull and routine tasks are done by machine.

generated at twice the pace of the past decade" (Ibid.).

The fastest-growing geographical areas for jobs will be the Southeast and Southwest, especially Colorado and Arizona. By 1985, the Southwest will lead all other regions by adding nearly five millions jobs. The Far West, the traditional leader, will add over four million. In the East, job growth will be greatest in Florida and Maryland.

Jobs with the fastest growth rate will be in government-sponsored health and human services. They will grow with the prospect for a program of national health insurance. Projections remain high for occupations in electronic computers (repair and service), industrial equipment, air conditioning, refrigeration and heating, and transportation equipment (Buchen, 1974: 183).

Assuming the growth of education, affluence, leisure time, and government subsidies of people and business, the optimists maintain the future will present broader choices and open new alternatives to working. Individuals will be freed to pursue jobs and leisure activities of their own choosing. Perhaps the quality and meaning of work will thereby increase. These future trends are already becoming evident. As Levitan and Johnston wrote, "The trend, which is only emerging as a trickle now, is likely to swell as time goes on" (1973: 160).

Changes in social values will alter the nature of work. Values and organizational goals will stress "autonomy, diversity and acceptance." Achievement, though still important, will no longer be our central aim. The worlds of work and nonwork will come closer together, and eventually merge. People's search for self-actualization will find an easier and more open expression in work (Dunnette, 1973: 91).

Job opportunities for women, blacks, and youth should continue to improve if we make a firm commitment to equal employment. A study on future occupational needs points out that "the increase in occupational aspirations of minority groups, of women and, more generally, of all youth coming from lower-income or disadvantaged backgrounds—have acquired sufficient momentum that they can and should be considered as irreversible forces in our society" (Wool, 1976: 8). Whether society in the future will recognize those aspirations is debatable and problematic.

Marvin Dunnette and others (1973: 91–94) optimistically have suggested where and why future jobs will be created. They believe the following new careers and areas will (or should) be developed:

Technology. Technology has inaugurated a new resource-conservation industry. Preserving wildlife, protecting green space, recycling metal, paper, wastes and water, and controlling air and noise pollution will provide new jobs. Other inventions, some not even on the drawing board yet, will create millions of new jobs.

Education. Only 50 percent of American high schools provide professional counseling and vocational guidance to students. The need for counselors, professional and paraprofessional, will grow in the future.

Unemployment and Underemployment. Perhaps the only dark shadows over the future of work as underemployment and unemployment. Industry, government, and unions must take more deliberate steps to alleviate and prevent massive unemployment. As the boxed material by James O'Toole suggests, not just unemployment but underemployment may be a serious social problem in the future.

Rural Areas. They will need more outreach or "extension" workers, who must understand concepts of administration, agriculture, and marketing. Experts will be needed in technical and leadership training. For example, coordinating various systems of transportation for a rural area could be a full-time job.

Recreation. As more leisure time emerges, many new jobs will occur in recreation. Total employment in management of recreation is expected to reach nearly a million-and-a-half by 1980. Jobs in the forest and park services should expand as more people visit these areas. Already there is a great demand for recreation workers in many different capacities. More will be needed in the future to organize and supervise individual and group activities. People will be needed to staff physical, social, and cultural programs in homes for the aged, hospitals, community centers, playlots, and even in industry where recreational activities are provided.

Community Services. There is a great unmet need for community services in America. These include jobs in law enforcement, day-care centers, employment services, family counseling, and others. As more women enter the workforce, jobs will open up for professional and paraprofessional child care. Some feel the challenging teaching jobs of the future will be in day-care centers, not in the schools.

Health Care. Medical and health-care educators and aides, as well as doctors and nurses, will be in greater demand. Health care should be our leading growth industry in the 1980s, especially as we adopt a national system for funding such care. Paraprofessionals and college graduates will be needed to teach outpatients how to use medication and to recognize symptoms of common diseases; to do follow-up surveys and studies on former patients; to provide and coordinate transportation to and from medical facilities; and to hear patients' complaints and reassure them. Hospitals will need more people to interview and welcome incoming patients and to give them more attention than they now receive. College graduates educated in social gerontology and medical sociology will be in greater demand.

Conservation and Pollution Control. Our natural environment will require even greater attention. Rivers, lakes, air, and workplaces are all

---

UNDEREMPLOYMENT: A PRESENT AND FUTURE SOCIAL PROBLEM
James O'Toole

A portentous social pattern is beginning to emerge in many industrialized nations. In socialist and capitalist economies alike, increasing numbers of highly qualified workers are unable to find jobs that require their skills and training. Thus, a large and growing number of individuals are forced to take jobs that can be performed just as adequately by workers who have far lower levels of education....

And the effect trickles down the occupational scale.... Finally and predictably this process of job displacement reaches its full force at the bottom of the occupational ladder where poorly educated workers are often knocked off the last rung. Where Marx had forecast that mass unemployment would become the salient characteristic of labor markets in advanced economies, it is now clear that underemployment—working at less than one's full productive capacity—is more accurately the hallmark of work in industrial societies....

There is ... a growing refusal of the 80 percent of the population (the "masses" who have bad jobs) to accept the right of the elite to its special privileges.... Social observers ... have all seen signs of potential conflict between those who have bad jobs and those who have good jobs.

Source: James O'Toole, "The Reserve Army of the Underemployed," *Change* 7, 4 (May 1975): 26.

polluted. Thousands of workers will be needed for tasks of pollution control, waste treatment, and forestry. Testers, inspectors, environmental educators, researchers, and sanitation and health workers will all be needed to help clean up the environment.

Planning. Planners for cities, towns, and regions will be needed. Planners in industry who can envision markets, values, and consumer needs will also be in great demand. In fact, planning at all levels is truly the wave of the future; and many new careers and jobs will be riding the crest of that wave.

Most of these new jobs will call for imagination, initiative, and ingenuity and will be less routine and alienating. Rather than merely produce things, the new jobs will be more concerned with people's environment, health, safety, and needs.

Urban and Rural Development. Over eight million substandard housing units exist today, and must be replaced or rehabilitated at prices people can afford. This need will provide jobs and income for the unemployed and serve as a training ground for skilled trades. Maintaining homes for the 22 million elderly will be the source of new jobs in the future.

SUMMARY

We have examined the economic concentration of wealth and power by large corporations from the perspective of radicals, liberals, and conservatives. We have also explored the meaning and significance of work in the lives of people. We particularly noted C. Wright Mills's ideas about the power elite and the concentration of power in our society. We have discussed many problems involving the links of power among business, the military, and the government, as well as problems at the workplace. These include:

> the routine and specialized nature of work, leading to alienation, dissatisfaction, and decline of the work ethic
> automation and technological change
> unfavorable physical conditions of work; dangers from chemicals, asbestos, noise, and unsafe work environment
> inequality in jobs and in pay for women and minority-group members
> unemployment and underemployment

We explored the degree and extent to which business concentration permeated and influenced the operation of government and the military, and how government spending is used to benefit large corporate enterprises. We suggested several causes underlying problems of work and the power of corporations, including:

> value conflicts between our culture and the techno-economic system of work, especially between individual freedom and organizational efficiency; also, changes in cultural attitudes toward success, security, sex roles, social rights, and efficiency
>
> a serious cultural lag between changes in workers' expectations and traditional work institutions
>
> the structure, organization, and profit motive of our economy and industry, especially the concentration of capital and wealth in the hands of large corporations

We reviewed several proposals for changing our economic system and for solving problems of work. These include:

> a system of socialism to ensure everyone an adequate standard of living and a job
>
> buyer, service, and production co-ops
>
> federal chartering of corporations and establishment of government-owned businesses, as advocated by liberals Mintz and Cohen
>
> enforcing antitrust laws, strengthening federal regulatory agencies, and establishing a consumer agency
>
> breaking up or divesting large corporations, such as oil firms, so they could not control the market

Liberal and conservative proposals for ameliorating problems of work include job enrichment and enlargement, flexible work hours, worker participation in decision making, profit sharing, creating of new "people work" jobs, and federal support for new jobs and work-satisfaction experiments. To questions of job safety and health, inequality, and unemployment, we proposed properly financed and enforced laws, government-funded jobs for all, and tax incentives for business.

The future will hold greater choice, autonomy, and diversity in jobs, as well as perhaps greater job opportunities for women and minorities (as we move from blue-collar work to more white-collar and service jobs). Job demand will increase for higher-status jobs (mostly white-collar), while a possible shortage of those willing to take lower-status jobs might develop because of a decline in the youth population, starting in the 1980s. New jobs can be expected in technology, education, urban and rural development, recreation, community services, health care, conservation and pollution control, and planning. Unemployment and underemployment, however, is a work problem that *may* persist, for we must soon find a way to provide twice as many new jobs per week as were needed only a few years ago.

CAREER OPPORTUNITIES

Management Trainees.

The best opportunity for a starting position in industry is usually as a management trainee. A firm trains the college graduate in its policies, procedures, and operations. Usually a trainee will rotate through a number of staff positions before being placed in a fixed position, based upon the corporation's needs and the graduate's interests and abilities. Such openings are usually available on a competitive basis in retailing, insurance, banking, and large manufacturing firms. A variety of academic backgrounds are considered, although some concentrations in accounting, business administration, economics, and social sciences improve one's chances. For further information write to: American Management Association, 135 West 50th Street, New York, New York 10020.

Marketing Researchers.

Researchers analyze data on products and sales, make surveys, and conduct interviews. They prepare sales forecasts and make recommendations on product design and advertising. College courses valuable as preparation for such jobs include research methods and statistics, psychology, sociology, economics, and English composition. Knowledge of computers is helpful, since sales forecasting and distribution data are generated from computers. For further information write to: American Marketing Association, 230 North Michigan Avenue, Chicago, Illinois 60601.

Personnel and Labor-Relations Specialists.

They assist management in making better use of employees' skills, and help employees find greater satisfaction in their jobs and working conditions. A sociologist's understanding of complex organizations and social relations in dealing with people is essential to the job. The larger the firm the more specialized the function handled—safety, testing, fringe-benefit review, and so on. For a starting position, the small firm provides the best opportunity in handling almost all aspects of personnel. Opportunities in federal, state, and county government should not be overlooked. A variety of college courses and majors, including the social sciences, are useful. For further information write to: The Public Personnel Association, 1313 East 60th Street, Chicago, Illinois 60637.

REFERENCES

Baran, Paul and Paul M. Sweezy
    1968 Monopoly Capital. New York: Modern Reader Paperbacks.
Beitz, Charles and Michael Washburn
    1974 Creating the Future: A Guide to Living and Working for Social Change. New York: Bantam Books.

Bell, Daniel
    1974   The Coming of Post-Industrial Society. New York: Basic Books.
    1976   The Cultural Contradictions of Capitalism. New York: Basic Books.

Berger, Briggitte
    1976   "The Coming Age of People Work." Change 8, 4 (May): 24–30.

Bishop, Jerry E.
    1976   "AFL-CIO Aide Charges Delay in Reports on Exposure to Cancer-Causing Agents." Wall Street Journal (March 30): 6.

Braude, Lee
    1975   Work and Workers: A Sociological Analysis. New York: Praeger.

Brodeur, Paul
    1974   Expendable Americans. New York: Viking.

Buchen, Irvin
    1974   "The Job Market, 1975–85." Intellect 103, 2361 (December): 183.

Burnham, David
    1976   "Rise in Birth Defects Laid to Job Hazards." New York Times (March 14): 42.

Campbell, Angus C. and Philip E. Converse, eds.
    1972   The Human Meaning of Social Change. New York: Russell Sage Foundation.

Cassidy, Joseph
    1973   "Research Firm Finds . . . 8 Americans in 10 Are Unhappy and Frustrated in Their Jobs." National Enquirer (August 19): 7.

"Challenge to U.S.: 72,000 New Jobs Needed Every Week." U.S. News & World Report 80 (June 28) 20–22, 1976.

Comer, James P.
    1975   "The Hidden Costs of Unemployment." New York Times (June 9): 31.

Deans, Ralph C.
    1973   "Productivity and the New Work Ethic." Pp. 3–20 in Hoyt Gimlin, ed. American Work Ethic. Washington, D.C.: Congressional Quarterly.

Dembart, Lee
    1976   "Health Problems Traced to Jobs." New York Times (March 17): 23.

Dolbeare, Kenneth M. and Patricia Dolbeare
    1971   American Ideologies. Chicago: Markham.

Domhoff, G. William
    1971   The Higher Circles. New York: Random House.

Dulles, Foster Rhea
    1960   Labor in America. 2nd rev. ed. New York: Crowell.

Dunnette, Marvin D.
    1973   Work and Nonwork in the Year 2001. Monterey, Calif.: Brooks / Cole.

Economic Policy Committee, AFL-CIO
    1976   "The Continuing Recession." American Federationist 83, 3 (March): 14–19.

"Economic Storm Clouds." New York Times (December 23): 24, 1975.

"Environment Blamed for 60% of Cancer." Philadelphia Evening Bulletin (February 27): 7, 1976.

Faulkner, Harold U.
 1954 American Economic History. 7th ed. New York: Harper & Brothers.

Fernandez, Ronald
 1975 The Promise of Sociology. New York: Praeger.

Final Report of the Forty-Third American Assembly
 1973 The Changing World of Work. Harriman, N.Y.: The American Assembly.

Florman, Samuel
 1976 "The Job Enrichment Mistake." Harper's 252, 1512 (May): 18–25.

Freitag, Peter
 1975 "The Cabinet and Big Business: A Study of Interlocks." Social Problems 23, 2 (December): 137–52.

Friedman, Saul
 1975 "Troubles Multiply for the Jobless: Report from Flint, Mich." Philadelphia Inquirer (September 11): 16-D.

Galbraith, John Kenneth
 1971 The New Industrial State. 2nd ed. New York: New American Library.

Garfinkel, Irwin and Robert Plotnick
 1975 "Poverty, Unemployment, and the Current Recession." Public Welfare 33, 3 (Summer): 10–17.

Gimlin, Hoyt, ed.
 1973 American Work Ethic. Washington, D.C.: Congressional Quarterly.

Gooding, Judson
 1970 "Blue-Collar Blues on the Assembly Line." Fortune 82, 1 (July): 69–71; 116–17.

"Hearing Airs Alleged Mine Safety Violations." Allentown Morning Call (March 25): 18, 1976.

Hoult, Thomas Ford, ed.
 1975 Social Justice and Its Enemies. New York: Wiley.

"How to Find Jobs for All — Big Debate of the '70s." U.S. News & World Report 80, 12 (March 22): 63–65, 1976.

"Jobless Rate Remains at 7.5 Percent after Declining for Five Months." Allentown Morning Call (May 8): 3, 1976.

"Job Satisfaction: Is there a Trend?" Manpower Research Monograph No. 30, U.S. Department of Labor. Manpower Administration. Washington, D.C.: U.S. Government Printing Office, 1974.

"Jobs Plan Extension Approved by Panel." Allentown Morning Call (May 7): 8, 1976.

Kahn, Robert L.
 1972 "The Meaning of Work." P. 182 in Angus C. Campbell and Philip E. Converse, eds. The Human Meaning of Social Change. New York: Russell Sage Foundation.

Klein, Deborah P.
 1975 "Women in the Labor Force: The Middle Years." Monthly Labor Review 98, 11 (November): 10–16.

Kranzberg, Melvin and Joseph Gies
 1975 By the Sweat of Thy Brow: Work in the Western World. New York: Putnam.

Kutscher, Ronald
    1976 "Revised BLS Projections to 1980 and 1985: An Overview." Monthly Labor Review 99, 3 (March): 3–8.

"Labor's Outreach Efforts Swell Apprenticeships for Minorities." AFL-CIO News 20, 24 (June 14): 5, 1975.

Lasson, Kenneth
    1971 The Workers: Portraits of Nine American Jobholders. New York: Grossman.

"'Last Hired, First Fired' Decision Is Sent Back for Reconsideration." Allentown Morning Call (May 25): 3, 1976.

LeMasters, E. E.
    1975 Blue Collar Aristocrats: Life-Styles at a Working Class Tavern. Madison: University of Wisconsin Press.

Levison, Andrew
    1975 "The Rebellion of Blue Collar Youth." In Peter Wickman, ed. Annual Editions: Readings in Social Problems 75/76. Guilford, Conn.: Dushkin.

Levitan, Sar and William B. Johnston
    1973 Work Is Here to Stay, Alas. Salt Lake City, Utah: Olympus.

Lyons, Richard
    1976 "House Counts Its Assets and Totes Up 22 Millionaires." Allentown Sunday Call-Chronicle (January 4):A-10.

McCord, William and Arline McCord
    1977 American Social Problems. St. Louis: Mosby.

McNall, Scott
    1975 Social Problems Today. Boston: Little, Brown.

McVeigh, Frank J.
    1962 "The Good Old Days." Voice of the Cement, Lime & Gypsum Workers International 25, 10 (October): 29–31.

Mills, C. Wright
    1956 The Power Elite. New York: Oxford University Press.
    1958 "The Structure of Power in American Society." The British Journal of Sociology 9, 1 (March): 23–38.
    1951 White Collar: The American Middle Classes. Fairtown, N.J.: Oxford University Press.

Mintz, Morton and Jerry S. Cohen
    1971 America, Inc. Who Owns and Operates the United States. New York: Dell.

"More Risk Cited in Asbestos." Philadelphia Evening Bulletin (February 27): 4, 1976.

Mueller, Eberhard
    1973 "Humanizing Industrial Society." Worldview (April): 40.

"Multinational Corporations in World Development: Summary." New York: United Nations, 1973.

Oravec, John
    1976 "OSHA Seeks Improved Showing under First Professional Chief." AFL-CIO News 21, 21 (May 22): 9.

Parker, Stanley
    1971 The Future of Work and Leisure. New York: Praeger.

Parrish, John
1975 "Women in Professional Training—An Update." Monthly Labor Review 98, 11 (November): 49-51.

Perrucci, Robert and Marc Pilisuk
1971 The Triple Revolution: Emerging Social Problems in Depth. Boston: Little, Brown.

Piel, Gerald
1961 Consumers of Abundance. New York: Fund for the Republic.

Porter, Sylvia
1976 "Flexible Work Schedules Spreading." Allentown Morning Call (June 4): 26.

Press Associates, Inc.
1976 "Washington Window." AFL-CIO News 21, 10 (March 6): 5.

"Proposals to Break Up Major U.S. Oil Companies." Congressional Digest 55, 5 (May): 131, 1976.

"Proposed 'Horizontal Divestiture' Legislation Pending in Congress." Congressional Digest 55, 5 (May): 135, 1976.

Quinn, Robert P. and Martha S. Baldi de Mandilovitch
1977 Education and Job Satisfaction: A Questionable Payoff. National Institute of Education, U.S. Department of Health, Education and Welfare. Washington, D.C.: U.S. Government Printing Office.

Reinkin, Tom, ed.
1975 "Students Discontented with Business." Gallup Opinion Index, No. 123 (September): 12-24.

Rodgers, William H.
1973 Corporate Country: A State Shaped to Suit Technology. Emmaus, Penn.: Rodale.

Rosow, Jerome M., ed.
1974 The Worker and the Job: Coping with Change. Englewood Cliffs, N.J.: Prentice-Hall.

Rothschild, Emma
1976 "Auto Production—Lordstown." Pp. 329-41 in Jerome Skolnick and Elliott Currie, eds. Crisis in American Institutions. 3rd ed. Boston: Little, Brown.

"Ruling Gives Black Job Bias Victims Special Seniority." Allentown Morning Call (March 25): 10, 1976.

Rutledge, Philip J.
1975 "The Recession and Urban Population." Public Welfare 33, 3 (Summer): 18-25.

Scarpitti, Frank
1977 Social Problems. 2nd ed. New York: Holt, Rinehart and Winston.

"Seniority Squeezes Out Minorities in Layoffs." Business Week (May 5): 66, 1975.

"Severe Joblessness Persists in Nation." AFL-CIO News 12, 19 (May 8): 1, 1976.

Shaffer, Helen B.
1973 "Four Day Week." In Hoyt Gimlin, ed. American Work Ethic. Washington, D.C.: Congressional Quarterly.

Shearer, Lloyd
- 1976 "Facts and Figures: Intelligence Report." Parade Magazine (January 4): 7.
- 1976 "The Next 20 Years: Intelligence Report." Parade Magazine (February 15): 5.

Shenker, Israel
- 1973 "College Head's Sabbatical: 2 Months at Menial Jobs." New York Times (June 10): 1, 29.

Sheppard, Harold and Neal Q. Herrick
- 1972 Where Have All the Robots Gone: Worker Dissatisfaction in the 70's. New York: Free Press.

Shevis, James
- 1976 "10.5% 'Real' Jobless Rate Refutes Recovery Claims." AFL-CIO News 21, 11 (March 13): 1–2.

Shiskin, Julius
- 1976 "Employment and Unemployment: The Doughnut or the Hole?" Monthly Labor Review 99, 2 (February): 3–10.

Shostak, Arthur
- 1969 Blue-Collar Life. New York: Random House.
- 1974 Modern Social Reforms: Solving Today's Social Problems. New York: Macmillan.

Slocum, Walter L.
- 1974 Occupational Careers: A Sociological Perspective. 2nd ed. Chicago: Aldine.

Sullivan, Brian
- 1976 "Science Finds Technical Advances Often Bring Concealed Hazards." Allentown Sunday Call-Chronicle (January 25): D-8.

"Survey Shows 19% Gain for Corporate Earnings." AFL-CIO News 22, 6 (February 12): 1, 7, 1977.

"Swedish Style of Building Cars Doesn't Sway American Group." Allentown Morning Call (January 7): 23, 1975.

Swift, Pamela
- 1975 "Keeping Up ... with Youth: Conservation Employment." Parade Magazine (December 28): 6.
- 1976 "Keeping Up with Youth: Youth and Unemployment." Parade Magazine (April 11): 15.

Terkel, Studs
- 1974 Working: People Talk about What They Do All Day and How They Feel about What They Do. New York: Pantheon.

Tilgher, Adriano
- 1965 Homo Faber: Work through the Ages. Chicago: Regnery.

"Toward a Military Welfare State." Saturday Review (October): 26, 1973.

Turner, Jonathan
- 1972 American Society: Problems of Structure. New York: Harper & Row.

"U.N. Department of Economic and Social Affairs Reports on Multinational Corporations." The Delegates World Bulletin 3, 14 (August 20): 757, 759, 1973.

U.S. Department of Labor
  1974 "Job Satisfaction: Is There a Trend?" Monograph No. 30, Manpower Administration. Washington, D.C.: U.S. Government Printing Office.
  1976 "Employed Persons by Occupational Group, Sex and Age." Employment and Earnings 22, 10 (April): 32–33, 58.

Wallick, Franklin
  1972 The American Worker: An Endangered Species. New York: Ballantine.

Walton, Richard E.
  1972 "How to Counter Alienation in the Plant." Harvard Business Review 50, 6 (November/December): 70–81.
  1974 "Innovative Restructuring of Work." Pp. 145–76 in Jerome M. Rosow, ed. The Worker and the Job: Coping with Change. Englewood Cliffs, N.J.: Prentice-Hall.

Weaver, Paul
  1976 "Noise Regulation Strikes a Sour Note." Fortune 93, 3 (March): 159–66.

"When Workers Help Call the Tune in Management." U.S. News & World Report 80, 19 (May 10): 83–85, 1976.

Williamson, John B., Jerry F. Boren, and Linda Evans, eds.
  1974 Social Problems: The Contemporary Debates. Boston: Little, Brown.

Winpisinger, William W.
  1973 "Wage, Benefit Improvements Still Best Way to Enrich Jobs." AFL-CIO News (January 13): 5.

Wool, Harold
  1976 "Future Labor Supply for Lower Level Occupations." Monthly Labor Review 99, 3 (March): 22–31.

Work in America. Cambridge, Mass.: MIT Press, 1973.

Yankelovich, Daniel
  1974 "The Meaning of Work." Pp. 19–48 in Jerome M. Rosow, ed. The Worker and the Job: Coping with Change. Englewood Cliffs, N.J.: Prentice-Hall.

Zietz, Dorothy
  1969 Child Welfare: Services and Perspectives. 2nd ed. New York: Wiley.

SUGGESTED READINGS

Ashford, Nicholas A. Crisis in the Workplace: Occupational Disease and Injury: A Report to the Ford Foundation. Cambridge; MIT Press. 1976.

  A detailed report on the legal, political, social, and technical problems in occupational health and safety. A new look at an old environmental problem.

Cornuelle, Richard. De-Managing America: The Final Revolution. New York: Vintage. 1976.

  Looks at the revolution in values that rejects bureaucratic management as unworkable. It is conservative in tone but points up the limits of the social sciences and centralization for solving our social ills.

Horowitz, Irving, John Leggett, and Martin Oppenheimer, eds. American Working Class in the 1970s. New Brunswick, N.J.: Transaction Books. 1977.

A good summary of contemporary social problems surrounding the life, work, and work-a-day world of blue-collar America.

Nader, Ralph, Mark Green, and Joel Seligman. Taming the Giant Corporation. New York: Norton. 1976.

Details the excesses of large corporations, the power they wield, and how that power can be controlled by "federal chartering."

Solomon, Lewis D. Humanizing the Corporation: An Experiment in Social Planning. New Brunswick, N.J.: Transaction Books. 1976.

Using an interdisciplinary approach, the author examines various alternatives for making the corporation more humane. An authoritarian and bureaucratic work environment is rejected as harmful to both organizations and employees.

Periodicals Worth Exploring

Academy of Management Journal
Academy of Management Review
Administrative Science Quarterly
Business and Society
Challenge
Dissent
Fortune
Harvard Business Review
Journal of Business
Journal of Consumer Affairs
Journal of Economic Issues
Monthly Labor Review
Quarterly Review of Economics & Business
Sociology of Work and Occupations

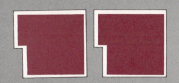

Problems of the Medical and Health-Care Institutions

DEFINITIONS OF THE PROBLEM
Medical care: a social right or a privilege?
"Idealized model" of medical care v. the "reality model":
a) Medical care from solo-practice private doctors, paid for by fee.
b) A structured, interrelated system dominated by three large social institutions (medical empires, the financing-planning complex, the medical-industrial complex).

Conservative government officials and doctors:
a) Lifestyle
b) Little connection between medical care and longevity.

The consumers' definitions of the problems:
a) Lack of access to and maldistribution of doctors.
b) Excessive costs.
c) Dissatisfaction with the competence and quality of health care, especially among minorities and poor.

INCIDENCE AND PREVALENCE OF THE PROBLEM
Lack of doctors in "primary care."
Shortage in rural areas.
The $118-billion health industry, employing over 4 million persons:
a) Over 10 years a 102 percent increase in cost of health care.
b) Average hospital stay cost over $1,000 in 1975.
c) Rising cost of malpractice insurance.

Competence and quality of care criticized:
a) Cornell University study (2.5 million unneeded operations).
b) University of Florida and Ohio State Univ. medical schools report on unneeded antibiotics.
c) Federation of State Medical Boards — 16,000 doctors "unworthy of licenses" but only 66 revoked.
d) Other studies on quality of health care.
e) Health care of poor and racial minorities.

CAUSES OF THE PROBLEM

Norms and values demanding more and better care; many social problems are now "medicalized."

Structure and organization:
a) Large institutions with concentrated power, prestige, and wealth.
b) Profit and power often pursued at expense of patients and consumers.
c) Medical schools more research-oriented than improving delivery of health care.

Financial fraud and waste cheating the public.

PROPOSED SOLUTIONS TO THE PROBLEM

National health insurance.
Health-maintenance organizations.
Consumer-control and radical restructure of system.
Reforms of medical schools and redistribution of new doctors.
Use of paraprofessionals and medical "extenders."
Medicaid-Medicare reforms.
Regional planning of health care.

FUTURE OF THE PROBLEM

More technology: computer information analysis; transportation.
Right to health with social controls on individuals.
More regulation; expansion of health industry.
A five-year plan for health.
Government unable to control power and wealth of medical system.

SUMMARY

> The medical establishment has become a major threat to health.
>
> Ivan Illich, "Medical Nemesis," *Time,* June 28, 1976:66.

Robert Deindorfer, a New York writer, visited London one summer with his family. His four-year-old son became seriously ill and spent three days in a hospital. He had numerous tests and intravenous feeding. He was in a private room, and his mother and father were given a room to be near him. The hospital bill at the end was $7.80—for the parents' meals.

This was not a unique experience for Americans who visit England. Many have discovered, to their amazement, that in emergencies they can receive free medical care under the National Health System, even though they have no choice of a doctor.

The experience of Englishmen taken ill while visiting the United States is not exactly the same. Reginald Forrester, a British businessman visiting New York, became ill and was rushed to a nearby hospital in desperate condition. The hospital would not admit him until it obtained a guarantee that his hospital bills would be paid. Mr. Forrester died 16 days later, and Mrs. Forrester was given a bill for $12,000 (Blumenthal and Fallows, 1976:202).

This story illustrates what most of us know—our health-care delivery system is "sicker" than the people it is supposed to serve. Although we as a society spend more money for health care than any other nation, we have a crisis in providing health care. The symptoms are clear. We stand fifteenth in the world in our infant-death rate. Even our life-expectancy rates are lower than those of most European countries. Doctors are not available to millions of persons especially at night, on weekends, or in their homes. Hospitals and medical care are not accessible to all equally, especially in inner-city slums and in rural areas. Costs are astronomical and are still increasing. People are dissatisfied with the impersonal, incompetent, bureaucratic treatment they often receive when sick.

DEFINING THE HEALTH-CARE PROBLEM

Most of us know that something is wrong with our medical-care system. Some experts have called it a health crisis, for lives are at stake. Providers and consumers each have their own conception of the problem. Most people feel that good medical care should be everyone's right. The right to life assumes the availability of medical care for all.

But others—sometimes doctors, and particularly the American Medical Association—have traditionally defined medical care as a privilege, not a right. It is a privilege that people must purchase from a "private" physician. Such a view of medical care protects the freedom of independent professionals and elite and ensures a private doctor-patient relationship.

To some scholars, this interpretation of health care is the root cause of the crisis.

> Even when we have taken steps to improve medical care for the poor, as under Medicaid, or for the self-supporting, as under voluntary health insurance plans, we have used a systematized flow of money simply to purchase the services of physicians or hospitals in the open market. We have not organized the provision or "delivery" of health services in the way that other services deemed essential to society have been organized, such as education or protection against "fire" (Roemer, 1971:31).

On the other hand, those who define medical care as a right consider medicine as a social good, not a private commodity. According to Daniel Bell, social goods are not "divisible" into individual items of possession (such as one's private doctor), but are a community service. For example, schools, police and fire protection, parks, highways, and waterways are all social goods. They benefit everyone, not only those who can afford to pay for them. They are subject to community and societal control, not the wishes of the professionals or organizations supplying the service.

Another interpretation of modern health care centers around an "idealized model" of medicine and doctors, in contrast to a "reality model." In defining health care, those who use the idealized model (a nostalgic caricature of medicine) provide a standard diagnosis of the crisis and what must be done about it. Those who employ the reality model of the system (or nonsystem) end up with a Millsian diagnosis of the problem and its solution. Let us examine these two conflicting definitions.

The Idealized Model of Health Care

The idealized model of health care is built upon free-enterprise assumptions about doctors, hospitals, patients, and health-equipment providers. Sociologist Monroe Lerner describes this model of the doctor-patient relationship as one in which the doctor is a general practitioner, a family physician. He works alone (a solo practitioner) out of his own office (usually his home) and is able to give first-rate primary care when someone is sick. He provides help at his office or, in serious illness, will visit the patient's home. Such a doctor is concerned about the whole person, is friendly, and is fully competent.

A good general practitioner expects his patients to consult him for health maintenance as well as when they are seriously ill. A good doctor also refers patients to specialists whose skills he knows and whose judgments he trusts. He willingly gives his services to all who need them—rich and poor, white and black. He is motivated by the ancient Hippocratic Oath; an ethical and moral concern for his patients' well-being guides his every action. The physician is answerable to no one but his oath, and the patient is free to accept or reject his services and suggestions. Lerner describes this as a thing of the past:

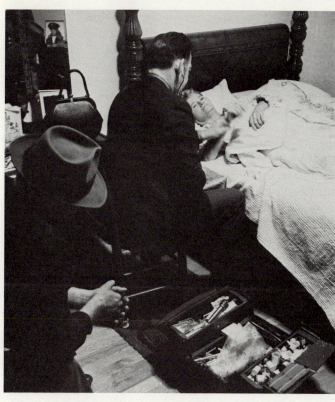

Traditionally the family doctor made house calls and took an interest in the whole person and the family. Today most doctors find it impossible to make such calls, and many people thus seek emergency care at a hospital.

The patient in this idealized model selected his physician on the basis of "free choice"; if dissatisfied, he could always choose another physician. Because of this, the physician tried very hard to please his patient. He charged on a fee-for-service basis, discriminating only in accordance with the patient's income. Thus, he charged the poor little or nothing, and gave much free service in the hospital. The doctor made up for this in Robin Hood fashion by "soaking the rich" (1971:301).

Underlying such a model are assumptions about the patients being treated. First, it assumes that patients can pay for their medical care either directly or indirectly, through insurance, union, or employer health plans. Generally, medical providers are paid fees for service by the patient or a third party. The idealized model also assumes that patients can obtain care whenever they need it and that they are able to perform a good deal of self-diagnosis and care. Patients must make frequent decisions about whether they need medical care and which doctor they should see. It further assumes that most patients are basically healthy and are likely to remain so. When a person thinks or feels that something is wrong he goes to a primary-care physician (generalist or internist) and gets better.

In the idealized view, hospitals, too, have a specific role. They are used whenever a person is seriously injured, critically ill, or about to die. The hospital has traditionally been looked upon as a place to which the doctor sends a patient when he can do no more for him. It is often a place to die. Drugs and medical equipment are used when absolutely necessary, but for the most part it is the skill and ability of the private family doctor that really makes the difference between getting better or remaining sick, or between living and dying.

Those who accept the idealized model see problems in the present trends of health care, but give a standard diagnosis. They say that health care is the only major American industry that is still run by small businessmen (doctors). Our health-care system, with its thousands of private doctors, is still in the era of the corner grocery store; and this is not only inefficient and costly, but also, at times, uncoordinated and chaotic. For example, some areas have too many hospitals and doctors, while others have none. Suburbs fare much better than inner-city slum areas or rural counties. The health-care structure is so chaotic, so uncoordinated, that many persons supporting the idealized model call it a nonsystem. To cure what ails health-care delivery, we must turn it into a genuine system. Doctors should form panel or group practices, and hospitals and medical schools should be linked together in regional networks to plan more efficiently for the medical needs of an entire region. According to believers in the idealized model, "more money, more planning, more coordination" is the standard prescription for our health-care system (Health Policy Advisory Center, 1975:46).

The Reality Model of Health Care

Followers of the reality model of our health-care system define the problem quite differently. They offer a new diagnosis of the situation, similar to C. Wright Mills's approach. Years ago, private family doctors may have dominated the practice of medicine, but not today. Many people do not even have a private physician. As medical sociologist Eliot Freidson notes: "The nostalgic and sentimental image of the old-fashioned family doctor whowas all things to all men is based upon a fleeting period in history when folk practice had declined but medical specialization was still in an incipient state" (in Freeman et al., 1972:344). For a great many people, particularly in central cities, the hospital clinic and emergency ward have become their doctors.

The realists point out that health care is dominated today by large powerful institutions. These institutions are hospitals, medical schools, drug firms, health-insurance companies (like Blue–Cross–Blue–Shield), health-planning agencies, and research and testing laboratories. Nine out of 10 health-care workers today are not doctors, but specialists in large institutions—nurses, dietitians, x-ray technicians, orderlies, lab technicians, health educators and planners.

The Medical "Empires"

There are three major parts to our present medical-care system—the "medical empires," the "financing-planning complex" and the "medical-industrial complex."*

The medical empires include medical schools, medical centers, and large hospitals. They control the medical resources for a wide region, through vast networks of connections and affiliations. For example, through affiliations (contracts to provide professional personnel), Albert Einstein Medical College and its close ally, Montefiore Hospital, control medical resources in the Bronx, New York—city and private hospitals, state mental hospitals, neighborhood clinics, and even experimental projects to improve health care in ghetto areas. Two thousand of the 2,400 hospital beds in the Bronx are controlled by Einstein, and 2,000 of the 2,700 doctors in the Bronx are affiliated with Einstein.

All across the country, medical empires have sprung up: Harvard Medical School in Boston, Johns Hopkins in Baltimore, the University of Pennsylvania and Jefferson Hospitals in Philadelphia, Case Western Reserve in Cleveland, and the University of Washington Medical School in Seattle. Everywhere the results are the same: the system provides excellent, even luxurious care for the wealthy; mediocre or bad care for the middle class, and "guinea pig" or custodial care for the poor. For example, a poor person living in the Bronx would be sent to the city-owned, run-down Lincoln Hospital. A wealthy patient with a private doctor would probably enter Einstein College or Montefiore Hospital.

The Financing-Planning Complex

The second part of the health-care system is the financing–planning complex. The key aspect here is the multibillion-dollar Blue–Cross–Blue Shield operation, through which 45 percent of Americans receive hospital care. Blue Cross pays over half of all hospital income; in New York City it pays 75 percent of all hospital bills. It is closely associated with big hospitals, and because it has a near monopoly on health insurance, Blue Cross helps set health policy in America. Its elite board of directors and top officers advise presidential and congressional committees. Together with big hospitals, they establish and run area-wide comprehensive health-planning agencies, started by law in 1975.

Blue Cross itself is dominated by the major hospitals. Half of all regional Blue Cross directors are hospital administrators. The hospital administrators and the health consumers (the public) often have different interests. Consumers want high-quality, low-cost, necessary health care. On the other hand, hospital heads are often more interested in expansion

---

*These terms and the analysis that follows are based upon "Your Health Care in Crisis" by the Health Policy Advisory Center. Pp. 45–48 in Cheever, 1975.

and prestige gained by acquiring well-known researchers, sophisticated medical equipment, and new and larger buildings.

The Medical-Industrial Complex

The third part of the health system is the medical-industrial complex. A relationship also exists between the health-care providers (doctors, hospitals, and medical schools) and companies that make money from people's sickness (drug corporations, hospital suppliers, hospital-construction companies, insurance companies, nursing homes, and laboratories). Health care is one of our largest, fastest-growing businesses. Any stockbroker will tell you that health stocks are a good buy. For example, drug companies have consistently been among the top money-makers in America. During the last 10 years they have ranked among the first three in profits for all American industries. They received over $10 billion in 1975 for helping doctors and patients relieve thousands of ailments, major and minor, real and imagined. Hospital suppliers, who sell hospitals and doctors anything from sheets and towels to bedpans and surgical instruments, make annual profits of over $500 million. Nursing homes are now a $9-billion business, thanks to federal compensation for all "reasonable costs" of doing business.

Several nationwide chains of hospitals and nursing homes are run by businesses such as the Holiday Inns and Minnie Pearl Fried Chicken. If families will not care for the aged, our free-enterprise system will move in to fill the need, and make a profit.

The commercial insurance companies and banks that back hospital-construction firms make millions of dollars every year. Of course, doctors, particularly specialists, are still among our highest-paid professionals.

Everyone in each part of the system makes a good living from people's illness and death. Their needs and goals are interdependent. Medical empires require the manufacture of expensive equipment and the presence of large construction firms. Of course, only large institutions can afford the expensive products of the medical-equipment and drug manufacturers; these institutions, in turn, need the stable and generous financing of Blue Cross and other medical insurers. Top drug-company and medical-equipment executives sit on hospital boards of trustees and serve on the boards of large medical schools and centers. Doctors own stock in hospitals and hospital-supply companies.

The best thing about the modern health business is that profits are certain. Blue Cross, the states' Medicaid program for the poor, and Social Security's Medicare system hand hospitals and doctors a virtual blank check to fill out. The hospital, in effect, tells Blue Cross what its expenses are, and Blue Cross pays the bill. Some cost controls exist, but they have proved ineffective in holding down most hospital costs.

Some hospital costs are necessary for the patients' well-being, but according to research of the Health Policy Advisory Center, "they also may be 'necessary' for the purchase of seldom-used and expensive equipment that was available in another hospital across the street; for plush offices and high salaries for doctors and hospital administrators; for expenses incurred in fighting off attempts by unions to organize workers; or for hiring public relations firms to clean up the hospital's poor image in the community" (1975:48).

The three health institutions—medical, financial-planning, and suppliers—as well as doctors, all get rich; the patient and taxpayer pay the bills.

Conservative Views of Government Officials and Physicians

Another definition of the problem comes from conservative government officials and doctors. Some government officials and doctors see no serious social problem connected with medical care. They consider our system of care the best in the world. According to this concept, the individual's lifestyle is the cause of ill health and death. For example, Dr. Theodore Cooper, assistant secretary for health, said that "much improvement in health status could come from individual action." According to Dr. Cooper, bad health comes from excessive use of alcohol and tobacco, lack of proper exercise, and poor diet. These all contribute to high rates of cancer, heart attacks, lung ailments, and kidney and liver diseases ("U.S. Lifestyle . . . ," January 13, 1976:1). Indiscriminate sex spreads venereal diseases, which have reached epidemic proportions.

In addition, Dr. F. Paul Wilson stresses that "a staggering number of us die from causes unrelated to disease." Accidents are the most common cause of death through middle age in the United States; about 50,000 die each year from highway accidents alone (1976:89). The major health hazards—heart attacks, strokes, and cancer—are related in part to lifestyle, such as rich diets, smoking, overweight, and lack of exercise. Hence we must improve our lifestyles, not our medical-care system, if we want better health in America.

Along similar lines, Rick J. Carlson, a lawyer who has studied illnesses and our medical-care system, has concluded that "medical care has very little to do with health." As this becomes clearer to the public, the medical-care system as we know it—which generally treats symptoms, not causes—will be abolished in favor of preventive care and health maintenance. So there is really no problem except the present system itself, which has little effect on health (Carlson, 1975).

In 1967 Dr. W. H. Forbes explored the relationship between national spending for health and actual results. He concluded that spending twice as much for health care would not have a different effect on how long people live from spending half as much (Abelson, May 1976:619). One detailed study calculates that the fullest and most efficient use of our present medical system would reduce deaths by no more than six percent below present levels (Palmore and Luikart, 1972:142). Hence, our present system of doctoring is not so related to living or dying as we may believe.

Consumers' Views

How does the consumer of health-care services define this social issue? At first, a person's problems with medical delivery are perceived as personal ones. He cannot get a doctor out to make a house call when a family member is sick. A new resident in town cannot find a doctor who will accept new patients, or perhaps there are no doctors in town. If a person calls his doctor when seriously ill, he may hear only the answering service. When a person goes into the hospital the costs to him (even with insurance) are unbelievably high. Sometimes the quality of care received is not satisfactory to the patient.

Gradually millions of persons begin to have the same or similar experiences. A personal problem becomes a social issue, defined by the consuming public and sociologists as:

> lack of availability and maldistribution of doctors in certain areas
>
> excessive costs
>
> dissatisfaction with the competence and quality of health care, especially among the poor and minorities

The Doctor Shortage. There is a serious shortage of doctors in the United States. They are not readily available for many people. General practitioners who administer "primary care" have declined. Many of our graduating doctors become specialists, as well as researchers, teachers, and industrial or public-health doctors. With Medicare and Medicaid and hospital insurance, demand for health care is far greater than doctors are able to provide (Bornemeier, 1971:60).

In 1976, the Senate Labor and Public Welfare Committee, considering a health manpower bill, reported that although fewer than half our doctors rendered primary care, such doctors could serve about 85 percent of all health-care needs. Too many become surgeons and specialists of another kind. Senator Edward Kennedy pointed out: "This is a problem which is national in scope. It has existed for decades. It is growing worse, not better" ("Should Federal Government Allocate Residencies?" June 5, 1976:1435).

The geographical distribution of physicians is uneven. Some states have more than 1,000 persons for each doctor, while others have about 400. Dentists, nurses, and other health professionals are clustered in urban areas (Endicott, March/April 1976: inside front cover). For instance, Wyoming, a rural state, has a doctor-to-population ratio that is 62 percent of the national average. The variation in the physician-patient ratio is greater between different areas of the United States than between the United States and some underdeveloped countries, such as Pakistan. Residents of slums in New York and Chicago are as short of doctors and health services as their relatives in Mississippi (Ehrenreich and Ehrenreich, 1971:4). Some 130 counties have no doctors practicing within their borders (Blumenthal and Fallows, 1976:204). Such small, rural communities set up recruiting booths at medical conventions, thus demonstrating the gravity of the problem.

Excessive Costs. Everyone considers the rapidly increasing cost of medical care a serious social problem. Between 1965 and 1976, all goods and services (*excluding* medical care) increased 76 percent, while medical-care costs rose 102 percent ("Behind Those Skyrocketing Health-Care Costs," May 10, 1976:68). Inflation (the general rise in the cost of all goods and services) is only part of the explanation. Another reason is that doctors and hospitals have a virtual monopoly of the health industry. Real price competition and cost-cutting programs do not exist.

In addition, government- and employer-paid Blue Cross and other insurance plans subsidize doctors and hospitals, Medicaid and Medicare actually benefit the wealthy more than the needy, and they add to the cost of medicine. A report by the President's Council on Wage and Price Stability says the American patient has "little or no chance to shop around for better or cheaper alternatives to the course of treatment that his physician prescribes." The Council calls this situation a "major public-policy problem."

The Quality of Care. The competence of doctors and the quality of care received are growing social problems. Dr. Allen Swartz, Director of Pharmacy at the University of California in Los Angeles, said that more than 100,000 serious errors are made daily in prescribing, preparing, and dispensing drugs. These mistakes cause thousands of deaths among hospital patients every year. A doctor in a Midwest hospital made an error in computing the dosage of a drug, and the patient lost his leg as a result; a nurse in New York accidentally switched hypodermic needles, and a woman almost died. A prominent West Coast surgeon ordered a wound washed out with an antibiotic solution. This reacted negatively with the patient's anesthetic, and his breathing stopped to the point of death ("Is Your Hospital Drug-Wise?" December 1975:19). A middle-aged man entered a leading New York hospital for the replacement of a heart valve. When he was taken off the heart-lung machine after his operation, his circulation failed and he died minutes later. An autopsy showed that the surgeon had put the heart valve in backwards, preventing blood from flowing through the heart (Brody, January 27, 1976:19). The patient was one of the more than 250,000 persons who died shortly after surgery in 1975.

Dr. Alan E. Nourse writes: "We also have physicians who have been practicing medicine without interruption for the last 60 years without once opening a textbook or journal or submitting to an examination since they were first licensed to practice" (1976:92). In addition, about 2,200 hospitals (nearly one-third of all hospitals) fail to meet the minimum standards of safety and adequacy of patient care required by the medical profes-

> **MEDICINE MAY BE DANGEROUS TO YOUR HEALTH**
>
> Some people, perhaps more trusting of doctors, never ask for an explanation until they have to in sheer self-defense. Residents of Manhattan's lower east side tell the story of the woman who was admitted to a ward at Bellevue for a stomach operation. The operation was scheduled for Thursday. On Wednesday a nurse told her she was to be operated on that day. The patient asked why the change. "Never mind," said the nurse, "give me your glasses." The patient could not see why she should give up her glasses, but finally handed them over at the nurse's insistence. Inside the operating room, the patient was surprised when she was not given general anesthesia. Although her English was poor, she noticed that the doctors were talking about eye cancer, and looking at her eyes. She sat up and said there was nothing wrong with her eyes—her stomach was the problem. She was pushed back on the operating table. With the strength of panic, she leaped up and ran into the hall. A security guard caught her, running sobbing down the hall in an operating gown. She was summarily placed in the psychiatric ward for a week's observation.
>
> Source: Barbara Ehrenreich and John Ehrenreich, *The American Health Empire: Power, Profits and Politics* (New York: Vintage Books, 1971):10–11.

sion's Joint Commission on Hospital Accreditation. Despite this, there are no restrictions on the medical and surgical procedures these hospitals practice (Rensberger, January 26, 1976:1).

Minority Groups and Medical Care Quality

The quality and competence of medical care is questioned by millions of patients today, especially by the poor and minority-group members. Their inadequate medical care is well documented (Ehrenreich and Ehrenreich, 1971). Access to doctors and hospitals is limited (Scarpitti, 1977:280–81); infant death rates of blacks, Puerto Ricans, chicanos, and American Indians are often twice as high as those of whites (Thomlinson, 1976:158); and life expectancy of these groups is less than for most Americans (Petersen, 1975:223). Many hospitals in the South are still unofficially segregated or "highly selective." White "references" and connections are needed before blacks are admitted to predominantly white hospitals. In the West, thousands of Indians on reservations are left without doctors or hospitals. Special federal programs to improve health-care delivery on Indian reservations have been slashed back in recent years.

In the North, health facilities are available on a somewhat more equal footing. Even so, nonwhites experience a different kind of medical care. They are treated at a large hospital clinic rather than at a private doctor's office. Here one finds that institutional racism is a "built-in feature of the way medicine is learned and practice in the United States" (Ehrenreich and Ehrenreich, 1971:14). Young doctors, interns, and residents get their training by practicing on hospital-ward and clinic patients, usually nonwhites. Later they make their money by serving paying clients, usually white. Thus, white patients are customers, whereas black patients are teaching material. White patients pay with money, blacks with their dignity and comfort. Clinic patients at the hospital affiliated with Columbia University Medical School found this out in a very painful way. They complained that they were never given novocaine when having a tooth filled or pulled. It was learned this was an official policy: "The patient's pain is a good guide to the dentist-in-training—it teaches him not to drill too deep. Anesthetic would deaden the pain and dull the intern's learning experience" (Ibid., 14–15).

In addition, ghetto hospitals have a reputation as racist because they serve as police strongholds in the community. "In the emergency room, cops often outnumber doctors. They interrogate the wounded—often before the doctor does, and pick up any vagrants, police-brutality victims, drunks or addicts who have mistakenly come in for help," notes the Ehrenreich's study for the Health Policy Advisory Center in New York City (Ibid.).

Some persons, especially minorities, must wait for hours before receiving proper medical treatment.

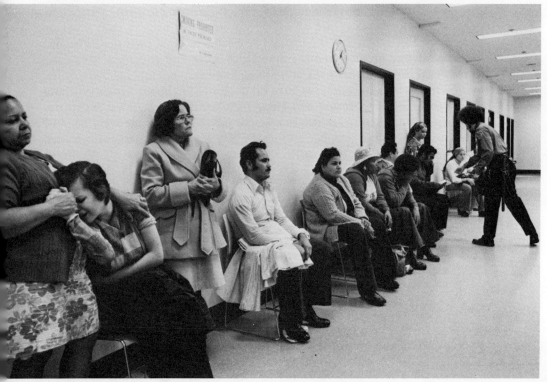

Illes Peress/Magnum.

INCIDENCE AND PREVALENCE OF THE HEALTH-CARE PROBLEM

Every day three million Americans go out in search of medical care. Some find one of the 338,000 doctors; others are not as lucky. Doctors manage to see 2,300,000 patients a day, over 50,000 of them by house calls. Another 20 million Americans ought to seek medical care, but they are not healthy enough, rich enough, or enterprising enough to try. If they are poor, they will probably seek help in the emergency room of one of our 7,000 hospitals. On any one day, over one million patients are occupying beds in our hospitals, and another million are living out their last years in a nursing home. In a year's time, over 35 million persons will have been admitted to a hospital, about 16 percent of our population.

The Doctor Shortage

The incidence and prevalence of the doctor shortage is evident. One estimate puts the nationwide shortage at about 50,000 doctors. Geographical distribution of physicians is uneven. In large metropolitan areas, especially suburbs, there are about 500 persons for each doctor, whereas there are more than 2,000 persons per doctor in rural counties. The two areas with the greatest shortage are rural areas and poverty areas of the inner city, especially in black and Spanish-speaking neighborhoods. Some 5,000 towns and 107 counties have no doctor at all; about 144 more counties have only one (Horton and Leslie, 1974:601). These are mostly rural counties. In the United States as a whole are 165 doctors for every 100,000 persons. In Washington, D.C., there are 371 per 100,000 persons, while in Mississippi and Alaska, only 78. One area in Brooklyn's Bedford-Stuyvesant contains only one doctor for a population of 100,000 (Ehrenreich and Ehrenreich, 1971:4).

Considering a bill to have medical students work in understaffed areas, the Senate Labor and Public Welfare Committee observed:

> Despite an increased supply of doctors ... rural and inner-city areas continue to experience physician shortages ... And the doctor-to-population ratio in metropolitan areas is still more than twice that in rural areas. ...
>
> Like the geographical maldistribution problem, the specialty maldistribution problem has worsened over the past 20 years. ... Over the past decade, while the federal government spent more than $3.5 billion for health manpower programs, these [doctor maldistribution] problems have grown worse ("Senate Bill ...," June 5, 1976: 1433).

THE DOCTOR JUST WON'T COME OUT

Chicago is the medical capital of America. It is the headquarters of the American Medical Association, with an annual budget of $34 million. Chicago has 80 hospitals and five medical schools. But in the West Side ghetto, with 300,000 people and disease rates three to four times the national average, people have to travel miles and wait for hours for access to one charity hospital that must take them in—Cook County, the nation's largest general hospital.

Cook County, on the day of our visit, was bursting at the seams. More than a thousand persons daily crowd into its registration and emergency room for treatment. They are not necessarily emergency cases, but for many it is the only way to see a doctor. Many, discouraged by the wait, leave before they are attended. Others, who need a hospital bed, are sent home because no hospital bed is available. For those who are admitted, there may be waits of three to four hours for x-rays, even in emergencies. They are crowded into medical wards where there is one registered nurse for a hundred patients. Of those admitted, one out of every six dies.

... There are few hospitals that will take the poor.... Frank Brown is a community-health worker in Kenwood-Oakland, a community that has one doctor for every 15,000 people—less than one-tenth the national average. Brown became a health worker when his daughter died because he couldn't get her into a nearby hospital in time to save her.

... "Let me ask you this—isn't it the obligation of public assistance to send in medical help when a person is quite ill? She needs to see a doctor now—right now! You know, I've been calling for about an hour-and-a-half and, you know, everyone has the same story that the doctor just won't come out...." The doctor did not come to Mrs. Montgomery that day. Nor did an ambulance come to the home of Mrs. Laura Hayes, whom Brown found with a doctor's note saying that she needed immediate hospitalization. Nor did any help come in time to two other homes, where persons were found dead.

"We're already a sick society," says Brown, "and we'll become a sicker society simply because people just don't care. They're more interested in perpetuating wars, more interested in getting to the moon. They just aren't interested in people's health."

Source: Daniel Schorr, *Don't Get Sick in America* (Nshville, Tenn.: Aurora, 1970), 44–48.

Rising Costs

The most prevalent social problem confronting our health-care system is rising costs. Good health care has actually been placed out of the reach of millions. According to the Social Security Administration, in 1975 only eight percent of hospital costs were paid for directly by the patient. The remainder of the money came from the government, private health insurance, and philanthropic funds. About 38 million Americans have no insurance at all. A critical or chronic illness can cause bankruptcy almost overnight, with or without insurance. For example, a

Middle- and upper-class Americans enjoy excellent, though expensive, medical care in luxurious modern hospitals.

year-long study at the Massachusetts General Hospital revealed that 226 critically ill patients in its intensive-care unit were charged an average of $14,304 each for treatment. Each of the patients spent an average of 35 days in the hospital. A follow-up study showed that almost 75 percent of the patients died within a year after receiving the expensive care ("Critically Ill Patients...," June 15, 1976:10).

Figure 11-1 shows the distribution of the $118 billion spent for health care in 1975, as well as the trend in rapidly climbing costs.

Public spending for health care in 1975 reached almost $50 billion, or 42 percent of such spending. Most public spending was on two government health programs, Medicare and Medicaid. In 1976 an estimated 24.3 million persons were insured under Medicare, and over 13 million received some kind of benefits when sick. Over 23 million persons received Medicaid benefits in 1976. Medicare and Medicaid together cost around $40 billion in 1977, nearly seven times as great as when the program was begun in 1967. Figure 11-2 shows how their costs have skyrocketed in 10 years.

Medical malpractice insurance is also driving up the costs of medicine. Part of the explanation is that medical care has improved so much that patients expect much more of it today. If they do not get better,

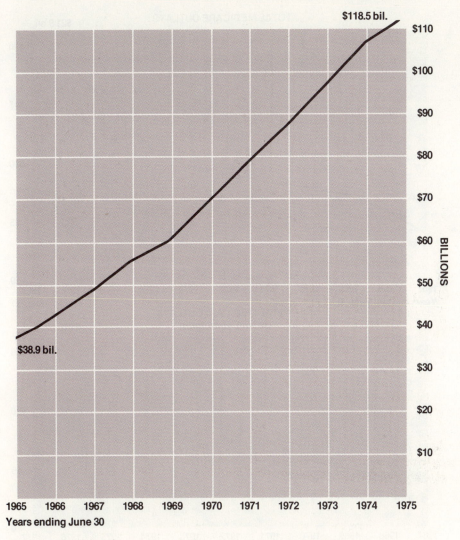

figure 11-1 WHAT LIES BEHIND OUR SKYROCKETING HEALTH-CARE COSTS?

Source: President's Council on Wage and Price Stability, U.S. Dept. of Health, Education and Welfare, U.S. Dept. of Labor.

or if a relative dies, they sue the doctor or hospital. More than 20,000 malpractice suits were brought against doctors in 1975, three times as many as in 1965 (Bromberg and Hotchkiss, Summer 1975:34). Juries in recent years have awarded large malpractice settlements to people suing doctors. For example, in 1969 California had only three cases involving a malpractice award or settlement of $300,000 or more. In 1974 there were 34 such cases, and 24 in 1975. The state's first malpractice case resulting in an award of one million dollars or more occurred in 1969; since then

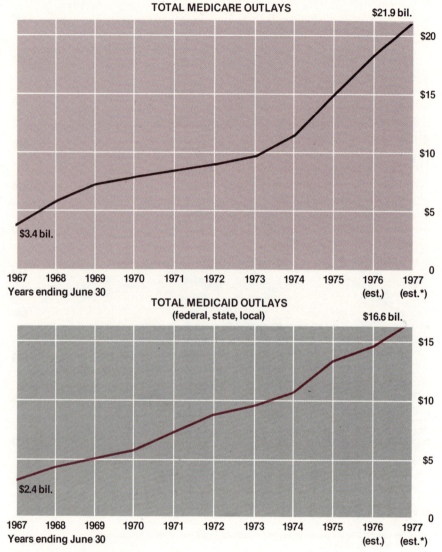

figure 11-2 SHARP INCREASES IN MEDICARE AND MEDICAID COSTS

★ Year ending September 30.

Source: U.S. Office of Management and Budget; Dept. of Health, Education and Welfare.

there have been 22 more, 14 of them after January 1974 (Rubsamen, August 1976:19).

This new trend drives up the cost of malpractice insurance, which most doctors must buy. In turn, these mounting premium costs are added to the patients' medical and hospital bills. A 1976 government report from the U.S. Public Health Services estimated that malpractice insurance premiums for doctors and hospitals add about "$15 per bed each day to hospital rates and $2 billion to national health care costs" ("New Plan," September 8, 1976:1).

Competence and Quality of Care

There is another important part of the explanation for higher premiums. The competence of doctors and quality of care are being challenged by millions of patients experiencing inadequate or improper care. A Cornell University study reports that nearly two-and-a-half million unnecessary operations are performed each year (Rensberger, January 25, 1976:1). Dr. Sidney Wolfe of the Public Interest Health Research Group estimates that unnecessary operations cost close to $5 billion a year and kill almost 16,000 patients (Shearer, September 7, 1975:7). More than 250,000 of the nearly 18 million Americans who underwent surgery in 1975 died during or shortly after it, according to the National Center for Health Statistics.

Studies at the University of Florida and Ohio State University medical schools estimate that 10,000 patients die from or have a potentially fatal reaction to unrequired antibiotics. The Federation of State Medical Boards estimates that 16,000 physicians (about five percent of the total) are unworthy of their licenses. Yet state licensing agencies revoke only about 66 licenses a year. These incompetent doctors treat about seven-and-half million patients a year.

Dr. Avedis Donabedian, professor of health-care organization at the University of Michigan, believes the biggest problem in medicine comes not from the five percent who are "thoroughly incompetent," but from the much larger body of average doctors who, for various reasons, do not practice the best medicine they can. According to Donabedian, "There is much evidence to indicate that the quality of care available under many circumstances falls far below acceptable standards" (Rensberger, 1976:1).

Whether the problem is unnecessary surgery, the wrong drugs, or incompetent doctors, evidence has accumulated that poor medical care is a bigger problem than most medical authorities suspected. According to a major study sponsored by the nation's leading surgical groups, much unnecessary surgery is being performed, and too many new surgeons are being trained each year. The likely result is that at least some surgeons make work for themselves by doing unnecessary operations. The rate of "elective" surgery (the patients make the final decision) in the United States is the highest in the world. In 1974, 78 elective operations were performed for every 1,000 persons (Brody, January 27, 1976:19).

Quality of Care for Minorities

The poor and minority groups generally suffer most from lack of proper health and medical care. Life expectancy for blacks is about seven years less than for whites. Minority-group children, especially blacks, Spanish-Americans, and American Indians, die at a rate usually twice as high as whites. In fact, the United States as a whole ranks fifteenth in the world for deaths of children during the first year of life.

The health of the poor is worse than that of other groups. Almost 60 percent of those in poverty have more than one disabling condition, compared with about 24 percent of the nonpoor. Poor men lose about 10 days of work each year because of ill health or disability, compared with nearly five days for others (Strauss, 1975:333). Those with low-income make fewer visits to a doctor each year, because of the costs, physician shortages, long waiting lines, and (perhaps out of necessity) greater tolerance of illness. In 1974, 17 percent of the poor had not seen a doctor within two years. Yet the poor spend a greater percentage of their meager income on health care than those better off (Endicott, 1976:inside front cover).

Minority persons and our urban poor are forced to visit overcrowded and inadequate public hospitals. In New York City, the Commissioner of Health estimates that in 1968, 13,000 poor died because adequate medical care was not available to them. Chicago has about 80 hospitals and medical schools; yet the 300,000 residents of the West Side ghetto have only one hospital available. More than 1,000 patients a day must go to Cook County General Hospital. Disease rates reported from that area are three

The poor and minorities encounter overcrowded clinics and inadequate medical-care delivery in their neighborhoods or areas.

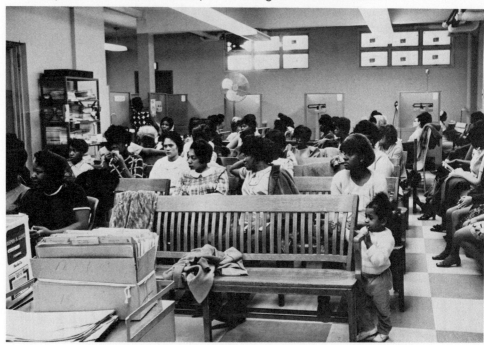

Credit: Robert Goldstein.

to four times the national average (Schorr, 1970:44–45). In Philadelphia, the blacks and the poor use Philadelphia General Hospital. In 1976 the city proposed to close it down because it "costs too much to operate" ("Issues in PGH March," February 25, 1976:18). Some 2,500 persons protested its closing and argued that "it is needed to serve patients unwanted elsewhere—the poor, the drug addicts, the rape victims, as well as the bloodied victims of violence and accidents who make PGH's emergency ward the busiest in the city" (Ibid.). In a court battle to prevent its closing, a lower court judge ruled that "the city is not legally obligated to operate a municipal hospital" (Ibid.).

The fight continues in America for decent health care for the poor and minority group people.

CAUSES OF THE HEALTH-CARE PROBLEM

The causes of the problems of medical care are our value system, the structure and organization of our medical system, and financial fraud and waste.

Our Value System

Problems in the health-care system stem from its successes rather than its limitations or failures. In the past 30 years or so, as modern technology and wonder drugs have enabled us to save lives and relieve pain, which are primary values, public demand for medical services has grown. In 1950 we had about 150 million people; today we have over 216 million. So demand for the services of doctors and hospitals has grown. Our social values and norms tell us that if we are sick or ill we should see a doctor or go to the hospital. This has further increased our demands on the health-care system.

At the same time, due to our value system, more and more personal and social problems have become medically defined. As Rick Carlson notes in *The End of Medicine,*

> medicine has deeply penetrated society. Many judgments made by medical practitioners are heavily weighted with moral considerations. A growing list of social "problems," including aging, drug use and addiction, alcoholism, pregnancy and genetic counseling, have been or are becoming "medicalized" (1975:44).

Sociologist Irving Zola argues: "The list of daily activities to which health can be related is ever growing, and with the current operating perspective of medicine seems infinitely expandable" (Ibid., 45). This expansion of medicine occurs, in part, because many activities such as drinking, sex, and eating are governed by social norms and our value system. As individuals fail to adhere to society's norms, their deviance is interpreted as an illness (Conrad, 1975: 12–21). In such an approach, says David

Mechanic, a medical sociologist, society "seeks to identify an underlying disorder . . . that explains the apparent deviant manifestations, and thus introduced into the medical model, these behavioral syndromes are increasingly identified as diseases" (Ibid., 45).

With such an expansion of medicine into problem areas formerly reserved for the police, sociologist, or clergy, people become more dependent on doctors, drugs, and hospitals. The penetration of the health profession into everyday life, according to Zola, gives doctors and hospitals new power in areas that patients formerly controlled (e.g., dieting). It makes the patient more powerless and dependent upon the existing medical system than in the past; it overloads the system, and hurried, poor-quality care is the result. It is often very difficult to serve the masses and satisfy the individual.

Structure and Organization of the System

The reality model of medical and health care in our society is one of the roots of our problems. As noted, years ago the private physician, in a kind of "cottage industry," dominated the health-care system from his office or home. Today, however, it is dominated by a large corporate structure and by institutions—hospitals, medical schools, research labs, drug firms, health-insurance corporations, and large agencies. These corporate institutions are motivated by a drive for profit and power. Such power elites often pursue their own vested interests, rather than those of the patient, the consumer of health care.

To understand how this highly structured and organized system of medicine lies at the heart of the problems discussed, we must examine how the system came about and how it causes problems. The system became more highly structured after World War II because of changes in medical technology and in funding for hospitals and surgeons by Blue Cross–Blue Shield. Once the system became a modern industry, health-care corporations grew in size and in concentrated power, prestige, and wealth. A vast influx of federal funds encouraged that concentration. During the 1950s and early 1960s, the government spent billions of dollars for research at medical schools and their affiliated hospitals. After Medicare and Medicaid appeared in the late 1960s, "vast sums of money, ostensibly for patient care, poured virtually without government controls into hospitals and other health-care institutions" (Kotelchuck, 1976:xii). With power and money at their disposal, elite medical centers absorbed and merged with public and smaller private hospitals through affiliation agreements. Such medical-school systems pursue their primary goals of profits, research, and education; their secondary concern is with public access to excellent health care. The dynamics of scientific research and medical education are different from delivery of health care to all. Sometimes the interests of these "medical corporations" and the public do coincide, as in the case of antibiotic drugs—a research discovery that

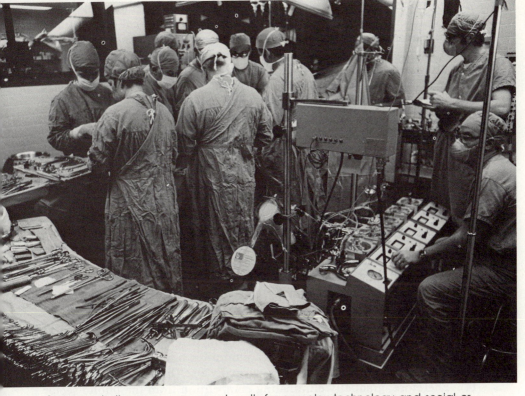

Surgery, whether necessary or not, calls for complex technology and social organization.

benefited millions. More often, the interests of the organization conflict with good (and humane) medical treatment. For example, conflicts arose in the case of the "infamous Willowbrook experiments [in which retarded children serving as experimental subjects were injected with live hepatitis virus], in the use of inadequately tested drugs on humans in a headlong rush for experimental results, or in the mundane, but equally significant organization by hospitals of dozens of specialty clinics that suit the needs of students and researchers but that may confuse, discourage and sometimes mistreat the patients" (Ibid., 2–3).

Although medical-school corporations have made contributions to patient care, their pursuit of research and teaching has made them the centers of power and wealth they are today. The system rewards and grants power to researchers, who are considered the elite members of the medical profession. The system encourages new medical students to become medical research scientists rather than practicing physicians.

Most medical care today is concentrated in large hospitals and medical centers. Less than 30 percent of health spending goes for private doctors; most of the rest goes to institutions. More than nine out of 10 health workers are not doctors at all; they are the nurses, x-ray technicians, dietitians, orderlies, and others needed to run the giant medical corporations. The concentration of medical resources in hospitals makes them less accessible to patients. Hospitals and medical centers may be located in wealthy suburban communities or in more affluent sections of cities. In emergencies, when time may mean loss of life, not everyone has ready access to such facilities. In many cases, a person's needs for medical treatment might be better served by a doctor in his office or at a neighborhood facility rather than at a centralized location. Home care is an option that is rarely ever considered by the elite decision makers. The patient's wishes, feelings, and concerns must take second place to the preferences and conveniences of the corporate system.

The way in which the system is financed causes some of the problems, especially rising costs. Blue Cross, founded by hospitals and dominated by powerful hospital interests, has tilted and directed the entire medical-care system toward hospitals. Whatever the circumstances or needs of patients, Blue Cross pays only for hospital care; thus hospital care is what a person must receive if he wants his medical care paid for. Even government programs, such as Medicare and Medicaid, favor hospital care over other types of care a patient may receive.

Nowhere is the power and profit motive of the corporate medical system more evident than in its efforts to convince counties and cities to close their public hospitals. Many communities now have private hospitals with more beds than they can normally use (Ensminger, 1976:413–14). Therefore, gradually eliminating competition from the public sector will force consumers to use their services, and the government will pay the bills at these private hospitals. In California alone, 12 out of 50 county hospitals have been closed or sold; 10 or more, according to one study, are likely to disappear shortly. New York City has started plans to close or lease up to seven of its municipal hospitals. In Florida, Massachusetts, North Carolina, and Wisconsin, public hospitals, formerly open to the needy and poor, have fallen into private corporate hands (Blake and Bodenheimer, 1976:331).

Even when powerful medical schools take over county hospitals, the poor and powerless are often the victims. For instance, when the University of California Medical School at Davis, California, took over the county hospital in Sacramento in 1972, part of the transfer agreement stated that "the University would reserve the right to refuse care to any patients, particularly to patients the cost of whose care is not guaranteed by the county." University of California Vice-Chancellor Elmer Learn admitted: "We can't deprive a student of his education to finance a patient who can't pay" (Ibid., 349). The same situation occurred in San Diego when the University of California took over the county hospital there. As reported by Blake and Bodenheimer, "no one has yet made any provisions for the medically indigent, many of them Mexican-Americans. . . . Some patients are simply turned away" (Ibid., 338).

Financial Fraud and Waste

The last cause underlying the medical-care issue is financial. Too much financial fraud and waste exist, especially since third-party funding (Blue Cross–Blue Shield, government plans such as Medicaid and Medicare, and other private insurance programs) pays for the hospital and doctor bills. Such fraud and waste are well documented and exist on a scale more vast than most Americans ever suspected. A wide range of financial abuses is involved. Investigations reveal that bill padding by doctors, kickbacks by medical labs, and massive swindles by nursing-home operators cost the public millions of dollars every year.

These abuses may be only the tip of the financial iceberg. Federal officials estimate that tax-supported health-care losses from fraud approach one dollar for every $10 spent ("Billions in Medicaid...," 1976:18). That would mean more than $3 billion a year in programs that cost nearly $33 billion in 1976. The congressional Special Committee on Aging learned that "kickbacks, fraudulent billing and overpayments involving a few medical laboratories waste almost $1 out of $5 paid out for Medicare and Medicaid lab services" ("Fraud, Waste Cited...," February 17, 1976:18). The Senate report noted that "kickbacks are so rampant that laboratories are almost barred from obtaining a Medicaid account unless they offer a kickback" to doctors ("Probes Revealing Fraud...,"

"THERE! I THINK WE GOT IT ALL.... CLOSE THE WALLET, DOCTOR."

Credit: Chicago Tribune–New York News Syndicate.

March 2, 1976:31). For example, a medical lab in Illinois routinely gave tests that were never ordered, altered bills, and inflated prices of Medicaid patients. State investigators, posing as the operators of a new clinic, were offered kickbacks of up to 50 percent by several such labs ("Billions in Medicaid Ripoffs," March 22, 1976:18).

The government is paying some doctors more than $100,000 a year to provide mostly routine care for patients dependent on artificial-kidney machines. Under the program, a doctor who has 45 kidney-machine patients could receive $103,680 of the taxpayers' money. In addition, he bills his patients for an additional 20 percent, because the government pays only 80 percent of what a doctor can charge. About 20,000 persons now receive artificial-kidney treatments under the federal program ("High Doctor Fees . . . ," September 10, 1975:11).

Even the federal medical program to help Armed Forces dependents is wasteful. Congressman Les Aspin reported that the military's health program is wasting millions of tax dollars through failure to adopt changes first recommended by the General Accounting Office in 1971. He provides three examples of how money was wasted:

> Medical equipment was bought at inflated prices from civilian rather than government suppliers. Beds bought for $397 each could have been gotten for $221.
> A hearing aid bought for $350 from a civilian supplier would have cost only $110 from a government supplier.
> Instead of paying $220 to $445 for devices to control bed wetting, the military health program could have had them for only $20 to $35 ("Health-Plan Waste . . .," January 12, 1976:3).

PROPOSED SOLUTIONS TO HEALTH-CARE PROBLEMS

Many proposals and attempts to solve the problems are possible. National health insurance, health-maintenance organizations, a more consumer-controlled and radically structured system, reforms of medical schools, use of paraprofessionals, Medicaid-Medicare reforms, and regional, state, and local health planning have been proposed or are being tried.

National Health Insurance

One widely supported solution is some kind of national health insurance (NHI) program. Some program will probably be passed in 1978 or 1979. A Gallup poll in June 1975 found that health care ranked first among choices for federal spending. In 1977 more than half of those polled thought that health care should be one of the top three government priorities (Auerbach, April 7, 1976:13). American public opinion has been steady in its support for such legislation since 1971. What is not agreed upon is what kind of bill should be passed ("Poll Finds ...," September 28, 1974:6).

Here are some of the questions raised by proposals for national health insurance:

> How much of society's resources should be spent on health care?
>
> Should we try to guarantee absolute equality of health care or just a minimum level and standard of care?
>
> How should the costs of such a program be shared? Should workers and employers be taxed through Social Security taxes; should the money come from the federal treasury; or should a combination of both sources be used?
>
> Who will administer it—the private insurance sector (like Blue Cross–Blue Shield), a public agency (such as the Social Security Administration), or the Department of Health, Education and Welfare; or should a new federal agency be created to run it?
>
> How will costs be held down?
>
> Will consumers of health care have a voice in how the new system will operate?
>
> Will ultimate control still be in the hands of the medical establishment, the system that has failed to control costs in the last 10 years or more?

In a detailed analysis of four prototype national health insurance bills, Dr. Bridger Mitchell, a senior economist for the Rand Corporation, and Dr. William B. Schwartz, Chairman of the Department of Medicine at Tufts University, predicted that any NHI program would be funded by a combination of tax dollars and out-of-pocket payments by patients.

The 1976 Democratic Platform recommended "a combination of employer-employee shared payroll taxes and general tax revenues" ("Democrats NHI Plank ...," June 21, 1976:1). It also recommended a plan with "built-in" cost and quality controls. Hospital and doctor rates for services should be set in advance. Most physicians strongly oppose government setting of doctors' fees and hospital bills, though the Carter Administration has proposed controlling both (Lyons, April 27, 1977:1). Existing programs such as Medicare and Medicaid state that all reasonable charges, with certain exceptions, will be paid by the government.

According to liberal advocates of NHI, an effective plan should have the following elements:

> access to health care as a matter of right
> a comprehensive single standard of benefits
> incentives for reform of the delivery system
> built-in quality control

strong cost control
small administrative costs
strong consumer representation
equitable and progressive financing ("Financing Health Care," June 19, 1976:4)

David Mechanic insists that to break the doctors' hold on the health-care system, the government must regulate doctors' fees, review committees must reduce unnecessary surgery, and the government must subsidize the training of more family physicians (Fogg, December 16, 1975:19).

Health-Maintenance Organizations

Another proposed solution to expensive medical care is prepaid group-practice organizations. Under such arrangements, doctors become employees of the organization and receive a fixed salary rather than fees-for-service. Members of such plans pay the same annual premium whether they are well or sick. The money goes toward the doctors' salaries, rather than to an insurance company.

The federal government has tried to encourage such health-maintenance organizations (HMOs). In 1976 Congress authorized about $250 million to encourage new HMOs. In addition it changed some of the rules, such as allowing doctors to devote 35 percent of their time, instead of 50 percent, to the HMO. The HMO pools money from people when they are well so that good medical care will be available to them and their families when illness occurs. The pioneer example of HMO care is the Kaiser-Permanente Health Plan of California, begun in 1938 (Johnson, April 28, 1974:34–54). The Health Insurance Plan (HIP) of New York is another well-known HMO.

A Consumer-Controlled System

More money, more planning, and more coordination—even a plan for national health insurance—will not necessarily help our entrenched medical-care system based on power, prestige, and privilege. Government funding or better planning will make little difference "as long as control of the health system is left in the hands of those who make their fortunes and reputations from it" (Health Policy Advisory Center, 1975:48). The patients and consumers, those who use and pay for health care, must have a dominant voice in setting priorities of the health system.

Radical changes are needed to curb the concentration of power and wealth in our health-care system. The medical elites must be made more responsive and accountable to the people so that we can achieve more competent, personal care and a guaranteed right to care at a cost everyone can afford (Blumenthal and Fallows, 1976:202–8).

Medical-School Reforms

To remedy problems of the shortage and maldistribution of doctors, Congress has proposed legislation that would require 35 percent of new medical students to serve in an area that lacks doctors. They would serve at least two years in the area. Students who did not fulfill their obligation would be subject to stiff monetary penalties, and a medical school that did not meet its quota would lose federal aid.

The Carnegie Commission on Higher Education has made several recommendations for reforming medical schools:

1. The time required to become a practicing physician should be reduced from eight to six years.
2. The output of doctors should be increased by 50 percent by 1978.
3. An intermediate degree should be available to those who complete two years of basic science (the equivalent of the first two years of medical school); they would then choose between scientific research or becoming practicing physicians.
4. The federal government should subsidize the training of doctors through aid to medical students and schools.
5. A uniform level of tuition of $1,000 a year should be established for all schools (Kessel, 1975:373-75).

Some schools have initiated programs that shorten by two years the time required to become a doctor, but these are still exceptional.

In late 1975 the National Academy of Sciences Institute of Medicine sponsored a two-day seminar on medical care. The liberal faction of professionals called for greater use of paramedics and paraprofessionals. Under physician supervision, they would handle routine, chronic illnesses such as hypertension, and care for the old and terminally ill (Fogg, 1975:19).

These new paraprofessionals are labeled MEDEX and physicians' assistants. The MEDEX program, begun in Washington State, uses the talents of medical corpsmen who have left the military. They do tasks that take much of a doctor's time—taking blood pressure, temperatures, medical histories, and other routine aspects of physical examination. They can check on hospital patients to determine their progress. In the doctor's office they screen the incoming patients, leaving the physician free to devote more time to seriously ill patients.

Medicaid-Medicare Reform

To remedy the rising costs, waste, and fraud of Medicaid, Congress has proposed such legislation as the Medicare-Medicaid Administrative and Reimbursement Reform Act. It calls for—

creation of a Health Care Financing Administration and a special HEW Office on Fraud and Abuse provisions to add criteria for determining doctors' "reasonable charges"; this would equalize charges throughout the state and control fee increases

elimination of direct billing of Medicare patients; bills would be sent directly to the agency handling Medicare payments

lowering payment to pathologists to levels determined by the government

revision of Medicaid so that doctor services outside the hospital would be based on Medicare's concept of a "reasonable charge" instead of "usual, customary or reasonable fees"

The AMA opposes most of these provisions as interference with doctors, medical care, and the patient-physician relationship ("AMA Newsletter," June 21, 1976:15). The measure is still being studied by Congress.

Various states are adding investigators to explore Medicaid overcharges, fraud, and waste. HEW added 108 investigators in early 1976, compared with only one in 1975. In New York State, the Commission on Nursing Homes has called for a reform of Medicaid rates that would narrow the range of costs and eliminate payments for "deluxe service." Its "efficient-care standards" of payment, determined by computer, should save $40 to $50 million (Hess, April 8, 1976:24).

Regional Health Planning

To overcome the fragmentation of health services and avoid duplication of expensive equipment, authorities have proposed better planning on a regional basis and centralized medical centers. New regional planning for health services has been established under the National Health Planning and Resources Development Act of 1974. This law is already having a dramatic and significant effect on the delivery of health care services. It seeks to provide "a new unified approach to resolving the problems of access, cost, and quality of care . . ." (Rubel, January/February 1976:3).

The preamble to the law states that its purpose is "to facilitate the development of recommendations for a national health planning policy, to augment areawide and state planning for health services manpower and facilities, and to authorize financial assistance for development of resources to further that policy" (Ibid.). It creates a national network of local health systems agencies (HSAs), state health planning and developing agencies (SHPDAs), and state health coordinating councils (SHCCs). It also establishes the National Council for Health Policy within the Department of Health, Education and Welfare. A major emphasis is on participation in health planning by all segments of the health-care system—doctors, hospitals, Blue Cross–Blue Shield representatives, health educators, government, and consumers. Significant consumer and provider representation on local and state planning boards is required. A survey by Public Citizens Health Research Group, an advocate for a radically reformed medical care system, points to domination by the medical establishment of these planning boards. Even consumer representatives are often part of the medical power structure (Ensminger, 1976:414–18).

The law has the power to restrict unnecessary expansion of hospitals and medical services. For the first time, every state must establish and administer a "certificate of need" (CON) program, and will be forced to stop the development of unneeded services. Grants will be made to six states to study ways of regulating rates so as to control health-care costs. The Secretary of HEW, in cooperation with state governors, has designated health service areas (HSAs) in all but three states. Each designated HSA must have between 500,000 and three million persons (unless the area includes a Standard Metropolitan Statistical Area with more than three million inhabitants).

At present there are 202 health service areas in 47 states (the very small states were exempt from setting up HSAs) (Peterson, 1976:9). All health planning, hospital construction, allocation of medical personnel, and coordination of health services will be done within these regional HSAs. Figure 11-3 shows the health service areas in the Eastern United States.

All these suggestions, proposals, and laws aim to overcome the social, structural, and financial causes of health-care problems. No one measure can possible be a panacea for the social problems of the shortage and maldistribution of physicians, excessive costs, and incompetent, poor-quality care, especially for minority-group and low-income patients. Taken together, though, they might effectively produce a more efficient, effective, and humane system.

THE FUTURE OF THE HEALTH-CARE PROBLEM

Profound changes have occurred in medicine in the past 30 years; more will occur in the next 20.* Half the knowledge a physician needs today was unknown 10 years ago. We are well into the era of organ transplants and artificial organs. Sophisticated artificial limbs will be available in the future. Emergency vehicles are bringing the equivalent of an intensive-care unit to the scene of an accident or a heart attack. Some cancer may soon be brought under control. Health centers, community clinics, and drugs will serve as alternatives to the traditional hospital.

Biomedical engineering is still an infant field, but it has already changed the character of the hospital. Half the cost of a new hospital is now equipment and electrical wiring. The development of this equipment

---

*Unless otherwise cited, the information and insights in this section are from "Health Care in the Year 2000," a paper given by George S. Shields, MD, at the Futurology 2 Conference, June 12, 1973, at Mount Saint Joseph College, Cincinnati, Ohio.

11 PROBLEMS OF THE MEDICAL AND HEALTH-CARE INSTITUTIONS

476

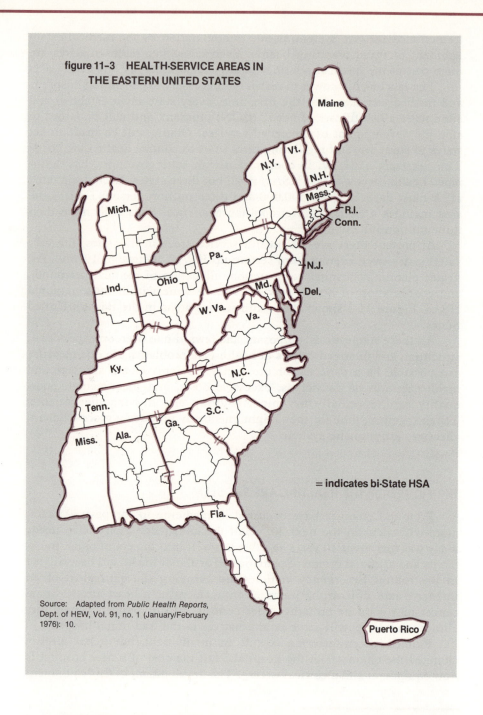

figure 11-3 HEALTH-SERVICE AREAS IN THE EASTERN UNITED STATES

= indicates bi-State HSA

Source: Adapted from *Public Health Reports*, Dept. of HEW, Vol. 91, no. 1 (January/February 1976): 10.

is so rapid that a new hospital will be obsolete in 20 years. Therefore hospitals of the future will be disposable or rearrangeable, with a central core connecting independent floors with movable partitions and movable exterior walls. Pneumatic linen and trash conveyors, monorail trucks directed by computer, a 25-mile-radius paging system, and computer information systems are all examples of current technology housed in modern hospitals. Technology will be exploited through the institutionalization of change in medicine, as it has been for decades in industry. The medical establishment will offer only weak resistance to change and will adapt rather than react, as long as it profits from such change.

Because medical decisions are dependent upon acquiring and analyzing information about the patient, information technology and the computer promise to play an important role in future medical practice. As our geographical mobility increases, the frequency with which a patient enounters a physician for the first time will increase. The physician can ill afford to spend increased amounts of time both in renewing his knowledge of new developments and in more extensive patient interviews. The handling of medical information must become more efficient, with the computer being used for diagnosis and to outline treatment proposals.

Modern transportation, computer technology and lessons learned in Vietnam about evacuation of the sick and wounded "will consign the contemporary system of medical care to obsolescence" (Ehrlich, 1973:72). Instead of trying to place a doctor in every neighborhood, teams of doctors will apply life-saving and health-saving equipment in centralized medical centers where patients can be brought quickly. In the future, most life processes will be monitored from a distance. The majority of diagnoses will be made without the doctor's being with the patient. Telephones and closed circuit television will permit the doctor to examine patients in their homes. Blood analysis and x-rays will be transmitted to medical centers, and only the most seriously ill patients will need to be transported to hospitals. Doctors, even more specialized, will be clustered in such medical centers, to which patients needing urgent care will be brought by helicopter or other emergency transportation (Ibid.).

The new systems of technological health care will bring less personal relations between doctor and patient, but more medical care will be offered to more people. Time-consuming reassurances, which some persons seek when visiting a doctor, will perhaps be provided by a new discipline or by medical paraprofessionals.

Immunization against contagious disease is well accepted. In the future, government-sponsored immunization programs will be required of all citizens. Multiphasic Health Testing (MHT) programs, using nurses and technicians to test all organ systems periodically, has been in wide use for nearly 10 years. There is no doubt that these programs are effective in detecting early disease in 85 percent of apparently healthy persons. Prospective (or predictive) medicine will identify the dozen or so health hazards for each patient's age, sex, and racial group, modified by any individual risk factors. An MHT examination to appraise individual health hazards will eventually be required for insurance purposes and perhaps even for eligibility to receive government-paid health benefits. We

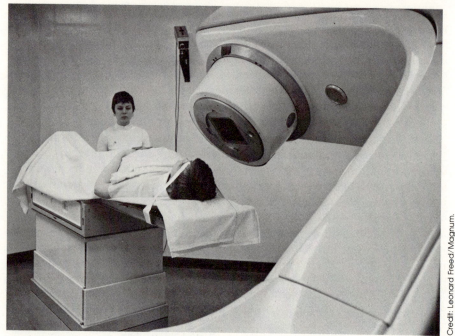

The future will bring more highly technical and sophisticated equipment that will improve the quality of care but will add to the increasing costs.

will have greater control over degenerative diseases and can expect some increase in life expectancy. Better health through earlier disease detection, as well as a healthier environment and lifestyle, will lead to a better life for many.

As patients, we will be much more knowledgeable about medical and health matters; indeed, we will be held responsible for our own health. Our basic right to health will be recognized; but also, under law, we will be obligated to remain as healthy as possible. Social controls will be placed on the individual to protect his own health. Cigarette smoking may be controlled, or a tobacco substitute used to protect the health of smokers and nonsmokers alike. Our health will be checked by frequent health-hazard appraisals and computer decisions, but we will have only infrequent contacts with physicians. As medical costs continue to rise, laws will control excessive, nonessential use of health-care resources; these restrictions will probably be enforced by economic penalties.

We are now seeing the first evidence of these changes in the Professional Standards Review Organizations (PSROs) under federally funded health plans (Wilson, 1976:90). Under the PSRO concept, first mandated by law in 1972, doctors organize themselves on a local basis to review and monitor the cost and quality of medical practice and services in their area. The failure of doctors to comply with standards set by the PSRO can result in being ineligible to receive payments from a government-paid medical program, such as Medicare or Medicaid. In the future, a PSRO could review all regional medical performance.

Most illnesses will be predicted in advance; we will belong to a health plan offering cradle-to-grave medical and health services; and we will never need to find a doctor because we will know our source of medical care through membership in an HMO association. We shall learn to treat ourselves for most minor illnesses.

Most medical care will be rendered through health-maintenance organizations (HMOs), which will include both hospital and ambulatory care. Each HMO will be responsible for all aspects of health and medical care for its own membership. Each will have a large computer, including a regional medical-data bank linked to a national network of medical-data centers. Even if we need care in a distant city, our complete medical records will be immediately available. Part of this record will be our private medical dossier and part will be public property. The privacy of our medical record will be limited, and in some circumstances our medical record will be accessible for other than medical purposes.

The health industry will expand to about $400 billion and about 10 percent of all goods and services by the year 2000. Because of the high cost of medical care, paid largely through tax-supported national health insurance, the physician's autonomy in medical decisions will be limited. Medical decisions requiring hospitalization, surgery, and other expensive therapy will be monitored and subject to review before they are implemented. Both the quality and cost of medical care will be regulated, much as public utilities are regulated today. The patient's medical record will be checked against a set of decision rules in the computer, and medical decisions will be made with due consideration for limited resources.

Government Medical Planning

For the near future, the federal government has a five-year health plan. It represents the U.S. Public Health Services' blueprint for dealing with major health problems between 1978 and 1982. Issued in a report, *Forward Plan for Health*, the plan seeks a "major attack on cost escalation as the factor now driving national health policy" ("New Plan ...," September 8, 1976:1). It emphasizes more use of preventive services, improved quality of care, and more research on medical malpractice. Cost of malpractice insurance in 1976 amounted to the equivalent of $15 per bed each day added to hospital rates and $2 billion to national health care costs, the report stated.

To control future health-care costs, the report noted that Congress is considering changes in Medicare and Medicaid policies and benefits. It mentioned the specific possibility that all doctors will be required to accept reasonable fees for treating elderly Medicare patients. At present only about half the doctors in the United States accept Medicare patients who do not pay the doctor directly. The report also suggested eliminating Medicare's requirement that a patient be in the hospital at least three days before he can be admitted to a nursing home. Increased coverage for mental-health treatment and clinic services was also proposed.

This all suggests that the power and privilege that doctors and hospitals enjoy today may be more closely controlled by government. Whether such control will basically change the power and profits that large hospitals and medical-school complexes have amassed remains an open question. If private business corporations are used as a model of the future, it is highly doubtful whether the federal government will be successful in changing or altering the power and position of our medical establishment.

SUMMARY

It is often said that our health-care system is sicker than its patients. Our view depends on how we define the social problems of medicine and of health-care institutions. Some define medical care as a social right; others as a privilege we pay for. Conservatives who adhere to the idealized model say that we can receive the best medical care from private doctors freely chosen and paid for on a fee-for-service basis. The reality model, following the radical approach, interprets the situation as a highly structured, interrelated system dominated by three large institutions—medical empires (medical schools and hospitals), the financing-planning complex (e.g., Blue Cross–Blue Shield), and the medical-industrial complex (drug firms, suppliers, and construction firms). The whole profitable and powerful system is paid for by taxpayers and patients.

The public views the delivery of medical care as very problematic. The three major social issues of medicine and health care are: lack of access to and maldistribution of doctors; excessive costs; and incompetent, poor-quality health care. These problems are especially acute for the poor and the minorities. Some conservative government officials and doctors consider our health-care problems as personal ones related to our lifestyles: excessive use of alcohol and tobacco and lack of proper diet and exercise. Some argue that medical care has little to do with our longevity.

The incidence and prevalence of these problems are growing more severe. In large metropolitan areas there are 500 persons for each doctor, but more than 3,000 persons in rural counties. Some areas have no doctors. Between 1966 and 1976, medical-care costs rose 102 percent, while all other goods and services increased 76 percent.

The chief causes of medical-care problems are our value system, the structure and organization of the system, and financial fraud and waste. Our norms and values demand more and better medical care, and more personal and social problems are being interpreted medically. Structurally, medicine grew from a kind of cottage industry (the doctor's home and office) to a modern industry dominated by large institutions with concentrated power, prestige, and wealth. Aims of centralized medical-school complexes are directed more at basic research and science than at improving the delivery of health care. Other medical institutions pursue profit and power, often at the expense of the patient. Excessive waste and fraud, especially in government-funded programs, drives up health-care costs.

The many proposals for dealing with our health-care problems include national health insurance, health-maintenance organizations, reforms of medical schools, redistribution of new doctors, use of paraprofessionals, Medicaid reforms, and government planning and coordination of health care on a regional basis.

Future changes in health-care institutions will entail technology and centralization of services. Although our right to good health will be recognized, social controls will be placed over individual lifestyle and use of medical facilities. As costs continue to rise, more health organizations will appear, along with greater government regulation of the entire system. Nevertheless, it is doubtful whether government will be able to contain the profits or power of the medical system.

CAREER OPPORTUNITIES

Health-Services Administrators and Assistants.

Medical and health care is provided by various-size organizations. Each of them requires effective management. Administrators, nearly half of them women, coordinate the various functions and activities needed to make a health organization work. They form decisions on need for additional staff or equipment, space requirements, and budget. Some administer in-service training programs and provide nursing and food services. They must also maintain a good working relationship with civic groups. For further information write to: National Health Council, Inc., 1740 Broadway, New York, New York 10019.

Medical-Record Administrators and Assistants.

All health-care facilities keep medical records on each person, as well as overall reports on use of medical services. Systems must be developed for documenting, storing, and retrieving medical information. The medical-record staff processes and analyzes records and reports, compiles medical statistics required by state and national health agencies, and conducts research to evaluate patient care and use of resources. For a sociology major with good training in research methodology and statistics, this would prove a good entry-level job with excellent opportunities for advancement. For further information, write to: American Medical Record Association, 875 North Michigan Ave., Chicago, Ill. 60611.

Medical Sociologists.

These professionals study and analyzes the structure, functions, and system of health and medical care and how human behavior is affected within that social system. A background in sociology (usually an advanced degree) is required, and an understanding of social systems analysis is helpful. In recent years opportunities in medical sociology have expanded as more attention and money have been devoted to our system of delivering medical services. As demand grows for health planning, so will the need for well-educated medical sociologists. For further information write to: American Sociological Association, 1722 N St., N.W., Washington, D.C. 20036.

REFERENCES

Abelson, Philip
1976 "Cost-Effective Health Care." Science 192, 4240 (May 14): 619.
Altman, Laurence K.
1976 "Physician Scores Manpower Plan." New York Times (April 6): 15.
"AMA Newsletter." American Medical News 19, 25 (June 21): 15, 1976.
Auerbach, Stuart
1976 "Health-Insurance Issue is Politically Alive and Well." Allentown Morning Call (April 7): 13.
"Behind Those Skyrocketing Health-Care Costs." U.S. News & World Report 80, 19 (May 10): 71, 1976.
"Billions in Medicaid Ripoffs: Can Anyone Stop It?" U.S. News & World Report 80, 12 (March 22): 18–19, 1976.
Blake, Elinor and Thomas Bodenheimer
1976 "Hospitals For Sale (and Other Ways to Kill a Public Health System)." Pp. 330–34 in David Kotelchuck, ed. Prognosis Negative: Crisis in the Health Care System. New York: Vintage.
Blumenthal, David and James Fallows
1976 "Health: The Care We Want and Need." Pp. 202–8 in Jacqueline Scherer, ed. Annual Editions: Readings in Sociology 76/77. Guilford, Conn.: Dushkin.
Bornemeier, Walter
1971 "Rx for the Family Doctor Shortage." Pp. 59–64 in Stephen Lewin, ed. The Nation's Health. New York: Wilson.
Brody, Jane E.
1976 "Surgery's Hidden Side—the Incompetents." Allentown Morning Call (January 27): 19.
Bromberg, Myron and Anita Hotchkiss
1976 "Medical Malpractice: Diagnosis and Cures." Bar Journal: New Jersey State Bar Association. (August): 34–39.
Carlson, Rick J.
1975 The End of Medicine. New York: Wiley.
Cheever, Julia
1975 Your Community and Beyond: An Information and Action Guide. Palo Alto, Calif.: Page Ficklin.
"Child Health Care Held U.S. Scandal." Allentown Morning Call (June 12): 1, 1976.

Conrad, Peter
    1975 "Medicalization of Deviant Behavior." Social Problems 23,1 (October): 12–21.

Cordtz, Dan
    1971 "Change Begins in the Doctor's Of!ce." Pp. 64–70 in Stephen Lewin, ed. The Nation's Health. New York: Wilson.

"Critically Ill Patients Charged an Average of $14,300 by Hospital." National Enquirer (June 15): 10, 1976.

"Democrats' NHI Plank Backs No Specific Bill." American Medical News 19, 25 (June 21): 1, 8, 1976.

Ehrenreich, Barbara and John Ehrenreich
    1971 The American Health Empire: Power, Profits and Politics. New York: Vintage.

Ehrlich, George
    1973 "Health Challenges of the Future." Annals of the American Academy of Political and Social Science 408 (July): 70–82.

Endicott, Kenneth
    1976 "U.S. Health 1975." Public Health Reports 91, 2 (March/April): inside front cover.

Enos, Darryl
    1976 "Blacks, Chicanos and the Health Care System." Pp. 242–62 in Don Zimmerman, D. Laurence Wieder, and Siu Zimmerman. Understanding Social Problems. New York: Praeger.

Ensminger, Barry
    1976 "The $8-Billion Hospital Bed Overrun: A Consumer's Guide to Stopping Wasteful Construction." Pp. 413–19 in David Kotelchuck, ed., Prognosis Negative: Crisis in the Health Care System. New York: Vintage.

Fein, Rashi
    1975 "Health Care Cost: A Distorted Issue." The American Federationist 82, 6 (June): 13–17.

"Financing Health Care." AFL-CIO News 21, 25 (June 19): 4, 1976.

Fogg, Susan
    1975 "National Health Care: The Liberals Viewpoints." Long Island Press (December 16): 19.

"Fraud, Waste Cited in Health Care." Allentown Morning Call (February 17): 18, 1976.

Freidson, Eliot
    1972 "The Organization of Medical Practice." P. 341 in Howard E. Freeman, Sol Levine, and Leo Reeder, eds. Handbook of Medical Sociology, 2nd ed. Englewood Cliffs, N.J.: Prentice-Hall.

Gorwitz, Kurt and Ruth Dennis
    1976 "On the Decrease in the Life Expectancy of Black Males in Michigan." Public Health Reports 91, 2 (March/April): 141–45.

Haggard, Howard W.
    1929 Devils, Drugs and Doctors. New York: Harper & Brothers.

"Health Fund Cuts Pushing New York to Brink of Crisis." American Medical News 19, 24 (June 14): 1, 15, 1976.

"Health-Plan Waste Hit by Aspin." Allentown Morning Call (January 12): 3, 1976.

Health Policy Advisory Center
    1975 "Your Health Care in Crisis." Pp. 45–48 in Julia Cheever, ed. Your Community and Beyond: An Information and Action Guide. Palo Alto, Calif.: Page Ficklin.

Hess, John
    1976 "Moreland Panel Proposes Reform of Medicare Rates." New York Times (April 8): 24.

Hicks, Nancy
    1976 "HEW Escaping Ford's Budget Cutting with Help of Congress and Because of Inflated Costs." New York Times (January 12): 12.

"High Doctor Fees Cited for Kidney Patients." Allentown Morning Call (September 10): 11, 1975.

Horton, Paul and Gerald Leslie
    1974 The Sociology of Social Problems. 5th ed. Englewood Cliffs, N.J.: Prentice-Hall.

Illich, Ivan
    1976 Medical Nemesis. New York: Pantheon.

"Inquiry to Determine Whether the AMA Curbs Health Care." New York Times (April 15): 36, 1976.

"Issues in PGH March." Philadelphia Evening Bulletin (February 25): 18, 1976.

"Is Your Hospital Drug-Wise?" Voice of Cement, Lime & Gypsum Workers International 38, 12 (December): 19, 1975.

Johnson, Sheila K.
    1974 "Health Maintenance: It Works," The New York Times Magazine (April 28): 34–54.

Kessel, Reuben
    1975 "Higher Education and the Nation's Health." Pp. 372–83 in Rose Giallombardo, ed. Contemporary Social Issues. Santa Barbara, Calif.: Hamilton.

Kessler, Richard
    1976 "Accelerated Medical Education." Journal of the American Medical Association 235, 24 (June 14): 2629.

King, Lester S.
    1958 The Medical World of the Eighteenth Century. Chicago: University of Chicago Press.

Kotelchuck, David, ed.
    1976 Prognosis Negative: Crisis in the Health Care System. New York: Vintage.

Lerner, Monroe
    1971 "Health as a Social Problem." In Erwin O. Smigel, ed. Handbook on the Study of Social Problems. Chicago: Rand McNally.

Lewin, Stephen, ed.
    1971 "Revamping Our Medical Schools." Pp. 24–25 in Stephen Lewin. The Nation's Health. New York: Wilson.

Lyons, Richard D.
    1977 "Doctors May Hit Ceiling Over Ceiling on Fees." Allentown Morning Call (April 27): 1.

"Medicaid Turnover Ford Goal." Allentown Morning Call (January 15): 15, 1976.

"Medicare Payouts Nearly $20 Million." Allentown Morning Call (February 26): 1, 1976.

Mitchell, Bridger and William Schwartz
1976 "The Financing of National Health Insurance." Science 192, 4240 (May 14): 621-29.

Morland, J. Kenneth, Jack Balswick, John Belcher, and Morton Rubin
1975 Social Problems in the United States. New York: Ronald Press.

"New Plan Emphasizes Medical Cost Controls." Allentown Morning Call (September 8): 1, 1976.

Nourse, Alan E.
1976 "The Controversy over National Health Insurance." Social Education 40, 2 (February): 88-92.

Palmore, Erdman and Clark Luikart
1972 "Health and Social Factors Related to Life Satisfaction." Journal of Health and Social Behavior 13 (March): 68-80.

Peterson, Roland L.
1976 "The Designation of Health Service Areas: HSAs." Public Health Reports 91, 1 (January/February): 9-18.

"Poll Finds Public Backs Health Security System." AFL-CIO News (September 28): 6, 1974.

"Probes Revealing Fraud by Doctors." Allentown Morning Call (March 2): 31, 1976.

Rensberger, Boyce
1976 "Doctors View Unfit Physicians as Big Problem, Threat to Lives." Allentown Morning Call (January 26): 1.

Roemer, Milton I.
1971 "Nationalized Medicine for America." Transaction 8, 11 (September): 31.

Rubel, Eugene J.
1976 "Implementing the National Health Planning and Resources Development Act of 1974." Public Health Reports (January/February): 3-8.

Rubsamen, David S.
1976 "Medical Malpractice." Scientific American 235, 2 (August): 18-23.

Scarpitti, Frank R.
1977 Social Problems, 2nd ed. New York: Holt, Rinehart and Winston Inc.

Schorr, David
1970 Don't Get Sick in America. Nashville, Tenn.: Aurora.

"Senate Bill Puts Controls on Doctor Training." Congressional Quarterly 34, 23 (June 5): 1433-35, 1976.

Shearer, Lloyd
1975 "Unnecessary Surgery: Intelligence Report." Parade Magazine (September 7): 7.

Shields, George S.
1973 "Health Care in the Year 2000." Paper presented at Futurology 2 Conference, June 12, 1973. Mount Saint Joseph College, Cincinnati, Ohio.

"Should Federal Government Allocate Residencies?" Congressional Quarterly 34, 23 (June 5): 1435, 1976.

Shryock, Richard H.
1966 Medicine in America: Historical Essays. Baltimore: Johns Hopkins Press.

Stevens, Robert and Rosemary Stevens
1974 Welfare Medicine in America. New York: Free Press.

Stoler, Peter
1976 "**Medical Nemesis** by Ivan Illich, Review." Time (June 28): 64–66.

Strauss, Anselm
1975 "Medical Ghettos." Pp. 331–39 in Paul Horton and Gerald Leslie, eds. Readings in the Sociology of Social Problems. 2nd ed. Englewood Cliffs, N.J.: Prentice-Hall.

Thomlinson, Ralph
1976 Population Dynamics: Causes and Consequences of Work Demographic Change. New York: Random House.

"Unnecessary Surgery Disclosed by Probers." Allentown Sunday Call-Chronicle (January 25): A-4, 1976.

"U.S. Lifestyle Key Health Hazard, Report Says." Allentown Morning Call (January 13): 1, 1976.

Wilson, F. Paul
1976 "The Controversy over National Health Insurance." Social Education 40, 2 (February): 88–91.

SUGGESTED READINGS

Barrett, Stephen and Gilda Knight. The Health Robbers. Philadelphia: Stickley, 1976.
An exposé of health frauds, from phony sex clinics to dubious dentistry; from food fads to the water we drink.

Enos, Darryl D. and Paul Sultan. The Sociology of Health Care: Social, Economic and Political Perspectives. New York: Praeger. 1977.
An excellent overview of the health-care system, how it operates, current directions of change, and prospects for the future. It integrates very well the perspectives of various disciplines, while maintaining a sociological analysis of our health-care system.

Illich, Ivan D. Medical Nemesis: The Expropriation of Health. New York: Pantheon. 1976.
A critique of the existing medical-care system that supports the basic point that modern medical- and health-care systems cause more illness than they cure.

Kane, Robert L. et al., eds. The Health Gap: Medical Services and the Poor. New York: Springer. 1976.
Representative and important readings on the nature of this social problem and divergent outlooks for the future.

Kotelchuck, David., ed. Prognosis Negative: Crisis in the Health Care System. New York: Vintage. 1976.
The Health Policy Advisory Center examines the industrialization of the health-care system, its impact on patients and health-care workers

(professionals and nonprofessionals), and the economic and social forces shaping the system.

Maxmen, Jerold S. The Post-Physician Era: Medicine in the 21st Century. New York: Wiley-Interscience. 1976.

Computers and the "medic" (through TV and computers) will make doctors, as we know them, obsolete. Some novel views are presented.

Periodicals Worth Exploring
Journal of the American Medical Association (JAMA)
Journal of the American Public Health Association
Journal of Health and Social Behavior
Social Security Bulletin
Social Work in Health Care

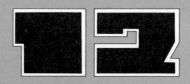

Labeling and Treating Mental Illness

DEFINITIONS OF THE PROBLEM
Two conflicting models of mental illness:
a) The disease–medical model (based on deviance, labeling, and treatment). Classifications of mental illness—as neuroses and psychoses.
b) The social-model (Szasz and Scheff), based on problems of living.
Sociological perspective of problems in institutional care:
a) Dual system for poor and nonpoor.
b) Violations of personal and civil rights.
c) Abusive and inadequate care.
d) Little or no aftercare.

INCIDENCE AND PREVALENCE OF THE PROBLEM
Mental hospitals being replaced by community clinics.
Treated episodes of mental illness are three times as great as in 1955.
Labeling by social class and other social factors affecting prevalence.
The system for treating mental illness.

CAUSES OF THE PROBLEM
Physiological (biochemical) theories.
Psychological theories (Freudian and learning theories).
Sociological theories (labeling, "strain," and social-structure theories).

PROPOSED SOLUTIONS TO THE PROBLEM
Physiological-medical solutions (drugs, electroshocks, and psychosurgery).
Psychological solutions (psychoanalysis and behavior modification).
Social solutions (family therapy, therapeutic communities, and community-health programs).
Restructuring the system.

FUTURE OF THE PROBLEM
Dominance of disease-medical model.
Improved future for mentally ill.
Future goals of National Mental Health Association.
Improved public attitudes.

SUMMARY

> If the Wizard of Oz had had modern behavioral modification techniques in his bag of tricks, the cowardly lion might well have been lobotomized, the tin woodman tranquilized, and the scarecrow treated with operant conditioning.
>
> "Commentary," **Mental Health,** Spring 1975:2; attributed to Judge David L. Bazelon.

Who is crazy, insane, or mentally ill? Who is normal, sane, and mentally healthy? One experiment answers: "Who knows?" This experiment, by Stanford psychology professor D. S. Rosenhan, showed that the labels "sane" and "insane" are arbitrary. He and seven others gained admission to 12 different mental hospitals in five states on the East and West coasts. They all reported hearing voices that said "empty," "hollow," or "thud." All used false names and occupations, but everything else about themselves they revealed truthfully. One was diagnosed as manic-depressive, the other seven as schizophrenic. While in the hospital they acted naturally, speaking to patients and staff normally. They spent between nine and 52 days in the hospital (19 days on the average). All but one were released with the diagnosis schizophrenia in remission; that is, they were getting better. While in the mental institution, they were treated like the other patients. All together the eight researchers were given nearly 2,100 pills.

The staff apparently thought that if a person was confined, he or she must be mentally ill; so the "patients'" most normal actions or explanations were interpreted as symptoms of their illness. For example, one psychiatric nurse, on seeing that one researcher often took notes, recorded that the patient "engaged in writing behavior." But more serious things happened, as Rosenhan reports:

> Often enough, a patient would go "berserk" because he had, wittingly or unwittingly, been mistreated by, say, an attendant. A nurse coming upon the scene would rarely inquire even cursorily into the environmental stimuli of the patient's behavior. Rather, she assumed that his upset derived from his pathology, not from his present interactions with other staff members.... But never were the staff found to assume that one of themselves or the structure of the hospital had anything to do with the patient's behavior (January 19, 1973:253).

Although nearly a third of the regular patients detected almost immediately that the researchers were normal, not one of the staff members discovered that the pseudopatients were sane.

When the staff of one mental hospital heard of this experiment, they asserted that no such errors were likely to happen at their hospital. Rosenhan replied by saying that sometime during the next three months he would send one or more researchers who would try to get admitted. During the next three months at that mental institution, 41 out of 193 patients admitted were judged to be impostors by at least one staff members—even though Rosenhan had sent no one (Ibid., 250–58).

Rosenhan's study suggests that our society labels a wide range of behaviors mental illness. Psychiatrists cannot agree on what mental illness is, what causes it, and what cures it. But they do suggest that our social institutions and systems for helping the mentally ill often make them worse.

There are almost as many explanations for the causes of mental illness as there are social scientists interested in the phenomenon. Their reliance on so many conflicting theories indicates that social scientists are far from sure about what causes mental illness, and that no one cause (or theory) is able to explain all types of mental illness.

DEFINITIONS OF MENTAL ILLNESS

There are two major, conflicting views of mental illness. The dominant one, built on deviance theory, holds that it is a disease and should be treated as such. Certain symptoms can be diagnosed; these can be classified for the type and severity of the disease involved; and plans of treatment can be prescribed by a psychiatrist to help or cure the patient. This disease–medical model is best summed up as follows:

> It is widely believed today that just as some people suffer from diseases of the liver or kidney, others suffer from diseases of the mind or personality; that persons afflicted with such "mental illness" are psychologically and socially inferior to those not so afflicted (Szasz, 1970:xv).

Psychiatrist Karl Menninger maintains that "all people have mental illness of different degrees at different times" (1963:32). The disease–medical model of mental illness seems to be well institutionalized in our society and culture. Even such psychiatric terms as neurotic, psychotic, schizophrenic, and paranoid are an integral part of our language.

The other definition of mental illness is what we shall call the social model. Its advocates argue that symptoms diagnosed as mental illness should actually be considered problems of interpersonal behavior, as unsolved difficulties of living with others and oneself in society. The disease diagnosis, they charge, labels a social rule-breaker as a deviant who then becomes cruelly stigmatized. A psychiatric diagnosis of mental illness, unlike diagnoses in other areas of medicine, affects those labeled as such and becomes a self-fulfilling prophecy. In addition, the social model stresses the social processes involved in the recognition, commitment, and treatment of the mentally deviant.

The Disease-Medical Model

Millions of dollars are spent each year to treat people on the assumption that they suffer from an ailment that can be alleviated or cured by medical or clinical procedures, as with any other disease. Mental patients themselves often maintain that something is physically and emotionally wrong. Clifford Beers, a pioneer in the mental-health movement, described his condition: "My brain was in a ferment. It felt as if pricked by a million needles at white heat. My whole body felt like it would be torn apart . . ." (1921:17). The nervous breakdown of Sylvia Plath, a young poet who committed suicide, has been described as "a bell jar which descended over her and which provided a distorting lens through which she saw her world and the people in it. She knew something was wrong with her mind and this terrified her" (Morland et al., 1975:425).

The disease–medical model emphasizes that mental illness is real; it has physical and emotional causes and effects. It cannot be dismissed, as the social model suggests, as merely a label or as a lack of interpersonal skills needed to cope with life. At the same time, the disease–medical approach accepts the possibility that the problem may stem from biological, environmental, or internal psychological dysfunctions (Buss, 1966). It tends to disguise or disregard larger structural problems of society itself, or the system used for treating people labeled "mentally ill."

The disease–medical practitioners have developed elaborate systems for classifying and defining types of mental illness in order to identify symptoms and treat the patient. Although there is no real consensus between cultures or psychiatrists on how one knows absolutely what ailment a person may have, there is a general agreement on broad classifications. In the United States, mental illness is divided into two main types, neuroses and psychoses. Neurotic behavior is considered less serious than psychotic behavior; a person with a neurosis is better able to function in the real world. In practice, however, it is often difficult to set a borderline between normal and neurotic or between neurosis and psychosis. Let us look at these two classifications of mental illness.

Neuroses. We all have things that worry us or make us anxious. When the intensity of worry or anxiety is great enough to impair a person's ability to interact with others or carry on normal functions, such behavior is labeled neurotic. Neurotics frequently report being worried, having excessive fears, experiencing pain, or feeling compelled to act in a certain way. People under stress report some of the same symptoms, but they usually vanish when the stressful situation ends. With neurotics, however, the symptoms persist or return periodically. Various neuroses include depression, hypochondria (constant feeling of illness), obsessive neurosis (compulsive behavior; e.g., washing one's hands frequently), phobia (an unreasonable fear), and psychosomatic illness (emotionally caused headaches, rashes, ulcers, etc.).

Psychoses. Psychotics experience a sharp break with reality. They act in a way that is out of keeping with situations in the real world. Reality is distorted—they hear or see things no one else does—and they are wholly

Mental depression, despair, and conditions leading to neurosis or psychosis can be found in any large community today.

unable to function in society. The psychotic is more likely to be put in a mental hospital, usually because his behavior becomes uncontrollable and intolerable to his family and friends. It is not unusual for a patient diagnosed as psychotic (particularly if he is old or poor) to be permanently put away. In fact, there are probably as many psychotics living in the community as in mental hospitals (Pasamanick, 1961:59-63).

The disease–medical practitioners recognize two broad types of psychosis, organic and functional. Organic psychoses have physical causes—damage to the brain cells from injury, tumors, syphilis, alcoholism, and senility. Functional psychoses have no clearly defined physical cause and are assumed to have a psychological basis.

There are three main subtypes of functional psychosis: schizophrenia, affective psychosis, and paranoia.

Schizophrenia is the most widespread label applied to psychotics, accounting for over 50 percent of all chronic mental-hospital cases. Contrary to conventional wisdom, schizophrenia does not mean that a person has a "split" personality. The schizoid has only one personality; it is split only in the sense that his feelings and thoughts are not integrated together. There are several types of schizophrenia, of which the most common are simple schizophrenia (general withdrawal from reality), hebephrenic schizophrenia (hallucinations and seclusion), catatonic schizophrenia (in a stupor and immobile), and chronic undifferentiated schizophrenia (symptoms not clear and cannot be otherwise categorized).

Affective psychoses are marked by disturbances of mood or feeling, usually in extremes. Two types are manic-depressive psychosis and involutional melancholia. Classic symptoms of manic-depression are violent swings from extreme happiness and elation to extreme depression. The cycles of moods vary in length and regularity, but the depression usually lasts longer than the elation. Involutional melancholia also includes chronic depression, but it differs from manic-depression in that it generally occurs during menopause.

Paranoia classifies those who are extremely suspicious of others and imagine they are being persecuted by someone, real or unreal. For instance, a person may believe that secret agents from a foreign country are trying to kill him. Paranoia usually focuses on one or two concerns, and no logical arguments based on reality can convince the person that he is not in danger. Often, other behavior patterns tend to be normal and the person may otherwise be realistic (Buss and Buss, 1969:3, 5).

Shortcomings of These Diagnoses. The diagnoses of these neuroses and psychoses are based on major symptoms, but often these symptoms tend to be unreliable over time. Persons may exhibit symptoms of several classifications at the same time or consecutively. Agreement among psychiatrists rarely exceeds 50 percent on what form of psychosis a person suffers from, or even whether he is psychotic. Social-class factors often enter into the diagnosis. The concepts used in interpreting symptoms of schizophrenia are also "vague, amorphous, and abstract" (Camenietzki and Abbot, March 1976:118). As Rosenhan observed, "we have known for a long time that diagnoses are not useful or reliable . . ." (1973:251). Yet the disease–medical approach continues to use the broad, general classifications of mental illness, despite their shortcomings.

The social-model advocates, such as Thomas Szasz and Thomas Scheff, argue that the lack of agreement among psychiatrists on the symptoms and diagnosis of mental illness makes the disease-medical model extremely suspect. In common physical diseases there is considerable agreement on symptoms, diagnosis, treatment, and understanding of how the treatment works. With mental disorders, however, there is little agreement on appropriate treatment or on how methods such as shock treatments actually work.

The Social Model

There are other perspectives that advocates of the social model have about those labeled mentally ill. Thomas Szasz, M.D. and specialist in psychiatry, in *The Myth of Mental Illness* (1961) and *The Manufacture of*

Madness (1970), argues that there is no such physical disease as mental illness. He does not deny that behavior labeled as mental illness exists, but he contends that these behaviors are actually "a problem in living." He maintains that mental disorders can only be fully understood within the social conditions that create them. They are deviations from accepted social, legal, and moral norms—"defective strategies" for dealing with life's problems.

The mentally "ill" behave as they do because they have no better way at the moment for handling their problems. They communicate to others in the "language of illness" because they feel it is useful and helpful to themselves. It may draw people's attention to them and their problems when they have been ignored by people. The psychiatrist, then, is not a doctor of medicine; he becomes an interpreter of social norms, who often penalizes those whose "strategies for interpersonal relations" he interprets as defective. Szasz feels that the disease model of mental illness, which may have been useful in the nineteenth century, is today "scientifically worthless."

Thomas Scheff points out that if a person violates social norms, he is labeled a deviant. Society takes certain "residual norms" so much for granted that these are considered normal. For example, one does not talk to another person who is not present. When these "residual norms" are violated, onlookers become upset and frightened by such behavior. They consider that a person who violates such norms has lost his senses, and they label him as mentally ill.

Thereafter the labeled person can follow certain rules (in any culture) to be considered mentally sick. Accepting the label and following the rules gives the person an opportunity to withdraw into a socially acceptable sick role. He now has a chance to relinquish all personal responsibility for his actions. But once labeled, a person cannot easily shed the stigmatizing terms "mentally ill," "insane," and "crazy." Mental illness is thus a form of learned behavior and labeling (Scheff, 1966).

Karl Menninger (1963) suggests that mental illness should not be defined as a thing, such as a disease, to which a label is attached. It is a way of behaving, and the behavior should be described without calling it neurosis, psychosis, schizophrenia, or paranoia. Menninger tells the story of a college senior who, under great academic pressure and stress, began to write strange letters home, miss her classes, and suffer academically. The college psychiatrist recognized her confusion and depression and advised her to "dropout" of school for a time. Instead of labeling the student as mentally ill, he attributed her difficulty to excessive stresses and said she could be helped with proper rest and treatment. The student was treated, recovered, and eventually returned to finish her education. According to Menninger, if the student had been labeled psychotic, the reactions of others toward her and her own self-reaction would probably have been far different. Those who have mental disorders need help rather than "damning labels."

According to social scientist Erving Goffman, people who are socially defined as "different" either acquire a stigma that leads them to devise ways of behaving to conceal the blot on their social identity, or they act out the role prepared for them to protect themselves from the negative reactions of others. People defined as mentally ill may become mentally ill because society has left them little opportunity or few options to act in any other way (1963). This is the danger of labeling.

Statistical and Practical Definitions

There are two other minor, less controversial definitions of mental illness: the statistical and the practical, or functional.

The statistical definition is descriptive and devoid of most social values. Anyone who acts differently from the overwhelming majority is considered abnormal. The definition is based on the "normal distribution curve," which graphically illustrates how often a trait or behavior pattern occurs within the society.

The statistical approach provides a standard for what is normal, but it does not give a standard of mental health, because it does not say whether a dominant trait is mentally desirable or undesirable. As people's traits and behavior patterns change over time, abnormal behavior may later become normal. At one time, a single girl was considered abnormal if she had premarital sex. Today, many would consider her normal.

The functional definition of mental illness is based on the answer to the practical question, "Can the person function at home and on the job?" If the answer is yes, the person is mentally healthy; if the answer is no, he is mentally ill. Even if a person displays symptoms of mental illness, he will be accepted as normal if he continues to function well. The higher one's social position or social class, the more likely that eccentric behavior will be tolerated, since the social functions performed by the upper strata are respected.

Problems of the Mental-Health System

Many sociologists define the basic social problems of mental illness as the treatment system established in our society and the effects that system has on people. They distinguish four problems that attend our system for treating mental illness:

1. a dual system of care: one for the poor, the other for the nonpoor
2. commitment of the poor people to mental hospitals, thus violating their personal and civil rights
3. abusive hospital care and lack of proper therapeutic treatment
4. inadequate care after release from the mental hospital

Dual System of Care. There is a dual system of care for the mentally ill in America. Half of the persons who seek psychiatric care receive it from private psychiatrists. Since they commonly charge $50 or more per hourly session, their clients are quite well-to-do or at least middle-class.

According to Dr. Herbert Modlin, Director of the Department of Preventive Psychiatry of the Menninger Foundation, "Privately practicing psychiatrists see very few minority-group members, very few children, and very few poor people" (1976:153). William Ryan's mental-health survey of Boston revealed that the patients of private psychiatrists are drawn from an even smaller segment of the population than had been imagined. In Boston the great majority of those undergoing private therapy live in the very small "Back Bay" area of the city, which contains only 3 or 4 percent of the city's population. Its residents are mostly single, college-educated youth who come from other cities and now live near the Harvard Club, the Ritz Carlton Hotel, the Public Library, and the theaters that specialize in foreign films (1971:144–45).

Even patients treated in some community psychiatric clinics are not much different from patients in private treatment, although the fees are a bit lower. The poor and the black also come to these clinics in fairly large numbers, but an elimination process prevents them from getting help there. A study in New Haven, Connecticut, showed that lower-status patients underwent more "authoritative or compulsory forms of treatment, such as electro-shock, tranquilizers and confinement" (Jones, April 1975:26). A three-year study at Johns Hopkins Hospital found that community psychiatrists tended to refer better-educated, more affluent, white patients for psychotherapy. A study of 366 cases at the Yale Medical School produced similar results: about two-thirds of the upper-class patients were accepted for psychoanalysis, compared with less than one-third from the lower classes (Ibid.).

Violation of Personal and Civil Rights. Drs. Paul Adams and Nancy McDonald have documented how the mental-health system operates against the poor. The psychiatrist considers questions about the patient's motivation, "suitability for treatment," and "ability to profit from therapy." In answering his own questions, the psychiatrist is able to screen out many poor persons from the clinic (1968:457–63). He then refers them, or commits them against their will, to the state mental hospital, where a person's rights are often violated and the treatment received is commonly inadequate.

A federal court in 1976 declared unconstitutional Pennsylvania's law that commits prisoners to mental institutions. The court ruled that it did not provide prisoners with the same protection against "involuntary commitment" as it provided to other citizens ("Cuckoo's Nest," May 7, 1976:1). Earlier, another court had ruled that 2,000 children committed to Pennsylvania's mental hospitals without hearings should be released or recommitted ("High Court...," December 16, 1975:8). The court case, brought by the Mental Patients Civil Liberties Project, involved a boy who was committed "so his family could go on vacation" and a 14-year-old girl committed because "she didn't get along with her mother" ("Children," July 25, 1975:2).

The treatment received by Ken Donaldson has gotten widespread attention. Donaldson sued two doctors at a Florida state mental institution for violating his constitutional rights. He had been confined between 1957 and 1971, and a jury ruled that the two doctors were guilty of "intentionally and maliciously" holding him there against his will. On June 25, 1975, the Supreme Court, to which the doctors had appealed, ruled unanimously that "mental patients cannot be confined against their will without treatment if they are not dangerous and are capable of surviving outside the institution" (Bloss, Spring 1976:5).

Abusive and Inadequate Treatment. Donaldson describes his treatment while in the hospital:

> It was abuse. It's just like being driven around like a bunch of cattle.... There were 1,300 men in the department I was in.... They had ... only one or two attendants for up to 240 patients. If the attendant doesn't like you ... it can be really rough.... You didn't get a sharp razor blade [for shaving] if they didn't like you. They'd let 25 other men shave with the blade and then give it to you.... You took a shower just at certain times. They'd turn on the shower and drive everybody through like cattle.... [It was] very dehumanizing (Ibid.).

The caliber of professional treatment he received was also poor:

> My doctor wasn't a psychiatrist and very few of them in the state hospital were psychiatrists. In fact, one of the doctors that I sued, who had 1,300 employees working under him in the state hospital, was licensed as an obstetrician.... Most of my close friends died while I was in the hospital, just from the abuse, from the medications.... Doctors don't know what some of these medications do, in my viewpoint. They just give them because they know it does something. In the state hospital they don't really practice psychiatry (Ibid., 6–7).

Treatment of the so-called criminally insane is even worse. In 1971, five inmates were finally released from an Ohio mental institution for the criminally insane. The men had never been convicted of a crime, but had only been kept for observation. Yet the five had remained locked up for periods between 22 and 41 years. A new psychiatrist noticed them, considered them fit for release, and took up their cases. At the time, he estimated that there were "over 100 other patients in the same institution who were in a similar situation" (McKee and Robertson, 1975: 504).

Lack of Proper Aftercare. In recent years, the number of persons confined to large state mental hospitals has dropped. However, this has created a new problem: a lack of proper follow-up care after persons leave the mental institution. They are supposed to be cared for by new community-based aftercare agencies, but these are too few and too poorly funded to handle the flood of mentally ill patients (many not fully recovered) who have returned to the community.

Residents in Queens, New York, have expressed fears about area mental patients who have been released to unsupervised rooming houses. They wander "helplessly around neighborhoods, exposing themselves before women and children, urinating in public, riding up and down in automatic elevators" (Doll, Winter 1975:23). In California, former patients are placed in rundown hotels because they have no homes to which to return. They receive little if any care or help. On Long Island the story is the same: hundreds of former patients of state mental hospitals, many of them elderly, are housed in the community's rundown hotels. Lonely and abandoned, they spend their time walking up and down the boardwalks.

Nationally we are abandoning former patients in substandard, profit-making boarding homes supported by federal welfare programs. The boarding-house problems include many of the unsafe, unsanitary, and inhumane conditions found in nursing homes. These boarding homes and single-room hotels are unregulated by any state or federal mental-health rules; yet they have become dumping grounds for thousands of elderly mentally ill patients for whom no proper aftercare is provided.

Too often we return them to the mental hospital (where they undergo drug therapy), then push them out quickly, and so on over again. One investigation cited an example of 12 patients in Nebraska who were admitted and discharged from state mental hospitals a total of 127 times ("Probe Bares," 1976:1). This may help the income of the hospitals, but it does not help the persons involved. Such "ping-pong-ball" treatment of the mentally ill must stop if we expect to solve the problem.

INCIDENCE AND PREVALENCE OF THE MENTAL-ILLNESS PROBLEM

Government data on mental illness lags two or three years behind current conditions. Furthermore, there is a vast difference between "treated" rates and "true" rates of mental illness. "Treated" refers to persons who were undergoing treatment or who were treated for mental illness during a particular year. As psychiatry defines more behavior as mental illness and as society accepts the definitions, more cases will be reported. As Bruce and Barbara Dohrenwald observed: "The median rate reported by studies published in 1950 or later was more than *seven* times greater than that for studies published earlier, and this difference more likely reflected a broader definition of disorder than any real change in prevalence" (Stark, 1975:135).

table 12-1   SELECTED FACTS ABOUT STATE AND COUNTY MENTAL HOSPITALS

YEAR	TOTAL ADMITTED	NET RELEASES*	DEATHS IN HOSPITAL	RESIDENTS AT END OF YEAR
1955	178,003	N.A.	44,384	558,922
1970	393,174	394,627	30,804	338,592
1973	377,020	386,962	19,899	248,562
1974	374,554	389,094	16,597	215,573

*Difference between all admissions and all releases.
Source: National Institute of Mental Health, in The Word Almanac and Book of Facts, 1976: 967.

One certainty about mental illness is that the number of persons confined in state and county mental hospitals has dropped dramatically. Between 1955 and 1974, the number has declined by over 60 percent—from almost 559,000 to 215,573. Table 12-1 shows this downward trend. Today there are probably fewer than 200,000 such inmates.

During 1973 there were 5,475,000 patient-care episodes* in all mental-health facilities, a rate of 2,631 per 100,000 population. Of these episodes, 65 percent were outpatient, 32 percent were inpatient, and 3 percent were day-care. The total of episodes in 1973 was over three times as great as the 1.7 million episodes in 1955. Most treatment for mental illness today is on an outpatient basis and at community mental-health centers. Even inpatient care at a local hospital is for a short duration, compared with the long-time confinement in a state or county mental hospital in the past. Long-term decline of inpatient care and confinement is clearly illustrated in Figure 12-1 (Taube and Redick, February 1976:1).

This sharp change, however, does *not* represent a real decline in the prevalence or incidence of reported mental illness. Indeed, the annual number of inpatient episodes actually increased from 1.2 million in 1955 to 1.7 million in 1973 (Ibid.). The basic change has occurred in the places and programs providing treatment. With new programs, especially community clinics, and a quadrupling of mental-health professionals in the last 30 years, more persons are receiving help than ever before. About one in every 12 persons will spend part of his life in a mental institution. Nearly half of all hospital beds in 1973 were occupied by patients with alleged mental disorders. An estimated 5 million persons seek psychiatric help each year, half of whom go to private psychiatrists (Modlin, 1976:152). This indicates that about one person out of 40 seeks some kind of help for emotional problems. Many others, of course, fail to seek help.

*Number of recorded visits or confinements to mental-health facilities. A small disproportionate percentage of the population accounts for these reported episodes. Once a person is treated, the episode ends; thus if he returns later, it counts as a new episode. Hence, there are always many more episodes than mentally ill persons.

figure 12-1 PERCENT DISTRIBUTIONS OF INPATIENT AND OUTPATIENT CARE EPISODES IN MENTAL HEALTH FACILITIES, BY TYPE OF FACILITY: UNITED STATES, 1955 AND 1973

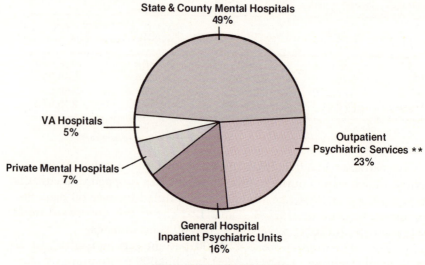

1955 (1.7 MILLION EPISODES)

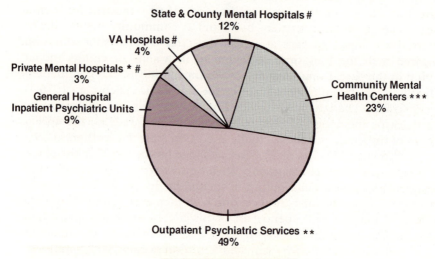

1973 (5.2 MILLION EPISODES)

* Includes residential treatment centers for emotionally disturbed children. Source: Division of Biometry, National Institute of Mental Health.
# Inpatient services only.
** Includes free-standing outpatient services as well as those affiliated with psychiatric and general hospitals.
*** Includes inpatient and outpatient services of federally funded CMHC s.

Source: Carl Taube and Richard Redick, "Provisional Data on Patient Care Episodes in Mental Health Facilities, 1973". Mental Health Statistical Note No. 127 (Feb. 1976) U.S. Department of HEW, ADRAMHA, Publication no. 76-158, p. 3.

Labeling by Social Class

A person's social class has a bearing on the likelihood that he will be labeled as suffering from a mental illness. Faris and Dunham, in Chicago in 1939, verified the differences between classes. Similarly, one of the most significant studies to point this out was Hollingshead and Redlich's 1958 study in New Haven. They studied all persons receiving psychiatric care over a five-month period and divided them into five social classes, from I (upper) to V (lower). The rates of treated mental illness per 100,000 persons in New Haven were as follows:

Classes I and II (Upper, Lower-Upper)	556
Class III (Middle Class)	538
Class IV (Working Class)	642
Class V (Lower)	1,659

The rate of treated illness for the lower class was some three times as great as for the upper classes. Much of this could be attributed to subcultural behavior that the more powerful higher classes label mental illness. In addition, the severity of the diagnosis was greater for the lower class. Whereas 35 percent of the upper-class illnesses were psychotic and 65 percent neurotic, 90 percent of the lower-class illnesses were labeled psychotic.

The study also revealed that the poor received much more "custodial care" in a state mental hospital. All of the rich received psychotherapy

There is often a thin line between being labeled mentally ill and just being socially isolated and lonely. One's social class affects how a person is labeled and treated.

Credit: Robert Goldstein.

from a private psychiatrist. A follow-up study 10 years later indicated that these same disparities persisted (Meyers and Bean, 1968).

A well-researched study of midtown Manhattan in 1965 by Srole and others from Cornell University found that the lower-class person was under much greater mental stress, and that the sheer number of stress factors was more important than the quality of stresses. As stress after stress impinges upon a person over time, he becomes more likely to suffer from mental illness. The lower class had a mental-health risk almost 40 percent greater than that of the upper class (Harrington, 1963:122–23). This is attributed to a social structure that often makes it difficult for the poor to obtain equality, equity, and power.

Labeling by Other Social Factors

Other social factors also affect the rate of mental illness and treatment:

> Race and minority-group status: Rates are higher for blacks and Puerto Ricans than for whites.
> Sex: Males generally are more frequently treated for mental illness than females.
> Marital Status: Rates are always lowest for the married, as compared with the single, divorced, or separated.
> Age: Generally those between 25 and 44 are disproportionately represented in mental hospitals, and as having schizophrenia diagnosis.

Figure 12-2 shows the admission rates to mental hospitals by age, race, and sex. Most of the figures relied upon to measure the seriousness of the mental-health problem are based on figures supplied by mental-health facilities. However, field surveys indicate that while one out of four persons reports having emotional problems severe enough to require professional help, only one in seven actually seeks any kind of professional help (usually from a family doctor or clergyman) (Scarpitti, 1974:315).

The System for Treating Mental Illness

We have over 20,000 psychiatrists, 235 state and county hospitals, and 2,500 outpatient clinics. Psychiatric facilities are usually found in many general hospitals across the country. Hence, more and more persons are getting some kind of psychiatric care. In some cases the number of staff persons to patients is not good. State and county hospitals have the poorest ratio, while private nonprofit mental hospitals have the best ratio. In 1975, the National Institute of Mental Health reported that for the first time in the history of the state mental-hospital system, there was the equivalent of one full-time staff person for each hospitalized patient (Flanagan, Summer, 1975:19). This improvement, though, is one cause of higher prices in

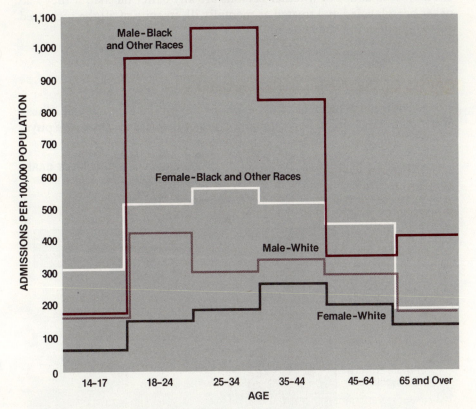

figure 12-2 ADMISSION RATES TO MENTAL HOSPITALS BY AGE, RACE, AND SEX, 1970

Source: Executive Office of the President; Office of Management and Budget, *Social Indicators,* 1973 (Washington, D.C.: U.S. Government Printing Office, 1973): 13.

The breakdown of statistics on admissions to state and county hospitals by race and sex confirms the evidence that mental disorder and hospitalization are linked to socioeconomic factors.

this field. In 1971 our society spent over $25 billion on mental illness; by 1974 it cost us nearly $37 billion. Today it is even higher. Only about a quarter of the increase between 1971 and 1974 was due to inflation. Vested interests on the part of professionals who run the mental-health system's institutions, clinics and centers, as well as hospitals, account for a great deal of increased costs. Only about 40 percent of all money spent on our mental health system goes directly to care for patients (Levine and Willner, February 1976:1). Figure 12-3 shows how and where this money was spent. Over half of direct costs for patients were spent in nursing homes and large public mental hospitals.

The annual expense per patient in state and county mental hospitals in 1974 was $11,277, compared with $5,435 in 1970 (1976:967). In Pennsylvania the yearly cost of maintaining a patient in a state mental hospital increased from $2,000 in 1966 to $17,000 in 1976 (Livingood, May 28, 1976:1). It is doubtful whether persons are any better off than if they had never been labeled and treated as mentally ill, in spite of all the increased costs for operating the system.

CAUSES OF THE MENTAL-ILLNESS PROBLEM

No one cause or theory fully explains the problems of mental illness or its treatment system. Several major types of theories or causes are phys-

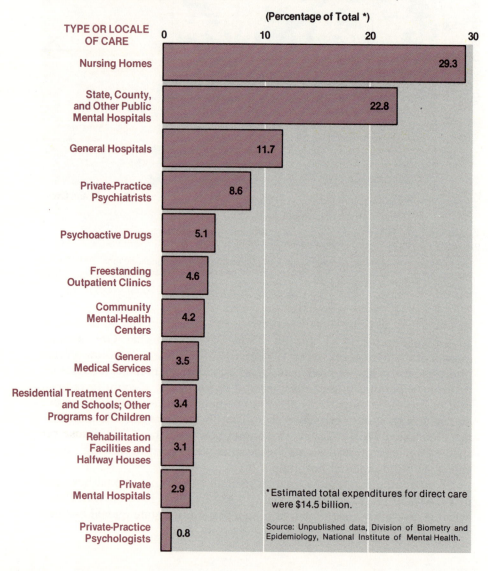

figure 12-3 PERCENTAGE DISTRIBUTION OF EXPENDITURES FOR DIRECT CARE OF THE MENTALLY ILL BY TYPE OR LOCALE OF CARE, 1974

*Estimated total expenditures for direct care were $14.5 billion.

Source: Unpublished data, Division of Biometry and Epidemiology, National Institute of Mental Health.

iological, biochemical, psychological, and sociological. Let us examine each of these in turn.

Physiological Explanations

The physiological causes of mental illness include genetic and biochemical factors. Most genetic studies of mental illness have focused on the cause of schizophrenia, though in the past all mental illness (or feeblemindedness, as it was called) was linked to biological inheritance. The assumption of the genetic theorists is that the gene or genes responsible for the development of schizophrenia are specific to the disease, while environmental factors are nonspecific and not *directly* related to it. Thus, a specific gene or genes must be present for schizophrenia to develop, although environmental factors might also be necessary.

This theory remains problematic, since no particular gene or combination of genes has been identified with schizophrenia. There is not yet a convincing argument for all schizophrenia. Studies of adopted children whose mothers were schizophrenic do not provide clear evidence to support a theory of genetic transmission of the disease.

Biochemical Explanations

Biochemical theories try to attribute mental illness to the presence or absence of certain chemicals in the body or brain. For example, in 1972 at Lafayette Clinic and Wayne State University in Detroit, Dr. Jacques S. Gottlieb, a psychiatrist, and Dr. Charles Forhman, a biochemist, discovered an enzyme deficiency in the brains of schizophrenic patients. The absence of the enzyme, Anti-S Protein, causes production of an excessive amount of chemicals called methylated idoleamines. These excessive chemicals are known to have mentally disturbing and mind-altering effects ("Schizophrenia's Cause Found," May 5, 1972:1). In 1973 Wise and Stein reported the absence of an enzyme, dopamine-B-hydroxylase (DBH), in the brains of 18 schizophrenic patients, compared with its presence in 12 normal brains. The enzyme was believed to be connected with the organization and control of goal-directed behavior. Another study of brain specimens by Wyatt and others found no significant differences in the amounts of DBH in brains of nonschizophrenics as compared with those of schizophrenics (Morland et al., 1975:436).

Recent experiments have discovered that "neurotransmitters," chemical links between nerve neurons that make motions or thoughts possible, are produced by environmental and social factors as a potential cause of depression. The researchers report:

> Through several years of experiments, we have succeeded in showing how environmental factors can yield some of the same chemical changes thought to be important in depression, and how these chemical changes can cause behavior abnormalities.

> We thus find that there is a pathway from the environment to behavioral disturbance that passes over a chemical bridge. The chemical substances that form this bridge are called neurotransmitters (Weiss et al., December 1974: 59).

This suggests that biochemical explanations for mental illness cannot be totally divorced from social and environmental forces in a person's life. Two research psychologists, Joseph Schildkraut and Seymour Kety, have hypothesized that a depletion of one neurotransmitter—norepinephrine—causes depression.

Biochemical theories are problematic because hospitalized patients have diets and experiences different from those of most persons. For example, many smoke frequently, get little exercise, and usually have long histories of drugtaking. Any of these factors could alter a person's biochemistry; in addition, biochemical theory may be confusing effect with cause. Extreme emotional and physical stresses involved with being committed to a mental hospital and labeled as emotionally ill can also *cause* changes in biochemical functioning. The system devised for treating mental illness often makes normal people worse.

Psychological Explanations

The psychological theories of mental illness include Freudian early-childhood experiences (psychoanalytical theory), family interaction, and learning theory.

Freudian Psychoanalysis. Freudian, psychoanalytical theories, in particular, go to the base of personality formation and functioning. Our early childhood experiences, especially our relationships with our parents, explain much of diagnosed mental ailments in terms of unresolved internal conflicts.

Personality disorders may result from our defective early experiences. Perhaps an abnormal fear of death haunts us to the extent that we cannot think or function. This fear may stem from the loss of a parent at a very early age. Or we may have had sexual experiences as children that make it difficult to function as a sexually normal adult. The Freudian, psychoanalytical approach assumes that the past, especially when repressed in our unconscious, determines our present and future. A person might become emotionally fixed at an early stage of development. The solution for the psychiatrist is to raise our memories and experiences to a conscious level, so that we can confront and resolve them.

Family Interaction. Bateson, Fidz, and Wynne-Singer have extensively explored the connection between family interaction and schizophrenia. Gregory Bateson, for example, has argued that children are often in a "double-bind" situation that leads to mental illness. In such a situation, the individual receives two contrary messages. For example, the

Some persons labeled as mentally ill only have problems of adjustment due to childhood fixations or regressions.

father says he will respect his son if he "acts like a man" but will punish him whenever he asserts himself. Often another family member is involved and manipulates the situation for his own ends. If interaction consistently follows this double-bind pattern, the victim becomes intellectually and emotionally confused. One way out is to adopt the role of a mentally sick person; by doing so, he is no longer obligated or expected to interact with family members in a normal fashion (Bateson et al., 1956:251–64).

Learning Theory. Learning theorists try to discover how each person acquires appropriate or inappropriate behavior. In examining mental illness, the therapist would try to uncover how the patient has acquired the present deviant behavior and which environmental factors are reinforcing it. The underlying assumption of learning theory is that abnormal behavior is learned in the same way as any other behavior—through stimulus-response, or operant conditioning, a learning procedure in which spontaneous behavior is reinforced. The mentally ill learn deviant behavior because their social or physical environment in some way rewards or reinforces these behaviors.

Learning theory, then, sees mental illness as a series of maladaptive behaviors and problems in interpersonal relations. The symptoms are not manifestations of inner conflicts, but the disorders themselves. Therefore, unlearning or counterlearning patterns of behavior is the key to mental health. The person's responses to external stress and tension must be made more socially acceptable, not rewarded or reinforced. Mental-hospital care and our related social institutions, on the other hand, often encourage and reinforce maladaptive responses by insisting that the patient is sick and abnormal.

Sociological Explanations

The sociological or sociocultural causes of mental illness include the social-process, or labeling, theory of Scheff, Laing, and Szasz; the strain theory; and the social-structure theory.

Labeling Theory. The theories of Scheff and Szasz, mentioned earlier, examine the effects of diagnosing and labeling persons as mentally ill. As a result of such labeling, these persons are treated differently, which only makes their situation worse. Psychiatry often labels as mental illness normal emotional upsets and human reactions to trying or tense life situations that will eventually change. R. D. Laing maintains, similarly, that mental illness results from labeling and is merely a temporary "special strategy that a person invents in order to live in an unlivable situation." Furthermore, "There is no such 'condition' as schizophrenia, but the label is a social fact. . . . The person labeled is inaugurated not only into a role but into a career of patient" (Laing, 1967:78–79). This may be good for the psychiatrists' business or for mental hospital administrators but such labeling stigmatizes the normal person.

The social-process (labeling) theories of Scheff, Szasz, and Laing have been attacked by those who adhere to the psychoanalytic theory. For example, sociologist Walter R. Gove maintains that the labeling theorists exaggerate the effect of labeling (inside and outside the mental hospital), as well as the degree to which formerly mentally ill persons suffer from a social stigma. Gove and others focus on why a person commits the deviant acts that invite the label of mental illness. Studies show, for example, that families, rather than impose a label, go to great lengths to deny that a member's behavior is deviant. Moreover, many persons voluntarily admit themselves to a mental hospital; they label themselves as mentally ill before anyone else does. In Gove's analysis, the evidence suggests a cause-effect relationship opposed to that of the labeling theorists. Although labeling may have a long-term impact on a person's behavior, in the short run it is the person's behavior that causes the expectations of and labels from those around him (Gove, 1970:873–80).

Strain Theory (Anomie). The strain theory holds that most persons conform to social norms, although intense pressures cause some to deviate. According to Robert Merton, the social source of these strain-producing pressures is the discrepancy between cultural goals and the social means to achieve those goals. Thus, many who encounter difficult or unequal access to socially acceptable means turn to antisocial ones. The mentally ill reject both goals and means and retreat from society.

Strain theory (anomie) especially explains the more severe forms of mental illness and the higher incidence of mental illness among the lower class.

Social-Structure Theories. C. Wright Mills and other sociologists look to various theories that find the source of mental illness in the social structure. Mental illness, according to these theories, is not an individual matter so much as a product of an unjust, oppressive society. Abnormal stresses and strains are imposed on us by the complexity, inequities, and pace of modern society. Dr. Harvey Brenner of Johns Hopkins School of Hygiene and Public Health has studied changes in the economy and in mental hospitalization over half a century. His study shows that economic declines or recessions lead to a marked increase in mental disorder. The results show a clear inverse relationship: as employment drops, mental-hospital admissions rise (Rice, August 1975:74, 76).

Psychiatrist Karen Horney asserted that neurosis is caused primarily by fears and conflicts experienced by those trying to live in a highly individualistic, impersonal, competitive, aggressive society. Modernization of our society has been bought at a high price.

Others argue that mental illness is induced by a repressive political and social order, and that radical social and political change is the only suitable therapy. In our repressive society, what we define as reality is lunacy and madness. Laing points out that those statesmen who boast that they have nuclear doomsday weapons and that a certain level of casualties is acceptable in a nuclear war are as divorced from reality as the severest case of mental illness. To be normal in an abnormal social structure produces madness of the highest order. As he wrote: "Normal men have killed perhaps 100,000,000 of their fellow normal men in the last fifty years" (Laing, 1967:100). An insane society cannot produce too many sane people. Those whom we call mentally ill may in fact be saner than most of the rest of us.

The social-structure theory attributes the basic problems in the mental-health field to the labeling process itself, the effects this has on people, and the deprivation of liberty that results when persons are confined or treated as "ill." Thomas Szasz, in "Justice in the Therapeutic State," points to most psychiatrists' "medical-therapeutic" perspectives on radical political change. He writes:

> Conflict among individuals, and especially between the individual and the State, is invariably seen as a symptom of "illness" or psychopathology, and the primary function of the State is accordingly the removal of such conflict by "therapy" — therapy imposed by force, if necessary. It is not difficult to recognize in this imagery of the Therapeutic State the old Inquisitorial, or the most recent totalitarian, concept of the State, now clothed in the garb of psychiatric treatment (1970:433–34).

In a highly structured and organized society, we fear and stigmatize as "abnormal" any behavior patterns that have the potential for questioning the system and how it operates. Such aberrant behavior may reject the given social order as unfair and unjust. It might slow down the productivity and consumption of the industrial machine, or, worse yet, ignite a revolution against the existing system. To forestall such a possibility, any behavior that deviates from the accepted norms of our society must be labeled as "mental illness"; the transgressor must be confined or "treated" until he is able to accept the existing power structure and society. Setting up an elaborate system to treat mental illness makes clear to everyone that any essential deviance from established social norms will not be tolerated.

PROPOSED SOLUTIONS TO MENTAL-ILLNESS PROBLEMS

Proposals for reducing the problems associated with mental illness depend upon the cause or theory used to explain it. The two contradictory theories behind most solutions are (1) mental illness exists as a disease, and persons suffering from it need treatment; and (2) it is a label arbitrarily applied to those with problems, and this system of labeling and treatment is the greater problem. Physiological theorists who view it as a disease favor medicine, surgery, and chemotherapy (drug treatment) as solutions to the problem. Advocates of psychological causes who interpret it as deviance perceive psychoanalysis, behavior modification, and other kinds of psychological and social therapies as solutions. Those who see social and structural sources as the main cause propose various organizational and social changes to restructure radically the present mental-health system. Those with vested interests in retaining their prestige, power, and profits in medicine and psychiatry recommend physical and psychological approaches. Those who see the problem of mental illness as essentially the way persons are labeled and treated advocate a radical restructuring of our entire social system. Most sociologists would support the social-therapy and restructuring approaches.

Let us look at many of these proposals in turn.

Physiological-Medical Proposals

The use of drugs has dramatically changed the treatment of mental disorders. Since 1954, when tranquilizers were first used in mental hospitals, former patients have returned in large numbers to the community. Many who might have spent the rest of their lives in mental hospital have been released. Many others were able to undergo psychoanalysis. The medical and physiological approaches include chemotherapy, electroshock and psychosurgery.

Chemotherapy. The two main drugs in this form of treatment are tranquilizers and amphetamines (antidepressants). Valium is the most widely used tranquilizer, while Benzedrine and Dexedrine are the leading amphetamines. Other drugs, such as Tofranil and Elavil, are used to relieve depression. About 20 million prescriptions for antidepressants are written each year, and are effective about 60 percent of the time. Hyperactivity in children is often treated with Ritalin or Dexedrine. Surprisingly, these stimulants seem to suppress symptoms of hyperactivity in children (Walker, December 1974:43). With government support, these stimulants have been used in schools to control hyperactive children. Nationally between 500,000 and two million schoolchildren are given various drugs for hyperactivity (Offir, December 1974:49), although warnings have been issued in the *American Journal of Psychiatry* that Ritalin should not be used to treat children under six since "safety and efficacy in this age group has not yet been established" (Walker, 1974:48).

Drugs often do not cure mental illness so much as mask or suppress the symptoms. Some sociologists have argued that this practice puts the mentally ill person into a chemical straitjacket, so that he can be controlled, manipulated, or ignored by psychiatrists.

Electroshock. Electroshock has been used as another physiological solution to mental illness. No official nationwide figures exist on how many persons receive electroshock treatment, but estimates range from 50,000 to 200,000 a year. In 90 percent of such cases, the treatments are administered in psychiatric institutions. Electroshock treatment has acceptance in the medical profession, even by psychiatrists who do not use it. Medical insurance plans, as well as state and federal health and welfare agencies, are more willing to pay for such therapy than for certain verbal therapies.

Psychiatrists admit they do not know how electroshock works. First experimented with in Fascist Italy during the 1930s, it is now used with an anesthetic and muscle relaxant to keep the patient still and reduce the physical convulsions. A bolt of electric current, of 70 to 150 volts, is sent to the brain from electrodes attached to the patient's head. The charge lasts from one-half to a full second. Depressive patients may receive from six to 12 separate shock treatments; schizophrenic, from 18 to 25 treatments (Friedberg, August 1975:20).

The use of electroshocks is extremely controversial. Patients often hate and fear it, complaining that it causes confusion and loss of memory. Neurologist John Friedberg in "Electroshock Therapy: Let's Stop Blasting the Brain" (1975), argues that "it causes brain damage manifested in such forms as severe and often permanent loss of memory, learning disability, and spatial and temporal disorientation" (Ibid., 19). An even more convincing argument is the death rate from electroshocks—one for every 1,000 patients, a high rate for any medical procedure. About 20 percent of such deaths are directly due to brain damage. Psychiatrists who use such treatments pay three to four times as much for malpractice insurance. In 1975 California passed a law restricting the use of electroshocks. Clearly, electroshock treatment should be used sparingly, if at all, to alleviate mental illness.

Psychosurgery. Psychosurgery severs or removes nerves in parts of the brain. The most well-known and controversial operation is the lobotomy, which severs the nerves in the frontal lobes of the brain. Used mostly on violent patients (a very small percentage of the mentally ill), it subdues them but also turns them into "living vegetables." Psychiatrist Peter Breggin maintains that all behavior surgery results in the "the loss of impulsiveness, spontaneity and imagination, but the psychic disturbances and their causes are not removed" ("Electric Scalpel," November 2, 1975:E-21). During the 1950s, some 50,000 lobotomies were performed but since then they have been restricted. Even now, however, about 500 are performed every year.

Psychological Proposals

Proposals based on psychological theories include psychoanalysis and behavior modification.

Psychoanalysis. Psychoanalysis remains expensive and time-consuming. Based on Freudian theory of unconscious, repressed childhood experiences, it does not work in all cases, though many benefit from it. Often people expect it to help, and the personality and techniques of the psychiatrist reinforce these positive expectations (Gillis, December 1974:92). Psychiatrist Allen Bergin, summarizing about a dozen studies covering nearly 1,000 cases of almost every kind, concludes that psychoanalysis helps 65 percent of those who use it (25 percent more than if left untreated), but harms 10 percent of the patients. His findings, comparing treated with untreated groups, are shown in Table 12-2. Untreated people, of course, were still in society, not isolated or forced to interact only with psychiatrists or mental patients. This finding gives some credence to the social model perspective that mental illness is merely "a

table 12-2 COMPARATIVE EFFECTS OF PSYCHOTHERAPY

UNTREATED GROUPS	EFFECT OF THERAPY	THERAPY GROUPS
40%	Improvement	65%
55	No change	25
5	Deterioration	10

Source: Allen Bergin, "Psychotherapy Can Be Dangerous," **Psychology Today**, 9. 6 (November 1975): 98. © 1975 Ziff-Davis Publishing Company. Reprinted by permission.

problem in living" and if people are not labeled "mentally ill" they will eventually overcome their difficulties or learn to accept them.

As we pointed out earlier, the poor and minorities often do not have access to psychotherapy; yet it is clear that many of them seek and could benefit from such aid. For example, a major study of 250 lower-class patients at the psychiatric outpatient clinic of Los Angeles General Hospital found that "52 percent expressed a desire for extended insight therapy" (Jones, April 1975:26).

Behavior Modification. A more recent outgrowth of psychological theories, particularly learning theory, has been behavior modification, or behavior therapy. Based on "systematic desensitization" and "operant conditioning," as developed by Joseph Wolpe, Andrew Salter, and B. F. Skinner, it seeks to change immediate external behavior rather than analyze complex internal motivations or emotions. It rewards and reinforces positive behavior, and has been used successfully in treating such problems as social withdrawal, delinquent acts, phobias, aggression, and social disruption. Psychologists G. Terence Wilson and Gerald Davison write the following about its effectiveness in alleviating mental illness: "The burgeoning evidence from well-controlled clinical research suggests that behavior therapy has been successful in treating the entire spectrum of psychiatric disorders and is clearly the therapy of choice in many areas" (1975:59).

Sociologists who oppose behavior modification have attacked it as "a mechanistic, totalitarian form of control that is imposed arbitrarily upon clients." They argue this method of changing human behavior often violates a person's human and civil rights. It has been abused in mental hospitals to control a person's behavior rather than cure him of psychic ills. Basics of life—food, security, warmth—have been withheld to induce and reinforce desired behavioral changes. Although the procedures of behavior modification may be abused, they work in changing behavior. To the extent that mental illness produces deviant or violent behavior, behavior modification may solve the problem by making the person's behavior more "normal."

Social-Therapy Proposals

Since most sociologists consider that the causes of mental illness stem from society itself, their proposals have a social focus. This recognition of social causes has led to development of family therapy, T-groups, therapeutic communities within hospitals, halfway houses, community mental-health programs, and preventive programs that emphasize good mental health.

Families, professionals, and the public have come to understand that the emotionally disturbed person is best treated in his own community. This has caused a reaction against the social isolation and insulation of

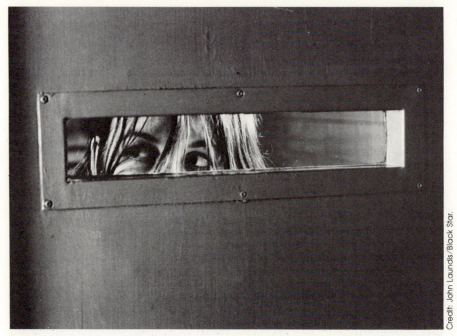

Confinement in mental institutions causes some persons to become worse, not better. Recent legislation has encouraged treatment of the mentally ill at clinics and community-treatment centers.

mental patients within state hospitals. Even if a person is temporarily confined to a distant hospital, community mental-health services will ease his return into normal life patterns. A good community mental-health program should include a variety of services and facilities—from outpatient psychiatric clinics to rehabilitative day centers and from sheltered workshops to halfway houses. Community services should ideally include the following:

> inpatient psychiatric services in general hospitals
> outpatient psychiatric clinics
> small, community mental hospitals organized as therapeutic communities
> rehabilitative day centers
> halfway houses
> sheltered workshops to prepare people for work
> day treatment or training centers for children
> residential treatment centers for emotionally disturbed children

All such services are needed for a comprehensive community health program. The first step would be funding and building more community health centers, since the number we have now is inadequate.

A victory for the mentally ill was scored in 1975 when Congress overrode a presidential veto of legislation that renewed for two years the Community Mental Health Centers Act. For two years the NAMH and other groups had sought to improve the law. Among other things, the law now provides for—

1. expansion of mental-health services to children and the elderly
2. screening of individuals before referral to state mental hospitals
3. a program of halfway-house services for those leaving mental-health institutions
4. follow-up care for those discharged from state mental hospitals (Flanagan, Summer 1975:18).

Restructuring the System

Sociologists who oppose a treatment system that often does more harm than good see a need to restructure and change the system, as well as society's attitudes toward persons who may appear different from us because of labeling.

One proposal is to work toward closing down all of our large state and county mental hospitals. They often serve more as prisons than as a source of help. Isolating patients from the rest of society and giving them no positive attention serves no social purpose. When persons leave such institutions, though, we must provide follow-up care and concern if we expect to help those who have been labeled and hurt by the traditional system of treatment. We have already closed some state mental hospitals; but we have only transferred the problem to the community, where the former patients receive not even custodial care. The very least we must do is to regulate so-called boarding homes so that basic attention and aftercare can be given to those who still suffer from the stigma of being labeled mentally ill.

Another solution is public education to remove, once and for all, the stigma of having been labeled mentally ill. In addition, we can restrict the use of confinement to only certain illegal behaviors and only for specified short periods of time with periodic reviews. Months instead of decades would define the upper limits to involuntary commitment to a mental institution (Steadman and Cocozza, January 1975:35).

Advocates of restructuring the present system also note that the social structure itself must be changed so that inequality, injustice, and powerlessness do not make it difficult or impossible for persons to deal with their problems of living. If our society produced a better life for all, we would have little reason to fear or label those who behave differently. A secure society usually has no need for creating scapegoats, as our present society has done. If we concentrate on creating a just society, many of the "daily problems of living" will be eliminated, and the need to label people as mentally ill will vanish.

THE FUTURE OF THE MENTAL-HEALTH PROBLEM

The disease–medical model of mental illness, with emphasis on deviance, labeling, and treatment, will dominate the future. Some current trends affecting changes in private psychiatric practice look toward more structuring of the system, but on a local or regional basis, rather than state or county as in the past. These changes are evident from four movements that have gained momentum in recent years, namely:

1. community mental-health centers
2. new health-maintenance organizations
3. professional standards review organizations
4. national health insurance (which should include payment for treating mental illness)

The community mental-health centers will lay the foundation for future mental-health care on a local basis. The basic elements of the CMHCs, according to Dr. Herbert Modlin of the Menninger Foundation, include:

availability of mental-health services for *all* citizens in a local geographical area (the catchment-area concept)

equal accessibility of services to all citizens (the outreach concept)

comprehensive services to fit all needs (the anti-procrustean concept)

continuity of services over time (the expanded-responsibility concept) (Modlin, 1976:156)

Others also see improvement in delivery of mental-health services in the near future, as government financing of national health insurance appears. They envision better medical planning, coordination between subsystems, an easier flow of patients from one treatment facility to another, and better evaluation of treatment results.

The goals of the National Association of Mental Health for the years between 1976 and 1980 have been formulated as follows:

Greatly increase research into the causes, prevention, and treatment of mental illness.

Make prevention as important as treatment in community mental-health services.

Push for establishment of a complete network of community mental-health systems by 1980.

See that community facilities are effective and responsive.

Ensure effective mental-health services for minorities and the poor.

Urge creation of appropriate alternate services for hospitalized patients

Work for improved long-term care for seriously ill children and adults.

Ensure that national health insurance includes realistic mental-health coverage.

Work for inclusion of mental-health needs in all local, state, and federal programs.

Undertake court actions aimed at protecting and strengthening patients' rights.

Support development of patient advocacy for children and adults.

Clearly define NMHA's role in occupational mental health.

Improve public attitudes toward mental illness (Flanagan, Spring 1976:19).

More Government and Technical Emphasis

Dr. Bertram Brown, Director of the National Institute of Mental Health (NIMH), makes several observations and predictions. He envisions vast increases in government spending on mental health and mental illness, especially for further research. He predicts, for example, a five to eight-fold increase in spending for the work of the NIMH (from $600 million to as much as $5 billion) within five years.

In coming years the federal government is likely to put greater stress on applied rather than pure research. Congress wants to direct research more toward preventing and treating disease than toward understanding it. The government will encourage practical, people-oriented research that will be "rapidly and broadly disseminated" (Culliton, June 1976:32).

Dr. Brown of the NIMH maintains that if the dominant ethic or value in the future is government or technical control of people, then such mental-health techniques as psychosurgery and drugs will become a powerful tool to intimidate, change, and control human behavior. On the other hand, if the future ethic is the cure and control of disease (not persons), psychosurgery and other mental-illness tools may become "a significant, though minor addendum" to medical science.

A whole range of social problems, including violence, crime, alcoholism, and drug addiction, will be included under the province of the medical and mental-illness fields. This trend already appears in the name of the federal agency chiefly responsible for mental health, the Alcohol, Drug Abuse, and Mental Health Administration. The present Community Mental Health Centers Act includes money for programs dealing with "the prevention and treatment of alcoholism and drug addiction and abuse" (Flanagan, 1975:18).

The NAMH has adopted the mental-health bell as its symbol. This 300-pound bell, cast from chains and shackles gathered from mental hospitals around the country, carries the inscription: "Cast from shackles which bound them, this bell shall ring out hope for the mentally ill and victory over mental illness" (Morland et al., 1975:415). By the next century or shortly thereafter, the hope of many social scientists in America is that the bell will toll out the last vestige of labeling people mentally ill.

SUMMARY

It is difficult to say who is or is not mentally ill. The disease–medical model—built on labeling, deviance, and treatment—and social model—built on radically changing the system—are two conflicting perspectives of mental illness. Those who accept the disease–medical model diagnose various neuroses and psychoses. Thomas Szasz and Thomas Scheff, proponents of the social model, consider that persons are labeled mentally ill because of behaviors that merely signify "problems in living" or "defective strategies for interpersonal relations." Mental illness, they argue, is an invention of society perpetuated by psychiatrists. Sociologists who adhere to the social-model perspective see social problems in the institutional system of mental care—especially a dual system of treatment (one for the poor, another for the nonpoor), violations of personal and civil rights, abusive and inadequate care, and little or no aftercare.

State and county mental hospitals and long-term confinement are being replaced by community clinics, although the number of treated episodes of mental illness is about three times as great as in 1955. Our society has over 20,000 psychiatrists and more than 2,500 outpatient clinics.

Alleged causes of mental illness are physiological (biochemical theories); psychological (Freudian, family-interaction, and learning theories); and sociological (labeling, the strain—anomie, and the social-structure theories).

Proposed solutions depend upon which perspective of mental illness is accepted—a disease to be treated or a label applied to persons with problems of living. The disease approach includes the physiological-medical therapies (drugs, electroshock and psychosurgery); the psychological therapies (psychoanalysis and behavior modification); the social therapies (family therapy, T-groups, therapeutic communities, halfway houses, community mental-health programs), and major changes in our social structure. Those who consider mental illness a problem of labeling and treatment advocate restructuring of the mental-health system.

The National Mental Health Association's goals, as well as the National Institute of Mental Health's predictions, foresee an improved future for treatment of mental illness, including increased funding, coordination of services, access for all, and prevention. They especially look for improved public attitudes toward those labeled as mentally ill.

CAREER OPPORTUNITIES

Psychiatric Social Workers.

These professionals work in an institutional setting, compiling and analyzing data about patients' social background and environment. Such a social profile helps an agency or psychiatrist to understand and analyze patients. They also keep families informed of the progress and needs of patients, collect and analyze statistical data, conduct case interviews, and perform administrative duties as part of a therapeutic team. Besides employment in mental-health clinics or hospitals, some work in halfway houses and group homes. Many work for such government agencies as the Veterans Administration, the Department of Defense, and the Public Health Service. Generally a Master's degree is needed to begin a practice, but a Ph.D. is expected for more responsible positions. For further information write to: National Commission for Social Work Careers, 600 Southern Building, 15th and H Sts., N.W., Washington, D.C. 20005.

Mental-Care Aides and Attendants.

They usually work under the direction and supervision of nurses and doctors. Although the job is considered semiskilled, it could develop a student's interest in psychiatry or in working with the mentally ill. This position provides direct contact and interaction with patients in mental hospitals. Working in this low-paying job often provides an overview of how a mental institution operates. For further information write to: National Association for Mental Health, 1800 North Kent St., Rosslyn Station, Arlington, Va. 22209.

Mental-Health Educators.

Many government-financed county mental-health and mental-retardation agencies seek mental-health educators. Some require a nursing degree, others experience in education; still others a degree in sociology or social science. Contacting other community groups and agencies to overcome the public's misunderstanding, stigmatizing, and fear of the mentally ill is an important aspect of the job. An ability to express positive attitudes toward mental health publicly is essential. The extent of government funding for mental-health programs will determine the future of this career. For further information write to: National Association for Mental Health, 1800 North Kent St., Rosslyn Station, Arlington, Va. 22209.

REFERENCES

Adams, Paul and Nancy McDonald
    1968 "Clinical Cooling Out of Poor People." American Journal of Orthopsychiatry 38, 4 (April): 457–63.

Bateson, Gregory, et al.
    1956   "Toward a Theory of Schizophrenia." Behavioral Science 1, 4 (October): 251-54.

Beers, Clifford
    1921   A Mind That Found Itself. 5th ed. New York: Longmans, Green.

Bergin, Allen
    1975   "Psychotherapy Can Be Dangerous." Psychology Today 9, 6 (November): 96-104.

Bloss, Mary E.
    1976   "Looking Back: An Interview with Ken Donaldson." MH 60, 1 (Spring): 5-9.

Buss, Arnold
    1966   Psychopathology. New York: Wiley.

Buss, Arnold and Edith H. Buss, eds.
    1969   Theories of Schizophrenia. New York: Atherton Press.

Camemetzki, Schalom and William Abbott
    1976   "How to Fail in the Treatment of Schizophrenic People: A Primer." Bulletin of the Menninger Clinic 40, 2 (March): 118-24.

"Children to Get Hearings on Being Institutionalized." Allentown Morning Call (July 25): 2, 1975.

"Coping with Depression." Newsweek 81, 2 (January 8): 51-54, 1973.

"'Cuckoo's Nest' Horrors Real." Allentown Morning Call (May 7): 1, 1976.

Culliton, Barbara
    1976   "Kennedy Hearings: Year Long Probe of Biomedical Research Begins." Science 193, 4247 (July 2): 32-35.

Doll, William
    1975   "Home Is Not Sweet Anymore." MH 59, 1 (Winter): 22-24.

"Electric Scalpel Burns Out Mental Disturbance." Allentown Sunday Call-Chronicle (November 2): E-1, 21, 1975.

Flanagan, Richard
    1976   "The Mental Health Association's Goals." MH 60, 1 (Spring): 19.
    1975   "Patient Care, Admissions and Children." MH 59, 3 (Summer): 19.
    1975   "A Victory for Mentally Ill." MH 59, 3 (Summer): 18.

Friedberg, John
    1975   "Let's Stop Blasting the Brain." Psychology Today 9, 3 (August): 18-23.

Gillis, John
    1974   "The Therapist as Manipulator." Psychology Today 8, 7 (December): 91-95.

Goffman, Erving
    1963   Stigma. Englewood Cliffs, N.J.: Prentice-Hall.

Gove, Walter
    1970   "Societal Reactions as an Explanation of Mental Illness: An Evaluation." American Sociological Review 35 (1970): 873-80.

Harrington, Michael
    1963   The Other America: Poverty in the United States. Baltimore: Penguin.

"High Court Stays Mental Health Rule." Allentown Morning Call (December 16): 8, 1975.

Jones, Enrico
  1975 "Psychotherapists Shortchange the Poor." Psychology Today 8, 11 (April): 24–28.

Laing, R. D.
  1967 The Politics of Experience. New York: Pantheon.

Levine, Daniel S. and Shirley Willner
  1976 "The Cost of Mental Illness, 1974." Mental Health Statistical Note No. 125 (February), U.S. Department of Health, Education and Welfare, ADRAMHA, DHEW Publication No. (ADM) 76-158.

Livingood, Ben
  1976 "Mental Patient Costs Skyrocketing in State." Allentown Morning Call (May 28): 1.

McKee, Michael and Ian Robertson
  1975 Social Problems. New York: Random House.

Menninger, Karl
  1963 The Vital Balance: The Life Process in Mental Health and Illness. New York: Viking Press.

Meyers, J. K. and L. L. Bean
  1968 A Decade Later: A Follow-up of Social Class and Mental Illness. New York: Wiley.

"Modern Life Is Too Much for 23 Million Americans." U.S. News & World Report (November 10). P. 100 in Anne Kilbride, ed. Readings in Sociology 76/77: Annual Editions. Guilford, Conn.: Dushkin, 1975.

Modlin, Herbert
  1976 "Organizational Changes in Mental Health Delivery Systems." Bulletin of the Menninger Clinic 40, 2 (March): 151–57.

Morland, J. Kenneth, Jack O. Balswick, John Belcher, and Morton Rubin
  1975 Social Problems in the United States. New York: Ronald Press.

O'Connell, Brian
  1975 "The Right to Know." MH 59, 2 (Spring): 11–13.

Offir, Carole Wade
  1974 "A Slavish Reliance on Drugs: Are We Pushers for Our Own Children?" Psychology Today 8, 7 (December): 49.

Pasamanick, Benjamin
  1961 "A Survey of Mental Disease in an Urban Population." Archives of General Psychiatry 5: 59–63.

"Probe Bares "Warehousing' of Aged." Allentown Morning Call (March 19): 1, 1976.

Rappaport, Jonas
  1975 "The Cutting Edge: Right to Treatment." MH 59, 2 (Spring): 8–10.

Rice, Berkeley
  1975 "The Worry Epidemic." Psychology Today 9, 3 (August): 74, 76.

Rosenhan, D. L.
  1973 "On Being Sane in Insane Places." Science 179 (January 19): 250–58.

Ryan, William
  1971 Blaming the Victim. New York: Vintage.

Sandifer, Myron G., Charles Pettus, and Dana Quode
    1964 "A Study of Psychiatric Diagnosis." Journal of Nervous Mental Diseases 139 (October): 350–56.

Scarpitti, Frank
    1977 Social Problems. 2nd ed. New York: Dryden Press.

Scheff, Thomas
    1966 Being Mentally Ill: A Sociological Theory. Chicago: Aldine.

"Schizophrenia's Cause Found: Treatment, Cure Could Follow." Allentown Morning Call (May 5): 1, 1972.

Srole, Leo
    1975 "Measurement and Classification in Socio-Psychiatric Epidemiology, Midtown Manhattan Study (1954) and Midtown Manhattan Restudy (1974)." Journal of Health and Social Behavior 16, 4 (December): 347–64.

Stark, Rodney
    1975 Social Problems. New York: Random House.

Steadman, Henry and Joseph Cocozza
    1975 "We Can't Predict Who Is Dangerous." Psychology Today 8, 8 (January): 32–35.

Szaz, Thomas
    1961 The Myth of Mental Illness: The Foundations of a Theory of Personal Conduct. New York: Harper.
    1970 "Justice in the Therapeutic State." Comprehensive Psychiatry 11 (1970): 433–44.
    1970 The Manufacture of Madness. New York: Dell.

Taube, Carl and Richard Redick
    1976 "Provisional Data on Patient Care Episodes in Mental Health Facilities, 1973." Mental Health Statistical Note No. 127 (February), U.S. Department of Health, Education and Welfare, ADRAMHA, DHEW Publication No. (ADM): 76-158.

Taube, Carl and Michael Witkin
    1976 "Staff-Patient Ratios in Selected Inpatient Mental Health Facilities, January 1974." Mental Health Statistical Note No. 129 (May), U.S. Department of Health, Education and Welfare, ADRAMHA, DHEW Publication No. (ADM): 76-158.

Walker, Sydney
    1974 "Drugging the American Child: We're Too Cavalier about Hyperactivity." Psychology Today 8, 7 (December): 43–48.

Weiss, Jay, Howard Glazer, and Larissa Pokorecky
    1974 "Neurotransmitters and Helplessness: A Chemical Bridge to Depression?" Psychology Today 8, 7 (December): 59–62.

Wilson, G. Terence and Gerald Davison
    1975 "A Road to Self-Control." Psychology Today 9, 5 (October): 54–60.

Witkin, Michael J.
    1975 "State and Regional Distribution of Psychiatric Beds in 1974." Statistical Note No. 118 (July), U.S. Department of Health, Education and Welfare, ADRAMHA, DHEW Publication No. (ADM): 75-158.

Wittman, Bob and John Clark
    1976 "Convicted Gay, 66, Cannot Find a Job Despite 2 Degrees." Allen-

town Morning Call (July 16): 1–2.
The World Almanac and Book of Facts: 1976. New York: Newspaper Enterprise Association, 1975.

SUGGESTED READINGS

Carter, Frances M. Psychosocial Nursing: Theory and Practice in Hospital and Community Mental Health. 2nd ed. New York: Macmillan. 1976.
Describes and analyzes the role of the nurse in relating to mentally ill patients, as well as coordinating that role with other professionals in a mental-health setting.

Dean, Alfred, Alan M. Draft, and Bert Pepper. The Social Setting of Mental Health. New York: Basic Books. 1976.
Describes advantages of therapeutic communities and mental-health services, and the shortcomings of typical mental-illness diagnoses.

Donaldson, Kenneth. Insanity Inside Out. New York: Crown. 1976.
Written by the man who brought his case to the courts after 15 years of mistreatment in a mental institution. Reforms within mental institutions were suddenly effected after he won his case in 1975.

Monahan, John. Community Mental Health and the Criminal Justice System. New York: Pergamon. 1976.
Examines the relationship between the community mental-health system and its use and abuse by the police and courts.

Peszke, Michael A. Involuntary Treatment of the Mentally Ill: The Problem of Autonomy. Springfield, Ill.: Thomas. 1975.
Provides good suggestions for meeting the needs of the mentally ill while protecting their freedom and rights.

Periodicals Worth Exploring

Adolescence
American Journal of Orthopsychiatry
Behavioral Science
Journal of Health and Social Behavior
MH
Psychology Today
Small Group Behavior

Sociologists have recognized that powerful social institutions and serious social problems transcend national boundaries to take on international scope and scale. Power elites and inequality transcend the societal and national boundaries. Two of our social institutions in particular, government and the military, which are closely interlocked, span the globe, so that what happens anywhere in the world today sends ripples to our own country. Many modern social problems have an international dimension. They involve questions of war and peace, as well as life and death for mankind. Racial conflict and suppression of blacks in South Africa are viewed on the livingroom TV of families in American cities and towns the same evening. The hijacking of a plane in the United States makes news all over the world almost while it is happening.

The social problem of big government and political power has not yet been resolved on an international scale. Large governments, particularly the "Big Three" (China, Russia, and the United States), must begin to realize that they cannot use their power and bureaucracies in any way they see fit. Russia learned that lesson during the Cuban missile confrontation in the early 1960s, and the United States learned the lesson in Vietnam in the late 1960s. The world hope is that China learned from both of those confrontations.

In the United States, the influence and power of the federal government expand with each passing year. They cause mistrust; problems of centralized bigness and bureaucracy that overlook individual human needs; excessive spending, especially for the military, that feeds the flames of inflation, builds up the arms race, and makes the military more powerful. Basic value conflicts over the dichotomies of centralization versus decentralization of power, order versus liberty, and security versus democracy remain unresolved in our society and throughout the world. Computers, closed-circuit TV, and data banks, could aid power elites in government to eventually create a totalitarian society in the United States. When C. Wright Mills wrote in 1950 about "power elites" and technology dominating the lives of persons in

International Dimensions of Social Issues

our society, perhaps even he did not realize the tremendous efficiency and effectiveness of such governmental social structures.

But Mills did correctly envision the path that military development and arms accumulation were taking. He saw how an arms race could lead to an ideology of "crack-pot realism" among the world powers to justify the irrational escalation and massive stockpiling of nuclear weapons. In his book **The Causes of World War III**, he envisioned how such "crack-pot realism" would lead inevitably to a thermonuclear holocaust for all mankind. He also correctly predicted how the military would become one of the dominant social institutions and would influence and control our other major institutions, especially government and the economy. His vision of the interlocking triumvirate of power elites in government, business, and the military, has indeed come true. The international dimensions of such concentrated power are frightening and in some ways hard for most persons to imagine.

Closely related to the international repercussions of our government and the military are the social problems of population and ecology. When a tanker shipping oil from the Middle East to feed our motorized and jet-fueled armed forces spills its oozy cargo along our seashores, the environment is instantly threatened. When nuclear waste or poison nerve gas from military weapons is stored underground and later leaks, our ecological system must bear the burden. Key industries geared for military and industrial production think little about polluting our air or water since they serve our needs for defense and for goods. Uncontrolled population growth and expansion in underdeveloped countries are also considered a potential threat to our position as one of the world's leading nations. Overpopulation could bring desperation and despair, leading to revolution or war. In such a situation our government and military have a vested interest. Helping less-developed countries to develop their economies and to control their populations in ways that will benefit the United States causes new social problems that transcend our national boundaries.

Big Government and the Military

DEFINITION OF THE PROBLEM
Conservative perspective.
Liberal perspective.
Radical perspective.

INCIDENCE AND PREVALENCE OF THE PROBLEM
Lack of trust in government.
Government employment and spending.
Government control by a power elite.
Government bureaucracy and paperwork.
Power and influence of the military.

CAUSES OF THE PROBLEM
Growth in our complex mass society.
Growth in bureaucracy and "state management" by the military.
A military culture.
Value conflicts:
a) Decentralization of power v. centralization.
b) Order v. liberty.
c) Security v. democracy.

PROPOSED SOLUTIONS TO THE PROBLEM
General revenue sharing.
Reforming Congress.
Proposals to aid consumers and public-interest groups.
The experimenting society.

Proposals for controlling the arms race.
Proposals to curb the military's power and defense spending.

FUTURE OF THE PROBLEM
Larger, more centralized government.
Use of "social indicators."
More government technocratic and professional elites.
Military power and arms.

SUMMARY

The world spends an average of $12,330 to arm each soldier but only an average of $219 to educate each school-age child.

From the report "World Military and Social Expenditures 1976," **Washington Post,** March 1, 1976.

If a foreign power really wanted to destroy this country, it could develop a chemical to destroy paper. That would bring us to our knees.

Attributed to Dr. Richard Brautigan, Superintendent of 11 district schools in El Centro, Calif., by David M. Alpern "Big Government," **Newsweek** (December 15, 1975): 35.

Several years ago the following story was making the rounds in Washington, D.C.:

> A young man lived with his parents in a low-cost public housing development. . . . He attended public school, rode the free bus, enjoyed the free lunch program. After graduating from high school, he entered the Army and after discharge kept his National Service Life Insurance. He then enrolled in Ohio University, using his GI benefits.
>
> Upon graduation, he married a Public Health nurse, and bought a farm with an FHA loan. . . . Rural Electrification Administration supplied lines, and a loan from the Farmers Home Administration helped clear the land; the government stocked a pond with fish and guaranteed him a sale for his farm products.
>
> He banked his money in an institution which a government agency insured for every depositor. . . . He signed a petition seeking federal assistance for an industrial project to help the economy of the area.
>
> About that time, he bought business and real estate property at the county seat, aided by an FHA loan; he was elected to an office in the local chamber of commerce. He wrote his congressman, protesting excessive government spending and high taxes: "I believe in individualism and oppose all Socialist trends. People should stand on their own feet," he concluded (Harris, August 7, 1976:6).

This story illustrates the fact that even those who oppose big government and the massive size and scale of our political institutions often benefit directly or indirectly from them. It also illustrates that government has so thoroughly permeated and penetrated society and its operations that we are often unaware of its presence or simply take it for granted, as did the young man in the story.

In this chapter we will explore the views of conservatives, liberals, and radicals on government size and bureaucracy, government spending, distribution of power, as well as the power and influence of the military.

DEFINING THE PROBLEMS OF BIG GOVERNMENT

The Conservative Perspective

After more than 200 years, our government as a social institution is under attack again, this time by Americans. Some see the federal government (and sometimes state and county governments) as too large, bureaucratic, powerful, "nosey," and wasteful of our money. Many Americans resent being told by Washington bureaucrats what to do and how to do it. They feel that matters are best handled by their local community, not the state or federal government. In our mass society, people no longer trust their government because it is often unresponsive to their wishes. Many feel that individuals should have a say through their own groups and organizations; in that way all voices and opinions are heard as part of our democratic, pluralistic society. These views of the situation are held by persons we label "conservatives." Conservatives argue that the size and number of federal programs and policies have grown astronomically during the last 15 years or so. As sociologist Max Weber pointed out many years ago, large bureaucratic organizations are impersonal and are governed by rigid rules, regulations, and procedures. Sociologist Robert Merton also noted that bureaucracies have many "dysfunctional" aspects that lead to "buck-passing," ritualistic behavior by bureaucrats, and a "displacement of goals" so that often very little ever gets done. Average citizens who need help are often treated impersonally, and their problems go unresolved. This "overregulation," say the conservatives, is hurting business, destroying competition, and raising prices.

The Liberal Perspective

The liberals, on the other hand, argue that the federal system is not so big or incompetent; in a society of nearly 220 million citizens, we need a central coordinator. Indeed, they say, its policies and programs have benefited society. Even internationally our society's interests must be represented and protected. As the late Michigan Senator Philip Hart told a meeting of the American Academy of Political and Social Science: "It should be remembered that it was not local and state governments but the national government which moved, however imperfectly, against pollution, poverty and discrimination. It was the national government, rather than the spirit of volunteerism, which sought to improve working conditions, started medicare, and is working on a national health plan" (Hart, 1973:97–98). Middle-class citizens have benefited from FHA mortgage loans, the GI bill, highway construction, and aid to education, to mention just a few programs.

Liberals concede that central power usually ends up in the hands of an elite, but there are often countervailing power groups that offset central control by big government. They maintain we must use big government to serve more persons—more common interests—instead of serving only the vested interests, such as big business or the military. We should change our national priorities so that the central government's power can benefit all persons.

The Radical Perspective

C. Wright Mills, in *The Power Elite*, asserted that our political and social system is dominated by a "power elite" who hold interchangeable positions in the political, economic, and military institutions. They all belong to the same social milieu and have similar educational and social experiences, and their decisions and actions are well coordinated (1956: 19-20). The really important decisions (or nondecisions) are made by this homogeneous power elite. Although conservatives and liberals offer conflicting theories of political pluralism—that is, participation in government and decision making by diverse groups—the radicals maintain that the elites control our entire system through their interconnecting links in government, the military, and the economy. Such institutions, especially government, must be radically restructured and the whole society changed to serve the needs and wants of the people. If necessary, violent revolution should be used to achieve the goal of a new democratic-socialistic society in which power and wealth would be diffused to most persons and the basic needs for food, clothing, shelter, and a job would be met.

Most of all, radicals point to instances of how the military has gained influence and control over the operation of government. This has led to a system of "state management" by the military, involving expenditure of billions of dollars, as well as management of large defense contracts and millions of employees. Every year Congress appropriates billions to feed a vast military machine, which soon becomes obsolete. Radicals point to how former generals or officers become top corporation officials, who then negotiate defense contracts with the Pentagon. Congressmen interact socially on a first-name basis with Pentagon and defense-contract executives. Congressmen from such states as Texas and Georgia depend on help from large defense contractors and military officials to gain reelection. In turn, the Congressman funnels more defense contracts into his home state.

Waste and Corruption

Another problem with big government, the radicals and others point out, is that it breeds waste and corruption. An example of such waste is the

Billions are spent each year on modern, sophisticated weapons of destruction that soon become obsolete. The arms race is both costly and wasteful.

Credit: Owen F. W./Black Star.

congressional practice of taking all-expense-paid trips to foreign countries, allegedly for fact-finding in conjunction with legislative duties. But recent detailed information, obtained by the *Washington Post* under the Freedom of Information Act, revealed that many Congressmen and their wives (or friends) have taken chauffeured jaunts, at public expense, to such spots as the Swiss lake country, the chateau regions of France, and the Taj Mahal in India ("Sky Still the Limit . . .," July 6, 1976:1).

The military also wastes money. It is top-heavy with "brass"—high-ranking officers. Top Pentagon officials are chauffeured in tax-financed limousines, and there are now more officers per lower-ranking enlisted men than ever before. The current ratio of one to one is inefficient, unnecessary, and wasteful. Waste is compounded when so much of what is made for the military is eventually scrapped, junked, or literally blown up. For example, Representative Les Aspin reports that under a Pentagon policy, 101 jet engines made by General Electric, costing from $100,000 to $150,000 each, were junked for $166 each ("$404,000 in Jet Engines...," February 17, 1976:2).

Waste in the military and government is often combined with corruption. For example, 38 top military officials, including nine admirals and 17 Air Force generals, accepted entertainment, including prostitutes, at a Maryland hunting lodge of the Northrop Corporation, a major aerospace defense contractor. According to one report, "the Northrop Corporation billed the government—and was routinely reimbursed for—at least $24,000 related to its Easton, Maryland, hunting lodge" (Gruenstein, 1975: 1). Congressional investigations revealed that similar entertainment is often provided for military brass almost routinely. Former Secretary of Defense James Schlesinger called such cases "only the tip of the iceberg" ("Pentagon Warns 38....," January 24, 1976:1).

Another symptom and symbol of corruption in government is the notorious "Hays-Ray Affair." For nearly two years, former Representative Wayne Hays of Ohio, then chairman of the House Administration Committee, kept on his staff Elizabeth Ray, who said she was paid $15,000 a year in public funds to serve as his mistress. As she admitted, "I can't type, I can't file, I can't even answer the phone" ("Rep. Hays's Employee...," May 23, 1976:A-10). While working for Representative Hays, Ms. Ray was never asked to do any congressional work and appeared at the House Office Building once or twice a week for a few hours. Hays originally denied Ms. Ray's charges, but later admitted some of them and resigned one of his committee chairmanships. He later decided not to run again for Congress.

INCIDENCE AND PREVALENCE OF BIG GOVERNMENT

Government is getting bigger every year. The conservatives argue that the public is fed up with "big government." In recent Gallup Poll surveys of the nation's "most important problems," big government has consistently been second or third on the list. In a 1975 CBS News poll, 39 percent cited "dissatisfaction" with government as a matter of "serious concern" (Alpern, December 15, 1975:34).

Lack of Trust in Government

Between 1970 and 1975 "Who's Who among American High School Students" surveyed 23,000 top high-school seniors across the country. The following results were reported from its 1975 poll:

> 81 percent believe that elected politicians lack honor and integrity (in 1972, before the Watergate cover-up was exposed, only 21 percent believed that).

73 percent believe most major political campaigns are crooked.

83 percent think our system does not provide equal justice for all citizens.

9 percent think that elected officials represent the voters adequately.

83 percent of the seniors eligible to vote said they would vote as independents since they were, at that time, disenchanted with the Republican and Democratic parties (Swift, May 25, 1975:12).

All this may represent an immediate reaction to Watergate, but it also represents a serious social issue about our lack of trust in big government.

A Market-Opinion Research Company poll reveals the following changes, as noted in Table 13-1, in the people's trust of the federal government between 1964 and 1974. The hope is that the Carter administration will overcome some of this lack of trust in government.

Government Employment and Spending

Federal, state, and local governments directly employ over 14½ million persons and annually spend well over half a *trillion* dollars. Government spending at all levels in 1976 accounted for 37 percent of the Gross National Product (value of all goods and service), whereas government's share in 1929 was only 12 percent. Figure 13-1 compares the federal government and state and local governments by payroll and number of employees. Government at all levels spends over $150 billion a year just for the salaries of its employees. Furthermore, the federal government alone is at least $700 billion in debt. Not counted in any of this are more billions in stocks and bonds issued by the Export-Import Bank and other federal agencies. For interest payments alone, the Feds paid out over $37 billion in fiscal 1976 ("National Debt...," July 5, 1976: 104). The federal gov-

table 13-1   COMPARISON OF THE PUBLIC'S TRUST IN GOVERNMENT

FREQUENCY OF TRUST IN FEDERAL GOVERNMENT	1964	1974
Always	14%	2%
Most of the Time	62	30
Some of the Time	22	64
Don't know	2	4

Source: Larry Martz, **Newsweek**, 86, 24 (December 15, 1975): 44.

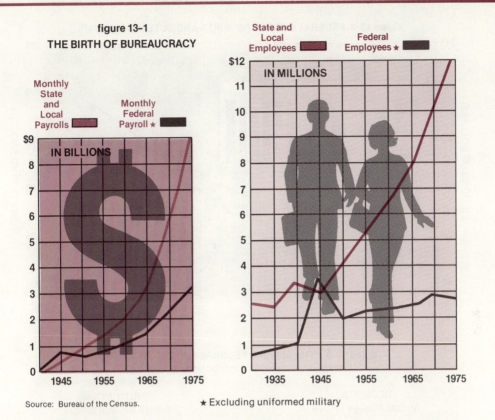

figure 13-1
THE BIRTH OF BUREAUCRACY

Source: Bureau of the Census.   ★ Excluding uniformed military

ernment owes 40 percent of the total debt to itself. The rest is owed to other government bodies, private corporations, banks, and individuals. The federal government also provides cash for about one-fourth of the spending of state and local governments.

Federal budget outlays for 1975 totaled over $315 billion and accounted for about 22 percent of our GNP (up from 18 percent in 1965). Figure 13-2 illustrates the annual federal budget receipts and outlays from 1960 to 1975. Meanwhile, Figure 13-3 shows where the money comes from and how it is spent. In the fiscal year ended June 30, 1976, our government had a deficit of $69 billion, and this was the seventh straight year a federal budget was in the red. This trend persists because government spending increases faster than the available revenue. For example, in the 10 years between 1966 and 1976, the GNP increased by 121 percent, but federal spending increased by 174 percent ("Balancing the U.S. Budget," August 2, 1976: 25). Federal spending reaches into almost every nook and cranny of our society.

Government Bureaucracy and Paperwork

Hundreds and thousands of agencies make up the federal bureaucracy. Political scientist Herbert Kaufman of the Brookings Institution

13 BIG GOVERNMENT AND THE MILITARY

538

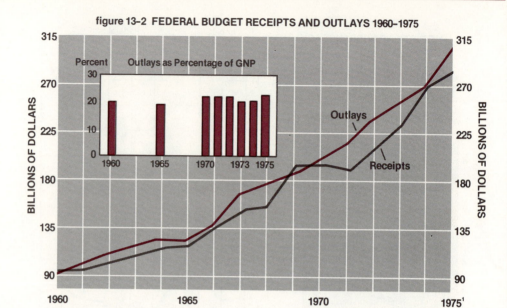

figure 13-2 FEDERAL BUDGET RECEIPTS AND OUTLAYS 1960-1975

[1] Estimate.

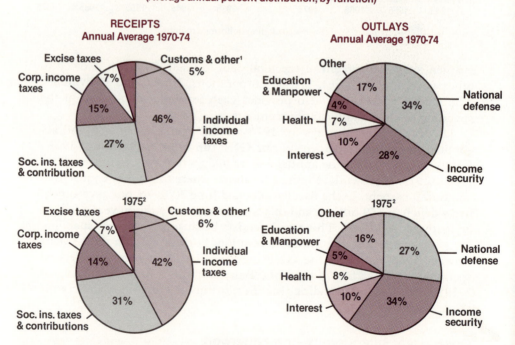

figure 13-3 THE ANNUAL FEDERAL BUDGET: 1970-1975
(Average annual percent distribution, by function)

[1] Other includes estate and gift taxes and other receipts.
[2] Estimate.

Source: Data from U.S. Office of Management and Budget.

Big government generates tons of paperwork that may or may not help to remedy particular social problems.

analyzed 175 federal agencies that existed in 1923 and found that 148 of them were still functioning 50 years later. Only 27 had gone out of existence, while 246 new ones were created ("Can't Stop Agencies' Growth...," May 23, 1976: 1). The same study reported that 53 executive-branch agencies and units were created from 1968 to 1972, more than during any other presidential term.

Such proliferation of agencies leads to waste, inefficiency, and paperwork. As former President Nixon pointed out:

> Nine different Federal departments and 20 independent agencies are now involved in education matters. Seven departments and eight independent agencies are involved in health. In many major cities, there are at least 20 or 30 separate manpower programs funded by a variety of Federal offices. Three departments help develop our water resources and four agencies in two de-

partments are involved in the management of public lands. . . . Six departments of the government collect similar economic information — often from the same sources . . . ("State of the Union Address," January 23, 1971: 12).

Figure 13-4 shows some of the *major* departments and independent offices in the executive branch alone.

Present government red tape and required paperwork add to the woes of local communities and private business. Constant change in government regulations makes rational business virtually impossible. For example, the state of California has filed a suit against the United States Department of Agriculture to ban any more changes in food-stamp regulations. The state charges that the food-stamp manual was rewritten every year from 1965 to 1968, rewritten again in 1972, modified 89 times by 1974, and revised 27 times between 1974 and early 1976. In 1975 alone there were 500 individual regulatory changes. One "reg" spells out when to use paper clips and when to use staples on food-stamp files (Martz, December 15, 1975: 44).

Nevertheless, a survey conducted for the Commerce Department by the business-oriented Advertising Council revealed that 56 percent of the population believe that "still more government regulation of some economic activities is required" (Alpern, December 15, 1975:34). In addition, people's experience with large bureaucratic agencies is not always as frustrating as conservatives would have us believe. A study by Robert Kahn and others indicates that most Americans who have contact and experiences with bureaucrats and bureaucracies are satisfied. Most persons generalize negatively about bureaucracies, "but their own experiences are far from the picture of pettiness and inefficiency that we have come to assume is real" (Kahn, et al., 1975: 66). Professor Kahn's study, based on a representative sample of 1,431 adults, described the quality of service they felt they received from a variety of federal and state agencies. The surprisingly favorable results are shown in Table 13-2. In addition, many persons said the bureaucrats were doing a good job. Table 13-3 shows the kinds of efforts the government staff persons made to help those who came to them for help.

Government Control by a Power Elite

How extensive is the power elite's control of government? Firm empirical research has verified the existence of a pervasive elite in big government. G. William Domhoff's *The Higher Circles* (1971) and David Halberstam's *The Best and the Brightest* (1972) refer to the organization called "The Council on Foreign Relations." It was formed in 1921 by members of the New York Social Register (a listing of rich families) and now limits its membership to 1,400 (half of whom must live in New York City). Since its inception, it has supplied the foreign-policy agencies of the federal government with many leaders. In the early 1960s the Kennedy

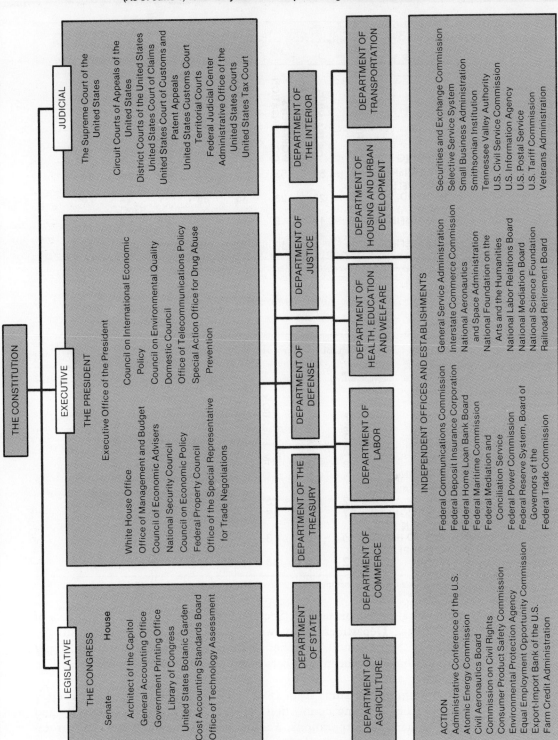

figure 13-4 THE GOVERNMENT OF THE UNITED STATES
(As of June 1, 1975. Only the more important agencies are shown)

Source: U.S. General Services Administration, National Archives and Records Service.

table 13-2 PUBLIC REACTION TO EFFORTS OF BUREAUCRATS TO SOLVE VARIOUS PROBLEMS

RATING	JOB FINDING	JOB TRAINING	WORKMEN'S COMPENSATION	UNEMPLOYMENT COMPENSATION	WELFARE	HOSPITAL/MEDICAL	RETIREMENT	TOTAL
VERY SATISFIED	35	51	53	35	27	49	64	43
FAIRLY WELL SATISFIED	26	23	23	36	34	9	24	26
SOMEWHAT DISSATISFIED	16	19	5	14	18	24	4	13
VERY DISSATISFIED	20	6	10	12	10	18	3	14

Source: Robert Kahn et. al., "Americans Love Their Bureaucrats." **Psychology Today** (June 1975): 69. © 1975 Ziff-Davis Publishing Company. Reprinted by permission.

tables 13-3 PUBLIC REACTION TO EXTENT OF BUREAUCRATS' EFFORTS TO HELP THEM

RATING	JOB FINDING	JOB TRAINING	WORKMEN'S COMPENSATION	UNEMPLOYMENT COMPENSATION	WELFARE	HOSPITAL/MEDICAL	RETIREMENT	TOTAL
MORE THAN THEY HAD TO	12	25	25	4	11	20	26	16
ABOUT RIGHT	57	57	15	71	59	49	61	57
LESS THAN THEY SHOULD HAVE	16	8	3	13	21	13	5	12
NO EFFORT AT ALL	12	8	13	8	7	18	1	9

Source: Robert Kahn et. al., **Psychology Today** (June 1975): 70. © 1975 Ziff-Davis Publishing Company. Reprinted by permission.

Administration appointees for Secretary of State, four senior members of the Defense Department, and two White House staff members all belonged to "the Council." Former Secretaries of State and other Cabinet members have also been members of the elite Council (Fernandez, 1975: 137–38).

A longitudinal study from 1897 to 1973 by sociologist Peter Freitag demonstrates a strong connection between U.S. Cabinet Secretaries and major American corporations. Freitag used the term "interlock" to describe the situation in which the same person served in the Cabinet and as

No matter how informal or folksy a president may be, elites behind the scenes wield vast power that affects millions. The public's trust or distrust of big government usually reflects its attitudes toward the president in power.

a top officer, director, or lawyer in a major corporation before or after serving in his government post. Freitag's figures revealed that 62 percent of Cabinet heads were corporate directors or officers, 14.1 percent were corporate lawyers, and 11.7 percent were lawyers with possible connections to business corporations. In all, only 12.2 percent of the top Cabinet officials were not "interlocked" with major corporations (December 1975: 141).

There was no significant difference in the percentage of "interlocks" between Republican and Democratic administrations. Freitag concludes that "this study casts heavy doubt upon the pluralist perspective and provides evidence which makes the elitist position more tenable" (Ibid., 151). Wealth and power go together in big government, not only in the executive branch, but also in the legislative. A report released in 1976 showed that at least 22 millionaires were serving in the Senate and possibly a larger number in the House of Representatives. Thus, the interests of the wealthy are well represented in the Congress (Lyons, January 4, 1976: A–10).

Even when we look at the election of convention delegates by the two political parties, a concentration of high socioeconomic status is evident. An Associated Press survey of the 1976 Democratic Convention showed the following profile:

1. Exactly half the delegates had earnings of more than $25,000 a year (an income reached by only 11-1/2 percent of the public). Only 7 percent of the delegates earned less than $10,000 a year.
2. Four out of every five delegates had attended college, and only 2 percent had less than a high-school education (though one-third of all Americans do not finish high school).
3. Women held 33 percent of the delegate seats, though women represent over half our population (Witt and Barnes, July 11, 1976: A-10).

Clearly, the delegates who elect our presidential candidates are not representative of the majority. Delegates to the 1976 Republican Convention displayed an even more elite profile—again very rich, well-educated, and predominantly male.

In the judicial branch, the hope is that justice can be obtained for all. However, a recent Supreme Court decision makes that prospect rather dim. For a decade or so, a "public-interest" movement represented the rights of poor and middle-class persons who could not afford a lawyer or the expense of an extended law suit. Rights of mental patients, and environmental issues, for example, were advanced because of an array of public-interest law suits. But a Supreme Court ruling in 1975 (*Alyeska Pipeline Co.* v. *Wilderness Society*) forbade judges to grant fee awards to lawyers who, in effect, represented the public interest. These lawyers had sought to enforce laws that the federal and state authorities could not. In the past, the fee award came from the losing parties, usually government agencies, and covered the costs of preparing the cases. After the ruling, however, public-interest attorney David Ferleger estimated that his project lost at least $100,000 in fee awards. Now his highly successful and useful public-interest law project is in danger of going out of business (Leary, July 18, 1976: B-21).

Power and Influence of the Military

Power and influence in Washington are exerted by federal bureaucratic agencies to pass the laws that they favor. One of the most effective lobbying groups has been the Pentagon. The military's power and influence, as well as its budget for arms and defense spending, have increased dramatically in the last 20 years. The military and its defense weapons take about one-third of the federal budget and about 70 percent of national revenue each year. The defense budget is well over $100 billion, and is expected to rise to about $150 billion in the near future. Figure 13-5 illustrates how defense spending has increased over the past 40 years.

Between the start of World War II and 1976, military spending cost American taxpayers $1.3 trillion. The increases in defense spending are often at the expense of social and health programs. For example, in January 1976 former President Ford proposed that Congress

> end the Public Service Employment Program
> eliminate funding for waste-water treatment
> cut back on water-pollution control
> end summer-jobs programs for 100,000 youths
> drop community nutrition programs for the elderly

At the same time, the President called for

> the addition of 4 new fighter wings to the Air Force
>
> 15 new naval ships, including 3 nuclear-powered submarines and 8 guided-missile frigates
>
> production of the B-1 bomber force, the Trident submarine fleet, the cruise missile system, and an entirely new ICBM system
>
> production of the XM-1 Battle Tank, new F-16 fighter jets, and a new attack helicopter

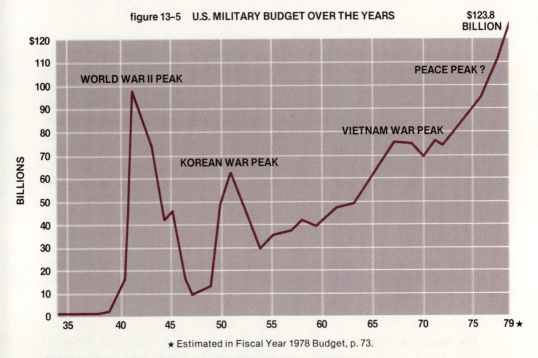

figure 13-5 U.S. MILITARY BUDGET OVER THE YEARS

★ Estimated in Fiscal Year 1978 Budget, p. 73.

Source: OASD (Comptroller) Budgets of the U.S. Reprinted by permission of the Coalition on National Priorities and Military Policies.

The Pentagon and the military play a powerful economic and social role in Washington and in the world, no matter which political party is in power.

the beginning of research and development for a new Army tank, a new transport helicopter, a new F-18 air-combat fighter jet, and a new air-defense system

Furthermore, the Defense Department had a surplus of nearly $85 billion on hand by the end of fiscal 1977. At the same time that military and defense spending increased by 20 percent, federal aid to cities and states declined by 30 percent. Also, total cost-overruns incurred by our weapons systems programs came to $38 billion (Pollack, 1976: 2).

In 1974, the Department of Defense owned property worth $228 billion ($178 billion at home and $50 billion overseas) (U.S. Bureau of the Census, 1975: 320). They let out $37.7 billion in contracts and accounted for payrolls of almost $25 billion. Over two million men and women are in the Armed Services, while another one million are employed by the Defense Department; these account for 37 percent of all federal civilian employees (Ibid., 321). These same employees take almost 65 percent of the federal payroll.

The Nuclear Arms Race

Our nuclear weapons are numerous and are deployed almost worldwide. We have 7,000 tactical nuclear weapons in Europe alone, and

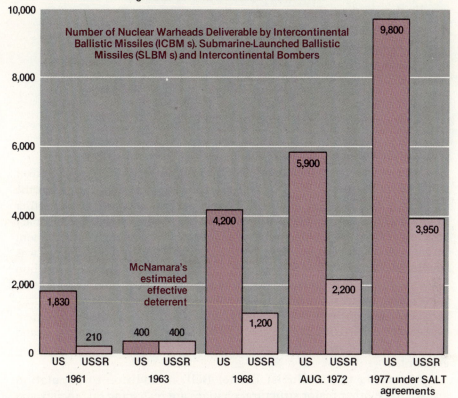

figure 13-6 THE NUCLEAR ARMS RACE

Source: Reprinted by permission of SANE, a Citizen's Organization for a Sane World.

about 600 more in South Korea (King, April 17, 1976: 21). Admiral Gene La Rocque, head of the Center for Defense Information, told Congress that the megatonnage of Russia and the United States has so increased that the combined impact of both nations is equal to over one million bombs of the type that destroyed Hiroshima ("New A-Bomb Peril...," September 11, 1974:10). The American government began the SALT (Strategic Arms Limitation) talks with 4,000 nuclear warheads, ended the first round of discussions with 7,000 warheads, and later planned to limit its arsenal to around 10,000 (Wickersham, April 17, 1976: 23). Figure 13-6 demonstrates how both American and Russian nuclear stockpiles have grown.

CAUSES OF BIG GOVERNMENT AND MILITARY POWER

We will examine four main causes behind bigness in government and power of the military stemming from it.

1. a large, complex, mass society and social structure produc-

ing needs that must be met by some social institution, usually the government
2. growth of bureaucracy and "state management" by the military in modern society
3. a military culture
4. value conflicts focusing on centralized v. decentralized power, order v. liberty, security v. freedom.

Our Complex Mass Society

We live in a large society of over 216 million persons, spread out over 3,000 miles coast to coast. It is a much different kind of society from the one with which we started in 1776. People were isolated from one another in small communities and rarely traveled great distances. The ordinary citizen's concern with government was local and parochial. If government in general was small and decentralized, it was because our society was small and localized. But our society has now grown to over 216 million persons. A rural, dispersed people needed few government services in those days, whereas millions of people need services today. Necessary services, such as roads, water supply, sewerage, and schools, cost a great deal of money ($18,000 per person in 1970). This growth in population and in their needs, among other reasons, explains the existence of large government.

According to sociologist Daniel Bell, in addition to population growth three other major structural changes are reshaping our society and account for the bigness of government today: a national society, a communal society, and a postindustrial, international society. We have become a national society in only the past 50 or 60 years. During the economic Depression of the 1930s, the federal government had to fashion national social structures to control and manage a fledgling national economy that had collapsed. The federal government set up national mechanisms to regulate labor-management relations, transportation, communications, fiscal and monetary matters, and the securities and exchange market. Today government is attempting to create new national mechanisms to meet people's needs nationally in health, welfare, and education.

Second, we have become a communal society. Because of our numerical and technological growth, we have become aware of common dangers from a polluted environment. This has produced a need for a social institution to regulate air and water pollution, solid-waste disposal, and recreational space. These tasks logically fall to government, especially on a national or regional level. We are also much more aware of the just claims on the community and nation by disadvantaged groups—the aged, women, the culturally deprived, and the racially segregated. For these reasons, too, the role of government has been enlarged and expanded.

Third, we are becoming a postindustrial, international society. No longer are we simply a blue-collar, manufacturing society. Over 60 percent of the workforce renders services instead of making goods. This has meant more white-collar jobs and a new emphasis on education and training for a larger, more complex, interdependent society. To fund and finance such education and training, we require additional government monies.

According to Margaret Mead, we now live in a "global village." Our government involves itself in economic, military, and other power relationships on an international scale. No longer can any central government operate solely on a national level. So, according to Bell, "It is the simultaneous convergence of these four structural changes—the demographic transformation, the creation of a new, tighter-knit national society, the development of a communal society with new claims, and the emergence of a post-industrial [international] society with new educational requirements"—that have posed social problems for government and our society (Bell, September 30, 1973: F-10).

The Growth of Bureaucracy

An integral part of our growth toward becoming a national society with a large central government has been the growth of bureaucracy in all our social institutions. Max Weber predicted and saw the bureaucratiza-

Government bureaucracies often become so large and complex that the individual and his needs are ignored or forgotten.

Credit: Benyos/Kaufman from Black Star.

tion and rationalization (definite means worked out to reach definite goals) of modern society. Writing at the beginning of the twentieth century, Weber described the forms and processes by which spontaneous, traditional, and informal ways of doing things would be replaced by logical, calculated rules and procedures. To achieve this "disenchantment of the world," a new social form called bureaucracy would become the dominant social and technical form. He saw the growth of modern bureaucracy as inevitable, even essential, for democracy to flourish. He saw it as a social structure or system that would treat all people fairly and impartially (though impersonally) and would eliminate personal capriciousness or prejudice from business decisions. Favoritism and autocracy would be checked and controlled by bureaucracy, he argued. He saw the functionality that bureaucracy could have for mass societies. Yet he saw the ways in which a bureaucratic government or organization could control the lives of people very efficiently and effectively. The great paradox (which even de Tocqueville envisioned) was that as a society strove for greater equality and services from government, it would inevitably create the need for large bureaucracies to control the economy and provide the necessary social services. To do this efficiently would put restraints on individuals' goals and expression.

Other sociologists, such as Robert Merton and Amitai Etzioni, saw the dysfunctions of bureaucracy. They noted how bureaucracies were often inefficient, encouraged "buck-passing" and red tape, stuck to obsolete rules, and tended to resist change. Popular critics of bureaucracy, such as C. Northcote Parkinson and Laurence Peter, described other inefficiencies of bureaucratic structures. For example, Parkinson coined "Parkinson's Law"—in any bureaucracy, "work expands to fill the amount of time available for its completion" (1957). Lawrence Peter, in his famous "Peter Principle," maintained that in any bureaucracy, "every employee tends to rise in the hierarchy to his own level of incompetence"(1969). According to this theorem, a person who does a competent and capable job in a bureaucracy is generally promoted out of it until he reaches a job beyond his capacity, where he tends to remain.

But whether a bureaucracy is functional or dysfunctional for society and government, such a social structure is clearly a reflection of our own mass society. As the French social critic Jacques Ellul points out: "We must not condemn the bureaucracy's expansion—its complexity is the mirror image of the nation's complexity and the diverse tasks entrusted to the state. Nobody can have exact knowledge of this vast machinery.... Nobody can grasp the whole, and in reality nobody controls it" (1967: 141–44).

"State Management" by the Military

The powerful members of our society seek to expand business and military management as a measure of peacetime success. The structure of the defense establishment makes expansion inevitable: the scope and scale of its decision power—the new "state management"—is the largest and most important management system in the world. It has about 15,000 members simply to apportion work assignments among subordinate managers (contract negotiators), and 40,000 members to oversee the work of thousands of subcontractors for defense items. Through expansion, the military has become "the largest industrial central administrative office in the United States—perhaps in the world" (Melman, 1976: 352). The military controls an industrial empire that may produce "as much as 30 percent of the total gross national product each year" (Turner, 1972: 176). The products of this state management are defense and deterrence, and it is supported by the large, powerful corporations that dominate our society and others.

The state-management system can expand because it does not have to compete in the open market to sell its goods, or compete in the financial market for funds. Since it is not competitive, it also does not have to worry about being efficient or cutting costs.

A Military Culture

As the Pentagon has expanded in size and wealth, a military culture has developed. More people come to accept and internalize the needs, purposes, and functions of the military. An elite status has accrued to professional officers in America, although tarnished for a while by the war in Vietnam. Such a culture is diffused to the larger society because the military is a complex organization that is functionally interdependent with the business and civilian sector. The two sectors are closely interrelated economically, socially, and politically. As Kurt Lang observes, "The civil-military distinction is temporal rather than structural in a system that requires all men to equip themselves at the proper time in response to a call to war. In that case, participation in military activity is simply an outgrowth of membership in the community" (1972: 83). This accurately describes the situation in the United States, in which millions of civilians at one time or another have served or will serve in the military. Today even women are being assimilated into the military culture.

Decentralization Versus Centralization

From the very start of our nation, most governmental functions were handled at the local and state level. Such a decentralized system originally grew from the notion that the federal government would perform best when its functions were limited to those specified in the Constitution—defense and security, coinage of money, regulation of trade, and a few other "housekeeping" duties. The last amendment of the Bill of Rights (Article X) specifically stated: "The powers not delegated to the United States by the Constitution, nor prohibited by it to the States, are reserved

Many Americans feel that armaments and weapons must continually be added to our armed forces, regardless of cost overruns or inefficiencies.

to the States respectively, or to the people." Such values as these, codified into the Constitution, have always been the basis for arguing that the Federal government is too big, has too much power, and interferes in the lives of the people. It is this underlying value that gives "states' rights" plausibility and respectability even when used to cover up "states' wrongs." Reinforcing the notion of decentralized power in government are our conservative economic values of "laissez faire," that private enterprise should be free to operate and function without government intervention or regulation.

At the same time, however, many liberals and others saw the need for a central government to overcome the disunity, vested local interests, fragmentation, and weakness in dealing with foreign governments. As we expanded westward, we saw the need for a federal army to protect settlers and "win the West" from Spain and the Indians. As various parts of the country became linked by the railroad (built on federal land given over for that purpose), more people saw the need for better coordination of activities by a central government in Washington. When private laissez-faire corporations ignored the rights and interests of people, the people turned to Washington for help. Local and state governments were too easily controlled by the wealthy to expect any real remedy of society's problems from these levels of government. Hence we developed the new value of depending upon the central government to help out whenever a problem arose.

Even today so-called private enterprise recognizes the economic value of turning to the central government for help. For example, the federal government has loaned millions of dollars to Lockheed Aircraft, has financed sophisticated space-communications systems for private firms such as ITT, and has paid large corporate farms billions of dollars for *not* growing crops.

Order Versus Liberty

Order versus liberty has always been a conflicting value in our society. Our government was designed to give people as much liberty as possible, congruent with reasonable social order. But in recent years federal agencies, in their zeal to preserve "law and order" at all costs, have resorted to wiretapping, surveillance, and spying on our own citizens. All of this government activity has infringed on the liberty and rights of its citizens. To establish more order, Congress in recent years has appropriated billions of dollars for the Law Enforcement Administration Agency. This federal agency, established in 1968, is primarily interested in arming state and local police with better weapons and equipment, instead of developing community liaison groups and programs.

Security Versus Democracy

"National security" has become a code phrase to justify and rationalize virtually any action by federal government. Even if it deprives other nations or groups of their freedom, security has become an important value to many, both government officials and others. Overemphasis on national security has led the government to spend over $100 billion a year on "defense." This spending severely curtails our freedom to spend some of that money on more pressing domestic and international social problems.

PROPOSED SOLUTIONS TO PROBLEMS OF BIG GOVERNMENT AND THE MILITARY

Proposed solutions to the problems of big government and the military establishment depend upon the persuasion—conservative, liberal, or radical—to which the group adheres. The conservative solution is to decentralize most government operations so that decisions are made at the state and local level. The liberal answer is to federalize most programs, policies, and procedures so that decision making is handled by the government in Washington. Others, both conservatives and liberals, see the solution as a relative balance of power between the federal government and state and local governments, as well as increased efficiency in government agencies. Radicals, of course, advocate revolutionizing the whole governmental and military system so that it serves the needs of all instead of the powerful alone.

General Revenue Sharing

A conservative solution with the potential for balancing the power between the central and local governments is General Revenue Sharing (GRS). Under this legislation, first passed in 1972 as the State and Local Fiscal Assistance Act, the federal government returned $30.2 billion in taxes to states and local communities. Although the law required states and localities to use the money in nine "priority categories," they were actually able to use the money pretty much as they saw fit. Through GRS, "many decisions about what to do and how to do it were transferred to state and local governments" (Lovell, 1976: 211). The political scientist Paul Dommel suggests that GRS represents not so much a decentralization of policy making but "a policy of decrementalism"—reversing federal policy directions. GRS begins a key step toward reducing the federal government's decision-making role and turning more money and decision making over to state and local officials. According to Dommel, GRS represents "an effort to develop a new national consensus that believed that federal efforts to solve social problems had failed, that the national government had been inept and inefficient, and that state and local bureaucracies can do a better job than the national bureaucracy" (Ibid., 212). Nevertheless, many are still not convinced that GRS, or other programs to decentralize government, will solve our major social problems. And some argue that these efforts may just make them worse.

Reforming Congress

Many persons (conservatives and liberals) are convinced, however, that government reform is needed, in both Congress and the executive branch, to restore the public's trust in the honesty, openness, and efficiency of government. Many scholars and congressmen themselves have made suggestions, some of which have been adopted, to improve these aspects of Congress. According to political science professor Charles Jones, three things are needed to improve the functioning of Congress. "Access, debate and conclusion—those functions constitute my short list of what ought to be happening in Congress" (Jones, 1975: 269). To achieve these changes, Professor Jones offers six proposals:

1. Provide for more formal nomination and campaign procedures in electing party leaders.
2. Increase the authority of party leaders to control legislative production in Congress, including methods by which legislation can be acted on in committees (e.g., careful monitoring of committee progress on major legislation; authority to withdraw legislation from a committee).

3. Require an end-of-session review of the legislative record of party leaders before a caucus of party members from both houses. Such a session should provide for debate of the record and be open to the press and the public.
4. Commission a study of the efficiency and effectiveness of the existing party structure in each house—directed by an independent agent but including members of both parties and houses.
5. Expand the Congressional Research Service and the Office of Legislative Counsel; establish Offices of Congressional Committee Organization and Administration; and reduce the size of existing committee staffs.
6. Review the existing research capabilities for congressional political parties; possibly increase staff available for that purpose; make party leaders directly responsible for the use of research staff; and require periodic reporting by party leaders in caucus (Ibid., 272).

In addition, the late liberal senator Philip Hart (Mich.) proposed three steps for restoring public confidence:

1. Eliminate one source of distrust that plagues an office seeker even before he is elected: the need to raise campaign money.
2. Congress must reform its handling of federal spending proposals.
3. Educators and the media should spend more time discussing the problems of Congress and the importance of keeping Congress viable (1973: 99).

In 1976 both the House and Senate set up new Budget Committees, using procedures similar to what Senator Hart and others had proposed. These committees will be responsible for setting income and spending ceilings, which will then be adopted by a congressional resolution. For the first time, Congress can see the overall cost and effect of voting on separate appropriation bills (Gardner, January 17, 1976: 73).

Proposals to Aid Consumer and Public-Interest Groups

To make the government more responsive to the people, liberals have proposed a Consumer Protection Agency (CPA). This agency would represent consumer interests before other federal agencies and courts, and act as a clearinghouse for consumer information (Gardner, January 17, 1976: 74). To offset this proposal, former President Ford offered a counterproposal, which would require 17 federal departments and agencies to develop "consumer representation plans" designed to give the public "a greater voice in the federal decision-making process" (Crewdson, February 14, 1976: 330). Nationwide hearings have been held on this counterproposal, and the plan is still tentative. If adopted, it would create special consumer-complaint offices and simplify government procedures and forms to reduce the public's confusion. Kathleen O'Reilly of the Consumer Federation of America calls the counterproposal "stale and ineffective."

Senate liberals have introduced an even more significant bill (S 2715), which would authorize all federal agencies to pay the expenses of private individuals or groups that participate in agency proceedings and present viewpoints that would otherwise go unrepresented. It would also allow judges to award cost and attorney fees to persons or groups that successfully challenge agency actions. If passed, this bill would help public-interest groups to regain funds needed to challenge unfair laws in the courts (Ibid., 329).

Existing liberal public-interest groups—such as Ralph Nader's Center for the Study of Responsible Law and Nader's Raiders—as well as public-interest research groups and John Gardner's Common Cause group, need more public support and money if they are to solve the problem of large, bureaucratic, unresponsive government.

The "Experimenting Society"

One other important solution for better government, proposed by Northwestern University Professor Donald T. Campbell, is the "experimenting society." He observes that in government-funded programs, we experiment with new procedures and techniques, but often fail to evaluate them rationally. He states:

> We spend billions to explore innovations, and only a few dollars to see if they're worth anything. . . . Our political and bureaucratic rigidity complicates the problem. To try something new you have to promise the moon. If you merely produce a few stars, everyone is disappointed. So we've created a conspiracy to avoid solid, honest results (Tavris, September 1975: 47, 52).

To remedy this present situation, Campbell suggests, we must create an experimenting society. This society would vigorously try out solutions to social problems, evaluate outcomes, propose alternatives to see whether they work better, and then retain sound, workable programs. In its research and evaluation of programs, we would encourage honesty, open criticism, and a willingness to change in the face of new evidence. Instead of ending government funding after a year or two if a new program has not measured up to expectations, we might say: "If the program doesn't work, we will increase your budget 25 percent and support you in having another go at the problem" (Ibid., 52). Even the way in which government programs are evaluated should be changed. Evaluation research, according to Campbell, should become more of a do-it-yourself folk science so that "we move in the opposite direction from government control and totalitarian centralization." We should tap more private sources of money for scientific experiments, rather than depend so heavily on federal financing.

The basic radical solution to the problems of big government is to change the social structure and political system in such a way as to make them represent the common good, without concern for the rich or wealthy. We should make local and regional areas more responsible for solving their own social problems under central government directives and five-year plans. The hope of the radicals is that a revolutionary government would give citizens a much greater chance to participate directly in the decision-making process of government.

Proposals for Controlling the Arms Race

As long as America's belief in the Communist threat persists, most Americans will not regard the arms race, the military's power, and larger defense budgets as a major social problem.

American and Russian peace agreements to limit arms have grown in recent years; the latest Strategic Arms Limitation (SALT) Agreement was signed in 1976. This, together with our country's official policy of detente, should help to reduce the fear of the Russians and communism as a real threat. Further disarmament agreements, especially those limiting the number and kinds of weapons on both sides, could further reduce our fears.

The arms race escalates as Russia and the United States vie for supremacy rather than sufficiency in weapons. Some kind of disarmament is needed to slow down the arms race.

A liberal proposal to speed up this process is called a "strategy of American initiatives," first advocated by Amitai Etzioni in the 1960s. It is designed to set an example of deescalation and to offer incentives to other nations for small (but important) steps to reverse the arms race and build the structures of peace. The idea behind the initiative approach is for the United States to take unilateral action toward arms restraint or reduction that would not endanger American security but would serve to reduce tensions and build trust. As an additional incentive, we would announce that if the Russians did the same, we would then take another initiative toward peace. President Carter's decision not to produce the B-1 bomber was a step in this direction.

Robert Pickus, in his book *To End War*, and Roy Prosterman, in *Surviving to 3000*, suggest a strategy not only to reduce threats and create trust, but also to increase world pressures for reciprocation by Russia. Their solution is an eventually disarmed world under law, in which international disputes would be resolved without war or its threat. To do this, alternative social organizations and mechanisms must be made available and used. The United Nations, though its record in avoiding war is imperfect, can be a foundation for developing such mechanisms.

A similar proposal is to increase the funding, functions, and staff of the U.S. Arms Control and Disarmament Agency. The new amendments to the Arms Control and Disarmament Act of November 1975 are a step in the right direction. They require that proposals for major weapons systems be accompanied by an "arms control impact" statement. The statement must examine the impact of such a program on policy and negotiations toward arms control and disarmament. Further, the agency should research and draw up specific proposals for slowing down the arms race. It should formulate plans for "initiative strategy," including how the United States could respond to specific Soviet initiatives to foster peace. Last, it should develop in-depth plans and incentives to convert our massive defense industry back to more peaceful production and pursuits (Rose, 1975: 14).

Since defense against missiles and lasers is nearly impossible (we have virtually given up the idea of fallout shelters), some liberals advocate we should seriously consider eliminating some fixed-site ABM and ICBM missiles. "There is wide agreement among arms control specialists that nothing would promote strategic stability more than to begin phasing out most, if not all, ICBMs . . ." ("Beyond Vladivostok," April 1975: 131). As we enter the age of the laser as the "ultimate weapon," the need for missiles will not be great. To begin eliminating them will not seem too farfetched—and it will save a lot of money. The Federation of American Scientists (FAS) has proposed that the superpowers eliminate all their ICBMs in "three successive five-year agreements, with one-third of these forces being destroyed during each phase" (Ibid., 131). The destruction could be readily verified by the reconnaissance satellites now in operation to detect them.

Proposals to Curb the Military's Power and Defense Spending

A vital proposal to curb the military's power in government and decelerate the arms race is for Congress to exert more control over military spending. In America, money and power go hand in hand. Dr. Ralph Lapp, a widely known scientist who opposes the arms race, suggests that "Congress and the public should assume an instrumental role in the formulation of defense policies and decisions regarding weapons procurement, thus taking the total decision making out of the military's hands" (1972: 12). The congressional budget process and review system, set up in 1976, is a step in the right direction. Yet even under such a system, the Pentagon's budget request was hardly changed, while some social programs were cut ("Dissenting Views . . . ," April 9, 1976: 127–31). According to liberals and radicals more stringent social and government control of large corporations and our economy is needed before the military's power is reduced. The display box illustrates the liberal views of Representative Elizabeth Holtzman.

Brookings Institution's Proposals. The Brookings Institution proposes three alternative ways of cutting the defense budget. The first option would reduce waste. The plan would serve present military purposes, but at far lower cost. Large economies can be made in defense costs without modifying America's concept of its interests or affecting its present military capabilities. The major cut would be in strategic forces, in which there would be a more moderate pace of modernization, with elimination of marginal forces. There would be moderate reductions in support services and reserve forces, along with changes in military pay policies. This plan would keep the defense budget at the fiscal 1974 level (about $100 billion) for the rest of the decade, and would save almost $10 billion in 1978.

The second Brookings plan modifies the first. It proposes that commitments in Asia be limited to Japan, that American forces in Europe be geared only to a short war, and that land-based missiles be gradually dismantled, thus changing both the political and military missions of the American forces. It further proposes that the United States maintain a strong alliance with Japan based on mutual confidence and cooperation, disengage itself from commitments to the defense of Southeast Asia (as it did in 1977), and reduce its Pacific forces only to those necessary for an alliance with Japan. In 1977, the South East Asia Treaty Organization (SEATO) came to an end, and President Carter announced gradual withdrawal of American troops from South Korea within five years. Land-based missiles would gradually be eliminated and reliance would be placed on bombers and submarine-launched missiles. Conventional ground forces would also be cut by one-third. This plan would reduce the defense costs by 1980 by an average of $12 billion a year. By the end of the decade, the defense budget would decline from six percent to four-and-one-half percent of the GNP.

DISSENTING VIEWS OF REPRESENTATIVE ELIZABETH HOLTZMAN

I cannot support the First Concurrent Resolution on the Budget for the fiscal year 1977, because it fails to deal with the most serious problems and locks the Federal government into military expenditures that will shortchange domestic needs for many years to come.

The Committee proposes to increase military spending by $11.8 billion in budget authority over fiscal 1976 levels. This is the largest peacetime increase in our history. It includes a 21 percent increase in weapons purchases: $3.6 billion to offset inflation and $8.3 billion for real growth. This is by far the largest real-program growth in the federal budget. The result is a budget in which military spending accounts for one-quarter of all spending, almost 50 percent of all federal revenues not earmarked for trust funds, and 70 percent of all "controllable outlays."

Defense Department arguments boil down to a plan for increased military spending allegedly to meet Soviet increases. The fundamental fact remains, however, that the U.S. nuclear deterrent is second to none, and that overall Russian military strength does not and will not surpass our own.

The Committee noted that the Defense Department now has about $70 billion in unexpended balances on hand. Under this resolution, the unspent funds will rise to $84 billion by the end of fiscal 1977. If the Defense Department cannot spend the money it already has, and if it cannot spend the new money it is getting, why is this new money needed?

If, as many members of the Budget Committee recognized, increased defense spending has no military justification, why has it been approved? The answer given was to "send a message"—that a weak President worried about a right-wing political challenge is willing to panic this country, this Committee, and the Congress into a pointless arms race and a dangerous neglect of national problems. That message, I fear, offers far more comfort than concern to our adversaries.

Source: House Report 94-1030 (April 9, 1976): 127-28.

The third Brookings Institution plan is based on an exclusive reliance on nuclear forces to avoid war. The concept is that the consequences of nuclear war are so catastrophic that the essential interests of the United States can be safeguarded at a far lower cost by relying more heavily on nuclear forces. Hence, in response to any attack on its allies, the United States would rely on the threat of nuclear weapons, including the new neutron bomb (which kills people but leaves property and buildings unharmed). The deployment of antiballistic missiles and air defenses would increase the costs of strategic forces, but the general budget would decrease sharply and steadily because other general-purpose forces would decrease. The budget would be one-third less than it is now. By 1978 the savings would be $38 billion.

Liberal Seymour Melman has proposed an even more far-reaching plan. According to Melman,

> to remedy decay in American life we must demilitarize. A defense budget should be adequate to pay for men and equipment needed to implement a particular military security policy. If our security policy is aimed at defense (nuclear deterrence, competence to guard our country, and capacity to contribute to international peace keeping) our budget is too high. We do not need the capability to fight a nuclear war and two other wars at the same time, just commitment to the three above defenses (Melman, December 1973: 73).

His plan would allow us to decrease our manpower to one-fourth of what it is now. It requires operation of a nuclear-deterrence force until there is a better controlled agreement on disarmament. This proposal would thereby "make available the funds needed for economic and other rehabilitation in the United States" (Ibid., 73).

Melman argues that we should adopt such a policy because it profoundly serves the needs of the people. If the Soviets do not follow and

American nuclear rockets can be delivered from or to practically any spot on earth.

Credit: Owen F. W./Black Star.

instead pile up nuclear-overkill security and forces, this would only serve to drain Soviet resources and impose a heavy burden of economic privation on the Soviets. He states: "We must overcome the fears we feel if we are not out-doing the Russians weapon by weapon and technology by technology" (Ibid., 74).

Finally, radicals and liberals contend we need a more massive and representative peace lobby and social movement to *demand* alternative spending for domestic needs. Such forces are needed to weaken and offset the power of the promilitary and defense-interest groups. Thus, Congress and the public are one major part of the answer to what can be done to solve the social problem of the military and the arms race.

THE FUTURE OF BIG GOVERNMENT AND THE MILITARY

As our government begins its third century, its trends are fairly clear. The popular view is that we will have more of the same; federal control of the economy and society will become further institutionalized. According to this scenario, most of our social needs and problems will be directly touched by government programs and funding. Even if decentralization were to occur, it would probably occur within guidelines set by the central government. For example, many federal programs now *require* local community participation before a city or community can receive federal funds. There is no reason to believe that this process of federal guidelines for local communities will somehow reverse itself. If anything, the future outlook is for more (not less) local community dependence on the federal government. Indeed, some financially hard-pressed states will actively seek federal assistance, as several large corporations have already done.

Four Developments in Federal System

Liberal Senator Daniel P. Moynihan, college professor and former presidential advisor, saw four developments in the late 1960s converging in a manner that is "likely to add stability to the federal system . . ." (1969: 169). Nothing has happened since his predictions were made to change these developments, except to strengthen their likelihood. First, the nationalization of public policy will continue, paralleling our continued development as a genuine national society. If there are still many local "problems," there are fewer and fewer specifically local social "issues." A consensus has been reached (implicitly by silence or explicitly by design) that the important national issues will be dealt with in national terms by the national government. For instance, conflicts between white suburbs and black cities will be arbitrated, mediated, or resolved at the federal level. Executive, legislative, and judicial branches will all play a role, as the courts are now doing in matters of housing and education.

Second, despite the periodic hue and cry about federal spending, states and localities will continue to look to Washington for financial aid and grants. Unless the taxing mechanisms and power of state and local communities are changed, federal money will continue to dominate our economy, society, and lower-level governments. Third, grants-in-aid will persist, and a maze of federal programs will periodically be consolidated and coordinated into larger, more general programs.

Fourth, the diffusion and adoption of the middle-class ideal of public participation in government decision-making will add a certain democratic veneer to centrally determined decisions. Often the public's views will be heard on how best to implement a course of action locally on a goal that has already been determined in Washington. Of course, this does not guarantee more efficient or higher-quality decisions at a local level, since the more persons involved the more difficult it is to decide on what to do.

Six Themes in Government

With these four developments as a backdrop, Moynihan envisions six themes in government during the last part of the twentieth century. The President will oversee:

"Wedding Cake" Federalism. A multitiered system of bureaucracies and governmental units. At every level, federal funds "will provide much of the cake and most of the icing."

New Varieties of Government. Special-purpose governments will multiply to meet technical and social needs. Already hundreds of special "authorities" exist on county and regional levels—bridge and transportation authorities, water-sewage districts, air-pollution control units, and so on. Thousands more will be formed as a way of raising money (by floating bonds) for special needs and of tapping federal funds. Some special units will be created directly by the federal government or by federal legislation. We already have 489 areas agencies on aging set up in a national network. This is the wave of the future.

Metropolitanism in Education. For the last 50 years or so, school districts have been steadily consolidating into very large districts. Despite oratory about the sacredness of the neighborhood school, educational districts of the future will be boundaries across city and county lines (with or without busing for racial balance).

National Social Accounting. In the past the emphasis in government has been to develop indicators capable of understanding, predicting, and directing economic events. Their influence today is clear and pervasive. The rest of the twentieth century will see more government interest in developing and using a "system of social accounting." Such social indicators will enable the federal government to "comprehend, predict and direct social events," just as it presently does with the economy. Moynihan envisions that this "will probably be the most powerful development of the last third of the century..." (Ibid., 173). In addition the technique of simulating social processes—through "demonstration projects" or by computer—will lead to full-scale, controlled social experiments by government. These might include adoption of Campbell's "experimenting society" or the creation of isolated, government-run communities (what Alvin Toffler calls "enclaves of the future") to experiment with various forms of social organization, transportation, education, socialization, communication, and government participation. Just as business tests its products in a market-test area, so government could experiment in small communities with new social ideas before the entire nation was subjected to them.

The Quest for Community. In the future, government programs that promote a sense of community, such as beautification, conservation, preservation, and so forth, are likely to be given priority. Such a federal effort would help to develop local activities and uniqueness.

The Rediscovery of the Market. As government tries to do more, it will discover it accomplishes less. The limitations of large size and scale will become increasingly evident. And just as large corporations subcontract part of their work to small businesses and shops, so also the federal government (as it does today) will subcontract some of its activities to private consulting firms and other private organizations. All this could lead to what Charles Lindblom called the "rediscovery of the market" as a means of reaching social objectives. For example, a profit-making organization could run a chain of junior colleges or special retraining programs, under contracts with the federal, state, or county government. Contracts would be paid on a strict performance-and-results basis, although profit-making organizations will sometimes fail, as do government agencies.

New Elites in Government

Daniel Bell sees the rise of new elites in government based on knowledge of military, economic, and social planning. As Bell points out: "The members of this new technocratic elite, with their new techniques of decision-making ... have now become essential to the formulation and analysis of decisions on which political judgments have to be made, if not to the wielding of power" (1973a: 362). Political office holders will depend more and more upon technical experts and professionals. Congressmen and Presidents will even seek technical advice on how best to use TV and when to avoid it. Television coverage of government meetings, including deliberations of legislative bodies, should occur before the year 2000. This will enhance the public's perception of the importance of government (Ornstein, 1975: 252).

Although these new elites will emerge, the nature of the political system—as the social institution that mediates or controls conflicting interests—will not change essentially. However, government will take on even more roles and functions than it assumes today. For example, we saw in the 1960s and early 1970s how quickly the federal government moved into areas of population and environmental control. In the future the government will respond even more quickly once social problems or issues are identified.

Hence, the relationship between technical and political decisions will become one of the critical and crucial problems that government and the public will have to resolve. Part of this conflict will emerge out of greater public insistence on more of a voice in matters and decisions that directly affect their lives. The insistence on participation is a reaction, according to Bell, against "professionalization" of society and the technocratic decision making of a postindustrial society. The public is often more sensible and sensitive than the technical experts, as the Vietnam and environmental issues have shown. Yet Bell warns that decentralization of power to permit greater community participation is far from a panacea.

Lastly, Bell sees a democratization (through public participation) of bureaucratic agencies and their operations. He predicts that the traditional bureaucratic agency based on hierarchy and central control will be replaced by new forms of less bureaucratic social organization.

The Future of Arms and the Military

The future seems likely to follow one of two roads. One is paved with more of the same—greater defense spending, increased military power, newer weapons, and continued mutual distrust (if not hostility) between the superpowers, culminating in a nuclear holocaust. That road is wide and open, and it is the general direction in which our nation has traveled for the last 35 years. The second road is straight and narrow. It calls for new ideas and ideologies. It means dropping the defense ideology and substituting a new peace ideology. It means moving from mutual assured destruction (MAD) to mutual accommodation and, from there, eventually to mutual cooperation. We have present and past models for such future cooperation, such as the joint space flights, SALT talks, and continuing détente. This second road does not require complete disarmament, but means a reduction of arms to a level for reasonable and rational defense.

One thing is certain about the near future. We will experience larger defense spending. Military spending for 1978 is only a down payment on future expenditures. The current budget will fund only the first step of several major weapons systems, such as the Trident submarines, cruise missiles, and a huge shipbuilding effort. These programs alone will cost $90 billion over the next five years. By 1981, defense spending is projected to exceed $130 billion ("Dissenting Views. . . .," April 9, 1976: 131).

Ruth Leger Sivard, economist and author of *World Military and Social Expenditures, 1976,* responded to the question of whether she sees significant hope for human survival:

> I would say I haven't seen any. The negotiations that have taken place and are still going on aren't cast in a way aimed at reducing the threat or the burden of arms. There has been no saving of money by anyone, even through treaties that have already been achieved. There has been no reduction in the nuclear force — in fact it grows ("An Economist Looks . . .," June 1976: 3).

As the arms race escalates, it is not too far-fetched to envision a central government controlled and manipulated by a malevolent or benevolent presidential dictator or military leader. We came too close to something similar in the early 1970s, before Watergate and its implications were revealed. The current hope is, however, that the Carter Administration will control the power of our military, reduce needless spending (as was done with the B-1 bomber in 1977), yet not weaken our defense

The military now has the nuclear power to blow up the world.

posture. At the same time, it is hoped that a new foundation will be set for a just and lasting peace among all nations.

SUMMARY

Big government poses, and attempts to solve, many problems. Conservatives, liberals, and radicals differently define the situation of big government, bureaucracy, spending, distribution of power, and military power and influence. Conservatives feel that government is too big and interferes with business and with people's lives. They assert that government is too bureaucratic, spends too much money, has too much centralized power, and that local communities should be given more decision-making power. Liberals feel big government is necessary and effective, and although its power may be in the hands of an elite, other countervailing groups control the elites and military. Radicals think our whole system of government and power should be changed, by revolution if necessary, so that the people's needs are met.

As government has grown in size and power, the people's trust in big government has declined. Underlying causes for the growth of government have been:

- a growth in the size and population of our complex mass society, whose essential needs are met by government
- a growth in all bureaucracies as a modern "social form" for carrying out activities—including government (as predicted by Max Weber) and "state management" by the military
- a military culture that has led to increased power and influence for the military
- value conflicts, present since the formation of our central government, such as decentralization of power v. centralization, order v. liberty, and security v. democracy

Conservatives see General Revenue Sharing as a possible solution to the problems of big government. Reforms have been proposed and made in the operation of Congress to produce greater popular access to legislators, better handling of the budget, and quicker conclusion of its business. The "experimenting society" has been advocated as a way to try out new social forms of government and solutions to our social problems. A "strategy of initiatives" and three plans by the Brookings Institution have been suggested as ways to control the arms race and curb the military's defense spending.

Future government operations will be larger, more centralized, and will affect more areas of our society. The central government will use a system of "social indicators" to predict and control social problems and other social activities. Technocratic and professional elites will dominate future governments, and the power of the military could grow unless checked soon. These trends have the potential for creating a totalitarian society. Thus, vigilance remains the price of liberty.

CAREER OPPORTUNITIES

Regulatory Government Inspectors.

The federal government is our society's largest employer. Regulatory inspectors help ensure observance of the laws and regulations governing health and safety. Various fields employing regulatory inspectors include: immigration, customs, aviation safety, wage and hour compliance, alcohol, tobacco and firearms control, and occupational safety. Sanitarians, working primarily for state and local governments, perform a variety of inspection duties to ensure that food and water meet government standards, and that waste control is handled properly. The federal government requires a passing score on the Professional and Administrative Career Examination (PACE) for most inspector occupations. These jobs are expected to increase faster than the average of other occupations through the 1980s. For further information write to: The U.S. Civil Service Commission, Washington, D.C.

Political Scientists.

They study the functions and workings of government, much as a sociologist. The usual opportunities for those with a Master's degree or a Ph.D. are teaching positions at a college or university. Some 20 percent work in government, research bureaus, civic and taxpayers associations, and very large business firms. Some work overseas for agencies of the Department of State, particularly the Foreign Service and the Agency for International Development. Some are also employed by the United States Information Agency. Methods of social-science research are important for anyone aspiring to be a political scientist. For further information write to: American Political Science Association, 1527 New Hampshire Ave., N.W. Washington, D.C. 20036

Positions in State, County, and Local Government.

Good opportunities exist for students of sociology with research skills and knowledge of urban planning, redevelopment, and community problems. A background in demography (population) would also be helpful. Summer employment with a government planning commission or agency would be a step toward a full-time government position. Civil service tests are usually required for state and county jobs. For further information write to your state Civil Service Commission.

REFERENCES

Alpern, David
1975 "Big Government." Newsweek 86, 24 (December 15): 34–41.
"Balancing the U.S. Budget: Why an Impossible Dream?" U.S. News & World Report 81, 5 (August 2): 25–26, 1976.

Bell, Daniel
- 1969 Toward the Year 2000: Work in Progress. Boston: Beacon Press.
- 1973 "America and the Future of Man." Allentown Sunday Call-Chronicle (September 30): F-10.
- 1973a The Coming of Post-Industrial Society: A Venture in Social Forecasting. New York: Basic Books.

"Beyond Vladivostok: The Feasibility and the Politics of Arms Reduction." Science 188 (April 11): 130–33, 1975.

Bridgewater, William and Seymour Kurtz, eds.
- 1970 "United States: The States in Union." The Illustrated Columbia Encyclopedia, Vol. 21. New York: Columbia University Press.

"Can't Stop Agencies' Growth, Study Shows." Allentown Morning Call (May 23): 1, 1976.

Crewdson, Prudence
- 1976 "Bill Would Finance Presenting of Public Views." Congressional Quarterly Weekly Report 34, 7 (February 14): 329–31.

"CIA Seen Influencing News Reports," Allentown Morning Call (February 9): 1, 1976.

D'Antonio, Dennis
- 1976 "Incredible 15,000 Lobbyists Seek Special Favors in Washington—Outnumber Congressmen 28 to 1!" National Enquirer (June 15): 24.

"Dissenting Views of Hon. Elizabeth Holtzman." House Report 94-1030 (April 9): 127–31, 1976.

Domhoff, David
- 1971 The Higher Circles. New York: Random House.

Donner, Frank
- 1975 "Political Intelligence: Cameras, Informers and Files." Civil Liberties Review (Summer). Also in Thomas Hoult, ed. Social Justice and Its Enemies. New York: Wiley: 444–53.

"A Drive to Hold Down Growth of 'Big Government.'" U.S. News & World Report 72, 25 (June 19): 78–80, 1972.

Drucker, Peter
- 1975 The Practice of Management. New York: Harper & Row.

"An Economist Looks at the Arms Race: 'The Issue Is More than Military Superiority.'" Transition 3, 3 (June): 1–4, 1976.

Ellul, Jacques
- 1967 The Political Allusion. New York: Knopf.

"FBI Headquarters Linked to Burglaries." Allentown Morning Call (July 9): 3, 1976.

Fernandez, Ronald
- 1975 The Promise of Sociology. New York: Praeger.

Fisher, Louis
- 1976 President and Congress: Power and Policy. New York: The Free Press.

Forestall, William, ed.
- 1976 "Who Really Runs Local Governments?" American City & County 91,4 (April): 128.

"$404,000 in Jet Engines Market to Be Scrapped." Allentown Morning Call (February 17): 2, 1976.

Freitag, Peter
1975 "The Cabinet and Big Business: A Study of Interlocks." Social Problems 23, 2 (December): 137–52.

Gardner, Judy
1976 "Ford to Draw Battle Line with 1977 Budget." Congressional Quarterly Weekly Report 34, 3 (January 17): 71–74.

Goldman, Peter and Gerald Lubenow
1975 "Mr. Small-Is-Beautiful." Newsweek 86, 24 (December 15): 47, 50.

Gruenstein, Peter
1975 "Prostitutes Hired to Entertain Pentagon Aides." Allentown Morning Call (November 1): 1.

Halberstam, David.
1972 The Best and the Brightest. New York: Random House.

Halloran, Richard
1977 "Poll Reveals Congressmen Got Gifts from S. Korea." Allentown Morning Call (July 11): 1.

Harris, Louis
1973 The Anguish of Change. New York: Norton.

Harris, Sydney
1976 "The Popular Thing: Be 'Antigovernment.'" Allentown Morning Call (August 7): 6.

Hart, Philip
1973 "The Future of the Government Process." Annals of the American Academy of Political and Social Science 408 (July): 94–102.

Hendelson, William H., ed.
1973 "Congress of the United States." Funk & Wagnalls New Encyclopedia, Vol. 6. New York: Funk & Wagnalls.
1973 "President of the United States." Funk & Wagnalls New Encyclopedia, Vol. 19. New York. Funk & Wagnalls.

Herman, William
1976 "Deregulation: Now or Never! (Or Maybe Someday?)." Public Administration Review 36, 2 (March/April): 223–28.

"House, Senate Conference Agree on 'Sunshine' Bill." Allentown Morning Call (August 7): 3, 1976.

"Humphrey Bill Declared Private Enterprise Threat." Allentown Morning Call (January 30): 41, 1976.

1975 "House of File Cards." New Repubilc (March 15): 1.

Jones, Charles
1975 "Somebody Must Be Trusted: An Essay on Leadership of the U.S. Congress." Pp. 265–76 in Norman J. Ornstein, ed. Congress in Change: Evolution and Reform. New York: Praeger.

Jun, Jong S.
1976 "A Symposium: Management by Objectives in the Public Sector." Public Administration Review 36, 1 (January/ February): 1–5.

Kahn, Robert, Barbara Gutek, Eugenia Barton, and Daniel Katz
1975 "Americans Love Their Bureaucrats." Psychology Today 9, 1 (June): 66–71.

"Kentucky Lawmaker Asks Hays to Quit." Allentown Morning Call (May 28): 10, 1976.

Kroeger, Naomi
   1975 "Bureaucracy, Social Exchange and Benefits Received in a Public Assistance Agency." Social Problems 23, 2 (December): 197–208.

Lang, Kurt
   1972 Military Institutions and the Sociology of War: A Review of the Literature with Annotated Bibliography. Beverly Hills, Calif.: Sage.

Lapp, Ralph E.
   1972 "Pentagon Buck-Passing." New Republic (June): 7–12.

"The Last Word on Intelligence." New York Times Magazine (May 2): 1, 1976.

Leary, Mike
   1976 "High Court Ruling Stunts Growth of Public Interest Law Movement." Allentown Sunday Call-Chronicle (July 18): 13–21.

Lewis, Anthony
   1976 "The Church Committee: A Return to Basics." New York Times Magazine (May 2): 1.

Lovell, Catherine
   1976 "The Future of the Intergovernmental Process." Public Administration Review 36, 2 (March/April): 211–16.

Lyons, Richard
   1976 "House Counts Its Assets and Totes Up 22 Millionaires." Allentown Sunday Call-Chronicle (January 4): A-10.

Martz, Larry
   1975 "How It Really Works: Rules, Rules," Newsweek 86, 24 (December 15): 44.

Melman, Seymour
   1973 "All the Muscle at One-Third the Cost." Sane World Quarterly (December): 73–74.
   1976 "Pentagon Capitalism: The New Power Center in the United States." Pp. 35–58 in James Henslin and Larry Reynolds, eds. Social Problems in American Society, 2nd ed. Boston: Holbrook Press.

Michels, Robert
   1962 Political Parties. New York: Free Press.

Moynihan, Daniel
   1969 "The Relationship of Federal to Local Authorities." Pp. 169–76 in Daniel Bell, ed. Toward the Year 2000: Work in Progress. Boston: Beacon Press.

"National Debt: Skyrocketing Toward $1 Trillion." U.S. News & World Report 81, 1 (July 5): 104, 1976.

"New A-Bomb Peril Cited." Allentown Morning Call (September 11): 10, 1974.

Ornstein, Norman J., ed.
   1975 Congress in Change: Evolution and Reform. New York: Praeger.

Ott, Carol J.
   1976 "Ban Sought on Closed Advisory Sessions." Congressional Quarterly Weekly Report 34, 12 (March 20): 646–47.

Parkinson, C. Northcote
   1957 Parkinson's Law. Boston: Houghton Mifflin.

"'Peanut Giveaway' to Cost $142 Million." Allentown Morning Call (March 28): 2, 1975.

"Pentagon Warns 38 in Northrop Probe." Allentown Morning Call (January

24): 1, 1976.

Peter, Lawrence and Raymond Hall
   1969 The Peter Principle. New York: Morrow.

Porter, David and Eugene Olsen
   1976 "Some Critical Losses in Government Centralization and Decentralization." Public Administration Review 1, 36 (January/February): 72–84.

"Rep. Hays's Employee Says She's Paid to Be Mistress." Allentown Sunday Call-Chronicle (May 23): A–10, 1976.

Rose, William M.
   1975 "Let's Reverse the Arms Race." War/Peace Report 13, 3 (1975).

Scarpitti, Frank
   1977 Social Problems. Hinsdale, Ill.: The Dryden Press.

Schlesinger, Arthur
   1973 The Imperial Presidency. Boston: Houghton Mifflin.

Schorr, Burt
   1975 "When Carol Foreman Talks Consumerism, Congressmen Listen." Wall Street Journal (April 9): 1, 27.

"Sky Still the Limit on Congress's Foreign Travel." Allentown Morning Call (July 6): 1, 1976.

Spekke, Andrew A.
   1976 "America: The Next 200 Years." Intellect 105, 2376 (July–August): 49–50.

"State of the Union Message to Joint Session of Congress" (January 22) quoted in the New York Times (January 23, 1971): 12, 1971.

Stewart, Albert
   1976 The Troubled Land. New York: McGraw-Hill.

Swift, Pamela
   1975 "Disenchanted Youth: Keeping Up ... with Youth." Parade Magazine (May 25): 12.

Travis, Carol
   1975 "The Experimenting Society: To Find Programs That Work, Government Must Measure Its Failures." Psychology Today 9, 4 (September): 47–56.

Turner, Jonathan H.
   1972 American Society: Problems of Structure. New York: Harper & Row.

U.S. Bureau of the Census
   1975 "Federal Government Finances and Employment." Sec. 8 of Statistical Abstract of the United States: 1975 (96th ed.) Washington, D.C.: U.S. Government Printing Office.

"Why Small Business May Find Federal Aid Harder to Get." U.S. News & World Report 80, 18 (May 3): 67, 1976.

Witt, Evans and Dick Barnes
   1976 "Demo Convention Delegates Still Mostly Male and White." Allentown Sunday Call-Chronicle (July 11): A–10.

SUGGESTED READINGS

Goldsmith, William M. The Growth of Presidential Power: A Documented History. New York: Bowker. 1975.

A documentation and analysis of the 200-year evolution of presidential power from Washington to Nixon.

Guttman, Daniel and Barry Willner. The Shadow Government. New York: Pantheon. 1976.

Through "contracting out" its work, the federal government relinquishes some of its public decision-making power to elite, private management consultants, "experts," and think tanks. Private interests usually benefit from it all.

Lodge, George. The New American Ideology. New York: Knopf. 1975.

Norms of individualism and decentralization, which shaped early America, are being replaced by group norms and centralized government planning. The book sees the drift toward communitarianism and collectivism as inescapable.

Richardson, Eliot. The Creative Balance. New York: Holt, Rinehart and Winston. 1976.

Analyzes government in terms of a series of historical balances: individuality v. community; liberty v. equality; centralization v. decentralization. It focuses on broad public issues and possible solutions.

Rieselbach, Leroy N. Congressional Reform in the Seventies. Morristown, N.J.: General Learning Press. 1977.

Discusses why the executive branch rather than Congress has initiated meaningful public policy; examines "new breed" legislators and the future of Congress based on "majoritarian democracy."

Periodicals Worth Exploring

Administration & Society
Administrative Science Quarterly
American City and County
American Journal of Political Science
American Political Science Review
American Politics Quarterly
Annals of American Academy of Political and Social Science
The Bureaucrat
Dissent
Foreign Policy
Government Finance

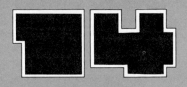

Problems of Ecology and Population Growth

I. DEFINITIONS OF THE ECOLOGICAL PROBLEM
International dimension of the problem.
"Doomsday" and "minimalist" definitions.
Misuse and abuse of air, water, land, and natural resources.

INCIDENCE AND PREVALENCE OF THE PROBLEM
Recent increase in attention to the problem.
Synergistic, threshold, trigger, and time-lag effects.
Increase in the incidence and prevalence of the problem.

CAUSES OF THE PROBLEM
Population increase.
Industrialization and affluence.
Changes in product technology.

PROPOSED SOLUTIONS TO THE PROBLEM
New laws to solve the problem.
Actions taken by government.
Actions of society.

FUTURE OF THE PROBLEM
Alternate resources and sources of energy.
New orientation in our norms and values about technology.

II. DEFINITIONS OF THE POPULATION PROBLEM
Aggravation of the ecological problem.
Problems of population increase and decline in developed and less-developed countries (LDCs)

INCIDENCE AND PREVALENCE OF THE PROBLEM
U.S. added 100 million people in 50 years; over 70 percent of our population lives on 2 percent of our land.
Difference in population growth between 2- and 3-child families.

CAUSES OF THE PROBLEM
Industrialization and urbanization.
Decline in death rate in LDCs.
Traditional values.

PROPOSED SOLUTIONS TO THE PROBLEM
Recommendations of the U.S. Population Commission.
Population control and economic growth in LDCs.

FUTURE OF THE PROBLEM
Massive aid needed now if LDCs are to control population and grow economically.
Totalitarian means to control population may be wave of the future.

SUMMARY

The first law of ecology: Everything is connected to everything else.
The second law of ecology: Everything must go somewhere.
The third law of ecology: Nature knows best.
The fourth law of ecology: There is no such thing as a free lunch.

Barry Commoner, "The Closing Circle," **The New Yorker** (September 25, 1971): 60, 68, 70, 76.

Long before Columbus came to the New World, the people who lived here respected and revered the earth. They called it their mother. The white man came with a different concept: he should use and conquer the land and use it as he will. He came to think of himself as the master of mother nature. The wilderness was limitless; why worry about how we used it?

What made us realize that man must eventually pay for environmental degradation and pollution? Are we running out of resources? What steps can man take to undo the damage he has done to the earth?

I. DEFINING THE ECOLOGICAL PROBLEM

There are conflicting ways of looking at ecology as an international social problem. On one extreme is the doomsday school, which holds that it is too late to solve the problem. On the opposite side, the minimalist school views our concern as a diversion from the real social problems—poverty, civil rights, and war (Jacoby, 1971:165).

Some conservatives, as distinguished from liberals, consider industrial output and the growth of profit and social power as the main priority for any society—regardless of the cost to the environment. In an interview with 270 top business executives conducted for *Fortune* by Daniel Yankelovich, seven out of 10 did not believe the environment directly affects their own health or that of their families (Editors of Fortune, 1970:56). A group of executives heading up the mass media did not define the issue as critical or as important as other social problems (Althoff et al., 1973:672).

Still other conservatives view control of environmental problems as interference with economic and industrial progress. In talking about the Sierra Club, an environmentalist group, one Ohio businessman said:

> I think that group has gone crazy. If you listen to them we'd have no industry at all—just forests and streams. They'd rather have sand dunes than huge new mills to serve the needs of the entire Middle West. That doesn't make sense to me (Diamond, 1970:59-60).

Other groups, as well as liberals and radicals, sense that environmental pollution of all sorts and exhaustion of resources are inevitably results of our growth-oriented, technological society. These groups are calling for a no-growth economy and society. To them, zero population growth should mean zero economic growth (Olson and Landsberg, 1973). John Hardesty refers to this concept as the "stationary-state" position (1974:13).

The Balanced-System Definition

So the basic problem we all face with ecology as a social problem is how to build an ecologically sound society without destroying our economy. Our environment is an ecosphere or biosphere. It consists of air, water, land, and the sun, together with all living things dependent on them and on each other. The ecosphere—"the home that life has built for itself on the planet's outer surface" (Commoner, 1971:11)—includes the relationships between all living things and the delicate physical environment shared by all. A "food chain" is part of the system; it contains every element needed to sustain life. Oxygen, nitrogen, and carbon all go through cycles of use and reuse. Each part of the system is symbiotically related and balanced.

Any part damaged or destroyed can hurt the whole system. For instance, on a small Atlantic island near Bermuda live 100 endangered petrel birds. They never leave the area, since they have plenty of fish nearby. Yet a gentle dust, blown by the trade winds from North African farms 3,000 miles away, contains the remnants of the chemical DDT. It settles on the ocean and poisons the fish on which the petrels feed. The birds' eggs no longer hatch; thus the petrels are close to extinction (Perlman, 1969:25).

The New Awareness

An awareness of this balance in nature and the role that human beings play in upsetting it dawned with overdue suddenness on most Americans in the late 1960s and early 1970s. This new, widely accepted concept of the environmental social problem involves man's international connections and relationships to the ecosystem. As Barry Commoner, biologist and leading environmentalist, defines the problem:

> We have come to a turning point in the human habitation of the earth. The environment is a complex, subtly balanced system, and it is this integrated whole which receives the impact of all the separate insults inflicted by pollution. Never before in the history of the planet has its thin life-supporting surface been subject to such diverse, novel, and potent agents. I believe that the cumulative effects of these pollutants, their interaction, and amplification, can be fatal to the complex fabric of the biosphere. And because man is, after all, a dependent part of this

system, I believe that continued pollution of the earth, if unchecked, will eventually destroy the fitness of this planet as a place for human life (Commoner, 1966:122).

This definition of the problem recognizes not only the adaptations that the natural environment has made to the various species, but also the necessity for us to make adaptations and adjustments to this environment.

Two other differences appear in defining the ecological problem. These involve the concepts of pollution and resources.

We could accurately say that a pollutant is "a substance in the wrong place in a concentration which is harmful" (Beckerman, 1974:98). With this definition in mind, we can note that pollution does not depend solely on our actions. Much pollution occurs naturally; even natural radioactivity exists, and many natural chemicals are contained in "pure" water.

We must decide how to evaluate resources. Are they to be defined in physical terms, based on their currently known limits, or in social terms, based on currently unknown limits? Most geologists and biologists think of resources in the first way (physical and known). Some economists and a few social scientists view them in the second way (social and unknown).

Frank Notestein defines resources in the latter way. He observes:

> Basically resources are not material; they are socially defined. Coal did not become a resource until a few centuries ago. It is barely one hundred years since petroleum had any but medical and magical uses. . . . We have only one non-renewable resource, and that is space. Otherwise mankind's basic resources are knowledge and skill, mainly of the organizational kind (1971:33–34).

When evaluating our resources, it is useful to distinguish renewable from nonrenewable resources. Renewable resources—for example, the sun, wind, tides, and rain—maintain a roughly stable potential, regardless of use. For this reason solar power is often considered as an answer to our energy needs (Hammond et al., 1973:61–66). Nonrenewable resources—coal, oil, and gas—normally cannot be replaced. Some resources, such as soil fertility, are renewable if properly managed, but may be so depleted by inadequate care that they become nonrenewable. New resources are discovered or developed when shortages begin to be evident. The boxed item suggests what might happen as new resources are tapped.

The problems of ecology and the environment are undoubtedly not as insoluble as the doomsday group maintain, nor as unimportant as the minimalists contend.

INCIDENCE AND PREVALENCE OF THE ECOLOGICAL PROBLEM

The problems of ecology and the environment include

1. air pollution

> **580**
>
> ## AN OIL SURPLUS?
> ### Sheldon Novick
>
> Not all our resources are running out as fast as we may have believed. The Alaska Pipeline will produce a serious surplus of oil on the West Coast of the US by 1978. Production of the oil may have to be cut back or the surplus exported, the Federal Energy Agency (FEA) revealed (Wall Street Journal, March 18). Export of the oil is prohibited by statute, however, without special congressional authorization. The FEA therefore wants to use gas pipelines being abandoned in the Southwest to ship oil to the Midwest. The peak flow of oil from Alaska will be 1.2 million barrels per day, about twice what the West Coast will be able to absorb at present prices.
>
> Source: Sheldon Novick, "Spectrum," *Environment* (June 1976):22.

2. water pollution
3. degradation of land and soil by solid waste
4. exhaustion of resources

Let us examine each of these aspects in turn.

Air Pollution

According to one estimate, about 264 million tons of pollutants were put into the air in the United States in one year. In Los Angeles alone, waste hydrocarbons from cars and trucks reach 1,720 tons per day. Meanwhile, the levels of "particulate" pollution in Japan are between two and four times as high as in the United States. Particulates are solids and liquids suspended in mid-air, chunks of dirt, acid, sulfates, nitrates, and metals. In such a heavily industrialized and urbanized area as Japan, severe problems occur. A few years ago, particulates in the air over Tokyo caused 22 schoolgirls playing handball to collapse in heaps. The situation has gotten so bad that people wear gauze masks; in some of Tokyo's most polluted streets, oxygen-vending machines have been installed so that people can continue to breathe with the help of pure oxygen ("Pollution...,"1973:43). In Pittsburgh recently, an air-pollution alert shut down steel mills and other factories for 24 hours.

Transportation vehicles, especially cars, contribute about 55 percent of air pollutants. In Los Angeles, cars account for as much as 80 percent of some pollutants, such as nitrogen oxides (Commoner, 1971:73). Industry, especially power plants, produces about 81 million tons of pollutants. The remainder comes from burning solid wastes, farm refuse, coal wastes, and other trash.

Much of our manmade pollutants is thinned out and blown away by the wind, making air pollution a national and international problem. For instance, Detroit's pollution reaches into Canadian forests, while polluted air circles the earth from Italy to Russia, and from Japan to Africa.

Lead, mercury, fluorides, nitrates from fertilizers, and chlorinated hydrocarbons add to air pollution. Recently a new kind of chlorinated hydrocarbon compound, called PCBs, has been found to be a serious pollutant ("EPA Starting Major Effort," 1975:2). PCBs render several species of fish incapable of reproducing and threaten fishing grounds. High levels of PCBs constitute a threat to fish life in the Hudson River and add to environmental pollution there. The combined effects of air pollution around the world "menace the survival of no less than 280 mammal, 350 bird, and 20,000 plant species" (Editors of the Ecologist, 1972:16).

The Environmental Protection Agency estimates that air pollution costs us at least $12 billion a year, including $5 billion in medical bills for treating those who breathe polluted air. The National Science Foundation reports that at least 4,000 persons die from pollutants from auto exhausts each year, and thousands more die from industrial pollutants.

Air pollution has such adverse effects on our health that the ecology movement began as a protest against this pollution by industry.

The Federal Power Commission says that fumes from coal-operated power plants without pollution controls could claim 25,000 lives in the next five years. Unless we halt destruction of the ozone layer in the atmosphere by jet planes (and possibly aerosol sprays), scientists estimate that within 30 years, 90,000 more persons will develop skin cancer and 10,000 other cancer cases a year will develop (Edson, 1975:34).

Fallout from testing of nuclear weapons, as well as possible radiation in the future from power plants that use nuclear energy, is a growing health hazard (Meadows, 1974:75–78; Cohn, 1969:B-1). Paul Ehrlich reports that nuclear-weapons fallout "may have been responsible for up to 12,000 genetically defective babies and 100,000 cases of leukemia and bone tumors" (Ehrlich and Ehrlich, 1970:137).

Water Pollution

For most of man's stay on earth, nature has purified and recycled water. But since 1850 the world's population has grown nearly four-fold, and the population of the United States has almost tripled since 1900. Industry has multiplied, and the use of water has soared. We are now using water much faster than nature can recycle or purify it.

Every day, city sewers discharge into our rivers, lakes, streams, and oceans 40 billion gallons of effluent—after various degrees of treatment, or none at all. Every day the city of Philadelphia dumps 30 million gallons of raw sewage into the Delaware River ("Rep. Florio Seeks Ban . . .," April 11, 1975:13). Our industries alone annually discharge at least 125 billion gallons of effluent; farms account for another 50 billion gallons.

About 90 percent of America's streams and rivers are polluted. This includes the water we drink. Between 1961 and 1970, 130 officially recorded outbreaks of disease were attributed to polluted drinking water, affecting over 16,000 persons. According to the U.S. Public Health Service, several million persons are drinking water containing fecal bacteria and other pollutants. Even water supplies percolating underground sometimes encounter solid-waste-disposal sites, thus contaminating our underground water supply. Sidney Brown, Executive Director of the Pennsylvania Coalition of Health Consumers, writes:

> When unsuspecting people draw "clear" water from their kitchen tap, they anticipate pure potable water, but in reality they are ingesting more chemicals than one would find in the corner drug store. There is good reason to suspect that these chemicals increase the incidence of congenital abnormalities, infant mortality and the overall death rate, not to mention the impact upon our health care and delivery cost. These harmful effects occur particularly among poor people who are undernourished and defenseless . . . ("Drinking Water Safety Debates . . ." April 11, 1975:18).

The oceans have become an international sewer. Each year the United States alone dumps 48.2 million tons of waste into them. Underwater explorer Jacques Cousteau has stated, "The oceans are in danger of dying. The pollution is general. Fish have diminished by 40 percent in 20 years" ("The Dying Oceans," 1970:64).

Solid Waste

Solid-waste disposal on the land is growing to epidemic proportions. Each year in the United States, we must dispose of 55 billion cans, 26 billion bottles and jars, 65 billion metal and plastic bottle caps, 200 million tons of trash and garbage, 10 million tons of iron and steel as scrap, and 3 billion tons of waste near mine sites. About 60 million tons of solid wastes are dumped illegally in New York City alone, not including the 50,000 autos abandoned there every year (Ehrlich and Ehrlich, 1974:159).

Because of our reliance on technology, the total waste disposal, including all industry, "becomes the equivalent of the human wastes of 102.3 billion people" (Stewart, 1976:41). Our solid wastes have been doubling every 10 years, and we pay over $4.5 billion a year to get rid of them.

Good farm land and soil are sold for large housing developments or are paved over as highways. In addition, about three billion tons of topsoil

Air, water, and waste pollution continually degrade the environment and upset the ecological balance.

Credit: Horst Schäfer/Photo Trends.

erode from farm lands each year. Consequently, heavy doses of fertilizers are needed to enrich poorer lands, and often the nitrate fertilizers must be strengthened until they become detrimental to the environment. As Barry Commoner puts it, the farmer becomes "hooked" on nitrates. Health hazards mount as fertilizers and pesticides clinging to eroded soil pollute our streams and rivers (Natural Resources Defense Council, 1975:5).

Four additional factors are increasing the ongoing environmental degradation. These four factors, according to Ehrlich and Holdren, are synergistic effects, threshold effects, trigger effects, and time-delay effects.

Synergism is the interaction of two or more factors that yield a total effect greater than the result of each acting alone. For instance, sulphur dioxide (from coal-burning plants) and asbestos particles (from a car's brake linings), acting synergistically, could induce lung cancer.

A threshold effect is the ability of the environment to withstand pollution. At levels of pollution below a certain threshold, many kinds of pollution can "naturally" be absorbed by the environment without adverse effects. But when the threshold is exceeded, nature's system can become overloaded. Rivers in the early nineteenth century could easily absorb the sewage and industrial wastes. Today their thresholds have been exceeded, so that nature can no longer accommodate man's technological society.

In the trigger effect, an environmental balance is upset by a relatively small manmade factor. For example, as a result of filling the reservoirs behind large dams, earthquakes may be triggered. Or jet-plane exhaust may weaken the ozone layer, which screens the earth against ultraviolet radiation.

Time-delay is a situation where the cause of problems may precede the effect by years or even decades. Persons who once worked in or lived near factories making polyvinyl chloride are now suffering from liver cancer, many years later. Exposure to radiation today may produce cancer 20 years from now (Ehrlich and Holdren, 1971:25–27).

Exhaustion of Resources

It is well known that although the United States contains only about 5 percent of the world's population, we use about 40 percent of its resources. Barry Commoner points to the reasons behind resource exhaustion. In a finite world, "mineral resources, if used, can only move in one direction—downward. . . . Unlike people, mineral resources are nonrenewable" (1971:121).

The Council on Environmental Quality reports:

> Even taking into account such economic factors as increased prices with decreasing availability, it would appear at present that the quantities of platinum, gold, zinc, and lead are not sufficient to meet demands. At the present rate of expansion . . . silver, tin, and uranium may be in short supply even at

table 14-1		NONRENEWABLE NATURAL RESOURCES: YEARS BEFORE THEY ARE EXHAUSTED	
RESOURCE	YEARS	RESOURCE	YEARS
ALUMINUM	100	NATURAL GAS	38
COBALT	110	NICKEL	150
COPPER	36	PETROLEUM	31
GOLD	11	PLATINUM GROUP	130
LEAD	26	SILVER	16
MANGANESE	97	TIN	17
MERCURY	13	TUNGSTEN	40
MOLYBDENUM	79	ZINC	23

Source: Donella Meadows, et al., *The Limits to Growth*, 2nd ed. (New York: Universe, 1974): 56-58. A Potomac Associates Book. Reprinted by permission.

higher prices by the turn of the century. By the year 2050, several more minerals may be exhausted if the current rate of consumption continues ("First Annual Report . . .," 1970:158).

The MIT study *Limits to Growth* lists 19 of the most important mineral and fuel resources for today's industry. Of these 19, 12 will be exhausted in less than 100 years; four more will be gone in 200 years (1974:56–58). Table 14-1 lists these 16 resources and the number of years left (at their current rates of use) before they are exhausted. The figures are based on known world reserves in 1970, according to the Bureau of Mines.

We can expect that resource exhaustion will spread and increase as the less-developed countries (LDCs) begin to industrialize; for they will need and demand the same scarce mineral resources that we use so freely today.

As we seek new ways for developing resources, this may only add to environmental pollution. For example, the big oil spill off Santa Barbara a few years ago came from a ruptured offshore drilling rig. Now we have begun to drill for oil in the Gulf of Mexico and off the shores of New Jersey, Delaware, and Maryland (Froelich, 1975:9).

CAUSES OF THE ECOLOGICAL PROBLEM

Most social and physical scientists attribute the ecological problem to three chief causes: population growth, the spread of industrialization and affluence, and a change in product technology (Commoner, 1971:125–77; Ehrlich and Ehrlich, 1972:145; Jacoby, 1971:161–63). Let us look at these three culprits.

Pollution of the ocean by oil tankers destroys beaches, fish, and birds. This scene shows the attempt to clean up an oil spill in Santa Barbara, California.

Population Growth

As we will point out later in this chapter, the United States has added almost 100 million persons to its population in the last 50 years; and it continues to add about one million more each year. Such growth in population helps to explain the increase in air, water, and land pollution in recent years.

The problems of pollution have been severest in the city. The worldwide trend toward congested urban centers puts extreme pressure on the ecological system. Traffic, crowding, and noise pollution add to the problems of air, water, and land pollution. Although the population and population density of our central cities are declining, the largest numbers of people still reside in metropolitan areas; and since cities and suburbs are symbiotically connected, the pollution problems remain.

The conventional wisdom is that population growth is the primary and principal cause of environmental pollution. This assumption is being seriously questioned today, because population increase has accounted for only 20 percent or less of the increase in pollution since 1946 (Commoner, 1971:176). Population is a contributing factor, but not as much as we may have assumed in the past.

The Spread of Industrialization and Affluence

Rising income and spreading industrialization have resulted in an increased demand for environmental amenities. We demand air-conditioned offices, restaurants, and homes; central heating; and paved superhighways and streets. Cars remain the most popular method of transportation for business and pleasure. As we attempt to meet consumer demands for comfort and convenience, we encourage environmental deterioration (Ehrlich and Ehrlich, 1972:3).

A value imbedded in our industrial system is to make a profit, regardless of the social costs involved. Large, powerful, and wealthy corporations continue to pollute our air and water, in their efforts to market products that earn them a substantial profit. Until we, through government or environmental groups, are able to check the power and influence of our large corporations, as well as throw-away habits of affluent citizens, pollution and environmental degradation will continue.

Change in Product Technology

The third cause, and what Barry Commoner and other environmentalists consider the main cause, is the rapid change in our product technology. Soap makers and consumers have switched to detergents. Farmers use more pesticides and chemical fertilizers and no longer grow food organically. Detroit now turns out millions of big, powerful cars that damage the environment and deplete our oil reserves. We have switched to flip-top beer and soda cans and nonreturnable bottles, and we fill our homes with an endless supply of electrical gadgets, which usually wear out in a few years. Barry Commoner concludes:

> The overall evidence seems clear. The chief reason for the environmental crisis that has engulfed the United States in recent years is the sweeping transformation of productive technology since World War II. The economy has grown enough to give the United States population about the same amount of basic goods, per capita, as it did in 1946. However, productive technologies with intense impacts on the environment have displaced less destructive ones. The environmental crisis is the inevitable result of this counterecological pattern of growth (1971:177).

PROPOSED SOLUTIONS TO THE ECOLOGICAL PROBLEM

The response to the many threats to our environment is a classic example of how collective action results once a situation is labeled as a

The automobile not only pollutes the air when running, but continues to be a blight on the landscape when discarded. A change in product technology is needed to ensure less pollution of the environment.

serious social problem. Real progress has already been made in cleaning up the environment. The 1976 Report of the White House Council on Environmental Quality reported the following progress:

> Air quality has improved "greatly" since the Clean Air Act was amended in 1971. Between 1971 and 1976 there were "14 percent fewer solid particles and 25 percent less sulfur dioxide reported in the nation's air."
>
> Steps against water pollution have shown "encouraging progress." Only 3 percent of the 87 government water-monitoring stations across the country reported levels in the "poor" or "severe" categories, compared with 16 percent in 1971.

The Annual Report of the Environmental Protection Agency(EPA) reveals that the nation's waters are becoming cleaner, although some areas still face serious pollution problems. It reported:

> Of 32 states that made an overall evaluation of the waters within their boundaries, 23 found them to be "good," and a few have met the 1983 goal of having "swimmable rivers."

Reduction of water pollution has been achieved, not only through waste-water treatment but also through federal controls over pesticides ("U.S. Clean Up Waters, ..." May 11, 1976:1). Even some endangered animal species are beginning to make a comeback, among them the peregrine falcons, blue whales, and timber wolves.

Even some noted environmental critics are beginning to report some progress in solving the problems of a degraded environment. Dr. Rene J. Dubos, Professor Emeritus of Microbiology at Rockefeller University, now sees that:

> Air pollution has decreased in many areas, and there has been "marked improvement" in our rivers and lakes. Federal allocation of money to cities to build sewage-treatment plants has risen sharply, from $1.6 billion in 1973 to $6.2 billion in 1977.
>
> Vigorous research programs are developing new sources of energy and less wasteful ways of using energy.
>
> Practices of recycling are being introduced into technological operations. Garbage is being recycled for use as a source of power and electricity in some cities.
>
> Many members of the upper and middle class are beginning to recognize the merits of a less consumptive society. These changes in attitudes will lead to the downgrading of certain technologies and foster the development of less environmentally degrading ones ("World May Beat Its Ills," February 15, 1976:8-20).

We have also improved our sudsy, polluted streams. Detergents and soap powders once caused suds and bubbles to appear in our waterways and streams. The "hard" detergents contained a chemical called ABS, which caused them to retain their sudsing action long after they had been used. Then industry researchers, aided by federal and state agencies, produced the biodegradable chemical LAS, which produces a sudsing action that is quickly broken down by biological bacteria and other forces. In this case, the same industry that caused the problem also helped to solve it ("Whatever Happened to America's Sudsy Streams," July 19, 1976:68).

Nevertheless, we have by no means solved our environmental problems. The Environmental Quality Index, designed by the National Wildlife Federation in 1969 to measure our progress in cleaning up the environment and preserving our ecological balance, reflected both good news and bad news in 1976. Environmental quality in the United States declined slightly in 1976, despite progress in areas of air pollution and forests. The Index assessed seven major environmental indicators—air, water, mineral resources, wildlife, living space, forests, and soil conditions. Five of the indices continued to decline, while air quality and forests improved. The trends produced a combined figure of 350 on a scale of a possible 700. By this measurement on an index from 0 to 100 we are at the

590

50 mark, halfway toward our goal of having a good environmental quality. The report also summarized the pluses and minuses of our efforts to solve our ecological and environmental problems ("The Year of the Invisible Crisis," February/March, 1977: 17–31).

Air. The original clean-air goal was May 31, 1975. By then, under the law, air pollution was to have been reduced to levels "safe enough to protect the public's health." But despite the gains made since the Clean Air Act of 1970 took effect, 65 percent of all regions across the United States reported pollution "in excess of the national standards" ("'76 EQ Index...," February/March 1976:20–21).

Water. Here the clean-up program was also running behind schedule. Only a portion of the $18-billion federal sewage-assistance grants had been disbursed by 1977. In the most populated and polluted areas some $7 billion "still has not been spent even though it is needed at the local level" ("The Year of the Invisible Crisis," February/March 1977:29). The EPA conceded that "some 9,000 communities serving 60 percent of the country's population" will not be able to meet the 1977 deadline for installing two-stage sewage treatment plants ("Environmental Quality," January 19, 1976:1). In addition, the EPA had issued 26,000 industrial permits for dumping limited wastes into our nation's waters, but spot checks of firms revealed that "two out of three were in violation" of the permit (1976:26).

Minerals. Oil-reserve estimates by the United States Geological Survey were revised sharply downward from between 160 and 320 billion barrels to only 50 billion in 1976. By 1977 we were more dependent on Arab countries for oil than before the 1973 embargo. However, demand for gasoline rose only one percent in 1975, compared with five percent between 1968 and 1973. Smaller cars with better mileage are now in wider use, and in 1977 crude oil began flowing through the Alaskan pipeline. Also, coal reserves continue to grow as a result of extensive mining. Petroleum imports are expected to rise from 41 percent today to as much as 60 percent before 1980..." ("The Year of the Invisible Crisis," February/March 1977:22).

Wildlife. In 1976 America's endangered species list contained 170 entries, compared with 120 in 1974. Nearly 1,700 plants are under consideration for inclusion on the list. The biggest loss came in habitat land for animals. About 1.2 million acres were converted from rural to urban use in 1975, but 86,000 acres were added to our national refuge for animals ("'76 EQ Index...," February/March 1976:18).

Living Space. In 1976 more than a million acres of rural land was lost to development ("The Year of the Invisible Crisis," February/March 1977:30). Urban development alone took over 750,000 acres. In 1975, highways and airports took 130,000 acres, and reservoirs and flood control 300,000 acres of rural land. Despite a $2.3-billion allocation to buy land for national parks, recreational areas, and wildlife refuges, only $118 million has been requested by the government and only 11 rivers (or parts of them), out of the 100 envisioned, have been protected under the National Wild and Scenic Rivers Act of 1968 ("'76 EQ Index...," February/March 1976:28).

Forests. More timber is being grown and we are using it more efficiently. Congress is spending much more money for reforestation—$51 million in 1975 alone—to replant 400,000 acres; but the Forest Service in 1977 had a backlog of about 2.5 million acres to replant. The United States Forest Service now has a master plan—the program to manage and assess the nation's renewable resources—for achieving specific conservation goals. The new National Forest Management Act of 1976 controls massive "clear cutting" of wood in national forests, restricts logging on stream banks and steep slopes, and emphasizes habitat improvement and reforestation ("The Year of the Invisible Crisis," February/March 1977:27).

Our development of highways and roads across forest land leads to soil erosion, less green space, and degradation of the environment.

Soil. One-half of our cropland is adequately protected against soil erosion, compared with only about one-third in 1965. But we are still losing 3.5 billion tons of soil each year to erosion, and over one million acres each year are lost to developers. Because of critical world food shortages, farmers were exhorted to plow up nine million acres of new land—five million acres of soil-bank reserves and four million acres of grasslands and woodlands. We are losing rich farming soil at an alarming rate ("'76 EQ Index . . . ," February/March 1976:24).

For whatever progress we have made in solving our environmental problems, conservationists (whether conservatives, liberals, or radicals) deserve much credit for calling this serious social issue to the attention of social scientists and others.

Other Proposals

Clean Air Act amendments to extend deadlines (for the third time) on auto-emission and industrial-pollution standards have been proposed. At the same time, they would impose new and more effective pollution-control requirements on industry.

Congress has passed bills that would fund a five-year, $160-million program to develop and demonstrate electrically powered cars suitable for mass production. Such a development would curtail our use of gasoline and save our dwindling oil reserves.

In 1976 new authority was granted to the EPA to regulate some 65 toxic chemicals. Toxic-substance legislation, after being held up in Congress for well over six years because of pressure from vested-interest groups, was passed. It bans the manufacture of PCBs by 1978 and gives the EPA power to police any other "potentially dangerous" new chemicals ("The Year of the Invisible Crisis," February/March 1977:29).

But even tough laws will not solve the problem unless they are enforced by the Environmental Protection Agency (EPA). For example, in 1976 three top EPA lawyers resigned, charging that the agency was failing to vigorously enforce laws controlling the use of pesticides and other cancer-causing chemicals. They attributed the laxity in enforcing the law to conservative business and congressional pressure (Novick, April 1976:21).

New Sources of Energy and Conservation

A solution to the problem of our biosphere lies in developing new sources of energy and in conserving scarce raw materials until new ones can be found. We have already alluded to steps taken to cut back on the use of gasoline-burning cars. We have begun to utilize nuclear power as a new source for generating electricity but there are dangers involved, especially in disposing of nuclear waste material. Some 58 atomic electric generating

In addition to industrial and auto pollution, people themselves add to our ecological problems by littering the landscape. Tougher laws with strict enforcement are needed to stop the public and industry from polluting.

plants accounted for about 8 percent of our generating capacity in 1975. More are planned for the future, though costs and public opposition to them are mounting (Novick, April 1976:24). In moving toward new energy sources, such as nuclear power, it becomes clear that there are ecological risks and costs involved in that new source of energy. But it offers a partial (though not perfect) solution of the problem concerning resources and sources of energy.

Another virtually untapped source of energy is the sun. We are on the threshold of developing this renewable resource, and the potential for solving some of our environmental problems by tapping it is vast. Utility officials estimate that solar energy could provide only 10 to 20 percent of our electricity and that other means of generating electricity will be needed. However, the electric utilities have a vested interest in discouraging the public from using "free" solar energy.

Congress recently appropriated an additional $95 million for solar-energy development, boosting total funds for solar-energy development to over $308 million. With these funds, the Energy Research and Development Administration (ERDA) is carrying out the federal government's policy of developing solar power as a source of long-term energy supplies. The ERDA's total fiscal 1977 budget is over $5 billion, all aimed at helping our society to develop new materials, minerals, and energy sources ("Public Works, Energy Funds," June 19, 1976:1609). These new ways of generating power include a nuclear "breeder reactor" (which creates more energy than it consumes), wind power, use of the tides, geothermal energy, and laser beams.

A clear possibility for strengthening our depleted mineral resources is mining from the sea. The United States is already committed to this type of mining, and the technology is already available. At a Law of the Sea Conference in 1976, the United States announced that we intend to mine the deep-sea beds of the ocean. There is also a wealth of strategic metals—especially nickel—contained in small rocks, or nodules, two or three miles down on the ocean floor. Bills now in Congress would authorize American companies to start mining soon (Hofmann, August 14, 1976:3). We are also beginning to "farm" the ocean, growing giant sea kelp 60 miles west of San Diego ("The 4-H Frogmen," September 23, 1974:107).

Some proposed solutions will require major adjustments for business and many Americans in the way we consume and waste, and in the way we mistreat our environment. Pollution control will cost money, and ideally the industry or person doing the polluting should pay; yet it is likelier that costs will be passed on to taxpayers and consumers. Some jobs in private industry may be lost in the interest of the public's health and well-being. Many items taken for granted will become luxuries, and we must develop a willingness to conserve and recycle (Turner, 1976:318).

Radicals argue that nothing more than a major revamping of our entire profit-oriented economic system will remedy the situation. As long as corporations can produce at a profit, the pollution or waste by-products they create does not interest them. If costs of pollution are passed on to consumers or taxpayers (via government) private capitalists will continue to exploit and degrade the public's air, water, land, and environment.

THE FUTURE OF OUR ENVIRONMENT

In the late 1960s and early 1970s, most research and writing about our ecological and environmental future were very grim. This outlook was fostered by issuance of the first Club of Rome Report, *The Limits to Growth*, in 1972. The report projected that within 100 years most of the world's nonrenewable resources would be exhausted unless something was done quickly (Meadows et al., 1974). In 1973 a refutation in *Models of Doom* offered a more balanced perspective from an interdisciplinary team of physical and social scientists at the University of Sussex, England. The scientists pointed out that in *The Limits to Growth* study, Meadows emphasized that only about one-tenth of one percent of the data on the variables required to construct "a satisfactory world model is now available"

(1973:8). Underlying assumptions and omissions from the original study left much to be desired, even though all the data, real and projected, were fed into the computer. Two later Club of Rome reports moderated the views of the original study, and a somewhat more balanced view of the future is beginning to emerge.

For instance, we have some reasons to doubt so-called shortages of natural gas or gasoline. Often, our resources are controlled by large, powerful corporations that derive great economic advantage in "creating" such shortages. As economist Wilfred Beckerman observes, "The usual estimates of known reserves of raw materials (namely those published by the U.S. Bureau of Mines) are 'conservative contingency forecasts by the exploration companies and they are related to a certain price: if the price is higher, more resources can be exploited commercially'" (1974:174). Even the estimates of oil reserves by the Geological Survey were influenced by oil-industry pressure and persuasion. Thus, within a few months' time the United States "lost" 210 billion barrels of oil merely because the Geological Survey was convinced to switch to a new way of estimating reserves that "resembles those of major oil companies" ("Geological Survey...," July 18, 1975:200).

Use of new technology and new sources of minerals, such as the ocean floor, will ensure an ample future supply. For example, one economist estimates by the year 2000, deep-seabed mining could provide the United States with all our requirements for manganese, cobalt and nickel, with plenty left over for export ("Geological Survey...," July 18, 1975:200). Economist Wilfred Malenbaum points out that new mineral deposits will continue to be discovered in the future. He notes: "Today known reserves of ores—in the noncommunist world—are almost 15 percent higher for zinc than they were in the 1950s. The copper reserves have increased by two to three times; for lead they have doubled; for chromium, they have become almost four times higher. Even for petroleum known reserves in 1970 were 33 times annual production—a higher multiple than pertained in 1950" (1973: 41).

Nevertheless, we need more than energy and natural resources if we are to cope effectively with environmental degradation. We need a new orientation in our values and attitudes about technology and in our use of the environment. In his book *Small Is Beautiful* (1973), E. F. Schumacher may have an answer to the question of how we move to an ecologically sound society without destroying our economy. He describes several requirements of a new "intermediate" technology:

> We need a "new orientation of science and technology towards the organic, the gentle, the non-violent, the elegant and beautiful."
>
> We must look for a technological revolution that will reverse our present detrimental and harmful use of technology.
>
> These machines and methods must be cheap enough to be accessible to almost everyone, suitable for small-scale opera-

tions, and "compatible with man's need for creativity" (Wade, July 18, 1975:199).

If, instead, we consistently use our present technology in an ecologically destructive manner, our own destruction is eventually ensured. If we reach the limits to growth, we could relapse into a Hobbesian universe of the war of all against all, followed, as anarchy has always been, by dictatorship of one form or another. This is precisely the direction in which Robert Heilbroner sees the world moving, as it attempts to control its technology, environment, and population (1974). Even if we remedy our environmental situation through economics and technology, we will still have other problems. To conserve our resources, control our environment, limit our technology, and check our population, we must inevitably place "tight controls on human behavior" (Ophuls, 1976:250). It is not accidental that the one country that has recently embarked upon a forced sterilization program is India: a former democracy that for a time became a dictatorship. We will make progress toward effectively controlling our environment, but it may be at a very heavy price. As C. S. Lewis once noted: "What we call Man's power over Nature turns out to be power

Future use of solar power and windmills to generate electricity and heat homes, as in this experimental house, will reduce our society's reliance on oil and other scarce resources.

exercised by some men over other men with Nature as its instrument" (Ibid., 251).

II. DEFINING THE PROBLEM OF POPULATION GROWTH

One of the factors affecting the limits to growth, exhausting our natural resources, and aggravating our ecological and environmental problems is world population growth. The two social problems—ecological degradation and population growth—are intertwined and connected. Another 190,000 persons are added to the world's population every day. It took 80 years to go from a world population of one billion in 1850 to two billion by 1930; 30 years to reach three billion in 1960; and only 16 years to go over the four-billion mark in 1976.

How does the United States fare in relation to this international social problem? Could it be that not only the poorest nations, but also the richest, suffer from too many people being added too fast, taxing too many resources too quickly? Is it possible that no matter what we do in the less-developed countries (LDCs) in the next two decades or so, famine and other disaster will occur?

Population growth affects virtually every social institution—from the family to the school, and from the economy to religion. Population growth (or decline) comes from three major social processes: fertility (births), mortality (deaths), and migration (movement in or out of an area). The relation between these three demographic (refers to study of population) variables determines what happens to a society's population growth. Some define the population problem in terms of absolute numbers—just too many people, especially in comparison with the past. These writers point to the rate of growth in world population in recent years. Others consider it a problem of concentration and distribution of population. In the United States, for example, over 70 percent of our population lives in urban areas, on only about 2 percent of our total land area. This high density aggravates, if it does not cause, pollution of our air, water, and open areas referred to earlier. Worldwide, Asia (especially China and India) accounts for over half the globe's people.

Some consider that the problems of population growth are much more critical for less-developed countries (hereafter referred to as LDCs). For them it involves questions of life and death. Can such nations produce enough food to feed their starving millions? India is a classic example of this situation. Although food production has increased about one percent or more a year, its population has been growing by two percent or more a year (Gavan and Dixon, 1975:548).

Looking beyond such crisis settings, the Presidential Commission on Population Growth and the American Future argued in 1972 that every society has a population problem. It noted that "this country, or any country, always has a 'population problem' in the sense of achieving a proper balance between size, growth, and distribution on one hand, and the quality of life to which its citizens aspire on the other" (Population and the American Future, 1972:3).

At the extremes of the issue are those social scientists who say we need more people, not fewer, to be economically healthy, and those who argue that we must cut our population in half.

We must distinguish between "family planning" as a means of curbing population and "population control" as a means of remedying the problem. Conservatives, liberals, and radicals disagree on just what measure is best. Ideologically, family planning entails a free choice on the part of individuals to have as many, or as few, children as they desire. Paul Ehrlich, Garrett Hardin, and other liberal and radical advocates of "population control" argue that voluntary family planning is not enough (Berelson, 1969). Governments must embark upon institutionalized programs designed to motivate or coerce, to ensure that couples have no more than two children. In some instances, economic incentives could be given to induce social cooperation. In other cases, mandatory laws would require that family size be limited. Hardin and others, following a "life-boat ethics" approach, argue that food should be denied to nations that have no effective population-control program. Population control is needed, the advocates argue, because the problem is so grave that freedom of individual choice in family size is a luxury societies can no longer afford.

INCIDENCE AND PREVALENCE OF POPULATION GROWTH

By the year 2000, the earth will have to support between six and seven billion persons. In the United States itself, the problem is not severe, but the increase in numbers is just as dramatic. When we took our first census in 1790, nearly four million persons were counted. Our population grew steadily over the years as sanitation, medicine, and life expectancy im-

table 14-2 POPULATION PERSPECTIVE IN TWENTIETH-CENTURY AMERICA

	AROUND 1900	AROUND 1977
POPULATION	76 million	216 million
LIFE EXPECTANCY	47 years	70 years
MEDIAN AGE	23 years	28 years
BIRTHS PER 1,000 POPULATION	32	14.7
DEATHS PER 1,000 POPULATION	17	8.9
ANNUAL GROWTH	1-3/4 million	1 million
GROWTH RATE	2.3 percent	0.7 percent

Source: Adapted and updated from Report of the Commission on Population Growth and the American Future (New York: Signet, 1972):11.

proved. In 1917 we reached 100 million persons, and a half-century later, we reached 200 million. By the end of 1976, we had over 215 million persons (Population Reference Bureau, April 1976:8). We should reach 300 million persons sometime well after the year 2000, and then population should begin to decline. Table 14-2 shows what has happened to our population between 1900 and 1977.

In the United States, the number of children per family has been declining since 1800, when women bore an average of seven. During the Depression of the 1930s, our birthrate fell to an all-time low. Women had only about two children in 1936. After World War II, families suddenly had an average of nearly four children. In 1976, women were bearing fewer than two children. For the five years 1972 through 1976, our birthrates were below the replacement level (an average 2.1 children).

The Presidential Commission on Population Growth and the American Future summed up the situation:

> The United States today has a declining birth rate, low population density, enormous amounts of open space and population leaving the central cities—but that does not eliminate the concern about population ("Themes and Highlights . . . ," 1972:1).

Nearly 100 million people have been born in the United States in the last 50 years. Our total population, as 1978 began, stood at about 218 million people. The outlook is for anywhere from 245 to 287 million people by the year 2000, less than 25 years from now (Bouvier, 1975:23). Shortly after that we should reach 300 million people.

The addition of one more child per family can spell the difference between population stability and increase. But every human life is important.

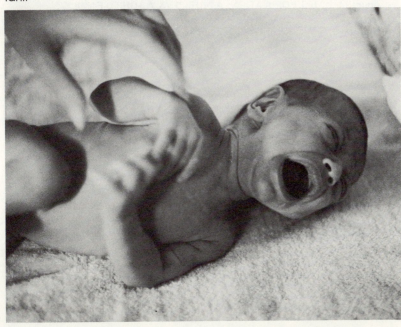

Credit: Shelly Rusten/Black Star.

600

Despite our declining birthrate, our numbers are now so vast and our death rate so low that our population is still growing by about one million a year. In addition, our largest generation of potential parents is coming of age, and their numbers will continue to grow. For instance, in 1975 there were about six million more women in the prime childbearing ages, 20 to 29, than in 1970. By 1985, there will be another five million in that age group, or 11 million more potential parents than in 1970 (U.S. Bureau of the Census, 1971:3). Unless we achieve a delay of childbearing or a smaller family size, we will be faced with many more births in the near future. Hence, the birthrate could swing upward just as abruptly as it dropped during the early 1970s.

Even a one-child difference in average family size makes an enormous difference over the decades. If the young mothers of the 1970s—and their daughters after them—bear only two children each, we will approach zero population growth—a stable or stationary population. Our population would reach about 271 million by the year 2000, and 350 million in 2070. If, instead, couples have three children, the population will reach 322 million in only 25 years, and over 900 million by 2070 (Planned Parenthood—World Population, 1972:3). Figure 14-1 plots the difference in population growth over the next century between two- and three-children families.

Population Growth in Less-Developed Countries (LDCs)

Most of the world's population growth will occur in so-called less-developed countries (LDCs) in Asia, Africa, and Latin America. By the

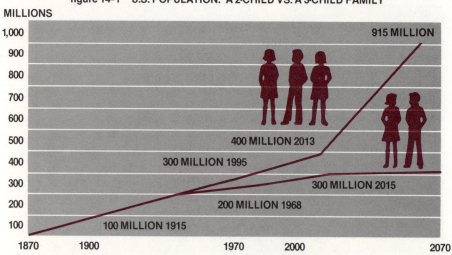

figure 14-1 U.S. POPULATION: A 2-CHILD VS. A 3-CHILD FAMILY

Source: U.S. Bureau of the Census, prepared for the Commission on Population Growth and the American Future.

INCIDENCE AND PREVALENCE OF POPULATION GROWTH

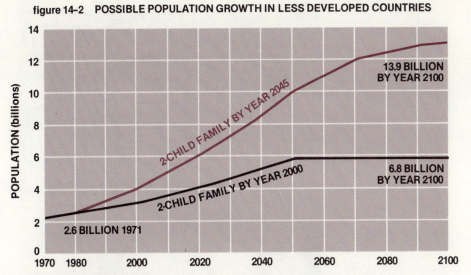

figure 14-2 POSSIBLE POPULATION GROWTH IN LESS DEVELOPED COUNTRIES

Source: Tomas Frejka, Population Council, *New York Times Supplement* (April 30, 1972): 16. Reprinted by permission of the author.

year 2000, 75 to 80 percent of the world's population will live in such developing societies.

What is usually not understood is the explosive potential of population growth in the LDCs. The growth rate of most developing countries is about 2 percent a year. Thus, their populations will double in about 35 years. For example, at Mexico's current 3 percent rate of population growth, it would have over two billion persons 100 years hence, compared with its present 64 million. Even if the LDCs unexpectedly reduced their reproduction rate to an average of two children per couple, "the present population in the developing world of 2.6 billion would increase more than five-fold to nearly 14 billion" by the year 2100 (McNamara, 1972:16).

Population will not stop growing in LDCs even when a two-child average family is reached. The population will continue to grow for another 60 to 70 years beyond that point. So the sooner we apply solutions to control population, the better, for progress will be slow. As Figure 14-2 illustrates, if we reach a two-child family by 2000, rather than by 2045, the LDCs will have to support about 7 billion fewer persons by 2100. Each decade of delay in controlling population in LDCs will lead to an ultimate population some 20 percent larger than if it had been controlled.

With an increase in population in developing nations, a whole series of social problems emerges. Overcrowding in large cities grows; starvation, malnutrition, and hunger become commonplace; unemployment and underemployment reach critical points; poverty becomes a way of life; social stress and tension mount; and economic development and political stability become unlikely under the massive weight of a growing population (Ehrlich, 1971).

In many less-developed countries (LDCs), children get barely enough food to survive.

Recent reports and figures offer some slight hope that world population growth, including that of some developing nations, is beginning to slow down. Nevertheless, the situation will, by the very nature of population dynamics, get worse before it gets better.

Dr. R. T. Ravenholt, director of the population program for the Agency for International Development (AID), pointed to some signs, seen in Table 14-3, that the *rate* of world annual population growth was slowly beginning to decline. He concluded that by concerted action on some of the solutions (mentioned later in this chapter), we should be able to reduce the world birth rate to below 20 persons for every 1,000 (from its 1974 level of 29), and the world-population growth rate to below one percent by 1985 (from its 1974 rate of 1.66 percent) by 1985.

A second recent report showing promising signs comes from the United Nations. The report compared the actual 1970 world population with what had been estimated two years earlier, and reported that "for the first time in the experience of the United Nations, estimated population trends had to be revised downward . . . " (UN Report, 1975:9). The world's population had been overestimated by 22 million.

Another study, the Worldwatch series on "World Population Trends," showed a world drop in the growth rate from 1.90 to 1.64 percent.

table 14-3

WORLD POPULATION PICTURE

	1965	1974
WORLD POPULATION TOTAL	3.2 billion	3.945 billion
AVG. WORLD BIRTHRATE	34 per 1,000	29.0 per 1,000
AVG. WORLD DEATH RATE	14 per 1,000	12.4 per 1,000
ANNUAL POPULATION GROWTH RATE	2 percent	1.66 percent
ANNUAL INCREMENT IN PEOPLE	79 million	66 million

Source: R.T. Ravenholt, "World Population Crisis and Action Toward Solution," November 21, 1975: 4, 9.

table 14-4

	BIRTHS PER 1,000 POPULATION		
	1960–64 avg.*	1970*	1995–2000†
CEYLON (SRI LANKA)	35.2	29.4	18.7
CHILE	35.3	26.6	19.8
COLOMBIA	39.2	31.4	26.9
EGYPT	42.6	34.9	28.3
GUATEMALA	47.7	39.9	32.7
IRAN	40.2	39.6	31.0
SINGAPORE	35.6	23.0	14.9
TAIWAN	37.2	28.1	21.0
THAILAND	36.9	32.6	29.1
TUNISIA	46.2	36.2	29.2
VENEZUELA	44.3	38.1	26.4

Sources: *Statistical Bulletin, Metropolitan Life, June 1972:9, derived from UN sources.
†Projected average from U.N. Report, 1975:24–25.

Lester Brown, Worldwatch Institute President, stated: "The apparent decline in the birth rate of China between 1970 and 1975, the most rapid of any country on record, . . . dropped from an estimated 32 to 19 [per 1,000] in a five-year period . . ." (Brown, September 1976:7). Whatever the reasons, Table 14-4 shows what has happened to birthrates in several LDCs, especially where birth-control programs have been applied.

CAUSES OF THE PROBLEM OF POPULATION GROWTH

As we have mentioned, the current rapid rate of population growth is a new phenomenon. Why is it occurring now?

Three major, interconnected causes are behind the population problem: industrialization and urbanization, a rapid decline in the death rate, and cultural norms and values favoring large families.

Industrialization and Urbanization

During the nineteenth and twentieth centuries, the United States began to experience a revolution in industry and an unprecedented concentration of people in cities. Production of food, clothing, and shelter was achieved on a scale never imagined in a subsistence agricultural society. These revolutions began to affect the size of our population. We could support more people because we now had the ability to produce more food and goods to maintain them, even above subsistence level. During the nineteenth century, knowledge of public sanitation and medicine grew, and cities began to have improved water systems. These factors led to a sharp drop in death rates. More persons were alive to have children, producing further population growth. It was not until the latter part of the nineteenth century and early twentieth century that Americans became conscious of the advantages of a smaller family. When they did, birthrates began to decline. Thus, our urbanization and industrialization both caused and alleviated population growth. In the early centuries of industrialization and mass urbanization, population grows; but in the later stages, as more rural residents move to the city, they begin to understand that children are less of an economic asset and more of a liability (Thomlinson, 1976:20–21). As women begin to find employment outside the home, they tend to have fewer children. As families seek to move up the social-class ladder, they come to appreciate that the fewer children they have, the better their chances for advancement in an urban, industrial society.

Rapid Decline in Death Rate

The industrialized world's rapidly declining death rate is best explained by the demographic-transition theory. Before the Industrial Revolution, the brutally harsh conditions of life kept populations in balance. Birthrates were extremely high, but so were death rates (Coale, 1974:41–51). With the advent of industry and large cities came the first real population increase. With industry emerged modern science, which helped to break the pattern of high death rates that had successfully kept population from growing significantly. Vaccination, as well as advancements in sanitation and medicine, improved people's chances of surviving, especially babies' and young children's. Combined with better technology for raising food and better transportation for distributing it, socioeconomic forces were set in motion to lower death rates dramatically.

As death rates started to fall, fertility remained at traditionally high levels for several generations. This widening spread between high birthrates (about 40 to 45 per 1,000 population) and lower death rates (about 10 to 15 per 1,000) produced a demographic gap. It is this gap (*not* increased birthrates) that is causing a population explosion in the LDCs. A long period of transition (several centuries) occurs before population is finally balanced by *low* birth and death rates. In Western nations it took over 100 years to close the gap (Stockwell, 1968:175).

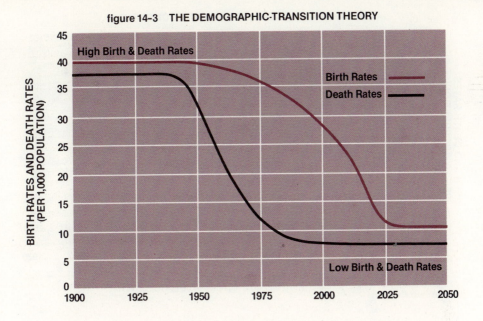

figure 14-3   THE DEMOGRAPHIC-TRANSITION THEORY

Figure 14-3 illustrates this demographic-transition theory, which it is assumed will apply to many LDCs in the future.

The basic cause of population growth in such countries is that most are still going through their period of transitional growth (from high birth-rates to low birth rates and death rates). Less than half of the world's people have completed this transition. To make matters worse, the base population in developing nations is much larger than it was when Western countries started their transition. Furthermore, the developing countries, with our help, make immediate use of modern medicine, insecticides, and sanitation, whereas Western nations, using these techniques in their infancy, required many years to bring about a substantial lowering of the death rate. But in developing nations, with modern means available, the death rate is cut in half in a short time.

The classic example of this occurrence in LDCs is Ceylon (now Sri Lanka). That country's death rate was cut almost in half in the *one year* between 1946 and 1947. With technical assistance from the United Nations, Great Britain, and the United States, the rural areas were sprayed with DDT, which killed mosquitoes and other disease-carrying insects. As a consequence, malaria and other childhood diseases dropped overnight. We should note, too, that before its sharp decline in deaths, Ceylon was a food-exporting nation with an economic surplus. Today, Sri Lanka must import food to feed its people, and must borrow money to maintain its economy.

Figure 14-4 compares the difference in progress made by Sweden and Sri Lanka in closing the gap between births and deaths. Sri Lanka, as the

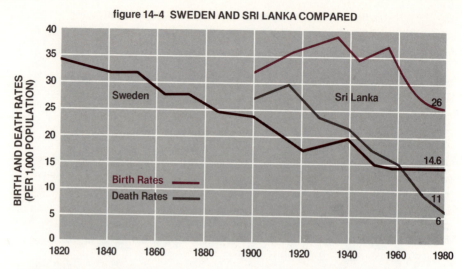

figure 14-4 SWEDEN AND SRI LANKA COMPARED

Source: Adapted from Kingsley Davis, "Population," *Scientific American* (September 1963): 70. Estimates for 1980 from U.N. Projections, March 1975. Reprinted by permission of W.H. Freeman and Company.

figure shows, has widened its gap since the late 1940s, while Sweden has almost closed it entirely.

Why do birthrates of the LDCs remain high for so long, prolonging the period of demographic transition? The answer lies in the third cause of the population problem—cultural norms and values.

Cultural Norms and Values Favoring Large Families

The traditions and values of many societies encourage young men and women to marry at an early age. Most women in LDCs thus define themselves solely in terms of their childbearing and childrearing roles. Often no other alternative role is even available. As long as this cultural norm persists, population will continue to rise.

A related value is the large-family ideal. In some cultures this ideal is reinforced by traditional ideas of "machismo," or manliness, which is proven by the number of children a man produces. This cultural value stems from centuries of high death rates among infants and children. Hence to ensure that a son lives to carry on the family's name and occupation, the man fathers many children. Even though infant death rates have declined sharply, a cultural lag persists between the values of traditional cultures and population growth.

Traditional, manual methods of agriculture also demand large families to work the fields. As long as cultural norms persist against using modern technology—be it plows or irrigation—populations will grow. Some cultures believe a metal plow will poison the soil; so they stick to the inefficient *wooden* one. In a subsistence agricultural society, more children mean not only more mouths to feed, but also more hands to help on the farm.

Another cultural norm and value is ignorance of or indifference to the consequences of having many children. In some cultures men and women are unaware of the connection between sexual intercourse and having a child. Hence, they see no need to use birth control. Even a traditional, natural way of allowing some time to pass between pregnancies has recently been changing in the LDCs. More and more women, especially as they move from farms to cities, have discontinued breast feeding their children. This traditional practice had acted somewhat to control the natural fecundity of the woman; for nursing mothers, ovulation is delayed anywhere from 10 weeks to 26 months. As the cultural practice changes, couples should be made aware of the consequences (Horsley, 1973:4). So cultural norms and values work against controlling family size and perpetuate the population problem.

PROPOSED SOLUTIONS TO THE PROBLEM OF POPULATION GROWTH

Let us look at some proposals that have been made for dealing with the problem of population growth, first in the United States, then in LDCs.*

Proposals for the United States

In 1972 the Commission on Population Growth and the American Future recommended that the federal government enact a population-education act to assist school systems in planning and implementing population-education programs. These would further enlighten our younger generations about the importance of responsible parenthood. The Commission also recommended widespread availability of sex education through the media, child- and maternal-health programs, adoption of the Equal Rights Amendment, liberalized abortion, contraceptives for teenagers, reduction of illegal immigration, development of national population-distribution guidelines, and the creation of a population growth and distribution office within the executive branch of the federal government, to act as a national coordinator of population policies. Conservatives, including then President Nixon, strongly opposed the proposals for liberalized abortion and contraceptives for teenagers as methods of curbing population growth.

---

*Much of the research and first-draft writing of the remainder of this chapter were done by Bryan Zeiner, an advanced sociology student at Muhlenberg College.

Economic deterrents have also been proposed as a way of motivating couples to limit family size to two children. It has been proposed that those with two or fewer children be given a tax break, instead of economically rewarding those who have many children, as is now the case.

Another radical proposal is to cut the American population in half, to about 100 million people. This idea, which would take over a century to achieve if each family had only one child, has been advocated by Donald Mann, president of a group called Negative Population Growth (NPG) (Loercher, June 2, 1975:30). Conservatives and some liberals see economic danger and disaster in such a drastic decline in our population.

Proposals for LDCs

In the LDCs, many programs are underway to help solve the problem. Two Asian nations, China and Pakistan, have taken steps to deal with the problem. In China, married women with at least two children must carry an oral contraceptive called the "paper pill" (made cheaply with dissolvable paper) at all times. They are asked to share them with any other females they meet who are without a pill (Population Reference Bureau, December 1975:7). China also practices and relies upon substantial sexual abstinence, as well as delays in the age of marriage and childbearing. In addition, there is wide use of conventional forms of birth control, including abortion in some cases. The Chinese are highly organized and socialized to accept the government's policy of controlling population.

Pakistan is engaging in a Contraceptive Inundation Scheme. The plan is a subsidized sales activity using both shops and door-to-door distributors in 40,000 villages to sell contraceptives at two-and-a-half cents for a monthly supply of birth-control pills. Some 700 clinics employ female high-school graduates to insert intrauterine devices (IUDs) and dispense pills. Birth-control programs operate in 400 government hospitals, and 2,000 doctors distribute free contraceptives to their patients (Population Reference Bureau, 1976:12).

In 1974, 141 nations adopted a World Population Plan of Action to promote economic development and improve the quality of life. The LDCs expressed more interest in fostering economic development than in population control, while the developing countries were more interested in seeing them establish programs of population control. Although member countries dropped specific goals to curb population growth from the original draft, the final plan did endorse the principle of family planning. The plan also recognized the interrelationship between economic development and population control.

At the International Women's Year Conference at Mexico City in 1975, 133 countries noted the close relationship between birth rates and women's rights. The group's Plan of Action stressed the importance of family planning to women's status:

> Individuals and couples have the right freely and responsibly to determine the number and spacing of their children and to have the information and means to do so. The exercise of this right is basic to the attainment of any real equality between the sexes ... (Population Reference Bureau, April 1976:23).

Yet at the IWY Conference, too, the emphasis of LDCs was on shaping a new economic order, while the United States stressed liberalizing the rights of women. Consequently, statements adopted by the United Nations or its international conferences (such as the IWY) tend to be political compromises between nations and, like party platforms in the United States, are usually not taken very seriously. Yet most demographers from the developed countries feel that a society cannot have effective economic and social development until it effectively controls its population growth.

In attempting to solve the problem of overpopulation in LDCs and the United States, we must not curtail individual rights and liberties. Failure to protect a family's or group's freedom of choice about how many children they do or do not want may result in totalitarian programs. Although such programs may control population, some conservatives maintain that it will do so only at the price of individual liberty. For instance, in Maharashtra Province (in which Bombay is located), a compulsory-sterilization bill was passed in 1976, requiring that married men with three living children be sterilized. Dr. D. N. Pai, Director of Bombay's Family Planning, and a vocal advocate for compulsory sterilization, responded to criticisms: "If some excesses appear, don't blame me.... You must consider it something like a war. There could be a certain amount of misfiring out of enthusiasm. There has been pressure to show results" (Kamm, August 13, 1976:A-8).

An amendment to a foreign-aid bill in 1977 prohibited the use of foreign-assistance money "for the performance of involuntary sterilization as a method of family planning" and to "coerce or provide any financial incentives to any person to practice sterilization" (Rosoff, May 27, 1977:2). United States Representative Robert Young, speaking to ban such sterilization, pointed out that among "uneducated people" in LDCs, a "very thin line" exists between voluntary choice and forced submission to sterilization.

THE FUTURE OF POPULATION GROWTH

Our concern over the growing world population is not only over the numbers per se, but also over the social, ecological, political, and physical changes that may result from too many more people too soon.

The Future for the United States

As we mentioned earlier, America's future population is not completely predictable. Even though many females are entering the childbear-

610

ing years and could increase the total number of births (even with a low fertility rate), the United States is very close to achieving a stable population base, at which births and deaths will be practically equal. Some demographers call this drastic growth reduction the "birth dearth." They predict that a zero or negative population growth would severely lower America's per capita output. The United States has prospered from rapid population and industrial growth in the past, and it is doubtful whether such advancements of mass production and consumption could have been made without an increasing population. It is by no means certain, however, that the United States must continue to increase its population in order to provide future generations with a higher standard of living. The point at which social benefits exceed social and ecological costs may have been reached.

Another argument for curbing America's future population growth is that by doing so we can forestall depletion of our resources. If the American people were to grow to 300 million or more by the year 2000, without changing our consumption habits, we would be faced with serious material shortages. Of course this does not mean that all our nation's energy and resource needs will be fulfilled if we reach Zero Population Growth, a stable population that we could achieve 60 years after we reach an average

The baby-boom children of the 1950s are now coming of age in the United States. The number of children they decide to have will determine whether we will have a growing or stable population in the decades ahead.

of 2.1 children per reproductive woman. Some scholars, such as Mancur Olson and Hans Landsberg, see Zero Economic Growth as a solution to problems caused by a large population. ZEG involves restructuring of values away from large-scale technology, consumption, and use of resources.

The Future for LDCs

How fast are the less-developed nations growing, and what are the indications for the future? In mid-1976, the United Nations reported that Latin America's population was growing at 2.8 percent annually, Asia's at 2.0 percent, and China's at 1.7 percent (Myers, April 1976:n.p.). When we realize that these areas contain over two-thirds of the world's peoples, we can see why such percentages of growth become frightening.

China, with between an estimated 800 million and one billion persons, was the subject of a study by William Brinton and several other researchers. They constructed a model of growth in China from 1953 to 2103. The model took into account China's conditions and its policies of development. Even though China has made remarkable progress in controlling birth rates, the researchers concluded that if early-1970 rates continued, China's population would continue to grow for another 50 years, even though fertility rates would probably decrease further. The model predicts a decline of China's resources, industrial shutdowns, and famine, before its population begins to decline. Only a two-child average family size by 1985 (which it may achieve), together with achievement of its proposed industrial output for 1990 and a change of technology favoring renewable resources, could prevent future calamity (Brinton, 1974:133–41).

World population stabilization will not come quickly. Even if the world's reproduction rate dropped in a few years so that we only replaced our existing population, the net population increase would still be large enough to push the world's population to 5.6 or 5.7 billion by the year 2050. And if it takes 70 years to reach zero population growth, by 2050 we could have 13 billion persons (Frejka, 1973:52–53).

Although a positive relationship exists between low birth rates, low death rates, and a higher standard of living, the problem of how to improve the standard of living for most LDCs remains to be solved. At present, a wide per-capita-income gap exists between the developed countries and the underdeveloped countries, and it is widening at an alarming rate. In short, the rich get richer as the poor get poorer. If population is to be curbed in the LDCs they need massive economic aid from developed nations to increase the process of industrialization.

Perhaps the whole question of curbing future population growth and solving related problems is best summed up in these words:

> The essence of the population problem—so far, at least—is not that mankind has propagated too many children but that it has

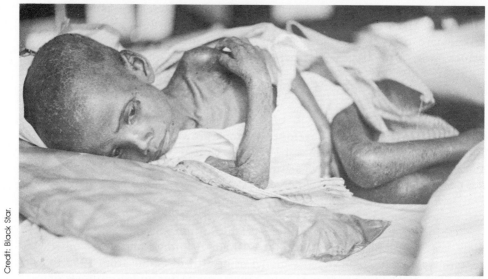

Both disease and malnutrition take a daily toll on human life in LDCs today. Will tomorrow be any different?

The inequality of wealth in the world produces a situation in which some nations spend billions on vehicles and weapons that consume natural resources and pollute the environment, while children of other nations go hungry.

failed to organize a world in which they can grow in peace and prosperity. Rich nations and poor alike have grossly misused that world's resources, both material and intellectual, neglected them, wasted them, and fought each other over how to share them. Thus, the basic question is not how many people can share the earth, but whether they can devise the means of sharing it at all ("Population Explosion," 1971:59).

Demographers, such as Kingsley Davis, feel the question is not *whether* the less-developed countries will share in the wealth of the world through industrialization and urbanization, but *when*. Likewise, the question is not *whether* LDCs will control their population growth but *how* and *when*.

SUMMARY

Although ecology and population are serious international issues, we have viewed them as neither doomsday issues nor as ones to be minimized. We recognize that all people are connected internationally to one giant ecosystem and biosphere—the earth. Our resources are both renewable and nonrenewable, and we must learn to use both kinds more effectively.

The four aspects of the ecological issue are misuse and abuse of the earth's (1) air, (2) water, (3) land, and (4) resources. Synergistic, threshold, trigger, and time-lag effects all increase the prevalence of the problem. Some figures show exhaustion of our resources; others show just the opposite.

Some causes of the ecological problem are population growth, the spread of industrialization and affluence, and changes in product technology.

Some progress has been made in improving our environment, usually because of new laws and action taken by society and the government. Much remains to be done, especially where large corporations continue to pollute in order to make a profit. We should develop alternate resources and sources of energy, as well as a new orientation in our attitudes and values about technology and our use of the environment.

Success or failure in dealing with our physical environment depends a great deal on what happens to our population growth. In the United States we added 100 million persons to our population in 50 years, and have over 70 percent of our population on two percent of our land. This has aggravated the environmental problems caused by technology and industry. Developed nations, such as the United States, now have declining birthrates, but population is still rapidly growing in LDCs.

The difference between a country's averaging a two-child and a three-child family will make a big difference in population in 100 years. For each decade LDCs delay in controlling their population, their growth will be 20 percent greater than if controlled. Due in part to China's efforts in cutting its birthrate in five years from 32 per 1,000 population to 19, the world is just beginning to control its population growth. But much remains to be done as long as the underlying causes (industrialization and urbanization, decline in death rates, and traditional values favoring large families) persist. A consensus must be worked out between developed countries and LDCs before economic aid and development is forthcoming. The priority of the United States as a world power is population control in LDCs; the LDCs' priority is economic development. Totalitarian means to control population may be the wave of the future in LDCs, according to Robert Heilbroner. India, with its experience with forced sterilization, may be a model of how other LDCs may move in the future, unless individual choice of family size is protected.

CAREER OPPORTUNITIES

Foresters.

A professional forester is a graduate of a four-year university-level school of forestry, and usually has a bachelor's degree (including sociology or social science). Some foresters combine three years of liberal arts education with two years of professional education in forestry and receive a master of forestry in five years. There are 39 schools of forestry in the United States, accredited by the Society of American Foresters. They are trained to preserve and replant our forests, and to protect natural terrain from erosion and environmental degradation. For further information write to: Society of American Foresters, Wild Acres, 5400 Grosvenor Lane, Bethesda, Maryland 20014.

Demographers.

Demographers are social scientists who study and analyze the size, composition, and distribution of population, as well as fertility, mortality, and migration rates. Using past and current trends, they make projections of the growth, composition, and nature of future population. They assist government and business by predicting the various impacts that certain populations will have on our economy and society. A good background in the research methods of sociology is essential. For further information write to: The Office of Population Research, Princeton University, Princeton, N.J.

Extension-Service Workers.

Extension-service workers are engaged with the rural population in (1) educational work to preserve the natural environment in agriculture, and in (2) community-resource development. They are employed jointly by state and land-grant universities and the Department of Agriculture. Persons with a wide range of skills and academic backgrounds (including sociology) are employed, although they must have a bachelor's degree in their field. Training in educational techniques is offered once a person is employed. The demand for these workers is expected to increase, particularly in economically depressed rural areas. For further information write to: U.S. Department of Health, Education and Welfare, Office of Education, Washington, D.C. 20202.

REFERENCES

I. Ecology and the Environment

"About Law on Sharing the Sea's Riches." U.S. News & World Report 81, 7 (August 16): 42, 1976.

Althoff, Phillip, William H. Grieg, and Francine Stuckey
   1973 "Environmental Pollution Control Attitudes of Media Managers in Kansas." Journalism Quarterly 50, 4 (Winter):666–72.

"Back from Extinction." Time (January 22): 75–76, 1973.

Beckerman, Wilfred
   1974 Two Cheers for the Affluent Society: A Spirited Defense of Economic Growth. New York: St. Martin's Press.

Bylinski, Gene
   1970 "The Long Littered Path to Clear Air and Water." **Fortune** 82 (October 1970): 112–15.

"Capsules/Demography: Birth Defects." Intercom 3, 11 (December): 12. Washington, D.C.: Population Reference Bureau, 1975.

Cohn, Victor
   1970 "Public Fights A-Power." Washington Post (October 19, 1969): 1. Pp. 52–57 in Grant McClellan, ed. Protecting Our Environment. New York: Wilson.

Commoner, Barry
   1966 Science and Survival. New York: Viking Press.
   1971 The Closing Circle: Nature, Man and Technology. New York: Knopf.

Crewdson, Prudence
   1976 "House Committee Files Clear Air Report." Congressional Quarterly Weekly Report 34, 23 (June 5): 1441–46.

Dasmann, Raymond
   1968 An Environment Fit for People. Public Affairs Pamphlet 421. New York: Public Affairs Committee.

"Drinking Water Safety Debate Is Continued." Philadelphia Evening Bulletin (April 11): 18, 1975.

"The Dying Oceans." Time 96 (September 28): 64, 1970.

Editors of the Ecologist
   1972 A Blueprint for Survival. Pp. 10–23 in William P. Lineberry, ed. Priorities for Survival. New York: Wilson.

Editors of Fortune
   1976 The Environment: A National Mission for the Seventies. New York: Harper & Row.

Edson, Lee
   1975 "Not with a Bang but a Pfffft." New York Times Magazine (December 21): 34.

Ehrlich, Paul R. and Anne H. Ehrlich
   1972 Population, Resources, Environment: Issues in Human Ecology. 2nd ed. San Francisco: Freeman.

Ehrlich, Paul R., and John Holdren
   1971 "Population and Environment." Pp. 21–30 in Daniel Callahan, ed. The American Population Debate. Garden City, N.Y.: Anchor.

"Environment Blamed for 60% of Cancer." Philadelphia Evening Bulletin (February 27): n.p., 1976.

"Environmental Quality Seen Declining in 1975." Allentown Morning Call (January 19): 1, 1976.

"EPA Starting Major Effort against Lethal Chemicals." Allentown Morning Call (December 23): 2, 1975.

First Annual Report of the Council on Environmental Quality. Washington, D.C.: U.S. Government Printing Office, 1970.

"The 4-H Frogmen." Newsweek (September 23): 107, 1974.

Froelich, Warren
   1975 "Four Governors Ask U.S. Check on Offshore Oil." Philadelphia Evening Bulletin (April 11): 9.

"Geological Survey Lowers Its Sights." Science 189, 4198 (July 18): 200, 1975.

Gist, Noel and Sylvia Fava
   1974 Urban Society. 6th ed. New York: Crowell.

Hammond, Allen L., William D. Metz, and Thomas Maugh
   1973 Energy and the Future. Washington, D.C.: American Association for the Advancement of Science.

Hardesty, John
   1974 "Economic Implications of Environmental Crisis." Society 12, 1 (November/December): 13–14.

Heilbroner, Robert L.
   1974 An Inquiry into the Human Prospect. New York: Norton.

Hill, Gladwin
   1973 Cleansing Our Waters. Public Affairs Pamphlet No. 497. New York: Public Affairs Committee.

Hofmann, Paul
   1976 "Kissinger Presses for Ocean Accord." New York Times (August 14): 3.

Horton, Paul B. and Gerald Leslie
   1974 The Sociology of Social Problems. 5th ed. Englewood Cliffs, N.J.: Prentice-Hall.

Jacoby, Neil
1971 "Policy Approaches to a Better Urban America." Pp. 160-79 in Clifton Fadiman and Jean White, eds. Ecocide — And Thoughts Toward Survival. Santa Barbara, Calif.: Center for the Study of Democratic Institutions.

King, Judson
1959 The Conservation Fight. Washington, D.C.: Public Affairs Press.

Knader, Laurence
1970 "Environmental Threat and Social Organization." Annals of the American Academy of Political and Social Science 389 (May): 11-18.

Lapedes, Daniel N., ed.
1976 Yearbook of Science and Technology: 1975. New York: McGraw-Hill.

McCaull, Julian
1976 "Storing the Sun: Scientists Institute for Public Information." Environment 18, 5 (June): 9-15.

MacGregor, Ian D.
1975 "Natural Distribution of Metals and Some Economic Effects." The Annals of the American Academy of Political and Social Science 420 (July): 31-45.

Malenbaum Wilfred
1973 "World Resources for the Year 2000." Annals of the American Academy of Political and Social Science 408 (July): 30-45.

Meadows, Dennis
1971 "What Are Man's Prospects: The Predicament of Mankind." Current (October): 3-9.

Meadows, Donella H., Dennis L. Meadows, Jorgen Randers, and William Behrens
1974 The Limits to Growth. 2nd ed. New York: Universe.

Mesarovic, Mihajlo and Eduard Pestel
1974 Mankind at the Turning Point. New York: Dutton.

Mumford, Lewis
1938 The Culture of Cities. New York: Harcourt Brace.

Natural Resources Defense Council, Inc.
1975 Your Dollars and Environmental Sense. New York: NRDC.

Notestein, Frank
1971 "Zero Population Growth: What Is It?" Pp. 31-43 in Daniel Callahan, ed. The American Population Debate. Garden City, N.Y.:Anchor.

Novick, Sheldon
1976 "Spectrum." Environment (April): 21, 24.
1976 "Spectrum." Environment (June): 22.

Olson, Mancur and Hans Landsberg, eds.
1973 The No-Growth Society. New York: Norton.

Organization for Economic Cooperation and Development
1976 "Paying to Pollute." Environment 18, 5 (June): 16–20.

Perlman, David
1969 "America the Beautiful?" Look 33 (November 4): 25–27.

Polanyi, Karl
1957 The Great Transformation. Boston: Beacon Press.

"Pollution: The Swedes Come Clean; Italy: Sewage in Your Eye; Japan: Where It Comes Down in Chunks; Russia: It's No Better over There." Pp. 43–44 in William P. Lineberry, ed. Priorities for Survival. New York: Wilson, 1973.

"Public Works, Energy Funds." Congressional Quarterly Weekly Report 34, 25 (June 19): 1609, 1976.

"Rep. Florio Seeks Ban on Philadelphia Sewage Plan." Philadelphia Evening Bulletin (April 11): 13, 1975.

"Reserve Mining Plant's Foes Seek 2-Year Limit on Pollution Cleanup." Wall Street Journal (March 28): 3, 1975.

Ridker, Ronald
1973 "The Impact of Population Growth on Resources and the Environment." Pp. 109–19 in Charles F. Westoff, ed. Toward the End of Growth. Englewood Cliffs, N.J.: Prentice-Hall.

"'76 EQ Index, EQ Summary: Where Is the Silver Lining?" National Wildlife 14, 2 (Feburary/March): 17–29, 1976.

Stanford, Neal
1970 "Project Seeks to Eliminate All Waste." Pp. 160–63 in Grant McClellan, ed. Protecting Our Environment. New York: Wilson.

Stewart, Elbert W.
1976 The Troubled Land: Social Problems in Modern America. 2nd ed. New York: McGraw-Hill.

Thomlinson, Ralph
1976 Population Dynamics: Causes and Consequences of World Demographic Change. New York: Random House.

"Toxic Substances Bill." Congressional Quarterly Weekly Report 34, 8 (February 21): 436, 1976.

Turner, Jonathan
1976 "The Ecosystem: The Interrelationship of Society and Nature." Pp. 292–322 in Don H. Zimmerman et al., eds. Understanding Social Problems. New York: Praeger.

"U.S. Clean Up Waters, EPA Reports to Congress." Allentown Morning Call (May 11): 1, 1976.

U.S. Commission on Population Growth
1972 Population Growth and the American Future. New York: Signet.

Vaden, Ted
1976 "Automotive Technology: Electric Cars." Congressional Quarterly Weekly Report 34, 25 (June 19): 1607–8.

Wade, Nicholas
1975 "E. F. Schumacher: Cutting Technology Down to Size." Science 189, 4198 (July 18): 199–201.

"Whatever Happened to America's Sudsy Streams." U.S. News & World Report 81, 3 (July 19): 68, 1976.
"World May Beat Its Ills." Allentown Sunday Call-Chronicle (February 15): B-20, 1976.
"The Year of the Invisible Crisis: National Wildlife EQ Index 1977." National Wildlife 15, 2 (February/March): 17-31, 1977.

Zeldin, Marvin
    1973 The Campaign for Cleaner Air. Public Affairs Pamphlet No. 494. New York: Public Affairs Committee.

II. Population Growth

Arriaga, Eduardo
    1970 Mortality Decline and Its Demographic Effects in Latin America. Berkeley: Institute of International Studies, University of Califonia.

Bell, Oliver, ed.
    1974 America's Changing Population. The Reference Shelf, 46, 2. New York: Wilson.

Berelson, Bernard
    1969 "Beyond Family Planning." Ekistics 27 (May): 288-91.

Bogue, Donald
    1967 "The End of the Population Explosion." The Public Interest (Spring): 11-20.

Bouvier, Leon F.
    1975 "U.S. Population in 2000 — Zero Growth or Not?" Population Bulletin 30, 5. Washington, D.C.: Population Reference Bureau.

Brinton, William, Gerald H. Rosenberg, and John Wolfe
    1974 "China: A Model of Growth for the People's Republic of China." Simulation, 23, 5 (November): 133-41.

Brown, Lester R.
    1975 By Bread Alone. New York: Praeger.
    1975a "The World Food Prospect." Science 190 (December 12): 1053-59.
    1976 World Population Trends: Signs of Hope, Signs of Stress. Worldwatch Paper 8 (September). Washington, D.C.: Worldwatch Institute.

Calhoun, John B.
    1962 "Population Density and Social Pathology." Scientific American 206 (February): 139-46.

Callahan, Daniel, ed.
    1971 The American Population Debate. Garden City, N.Y.: Anchor.

Callahan, Daniel
    1972 "Ethics and Population Limitations." Science 175 (February 4): 487-94.

Coale, Ansley
    1974 "The History of Human Population." Scientific American 231, 3 (September): 41-51.

Davis, Kingsley
    1973 "Zero Population Growth: The Goal and the Means." Daedalus 102, 4 (Fall): 15-30.

Dillon, Valerie Vance
 n.d. Will the Real Population Problem Please Stand Up: 1–6. East Brunswick, N.J.: Family Life Bureau.

Donovan, Robert J.
 1975 "Study Shows Familiarity Doesn't Breed Contempt." Allentown Sunday Call-Chronicle (December 21): A–13.

Ehrlich, Paul R.
 1971 The Population Bomb. rev. ed. New York: Ballantine.

Frejka, Tomas
 1973 The Future of Population Growth. New York: Wiley.

Friedrich, Otto
 1971 "Population Explosion: Is Man Really Doomed?" Time (September 13): 58–59.

Gavan, James D. and John Dixon
 1975 "India: A Perspective on the Food Situation." Science 188, 4188 (May): 541–49.

Heilbroner, Robert
 1974 An Inquiry into the Human Prospect. New York: Norton.

Horsley, Kathryn, ed.
 1973 "Nurturing Development." Interchange 2, 4 (November). Washington, D.C.: Population Reference Bureau.

Kamm, Henry
 1976 "India State Is Leader in Forced Sterilization." New York Times (August 13): A–8.

Keyfitz, Nathan
 1972 "Population Density and the Style of Social Life." Pp. 112–17 in Sue Reid and David Lyon, eds. Population Crisis: An Interdisciplinary Perspective. Glenview, Ill.: Scott, Foresman.

Loercher, Diane
 1975 "They Would Halve U.S. Population." Christian Science Monitor (June 2): 30.

McNamara, Robert S.
 1972 "A Burden on Development." In "Population: The U.S. Problem, the World Crisis." New York Times Supplement (April 30): 16.

McVeigh, Frank
 1976 "The Effects of the Changes in Women's Roles on Population Growth Internationally." Paper delivered at Cedar Crest College (April 1): 1–24.

Mamdani, Mahmood
 1974 "A Small Failure in Birth Control." Intellectual Digest 4, 5 (January): 66–67.

Mayer, Martin
 1976 "Growing Up Crowded." Commentary 60 (September 1975). Pp. 198–203 in Anne Kilbride, ed. Readings in Social Problems 76/77: Annual Editions. Guilford, Conn.: Dushkin.

Mesarovich, Mihajlo and Eduard Pestel
 1974 Mankind at the Turning Point. New York: Dutton.

Myers, Paul
- 1976 1976 World Population Data Sheet. Washington, D.C.: Population Reference Bureau.

Notestein, Frank
- 1970 "Zero Population Growth: What Is It?" Family Planning Perspectives 2, 3 (June): 20–24.

Oeschsli, Frank and Dudley Kirk
- 1975 "Modernization and Demographic Transition in Latin America and the Caribbean." Economic Development and Cultural Change 23 (April 3): 291–419.

Olson, Mancur and Hans Landsberg, eds.
- 1973 The No-Growth Society. New York: Norton.

Petersen, William
- 1975 Population. 3rd ed. New York: Macmillan.

Pimental, David, L. E. Hurd, A. C. Bellotte, et al.
- 1973 "Food Production and the Energy Crisis." Science 182, 16 (October): 448.

Planned Parenthood – World Population
- 1972 Population Boom or Bust? New York: Planned Parenthood Federation of America.

Population and the American Future
- 1972 The Report of the Commission on Population Growth and the American Future. New York: Signet.

Population Crisis Council and Planned Parenthood Federation of America.
- 1972 "Population: The U.S. Problem, the World Crisis." New York Times Supplement (April 30).

Population Reference Bureau
- 1975 "Capsules/General." Intercom 3, 11 (December): 7.
- 1975 "Census Forecasts Population to 2050." Intercom 3, 11 (December): 2.
- 1976 World Population Growth and Response: 1965–1975, A Decade of Global Action. (April). Washington, D.C.

Ravenholt, R. T.
- 1975 "World Population Crisis and Action Toward Solution." Paper presented at the Second Annual Meeting of the World Population Society's International Population Conference, Washington, D.C., November 21.

Rosoff, Jeannie L.
- 1977 "House OKs Overseas Family Planning Authorization after Sterilization Debate." Planned Parenthood–World Population Washington Memo (May 27): 2.

Safilos-Rothschild, Constantina
- 1971 "Children and Adolescents in Slums and Shanty-Towns in Developing Countries." New York: United Nations Economic and Social Council, United Nations Children's Fund.

Schumacher, E. F.

1973 Small Is Beautiful: A Study of Economics as if People Mattered. London: Blond & Brigu.

Stark, Rodney

1975 Social Problems. New York: Random House.

Stockwell, Edward G.

1968 Population and People. Chicago: Quadrangle.

Teitelbaum, Michael

1974 "Population and Development: Is a Consensus Possible?" Foreign Affairs (July): 742–60.

Themes and Highlights of the Final Report of the Commission on Population Growth and the American Future.

1972 Washington, D.C.: U. S. Government Printing Office.

Thomlinson, Ralph

1976 Population Dynamics: Causes and Consequences of World Demographic Change. New York: Random House.

Udry, J. Richard, E. Karl Bauman, and Charles J. Chase

1973 "Population Growth Rates in Perfect Contraceptive Population." Population Studies 27 (July): 365–71.

United Nations Report

1975 World Population Prospects, 1970–2000, as Assessed in 1973 (March 10). New York: Population Division, Department of Economic and Social Affairs.

U.S. Bureau of the Census

1971 "Projections of the Population of the United States by Age and Sex: 1970 to 2020." Current Population Reports. Series P-25, No. 470. Washington, D.C.: U.S. Government Printing Office.

Wheeler, Harvey

1968 Democracy in a Revolutionary Era: The Political Order Today. New York: Praeger.

World Population Plan of Action. Bucharest: United Nations World Population Conference, 1974.

SUGGESTED READINGS

I. Ecology and the Environment

Burchell, Robert W. and David Listokin. The Environmental Impact Handbook. New Brunswick: Rutgers University Press. 1975.

A guide to help citizens and professionals analyze and draw up environmental-impact statements, especially noting the human impact of the physical environment.

Cannon, James. A Clear View: Guide to Industrial Pollution. New York: Inform, Inc. 1975.

Acquaints citizens with rules and laws governing pollution, and with how to determine who is polluting and what can be done about it.

Carr, Donald E. Energy and the Earth Machine. New York: Norton. 1976.

Discusses and analyzes alternatives to present systems of energy; notes that there is abundant energy on earth if we apply technical competence and common sense.

Eckholm, Erik F. Losing Ground: Environmental Stress and World Food Prospects. New York: Norton. 1976.

As development takes place, less arable land remains available for food production at the same time that the need for food grows. Man must learn to make better use of his land and environment.

Toole, Kenneth R. The Rape of the Great Plains: Northwest America, Cattle and Coal. Boston: Little, Brown. 1976.

Documents environmental degradation caused by strip miners and cattle grazers in the western United States. Calls for conservation of grasslands and forests instead of indiscriminate economic exploitation of land.

Periodicals Worth Exploring

American Forests
Ecology Law Quarterly
Environment
Environmental Affairs
Environment and Behavior
Journal of Physical Education & Recreation
National Wildlife
Natural History
Oceans

624 Real Estate Review
Resources

II. Population

Brown, Lester R., Patricia McGrath, and Bruce Stokes. Twenty-two Dimensions of the Population Problem. Washington, D.C.: Worldwatch Institute. 1976.

One of the papers (#5) briefly summarizes 22 aspects of population growth, from climate change to water.

Freedman, Jonathan. Crowding and Behavior. New York: Viking Press. 1975.

Draws upon years of studying crowding in cities and finds that many variables affect people's reaction to high density of population. Concludes that crowding may not be as harmful to people as we often assume.

Kahn, Herman, William Brown, and Leon Martel. The Next 200 Years. New York: Morrow. 1976.

A plausible scenario for a growth world leading to plenty and prosperity. Authors feel that the current world-population rise is temporary and see 15 billion persons, and better living for all, by the year 2176.

Overbeek, Johannes. The Population Challenge: A Handbook for Nonspecialists. Westport, Conn.: Greenwood Press. 1976.

An interdisciplinary analysis of past, present, and future population growth, its determinants, and consequences. Focus is upon international problems: world food supply, overpopulation as a cause of war, energy and environment, economic growth, and aid to less-developed nations.

Population Reference Bureau. World Population Growth and Response: 1965–1975. A Decade of Global Action. Washington, D.C. 1976.

A valuable document covering population changes, policy actions, and program developments. Students and teachers can use it as a sourcebook for every nation of the world, including the United States.

Periodicals Worth Exploring

Demography

Development and Change
Growth and Change
Interchange
Population Studies
UN Chronicle
UNESCO Courier

Summary and Conclusions

In 1140 the little town of Weinsberg, Germany, was conquered by foreign invaders, who were ready to slaughter all the men of the village, with the women and children to be exiled. The commander of the enemy forces told the women that they could leave and carry away on their backs their most treasured and valuable possessions. The women looked at and rejected a wide variety of material goods. Then the women began to walk out of the town carrying on their backs their husbands, fathers, or brothers. The women of Weinsberg chose to be more concerned about people than possessions (Roselle, January 1976: 5).

Perhaps the social problems we have discussed and analyzed are primarily the results of our values and norms. Perhaps some social problems persist because of values—such as material wealth and success—that emphasize material goods rather than concern about people. Some evidence suggests that a new value system has begun to emerge among the young and will eventually affect even our older generations (Yankelovich, 1974: 5-11). A people-oriented value system could remedy some social problems, such as poverty and minority discrimination. But such a change in our value system must be translated into new social structures and social institutions to cope effectively with a myriad of social problems.

Throughout this book, we have attempted to show the many different ways social problems are perceived and different solutions proposed. Using a wide variety of sociological theories, from labeling to structural change, we presented perspectives of conservatives, liberals, and radicals.

These were not just ideologies about the political structure but reflected basic values and beliefs about society, the social order, and how social problems should be solved. We noted that all social problems occur and are experienced on three levels: the personal, the group, and the institutional level. We have looked at problems of crime and administration of justice, drugs and alcohol, and the family and sex-role behavior, recognizing that the individual's attempts to cope with his problems often become public or social issues. Groups interacting in their immediate milieu and relating with one another expose them to a wide variety of urban problems from poverty and discrimination to the concerns of the aging and the elderly. Social institutions, set up initially to solve or prevent social problems, sometime produce or exacerbate such problems for millions of persons, as we saw from the effects of education, the economic institutions, and our systems of medical and mental-health care. International dimensions of social issues became obvious as we explored the social institutions and issues of big government as well as of the military's influence and of ecology and population.

A fitting way to close would be to see what conclusions we can draw from our analysis of social problems and of their future.

CONCLUSIONS

The social problems we have examined are often not as discrete or separate as chapter headings might lead us to believe. For example, certain material on school busing for purposes of racial desegregation could have been analyzed in discussing the problems of education. Or we might have discussed job discrimination against women in the chapter on work. Social problems outside textbooks are often interwoven with numerous other issues. For example, like a color-coded wire that runs through the entire complex of an electrical panel, we could trace our *black* color-coded social wire through areas of crime, mental illness, drugs and alcohol, the family, work and unemployment, education, population, environment, urban and suburban problems, aging, health care, poverty, racism, the government and its spending, and other national and international problems. So the first conclusion we must draw about social problems overall is that they are all interrelated and interconnected *because* society itself is structured and organized in ways that produce social institutions, groups, and people that are socially interrelated and interconnected.

As long as different and competing groups exist in our society, we will always have different and conflicting definitions of all social problems, as we have illustrated in every chapter. It is equally important to remember that different definitions of the problem inexorably lead to conflicting solutions. As a matter of fact, in attempting to solve one social problem, we might unexpectedly add to or create another. For example, to alleviate hunger at home and abroad, we encouraged our farmers to increase their use of modern technology, such as gas-driven farm vehicles and chemical fertilizers. Although we have made good progress in supplying needy nations with food, we have developed an agricultural industry highly dependent on imported oil and large amounts of electricity. Also, our use of fertilizers may have helped us to grow more food per acre, but they are eventually washed into our streams and rivers, thereby adding to the chemical pollution of our water. So often proposed solutions to existing social problems cause new social problems.

We have created a social structure whose nature and magnitude we do not fully appreciate. The realities of our society and its institutions—especially their size and magnitude—are not quite comprehensible to our limited minds and life experiences. Just a few examples will suffice.

> In 1976 the United States put two unmanned space vehicles on the surface of our "neighboring" planet Mars, about 230 million miles from earth.
>
> Our national debt should soon reach one trillion dollars.
>
> One nuclear bomb has the explosive force of 20 megatons, equal to 20 million tons of TNT.

All of these facts or occurrences have been produced by our technology and social structure; they are hard to experience concretely or even imagine. Social philosopher Gunther Anders has summarized this situation:

> The basic dilemma of our age is that "We are smaller than ourselves," incapable of mentally realizing the realities which we ourselves have produced. Therefore we might call ourselves "inverted Utopians": while ordinary Utopians are unable to actually produce what they are able to visualize, we are unable to visualize what we are actually producing. . . .
>
> This inverted Utopianism is not simply one fact among many, but the outstanding one, for it defines the moral situation of man today. The dualism to which we are sentenced is . . . our capacity to produce as opposed to our power to imagine (1971: 174).

This is not only the *moral* situation of humans today, but also the *social* situation in which we live today. Our ability to conceive of and imagine the scope and scale of our social problems lags behind the reality of our problems.

Such a situation of not being able to fully grasp reality is accompanied by a separation of problem-definers from the problem itself. For example, some urban planner sitting in his comfortable office on the 25th floor of an air-conditioned high rise in the city (and living in a grass-covered suburban community where homes must be built on at least five acres of land) may make grandiose plans to change the face of the city by tearing down the old apartment buildings in neighborhoods the planner defines as blighted. But the black mother with four children living on welfare in a third-floor flat of the urban ghetto may have a different notion of how the city should be changed. While the planner might think in terms of getting rid of those ghetto third-floor flats, she might be thinking of that apartment as an economical, comfortable, and convenient home.

The point here is that neither the urban planner nor the black welfare mother has really any *firsthand* exposure to, or experience of, what the other's life is like. They live literally in separate worlds, and make decisions and form opinions without ever *once* seeing, smelling, feeling, or being in *physical contact* with the social reality of the other. Distance (physical and social) separates us all in our mass society. Our statistical knowledge and theories of how to spot and solve social problems become reified (abstract) instead of becoming acquainted with *the realities* of the social problem.

This example leads us to one further conclusion. Often the "solutions" offered for our problems involve new laws or better enforcement or funding of existing laws. This is not to deny that laws are helpful to a point in addressing social ills. The conclusion here, however, is that laws in and of themselves cannot solve social problems. For example, passage of the open-housing laws in the 1960s has not produced a racially integrated society. Outlawing certain acts as illegal has not remedied the problems of crime or delinquency. If we are to solve a problem, the people themselves, whenever and wherever possible, must prevent or work to alleviate them before they become too big to handle.

Overreliance on the federal government to solve all our social ills is not only unwise, but also unnecessary in some cases (Doughton, 1976). Society, not the state, must dominate the efforts to control and cure our social ills.

OUTLOOK FOR THE FUTURE

What about the future? Sociologist Arthur Shostak has offered some cogent, well-informed forecasts of what our social-reform agenda will look like tomorrow.* He sees five new developments:

1. The social-reform agenda in the next decade will differ substantially from anything in recent decades. Because of our declining population growth, the emphasis will shift from quantity to quality (large-scale programs funded by large budgets will be fewer). We will worry less about "how much" and worry more about "how." This will require a switch from government by program (or propaganda) to government by policy (or planning).

---

*The five forecasts that follow, as well as the reasons behind them, were originally formulated by Arthur Shostak and published as "Tomorrow's Reform Agenda," in the June 1973 issue of *The Futurist*, pp. 107–10.

2. The social-reform agenda in the next decade will be far more varied and eclectic. America frequently seeks novel approaches to problems of all kinds. A new international diffusion of ideas will be evident in the years ahead. Interest in the British system of drug maintenance and national health insurance has long intrigued social reformers and sociologists, if not the AMA. Ideas from the Israeli childcare approach, and little-publicized Japanese psychiatric (Morita) techniques and Canadian-European children's allowances might be adapted to America's needs in solving some of our social ills.
3. We will probably adopt fewer reforms in the near future than in the recent past. Two reasons explain this probable reaction. First, there is public and political disillusionment with the meager progress in overcoming such problems as poverty and discrimination. Second, because of widespread economic inflation, taxpayers, businessmen, and politicians are demanding "exacting cost-benefit analyses" of the various proposals for solving a problem.
4. Nearly all reforms that seek adoption will have to meet unprecedented computer-based tests. Proposals will increasingly be subjected to computer-simulation tests, which will be more precise, revealing, and exacting than any previous preliminary hurdle. Proposals also will be subjected to social-accounting or social-indicator evaluation. Progress has already been made on electronically gathering, storing, linking, and reporting social data, and the computer will dominate this effort in the future. Whether or not the United States sets up a national data inventory (or a five-year census), everyone is likely to know much more about each other. Such data banks and inventories will be at the fingertips of policy-makers to help them set priorities and choose among different plans to ameliorate our social problems. There are, of course, dangers in use of the computer, since even the most sophisticated computer simulations or evaluations are no better than the underlying assumptions of the human evaluator and the field data fed into the computer.
5. The lion's share of an evolving social-reform agenda will go—for the first time—to the private sector. If the public and Congress cut back on or prohibit further expansion of the federal government into solving social problems, we might turn to the private corporate structure as a means of dealing with such problems. As corporations need to find diverse investment and profit opportunities, some money from the federal government will be welcome, though most will be private funds. Whether private corporations can do as well as public agencies in solving social problems is still an open question.

If these five forecasts become reality, sociologists and other academics who formulate the theories and ideas about social problems will be required to produce more and better information and insights. They will also have greater opportunity to try innovative ideas in solving social problems. This should give us all reason for hope that we can do better in handling some of our social problems in the future.

Whatever the future may hold for society and its problems, sociologists are preparing to deal with whatever alternatives might arise. They are doing so through the methods of "futuristics"—various ways and means of gauging the future and making suggestions for retaining or changing social trends and social structures. There are distinct advantages for using futuristics as a way of anticipating society's future. Among other things, futuristics can help to

> identify new policy options
> identify important variables in a situation
> assign probabilities to various future events
> provide an early-warning system for social problems
> spot new opportunities in social and community development
> bring coherence to social policies that might otherwise be uneven, contradictory, or counterproductive
> raise the level of political dialogue in America, helping citizens to think in longer time perspectives (Shostak, April 9, 1976: 8).

Our hope is that sociologists will continue not only to analyze or envision a better future for all societies, but also to play an important role in creating such societies by pointing out the dangers and possibilities that lie ahead.

As C. Wright Mills stated:

> "Man's chief danger" today lies in the unruly forces of contemporary society itself, with its alienating methods of production, its enveloping techniques of political domination, its international anarchy—in a word, its pervasive transformation of the very "nature" of man and the conditions and aims of his life (1959: 13).

It is sociology's great promise and legacy to continually point out man's chief dangers and to seek to understand and overcome them.

REFERENCES

Anders, Gunther
 1971 "Theses for the Atomic Age." Pp. 172–81 in Bernard Rosenberg, Israel Gerver, and F. William Howton, eds. Mass Society in Crisis: Social Problems and Social Pathology. New York: Macmillan.

Doughton, Morgan J.
 1976 People Power: An Alternative to 1984. Bethlehem, Pa.: Media America.

Mills, C. Wright
   1959 The Sociological Imagination. New York: Oxford University Press.

Roselle, Daniel, ed.
   1976 "Wisdom of the Women of Weinsberg: Editorial Reflections." Social Education 40, 1 (January): 5.

Shostak, Arthur B.
   1973 "Tomorrow's Reform Agenda." The Futurist (June): 107–10.
   1976 "Looking into an Uncertain Future: Some Means, Problems and Possibilities." Paper delivered at 1975–76 Indiana-Michigan Conference of Danforth Associates (April 9), mimeographed.

Yankelovich, Daniel
   1974 The New Morality: A Profile of American Youth in the 70s. New York: McGraw-Hill.

SUGGESTED READINGS

Bell, Daniel. The Cultural Contradictions of Capitalism. New York: Basic Books. 1976.
> A book based on this leading intellectual's essays about culture, education, and politics in the past decade.

Kristol, Irving, and Paul Weaver, eds. The Americans: 1976. Lexington, Mass.: Lexington Books. 1976.
> Examines basic attitudes toward American institutions, including education and the role of the family. Recounts and reflects upon basic norms, values, and beliefs of modern society.

Rosen, Stephen. Future Facts: A Forecast of the World As We Will Know It Before the End of the Century. New York: Simon & Schuster. 1976.
> Based on the premise that future innovations and systems can be observed now in the embryonic state. Our observations should prepare us to accept and use these new social systems.

Periodicals Worth Exploring

American Journal of Sociology
American Scholar
American Sociological Review
Annals of the American Academy of Political and Social Science
The Center Magazine
Current History
The Gallup Opinion Index
Intellect
Public Interest
Saturday Review
Science
Scientific American
Social Forces
Social Problems
Social Service Review
Social Security Bulletin
Social Work
Society
Sociological Inquiry
Sociological Quarterly
Working Papers for a New Society

Index

Abbot, William, 495
Abelson, Philip, 453
abortion, 8, 147
Accelerated Rehabilitative Disposition (ARD), 64
ACTION, 334
Adams, Henry, 191
Adams, Paul, 498
affective psychoses, 495
affirmative-action programs, 295–96
affluence, ecology and, 587
After Divorce (Goode), 145
aftercare services, 37
Age Discrimination Employment Act, 331
ageism, 319–20
Agency for International Development (AID), 602
aggravated assault, 27, 28, 29
aging, *see* elderly
Aid to Families of Dependent Children (AFDC), 247, 248
air pollution, 548, 580–82, 588–90
Al-Anon, 117
Albert Einstein Medical College, 451
Alcohol, Drug Abuse, and Mental Health Administration, 519
alcohol use and abuse, 87–89, 106–21
   Alcoholics Anonymous (AA) and, 113, 116–17
   causes of, 114–15
   classification of disorders, 107
   classification of drinkers, 107–8
   cost of, 95
   defining, 106–10
   detoxification, 116
   family's role in rehabilitation, 115–16
   future of, 118–20
   halfway houses and, 117–18
   illnesses and deaths from, 95, 113, 114
   incidence of, 93, 110–14
   information programs and, 118
   as latent social problem, 4
   legal definitions of alcoholism, 110
   polydrug use and, 95
   prevalence of, 110–14
   proposed solutions to, 115–18
   social factors and, 112–14
   socialization to accept alcohol, 108–9
   treatment centers and, 117–18
   among youth, 110–12, 119
alcoholic psychoses, 107
Alcoholics Anonymous (AA), 113, 116–17
alienation from work, 401–2
Allport, Gordon, 270
Alpern, David, 535, 540
Althoff, Phillip, 577
Alvarez, Rodolfo, 282, 283
America, Inc. (Mintz and Cohen), 397–98
American Automobile Association, 202
American Bar Association, 56, 63
American Drugstore: A (Alcohol) to V (Valium). (Fort and Cory), 85
American Federation of State, County, and Municipal Employees, 211
American Indians, 269
   defining problem of, 268
   drug abuse by, 98–99
   education and, 360
   health care and, 456, 464
   institutional racism against, 284–85
   population of, 284, 297
   unemployment of, 284
American Journal of Psychiatry, 513
American Medical Association, 116, 447, 474
American Psychiatric Association, 107
American Society: Problems of Structure (Turner), 60
amphetamines, 86, 87, 512–13
Anders, Gunther, 629
Anderson, Jack, 198
anomie (strain) theory, 33, 133, 510–11
Anslinger, Harry J., 86
antabuse, 115
antagonist drugs, 103
antidepressants, 86, 87
antitrust laws, 39, 421
Apache Indians, 284–85, 330
apathy, bystander, 195–96
Arms Control and Disarmament Act of 1975, 558
Arms Control and Disarmament Agency, 558
arms race, 546–47, 557–58, 565–67
arrest statistics, 29–31, 48
Ashford, Nicholas, 409
Asians, 269, 273
Aspin, Les, 470, 534–35
Associated Press, 544
Associated Women for a Better Community, 158
Astin, Alexander, 368
athletic programs, 37, 39
Atkinson, A. B., 231–32
Atlanta, Ga., 31, 212
Attica State Prison, 58, 66
Auerbach, Stuart, 470
auto theft, 27, 28, 29
automation, 407–9, 418–19

635

INDEX

automobiles, 197–98, 202, 214, 217–18
aversion therapy, 119–20

Bachman, 362
Bachrach, Leona, 113
back-to-basics movement in education, 371
bail system, 51, 56–57
Baker, Russell, 25
Bakke, Allen, 269
balanced-system definition of ecology, 578
Baldi de Mandilovitch, Martha S., 403
Baldwin, Tom, 200
Bales, Robert, 131, 134
Baltimore, Md., 31
Banfield, Edward C., 191–92, 235, 276–77, 289
Baran, Paul, 428
Barber, Bob, 69
barbiturates, 86, 87, 88, 94, 95
Bateson, Gregory, 508–9
Baton Rouge, La., 212
Bean, L. L., 504
Becker, Howard, 34–35, 86
Beckerman, Wilfred, 579, 595
Beers, Clifford, 493
Beeson, Diane, 326
behavior modification, 58–59 68, 515
Bell, Daniel, 415, 428–29, 448, 548, 549, 564–65
Bell, Robert, 149
Berelson, Bernard, 598
Berg, Ivar, 351
Berger, Briggitte, 401, 426
Bergin, Allen, 514
Bergquist, William A., 368
Berkov, Beth, 144, 146
Bern, Sandra, 139
Bernstein, Arnold, 89
Bernstein, Jerrold, 120
Berry, David, 7
Best and the Brightest, The (Halberstam), 540
Biderman, Albert, 42
big-brother programs, 37
biochemical theories of mental illness, 507–8
biological theories of crime and criminals, 32
biomedical engineering, 475–77
Birch, David, 193
birth rates, 146–47, 599, 600, 603, 604, 610
bisexuals, 140
Bishop, George, 272

blacks
  busing and, 291–94
  causes of problems of, 286–90
  defining problems of, 267–72
  drug abuse by, 98–99
  education and, 240, 246, 279–80, 291–94, 359–60, 363–66
  future of problems of, 297–300
  health care and, 275–76, 456–57, 463–65
  housing and, 280–81
  illiteracy rates of, 360
  income of, 254–55, 276–77
  institutional racism and, 272
  job dissatisfaction among, 403
  job inequality and, 411–12
  life expectancy for, 463–64
  mental-illness labeling and, 504
  movement into cities, 273–75
  occupations of, 277–79
  police and, 48, 55
  political progress of, 281
  population of, 272–73, 297–98
  poverty and, 239–41, 254–55, 276
  in prison, 57
  unemployment of, 277, 414
  urban problems and, 194, 195, 199
Blair, John M., 421
Blake, Elinor, 468
Blane, H. T., 107
Blaxall, Martha, 152
Bloss, Mary E., 499
Blue Collar Aristocrats (LeMasters), 406
Blue Collar Life (Shostak), 405
Blue Cross, 451–52, 455, 466, 468, 469
Blum, Richard, 97
Blumenthal, David, 447, 455, 472
Blumstein, Alfred, 93
Bodenheimer, Thomas, 468
Boren, Jerry, 10, 11, 396
Bornemeier, Walter, 454
Bouma, Donald, 62
Bouvier, Leon, 42, 320, 326, 334, 599
Bradly, Nelson, 115–16
Bradshaw, Janice, 245
Braito, Rita, 245, 247
Brantingham, Paul, 36, 37
Braude, Lee, 402
Braun, Robert, 369
Brecher, Edward, 100
Breggin, Peter, 514
Brenner, Harvey, 511
bribes, 26
Brinton, William, 611
Brodeur, Paul, 410

Brodsky, Archie, 87
Brody, Elaine, 320
Brody, Jane E., 455, 463
Brody, Stanley J., 320
Bromberg, Myron, 461
Bronfenbrenner, Urie, 133, 156
Brookings Institution, 197, 559–60
Broom, Leonard, 232
Brower, Jonathan, 271
Brown, Bertram, 519
Brown, Claude, 97
Brown, Lester R., 603
Brown, Sidney, 582
Buchen, Irvin, 431
bureaucracy, 537, 539–41
  conservative perspective of, 532
  education and, 366–67, 371–72, 380–81
  future, 565
  growth of, 549–50
  liberal perspective of, 532–33
Burger, Robert, 324
Burger, Warren, 65
Burgess, Ernest, 189
burglary, 27, 28, 29, 113
Burnham, David, 411
Burns, Arthur, 427
bus transportation, 202, 203, 204, 218
busing issue, 291–94
Buss, Arnold, 493, 495
Buss, Edith H., 495
Butler, Robert, 315, 316, 326
bystander apathy, 195–96

Cadwallader, Mervyn, 134
caffeine, 89
Calhoun, John B., 195
California, University of, at Davis, California, 468
Campbell, Angus C., 287, 404
Camenietzki, Schalom, 495
Candy, Sandra, 327
Cardozo, Arlene Rossen, 132
Carlson, Norman, 61
Carlson, Rick J., 453, 465
Carnegie, Andrew, 242
Carnegie Commission on Higher Education, 154, 473
Carnegie Council on Policy Studies in Higher Education, 375, 377
Carter, Genevieve, 242
Carter, Jimmy, 558, 559
Carter Administration, 248, 249, 471
Case Western Reserve, 451
caseworkers, 39

636

INDEX

Casper, Jonathan, 52, 65
Cassady, Margie, 146
Cassidy, Joseph, 402
Castro, Bob, 283
catatonic schizophrenia, 494–95
Cathcart, John, 324, 328
Caudill, Harry, 246
Cavender, Chris C., 288
Census, U.S. Bureau of, 30, 146, 149, 200, 237, 240, 273, 274, 279, 282, 297, 326, 357, 359, 360, 375, 600
Center for the Study of Public Policy, 370
Center for the Study of Responsible Law, 556
Central Intelligence Agency (CIA), 24
centralization versus decentralization of government, 553
Ceylon, 605
Chafe, William, 157, 158
Chafetz, M. E., 107
challengers' views of family structure, 133–36, 141–43
Chambers, Carl, 107–8, 109n
charity, 37
Chein, Isidor, 97
chemotherapy, 512–13
Chevigny, Paul, 48
Chicago, Ill., 31, 211
Chicanos, *see* Spanish-Americans
childless (urban type), 190
"Children of the Law," 28
Chilman, Catherine, 245
China, People's Republic of, 597, 603, 608, 611
Chit Chat Farms, 115
chronic undifferentiated schizophrenia, 495
Churchill, Neil, 295
cities, *see* urban and suburban problems
Civil Rights Act of 1964, 166, 269, 295
Civil Rights Commission, 284, 292–93
Clean Air Act amendments, 588, 592
Cleveland, Ohio, 31, 212
Cloward, Richard A., 33–35, 246
Club of Rome Report, 594, 595
Coale, Ansley, 604
cocaine, 86–88, 93
Cocozza, Joseph, 517
codetermination, 424–25
cohabitation, 148–49, 164–65
Cohen, Albert, 35
Cohen, Jerry S., 397–98, 409, 420–21

Cohn, Victor, 582
Coleman, James S., 293–94, 362–64
Coles, Robert, 366
colleges
 enrollment in, 356, 375–77
 financial outlook for, 377
 funding for, 368–69
 proposed solutions to problems of, 374–75
 see also education
Columbia, Md., 209
Columbus, Ohio, 212
Comer, James, 415, 416
Coming of Age, The (de Beauvoir), 316
Commission on Civil Rights, 283
Commission on Non-Traditional Studies, 368
Committee for the Study of Incarceration, 64
Commoner, Barry, 578–80, 584, 585
communal families, 164
community-based corrections, 66–67
community health programs, 515–17
Community Mental Health Centers Act, 519
community relations, police and, 60
community service, future jobs in, 432–33
Comprehensive Employment and Training Act (CETA) of 1973, 251
Conant, James, 364
conflict theory
 changes in family structure and sex roles and, 156–58
 education and, 362
 focus of, 7
 work system and, 416–17
Congress, reform of, 554–55
Congressional Special Committee on Aging, 315
Conquest House, 101
Conrad, Peter, 465
consciousness raising, 167–69
conservation, 433–34, 592–94
conservative ideology
 administration of justice and, 45, 47, 52
 alcohol use and abuse and, 115, 118
 characteristics of, 10
 corporate power and, 396–97, 428–29
 crime and, 27, 36, 38, 39

drug use and abuse and, 86, 103
ecology and, 577
education and, 352, 362
the elderly and, 316–17, 331
family structure and, 132–33, 139–40
government and, 532, 552–55
health care and, 453
minorities and, 267–68, 290, 296
population growth and, 598, 607, 608
poverty and, 242–45, 251–53
urban and suburban problems and, 191–92, 208–10
work and, 405, 422–29
Consumer Protection Agency (CPA), 555
Consumers of Abundance (Piel), 426
control theory, 35–36
"Controversy," 38
Converse, Philip E., 404
Cooley, Charles, 191
Cooper, Theodore, 453
cooperatives, 420
Cornell University, 424, 463, 504
corporate power
 causes of problems, 418–19
 defining, 393–97
 economic concentration, 397–99, 418–19
 education and, 355–56
 government and, 394–96, 399–400, 420–21
 incidence of problems, 397–400
 military and, 394, 395
 prevalence of problems, 397–400
 proposed solutions to problems, 419–29
correctional volunteers, 37
corruption, police, 49
Cory, Christopher, 85, 95, 105, 111
Coser, Lewis, 235
cosmopolites (urban type), 190
Council on Environmental Quality, 584–85
"Council on Foreign Relations," 540
Councils of Governments (COGs), 212
counselors, 39
counterculture, drug, 86–87
courts
 bail system, 51, 56–57
 causes of problems, 59–61
 defining problems of, 49–52
 equality for women and, 167

637

INDEX

courts *(cont.)*
  future of, 68
  improvement of, 63-65
  incidence and prevalence of problems, 56-57
  plea bargaining, 51
  sentencing, 51-52, 60-61, 67
  treatment of poor and minorities, 49-50
Cousteau, Jacques, 583
Crewdson, Prudence, 555
crime, 23-44
  causes of, 31-36
  defining, 23-28
  future of, 42-43
  handgun control, 38, 40-41
  incidence of, 28-31
  as manifest social problem, 4
  police technology and, 39
  prevalence of, 28-31
  primary, secondary, and tertiary prevention and, 36-38
  proposed solutions to, 36-42
  recent stabilization of, 28-31
  relative definitions of, 23-24
  subcultures and, 28, 35
  theories of, 32-36
  types of, 24-27
  uniform laws and, 36
crime-location analysis, 37
"Crime Wave, The," 29-30
criminal-residence study, 37
Crisis in the Classroom (Silberman), 364
crowding, 57, 194-95, 201
cubic day, 424
Culliton, Barbara, 519
Cultural Contradictions of Capitalism, The (Bell), 415
cultural lag, 3, 417
culture of poverty, 243-45
Current Population Reports, 297
Currie, Elliott, 203
Cutler, Neal, 316

Dallas, Tex., 31, 218
Daniels, Roger, 272
Davis, Kingsley, 140-41, 613
Davison, Gerald, 515
Daytop Village, 101
de Beauvoir, Simone, 316
Deans, Ralph C., 405
Death at an Early Age (Kozol), 364
death rates, 603-6, 610
deaths, drug-induced, 94-95
decentralization
  of control over education, 373-74
  of government, 551-53
  decision making, shared, 424-25
Decter, Midge, 136, 161
defenders' views of family structure, 132-33, 136, 139-43, 147
Defense, Department of, 394, 399, 546
defense contracts, 395
defense spending, 534-35, 544-46, 553, 565-66
DeFunis, Marco, 269
delinquency, *see* crime
delinquency-specific social activities, 37
Dembart, Lee, 409
democracy versus security, 553
Democratic Socialism, 419-20
demogrant, 251-52
Dennis, Rugledge M., 271
Dennis, Wayne, 316
Denver, Colo., 31, 212, 218
dependent personality, 96-97
depressant drugs, 86, 87
DeRonde, Glen, 269
"deschooling" society, 372-73
detoxification, 116
Detroit, Mich., 31, 366, 581
deviant behavior theory, 8
Dewey, John, 191, 352
Diagnostic and Statistical Manual of Disorders, 107
differential-association theory, 33
differential-opportunities theory, 33-34
discrimination, 287-88
  defined, 270-71
  in education, 363-66
  in employment, 277, 278, 295
  by police, 48
  reverse, 268-69
  against women, 48, 151-54
  in union membership, 277, 278
disease-medical model of mental illness, 492-95
diversion from juvenile penal system, 39, 40
divorce, 144-46, 169
doctors, *see* health care; mental illness
Dixon, John, 597
Dohrenwald, Barbara, 500
Dohrenwald, Bruce, 500
Dolbeare, Kenneth M., 393, 428
Dolbeare, Patricia, 393, 428
Dole, Vincent, 103
Doll, William, 500
Domestic Council Drug Abuse Task Force, 105
Domhoff, G. William, 540
Dommel, Paul, 554
Donabedian, Avedis, 463
Donaldson, Ken, 499
Douglas, Jack, 231-33
Douthal, Strat, 47, 57
downwardly mobile (urban type), 190-91
Doyle, James, 69
Doyle, Nancy, 137, 154, 167
drinking, *see* alcohol use and abuse
drug-fiend definition of drug problem, 86, 89
drug use and abuse, 85-106
  antagonist drugs and, 103
  causes of, 96-100
  cost of, 95-96
  defining, 85-91
  drug-fiend definition of, 86, 89
  drug-induced illnesses and deaths, 94-95
  elements of, 90-91
  future of, 105-6
  heroin, 86-88, 93-95, 97, 106
  incidence of, 91-96
  marijuana, 8, 86-88, 91, 93, 95, 100, 104-6
  marijuana laws, 105
  methadone maintenance, 102-3
  outpatient treatment, 102
  personality factors in, 96-97
  pleasure and, 100
  polydrugs, 95
  prevalence of, 91-96
  proposed solutions to, 100-105
  social factors in, 97-100
  terminology, 85-90
  therapeutic communities and, 101
  total-drug-culture definition of, 87, 89-90
  types of drugs, 85-90
  youth-subculture definition of, 86-87, 89
Duberman, Lucile, 138, 163, 165, 169
Dubos, Rene J., 589
Dunham, 503
Dunnette, Marvin D., 431, 432
Dupont, Robert L., 93
Durkheim, Emile, 33

ecology, 577-97
  air pollution, 548, 580-82, 588-90

INDEX

balanced-system definition of, 578
causes of problems, 585-87
change in product technology and, 587
conservation of resources, 592, 594
defining problem of, 577-79
exhaustion of resources, 583-85, 590
future of environment, 594-97
incidence of problems, 579-85
new awareness of, 578-79
new sources of energy, 592-94
population growth and, 586-87
prevalence of problems, 579-85
proposed solutions to problems, 587-94
solid waste disposal, 548, 583-84
spread of industrialization and affluence and, 587
water pollution, 548, 582-83, 588-90
economic concentration, 397-99, 418-19
Edson, Lee, 582
education
 alcohol abuse and, 118-19
 American Indians and, 360
 back-to-basics movement in, 371
 blacks and, 240, 246, 279-80, 291-94, 359-60, 363-66
 bureaucracy and, 366-67, 371-72, 380-81
 busing and, 291-94
 causes of problems, 361-69
 conflicting values and, 362
 "deschooling" society, 372-73
 discrimination in, 363-66
 funding for, 367-69, 375, 377
 future jobs in, 432
 future of problems, 375-81
 metropolitanism in, 563
 poverty and, 240
 power and control over, 355-56, 373-74
 proposed solutions to problems, 369-75
 rising expectations and, 362-63
 Spanish-Americans and, 240, 282-83, 366
 voucher system and, 369-71
educational intervention programs, 37
Ehrenreich, Barbara, 454, 456, 457
Ehrenreich, John, 454, 456

Ehrlich, Anne H., 582, 583, 585, 587
Ehrlich, George, 477
Ehrlich, Isaac, 33
Ehrlich, Paul R., 582-85, 587, 598, 601
elderly, 313-39
 ageism and, 319-20
 attitudes toward, 317-19, 329-30
 causes of problems, 328-31
 defining problems of, 313-25
 economic plight of, 326, 327
 future of problems, 335-39
 health care for, 322
 housing for, 321-22, 333-34
 incidence of problems, 325-28
 income of, 320-21
 life expectancy and, 330-31, 335-36
 LIFE, program for, 333
 Meals-on-Wheels programs for, 333
 myths about, 313-17
 nursing homes and, 322-24, 326-28, 332-33
 population of, 325-26, 337
 poverty and, 240, 326
 prevalence of problems, 325-28
 proposed solutions to problems, 331-35
 retirement and, 313, 331-32, 336, 338
 social conditions of, 320-25
 Social Security System and, 239, 240, 253, 313, 319, 326, 331, 332, 337-38
 transportation for, 325, 334
electric shock therapy, 119-20, 513-14
Elesh, David, 242
Ellul, Jacques, 550
Emergency Employment Act of 1971, 427
Emerson, Ralph Waldo, 191
employee screening, 37
employment
 discrimination in, 277, 278, 295
 government, 536-37
 see also work
employment programs, 250-51
encounter groups, 115
End of Medicine, The (Carlson), 465
Endicott, Kenneth, 454, 464
Endres, Michael E., 336
energy
 future supplies of, 595
 new sources of, 592, 594

Energy Research and Development Administration (ERDA), 593-94
Ensminger, Barry, 468, 475
entitlement concept, 417
environmental conditions, drug abuse and, 98-99
environmental pollution, *see* ecology
Environmental Protection Agency (EPA), 411, 581, 588-89
Environmental Quality Index, 589, 592
Equal Employment Opportunity Act of 1972, 295
Equal Employment Opportunities Commission (EEOC), 167, 272
Equal Rights Amendment (ERA), 139, 166
Equality of Educational Opportunity (Coleman), 363-64
ethnic villagers, 190
Etzioni, Amitai, 550, 558
Evans, Linda, 10, 11, 396
executives, crimes of, 24-26
"experimenting society," 556-57
extramarital affairs, 149-50

Faherty, Robert L., 284
Fellows, James, 447, 455, 472
family, 131-74
 alternative forms of, 163-65
 birth rates, 146-47, 599, 600, 603, 604, 610
 causes of changes in, 154-59
 challengers' views of, 133-36, 141-43
 contemporary marriages, 134-35
 defenders' views of, 132-33, 136, 139-43, 147
 defining changes in, 131-42
 divorce and, 144-46, 169
 extramarital affairs and, 149-50
 future changes in, 169-70
 illegitimacy and, 146-47
 incidence of changes in, 142-51
 marriage rates, 143-44
 motherhood, 135-36
 prevalence of changes in, 142-51
 proposed solutions to changes in, 159-65
 role in alcoholic rehabilitation, 115-16

639

family (cont.)
  sex roles and, *see* sex roles
  working mothers, 150-51
family interaction, 508-9
family planning, 598, 608-9
Farson, Richard D., 173
Faust, Frederic, 36, 37
Fava, Sylvia F., 198
Federal-Aid Highway Act of 1973, 213
Federal Bureau of Investigation (FBI), 24, 27, 28, 42
federal chartering of corporations, 420
Federal Communications Commission, 421
Federal Housing Administration (FHA), 193, 194
Federal Housing and Community Development Act of 1974, 207, 208
Federal Power Commission, 582
Federal Reserve Board, 251
Federal Trade Commission, 421
Federation of State Medical Boards, 463
Feminine Mystique, The (Friedan), 161
Ferleger, David, 544
Fernandez, Ronald, 399, 542
Fisher, E., 137
Flanagan, Richard, 504, 517, 519
Florida, University of, 463
Florman, Samuel, 405-7
Fogg, Susan, 472, 473
Food and Drug Administration (FDA), 421
food stamps, 248, 249, 540
Forbes, W. H., 453
forcible rape, 27, 28, 29
Ford, Barbara, 195
Ford, Gerald, 292, 545, 555
Ford Foundation, 424
Forest Service, 591
Forestell, Bill, 197
forests, 591
Forhman, Charles, 507
Fort, Joel, 85, 90, 95, 105, 110, 111, 113, 114
Fortune, 577
Forward Plan for Health, 479
Francis, Polly, 315, 317
Freedman, Jonathan, 195
Freeman, Howard, 270, 289
Freidson, Eliot, 450
Freitag, Peter, 399, 542-43
Frejka, Tomas, 611
Freudian psychoanalysis, 508
Friedan, Betty, 157, 161
Friedberg, John, 513
Friedman, Robert, 271

Friedman, Rose, 232
Froelich, Warren, 585
Fromme, Lynette "Squeaky," 60-61
frustration-aggression theory, 32
Full Employment and Balance Growth Act of 1976, 250
Fuller, Richard, 3
functional psychoses, 494
Furstenberg, Frank, 131-32, 155

Gagnon, John H., 141, 171-72
Galbraith, John Kenneth, 232, 396, 398
Gallagher, Nora, 114
Gallup, George, 242
Gallup Poll, 113
gambling, 8
Gans, Herbert J., 190, 246
Gardner, John, 556
Gardner, Judy, 555
Garfinkle, Stuart, 153
Gault, Gerald, 24
Gavan, James D., 597
Gemeinschaft, 189
General Accounting Office (GAO), 324, 470
General Assistance (GA) programs, 247, 248
General Revenue Sharing (GRS), 554
Geological Survey, 590, 595
German, Deborah, 333
gerontology, 338
Gesellschaft, 189
Gibson, Robert, 322
Gilder, George, 132, 160, 161
Gillis, John, 514
Gist, Noel P., 198, 216
Gladwin, Thomas, 234, 235
Glaser, Daniel, 51, 98
Glazer, Nathan, 249, 269
Glenn, Norval, 316
Glick, Paul, 144, 145
Goffman, Erving, 497
Goldberg, Philip, 138-39
Goldmark, Peter, 215-16
Goldstein, Lee B., 145
Golenpaul, Ann, 273, 281
Golladay, Mary A., 368
Goode, William, 131-32, 144, 145, 155
Goodman, Mary Ellen, 286
Goodman, Robert, 159
Goodman, Walter, 293
Gottlieb, Jacques S., 507
Gove, Walter R., 510
government, 531-68
  bureaucracy, *see* bureaucracy

causes of problems, 547-53
complex mass society and, 548-49
Congress, proposal to reform, 554-55
conservative perspective of, 532
corporate power and, 394-96, 399-400, 420-21
decentralization versus centralization, 551-53
defining problems of, 532-35
developments in federal system, 562-63
education and, 355-56
employment, 536-37
"experimenting society" and, 556-57
future of, 562-67
general revenue sharing proposal, 554
incidence of problems, 535-47
lack of trust in, 535-36
liberal perspective of, 532-33
medical planning by, 479-80
mental illness and, 519
military's power and influence in, 553, 544-46
new elites in, 564-65
nuclear arms race and, 546-47, 557-58, 565-67
order versus liberty, 553
power elite and, 533, 540, 542-44
prevalence of problems, 535-47
proposed solutions to problems, 553-62
public interest groups and, 555-56
radical perspective of, 533
security versus democracy, 553
spending, 536-38
themes in, 563-64
urban and suburban problems and, 204, 210, 212
waste and, 532-35
government-owned enterprises, 420-21
Grambs, Jean d'resdes, 357
Grant, W. Vance, 356, 361
Greeley, Andrew M., 287
Green, Edward, 48
green space, preservation of, 206
Greenberg, Herbert, 402
Greene, Leonard, 252
Greene, Mark, 56
Griffin, Susan, 48
Grimes, John A., 194
Grimshaw, Allen, 271
Groder, Martin, 53

640

group marriage, 163–64
groupworkers, 39
Gruenstein, Peter, 535
guaranteed-income plans, 248
Gusfield, Joseph, 87, 158
Guthrie, Harold W., 254–55
Gutierrez, José Angel, 283

Halberstam, David, 540
halfway houses, 117–18
hallucinogens, 86, 87
Halsell, Grace, 273, 282
Hamilton, Charles V., 272, 281
Hammond, Allen L., 579
handgun control, 38, 40–41
Hardin, Garrett, 598
Harrington, Michael, 61, 231, 237, 243, 504
Harris, Louis, 55, 56, 317–19
Harris, Sydney, 531
Hart, Philip, 532, 555
Hartmann, Maria, 328–29
Harvard Medical School, 451
hashish, 86, 87, 91
Hays, Wayne, 535
Health, Education and Welfare, Department of, 295, 324, 327, 402, 473–75
health care, 447–80
  causes of problems, 465–70
  conservative views of, 453
  consumer-controlled systems for, 472
  consumers' views of, 454–56
  cost of, 455, 459
  defining problems of, 447–57
  doctor shortage and, 454–55, 458
  for the elderly, 322
  financial fraud and waste and, 469–70
  financing-planning complex, 451–52
  future jobs in, 433
  future problems of, 475–80
  health-maintenance organizations and, 472, 479
  idealized model of, 448–50
  incidence of problems, 458–65
  Medicaid-Medicare reform and, 473–74
  medical "empires," 451, 466–68
  medical-industrial complex, 452–53
  medical-school reform, 473
  minorities and, 275–76, 283, 456–57, 463–65

national health insurance and, 470–72
physical conditions of work and, 409–11
prevalence of problems, 458–65
proposed solutions to problems, 470–75
quality of, 455–57, 463
reality model of, 450, 466
regional health planning and, 474–75
structure and organization of system, 466–68
value system and, 465–66
see also mental illness
Health Insurance Plan (HIP), 472
health-maintenance organizations, 472, 479
Health Policy Advisory Center, 450, 452–53, 457, 472
health service areas (HSAs), 474, 475, 476
Heard, Alexander, 375
hebephrenic schizophrenia, 494
Hefner, Ted, 316
Heilbroner, Robert, 596
Henderson, Bruce, 141, 171–72
Henslin, James, 317
Herndon, James, 364
heroin, 86–88, 93–95, 97, 106
Herrick, Neal Q., 402
Herzberg, Frederick, 425
Hess, John, 474
Hess, Linda, 90
Heussenstamm, F. K., 24
Hickey, Joseph, 66–67
Hicks, Nancy, 292
Higher Circles, The (Domhoff), 399, 540
highway destruction of neighborhoods, 198
Hill, Margaret, 100
Hill, Robert, 275
Himes, Joseph S., 269
Hirschi, Travis, 35–36
Hofmann, Paul, 594
Holden, Constance, 53, 316
Holdren, John, 584
Holland, John, 189
Holt, John, 364
Holtzman, Elizabeth, 559, 560
home instruction, 378
homesteading, 208
homosexuality, 140–42, 172
Hoover, Eleanor, 149
Horn, Jack, 63
Horn, Patrice, 133, 145, 151, 156
Horner, Matina, 139
Horney, Karen, 511

Horowitz, Irving Louis, 205, 214
Horsley, Kathryn, 607
Horton, Paul B., 145, 194, 268, 458
hospitals, see health care; mental illness
Hotchkiss, Anita, 461
Hough, Joseph, 272
Hoult, Thomas Ford, 419
housing
  for blacks, 280–81
  crowding and, 194–95
  defining problems of, 193–94
  for the elderly, 321–22, 333–34
  future problems of, 216
  HUD programs for, 207–8
  institutional racism and, 289
  poverty and, 247
Housing and Community Development Act of 1974, 215
Housing and Urban Development, Department of (HUD), 207–9
Houston, Tex., 218
HOW (Happiness of Womanhood), 139
Howe, Louise Kapp, 158–59
Huber, Joan, 171
Hudson, Charles, 99
Humphrey, Hubert, 238
Humphrey-Hawkins Bill, 251
Hunt, Morton, 149
Hutton, William R., 333
Huyck, Margaret Hellie, 320
Hyer, Kathryn, 231, 233
Hyman, Herbert, 287

idealized model of health care, 448–50
ideologies, 10–11
  police, 60
  see also conservative ideology; liberal ideology; radical ideology
illegitimacy, 146–47
Illich, Ivan, 372–73
illiteracy, degree of, 360–61
illnesses, drug-induced, 94–95
income
  of blacks, 276–77
  distribution of, 238, 253, 254
  of the elderly, 320–21
  of Spanish-Americans, 276
income definition of poverty, 232, 233
income tax, negative, 248–50
India, 597, 609
Indian Removal Act of 1830, 284
Indianapolis, 212, 218

individualism, 242-43
individualistic conservatism, 10
industrialization
　ecology and, 587
　family structure and, 131, 154-56
　population growth and, 604
inequality, *see* poverty
Institute of Judicial Administration, 63
Institute for Research on Poverty, 244-45, 250
institutional education programs, 37
institutional racism, 271-72, 284-85, 288-89
institutional segregation, 319-20
Internal Revenue Service, 248
International Women's Year Conference, 608-9
involutional melancholia, 495

Jackson, Donald, 38, 52
Jacksonville, 212
Jacobs, James, 69
Jacobson, Lenore, 366
Jacoby, Neil, 577, 585
Jacoby, Susan, 324
James, Henry, 191
Japan, 559
Jefferson Hospital, 451
Jencks, Christopher, 362, 364
Jennings, William H., 245
Jensen, Arthur, 289
Jews, 269, 273, 299
job dissatisfaction, 402-5
job enrichment and enlargement, 422-24
job inequality, 411-12
jobs, creation of, 250-51
Johns Hopkins Hospital, 451, 498
Johnson, Lyndon B., 62
Johnson, Sheila K., 472
Johnston, William B., 408
Joint Commission on Hospital Accreditation, 456
Joint Economic Committee of the Congress, 419
Jonathan, Minnesota, 209
Jones, Charles, 554-55
Jones, Enrico, 515
Jones, Wyatt C., 270, 289
Jordon, Vernon E., 238
Julian, Joseph, 133, 146
"Just Community," Niantic, Connecticut, 66
justice, administration of, 44-70
　causes of problems, 59-62

courts, *see* courts
defining, 44-53
future of, 67-69
incidence of problems, 53-59
injustice definition of, 44-45, 47
lax-and-permissive definition of, 45-47
police, *see* police
prevalence of problems, 53-59
prisons, *see* prisons
proposed solutions to problems, 62-67
rehabilitation programs, improvement of, 65-67
Justice, Department of, 39, 50
juvenile delinquency, *see* crime
juvenile jails, 65
Juvenile Justice Standards Project, 63
juvenile prisons, 57

Kahn, Robert, 540
Kaiser-Permanente Health Plan of California, 472
Kamin, Leon, 289-90
Kamm, Henry, 609
Kantner, John, 148, 151
Kaplan, Roy, 245
Kart, Cary S., 327
Kastenbaum, Robert, 326-27
Kaufman, Herbert, 537, 539
Kennedy, Edward, 454
Kennedy Administration, 399, 540, 542
Kephart, William, 238
Kerner Commission, 62, 300
Kerr, Clark, 375
Kessel, Reuben, 473
Kids and Cops (Bouma), 62
Kilbride, Anne, 142
King, 547
King, Martin Luther, 289, 300
Kinsey, Alfred, 148, 149
Kiser, Clyde, 330
Kitano, Harry H. L., 272
Kitsuse, John, 11, 14
Klein, Deborah P., 151
Koch, John H., 198
Kohl, Herbert, 364
Kotelchuck, David, 276, 466
Kotler, Milton, 212-13
Kozol, Jonathan, 364
Kratcoski, Peter, 48
Kremen, Bennet, 403
Kuhn, Maggie, 316
Kupferberg, Herbert, 57, 158
Kutscher, Ronald, 413

La Rocque, Gene, 547
labeling theory, 8, 34-35, 510
Labor, Department of, 151, 153, 251, 254
labor force, 429-31
Labor Statistics, Bureau of, 233, 413, 429
Lafayette Clinic, 507
Laing, R. D., 510, 511
laissez-faire concept, 552
Lance, Bert, 26
Lane, Robert E., 242
Lang, Kurt, 551
Lapp, Ralph, 559
larceny, 27, 28, 29
Latane, Bibbe, 196
latent social problem, 4
Law Enforcement Administration Agency, 553
Law Enforcement Assistance Administration (LEAA), 30, 39, 57
learning theory, 509-10
Leary, Mike, 544
Lebergott, Stanley, 246
Leckachman, Robert, 251
Lee, Calvin B. T., 368
Lefcourt, Robert, 59
legal services, 56
Leinwand, Gerald, 218
LeMasters, E. E., 406
Lennard, Henry, 89
Lent, Norman, 200
Lerner, Monroe, 448-49
Leslie, Gerald R., 145, 194, 268, 458
less-developed countries (LDCs), population growth in, 597, 600-605, 608-9, 611-13
Levine, Daniel S., 505
Levison, Andrew, 401
Levitan, Sar, 238-39, 408
Lewin, Kurt, 425
Lewin, Roger, 247
Lewis, C. S., 596-97
Lewis, David L., 337
Lewis, Myrna, 315, 326
Lewis, Oscar, 243
liberal ideology
　administration of justice and, 44, 47, 53, 61, 62
　alcohol use and abuse and, 115, 118
　characteristics of, 10-11
　corporate power and, 396, 420-29
　crime and, 27, 36, 38, 39
　drug use and abuse and, 89, 98-99, 103
　ecology and, 578

education and, 351-52, 355, 362, 370, 373
the elderly and, 332
family structure and, 133-36
government and, 532-33, 552-56, 558-62
health care and, 471-72
minorities and, 290, 294-97
population growth and, 598, 607, 608
poverty and, 245-51, 253
urban and suburban problems and, 208-12
liberty versus order, 553
life expectancy, 330-31, 335-36, 463-64, 598
life-situation definitions of poverty, 234-37
Limits to Growth, The (Meadows et al.), 585, 594
Lind, C. George, 356
Lindblom, Charles, 564
Lineberry, Robert L., 204
Linn, Laurence S., 271
Lipset, Seymour, 271
Live-In-For-Elderly (LIFE), 333
living space, 590-91
Livingood, Ben, 506
Lockard, Duane, 192
Loercher, Diane, 608
Loftus, Joseph, 29, 30
Lombrose, Cesare, 32
Long, Larry, 43
Lopata, Helena Z., 136
Los Angeles, Calif., 31, 580
Lovell, Catherine, 554
LSD, 86, 87, 93, 95
Luce, Clare Booth, 137, 171
Lugar, Richard G., 204
Luikart, Clark, 453
Lundman, Richard, 39
Lupton, Andrew, 368, 369
Lyons, Richard, 399, 471, 543

McCary, James L., 170
McConahay, John B., 272
McCord, Arline, 398
McCord, William, 398
McCormack, Patricia, 151
McCormack, Kenneth, 353
McDonald, Frederick, 379
McDonald, Nancy, 498
Mace, David, 131
Mace, Vera, 131
McFarlane, Paul, 39
McGinnis, Thomas, 170
McGrath, Earl, 374-75
MacGregor, Douglas, 425
McKee, Michael, 56, 112, 499

Macklin, Eleanor D., 149
McNall, Scott, 7, 409
McVeigh, Frank J., 191, 276, 277, 278, 313, 380
Madsen, William, 267n, 282
Male and Female (Mead), 140
Malenbaum, Wilfred, 595
Maloney, Thomas, 30
malpractice insurance, 460-63
Manard, Barbara B., 327
Manchild in the Promised Land (Brown), 97
manic-depressive psychosis, 495
manifest social problem, 4
Manis, Jerome, 3-6
Mann, Brenda, 413
Mann, Donald, 608
Manufacture of Madness, The (Szasz), 495-96
Marburger, Carl, 353
Marcuse, Herbert, 97
marijuana, 8, 86-88, 91, 93, 95, 100, 104-6
marijuana laws, 105
market, rediscovery of, 564
Market-Opinion Research Company, 536
marriage
  alternative forms of, 165
  contemporary, 134-35
  future changes in, 169-73
  group, 163-64
  Mills on, 13
  polygamous, 164
  rates, 143-44
Marriages and Other Alternatives (Duberman), 163
Marston, Linda, 38
Martha Movement, 161
Martin, William, 108
Martinson, Robert, 52-53
Martz, Larry, 540
Marxism, *see* radical ideology
Marziani, Francis, 46-47
Maslow, Abraham, 69, 425
mass transit, 325
Mass Transportation Assistance Act of 1974, 213
Massey, Garth M., 243
Maugh, Thomas, 91
Mauss, Armand L., 95, 132
Mayo, Elton, 425
Maxwell, Eleanor, 330
Mead, Margaret, 140, 163, 165, 330, 549
Meadows, Donella H., 582, 594
Meals-on-Wheels programs, 333
Mechanic, David, 465-66, 472
MEDEX, 473
Medicaid, 452, 454, 455, 460, 466, 468-71, 473-74, 479

medical care, *see* health care
medical centers, 451, 466-68
medical-industrial complex, 452-53
medical schools, 451, 452, 466-68, 473
Medicare, 322, 452, 454, 455, 460, 466, 468, 469, 471, 473-74, 479-80
megalopolis, 201
Meissner, Hanna H., 242
Melia, Jinx, 161-62
Melman, Seymour, 551, 561-62
Menninger, Karl, 492, 496
Mental Health Centers Act, 102, 517
mental illness, 491-520
  abusive treatment and, 499
  biochemical theories of, 507-8
  causes of, 506-12
  definitions of, 492-97
  disease-medical model of, 492-95
  dual system of care and, 498
  future of problem, 518-20
  incidence of problem, 500-506
  labeling by social factors, 503-4
  lack of aftercare and, 500
  physiological-medical proposals for, 512-14
  physiological theories of, 507
  practical definitions of, 497
  prevalence of problem, 500-506
  problems of system for treating, 497-500
  proposed solutions to problem, 512-18
  psychological proposals for, 514-15
  psychological theories of, 508-10
  restructuring of treatment system, 517-18
  social model of, 495-97
  social-therapy proposals for, 515-17
  sociological theories of, 510-12
  statistical definitions of, 497
  system for treating, 504-6
  violation of rights and, 498-99
Merton, Robert, 4, 33, 232, 271, 510-11, 532, 550
mesomorphism, 32
methadone maintenance, 102-3
metropolitanism in education, 563
metropolitanization, 211-12

Mexican-Americans, *see* Spanish-Americans
Meyers, J.K., 504
Miami, Fla., 212
Michigan, University of, 402
migration, 199-202, 597
Milakovich, Michael, 27
Miles, Samuel A., 109
military
 arms race and, 546-47, 557-58, 565-67
 corporate power and, 394, 395
 culture of, 551
 defense spending, 534-35, 544-46, 553, 565-66
 education and, 355-56
 future of, 565-67
 health program of, 470
 power and influence of, 533, 544-46
 proposals to reduce spending, 559-62
 "state management" by, 550-51
 waste in, 534-35
military-industrial complex, 394
Miller, Harriet, 327
Miller, Jerome, 53, 65
Miller, S. M., 232, 235-37
Miller, Walter, 35
Mills, C. Wright, 8-9, 11-14, 35, 205, 393, 401, 450, 511, 533
Mines, Bureau of, 585, 595
Minneapolis, Minn., 206
minorities, 267-300
 affirmative-action programs for, 295-96
 American Indians, *see* American Indians
 blacks, *see* blacks
 causes of problems, 286-90
 court treatment of, 49-50
 defining problems of, 267-72
 discrimination, *see* discrimination
 drug abuse by, 98-99
 future of, 297-300
 health care and, 275-76, 283, 456-57, 463-65
 hierarchy of priorities and, 296-97
 housing and, 290
 incidence of problems, 272-85
 institutional racism and, 271-72, 284-85, 288-89
 in police departments, 62-63
 poverty and, *see* poverty
 proposed solutions to problems, 290-97
 prejudice and, 270-72, 286-87
 prevalence of problems, 272-85
 reverse discrimination and, 268-69
 school desegregation and integration and, 294-95
 segregation and, 280, 288, 289, 319-20
 Spanish-Americans, *see* Spanish-Americans
 subcultural differences and, 289-90
 symbolic racism, 272
Mintz, Morton, 397-98, 409, 420-21
Mitchell, Bridger, 471
Mitford, Jessica, 58, 59
mobile education, 379
Models of Doom, 594
Modlin, Herbert, 498, 501, 518
MOM (Men Our Masters), 139
Monanhan, Anthony, 195
Monopoly Capital (Baran and Sweezy), 428
Montefiore Hospital, 451
Moorehouse, Rebecca, 170
Morgenthaler, Eric, 375
Moritz, Owen, 337
Morland, J. Kenneth, 493, 507, 520
morphine, 94, 95, 106
Morris, Jan, 141
Morris, Norval, 47, 52-53, 69
Morris, Tom, 337
Morsell, John A., 300
Morshead, Richard W., 352, 353
motherhood, 135-36
Moynihan, Daniel P., 268, 562-64
Mueller, Eberhard, 425
Mueller, Marjorie, 322
multinational corporations, 398-99
Multiphasic Health Testing (MHT), 477
murder, 27, 28, 29, 113
Mushkin, Selma, 93, 103
Myers, Paul, 611
Myth of Mental Illness, The (Szasz), 495-96

Nader, Ralph, 323, 424-25, 556
Nader's Raiders, 556
Narcotics, Bureau of, 86, 91
Nashville, 212
National Academy of Sciences Institute of Medicine, 473
National Cancer Institute, 411
National Center for Educational Statistics, 356, 357
National Center for Health Statistics, 463
National Commission on Marijuanna and Drug Abuse, 85, 90, 91, 93, 99-100, 104, 106-7, 110
National Commission on Urban Problems, 193, 204, 280
National Committee for the Study of Incarceration, 53
National Council on the Aging, 313-14
National Council on Alcoholism, 107, 118
National Council on Crime and Delinquency, 63
National Council for Health Policy, 474
National Council of Senior Citizens, 333
National Crime Panel, 30-31
National Forest Management Act of 1976, 591
National Gun Control Center, 38, 40-41
national health insurance, 470-72
National Health Planning and Resources Development Act of 1974, 474
National Housing Conference (NHC), 216
National Institute on Alcohol Abuse and Alcoholism, 118
National Institute of Education, 403
National Institute of Mental Health, 504, 519-20
National League of Cities, 197
National Mental Health Association, 518-19
National Older Workers Program, 334
National Organization for the Reform of Marijuana Laws (NORML), 105
National Organization of Women (NOW), 157, 167-68
National Planning Association, 401, 429
National Resources Board, 400
National Retired Teachers Association Journal, 326
National Science Foundation, 581
national security, 553
National Security Act of 1947, 400

INDEX

national social accounting, 563-64
National Wildlife Federation, 589
National Women's Agenda, 163
natural resources
  conservation of, 592, 594
  defined, 579
  Environmental Quality Index of, 590
  exhaustion of, 584-85, 590
  future supplies of, 595
  mining from the sea and, 594
Natural Resources Defense Council, 584
Nature of Prejudice, The (Allport), 270
Navajo nation, 284
negative income taxes, 248-50
Negative Population Growth (NPG), 608
neighborhood delinquency-control groups and projects, 39
neo-Marxism, *see* radical ideology
Neugarten, Bernice, 316
Neuman, Nancy, 206
neuroses, 493
New Chastity and Other Arguments against Women's Liberation, The (Decter), 161
new towns, 209-10, 216
New York City, 31, 58, 59, 193, 196, 197, 198, 204, 206, 212, 214, 337, 464
New York Temporary Commission to Evaluate Drug Laws, 102
New York Times, The, 146, 152, 194, 352, 415
Newark, J.J., 31, 193
Nicholson, William, 411
nicotine, 86, 87
Nimkoff, Meyer, 325
Nixon, Richard M., 292, 539-40
nonpsychotic organic brain syndrome, 107
Notestein, Frank, 579
Nourse, Alan E., 455
Novak, Michael, 133
nuclear arms race, 546-47, 557-58, 565-67
nursing homes, 322-24, 326-28, 332-33
nutrition of the elderly, 322
nutrition-adequacy definition of poverty, 232
Nyswander, Marie, 103

occupational crime, 34
occupational distribution, changes in, 152-53
Occupational Outlook Handbook, 429
Occupational Safety and Health Act of 1970, 427
occupational sex-typing, 151-52
Odyssey House, 101
Oelsner, Lesley, 50
Ogburn, William, 3, 131, 417
Ohio State University, 463
Ohlin, Lloyd, 33-35
Olson, Mancur, 578, 611
O'Neill, George, 134-35
O'Neill, Nena, 134-35
open marriage, 134-35
opium, 86, 87
opium derivatives, 86, 87
Oravec, John, 427
order versus liberty, 553
O'Reilly, Kathleen, 556
organic conservatism, 10
organic psychoses, 494
organized crime, 26-27
Orlans, Harold, 379
Ornstein, Allan, 295
Ornstein, Norman J., 564
Other America, The (Harrington), 231, 243
O'Toole, James, 433, 434
Otto, Herbert A., 164, 170
outpatient treatment, 102
"Outreach" gang workers, 39
Overton, W. F., 107

Pai, D. N., 609
Pakistan, 608
Palen, J. John, 202, 214
Pallas, John, 69
Palmore, Erdman, 453
Palo Alto, Calif., 196
paramedics, 473
paranoia, 495
paraprofessionals, 473
Park, Robert, 189, 191
Parkinson, C. Northcote, 550
Parsons, Talcott, 131, 134
Pasamanick, Benjamin, 494
Peabody, Malcolm G., 206
Peele, Stanton, 87, 97
peer pressure
  crime and, 33
  drug abuse and, 99-100
Pennsylvania, University of, 451
Pentagon, 533, 544
"people-work" jobs, 426
Percy, Charles H., 320
Perella, Frederick J., Jr., 237

Perrucci, Robert, 4, 407
Perry, Erna, 94
Perry, John, 94
Perry, P. Wingfield, 315
personal troubles versus social issues, 12-14
  see also alcohol use and abuse; crime; drug use and abuse; family; justice, administration of; sex roles
personality factors in drug abuse, 96-97
Peter, Laurence, 550
Peterson, Charles, 144
Peterson, James, 315
Peterson, Roland L., 456, 475
Pettigrew, Thomas F., 268, 269, 274, 286, 290, 294
Philadelphia, Pa., 31, 206, 208, 212, 582
Philadelphia General Hospital, 465
Phoenix House, 101
physiological causes of mental illness, 507
Pickus, Robert, 558
Piel, Gerald, 426
Pilisuk, Marc, 4, 407
Pittsburg, Pa., 580
planning, future jobs in, 434
Plath, Sylvia, 493
Playboy Foundation, 149
plea bargaining, 51
pluralism, 10
Poe, Edgar Allan, 191
police, 45-49
  abuses by, 47-49
  causes of problems with, 60
  future of, 67-68
  improvement of, 62-63
  incidence of abuse by 54-55
  technology, 39
political "dirty tricks," 24
Pollack, Harriet, 61
pollution control
  future jobs in, 433-34
  see also ecology
polydrugs, 95
polygamous marriages, 164
population growth, 597-613
  birth rates, 146-47, 599, 600, 603, 604, 610
  causes of problem, 603-7
  cultural norms and values favoring large families, 606-7
  death rates, 603-6, 610
  defining problem of, 597-98
  ecology problem and, 586-87
  future of, 609-13
  government size and, 548

645

incidence of, 598–603
industrialization and, 604
in less-developed countries (LCDs), 597, 600–605, 608–9, 611–13
prevalence of, 598–603
proposed solutions to problem, 607–9
urbanization and, 604
Population and the American Future, 188
Population Reference Bureau, 599, 608
Portland, Ore., 31
postindustrial society, 428–29
poverty, 231–57
  blacks and, 239–41, 254–55, 276
  causes of, 241–47
  court treatment and, 49–50
  culture or subculture of, 243–45
  defining, 231–37
  demogrant proposal, 251–52
  of the elderly, 240, 326
  employment programs and, 250–51
  future of, 253–56
  guaranteed-income plans and, 248
  health care and, 464
  incidence of, 237–41
  income definition of, 232, 233
  individualism and, 242–43
  inequality definition of, 234
  life-situation definitions of, 234–37
  negative income tax proposal, 248–50
  prevalence of, 237–41
  as primary social problem, 3
  proposed solutions to, 247–53
  relative definition of, 232, 233
  social characteristics of the poor, 239–41
  social structure and, 245–47
  Spanish-Americans and, 239, 240, 276, 282–83
  unemployment and, 238, 240–41, 251, 254, 255
Poverty USA (Gladwin), 235
power elite, 533, 540, 542–44
Power Elite, The (Mills), 533
predelinquent screening, 37
prejudice, 270–72, 286–87
premarital sex, 148–49
Presidential Commission on Population Growth and the American Future, 330, 597–99, 607

Presidential Commission on Technology Automation and Economic Progress, 407
Presidential National Advisory Commission on Civil Disorders, 290–91, 297, 298
President's Commission on Law Enforcement and Administration of Justice, 56
President's Commission on School Finance, 368
President's Council on Wage and Price Stability, 455
President's National Advisory Commission on Criminal Justice Standards and Goals, 63, 65, 66
President's National Commission for Manpower Policy, 415
primary crime prevention, 36–38
primary social problems, 5, 6, 9
priorities, hierarchy of, 296–97
prisons, 45
  abolishment of, 65
  causes of problems, 61–62
  defining problems of, 52–53
  future of, 68–69
  prevalence of problems, 57–59
Procopio, Mariellen, 237
product technology, ecology problem and, 587
Professional Standards Review Organizations (PSROs), 478–79
profit sharing, 426
prosecution of truants and delinquents, 37
Prosterman, Roy, 558
Protestant work ethic, 242, 405–7
Protestantism, 4
psychoactive drugs, 86
psychoanalysis, 512
psychodrama, 115
psychological theories of mental illness, 508–10
psychoses, 493–95
psychosurgery, 514
psychotherapists, 39
Public Citizens Health Research Group, 474–75
public drunkenness, 113
Public Health Service, 463, 479, 582
public-interest groups, 555–56
public-service employment, 251
public welfare, 247–48, 253
Puerto Ricans, 269, 273, 281–84, 456, 504

Questions Divorced Catholics Ask (Young), 145
Quinn, Robert P., 403
Quinney, Richard, 7

Rabb, Earl, 271
racial minorities, *see* minorities
racism
  institutional, 271–72, 284–85, 288–89
  as primary social problem, 5
  symbolic, 272
radiation pollution, 582
radical ideology
  administration of justice and, 44, 47, 53, 63
  alcohol use and abuse and, 115
  characteristics of, 11
  corporate power and, 393–95, 419–20, 428
  crime and, 27, 36, 39, 42
  drug use and abuse and, 97, 118
  ecology and, 578, 594
  education and, 362, 373
  the elderly and, 330
  family structure and, 133–36
  government and, 533, 553–54, 557, 559, 562
  minorities and, 296–97
  population growth and, 598, 608
  poverty and, 245–47, 253
  urban and suburban problems and, 214–15
  work and, 401, 419–20, 428
radical nonintervention, 42
railroads, 202, 203
Rainwater, Lee, 254
Ramsey, Charles, 245, 247
rape, 113
rapid transit, 202, 213–14
Ravenholt, R. T., 602
Ravitch, Diane, 280
Ray, Elizabeth, 535
reality model of health care, 450, 466
Reasons, Charles, 86
recreation, future jobs in, 432
recreational programs, 37, 39
recreational space, 548
Redick, Richard, 501
red-lining, 194
Regan, Barbara, 152
regional health planning, 474–75
Regional Plan Association, 337
rehabilitation programs, 47, 52–53, 65–67

Reiss, Albert, 54–55
Reiss, Ira, 148
religious agencies, crime prevention and, 37
Rensberger, Boyce, 456, 463
Reston, Va., 209
restructuring theory, 8–9
Retired Senior Volunteer Program (RSVP), 334
retirement, 313, 331–32, 336, 338
revenue sharing, 554
reverse discrimination, 268–69
Rice, Berkeley, 511
Richards, Renee, 141
Richmond, 212
rising expectations, education and, 362–63
robbery, 27, 28, 29
Robertson, Ian, 56, 106, 112, 499
Robins, Lee, 99
Roby, Pamela, 232
Rodgers, William H., 419
Rodin, Judith, 196
Rodman, Hyman, 134
Roemer, Milton I., 448
Rose, Arnold, 286
Rose, Caroline, 286
Roselle, Daniel, 627
Rosenbaum, David E., 249
Rosenberg, Max, 371
Rosenfeld, Megan, 161
Rosenstein, Jean, 320
Rosenthal, Jack, 274
Rosenthal, Robert, 366
Rosenhan, D. L., 491–92, 495
Rosoff, Jeannie L., 609
Ross, Sid, 57
Rossi, Alice, 136
Roszak, Theodore, 366–67
Rothschild, Emma, 401, 408
Rowe, Alan, 233
Rubel, Eugene J., 474
rural areas, future jobs in, 432
Ryan, William, 8, 32, 242, 244, 246, 247, 268, 366, 498
Rydell, Charlene, 238
Rydell, Lars, 238

Saeta, Philip, 51–52
Sage, Wayne, 59
Sagi, Philip, 93
St. Louis, Mo., 31, 212
Salter, Andrew, 515
Saltman, Jules, 103
San Francisco, Calif., 212–14
Scammon, Richard, 277
Scanzoni, John, 147, 148
Scanzoni, Letha, 147, 148

Scarpitti, Frank R., 39, 142, 164, 456, 504
Scheff, Thomas, 495, 496, 510
Scheuerman, Kirk, 48
Schick-Shadel Hospital, 115
Schildkraut, Joseph, 508
Schiller, Bradley, 290
schizophrenia, 494–95, 507
Schlafly, Phyllis, 139
Schmidt, Wolfgang, 119
schools, *see* education
Schorr, Daniel, 459, 465
Schumacher, E. F., 595–96
Schur, Edwin M., 42
Schwartz, William B., 471
Science and Politics of IQ, The (Kamin), 289–90
Scott, Thomas, 212, 215
secondary crime prevention, 37
secondary social problems, 5, 6
security versus democracy, 553
sedatives, 86, 87, 93, 104
See, Carolyn, 144
Seeley, J. R., 192
segregation, 280, 288, 289, 319–20
Seligman, Ben, 232
Selznick, Philip, 232
Senate Labor and Public Affairs Committee, 454, 458
Senate Subcommittee on Internal Security, 91
senility, 315
sentencing, 51–52, 60–61, 67
separatism, 299–300
Severo, Richard, 236
sex
  changing attitudes toward, 158
  extramarital, 149–50
  premarital, 148–49
sex roles
  alternative forms of, 163–65
  causes of changes in, 154–59
  challengers' view of, 137–39
  consciousness raising among women, 167–69
  in contemporary marriages, 135
  defenders of female roles, 139–40
  equality for women, 165–67
  extramarital affairs, 149–50
  future changes in, 169–73
  homosexuality, 140–42, 172
  incidence of changes in, 148–51
  motherhood, 135–36
  occupational discrimination and, 153–54
  occupational distribution, changes in, 152–53

premarital sex, 148–49
prevalence of changes in, 148–51
proposed solutions to changes in, 159–69
traditional norms and values and, 160–63
unconscious ideology of women's inferiority, 138–39
women's liberation movement and, 156–58
work attitudes and, 417
working mothers, 150–51
Sexual Suicide (Gilder), 132, 160
sexism, *see* sex roles
Seymour, Kety, 508
Shabecoff, Philip, 292
Shaffer, Helen B., 424
Shanahan, Eileen, 237, 240
Shanas, Ethel, 327
Shank, John, 295
Shearer, Lloyd, 108, 113, 146, 148, 200, 463
Sheatsley, Paul, 287
Sheldon, William, 32
Sheppard, Harold, 402
Shevis, James M., 240
Shields, George S., 475n
Shock Probation, 64–65
Shostak, Arthur B., 209, 405, 422–23, 630–32
Sierra Club, 577
Silber, John R., 377
Silberman, Charles, 188, 268, 361, 363, 364, 367
Sim, R. A., 192
Simmel, Georg, 235
Simpson, George E., 271, 286
single-parent families, 164
Sivard, Ruth Leger, 566
Skinner, B. F., 515
Sklar, June, 144, 146
Skolnick, Jerome H., 203
Sloan, Irving J., 288
slums, 191
Slums and Suburbs (Conant), 364
Small Is Beautiful (Schumacher), 595–96
Smith, Alexander, 61
Smith, Fred, 188
Smith, Lillian, 286–87
social agencies, crime prevention and, 37
social change, work attitudes and, 417–18
social class
  alcohol use and abuse and, 113
  court system and, 51, 59, 60
  education and, 354–55
  mental illness labeling and, 503–4

social class *(cont.)*
  minority problem and, 289
  police discrimination and, 48
social disorganization theory, 7, 133
social drinking, 115
social institutions, 8–9
  the elderly and, 338–39
  poverty and, 245–47
  see also corporate power; government; health care; mental illness; military; work
social issues versus personal troubles, 12–14
social model of mental illness, 495–97
social pathology theory, 7
social problems, 1–14
  analyses and solutions of, 6–14
  definitions of, 3–6
  difficulties in definitions of, 3–4
  ideologies, 10–11
  lag between technological progress and solution of, 2–3
  new definition of, 5–6
  outlook for future, 630–32
  personal troubles versus social issues, 12–14
Social Security Administration, 232, 233, 247, 459
Social Security System, 239, 240, 253, 313, 319, 326, 331, 332, 337–38
social structure
  changes in family behavior and sex roles and, 158–59
  drug abuse and, 97
  poverty and, 245–47
  problems of, *see* elderly; minorities; poverty; urban and suburban problems
  restructuring theory and, 8–9
  see also social class
social-structure theories, 511–12
Sociological Imagination, The (Mills), 12–13
sociological theories of mental illness, 510–12
Soderlind, Sterling, 247
soil, 592
solar power, 579, 593–94, 596
Soleri, Paolo, 216–17
solid-waste disposal, 548, 583–84
Soltis, A., 108, 113
somatotomia, 32
Sowell, Thomas, 296
Spanish-Americans, 269
  defined, 281
  defining problems of, 267–68
  dispersion of, 282

drug abuse by, 98–99
education and, 240, 282–83, 366
health care and, 464
income of, 276
institutional racism and, 272
life conditions of, 282–84
population of, 273, 281–82, 297
poverty and, 239, 240, 276, 282–83
union membership of, 278
urban problems and, 195, 199
Spector, Malcolm, 11, 14
Spencer, Herbert, 242
Spokane, Wash., 206
Spradley, James P., 413
Sri Lanka (Ceylon), 605–6
Srole, Leo, 504
Stark, Rodney, 23, 28, 57, 500
State and Local Fiscal Assistance Act of 1972, 554
"state management" by the military, 550–51
Statistical Abstract of the U.S., 56
status frustration, 35
status offenses, 24, 63
Steadman, Henry, 517
Stedman, Murray, 191
stereotyping, 137
Sternlieb, George, 218
Stewart, Elbert W., 55, 237, 356, 583
Stewart, Maxwell, 188
stimulant drugs, 86, 87, 93, 104
Stockwell, Edward G., 604
Stouffer, Samuel, 232
strain theory (anomie), 33, 133, 510–11
Strategic Arms Limitation (SALT) Agreement, 547, 557
Strategy Council on Drug Abuse, 95, 105
Strauss, Anselm, 464
street crime, 24, 25, 29
subculture theory, 28, 35
subcultures
  crime and, 28, 35
  drug abuse and, 86–87, 99
  minority problem and, 289–90
  of poverty, 243–45
suburban problems, *see* urban and suburban problems
Sullivan, Brian, 411
Supplemental Security Income (SSI), 240, 247
Surviving to 3000 (Prosterman), 558
Sutherland, Edwin, 25, 33

Suttles, Gerald D., 191
Swartz, Allen, 455
Sweden, 605–6
Sweet, J. Stouder, 244
Sweezy, Paul, 428
Swift, Pamela, 137, 279, 427
symbolic racism, 272
Synanon, 101
Szasz, Thomas, 492, 495–96, 510 511

Taeuber, Alma, 280
Taeuber, Karl, 280
Tass, Leslie, 204
Taube, Carl, 501
Tausky, Curt, 245
Tavris, Carol, 556
Tax Reduction Act of 1975, 253
tax structure, revision of, 210–12
taxes
  the elderly and, 333–34
  loopholes, 396
  negative income, 248–50
  value-added (VAT), 251–52
technocratic elite, 564–65
technological change
  effect on workers, 407–9
  lag between solution of social problems and, 2–3
  urban and suburban problems and, 202–4
technology
  future of environment and, 595–96
  future jobs in, 432
Technology and the Changing Family (Ogburn), 131
technostructure, 396
teenage unemployment, 277, 283
Tennessee Valley Authority (TVA), 421
Terkel, Studs, 402
Terman, Lewis, 148
tertiary crime prevention, 37
tertiary social problems, 5, 6
theft, 27, 28, 29
therapeutic communities, 101
Thirty-Six Children (Kohl), 364
Thomas, W. I., 9–10
Thomlinson, Ralph, 456, 604
Thompson, Daniel D., 279, 280
Thompson, Warren, 337
Thoreau, Henry, 191
Tieman, Norbert, 217–18
To End War (Pickus), 558
tobacco, 88, 89, 93
Toffler, Alvin, 131, 378, 380, 564
Tonnies, Ferdinand, 189

Tokyo, 580
total-drug-culture definition of drug problem, 87, 89-90
Townsend, Claire, 323
Tracers Company, 145-46
traffic problem, 197-98, 201, 202, 213-14
tranquilizers, 86, 87, 93, 95, 104, 116, 512-13
transportation
 causes of problems, 201-4
 defining problems of, 197-98
 for the elderly, 325, 334
 future, 217-18
 proposed solutions to problems, 213-14
transsexuals, 140
transvestites, 140
trapped (urban type), 190-91
treatment centers, 117-18
Turner, Jonathan H., 290, 371-72, 394, 551, 594

underemployment, 412, 433, 434
Underwood, Kenneth, 353
unemployment
 of American Indians, 284
 of blacks, 277, 414
 government and, 427
 Mills on, 13
 poverty and, 238, 240-41, 251, 254, 255
 of Puerto Ricans, 283
 rate of, crime rate and, 33
 social repercussions of, 415
 teenage, 277, 283
 true prevalence of, 413-15
 of women, 414
unemployment-compensation benefits, 253
Unheavenly City, The (Banfield), 191-92
Unheavenly City Revisited, The (Banfield), 191-92
Uniform Alcoholism and Intoxication Treatment Act, 119
Uniform Crime Reports, 28, 29, 42, 45
uniform laws, 36
Union of Soviet Socialist Republics, 547, 557-58, 561-62
United Nations, 558, 602, 611
unmarried (urban type), 190
Upjohn Institute for Employment Research, 402
urban homesteading, 208-9
Urban Land Institute, 209
urban renewal, 193-94, 208-9

urban and rural development, future jobs in, 432
urban and suburban problems, 187-218
 bystander apathy, 195-96
 causes of, 198-205
 changes in family and, 131, 154-56
 crowding, 194-95, 201
 defining, 189-92
 financial, 196-97, 200, 210-12
 fragmentation of government and, 204, 210, 212
 future of, 215-18
 highway destruction of neighborhoods, 198
 homesteading, 208-9
 housing, *see* housing
 HUD programs and policies, 207-8
 incidence of, 192-98
 metropolitanization and, 211-12
 migration into and out of the city, 199-202
 new towns, 209-10, 216
 pollution, 586
 preservation of green space and, 206
 prevalence of, 192-98
 private corporations and developers and, 209
 proposed solutions to, 205-15
 radical proposals, 214-15
 special-interest structural forces and, 204-5
 structural decentralization and, 212-13
 tax structure and, 210-12
 technological change and, 202-4
 traffic, 197-98, 201, 202, 213-14
 transportation, *see* transportation
 urban types, 190-91
urbanization
 family structure and, 131, 154-56
 population growth and, 604

value-added tax (VAT), 251-52
value conflict approach, *see* conflict theory
Vatter, Harold H., 242
victimless crime, 25, 27
Vidich, Arthur, 4
Vietnam addicts, 99
Villemez, Wayne, 233

violence in prisons, 57-59
violent crimes, 27-30, 42
Vorenberg, James, 67
Voting Rights Act of 1965, 281
voucher system for education, 369-71

Wade, Nicholas, 596
Walinsky, Adam, 243
Walker, Sydney, 513
Wall Street Journal, 415
Waller, Chuck, 323-24, 328
Walton, Richard, 422
war, as primary social problem, 5
Warner, Lyle G., 271
Washington, University of, Medical School, 451
Washington Post, 534
Waskow, Arthur, 62-63
water pollution, 548, 582-83, 588-90
Watson, Peter, 271
Wattenberg, Ben, 277
Way it spozed to be, The (Herndon), 364
Wayne State University, 507
Weaver, Warren, 104
Webber, Melvin, 204
Weber, Max, 242, 532, 549-50
"wedding cake" federalism, 563
Weinberg, Kirson, 191
Weiner, Leon, 216
Weis, Kurt, 27
Weiss, Jay, 508
Weitzman, Lenore J., 288
welfare programs, 247-48, 253
welfare services, 37
welfare system, 247-48
Wheeler, Harvey, 336
White, Lucia, 191
White, Morton, 191
white-collar crimes, 24-26, 39
White House Conference on Aging, 331
White House Council on Environmental Quality, 588
Whitson, Dorothy, 200
Whitten, Philip, 106
Why Children Fail (Holt), 364
Wickersham, 547
wildlife, 590
Wilkins, Leslie T., 43
Wilkinson, Rupert, 118
Will, Robert E., 242
Williamson, John B., 10, 11, 231, 233, 396
Willner, Shirley, 505
Willowbrook experiment, 467
Wilson, F. Paul, 453

Wilson, G. Terence, 515
Wilson, James Q., 67
Winick, Charles, 97
Winpisinger, William W., 424
wiretapping, illegal, 24
Wirth, Louis, 189
Wise, 507
Wolfe, Sidney, 463
Wolfgang, Marvin, 30, 93
Wolpe, Joseph, 515
Woman at Home (Cardozo), 132
women
  alcohol use and abuse by, 112–13
  consciousness raising among, 167–69
  discrimination against, 48, 151–54
  equality for, 165–67
  family planning and, 608–9
  as heads of households, 240
  job dissatisfaction among, 402–3
  job inequality and, 411, 412
  mental illness labeling and, 504
  school staffing patterns and, 357
  unemployment of, 414
  see also family; sex roles
Wood, Nell, 354

Wooden, Kenneth, 45, 63
Wool, Harold, 429, 432
work
  alienation from, 401–2
  automation and, 407–9, 418–19
  causes of problems, 415–19
  decision making, shared, 424–25
  decline of work ethic, 405–7
  defining problems of, 397
  effective laws and, 427
  federal funding and, 426–27
  future of, 429–34
  incidence of problems, 400–415
  job dissatisfaction, 402–5
  job enrichment and enlargement, 422–24
  job inequality, 411–12
  "people-work" jobs, 426
  physical conditions of, 409–11
  prevalence of problems, 400–415
  profit sharing and, 426
  proposed solutions to problems, 422–29
  technological change and, 407–9
  unemployment and, *see* unemployment

work schedules, 424
Work in America, 402, 426
working mothers, 150–51
World Almanac, The, 144
World Population Plan of Action, 608
Worldwatch Institute, 602–3
Wright, Frank Lloyd, 191
Wright, James D., 38, 250
Wright, Sonia, 250

Yale Medical School, 498
Yankelovich, Daniel, 89–90, 416, 417, 577
Yarmolinsky, Adam, 374
Yette, Samuel, 298–99
Yinger, J. Milton, 271, 286
Young, Jim, 145
Young, Leontine, 134
Youth Conservation Corps, 429
youth-subculture definition of drug problem, 86–87, 89

Zeiner, Bryan, 607*n*
Zelnik, Melvin, 148, 151
Zietz, Dorothy, 24
Zimbardo, Philip, 196
Zola, Irving, 465, 466